PSALM STUDIES

VOLUME 2

SBL

Society of Biblical Literature

History of Biblical Studies

Leo G. Perdue
Old Testament/Hebrew Bible Editor

Number 3

PSALM STUDIES

By
Sigmund Mowinckel

Translated by
Mark E. Biddle

Volume 2

SBL Press
Atlanta

Copyright © 2014 by SBL Press

All rights reserved. No part of this work may be reproduced or transmitted in any form or by any means, electronic or mechanical, including photocopying and recording, or by means of any information storage or retrieval system, except as may be expressly permitted by the 1976 Copyright Act or in writing from the publisher. Requests for permission should be addressed in writing to the Rights and Permissions Office, SBL Press, 825 Houston Mill Road, Atlanta, GA 30329 USA.

Library of Congress Cataloging-in-Publication Data

Mowinckel, Sigmund, 1884–1965.
   [Psalmenstudien. English]
  Psalm studies / Sigmund Mowinckel ; translated by Mark E. Biddle.
     p. cm. — (Society of Biblical Literature History of Biblical Studies ; no. 2–3)
   Translation of: Psalmenstudien. Originally published in 6 v. Kristiania : Dybwad, 1921–24.
   Includes bibliographical references and index.
   ISBN 978-1-58983-508-5 (paper binding, vol. 1 : alk. paper) — 978-1-58983-509-2 (electronic library copy, vol.1) — 978-1-58983-510-8 (paper binding, vol. 2 : alk. paper) — 978-1-58983-511-5 (electronic library copy, vol. 2) — 9781589838017 (hardcover binding, vol. 1 : alk. paper) — 9781589838024 (hardcover binding, vol. 2 : alk. paper)
   1. Bible. O.T. Psalms—Criticism, interpretation, etc. I. Biddle, Mark E. II. Title.
   BS1430.52.M7213 2012b
   223'.206—dc22   2010021018

Printed on acid-free, recycled paper conforming to
ANSI/NISO Z39.48-1992 (R1997) and ISO 9706:1994
standards for paper permanence.

Contents

VOLUME 1

Translator's Note xi

PSALM STUDIES 1: 'ĀWEN AND THE PSALMS OF INDIVIDUAL LAMENT

Preface 3

1. The Path to the Core of the Term 5
    1.1. *Aun* and *Aun*-Doers: The Starting Point   5
    1.2. The *Aun*-Doers as Murderers   9
    1.3. The *Aun*-Doers as Robbers and Property Thieves   12
    1.4. *Aun* as the Cause of Illness   13
    1.5. *Aun* as the Art or Means of Soothsaying   16
    1.6. The Mysterious and Perfidious Activity of the *Aun*-Doers   18
    1.7. The Tongue and the Command as Means of the Man of *Aun*   20
    1.8. The *Aun*-Doer and Power   25
    1.9. Hand Movements and Other External *Aun* Techniques   28
    1.10. *Aun* = Magic   34
    1.11. The Etymology   35

2. Development 37
    2.1. General Meaning   37
    2.2. אָוֶן = Misfortune and Ruin Caused by Magic   38
    2.3. אָוֶן = Misfortune, Ruin   38
    2.4. Sorcery as a Type of Animosity toward God and Sin   39
    2.5. אָוֶן as a Designation for Illegitimate Cults   42
    2.6. Sorcery as "Lies" and "Deceit"   43

3. Magic in Israelite Popular Belief 63
    3.1. What Is Magic?   63
    3.2. Results   67

Contents

4. The Enemies in the Individual Psalms of Lament 81
    4.1. The Typical Statement of the Problem — 81
    4.2. Thesis: The Enemies Are the Magicians — 83
    4.3. The Evidence from Analogy: The Enemies in the
         Babylonian Psalms of Lament — 86
    4.4. The Direct Evidence — 101
    4.5. The Enemies in the Individual Songs of Thanksgiving — 129

5. The Individual Psalms of Lament as Cultic Psalms 139
    5.1. Did Cultic Individual Psalms of Lament Exist? — 139
    5.2. The Thesis: A Priori and Ex Analogia — 142
    5.3. Traces of the Cultic Purpose in the Lament Psalms — 144
    5.4. On the Religious Evaluation of the Lament Psalms — 161

6. The End of the Cultic Healing Rites 165
    6.1. The Reinterpretation of the Individual Psalms of Lament — 165
    6.2. The Causes — 171

PSALM STUDIES 2: YHWH'S ENTHRONEMENT FESTIVAL AND THE ORIGIN OF ESCHATOLOGY

Preface 175

PART 1: THE ENTHRONEMENT PSALMS AND THE FESTIVAL OF YHWH'S ENTHRONEMENT

1. The Enthronement Psalms and Their Interpretation 183
    1.1. The Material and Its Interrelationship — 183
    1.2. The Situation Presumed in the Enthronement Psalms — 185
        1.2.1. The Enthronement of the Earthly King — 185
        1.2.2. YHWH's Enthronement in the Psalms — 187
    1.3. On Early Attempts at Interpretation — 189
        1.3.1. The Interpretation in Terms of Contemporary History — 189
        1.3.2. The Eschatological Interpretation — 192
    1.4. The Cultic Interpretation — 195
        1.4.1. The Principle — 195
        1.4.2. The Cult as Drama of Creation — 197
        1.4.3. Traces of the Cultic Drama in Israel — 212
        1.4.4. YHWH's Enthronement Day: An Annual Festival — 214

Contents

2. YHWH's Enthronement Festival 223
   2.1. The Cultic Myth of the Festival   224
      2.1.1. The Myth of Creation and the Battle with the Dragon   224
      2.1.2. The Myth of the Battle of the Gods   230
      2.1.3. The Exodus Myth   233
      2.1.4. The Myth of the Battle of Nations   236
      2.1.5. The Judgment Myth   245
      2.1.6. Deliverance from Distress   257
   2.2. The Date of the Festival   260
      2.2.1. New Year's Day   260
      2.2.2. The Great Fall Festival   262
   2.3. The Rites of the Festival   268
      2.3.1. Introduction   268
      2.3.2. The Individual Rites and Their Significance   272
      2.3.3. YHWH's Entry   283
      2.3.4. Traces of Other Festival Dramas?   303
      2.3.5. The Processional Route   305
   2.4. The Mood of the Festival   306

3. YHWH's Dominion (Kingdom) 323
   3.1. The Gifts   323
   3.2. The Requirements   353
   3.3. Universalism and Nationalism   357

4. The Age of the Festival 365
   4.1. General Observations and Literary Attestations outside the Psalter   365
   4.1.2. The Age of the Various Enthronement Psalms   366
   4.1.3. The Probable Age of the Festival   378
   4.1.4. The History of the Festival   380

PART 2: THE ORIGINS OF ISRAELITE ESCHATOLOGY

1. The Problem and the Thesis 389
   1.1. The Cultic Day of YHWH's Enthronement   389
   1.2. The Problem: Gressmann, Gunkel, Sellin   395
   1.3. The Theses   400

2. Outline of the Argument 403

THE DAY OF YHWH

    2.1. The End of History = The Beginning of History 404
    2.2. The Day of YHWH Is the Day of Enthronement 404
    2.3. The Day of the Theophany and the Horrors of Revelation 417
    2.4. Natural Catastrophes and the Demise of the World 418
    2.5. The Time of Affliction and Deliverance from the Enemy 426
    2.6. Salvation and Disaster 434
    2.7. The Day of Judgment 439
    2.8. The Remnant 449
    2.9. The New Creation 454
    2.10. The Turn of Fate 458
    2.11. The New Covenant 459
    2.12. God's Worldwide Kingdom 461
    2.13. The Eschatological Meal 466
    2.14. The Messiah 467
    2.15. Summary 479

3. From Experience to Hope 483
    3.1. Conclusion 490

VOLUME 2

Psalm Studies 3: Cultic Prophecy and Prophetic Psalms

1. Introduction and Foundation 495
    1.1. The Problem 495
    1.2. Cult and Prophecy 497
        1.2.1. General 497
        1.2.2. The Seer and Priest 501
        1.2.3. The Priest as Mediator of Revelation 505
        1.2.4. The *Nābî'* as Minister of the Cult 507
        1.2.5. Form and Technique of the Cultic Oracle 515
        1.2.6. Cultic Prophecy and the Composition of the Psalms 517

2. The Individual Psalms 523
    2.1. Prophecies for the Great New Year's Festival 523
    2.2. Prophetic Oracles in Occasional Worship Services 557
    2.3. Royal Oracles 572
    2.4. Oracles in Private Cultic Procedures 592

Psalm Studies 4: The Technical Terms in the Psalm Superscriptions

Preface...599
Introduction...601

1. General and Specific Designations for Psalms and Cultic Songs.............603

2. Musical Terms...609

3. Indications of the Purpose of the Respective Psalm...............................617

4. Indications of the Cultic Procedures and Situations..............................625

Psalm Studies 5: Blessing and Curse in Israel's Cult and Psalmody

Preface...653
Introduction...655

1. The Blessing in Cult and Psalmody..659
   - 1.1. Blessing — 659
   - 1.2. The Blessing in the Cult — 666
   - 1.3. Psalms of Blessing — 683

2. The Curse in Cult and Psalmody...709
   - 2.1. Curse — 709
   - 2.2. The Curse in the Cult — 714
   - 2.3. Curse Psalms — 727

3. The Bipartite Blessing and Curse Formula in Cult and Psalmody............741
   - 3.1. The Bipartite Blessing and Curse Formula — 741
   - 3.2. Poetic Imitations and Echoes of the Scheme — 758

4. Conclusion: A Summary from the Perspective of the History
   of Religions..771

Addenda: Some of the Texts Discussed..777

Psalm Studies 6: The Psalmists

1. Introduction..783

2. The Purpose of the Psalms: Private or Cultic Songs 791

3. The Actual Psalmists 817

4. The Origin of the Pseudonyms 847

Index of Sources 869

Psalm Studies 3

Cultic Prophecy and Prophetic Psalms

1
Introduction and Foundation

1.1. The Problem

Among the Old Testament psalms one finds several in which the deity is introduced as the speaker, whether YHWH's answer follows more or less immediately after the lament and request, as in Pss 60 and 75, or whether the whole psalm is placed in YHWH's mouth, as in Ps 82 and the first part of Ps 110. In all these cases the form and style of the divine words are largely the same as in the prophetic literature. Sometimes the words sound very oracular, as in Pss 60, 2, and 110.

It is possible, of course, that we are dealing only with stylistic adaptations, with poetic fictions. A somewhat superficial consideration will always suggest as the likeliest assumption that the psalmists have given YHWH the word on paper fully aware that it is entirely a poetic fiction corresponding to no external reality.

One who has looked somewhat more deeply into the character of the poetry in the Psalter will hardly feel satisfied with this explanation. First, it is somewhat remarkable how relatively often direct divine speech to people occurs in these psalms, which, by nature, seek first to express human attitudes and ideas about and prayers to God. We are accustomed to assigning the singing of psalms to the sacrificial, not the sacramental, elements of the cult. Second, however, if we remember that the psalms per se were initially true cultic psalms, and if we make this otherwise self-evident postulate the starting point of explanation, we will soon find it in order that the sacramental elements of the cult are also represented in its poetry and music. God's involvement with people is no less solemn and musical art is no less valuable than people's prayers to God. In this case, however, one will more likely reach for the second possible explanation, that these YHWH sayings in the psalms express a cultic reality, that they correspond to an actual characteristic of ancient Israelite or Jewish worship.

As we will see, this was indeed the case. Only this assumption fully explains the characteristics of the psalms mentioned above.

A similar consideration brought Hermann Gunkel to conclude that there was a time in the cult of ancient Israel when the priestly promise of an audience in the name of the deity concluded the lament psalm by the sick person to be cleansed.[1] He started from the observation that the prophetic imitations of the communal laments, for example, Jer 14, fall into two major parts, as a rule: the request and the divine response. The second part corresponds in the psalms to "the assurance of being heard," a rather fixed component of the biblical lament psalms. "One may, accordingly, imagine that in the oldest lament ceremonies the prayer was pronounced first, whereupon the priest then proclaimed the response in God's name. This would correspond to Babylonian liturgies, for example."

Here Gunkel chose an idea, fruitful in many respects, but immediately laid it down again without pressing on to recognize the full reality. He could have had an Ariadne's thread of psalm exegesis here but spurned it because Wellhausen, Stade, and Smend had influenced him so strongly. In individual, specific psalms, he fell back into the views of earlier criticism according to which we have in the psalms private, noncultic outpourings of the heart. He understood the prophetic element in the psalm as the result of a dual imitation. First, the prophets imitated the psalmists in their prophecies and produced a mixed style in which the prophetic element was primary and authentic. Later the psalmists imitated this mixed style and adopted the prophetic element, now, however, as a literary form.

This thesis by Gunkel is, as has been said, influenced by his assumption that the current psalms, with a few exceptions, were not originally cultic psalms. In contrast, I am convinced that the situation was the converse. With very few exceptions, our biblical psalms were composed as cultic psalms. The prophetic element in the psalms, I believe, is not to be explained as an imitation but can only be comprehended on the assumption that we are dealing with true cultic psalms.

In order to answer this question, we must form a picture of Israel's worship services, with particular attention to their sacramental and prophetic aspects.

Our task will be to correlate Gunkel's hypothesis concerning the original meaning of the prophetic element in the Psalter, mentioned above, with what we know otherwise about the order of worship in Israel in order thereby to achieve confirmation or refutation of the hypothesis. Furthermore, we must examine whether the hypothesis is not valid in a much broader area than

---

1. Hermann Gunkel, "Psalmen," *RGG* 4:1935.

merely "in the oldest lament ceremonies." In any case—and Gunkel would probably have agreed—we must understand "lament ceremonies" not just as those occasions on which the community gathered to do penance because of common misfortune such as drought, famine, pestilence, and defeat but simultaneously as the cultic procedures undertaken to free individuals from the misfortune of illness, impurity, and sin. Such procedures belong to most of the Babylonian liturgies known to us. We will see, subsequently, however, that the prophetic word generally played a rather prominent role in the celebration of the Israelite cult. Finally, we face the task of investigating the individual prophetic psalms and correlating them with the resulting insight into Israel's celebration of the cult. We must attempt to explain them on the assumption of this very correlation.

The thesis to be tested below is this: the prophetic form of certain psalms reflects a cultic reality. In certain cases, the prophetic words, that is, the words given in a certain cultic situation as God's response to a request by someone who viewed himself and was viewed by his contemporaries as prophetically gifted, had a fixed place in the cult. Most, if not all, prophetic psalms in the Psalter are true cultic psalms to be explained in relation to this cultic practice.

We must consider the evidence for the thesis stated above as produced: (1) if we have shown from other reports outside the Psalter that there were actually such fixed cultic prophecies in ancient Israel, and (2) if we succeed in satisfactorily explaining the pertinent psalms in terms of this assumption. We must always proceed from the assumption that, if the psalms can be explained as cultic psalms, it is a self-evident postulate that they are such. First, the psalms were actually in use in the Jewish community as cultic psalms; second, since Gunkel, it is no longer necessary to demonstrate that the psalm originated from the cult. In fact, the psalms only became separate from the cult as Holy Scripture. Only as Holy Scripture did the cultic psalms also become private devotional psalms and undergo a complete reinterpretation. This reinterpretation had already been introduced, however, in the final phases of the temple cult.[2]

1.2. Cult and Prophecy

1.2.1. General

It is necessary, first, to gain insight into the relationship between the prophetic and the cultic.

If the prophetic passages in the Psalter presuppose a cultic reality, the communication of divine response must have had a fixed place in the cult.

---

2. See *Psalm Studies* 1, §4.

At first this appears somewhat unusual to us. We consider it obvious that the cult, and thus the cultic liturgies, must also have contained the sacramental element. But the concept that we usually associate with the word "prophecy" apparently does not coincide with the idea we have formed of the cult. We are accustomed to finding the "prophetic" as the opposite of the "cultic." At first glance, there seems to be an unbridgeable cleft between the fixed forms and formulas of the cult and the free inspiration of the prophet. Yet this relationship actually exists. It already appeared in Israel in the fact that the priest was often simultaneously the divine revealer (see below). The priest could communicate the revelation through technical means, such as the priest who administered the Urim and Thummim. But as an officeholder, he could also bear a special inspiration pertaining to the officeholder, conveyed through succession or through initiation into office. To whom God gives the office, to that one God also gives understanding, in this case, inspiration, the gift of prophecy. Thus, according to late Jewish belief, the high priest per se had the gift of prophecy (see John 11:51).

Statements above concerning the thesis, however, also clearly suggest that we do not take the word "prophetic" in the usual meaning of the word in the histories of Old Testament religion. The term "prophetic" is a formal term per se. In the language of theologians, however, it has usually attained quite specific content. The very circumstance that a formal term is usually, but not always, used with specific content is a contributing factor, I believe, to the significant wrangling over what was and was not "prophetic" in Israelite religion.[3] Various authors have employed this very word in a nonspecific and quite clearly, even to them, varying meaning. In this context, I do not understand how, at least usually, those tendencies, persons, and ideas in Old Testament religion, including the so-called writing prophets, are represented and how the favored ethical and anticultic, sometimes, indeed, even the personal, aspect of religion are emphasized. Here I take the word in its original formal sense. I understand a "prophet" here as one who, on commission of both the community and its deity, communicates in response to requests the necessary information in religious matters directly from a divine source by virtue of an unusual bestowal of power, one with certain knowledge of divine matters, whether he is inspired or can receive revelation, or has access to technical means through which he ascertains the will and instructions of the deity and can communicate the same in response to a question or a prayer. In this sense of the word, the prophet is not a private individual who happens to step forward. He is an

---

3. As, for example, in the question as to whether this religion was "prophetic" from its origins.

employee of society, a member connecting the two parties to the covenant, the community and the deity. In this sense, the religions of Babylonian-Assyria, Greece, and Syria/Asia Minor had their prophets. They were called priests, shamans, medicine men, and so on. Obviously, however, this alone says nothing about the value or lack of value of the various phenomena. Instead, this question depends everywhere on the religious and moral content the various forms have borne. In many places the prophetic institution contributed nothing to the further development of the religion to a higher level. In Israel, by contrast, for reasons that do not interest us here, it became the agent of some of the most important impacts in religious and moral development.

From the perspective of content, every cult consists of two elements, the sacrificial and the sacramental, as Christian liturgists have often stated. One could also say the human and the prophetic. It should be understood as though the two elements divide in a purely external manner into congregation and liturgist. The liturgist, the priest, can appear as the agent of both the sacrificial and the sacramental. The sacrificial elements are those actions and words in which the deity speaks to people and deals with them, such as blessings, responses to prayers, dedications, and sacraments in the proper sense of the word. To the degree that the cult consists of these two elements and contains speech and response, action and counteraction, it acquires a dramatic imprint and becomes a drama. To the degree that it intends and produces something—and it always does this—this drama is a creative act, a real, creative drama.[4]

In some form, the sacramental, the prophetic, is present in every cult. To the degree that it appears in the form of words, one can and must speak of prophetic words in the cult.

Since almost every cult, with the sole exception of certain truly Protestant tendencies, proceeds from the notion that the communication of such prophetic words cannot be accomplished by just anyone but that certain personal conditions are required, it is almost always the case that the cult has certain ministers whose task and privilege is to be agents of the cult's prophetic word. That is, the cult has special cultic prophets. The cultic prophet need not always have been a personality different from the actual liturgist. Liturgist and cultic prophet could be united in one person. In other cases, however, a particular cult has certain ministers who appear only or chiefly as cultic prophets. Then one distinguishes between liturgist, that is, the priest in the proper sense, and cultic prophet. As we will see, both forms occur in Israel.

---

4. See *Psalm Studies* 2, part 1, §1.4.2.

The personal conditions associated with the office of cultic prophet consist of a special equipping, a special empowerment or inspiration that makes one a bearer of the prophetic word. This equipping distinguishes cultic prophets from the laity, and, when cultic prophet differs from priest, it also sometimes differs from that of the priest. So it was in Israel, where the priest emphasized his hereditary qualifications and the cultic prophet, like the prophet in general, his free inspiration.

If the prophetic word appears as part of the cult, two situations are conceivable and attested. Only the appearance of the prophet needs to be fixed in the liturgy; every cult presses toward fixed "orderly" forms and sees them as a guarantee of its holiness and efficacy. The content and form of the words are left more or less to the authentic, spontaneous inspiration of the individual prophet. Alternatively, the content of the word may be fixed in the order of service. Then words proclaimed in the name of the deity witness to free, momentary inspiration only in terms of style and form. The transition between these two forms is fluid to the extent that it may often occur, even in the first case, that the content of the divine proclamation to be delivered was prescribed to the pertinent prophet. He must prophesy as the authorities want (see 1 Kgs 22:5–13). Only the precise poetic formulation of the words is left to the prophet.

If the psalms are actually supposed to be cultic psalms, and if, accordingly, we have psalms with cultic prophecies, then it is likely from the outset that we are dealing with divine sayings of the latter of the two types mentioned above. These proclamations in the name of YHWH through a prophetic spokesperson are probably to be regarded for the most part as passages determined by the worship order of an established, frequently repeated liturgy that was probably officially prescribed both in content and form. The divine response is not newly "inspired" each time but is prescribed by the order of worship. In worship, then, only the freely inspired prophetic form survives.

An intermediary form is also conceivable and likely. The situation can also be such that this or that prophetic psalm originated as the result of a spontaneous, subjectively authentic inspiration at a time when one left it to the free inspiration of the prophet to produce the formulation, and sometimes, perhaps, the content of the word, but that regarded this oracle as exemplary. Thus it later became a fixed component of certain cultic celebrations. This is quite certainly the case in Ps 60 (see below). I also have the impression that this circumstance prevails in most of the royal oracles.

Here the pious Bible reader may object that this idea, namely, that the production of prophecies that are both inspired and still prescribed in terms of content is the duty of the cultic prophets, would be a profanation of the psalms. It would amount to almost conscious dissimulation on the part of the pertinent poet. We must not suspect the sacred men of Holy Scripture of such. Now, the profanation of the psalms is not nearly as great as the Orthodox profanation inherent in the argument that a burning, fervent prayer from deep distress such as Pss 22 or 69 is no longer a proper prayer but a "prediction" concerning Christ. How the faithful were able to tolerate and bear this mockery of prayer life for centuries is simply inconceivable to me. If one considers somewhat more closely, however, one will see that the interpretation indicated above of the "prophetic" psalms in question does not result in their depreciation. If I am correct, it should first be noted that persons with prophetic gifts and inspiration had their place and profession in the fixed order of the cult and that these prophetic psalms—which stem then without question from the circle of the ministers of the cult—were composed by prophetically gifted individuals. The initial origin of the psalm may then be an "inspiration." In any case, they were written by those filled with the consciousness of their profession and their gift for proclaiming the will of God. Whether we share this conviction depends on the impression of personal authenticity that the individual psalms are able to elicit. It may be noted here that, in my view, it is precisely the prophetic psalms of the Psalter that take the lead when I sense even more of the authentic and personal experience in Pss 73, 122, 123, 126, 130, and 131, for example.

It should be said, second, that a distinction must be made between psychic origin and practical use. The later practical use cannot debase the origin. To the contrary, the lofty origin justifies the later practical use. Thus the Christian pastoral counselor, whether priest or lay, has a steadfast right to relate the "revelations" of Jesus that promised the forgiveness of sin to quite definite, specific individuals of Jesus' time to any Christians seeking assistance and thereby to maintain that today God speaks these words to you through me. In so doing one is neither a dissembler nor a deceiver, and the words of the Lord are not soiled.

1.2.2. The Seer and Priest

As I have already indicated, cultic prophecy assumes a firm connection between prophets and sanctuary or between the priestly and the prophetic profession and character.

It is well known that the priest gave definitive responses to certain questions, that is oracles. These oracles are the so-called *tôrôt*, singular *tôrâ*, the same word that would later become the comprehensive designation for the law of God. The priestly *tôrâ* have their own particular style.[5]

---

5. See Sigmund Mowinckel, *Ezra den skriflærde* (Kristiania: Dybwad, 1916), 98, 102, 111.

Notably, we do not encounter this priestly torah-style in the psalms but rather the *nābî'*-istic oracle style. The *nābî'* is the proper agent of divine revelations in Israel (see Deut 18:9–22).

Meanwhile, the seer (*rō'eh* or *ḥōzeh*; see 1 Sam 9:9) was incorporated into the *nābî'* with the passage of time. The seer's forms of revelation—visions, night visions, and dreams—were transferred to the *nābî'*.[6] As a loanword, *nābî'*, the root for which does not occur elsewhere other than in Assyria,[7] evidences non-Israelite origins. *Nābî'*-ism is a common Canaanite phenomenon. The role of seers, however, is genuinely Israelite, in all likelihood. The type of the seer in Samuel and Moses is a similar figure. Both were made into *něbî'îm* only in later tradition in accordance with the changed circumstances.

The ancient Israelite seer was simultaneously a priest. As has already been said, Samuel is typical. The redactional comment in 1 Sam 3:21 that calls him a *nābî'* does not belong to the original form of the tradition. This Samuel belonged from birth to the temple in Shiloh. He was the disciple and student of the priest Eli and his assistant in the priestly office; he tended the lamps of YHWH in the sanctuary. The account of the first revelation to Samuel is now abbreviated for the sake of the later legends that make him into a judge over all Israel. It was actually supposed to conclude with an account of Samuel's assumption of the priesthood after the death of his old teacher and the demise of his godless house.

Samuel's priestly status is also assumed in 1 Sam 9. He is very closely related to the sacrificial height, the *bāmâ*. No sacrificial meal takes place without him. He must first "bless" the flesh of the sacrifice. Blessing in the cult is a priestly task, however. Even the late accounts in 1 Sam 13:7b–15a and 15 are aware of Samuel's relationship to sacrifice.

Like Samuel, Moses is also a priest and seer. Numbers 12:6–8 puts him high above a *nābî'*; Samuel also stands higher than the *něbî'îm* who are subject and loyal to him (1 Sam 19:20). The passages that make him a *nābî'* are Deuteronomistic (Deut 18:15; 34:10; Hos 12:14). Like Samuel, Moses was introduced to priestly lore by his father-in-law, Jethro (Exod 18:14–23). He was the priestly mediator of the covenant between YHWH and Israel (Exod 24:8). He was the custodian of the sacred tent of revelation, the mobile sanctuary, and he took the concerns of the people and of individuals to YHWH (Exod 33:7–11). As priest, he was simultaneously a revealer to whom YHWH communicated his will. In the name of YHWH, he made legal and cultic decisions. Finally, his descendants became priests after him (Judg 18:30).

---

6. See Sigmund Mowinckel, "Om nebiisme og profeti," *NTT* 10 (1909): 192ff.
7. The word *nb'*, "to speak, proclaim." The divine name Nabi'u/Nabû is a derivative.

We also see elsewhere that the priests as such were still mediators of revelation in later historical periods. They bore the ephod and thus gave oracular responses (1 Sam 14:3, 18–19, 37, 41–42; 22:18).

We also find that seers were people who held official positions. David had his own seer at court (2 Sam 24:11). Holders of the office of seer, however, had little to do with independent inspiration. Their activity was priestly in nature.

This connection between "priesthood" and "prophecy" is, in reality, very ancient and, as has been said, quite widespread. We also find other traces of it on Semitic soil. In Assyria, there was a special priestly class called the *barû*, the "seers." As has long been noted, the Arabic equivalent of the Hebrew *kōhēn*, *kahîn*, which means "seer," also points to an original relationship. The relationship, or, more correctly, the identity of the two offices depends on the fact that the seer-priest was originally the one gifted with extraordinary power (manna) who by virtue of this endowment had both the insight to deal with the deity and the gift of "seeing," of soothsaying and working wonders—soothsaying and wonderworking also belong together in Israel. The priest Moses is the great wonderworker who did the most remarkable miracles with his wondrous staff (Exod 4:1–17; 7:14–25; 8:12–19), as did the *nĕbî'îm* (1 Kgs 17:7–24; 2 Kgs 1:9–16; 2:8, 14, 19–25; 3:16–20; 4–8).[8] The common Semitic word for priest, *kômar*, *kumra*, and the like—the fundamental meaning of which is "the hot one," that is, the one endowed with power[9]—also bespeaks the fact that the priest is the one endowed with power who through it can act both as seer and soothsayer under certain circumstances. We encounter the original Semitic type of priest in the unity of sanctuary guardians who were, under certain circumstances, both sacrificial priest and soothsayer (seer, prophet).

We find the same assumption that the endowment with power qualifies one both for the priesthood and for soothsaying and prophesying in the Israelite assessment of the monarchy. The king, the chief, was originally the one endowed with power above others—a concept replaced in historical Israel by the parallel that he was one possessed by YHWH's spirit. As such, he was both priest (1 Sam 13:9–10; 2 Sam 6:13–19; 1 Kgs 8:5, 14–64; 2 Sam 7:18; Ps 110:4) and revealer, one who was prophetically endowed (2 Sam 23:1–7) just as the chief Moses was.

We do not know whether in pre-Canaanite times there was already a division of the original unity into true priests, who were more ministers of the cult and administrators of the technical means of revelation, and seers,

---

8. It is better not to say "magical staff"; see *Psalm Studies* 1:63–67.
9. See Sigmund Mowinckel, "כמר בֹּמֶר," *ZAW* 36 (1916): 238–39.

who were especially ecstatically predisposed and whose chief or exclusive profession was manticism—in other words, whether one already distinguished between general endowment with power, knowledge, and capability, on the one hand, and specifically ecstatic and visionary endowment, on the other. The earliest historical Israel may have already distinguished between a priest and a seer. Actually, the name *rô'eh* already suggests this possibility. A word with this basic meaning may not have been the original term for a person whose chief vocation was cultic. Arabic *kahîn* only acquired this meaning in the course of development. Yet it can also be said that, at the most primitive stage of culture, the cult in the specific sense was not an everyday phenomenon. In everyday life, one needed the one endowed with power, the shaman, for example, more as a magician and manticist, more as a "seer" than as a leader of the cult. The minister of the cult, in the special sense, sometimes only developed from the "seer." To this extent, the name *rô'eh* may indeed have originally been the name for the "seer-priest" in Israel. In any case, the Moses and Samuel sagas demonstrate that it was still well known at that time that the *rô'eh* stood in a precise relationship with the cultic site.

The division of the originally unified clairvoyant priesthood into (sacrificial) priests and seers probably first took place under the influence of Canaanite *nābî'*-ism. The priests were still primarily oracle-givers in David's time, probably also on special occasions, as guardians of the sanctuary, the professional administrators of sacrifice. At roughly the same time, however, a certain division had already arisen. Some people at that time were described only as "seers," that is, oracle-givers ("Gad, David's seer," 2 Chr 29:25). The ascent of the great temple of the realm gave rise to the development of a special profession of cultic and sacrificial priest, which never, however, abandoned its connection to the Torah, with the mediation of revelation. The true seers, therefore, were rather soon thereafter transformed into the image of the *nābî'*. *Nābî'*-ism engulfed the old institution of seer but thereby became, in many cases, an institutional temple and cultic prophecy.

The original unity of priest and seer had two after-affects in Israel. First, in certain cases the priests in the later specific sense of the word, that is, the cultic priests, remained the revealers of the deity. Second, the heirs of the seers, the *něbî'îm*, adopted much of the original connection with cult and priesthood. Thus we also often find in later times priest and *nābî'* united in one person (Ezekiel, Jeremiah).

1.2.3. The Priest as Mediator of Revelation

It is often attested that the priests exercised prophetic functions. In serious and difficult situations, they are posed questions, to which they are supposed to give a divine response.[10]

We can distinguish between cultic, juridical, and future-oriented questions.

Haggai asks the priests one cultic question: If someone has carried sacred flesh in a fold of his cloak and the cloak accidentally touches something edible, does the food then become holy? The priests answer no (Hag 2:10–12). In Haggai's time, this question probably had a traditional response. At some time, however, someone must have obtained a direct divine response concerning similar cases.

When Exod 18:26 says that the elders issued rulings in all simple matters while all the difficult cases were presented to Moses, the assumption is that Moses presented the questions to YHWH and obtained his decision. We may imagine this priestly rendering of oracles in juridical cases ("judgments of God," ordeals) as a very frequent occurrence, especially if it was meant to discover the secret perpetrator of some crime. The account in 1 Sam 14:36–42 offers a comparison: Who has excited YHWH's wrath, a member of the royal house or one of the people? The guilty party is identified through the Urim and Thummim, which the priests administered.

Through the same means, Saul attempted to obtain an authoritative answer to the practical question, "Should I pursue the Philistines or not?" (1 Sam 14:37; see also 1 Sam 28:6; compare David in 1 Sam 23:2–5; 30:7–10). These are questions that actually refer to the future: their substance is "What will happen if…?" Thus one asks about the outcome before one marches to war or begins the battle: David asks, "Is it true, YHWH, that Saul will pass through here?" YHWH answers through the ephod bearer, that is, the priest, "Yes." "Will the men of Keilah hand my men and me over to Saul?" Answer, "Yes" (1 Sam 23:9–12). Or, "Should I pursue this band of robbers? Will I overtake them?" The priest's answer, "Pursue them, for you can overtake them" (1 Sam 30:7–8; see further 2 Sam 5:19).

If one notes the form of these questions, one sees that they are phrased such that a simple yes or no suffices in response. The answers given reflect this form. Things are no different in 1 Sam 30:7–10. Verse 8 is only an expansion of the simple yes inherent in the question. This agrees with what we know about the priestly means of rendering oracles. When the mediator is an officially appointed servant of the authorities or of society, the means of revelation

---

10. Inquiries involving the oracle: Judg 1:1; 18:6; 20:18, 27–28; 1 Sam 2:25; 14:18, 36, 41; 23:2, 9–12; 30:8–9; 2 Sam 2:1; 5:19, 28; Exod 22:7–8.

must necessarily be purely technical. The priest must have the means at hand by which he can evoke a response every time one is desired. The responses mentioned above are given by the priest who carries the ephod. The ephod, however, is not an idol or image of god, not even in ancient times, but some kind of container or garment related to the storage or the use of the Urim and Thummim (see 1 Sam 14:41–42 LXX; 28:6).[11] According to these passages, however, the Urim and Thummim are lots used in the rendering of oracles. With lots, the question could be posed as an alternative. The lot gave the briefest answer possible.

The example in 1 Sam 30:7–8 demonstrates, however, that the priest who announces the answer was not satisfied with giving a simple yes or no. He put the response in the style of the question; he gave it a richer form. We probably have a highly illuminating example of this phenomenon in 2 Sam 5:23–24. Here, too, the question was put to the lot on the analogy of David's other requests for an oracle, and, on close examination, the answer contains no more than what the priest could ascertain through the lot. The question must have been, "Shall I march against the Philistines, or should I fall upon them in ambush?" The lot answered, "You should set an ambush for them." The appropriate time for springing an ambush, however, is late in the night, near dawn. The dawn will be signaled, however, by the wind excited by the sunrise. The sound of the wind in the treetops will be perceived as the steps of God striding on the heights of the earth. The military chaplain knew all this very well. Instead of the simple "You should ambush them," he gave the answer a

---

11. Meanwhile, it has come to seem very likely to me that in the older sources ephod is indeed a designation for an idol image, as the older critics maintained. Of course, this was not the original designation for the idol but an application. It was probably originally the name for some article of the idol's clothing used when obtaining oracles. The article contained the oracular lot and *may* have been worn by the priest when giving an oracle. Because, in the consciousness of the one seeking the oracle, this article of clothing was the most important thing about the icon, the whole image bore this name (See Karl Budde, "Ephod und Lade," ZAW 39 [1921]: 1–42; Gressmann, *Auswahl*, 56–57; Georg Hoffmann and Hugo Gressmann, "Teraphim: Masken und Winkorakel in ägypten und Vorderasien" ZAW 40 [1922]: 75ff.; see esp. §8). Whether the original ephod was a coat or a loincloth, or perhaps a cloak containing a pocket for the lot, or perhaps only a broad band to hang around the neck (or the loins) to which the oracle pocket was attached, can hardly be determined and is also largely beside the point. I find the most recent conjecture by Gressmann (*Auswahl*, 107) that the ephod may have been "a carrying strap for the divine image" to be less likely, since the transfer of the word to the divine image itself seems quite unlikely to me. For the context above in the text, the question of the original meaning of the ephod is less important. It is certainly beyond question that, even in ancient times, the ephod was related to the giving of oracles and that "the fixed ephod" (= divine image) was an oracular divine image.

richer, more mythological form by indicating both the consequences and the self-evident grounds for the divine response, "Do not pursue them, but fall upon them from the rear and come upon them from the balsam trees. When you hear the sound of marching in the tops of the balsam trees, spring forth, for then YHWH has gone before you to smite the army of the Philistines."

1.2.4. The *Nābî'* as Minister of the Cult

The old Semitic seer-priesthood was suppressed on Palestinian soil by the Syrian and Canaanite *nābî'* role.

The fact that the *nābî'* role is not authentically Israelite in origin—if one understands "Israelite" as that which stems from pre-Canaanite times—is not generally acknowledged but should not be doubted. Enthusiastic and orgiastic prophecy—and that is the very core of ancient *nābî'*-ism—is a common phenomenon in Canaan, Syria, and Asia Minor, while we find nothing of this kind on the soil of pure Semitism. I refer here simply to the collection and examination of the material that Gustav Hölscher has undertaken.[12] The arguments given for the inner-Israelite origin of *nābî'*-ism are invalid. Some maintain that it must have arisen as a reaction against the specifically Canaanite because the *nābî'* wore the style of the wilderness period. The fur coat per se need not be traced to the wilderness period or a nomadic ideal any more than the ascetic lifestyle. The "magical" coat of the *nābî'* more likely refers to an orgiastic cult and the associated initiation sacrifice.[13] The fact that Amos 2:11 regards *nābî'*-ism as a gift of YHWH has no value as evidence, of course.[14] If the fusion of Israelite and Canaanite elements was, indeed, a fact, then everything valuable was naturally regarded as an endowment and gift of YHWH. The cooperation of the *nĕbî'îm* with Jehonadab ben Rechab (2 Kgs 10:15–21), also emphasized by Stade, and the *nĕbî'îm*'s zeal for YHWH, in general, are no more evidentiary. For whom should the Yahwistic *nĕbî'îm* be zealous, if not for the God by whom they were inspired? The fanatical adherents of Islam are not the Arabs but the Sudanese Dervishes. As those possessed by YHWH, the *nĕbî'îm* were naturally fanatical worshipers of YHWH. One expects such of any collabora-

---

12. Gustav Hölscher, "Zum Ursprung des israelitischen Prophetentums," in *Alttestamentliche Studien: Rudolf Kittel sum 60. Geburtstag dargebracht* (ed. A. Alt; BWAT 13; Leipzig: Hinrichs, 1913), 88–100. I had already assessed much of the material presented by Hölscher in "Nebiisme," 217–24, 358–60, and drawn the same conclusions as Hölscher.

13. See my "Nebiisme," 203–4, 227–37. Among today's Dervishes, too, the occasional practice is to prepare the garments of the Dervish order from the wool of the sheep brought by the novice and used as an initiation sacrifice (see ibid.).

14. Contra Bernhard Stade, *Biblische Theologie des Alten Testaments* (Tübingen: Mohr, 1905), 1:67.

tion inspired by the same fanaticism. But one cannot infer common origins from such collaboration. Indeed, the YHWH cult of the monarchial period, like the people Israel in the same period, originated only as a mixture of Israelite and Canaanite. Nonetheless, the people also perceived itself as a unity. The attitude of the later prophets, some of whom were not even actually proper *nĕbî'îm* (see Amos 7:14), toward the Canaanite elements of the cult is naturally not probative for its origin and original nature. In general, these prophets do not represent authentic and true *nābî'*-ism, were also usually rejected by the *nĕbî'îm* of their time, and were consequently engaged in constant polemics with them (cf. 1 Kgs 22; Jer 27–28).[15] Therefore, the appearance of the *nĕbî'îm* alongside Jehonadab ben Rechab by no means indicates that they react against the Canaanite per se but that, as YHWH *nĕbî'îm*, they struggle against the competition of the Baal *nĕbî'îm* and, as zealous YHWH worshipers, argue against the Baal cult. No one at that time could have distinguished "Canaanite per se" from "authentic Israelite," precisely because the two elements were already indissolubly melded with one another and constituted the unity of historical Israel. Consequently, we also see that everything that was considered valuable was spontaneously depicted as Mosaic, even such an undoubtedly "Canaanite" creation as the *mišpāṭîm* of the Covenant Code and the culture it presupposes. Obviously, as proponents of the "national religion," the *nĕbî'îm* were always "nationalist" in sentiment, in certain cases representing what can be considered the most sacred heritage of the patriarchs (e.g., Samuel in relation to Agag, 1 Sam 15:32–33), but that nation and that national religion was, in fact, the Canaanite and Israelite mixed nation and mixed religion. If the mixture simply existed and was no longer recognized as such by contemporaries, then its old practices and sanctuaries, no matter their origins, will have been venerated and guarded with equal zeal by all the elements incorporated into the mixture. The conflict between Saul and Samuel in 1 Sam 15 was between practical, political reason and blind, religious fanaticism, not between Canaanite and Israelite.[16] Thus, the fact that we first hear of *nĕbî'îm* under Saul is, undoubtedly, a matter of chance. Their origins were not connected with the uprising against foreign rule.

---

15. I emphasized, somewhat excessively, the contrasts between the *nĕbî'im* and the "writing prophets" in an early work and treated the most important texts (see "Profeternes forhold til nebiismen," *NTT* 11 [1910]: 126–38).

16. Contra Hans Schmidt, "Prophetentum, ältestes, bis auf Amos," *RGG* 4:1858–66. One may not base too much on the Ahijah legends in 1 Kgs 11:29–40. The account is Deuteronomistic. We know nothing about Ahijah's actual motives. Otherwise, one *nābî'* or the other could be found for every revolutionary or political act. For Ahijah, Israelite nationalism against Judahite foreign rule may have played a contributing role.

This *nābî'*-ism adopted from the Canaanites assumed much of the nature and the functions of the seer in the course of time, especially its connection with the temple and the cult. The situation could be expressed as follows: the old temple prophecy increasingly received the stamp of the *něbî'îm*.[17]

---

17. My view, that the seer-priest with the more technical and ecstatically contingent means of revelation was genuinely Israelite only to a minimal degree in contrast to the enthusiastic, spirit-possessed *nābî'* who was the Canaanite-Syrian type of the mediator of revelation, finds, it seems to me, analogical confirmation in Gressmann's observation in the essay "Teraphim" (133), mentioned above. He says, "while in Syria the bearers (of the divine image that gives oracles through 'hints') are usually explicitly described as inspired, we never hear of this in Egypt. The inspiration that surely makes the oracle even more credible is as entirely unnecessary as it is required for the lot oracle." In Israel, as we have seen, the seer, who had visions and dreams, and the priest, who administered the technical oracles, were actually often seen as inspired. It is beyond question, however, that equipping with the spirit "is by no means necessary" for these persons. When one finds them, nonetheless, they combine two originally quite independent forms of revelation, suggesting foreign influence. Now, we see at another point, according to Gressmann, that the inspiration of the spirit played no role among the Egyptians—and, according to Hölscher (see above in the text), we may add, among the ancient Arabs—but among the "Syrians," in contrast, a major role. Regarding the "oracle hint," Gressmann even deduces "that bearing the images of the gods for prophesying first became practice in Syria through Egyptian influence." According to Gressmann, this should probably be understood such that the giving of oracles by means of inspiration was the native practice among the "Syrians." Now, we surely will not go wrong to assume that the Israelites in pre-Canaanite times stood closer culturally to the Arabs and the Egyptians than to the "Syrians." On the other hand, a strong Canaanite influence through "Syrian" (Amorite and "Hittite") race and culture in pre-Israelite time is undeniable (see, e.g., Franz Böhl, *Kanaanäer und Hebräer: Untersuchungen zur Vorgeschichte des Volkstums und der Religion Israels auf dem Boden Kanaans* [BWAT 9; Leipzig: Hinrichs, 1911]). We can go further, however. It seems to me that Gressmann errs when he declares in connection with the statement above that, "in any case, prophetic excitement" is "more characteristic of the Semites than of the Egyptians." The error here lies in the word "Semites." In the time treated by Gressmann, which also comes into question for my topic, the "Syrians" were anything other than a pure "Semitic" race, from both physical and intellectual perspectives. The fact is that Syria and, as we also now know, Canaan were significantly infused by non-Semitic ("Hittite," "Aryan," "Indo-European") peoples and intellectual elements in very early historical and prehistorical times. We can say with all certitude—all the material assembled by Hölscher ("Zum Ursprung des israelitischen Prophetentums") implies it—that even orgiasm and the emphasis on inspiration belonged to these non-Semitic elements. In Asia Minor we find very strong emphasis on orgiasm and inspiration (see my "Nebiisme"). Gressmann mischaracterizes the difference between Egypt and Syria when he describes it as a difference between Egyptian and "Semitic" nature. Instead, the oracle system in Babylonia and Assyria and in Arabia shows us that the "Semites" stand alongside Egypt in this respect. The difference is rather one between Egypt and the Semites, on the one hand, and "Aryans" ("Hittites," in the broader

From the outset, the *nĕbî'îm* were not priests. The Old Testament always distinguishes between priests and prophets. Just as the priest is the administrator of the *tôrâ*, which is always primarily linked to the cult, the *nābî'* is the mediator of the divine *dābār*, regarded principally as independent inspiration (see Jer 18:18). According to the Priestly document, the *nĕbî'îm* were not permitted entry to the temple building proper. This prohibition reflects the old circumstance that from the outset they were not per se ministers of the cult in the more restricted and specific sense of the word, no *mĕšārĕtîm*. Thus, as we will see below, not all *nĕbî'îm* as such entered into the fixed institutional connection with the cult in which the old *rō'îm* and *ḥōzîm* stood. The *nĕbî'îm* of later times who worked as institutional cultic prophets were simultaneously regarded as Levites (singers) and may also in most cases have arisen from their ranks. Since the essence of *nābî'*-ism was always orgiasm,[18] the most likely assumption is that the *nĕbî'îm* were originally community representatives gripped by the ecstasy of the orgiastic delirium of the cultic festival and filled by the divine power to rave. Ideally and theoretically this should actually happen to the whole community. Along with the priest-seers, they were the true *religiosi* in the community who arose from the laity.

Nevertheless, or perhaps consequently, they were always closely connected to the sanctuaries. To this extent, they assumed a status analogous to the Galls in Hieropolis.[19] The *nĕbî'îm* were active at feasts and cultic procedures (1 Kgs 18:16–40; Jer 26; 28; 36). The first band of *nĕbî'îm* known to us came down from the *bāmâ* (1 Sam 10:5). The *nābî'* organizations were based at cultic sites, as at Ramah (1 Sam 19:19), Bethel (2 Kgs 2:3), Jericho (2 Kgs 2:5), and Gilgal (2 Kgs 4:38). Balaam must first build an altar and offer sacrifice before he can prophesy (Num 23:1–5, 14–16, 29–30). The *nĕbî'îm* are often mentioned along with the priests (Isa 28:7; Jer 4:9; 6:13; 14:18; 18:18; Mic 3:11; Zech 7:3). According to Jer 29:26, they were under the supervision of one of the temple priests. Jeremiah was a priest and a *nābî'* (Jer 1:1), as was Ezekiel (1:3). We will not go wrong to imagine that most of the later temple

---

sense of the word, or as one now wishes to put it), on the other. This understanding is also supported by another analogy. The mysticism of apparently orgiastic Persian Sufism, which depends on possession of people by God analogous to Old Testament spirit-possession, is acknowledged to be of non-Semitic, Iranian origins. The Old Testament emphasis on the spirit in contrast to technical means of revelation, which was, as far as we can see, singular in the entire "Semitic" East, is, therefore, "Aryan" in origins—taking the term "Aryan" quite broadly here for the time being, since we cannot more precisely determine the "Hittite" and "Indo-European" layers in the Syrian-Canaanite population. This would be a nice topic for "anti-Semitic" authors.

18. Cf. Mowinckel, "Nebiisme," 224ff.
19. Ibid., 224–25.

prophets may have come from the circles of the lower cultic personnel (see 2 Chr 20:14). This close connection with priests and the temple depended in part on the very fact that the old cultic prophets were suppressed by the *nĕbî'îm* or were transformed in the image of the *nĕbî'îm*. Thus the connection of the *nĕbî'îm* to the temple became institutional.

Without question, Jer 29:26 involves an institution of temple prophets. A passage in the Chronicler (1 Chr 15:22, 27), which has so far either been misconstrued or, in the best case, not understood at all, demonstrates that there was such an organized institution of temple prophets. These verses speak of Conaniah, the Levite, who was *śar hammaśśā'* (reading with LXX instead of *ysr bmś'*). Without betraying a trace of uncertainty, Gerhard Kittel translates "the leader of the bearers" and maintains, also without hesitation, that *maśśā'* can mean both "bearing" and "(musical) performance."[20] Immanuel Benzinger also thinks of bearing but knows quite well that *maśśā'* never means and cannot mean performance; he also acknowledges that, given the context, one would not even expect a comment about bearing or bearers.[21] The most clever is Buhl, who considers the phrase untranslatable in his Danish translation of the Old Testament. However, the sense of the phrase is quite clear. The chapter deals with the preparations for the ark-entry festival celebrated annually with a great procession.[22] In addition to sacrifice, singing, and music, the prophetic voice was also an element of this festival.[23] As Pss 132 and 81 indicate, these prophecies were sometimes fixed both as to content and form (see below). Thus 1 Chr 15:22, 27 is to be interpreted accordingly. The word *maśśā'* does not mean "burden" here but "oracle." Conaniah was "the leader of the oracle (system)." The passages shows us that the temple functionaries include some whose profession was to give divine statements, *maśśā'ôt*. They were organized like the other temple functionaries. They were headed by a leader, a *śār*, who "understood" the art of giving oracles (v. 22b). These temple prophets belonged to the Levites and, according to the context and verse 27b, to the singers (see also 2 Chr 20:14). This is quite natural. Prophetic ecstasy was induced by music (1 Sam 10:5; 2 Kgs 3:15). The revelations were sometimes made to music (Ps 49:2–36). As we will see, we have cultic oracles in the form of psalms. Thus we also find it quite in order that we are to seek the professional cultic prophets and the poets of the prophetic psalms among the temple singers. This agrees with circumstances in Babylonia. Here a priestly

---

20. *Die Psalmen* (HKAT 13; Leipzig: Werner Scholl, 1914).
21. *Die Bücher der Chronik* (KHCAT; Tübingen: Mohr Siebeck, 1901).
22. See *Psalm Studies* 2, part 1, §2.3.3.
23. See *Psalm Studies* 2, 172 and passim.

class bore the official name *barû*, "seers." The *maḫḫū*, the (raving) prophets, were also officially organized here.

In somewhat later times, the image of such temple prophets does not bear the character of the old seers but of *nābî'*-ism. Stated more precisely, in the main, it bore the characteristics of *nābî'*-ism but was influenced by certain characteristics of the seers. This situation mirrors the general process of development of matters in Israel: ancient Israelite visionary prophecy was absorbed and replaced by Canaanite *nābî'*-ism. Indeed, since antiquity the most important oracular media of the seer-priests were visions and dreams, on the one hand, and purely technical means (lots, etc.), of which we have already seen examples, on the other. The abilities of these people, from a primitive perspective, depended on the possession of a particular power: they were clairvoyants and visionaries, and they could also work wonders; they had, for example, the necessary "psychic force" to bless. The vision or the dream was probably the proper form of revelation even in terms of style at the time. *Nābî'*-ism set the tone later. This shift is evident in the following matters. Possession by the divine spirit, the *rûaḥ yhwh*, replaced the more indefinite gift of power. This change meant, however, that the enthusiastic form of prophetism suppressed the visionary and ecstatic form. The visionary, the ecstatic, was "beside himself." His soul, his "heart," left him for a while, sought out distant locations, and saw heavenly things (see 2 Kgs 5:26). He was caught up, and his alter ego stood listening in the heavenly council (see the night visions of Zechariah), or his soul went to some distant place (see Ezek 8:1–3; 11:1–2, 24–25). During this time the body of the seer lay rapt and as though dead in its usual place (Num 24:4). While Ezekiel's soul was in ecstasy in Jerusalem, his apparently lifeless body lay in Chaldea "in the presence of the elders of Judah" (see the description in Ezek 3:12–15). In contrast, a strange power has entered into the one possessed by the spirit; it has taken possession of him. He has become "enthused." Through his mouth speaks the spirit of YHWH. The *nābî'* also does wonders. He does so because the spirit is in him. Because the spirit that knows everything, the divine word, is "in him," he speaks true prophecies. Consequently, the form of revelation characteristic for the *nābî'* is the rhythmic word spoken by the spirit or by YHWH in which YHWH speaks in the first person. Thus the purely technical means of revelation (e.g., the lot) diminish. The *nābî'* always appears to observe the form of the free, spontaneous inspiration, even when he actually evokes it or quite dutifully proclaims words expected and required of him. Things that experience has proven to promote enthusiastic and orgiastic states appear as indirect means of revelation: music and dance (1 Sam 10:5–6, 10–13; 2 Kgs 3:15), loud, repetitive shouting, self-inflicted wounds (1 Kgs 18:26–29), handclapping and wild movements (Ezek 6:11; 21:19, 22), and so on. While, given the nature of his gift and his priestly office,

Introduction and Foundation 513

the seer was probably usually, if not always, an independent person, the first *nĕbî'îm* always appeared in groups and, for purposes of even greater intensity, induced the orgiastic delirium communally (1 Sam 10:5; 19:20; 1 Kgs 18; 22:6; 2 Kgs 2; 6:1–7; cf. *bĕnê hannĕbî'îm*, an expression that points to organization and communal life, 1 Kgs 20:25; 2 Kgs 2:3; 4:1, 39; 5:22; 6:1; Amos 7:14; the expression *nĕwāyôt* probably refers to a common dwelling, a kind of cenobium, 1 Sam 19:18–24). Thus, even the name *rō'eh* disappeared in later times. Then a mediator of divine revelations was always called a *nābî'*, even if he was not a member of the *nĕbî'îm* proper (Amos 7:14).

This does not mean that the older forms of revelation disappeared. It is known well enough that visions and revelatory dreams were also very popular forms of revelation among the *nĕbî'îm*. In reality, there is no psychological difference between ecstasy and enthusiasm. The actual psychic state of the seer and the *nābî'* were by and large the same. The boundaries of the concepts were also fluid in ancient Israel. Thus Ezekiel says that his visionary translation from Chaldea to Jerusalem was mediated by the spirit (of YHWH; Ezek 3:12, 14; 8:3; 11:1, 24). This spirit was sometimes depicted as a being who gripped him externally (Ezek 8:2–3) and sometimes conceived as the spirit that entered the prophet (Ezek 2:2; 3:24).

In addition to the free inspiration of the *nābî'*, at least in theory, certain purely technical means of revelation survived, such as the sacred lot. It seems, however, that these were reserved in later times solely for the priest in the proper sense of the word. That was the case at least for the Urim and the Thummim. The revelations of the *nĕbî'îm*, however, to the extent that they were subjectively authentic, were always mediated psychologically. The *nābî'* was regarded as permanently endowed with the spirit. As such, when he spoke *ex professo*, he always spoke on YHWH's commission. This explains the fact that the cultic prophet usually spoke *bona fide* and with the sense that he spoke on the basis of inspiration even when he was duty-bound to speak and sometimes even spoke words precisely prescribed by the cultic liturgy. In many cases, this consciousness will have even evoked in him certain psychic states that he understood as being possessed by the spirit and that permitted him to appear *bona fide*.

We may infer from several accounts that these temple prophets were obligated in certain cultic proceedings to give an oracle suited to the subject of the cultic celebration, indeed, in agreement with the belief and expectation of the majority of the congregation or of the authorities. Thus, for example, the four hundred prophets of Ahab assembled to give a prediction concerning the outcome of a military campaign on the day of prayer preceding it. Naturally they predicted just as most of the clergy in warring states now preach. In this regard, the Old Testament prophets are, for the most part, no better or more perfect than Catholic, Lutheran, Anglican, or Methodist priests and preachers. One also expected a favorable oracle from Micaiah ben Imlah and declared it a crime against the state and treason when he did not give one (1 Kgs 22). In Jer 28, too, the whole people assembled in the temple for a day of prayer. The issue was the planned rebellion against Nebuchadnezzar: Would it succeed or not? "O, YHWH, give us good fortune; O, YHWH, let it succeed!" Then Hananiah ben Azzur stepped forward. He knew his "state-church" obligation and task. "Thus says YHWH of hosts, the God of Israel, 'I will break the yoke of the king of Babel.'" The account in 2 Chr 20 is typical. The enemies of Judah have approached to attack. King Jehosophat calls for a great day of penitence and fasting. The whole community assembles in the temple. The king as priest and intercessor for the people pleads with YHWH for help. Obviously, this does not occur formlessly but in accordance with an established ritual. Based on the analogies above, it was also part of the ritual, of the "order of worship," for the Levite—a singer, see below—Oziel ben Zechariah to fall into ecstatic rapture. As we know from 2 Kgs 3:15; 1 Kgs 18:28, and 1 Sam 10:5, the *nĕbî'îm* knew technical means for inducing ecstasy. Naturally, in form it is free, unsought, spontaneous inspiration. Therefore, the Chronicler also says, "the spirit of YHWH came upon him" (1 Chr 20:14). In YHWH's name, the inspired singer promises the complete defeat of the enemies. Then the whole congregation falls on their faces to pay homage to YHWH. The festival concludes with a(n anticipated) hymn of thanksgiving.

In both this account and the passage treated above (1 Chr 15:22, 27), the pertinent cultic prophets are assigned to the Levites, more precisely, to the singers. Indeed, from the last passage one must conclude that, if the leader of the oracle system was one of the singers, then the same must have been true of the entire organization of the institutional cultic prophets. This corresponds to the views of the later, postexilic period, according to which no non-Levite could belong to the temple officials. The Priestly writer and Chronicler make even the Gibeonite wood-cutters and water-bearers into Levites. We must assume, accordingly, that the postexilic period included the cultic prophets in the ranks of the Levites (singers) in order to preserve their legitimacy. Thenceforth, they were singers first and prophetically gifted persons second. To the same degree that the cultic prophecies they were to present were linked to the order of worship (see above) and thus came to stand on the same level as the other cultic psalms, the difference between cultic prophets and ordinary singers was obscured until the perception that the cultic oracles were once the particular cultic task of a special profession was finally lost. Thus for the Chronicler, the Oziel ben Zechariah mentioned above was none other than a normal singer-Levite incidentally gripped by the spirit on this particular occasion so that he could announce YHWH's response. The Chronicler may have thought that this was a particular demonstration of YHWH's grace to the pious King Jehosophat.

Thus the institution of cultic prophecy gradually died out. The performance of certain long-fixed prophetic psalms took its place gradually and almost unnoticeably. All of the temple music was more or less the work of an admittedly very much diluted divine inspiration (1 Chr 25:1–3) in which the performance of the oracular psalms no longer stood out.

How early or late this took place can hardly be stated. The old institution of cultic prophecy, much more independent in terms of its essence and forms, certainly survived until the exile. This is evidenced by Jer 29:26 (cf. 20:1–6) and the fact that at that time many of the wholly independent *něbî'îm* still came from the ranks of the priests (Jeremiah, Ezekiel). But we still encounter prophets after the exile who appear entirely as temple prophets, in the first instance Haggai and Zechariah. It is particularly clear with Zechariah that almost all his picturesque language and his entire conceptual world originated in the cult: the candlesticks, the temple oil, the cultic curse, the purification rites (impurity born away by figures with bird's wings; cf. the bird in purification in Lev 14:6–7), the fast days, and so on. His highest goal was to see the temple completed and the cult resumed. In addition, he was also very much interested in the reconciliation of the two rival temple authorities, the governor and the high priest. It is most likely that the Zechariah in question was also from a priestly family.[24] Joel, too, most probably appeared as a cultic prophet (see below). Under Nehemiah, we still encounter *něbî'îm* who reside in the temple and appear in the dispute over religious policy to be totally partisan on the side of the priestly party, probably just as the temple *něbî'îm* in Jeremiah's time stood under the authority of the priests (Neh 6:10–14). It is a very likely assumption that these temple *něbî'îm* were simultaneously active in the official cult in some fashion. By all appearances, the Maccabean era, in contrast, had no institutional cultic prophecy, just as there was no longer any institutional prophecy (see 1 Macc 14:41), unless Ps 110 is "Maccabean," which I consider excluded, in part because it cannot be harmonized with the passage just cited.

1.2.5. Form and Technique of the Cultic Oracle

The means by which the priestly prophet learned the deity's response to a question or a request posed to him were also originally most certainly also

---

24. This resolves the apparent contradiction between Zech 1:1 and Ezra 5:1; 6:14. Iddo is not the personal grandfather of the prophet but the clan from which he came, identical with the Iddo of Neh 12:4.

technical in nature.²⁵ The giving of oracles through the Urim and Thummim mentioned above, the sacred lots, and the ephod indicate this clearly enough. Other legitimate oracular techniques seem to have been known. The psalm superscription ʿal šûšan ʿēdût in Pss 45:1; 60:1; and 69:1 may refer to a certain manner of obtaining cultic oracles (see *Psalm Studies* 4).

Many analogies suggest the assumption that obtaining oracles in Israel was connected somehow to sacrifice (cf. Babylonian and Assyrian hepatoscopy and Etrurian and Roman haruspicy and augury). The sacrifice of Balaam (Num 23:1–5, 14–16, 29–30) points to the connection between sacrifice and prophecy (cf. the report in the Golenischeff Papyrus concerning the sacrificial festival of King Zekar-Baal in Byblos).²⁶ Hieroscopy consists of learning the will of the deity from certain characteristics of the sacrificial animal (e.g., of the liver) or of the circumstances accompanying the sacrifice procedure, such as the ascent of the smoke, which were understood and interpreted as "signs." Genesis 4:4–5 indicates that such hieroscopy was also practiced in Israel. There were probably many such signs, not all of which, naturally, need have been connected with hieroscopy. In Ps 74:9, the people complain that it could no longer "see its signs," that is, the oracular signs favorable to it (the same expression occurs in Assyrian). To the contrary, they say, the prophets are silent. When Ps 86:17, an illness psalm of the usual type,²⁷ says, "Give me a sign for the good," it should certainly be interpreted in relation to the request, frequent in the Babylonian and Assyrian psalms, "Give me a good sign," and should most likely be related to a hieroscopic sign. Finally, any everyday event could become a mantic sign for the prophets.²⁸

Dreams also come under consideration as sources for cultic oracles and signs. The fact that the dream was a frequently occurring technique for the nābîʾ is well known.²⁹ Babylonian and Assyrian psalms frequently say, "Give me a good dream (one that promises salvation)."

Incubation is a special kind of dream oracle that must have been familiar to the cultic prophets. According to 1 Sam 21:8 and 1 Kgs 3:5–15, this form was known in Israel. The lament psalms may point to it a few times.³⁰

The account in 2 Chr 20:14–17 and the prophetic psalm in Hab 3 (see v. 16) demonstrate, however, that in the course of time the cultic prophets appro-

---

25. See Paul Volz, *Die biblischen Altertümer* (Cologne: Komet, 1914), 162–68.
26. See Hugo Gressmann, Arthur Ungnad, and Hermann Ranke, eds., *Altorientalische Texte und Bilder* (Tübingen: Mohr, 1909), 1:226 (final paragraph).
27. *Psalm Studies* 1:75, 149.
28. Ibid., 1:149.
29. See "Traum," *RGG* 5:1321.
30. *Psalm Studies* 1:158–61.

priated the freer forms and means of expression grounded in the inspiration of the spirit. The difference between the technical and the more psychologically grounded revelations of the *nābî'* is not sharp. Technical means could evoke psychic affects that the affected person would regard as signs of divine inspiration. An example of such a case would be when ecstasy was induced through external means such as music and dance and the ecstasy, in turn, produced mysterious psychic states or objectified the subconscious contents of the prophet's consciousness as divine inspiration. Thus the oracular forms intermingled. Everything was derived from the "spirit." One will even have claimed that the professional priest-prophets were also possessed by the spirit and, thus, as office-holders, received the gift of soothsaying. We have seen above that this belief was still vital in the Gospel of John.

1.2.6. Cultic Prophecy and the Composition of the Psalms
The examples treated above deal mostly with public days of fasting and prayer and with cultic inquiries prior to war and battle. In addition, the occurrence of the cultic oracle at a grand national religious festival is indicated (1 Chr 15). The prophetic psalms must have been inserted in this context.

We may already consider it proven that direct divine speech in the mouth of an official and authorized mediator of revelation on certain occasions in the ancient Israelite cult had its place in the liturgy of the respective day. We already know from the many cultic psalms that those liturgies had poetic and musical form, at least in part. Many psalms are cultic liturgies themselves. From the outset, the divine word of revelation in Israel had poetic, rhythmic, and metrical form. The same must have been true of the words of revelation in the liturgies.

A cultic liturgy in which various voices sound in rhythmic form, perhaps a psalm of lament, communal supplication, with a response by the cultic prophet in the name of the deity, then concluding with a thanksgiving, is, indeed, a psalm in the broader and Old Testament sense of the word. The psalms of the Psalter are by no means always uniform constructs in the sense that they permit expression only to one voice and attitude. Several of them are cultic and liturgical compositions, in fact, expressing several voices and attitudes.

The psalm compositions transmitted to us in which prophetic voices can also be heard will be examined from this perspective. It will be our task to seek cultic oracular psalms among the transmitted "prophetic psalms" and, in given cases, to demonstrate that they are such.

Here, however, we may also say a few words concerning the psalmists. It is inherent in the nature of the matter that the duty to write cultic psalms lay with the ministers of the cult. They will also have had an interest in the plentiful availability of such psalms. As is inherent in the nature of the matter, engagement with these psalms will also, undoubtedly, have resulted in many of the temple ministers having an appetite and gifts for such work.

Among the cultic ministers there is a class for whom we may presume a particular interest in the composition of psalms. This is the class of temple singers. They were responsible for providing the temple music, and we know that song and music always belonged together in that day. At least those songs sung in the name of the congregation, of the people, were sung, without doubt, by the professional singers. We can hardly go astray if we assume that the cultic songs of an individual, such as the lament psalms to be sung to accompany the rites of purification, were also sung, not by the respective sick person, but by the singers. There were surely not many of the common people with the skill to perform the cultic psalms in accordance with the tradition and precisely observing all the ritual details. Judging from all the analogies, the songs were not sung "from the music" but by memory. The laity cannot be expected to do this. Every ancient cult places great weight on the proper execution of all the prescribed details and finesse items. Nor will we go astray if we assume that most, if not all, of the old cultic songs were composed by men who belonged to the class of the temple singers. This class, after all, was involved with the cultic songs.

We know from the ancient Near East, however, that writing was attributed then to special inspiration. The poet was a divinely inspired person who had received a "supernatural" gift. We know from many indications that ancient Israel also shared this belief. The poet and the prophet were particularly close to one another then. The *nābî'* was always also a poet. In ancient times, his oracles always had rhythmic and metrical form (see the Balaam oracle and the blessings of Jacob and Moses). The ancient victory hymn in Judg 5 has been attributed to the prophetess Deborah. Only someone gifted prophetically could have composed such a song—so it was thought. Just as the prophet could see distant and future matters even "with closed eyes" (Num 24:3), so that his closed eye is, in reality, the sole truly "open" eye (Num 24:4), and just as he can hear the secret divine and heavenly voices with his opened ears (1 Sam 9:15; Isa 22:14), the poet of Ps 19A has heard the heavenly hymn that "is without speech and without words and inaudible (for human ears)." Just as the prophet was translated through music to an inspired state (see above), so also the poet (Ps 49:2–5). His ear becomes receptive so that he can receive the secret wisdom (*ḥokmâ, māšāl, ḥîdôt*) that stems from the deity and communicate it to humanity. To the tones of the harp, he communicates his secret lore. This very prophetic consciousness speaks from the introductory words of this psalm. A *maśkîl* is itself a cultic song that stems from such unusual empowerment, "ability," and knowledge and that, as a result, also has the correct impact.[31] Thus we also understand when the Chronicler employs the word *nibbā'* of the cultic functions of the singers (1 Chr 25:1–3) or even calls the singers *nĕbî'îm* (1 Chr 25:1, *ketiv*):[32] the singers themselves are prophetically gifted and exercise their art by virtue of prophetic inspiration.

If this is true, we should also suspect that the liturgies that evidence a prophetic consciousness in the specific sense of the word and that communicate direct divine revelations also originated among the temple singers. Conversely, however, there were also usually singers who appeared in the cult as inspired persons, as cultic prophets—or perhaps more correctly, who were obligated to appear as such on certain occasions. Indeed, as such they had the gift of singing and composing, that is, the gift of inspiration, of being possessed by the spirit, of prophecy. For ancient Israel, this was just as self-evident as it was for Mohammed: whoever can compose is inspired and can also prophesy under certain circumstances.

This conjecture is confirmed in the sources. The cultic prophet mentioned above, Oziel ben Zechariah, was a descendant of Asaph, according to 2 Chr 20:14; that is, he was one of the temple singers. Even the fact that we have so many prophetic psalms among the temple songs (see below) confirms that a close connection existed between psalmody and temple prophecy.

We have another source that confirms the connection between prophets, temple singers and psalmists: the book of Habakkuk. I place less weight here on the fact that Habakkuk was apparently a person very familiar with cultic psalmody and its forms. I only mention here that the first two chapters of his book have not only adopted isolated motifs from psalmody but appear in the form of a liturgy of lament and repentance with a complaint (1:2: "How long, YHWH?"), a description of the crisis (1:3–4), the honor motif (1:12–13), assurance of being heard (2:5–20), and a divine response (2:1–4), so that the attempt has even been made to understand the two chapters not as a prophecy with lament motifs but, conversely, as a repentance liturgy significantly influenced by the style and conceptual world of the prophets and composed by a prophet. More important in this context, however, is the fact that Hab 3 is an authentic psalm so markedly influenced by prophecy that is was surely composed by a *nābî'* (see 3:16). This psalm was used in the cult and was probably also written for cultic use—the cultic and liturgical information in verses 1 and 19 (see also 3:3, 9, 13) demonstrates this for us.

In terms of genre, the psalm is to be regarded as a mixture of prophecy and psalm of confidence. It begins as a psalm of confidence (3:2). The poet's

---

31. See *Psalm Studies* 4.
32. There is no need to alter the *ketiv* in these passages.

confidence rests both on YHWH's former mighty deeds (v. 2b) and especially on the fact that he has received a revelation (v. 16). The content of this revelation is communicated in verses 3–15. At the same time, however, we learn from this that the intention of the psalm is not that of a psalm of confidence in general. The declaration of confidence is based in a particular situation of distress in which the people and king, the whole "congregation," find themselves (vv. 12–14). Beneath the confidence, the request for help in distress sounds clearly and notably. The psalm intends to be a confident petition, a *tĕpillâ* (v. 1). The revelation received is not communicated directly here as a response to a request for transmission to the community; rather, in the form of a description of YHWH's coming to help, the poet expresses his thankful "assurance of being heard." The description, which speaks of YHWH in the third person at the beginning, shifts into the second person in verse 8, intensifying the impression that the description evokes, namely, that it was meant to have the effect of a confidence motif and an "assurance of being heard." All YHWH's great saving acts in ancient times and in the present, including those now expected, flow together here into one so that the question as to whether the prophet describes past or future should actually not even be raised. The poet wants to say, "You, who always do such things, will also surely save your people and its anointed this time." YHWH's intervention here is depicted in the conceptual forms of the enthronement myth: appearance for battle, battle with the primordial sea, new creation (the current time of distress is a time of chaos, of *tōhû wābōhû*, v. 17), "myth of the battle against the nations," deliverance from distress (see *Psalm Studies* 2, part 1, §2.1). The psalm concludes with the explicitly stated assurance of being heard and the anticipatory statement of thanks (vv. 18–19), as is so often the case in lament psalms and liturgies for days of prayer.

The *nābî'* Habakkuk is cited as the composer of this psalm, the same man whose prophecies in chapters 1–2 are so markedly influenced by psalm style, and there is hardly any reason to doubt the accuracy of this information. During my proofreading of this work, I first became aware of an essential confirmation of my hypothesis concerning the relationship between (temple) prophets and Levites, or singers. The superscript (v. 1) of the LXX legend of Bel and the Dragon contains a tradition concerning the genealogy of the prophet Habbukuk. He is called Αμβακουμ υἱοῦ Ἰησοῦ ἐκ τῆς φυλῆς Λευι. This is the very Habakkuk in which I found testimony to the accuracy of my view based solely on the nature of the prophecy attributed to him! The comment in LXX derives, naturally, from some midrash on Habakkuk or from an apocalypse circulating under his name. This does exclude the possibility that even such a document could have contained an accurate tradition concerning the prophet's father and profession. In actuality, there is very little reason to doubt the accuracy of the tradition. The psalm must be preexilic in any case, because it presupposes an anointed one, a king of Israel (v. 13). The distress of which the poet thinks is, thus, Assyrian domination. In the advance of the Chaldeans he sees the signs of the approaching great day of YHWH,[33] of the day of judgment and the day of the enthronement of Israel's God. We must imagine that the people, the "righteous"—Habakkuk is a nationalist prophet, probably sympathetic with Deuteronomisticism—encouraged on some occasion by the signs of the time, arranged a day of prayer in order to pray for the end of Assyrian domination, particularly despised after the Josianic reform. There may have been some particular political reason for doing so. On this occasion, the temple prophet and psalmist Habakkuk, who, accordingly, may have been one of the singers, composed the psalms (or one of them) to be performed and in it promised his people YHWH's assistance. The psalm was sung during one of the associated cultic proceedings as a psalm of petition with the intention "of putting YHWH in a gracious mood" (*lmnṣḥ*, actually, "in order to make [YHWH's countenance] radiant," see *Psalm Studies* 4).

If one wanted to deny the accuracy of the tradition in verse 1, one could object that the verse is still probative for our main thesis, because it demonstrates, in any case, that it was considered natural to find the poet of a prophetic cultic psalm among the *nĕbî'îm*. One would hardly do so if, in reality, such were not to occur with some frequency.

The book of Joel also points in the same direction. Here, too, the same mixture of psalm and prophetic style appears. Gunkel is probably correct that the first two chapters of the book "contain a liturgy performed in relation to a great plague of locusts."[34]

---

33. In this interpretation of the book of Habakkuk, I agree fully with Budde.
34. Gunkel, "Psalmen: 4," *RGG* 4:1934.

2

THE INDIVIDUAL PSALMS

2.1. Prophecies for the Great New Year's Festival

In *Psalm Studies* 2 I attempted to demonstrate that New Year's Day was celebrated in ancient Israel as the day of YHWH's enthronement. This day was one of the grand, apparently week-long, annual celebrations out of which the three independent festivals of New Year's, Atonement, and Booths later developed (in post-Deuteronomic times). Every New Year's Day, YHWH repeated his accession to the throne with all its real effects. In the ecstatic and shared events of the festival that greatly moved souls, one experienced YHWH's arrival, the bestowal of divine power, and the pledge of a blessed year bringing well-being in every respect.

A plethora of religious concepts, expectations, myths, and practices were entwined around YHWH's enthronement. Since cult in general is the repetition and revival of the fundamental saving realities, the entry into covenant that is the source of blessing, everything that happened when YHWH first ascended the throne and became king recurred on New Year's Day in the imaginations of the pious. He became king when he conquered chaos, divided the sea, and created the world. He repeated these acts when he conquered Egypt, divided the Reed Sea, "created" his people's world in Canaan, and entered into covenant with them. He repeated them when he made a covenant with David and chose Jerusalem as his dwelling "forever." Alternatively, the battle with chaos was imagined as a battle against human enemies who had attacked YHWH's city, whom YHWH vanquished and destroyed at the last moment, whereupon he established his kingdom of peace. YHWH's accession is an act of "judging." On that day, he "judges" the world, "vindicates" Israel, and "condemns" his opponents. Thus the day was conceived as a great day of judgment. Although the judgment and battle concepts intermingled, judgment became punishment. Thus one spoke of a judgment both on the gods and on the nations. For Israel, however, YHWH's advent meant deliverance from all distress, salvation, good fortune, wealth, fertility, victory, fame, and dominion over the nations. In YHWH's kingdom, Israel was to be the ruling people, YHWH's officials.

Thus the content of the day was envisioned as follows: YHWH comes, he reveals himself, greeted by the jubilation of nature and of the pious. He engages in battle against the enemies—in praxis, Israel's contemporary enemies and competitors—or cites them from his bench. The pagans and their gods are condemned, "shamed," at least "ideally," "in principle." Complete actualization will take place in the course of the year—that is, if Israel does not, as it has so often before, delay salvation through its sinfulness. In triumph, YHWH now marches to his palace, the temple on Zion, ascends to his throne, and is paid homage by his subjects. He determines the fate of the coming period. He makes a new covenant with his people in which he avouches them all salvation if they keep his commandments and walk "justly" according to his will. He "judges" the world, that is, puts it in a state of order corresponding to the "righteousness" rooted in the covenant.

Cultically, this matter of faith was not celebrated in the grand royal procession we learn something about from the description in 2 Sam 6. The ark was brought up to Zion in procession. YHWH's entry was portrayed dramatically through symbols and sacred acts, through the sacred "drama" of the cultic procession. The king, the priests, and the whole people were present and participated in the "cultic dance." Prophetic voices were raised, sacrifices were brought, hymns were sung, prayers prayed. The horns blared, the sacred temple music resounded. Ecstatic festival joy empowered the participants. In this psychic experience, they were assured of the reality of YHWH's gracious arrival.

A whole series of psalms—the enthronement psalms and among them several "prophetic" psalms—can be understood in relation to this situation.

Psalms 132; 89:29–38; 81; 95; 50; 82; 75; 87; 85; 14; and 12 will be treated here. Most of them have already been extensively analyzed in *Psalm Studies* 2 and will only be treated briefly here.

*

We begin with a few oracles incorporated into a more hymnic context. Other psalms, in which the oracle appears more directly as the divine response to a communal request, will follow.

We will begin, however, with Ps 132, which, as a prayer liturgy, actually belongs to the second group, since it is very informative concerning the course of an important section of the enthronement festival.

The essential statements about Ps 132 have already been made in *Psalm Studies* 2, part 1, §2.3.3, 287–95. It represents the text of a minor dramatic act performed at the procession of the ark on the day of YHWH's enthronement festival. The play is a repetition of the first festival procession with the ark when David brought it to the place he had prepared as YHWH's dwelling. The reigning king played the role of David. The psalm begins with the choir of singers remembering David's vow: he swore not to go to bed until he had found YHWH's whereabouts, that is, the unknown location of the ark after the Philistine wars. Now his men who had been sent out come and report, "We have found it in the fields of Yaar." "The ark is already there. Now, let us go up to the sacred place where it will reside from now on! Let us go up and kneel at YHWH's feet," the choir sings in the name of the congregation. While singing a departure song reminiscent of Num 10:34, the procession departs to go up to the temple.

According to 2 Sam 5, sacrifice was made "every six steps" on the way.[1] This was very likely the practice during the festival procession. It seems likely that the prayer for the king, the anointed, was offered (v. 10) after this sacrifice. May YHWH not "turn away his face," meaning, may he look upon the king graciously and impart to him all his blessings. The divine response follows in verses 11–18, spoken in the usual style of the prophetic oracle and undoubtedly communicated through the mouth of a prophet officiating at the cultic procedure. Entirely in prophetic fashion, the speaker reports YHWH's decisions, communicating this decision verbally. Thus YHWH speaks here in the first person. We should probably imagine that the prophet communicated the results of the hieroscopy. As in Ps 110, YHWH's decision takes the form of an oath:

> YHWH has sworn a sure oath to David—he will not withdraw it:
> "I will place on your throne a son of your body,
> and if they observe my covenant, the commandments that I teach you,
> then your sons will sit on the throne forever."

---

[1]. Regarding the sacrifice during the procession after a certain number of steps, one may compare the report by Capt. A. F. P. Harcourt concerning the festival of Bhunda in Nirmand in northern India, which recurs every twelfth year: "On the great day of the fair the statue [of the god Parasurama] is taken to the *Akarah* [= "a small court-yard adjacent to the temple"] and allowed to remain there one hour while all worship. A procession then winds round the temple, *and every ten or twelve paces a goat, then a sheep, and then a pig are killed*" (cited according to J. Ph. Vogel, "Note on the Nirmand Mask Inscriptions," *AcOr* 1 [1923]: 236). The meaning of 2 Sam 6 may also be that after every sixth step sacrifice was made.

This promise is grounded in the fact that Zion is the dwelling chosen and desired by YHWH himself: because the king dwells on Zion, where YHWH also wishes to dwell, he will be blessed:[2]

> For YHWH has chosen Zion; he desired it for his dwelling:
> "Here is my home forever; I dwell here. I have desired it to be so."

Since David recognized this wish of YHWH and brought him and the ark that represents him to the chosen place, he earned an eternal reward. Expressed more primitively, he brought the source of power into his house and can draw blessing from it perpetually. Consequently, blessing also depends on everything connected with Zion; the whole people that gathers around Zion as its capital will receive the richest divine reward:

> I will richly bless its[3] fruit, satiate its poor with bread.
> I will clothe its priests in salvation; its devout will rejoice aloud!
> Here I will cause the horn of David to sprout;
> I will ignite the light of my anointed.
> His enemies I will cloth in shame; indeed, his crown will shine upon him."

Rich, blessed harvest, salvation-giving priests who always do what is "right" (see v. 9), who thus mediate the divine salvation about which the pious can always rejoice, a powerful, fortunate king from the never-extinguished seed of David, victory over all enemies, shame for opponents, glory and honor for the anointed—this is the content of the divine promise. It is actually a royal oracle but thereby and simultaneously an oracle for the people that rests in the shadow of the blessing king (see Lam 4:20) and is blessed in his blessing—blessing is never the possession of an individual; it is the common possession of the clan, of the "house," in which every individual has a part, but the chief part goes to the "father of the household," the agent of the covenant, the trunk of the tree, who allows the blessing to flow to all branches and twigs. Thus we have treated this oracle here as a background for all the subsequent festival oracles.

---

2. The dwelling of the king, who incorporates the people, on Zion is therefore a guarantee that the blessing will be given to the people. This element is important for understanding Ps 132:5.

3. Zion's.

The prophecy inserted in Ps 89:20–38 is probably a cultic oracle of the same type as Ps 132:11–18.

In terms of content, the psalm is a public song of lament in which the king appears as the representative of the people. The complaint concerns the fact that YHWH has rejected his anointed, dealt with him in wrath, broken the covenant with him, and trod upon his crown in the dust. YHWH has destroyed all his[4] fortifications and cities; that is, he permitted and enabled the enemies to destroy them. Now the king and the people he represents lie open to all plunderers. He is defeated in battle; his throne, as the hyperbole puts it, has been cast down to the ground; his scepter has been taken from him. YHWH has heaped dishonor and shame on him and thereby "shortened the days of his youth." Like anyone affected by shame in the ancient Near East, he feels as though he has approached death through the "humiliation" of defeat and the inherent implications that he has been declared unjust. Thus, the king, the anointed, complains that Israel and thus he, too, has been overrun by the enemies and has suffered a severe defeat in war.[5] As a motive for the request for help in this distress, the former mighty deeds of YHWH in the creation and the people's confidence, which is drawn from these mighty deeds and never ashamed, in the just and faithful God, who has so far been the protector of the anointed, the kings of Israel, are mentioned first (vv. 7–19). Second, the supplicant reminds YHWH of his covenant with the anointed David and the

---

4. It is simply incomprehensible to me how one can have understood the fact that the cities and fortifications are called "his," the anointed's, as sufficient evidence that the anointed is identical with the people. What monarch does not speak of "his" troops and cities?!

5. Attempts to explain the psalm as postexilic (Rudolf Smend, "Über das Ich der Psalmen," *ZAW* 8 [1888]: 5–60; Stade, *Biblische Theologie*; Baethgen, *Psalmen*; Wellhausen, *Bemerkungen*; Buhl, *Psalmerne*; Kittel, *Psalmen*; etc.) have utterly failed. The psalm does not presuppose the fall of the monarchy but a harsh defeat of the monarchy together with the people. Indeed, the king appears as the subject of the prayer. "The anointed" does not mean the people but the king, as always. The argument based on vv. 41–42 is invalid (see n. 4 above). It is true, however, that the concerns of the king and the concerns of the people are understood to be identical. They were also identified in the ancient Near East, however, especially in war, distress, and danger. The same is true of the parallelism between "I" and "your servants" in v. 51. It demonstrates nothing more than that the Israelites and their king find themselves in the same difficult situation and have common interests. The assumption some seek to derive from Isa 55 that "in later times" the promises to David were applied to the people as heirs is also false. Isa 55:3–4 speak of a renewal of the covenant with David. A reestablishment of the Davidic house is presupposed as self-evident (see my *Der Knecht Jahwäs* [Giessen: Töpelmann, 1921], 35).

promises included in them to all later kings of the house of David (vv. 20–38). The promise that YHWH is believed to have given the house of David through prophetic revelation is cited here.

This oracle exhibits far-reaching agreement with the promise in Ps 132:11–18. They even agree that it is not a promise to David as an isolated individual—in the Israelite understanding, there were no isolated individuals at all—but to King David as he continues to live and, according to the promise, will always live[6] in his house, in his seed, his royal successors on the throne. This supports the notion that the oracle is not a promise actually given to the historical David—an assumption that would not be impossible per se, for why should such an oracle not be preserved in the temple archive and taken up by a later poet?—but a promise that applies to David surviving in the respective ruling king.

Usually the oracle is considered a poetic fiction spun from 2 Sam 7 by a poet or a later interpolator.[7] The value, not to mention the necessity, of this assumption is difficult to see. In view of the formal and substantive agreement with Ps 132:11–18, it is much more reasonable to assume that the poet adapted a cultic oracle pertaining to the king as such and stemming from a liturgy similar to Ps 132 and inserted it into his psalm.

Two grounds support this explanation. First, the agreement with Ps 132 already mentioned. The two oracles agree with respect to David, alive in the reigning king, in promising the ruling house everlasting existence, everlasting good fortune, and the everlasting grace of God, in grounding this promise in God's election of the delightful patriarch, and further in promising him and his sons victory over their enemies, good fortune, and success, but in making the promise dependent on whether the sons keep YHWH's covenant and observe his commandments as their father had done. Psalm 89 goes beyond Ps 132 only in promising God's grace and mercy in the event that the sons sin and go astray. If this should occur, YHWH will discipline them graciously and thereby bring them to repentance, but he will not remove his grace. This last circumstance itself suggests that we are not dealing here with an oracle from David's time—that ancient time could not provide the preconditions for this case: either the sons must prove to be "true" sons of the father, or they drag the family along in their well-deserved demise. We could well be dealing,

---

6. Buhl (*Psalmerne*) would be correct were his statement that the anointed is "not a historical figure but a concept" (more correctly, a reality) "represented by David" to refer, not to vv. 39–45 but to vv. 20–38 This does not, however, imply that this "concept" is simply identical with the people.

7. Duhm, *Psalmen*; Briggs, *Psalms*; Gunkel, "Königspsalmen"; Emil Balla, *Das Ich der Psalmen* (FRLANT 16; Göttingen: Vandenhoeck & Ruprecht, 1912), etc.

however, with a cultic oracle, in all likelihood with a New Year's Festival oracle such as Ps 132:11–18. The content of Ps 89:20–38 would be thoroughly suited to such an occasion, as the parallel in Ps 132 demonstrates.[8]

The second factor supporting our understanding is literary. As many of the more recent exegetes have seen, much speaks for the notion that the psalm was not written *uno tenore*. First, the change in meter is noteworthy: verses 2–3 are 3 + 3; verses 4–5, 3 +3; verses 6–16, 4 + 4; verses 17–46, 3 + 3; verses 47–52, apparently also 3 + 3. In addition, there is the hymnic introduction in verses 2–3, very unusual for a lament psalm, and the no less unusual position of verses 4–5, which seem to be related to verses 20–38. Attempts to explain these peculiarities are even less satisfactory, however. Not just any expansion or interpolation hypothesis is satisfactory. In terms of content, the psalm is nonetheless unified and well-rounded (see above). The fact that former mighty deeds and promises of God are employed as the motivation for being heard is not strange at all. The broad execution of this motive is noteworthy, however. It suggests that the poet should not actually be regarded as a poet in our sense of the word but as a compiler, a redactor of a cultic liturgy, and that he adopted the two motives from older poems. The notion that the hymnic section in verses 6–16, written in 4 + 4 meter, along with the introduction in verses 2–3, hardly suited for a lament psalm, may have been adapted from an older hymn celebrating the wonders of YHWH's creation seems an especially illuminating assumption. As we have seen, the creation hymn in verses 6–16 gives way toward the end to a blessing of the people whose God is YHWH and expresses confidence in YHWH as the guardian of Israel and, in particular, of the anointed. The 3 + 3 meter begins precisely here in verse 17. The "then" (*'āz*), which is unprepared and has no referent, cannot have been the original continuation of the creation hymn. In fact, verse 20a looks redactional. The isolated section in verses 4–5 must also have stood in some original relationship to the oracle in verses 20–38. Only verses 39–52 refer to

---

8. My understanding of the relationship between 2 Sam 7 and Ps 89:20–38 finds confirmation, I believe, in Gressmann's idea (*Auswahl*, 138–39) that we have in 2 Sam 7:8–17 a redaction of an older "royal song, similar to those transmitted to us in the Psalms." Almost without exception, the older critics regard 2 Sam 7 as the original passage, as it were, from which the poetic promises to the house of David, and especially Ps 89, arose. For them, this was also evidence for the late origin of the psalm. If Gressmann is correct, however—and I definitely believe so—then this is evidence that there were old royal oracles such as Ps 89:20–38 and that 2 Sam 7 is secondary in relation to them. Then, however, the close affinities between Ps 89:20–38 and 2 Sam 7 are not to be explained in terms of the psalm borrowing from the prose text. Instead, Ps 89:20–38 offers us evidence of the genre on which 2 Sam 7 depends and which it imitated. Thus, there is no ground for considering the psalm dependent on 2 Sam 7.

the actual situation of the lament psalm. Accordingly, the development of the psalm should most likely be conceived as follows: the poet wanted to compose a lament psalm in the name of the king for a penitential ceremony on the occasion of a military defeat. He wanted to set as the background of the lament the former positive experiences and YHWH's promises in order to provide the request for help with impressive motivations. He looked around in the temple's psalm collection and chose a few building blocks for the composition, namely, a hymn to YHWH as the creator God and the King of Israel now ascending his throne (see *těrûʿâ*, v. 16, which refers to the "cry of royal affirmation" in the enthronement festival; cf. Num 23:21; cf. *Psalm Studies* 2:221) and a (New Year's Festival) oracle to the royal house. The beginning of the creation hymn (in 4 + 4 meter) must have constituted the beginning of the composition. In order to mediate the transition from the creation to the former promises to the king, he wrote verses 17–19, which express the confidence of the people and the king in YHWH. He capriciously employed the 3 + 3 meter more familiar to him, however. In order to prepare for the following section, the former promises, he shifted a few verses from the oracle, verses 4–5, to the beginning of the hymnic section. Then, as a direct transition to the second section, he wrote verse 20a, a somewhat limping 3 + 3 meter, and continued with the oracle in 3 + 3 meter (vv. 20b–38). Following it, he freely composed the lament concerning the horrible current situation (vv. 39–46), likewise in 3 + 3 meter. He also wrote the last section, the request with lament motives that refer to the current situation. Here, however, the 3 + 3 meter is somewhat halting and interchanges with seven beat sections, which may be attributable, however, to later insertions into the text.[9]

If this understanding of the composition of the psalm is correct, the oracle was one of the poet's exemplars. It lends probability to our assumption that it originated in a liturgy similar to Ps 132.

Just as the cult in general is an act of covenant-making and commemoration, the great, major annual festival, the enthronement festival, is a repetition of the covenant between God and people.[10]

Psalm 132 presupposed this idea of covenant renewal. The divine blessing is promised to the people based on the covenant made with David. This cov-

---

9. The *lāneṣaḥ* in v. 47 can be removed and may have been taken from Ps 74:1 (cf. 79:5). The *kol* in v. 48 is to be stricken with Jerome. The phrase *běnê ʾādām* often constitutes a metrical foot. The *ʾădōnāy* may be stricken in v. 5 and in v. 51. Instead of *kol-rabbîm* in v. 51, it may be that one should read *kělimmat*. The *běḥêqî* is an incorrect gloss. In v. 52, both instances of *ʾăšer* are superfluous.

10. See *Psalm Studies* 2, part 1, §3.1, 327–29.

enant with "David" is made today with his "son," the ruling king as the natural representative of the people (see 2 Kgs 23:3).

This covenant with David is itself a repetition of the Sinai covenant. Thus we see in other psalms related to the enthronement festival that the renewal of the covenant is traced back to the exodus and the Sinai covenant (as in the parallels Ps 81 and 95).

We have also treated these two psalms in *Psalm Studies* 2, part 1, §3.1. By all appearances, they were performed in the temple after the entry. Both divide into two parts: introductory hymn and prophecy. The hymn praises the God now enthroned in the temple, who resides with his people again, the king, the one who has come, the creator who creates once again, the God of salvation who has come again to save, to shepherd his flock faithfully and justly.

A covenant is a bi-lateral matter, however. As at Sinai, so now YHWH also has requirements of his people on which the covenant must be based. This is what he tells his people at this moment through a prophet.

We may imagine that a brief pause for meditation occurred when the introductory hymn was ended—a moment of heightened solemn expectation. The people may even have knelt in worship before the throne of their God (Ps 95:6). There, however, a voice was suddenly audible. A figure appears before the eyes of the congregation. It stands as though rapt yet intent, as though listening to voices that reach its ear from the distance:

> I hear a voice that I do not recognize.

What will this mysterious person have heard that the others could not hear? He suddenly knows. The unknown voice becomes clear words. They form into sentences—and now he shares with the people what he has heard. Immediately after the first words, "I took the burden from your back," the people know who speaks. The speaker is an inspired cultic prophet of YHWH. Through him, YHWH himself speaks to his people and presents his requirements to them. YHWH reveals himself through him. Consequently, he begins with a self-presentation: I am the same God who liberated you from Egypt, who revealed himself at Sinai:

> I took the burden from your back, the basket from your[11] hands;
> when you cried out in distress, I heard you,
> in the caves of the thunder, listening to you.

---

11. Read *šikmĕkā* and *kappêkā* in v. 7; see v. 8.

Now, as then, the covenant will be established. God lays down the same requirements today as then:

> Pay attention, my people, I will show you; O Israel, listen to me:
> You shall have no other god, and you shall not bow to strange gods!

As at Sinai, we also hear now the name of the one God whom Israel should worship:

> It is I who showed you, and wanted to show you, my wonders then;
> I am YHWH your God, who brought you out of Egypt;
> I tested you at Meriba:[12] "Put my gifts in your mouth!"

The call to give heed already subtly alluded to the fact that Israel sometimes did not want to take instruction in past times. Now YHWH recalls the rebelliousness that Israel had already shown in the wilderness when YHWH first made his covenant with them. The covenant was broken then by Israel's sin and disobedience:

> Yet my people did not listen to me; no, Israel did not follow me.
> Then I abandoned the obdurate; they followed their own mind.

This suggests indirectly that since then they have often behaved in this fashion. YHWH has often graciously renewed the covenant, and each time Israel has broken it. Inherent in this idea is YHWH's theodicy in relation to the intense expectations of the festival. The sins of the people—or of certain individuals among the people—is the reason "the kingdom of YHWH" was unable to be fully effective in the course of the past year. How will it go this time? Should this not be the last? Should it not be possible now to make an enduring covenant? If that could only happen! Then the time of salvation, of eternal good fortune, would come for Israel, for the one who offers his covenant and his favor is YHWH, after all, the unique, the powerful, the gracious, the bestower of all blessing. Consequently, he now urgently admonishes:

> O that my people would only listen to me,
> that Israel would walk on my path;
> I would then soon bow his enemies and stretch my hand over them.

---

12. Transpose v. 8b before 11b with Duhm (*Psalmen*).

Today, however, YHWH may hope to find an obedient people. Consequently, the wish transforms into the cautious form of the promise:

YHWH's enemies will flatter him;
their time of forced labor should endure forever.
I will "satiate" him[13] with the power of the wheat
and nourish with honey from the rock!

The fact that we deal here not with free inspiration in the moment, outside the liturgical program, as it were, but with a regular element "tied to the order of worship" that only imitates the form of free inspiration, is suggested by the fact that we have precisely the same liturgical outline, the same ideas, the same arrangement, and to a degree some of the same expressions, only somewhat more briefly formulated, in Ps 95. Festival practice includes this element of the proclamation of these or very similar words by a prophet.

*

The belief that the YHWH who revealed himself in the festival reminds the people in a rebuke of their former unfaithfulness and admonishes them to faithfulness to the covenant and obedience, to fear of God and righteousness, has close affinities with another idea associated with this same festival, the judgment idea (see below on Ps 82). The admonition is an entry into judgment—just as any procedure that aims at the maintenance of the proper order, at the reestablishment of the internal and external "righteousness" of the people or of an individual, including good fortune, is a "judging" *mišpāṭ*.[14]

The judgment idea was developed forensically with specific reference to the nations. In principle, it is only a special form of the concept of the punishment of the enemies of YHWH and Israel. The concept of YHWH's admonition of the people is also combined with this judgment idea in the sense of punishment, discipline. Thus we also find in connection with the enthronement festival the idea that the coming, the appearance of YHWH in all his glory, is a "judgment" (*dîn*), indeed, a punitive and purifying judgment (*tôkaḥat*)—not just on the pagans but also on Israel (see *Psalm Studies* 2, part 1, §2.1.5). Here the later eschatological judgment ideas of the major prophets may have also played a role (see *Psalm Studies* 2:252–54; cf. 333). Thus the prophetic admonition attained the form of a judgment, that is, a chastisement

---

13. I.e., Israel.
14. See Pedersen, *Israel*, 348–52.

and admonition, and the coming of YHWH was described in the introduction to the statement, not as a coming of the king to ascend the throne, as had originally been the case, but as an appearance of the judge to judge.

Psalm 50 is to be understood on the basis of this assumption.[15]

---

15. Belatedly, I note in a passage in Carl Steuernagel's *Lehrbuch der Einleitung in das Alte Testament mit einem Anhang über die Apokryphen und Pseudepigraphen* (STL; Tübingen: Mohr Siebeck, 1912), 726–27, that tradition attests the affiliation of Ps 50 to the fall festival. According to the Talmud, Ps 50:16–23 was sung to accompany the Musaf sacrifice on the third day of the Festival of Booths. The Festival of Booths, however, is the true heir of the grand Fall and New Year's Festival that was simultaneously understood as the enthronement festival. The relationship to the Musaf sacrifice and the division of the psalm may be secondary. How would one have thought to associate Ps 50:16–23 with the Festival of Booths, however, if there had not already been some traditional connection between this psalm and this festival? Otherwise, nothing in these verses points to the Festival of Booths in the restricted sense. The actual relationship will be precisely that indicated in the text above whether the psalm was preexilic and was composed for the still united Fall and New Year's Festival or postexilic and meant for the Festival of Booths that still retained many of the concepts of YHWH's coming to ascend the throne (see *Psalm Studies* 2:260–68, 380–85).

Furthermore, I have something more to include here. I have heard from various quarters from my honored colleagues, sometimes by letter and sometimes orally, that in *Psalm Studies* 2 I have not assured the relationship of the enthronement songs to a specific festival understood as an enthronement festival. They agree fully with the interpretation of these psalms by means of the concept of God's enthronement. On this point, it should be said, first, that I have not postulated the festival in question. The well-known fall festival is involved. I have, however, attempted to demonstrate that notions concerning the coming of God to ascend the throne have also become associated with this festival. At the same time, the festival was the enthronement festival and was, indeed, celebrated with a procession involving the ark. Second, it would be more than a remarkable coincidence if those psalms that the talmudic tradition associates with the Festival of Booths and the New Year's Festival—and, without question, the old fall festival combined these two elements—are only those psalms that I defined as enthronement psalms in the broad sense and, as such, were associated with the fall festival. When I wrote *Psalm Studies* 2 (as can be seen on 261), I was aware only of the talmudic tradition concerning Pss 47 and 81. Later I became aware of the passage in Steuernagel (which can also be found in Buhl's commentary on the Psalms, but which I did not notice) and was led thereby to Jacob's investigations in *ZAW* 1896 and 1897. The Talmud associates the following psalms with the Festival of Booths: 29; 47; 50; 65; 81; 82; 94; 118 (b. Sukkah 53a); and the *ma'ălôt* [ascent] psalms. I have associated all of these psalms, with the sole exception of 94, with the fall festival. Can this concurrence depend solely on coincidence? That would be an entirely remarkable coincidence! What would have motivated later Judaism to connect Pss 29 and 82 with the Festival of Booths if there had been no related tradition or if the ideas that these psalms express, the idea of God's kingship, royal judgment, and enthronement (29:10), had not belonged to the Festival of Booths, i.e., if this festival itself had not also been understood as YHWH's royal festival?

The situation is YHWH's advent, an appearance in the temple in Jerusalem, whence his glory and majesty radiates over the earth. The poet betrays clearly enough the origin of his concept of the theophany situation. His introduction seems to be purely citations from enthronement psalms. YHWH appears on "Zion, the crown of beauty" (see Ps 48:3), the fire consuming before him (see Ps 97:3); he calls heaven and earth to witness (see Ps 97:4; the world as spectator of his majesty); reminiscent of the establishment of the covenant, he calls the people who are supposed to assemble before him and "be judged" now "those who make a covenant with me concerning sacrifices," and he reports the execution of the charge addressed to heaven and earth to invite the people to judgment in the following words. They are a somewhat unclear paraphrase of the words in Ps 19:2 and are also used in the enthronement psalm Ps 97:6:

Then the heavens announced his righteousness, that God is the judge.

All these allusions make it clear that the poet thought of YHWH's appearance in the temple in Zion at the enthronement festival to renew the covenant with the people and that he regarded this judgment scene as equivalent to YHWH's admonition at the establishment of the covenant.

Let me add that based precisely on this tradition, I am convinced that Ps 94 stands at the very center of the explicit enthronement psalms in the narrow sense and also belonged among the enthronement festival psalms. The psalm is not, in fact, an individual psalm, as I still thought in *Psalm Studies* 1. The demons and magicians about which it complains do not come under consideration here as oppressors of the individual but as afflicters of the people, i.e., as a universal evil (see vv. 5–6). The first-person subject here is the representative of the community. This style has a cultic and liturgical explanation: an individual steps forward and prays as the representative of the others, a role that in actual life the king probably exercised sometimes and the supreme (high) priest sometimes. To this extent, the older critical interpreters and, most recently, in the second edition of his Psalms commentary, Buhl have viewed this psalm more correctly than I. As a community prayer at the annual festival for protection against and the eradication of the sorcerers and demons (see *Psalm Studies* 1:68–70), Ps 94 should be associated with Pss 12; 14; 125; and 120 (see *Psalm Studies* 2:346–50 and below, 553–56). The divine designation in v. 2, "judge of the earth," points to the relationship of Ps 94 to the enthronement festival (see *Psalm Studies* 2:245, 254, 341, 343–44), as does the association of the apostrophized enemies with the powers of the underworld, i.e., chaos, in v. 20. The foundation of YHWH's kingship was, after all, his victory over those powers (see *Psalm Studies* 2:224–30).

In terms of content, the psalm has a rather didactic stamp, such that even Staerk included it, not entirely without justification, among the didactic songs.[16] Sacrifice constitutes the topic of instruction.

The psalm is not acultic, let alone anticultic. Admittedly, its stance is somewhat reserved regarding the value of sacrifice—but sacrifice is only one detail of the cult. In the view of the poet, even the sacrificial cult is necessary and justified because it is one of YHWH's commandments (see v. 16b)[17]— here, the poet's Jewish, probably postexilic, understanding is evident. Admittedly, the best sacrifice is the song of praise or the psalm of petition, if one is in distress, the psalm of thanksgiving if one has been delivered (vv. 15, 23). He knows something even more valuable than sacrifice, however, not that sacrifice is without value: the moral commandments that pertain to everyday life. His view of morality and sacrifice has been summarized briefly such that the one must be practiced without abandoning the other (see v. 8; if sacrifice had been disposable, he could not have God say, "I do not reprove you for your sacrifice, which you bring bounteously"). This concept of sacrifice has probably been influenced by the major prophets. It is significant, however, to find it represented in a cultic psalm and thus also by the temple personnel. Just as it was probably the priests who represented the overestimation of sacrifice, so is it the self-awareness and the religious assessments of the singers (and poets) who see the psalm as the true, best sacrifice.[18]

The polemic against the overestimation of sacrifice is rather vulgarly rationalist, even though the poet also occasionally found poetically spirited expressions for his ideas. Admittedly, God commanded sacrifice, and because of this commandment the poet need not reprimand the people; they make more than enough sacrifices. They forget, however, that God does not need sacrifice, for all the animals of the field and the forest and the flocks are his. Besides, God does not grow hungry; he does not drink the blood of the stag or eat the flesh of bulls. The best sacrifices are the psalm of petition and thanksgiving.

The poet clothed this instruction concerning sacrifice, prayer, and morality in the form of YHWH's cultic revelation for judgment on New

---

16. Willy Staerk, "Lyrik," in vol. 3.1 of *Die Schriften des Alten Testaments in Auswahl* (7 vols.; Göttingen: Vandenhoeck & Ruprecht, 1910–1915).

17. The commandments that the people have on their tongues (strike the awkward gloss in v. 16a with Duhm, *Psalmen*; and others) are the sacrifice commandments, in whose fulfillment they find comfort while rejecting the (actual and most important) commandments.

18. We know from Josephus that the priests and singers viewed each other with jealousy and that the singers ultimately obtained the rank of priest.

Year's Day—and I see no reason why he should not have meant his psalm for cultic use.

Instead of the admonition before the establishment of the covenant, he included a chastisement and an exhortation that he gave the name "judgment." Here we can easily see, however, that the judgment idea replaces the admonition to covenant fidelity in an only apparently inorganic manner. Despite the grandiose introduction and the ostentatious preparations for a grand judgment scene, there comes no actual judgment, only a chastisement and exhortation, an instruction concerning the relative value of sacrifice, an admonition to virtue and purity—in brief, YHWH appears and is satisfied with a reprimand instead of judgment.

Indeed, YHWH speaks harsh words against the people who, mollified by the sacrifice, consider themselves faithful to the law. They "count off YHWH's commandments and speak of his law," yet "hate his discipline and cast away his words." He accuses the people of tolerating thieves and adulterers in their midst; the people "walk with them and befriend them," he says harshly. He holds the people responsible for the evil words (of magic)[19] spoken in their midst: "your mouth indulges in evil; your tongue braids lies; you speak shameful things against your brother and insult the son of your mother." Despite the harsh words, it is still only a chastisement and warning. We hear nothing about YHWH really intervening against the evildoers and sinners. It is left to the people to exercise discipline in their own house and to remove the sinners from their midst—otherwise, things will go badly for them. YHWH does not tolerate such and will not keep silent about it.

The whole speech ends with a promise to the righteous. As an example of righteousness, verse 23 mentions singing psalms of thanksgiving, which is remarkable for a poet who does not value the sacrificial cult very highly. Despite all of this, his piety still involves much cultic piety. Thus, the poet-prophet has surrendered entirely to the old notion of the situation, the notion of the establishment of the covenant. Much as does Ps 81 and originally probably also Ps 95, he concludes with the conditional promise "whoever is just"[20]—or, in Ps 95, whoever has kept my commandments—"I will permit to see my salvation." Despite the "judgment," the covenant is reestablished, naturally, on the condition that Israel keep the law of God.

Judgment here is not to be taken so dreadfully seriously, then, as one might expect from the pompous introduction. There is no discussion of a judgment

---

19. For the meaning of the "evil tongue" and the "lying word," see *Psalm Studies 1*, §§1.7 and 2.6.

20. Read *wĕtam derek*.

such as Amos of Jeremiah might intend. The proclamation of punishment is ultimately rather promising. The prophet speaks of a judgment; his ideas range within the concept of the renewal of the covenant and the divine admonition customary on this occasion.

The poet is morally sober and idealistic. The commandments are to be observed—indeed, all of God's commandments, not just the simpler and the more external. He is concerned above all with a pure community. For him, the fact that the community tolerates evildoers in its midst, "runs with them and befriends them," is the great offense. If that does not change, the wrath of God will flare up without mercy. The poet is an optimist at the same time, however. Moral sobriety does not make him a prophet of judgment. He believes that an admonition will attain the objective. Above all, God is a gracious God, the God of salvation. Indeed, he comes to save when he reveals himself on New Year's Day—despite the form of the judgment scene.

The psalm is prophetic both in terms of form and content. The form is the old form of divine speech. In content, the poet betrays the prophetic consciousness to the extent that, for him, it is such a certain reality and not fiction that he presents YHWH as the speaker. He offers his very personal, if not original, ideas, and he is convinced that they are divinely inspired. Admittedly, we may not forget that he intended to compose for a very specific place in the liturgy and in a sense entirely determined by tradition. Such divine words should resound at the festival. One who could combine them in a psalm was proven by that very capability to be inspired by God. His authorization as a cultic prophet, as an inspired temple singer, was already inherent in his psalm's agreement with ancient sacred tradition.

Even though the psalm is also "prophetic," however, this does not mean that it can only be understood in relation to the thought world of the so-called major judgment and writing prophets. In the main, it stems from the conceptual forms and ideas of a cultic situation. Even in the condemnation of sacrifice, it differs significantly from an Amos, an Isaiah, or a Micah. They rejected external cultic procedures as they were generally practiced at the time, "the blubbering of the songs" no less than the smoking sacrifice (Isa 1:10–17; Amos 5:21–23). In contrast, our poet finds the cultic songs (and probably the related rites) beautiful and pleasing to God, the sacrifice, indeed, necessary, because they were obligatory, but not as valuable as the songs. To this degree, our psalm shares the standpoint of Pss 40; 51; and 69. It may be that the influence of the "prophetic," that is, of Amos's, preaching is evident here. The piety of our psalm is, nonetheless, temple piety, cultic piety. Thus, nothing prohibits the assumption that Ps 50 was composed in the circles of the temple singers and for cultic use.

Psalm 82 bears a certain similarity with Ps 50 in terms of arrangement and composition. Like Ps 50, Ps 82 also begins with an introduction that depicts the phenomenon of YHWH's theophany, although it actually only states the fact (v. 1):

> God (already) stands in the council of the gods;
> [YHWH] judges in the circle of the divine.[21]

There follow the words that he spoke upon his appearance—these, too, as in Ps 50, in the form of words of judgment. The difference with Ps 50 consists: (1) in the fact that in Ps 82 the gods of the world are the object of judgment, rather than Israel, as in Ps 50; and (2) in the fact that the judgment here is meant with all gravity and culminates in the proclamation of the death sentence for the gods. Judgment, conceived forensically here, is not understood as the intensification of an admonition and rebuke on the occasion of the covenant ceremony, but as a specifically Israelite form of the helpful activity of God. This activity maintains the covenant and the moral order of the world ($ṣedeq$) also expressed in the battle against, the "punishment" of, and the destruction of the powers hostile to the covenant, the covenant people, and their "rights." "Delivering" ("helping") and "judging" are synonymous ideas in Israelite thought. By helping and delivering (bringing salvation to) his people, YHWH "judges" both his people and its enemies. If attention is directed to the last point, the (punitive and destructive) judging of the enemies, and the idea is extended from the obvious forensic perspective, one immediately thinks of a particular act of YHWH that occurred under specific circumstances, such as the salvific appearance of God to ascend the throne, assume his reign, and vanquish his enemies—the "judgment myth" in the proper, forensic sense. I analyzed this origin of the judgment myth and its connection with the enthronement festival in *Psalm Studies* 2, part 1, §2, 245–57.

I also considered the content of Ps 82 and determined its relationship to the festival; I refer to the treatment there. Here mention will be made only of the fact that the psalm is apparently to be understood as a prophetic promise belonging to the fixed ritual of the festival, cast in the form of the prophetic chastisement and threat with sentence, mediated in the voice of a cultic minister. The content of the promise is condemnation (already underway in the

---

21. The oracles consist of 3 + 3 meter, each linked into strophes. The concluding prayer in v. 8 is 4 + 4, which may also be observed in the introduction, v. 1.

heavenly council while God ascends to the throne) of the cosmic powers that stand in the way of Israel's "right" and "salvation" and good fortunes, the gods of the pagan nations dethroned in Yahwism. In this form of the judgment myth, these gods have assumed the role of the chaotic power, "Rahab's helpers," in the creation myth (see v. 5). They became the destroyers of the cosmic order. If the primordial sea dragon once attacked the world and threatened thereby to return the cosmos to chaos—a "historification" of the chaos-creation myth known both in Babylonia and Israel and implied in and with the concept of the repetition of the saving realities—then the "gods" have now caused the pillars of the earth to totter again through their unjust rule ("false judging"). In and with YHWH's enthronement and his taking possession of all the countries and peoples of the earth (v. 8), however, the judicial proceedings and the condemnation of these powers take place in the heavenly council. We might say that the gods were already judged "ideally" and "in principle." For the community celebrating the festival, then, the oracle of this psalm contains God's comforting and uplifting promise. The gods are already judged. The faith of the community adds: we, the righteous, the people of YHWH, will experience the saving effects of this judgment in the course of the year just beginning. Consequently, the psalm also concludes with a request: may YHWH, who has now taken possession of the nations, arise and (henceforth) "judge" the earth, that is, execute the sentence through his active rule, restore order, "establish" justice, and assert Israel's rights.

*

The oracle in Ps 75 also deals with judgment against Israel's enemies. The enemies here are not the gods, however, but the pagan nations. Both the historical and political conditions in Canaan-Syria and the ever-increasing exclusivity of Israelite religion resulted in the fact that Israel's neighbors were almost always considered to be enemies. Israel lived in a world of enemies. The nations in general, the community of nations in general, are hostile to Israel. Protection against them, victory over them (*yĕšûʿâ*) became the first requirement for religion, for YHWH. We have seen in *Psalm Studies* 2 that, in addition to the chaos battle myth, the "battle against the nations myth" functioned as the festival myth of the enthronement festival. The precondition for YHWH's coming to rule is that the empirical world has again become a chaos of nations in which the pagan powers want to eradicate the righteous, the people of Israel, just as once the chaos dragon, the primordial sea, threatened the order of the cosmos. YHWH establishes the ground for his rule by once again forming a cosmos from this chaos, by reestablishing the moral order (*ṣedeq*), by defeating and destroying the pagan nations who have already attacked Jerusalem or who plan to (Pss 46; 48; 76), or as the judgment myth puts it: judges them. The battle against the nations myth and the judgment myth are only two forms of the same expectation, and both are rooted in the same cultic experiences and realities. The topic of the promise in Ps 75 is that this condemnation and punishment are to occur.

Like Pss 81 and 95, the psalm begins with a brief thanksgiving hymn. The precondition is that YHWH has now come (see Ps 76:2–4, which is related in content to Ps 75). Soon, therefore, the community may expect the great act of salvation that lays the foundation for his enduring rule. In advance, it sings the thanksgiving hymn to him for this:

> We thank you, O God, yes, we thank you—
> those who confess your name[22] recount your wonders.

As in Pss 81 and 95, the cultic prophet then steps forward and proclaims in mysterious, suggestive words the great, imminent—or perhaps better, immediate—wondrous acts of God. Through his mouth, YHWH himself speaks:

> "When I take the time, I will judge you righteously;
> the earth and its inhabitants may waver—I will establish your pillars firmly.
> I will say to the boastful, 'Do not boast!' to the evildoers, 'Do not raise the horn!
> Do not raise your horn aloft; do not speak impudently against 'the rock'!' "[23]

The relationship of the evildoers and fools to the "gods" in Ps 82 and the chaos monsters in the Tiamat myth still shines through in verse 4. Through their boastful and impudent behavior, the hostile powers have very nearly made a chaos of the cosmos; the pillars of the earth have been shaken. Now, however, YHWH comes to judge the righteous. He ends the fools' boasting and the evildoers' impertinence. Who can run headlong against the rock and come away without a cracked skull?

In what follows the prophet illuminates these mysterious words of the oracle. Subtly, YHWH's speech evolves into prophetic speech. Now comes the turn of events, for YHWH has already seized rule. No other powers of the world, neither human nor divine, can do anything at all. "Judging," worldwide rule in the full sense, is a matter reserved to YHWH alone:

---

22. Read *qōrĕ'ê bĕšîmĕkā*, BHK.
23. Read *baṣṣûr*, BHK following LXX.

Neither from east nor west, neither from the steppe nor "the mountains"[24]—
it is God who "judges"; he humbles one and elevates the other.

He will also take the government in his hands, and Israel already knows how the immediate future will take shape then:

For YHWH has a cup full of sparkling wine, full of intoxicating mixed drink,
and he gives it to one [after the other]; they must gulp it down to the dregs.[25]

The prophet may assume that all the details of the myth are known. He need not say here who the enemies, the rĕšāʿîm, are. We know from prophetic usage, however, that we have a form of the judgment myth before us, that the enemies are the nations of the earth (Jer 25:15–38), and that the concept of the poisonous cup as the penalty for those condemned to death lies in the background. Before the eyes of the prophet—and in the belief of the whole listening congregation—YHWH already stands with the poison cup in his hand and sends it to one after the other of the hostile nations. YHWH has come; the cup is already in his hand—therefore, the congregation rejoices and already sings the thanksgiving song. Just as the oracle is introduced by a hymn, so the choir of the congregation, the righteous (v. 11), enters, now that the prophet is silent, with a triumphant hymn inspired by the high emotions of the divine power already at work in the congregation, a hymn that expresses confidence in future victory and superiority:

I, however, will evermore "rejoice" and sing to the God of Jacob,
who smote the horns of the evildoers—
may the horn of the righteous rise high!

Why this psalm should be "eschatological" in the usual sense and not have its place in the cult is simply incomprehensible. Naturally, one need not assume that all the judgment oracles treated here were always announced sequentially on enthronement day. A degree of freedom must have governed the choice of oracle psalm for the day. It is, indeed, altogether unlikely that all the psalms we treated in *Psalm Studies* 2 as belonging to the enthronement festival were always performed at the same time in the festival. Various

---

24. Read ûmĕhārîm, BHK.
25. The last four words in v. 8 are a gloss.

times may have preferred and emphasized various forms of the myth and, accordingly, preferred and produced different psalms. I do not exclude the possibility that, given its ideas and the origin of the myth it reflects, Ps 75 belonged to the enthronement festival; in terms of its cultic function and use, however, it may have belonged to some other festival occasion. That is, I consider it possible that the psalm has quite specific historical enemies in view and was composed for a day of prayer preceding some war. If this should be the case, then a form of the enthronement myth will have been applied to a historical situation here. The oracle would then be intended to promise the people YHWH's royal and judicial appearance as the pledge of victory in the imminent war (see Ps 60). Even in this case, the psalm should be interpreted in terms of the cult and is incomprehensible without taking into account the enthronement festival and myth.

*

As we have seen in *Psalm Studies* 2, the idea of Jerusalem-Zion as the divine city and world capital plays a prominent role. One form of the enthronement myth, the "myth of the battle against the nations," recounts that YHWH lays the foundation for his reign and demonstrates himself to be king and emperor by appearing at the last moment and delivering his severely beset city. Since then, Zion has been the invincible city of God, the "mountain of God in the extreme north," YHWH's dwelling, in whose palaces the great king dwells as patron (Pss 46; 48; 76).[26] Occasionally the YHWH hymns become Zion's hymns: God is extolled through the praise of his glorious city. This reputation of Zion is proclaimed in the festival and also in the form of a YHWH-oracle in Ps 87. I have also discussed this psalm previously.[27] It refers clearly to the festival with the procession of the dancing and singing participants (v. 7). Its topic is Zion as metropolis, as the "spiritual" leader of the whole world. It is marked by its universalism, free of any fanaticism and exclusivity. All the nations of the world should be counted henceforth among YHWH's worshipers. Usually these enthronement festival songs maintain that henceforth YHWH and with him Israel is the lord, ruler, and master of the appalled, subservient, almost annihilated nations (Pss 46; 75; 76; 149). This passage, however, says that "from now on, all the nations will call Zion 'mother.'" All the nations will now become believing and enthusiastic worshipers of YHWH. The poet has YHWH proclaim these religious ideas through a solemn oracle:

---

26. *Psalm Studies* 2, part 1, §2.1.4, 236–44.
27. *Psalm Studies* 2, part 1, §3.3, 357–63.

> ⁶ᵃ YHWH consults the book of nations:
> ⁴ "I name as²⁸ my worshipers Rahab and Babel;
> there is Ethiopia, Tyre, and Philistia—
> one is born here, ⁶ᵇ another there.
> ⁵ᵃ (Only) Zion is called [mother], however:
> they are all born in her."²⁹

The poet does not explicitly state how he justifies the notion that the nations belong among YHWH's worshipers. Apparently, however, he does so in a manner similar to Deutero-Isaiah: the nations are converted through YHWH's mighty deeds and understand that the true God is only in Zion.

The fact that a different tone sounds in this oracle than the usual nationalistic one does not prohibit, of course, the psalm from being categorized as a cultic song. We have discovered, after all, that even Ps 50 is to be assigned to this category. It is remarkable how many strings the religion of Israel can play! Thus we also hear tones of individually shaded and personally appropriated religion in these cultic songs. Style and tradition are by no means everything, nor does an experience of the divine range merely within the forms and restrictions of the collective experience and of normal attitudes, thoughts, and ideas. Here someone experiences God in a new manner, one that awakens personally nuanced attitudes and thoughts. Based on such thoughts and attitudes, the cultic song composers, the singers and prophets of the temple, have also occasionally sung and had the congregation sing their "new songs." The piety of this cult is anything but uniform.

In a formal respect the liturgical nature of the cultic oracle is less clear in Ps 87. The oracle is not introduced expressly as such. Actually, YHWH is only introduced as speaking with himself in poetic fashion. At best, one can speak of this psalm as a poetic fiction. Thus we need not imagine its performance divided among several voices, perhaps choir, prophet, choir. The psalm may very well have been sung *uno tenore* by a single singer or choir (the Korahites, to whom belong, one notes, the two other Zion songs in Pss 46 and 48).

*

As mentioned above, the enthronement festival is identical with the fall festival. It was the main festival in ancient Israel and, as such, made room for all aspects and attitudes of the ancient popular religion. Quite naturally, not only

---

28. Actually "to."
29. Regarding the text, see *Psalm Studies* 2, part 1, 361.

were hymns sung at such a festival, but prayers were also offered. The congregation asked for everything that it needed to live, everything incorporated for the Israelites in the words "blessing," *bĕrākâ*, or "salvation," *šālôm*.[30] We have already dealt with a prayer liturgy of this king in Ps 132.

A few words of explanation must be added to our discussion of prayer psalms. The justification for the demarcation of a unique literary genre by this name seems disputed. Gunkel and, following him, Balla and Walter Baumgartner seem to want to acknowledge only the following four major genres: hymns and public thanksgiving psalms, public lament psalms, individual lament psalms, and individual thanksgiving psalms.[31] In contrast, Kittel speaks both of lament songs and prayer psalms; Staerk distinguishes between (public and individual) hymns and (public and individual) prayers (of thanksgiving and petition); he reckons the lament psalms to the latter category.[32] In the main, however, he wants to differentiate between cultic lyric (to which the old lament psalms are assigned) and "religious songs," that is, "religious poetry separated from the public or the private cult" ("Lyrik," 5, 228). He assigns to the latter category many of the psalms that Gunkel calls lament psalms.

In my view, if one wishes to define the genres of psalmody, one must always appeal to cultic poetry, as Gunkel also does in essence. Thus it seems certain to me that one may not insist, as Staerk does, in claiming for the cult only hymns and thanksgiving psalms, on the one hand, and "lament psalms" in the restricted sense, on the other. The cult was, in fact, richer. Even when dealing with the cult, one must distinguish between (public) "lament psalms," meant for a unique or regularly recurring cultic celebration (a day of penance), and "prayers" that did not pertain to a particular crisis but were prayed at regularly recurring festivals and dealt with the general needs of the community. The community did not need divine assistance only in particularly severe crises of some specific nature. The community always needed it. The cult consists chiefly of such procedures meant to secure divine blessing for all situations in the life of the community,[33] including blessing for everyday life, not just for the hour of danger and "distress" in the particular sense. As soon, however, as the divine was no longer understood as a "power" associated with things and procedures but as a person, as a free will, the prayers for the gifts of blessing and good fortune were added to the procedures. The power-producing formula became a prayer. One prayed, for example, for rain in the

---

30. See *Psalm Studies* 2, part 1, ch. 3.
31. Balla, *Das Ich*; Walter Baumgartner, *Die Klagegedichte des Jeremia* (BZAW 32; Giessen: Töpelmann, 1917).
32. Kittel, *Psalmen*; Staerk, "Lyrik."
33. *Psalm Studies* 2, part 1, §1.4.2.

regular cult not only when drought ruled. One prayed for victory, descendants, fertility, honor, and peace, in short, for God's benevolence, even when, viewed externally and superficially, the prayer did not seem particularly necessary. Without the cult and the related prayers, the blessing would diminish, the covenant would dissolve on its own, as it were—for gifts depend on the covenant,[34] and the covenant, like everything that exists, must be "renewed" in order to endure.

Thus it goes without saying that one should also expect prayer psalms among the cultic psalms of this community and that it is, therefore, imprecise for Gunkel, Balla, and Baumgartner to assign almost all the petitionary prayer psalms to the genre of "lament psalms." Among the petitionary prayer psalms of the Psalter there are also those that contain very little or nothing of what characterizes the "lament psalm": complaints and descriptions of distress.

Such community prayer psalms are: 12 (?); 14; 36 (?);[35] 53; 72;[36] 85; 94;[37]

---

34. Concerning covenant and gifts, see Pedersen, *Israel*, 296–304.

35. In Ps 36 we confront the same problem met in Ps 12 (see below): Is the supplicant an individual, the enemies magicians, and, thus, the psalm an individual illness psalm, or are the magicians here an insulting designation for the people's national enemies? The enemies are explicitly said to do magic (*'āwen*, vv. 4, 5, 13). In v. 10, does the supplicant (first-person singular, v. 12) include himself with other pious persons (first-person plural), or is he identical with a group? The confidence expressed in vv. 6–10 relates to YHWH's benevolent acts toward people (here the Israelites) in general. The request in v. 11 calls on YHWH's intervention to help the righteous and the pious in general. All of this can also be interpreted in terms of an individual, of course. The supplicant knows that his deliverance is comforting evidence of the deliverance of the pious in general and that, consequently, they feel that his concerns are their own. The collective interpretation finds support, in contrast, in the remarkable similarity of the first part with Ps 14 and in the fact that no mention is made of the actual suffering of the supplicant in the style of the lament psalms. Thus the decision remains uncertain.

36. An intercession for the king, perhaps related to his accession to the throne (see below, §2.3).

37. Pss 94 and 120 were added here during my proofreading of this work. Concerning Ps 94, see 534 n. 15 above. The proper understanding of this psalm also casts light on the problem treated below (553–54, 556) concerning Pss 36; 14 (= 53); and 12. Without question, Ps 94 depicts the enemies as sorcerers. On the other hand, as stated above, it is almost certain that they are envisioned and portrayed as oppressors of the whole people so that the subject of the psalm is the people or the community. It is entirely certain here that we are to seek the stated enemies among the people themselves (see v. 8 and cf. *Psalm Studies* 1:10 and 68–70). This circumstance excludes the possibility, however, of interpreting the sorcerers in Ps 94 as a "picturesque," spiteful designation for the national enemies and the psalm as an occasional lament psalm. Besides, there is testimony that it belongs among

106;³⁸ 120;³⁹ 121;⁴⁰ 122;⁴¹ 123;⁴² 125; 126; 130; 131;⁴³ 132. Psalms 90; 102;⁴⁴

---

the regularly repeated psalms and was sung at the fall festival. Thus we have the witness of tradition that community prayers against magicians and demons were components of the liturgies of the fall festival. This is significant for understanding Pss 14 and 36 (see n. 35 above). The expression "to change fate" in Ps 14 points to the fall festival. Nothing prohibits one from interpreting the psalm in analogy to Ps 94; that is, the magicians are meant literally, and the psalm is to be understood as a prayer for liberation from magicians in general. In Ps 36, the central section works wholly and entirely with the concepts of the Fall and enthronement festival. It is, therefore, best understood like Pss 94 and 14. From the outset, then, the same interpretation is also the most likely for Ps 12—if this psalm is to be understood as a community psalm. Here, however, the possibility of an individual interpretation should not be abandoned. Indeed, it is to be considered likely (of course, the magicians are meant quite literally).

Ps 94 shows us particularly clearly that the stylistic and cultic-liturgical classifications of the psalms do not always coincide. In the text above, I have advocated the propriety of the distinction between (occasional) community lament psalms and congregational prayers (that belong to the regular celebration of the festival). This distinction is liturgical, not purely stylistic. In general, however, this distinction coincides with a stylistic difference. In the prayers, the request is, indeed, the chief concern. Psalms in which the laments related to a specific crisis are the chief concern belong to the occasional cultic celebrations motivated by a specific crisis. As we have seen above in the discussion of Ps 85, however, some of the prayers are also rather significantly influenced by the complaints in the lament psalms. In Ps 94, we have a case where a regularly repeated communal prayer bears the full form of an occasional lament psalm. The situation is similar for Ps 93.

38. The actual purpose of the psalm comes to expression in v. 47. It is, like Ps 90, a prayer for liberation from the permanent distress of the postexilic period, although with no complaint. The great confession of sin (vv. 6–39) is to be regarded as a "repentance motif," intended to assure being heard. In terms of content, it belongs with Pss 90, etc. (see 557–58).

39. The same is true to a degree in Ps 120. The superscription indicates that this psalm belongs among the *ma'ălôt* songs, i.e., the fall festival songs. It was probably, however, originally a purely individual lament song (concerning evil magicians). It thus had nothing originally to do with a community cultic celebration. The superscription shows, however, that it was employed as a community festival prayer and probably as a prayer for assistance with all manner of enemies, perhaps sorcerers in the first instance (see *Psalm Studies* 1:170). Here, then, the form of the lament psalm in a communal prayer may depend on the reinterpretation of an original individual lament song. At any rate, this is the case in Ps 102 (see n. 44 below). The same is suggested concerning Ps 130 (n. 43 below). Now, another possible interpretation of the individual forms of several of the *ma'ălôt* songs seems likely to me. As shown in *Psalm Studies* 2:217–18 n. 75 with reference to Zimmern, *Zum babylonischen Neujahrsfest: Zweiter Beitrage* (BSGW, Philologisch-historische Klasse 70; Leipzig: Teubner, 1918), the Babylonian New Year's Festival included the king, in the figure of a penitent, reading certain prayers and psalms. I have shown in *Psalm Studies* 2 (passim) that in Israel, too, the king played an important role in the Fall and New Year's Festival. In that case,

106;[45] and 137 (see also Pss. Sol. 9), which were probably written for the annual repentance ceremony and petition for liberation from an enduring crisis,[46] stand on the boundary between prayers and lament psalms. Almost all of the congregational petitions mentioned above, it seems, were related to the great annual festival and have, consequently, been treated in *Psalm Studies 2* more or less thoroughly.

Only a few of the petition psalms are significant for our topic. Neither the cultic liturgy nor religious need suffices to raise merely a request on an occasion such as the great annual festival. Religion requires a response to a request, an assurance that the deity has heard. This answer cannot be given to the community in the community's cult in any fashion other than through the mouth of a cultic official or qualified individual who is generally believed to have the right and the ability to communicate answers in God's name. In ancient Israel, this means through a minister of the cult or priest who is prophetically gifted or equipped with "prophetic" skills.

---

however, the explanation of the first-person form in the prayers of many fall festival psalms (especially *maʿălôt* psalms) may very well be that we are dealing with songs placed in the mouth of the king or that he was supposed to recite. Here, then, Pss 120; 121; 130; 131 come under consideration, in particular (the latter is actually a psalm of confidence, to be understood as an indirect petition; see *Psalm Studies* 2:308–9), in addition to Ps 84 (see *Psalm Studies* 2:217–18 n. 75, 294), and perhaps also Ps 118, if it is preexilic (see *Psalm Studies* 2:297–303, 270–71, 368). Then the inclusion of Ps 120 among the *maʿălôt* songs involves no reinterpretation. The fact that the king appears as the representative of the people is obvious, despite the individual form of the prayer. This may be by far the most satisfactory explanation of the oscillating form of the *maʿălôt* songs.

40. See *Psalm Studies* 2:345–46.

41. A liturgy influenced by the style of the individual lament psalms. The speaker in v. 1 is the congregation or its representative, in vv. 8–9 the officiating priest (see *Psalm Studies* 5).

42. The speaker is the congregation or its representative. The psalm was influenced quite significantly by the style of the individual songs.

43. In the current text, the speaker in Pss 130 and 131 is the congregation. These psalms, however, apparently developed through a revision of an original individual psalm (see *Psalm Studies* 1, §6.1.2, 341).

44. In Ps 102, an original song of illness has been related to the suffering of destroyed Jerusalem and the supplicant reinterpreted as Zion. Accordingly, the interlude (vv. 13–23) was inserted (see *Psalm Studies* 1, §6.1.2, 342).

45. See n. 38 above.

46. There is evidence that Ps 137 was sung at the annual memorial on the 9th of Ab, and nothing contradicts the notion that it was also written for this day. Since Ps 90 does not mention a specific crisis but refers to the permanent crisis of the postexilic period, it is likely from the outset that it was written for a similar use (see also Zech 7:3, 5; 8:19).

We have a beautiful example of such a nonoccasional prayer liturgy meant for a regularly recurring cultic celebration in Ps 85. This psalm is neither an "eschatological" lament psalm, as Gunkel, Staerk, Buhl, and others think, nor a "historical" lament psalm. It does not complain about some specific "emergency" at all. It is a prayer for a good and blessed New Year.

Admittedly, it has certain features that give the appearance that it must have been composed in a specific emergency (vv. 5–7). If one considers only the words of complaint in these verses, one could be inclined to interpret the psalm either "historically" or, with Gunkel and Staerk, "eschatologically," that is, to seek to explain it in relation to the enduring crisis of the Jewish community and to understand the salvation it requests as *the* salvation, as the grand reconstitution of the end times. In contrast, however, the description of salvation in verses 10–14 is quite definitive. It says not one word about what, then, must have been the major issue: the liberation of the subjugated Israel from the pagan tyrants, the reconstitution of the nation and the state. The promise made here refers to the "salvation" of a blessed year. Accordingly, verses 5–7 are to be assessed as the stylistic influence of the lament song, as poetic hyperbole.

One of the peculiarities of the Israelite psyche is that, in prayer, when some gift or blessing is sought, one portrays oneself as humbly, as insignificantly, as oppressed, as suffering as possible (the "sympathy motif" in religious poetry). Israel and the Israelite would never be able, in our thinking, to bear his misfortune, his suffering, not even the lesser instances, with manly dignity, never proudly, with clenched teeth, to hold up his head in defiance of his fate. Just as our farmers in the period of the absolute monarchy also sometimes described themselves in petitions to the king or some other official, for example, as "the poor farmers, the poor people," and were usually also described as such by royal officials (especially pastors), even when, in reality, rather prosperous regions were involved and sometimes, in agricultural terms, rich people were also included—so the Israelite, when he wanted to ask God for something, also described himself as "poor," "afflicted," "oppressed," and the like. The common term *'ānî* or *'ānāw* combined the two meanings, "humble" and "afflicted, suffering, needy"; *'ebyôn*, "poor," is a common synonym for these words. In order to receive the greatest gift possible for the least price possible, one abandons pride and dignity and portrays oneself as insignificantly as possible. Israel was hardly so from the beginning. It also once knew the pride of the free bedouin. It became so rather early in the course of its history, however. The foundation may have already been laid in Egypt.

This peculiarity of character also affected Israel's religion. Humility, insignificance, self-abasement, and lying in the dust became virtues: God wants this of people. Only, do not be "haughty," for God loves to humble all who are "haughty." In addition, there is the passionate temperament of the orientals that always inclines toward exaggeration. If the soul of a people or an era is mirrored in its art, then ancient oriental art, both literature and inscriptions and graphic art, attest to how natural the exaggerations of these peoples and this culture were. With respect to Assyrian art, one may almost say that exaggeration was its most important aesthetic technique. Something similar, although perhaps less distinctly, is also true of the Israelites. If one comes into any distress, one cries aloud and feels and describes oneself as the most afflicted of all mortals. For this person, "crisis" is almost the same as a circumstance in which one needs or wants something. Then one moans and whines. Then one's soul is already in Sheol. The lament psalms offer evidence enough and to spare.

Thus it became almost a rule of style that both real distress and need of any kind were depicted with the strongest and most exaggerated expressions. Need should be portrayed as crisis, as deepest affliction; both the popular soul and practice and the rules of style promoted this practice.

With particular respect to Ps 85, all of this is joined by a final element that we will understand better if we examine Ps 126. Psalm 85 is a psalm "for peace and a good year." The foundation of the harvest blessing of the following year should be laid in the cult during the New Year's Festival ("the turn of fate" is related to the new year).[47] In the first instance, it deals with good rain in the coming winter. After the rain, the sowing can begin. Thus one is considered to have obtained the "blessing of heaven and *těhôm*," of the ground and field. In the agricultural and climatic conditions of Palestine, sowing is always a kind of wager. Drought, stunted growth, and famine are all too familiar realities. Thus one always sowed with anxious foreboding. The sower "goes out with tears," as it is said in poetic style (Ps 126:5). In addition, however, the most beautiful hope survives. When "the blessing" is there first, then the harvest can be very rich. "Hope" can never be suppressed. Anxious foreboding and radiant hope, "tears" and "laughter," dwell together in the soul of the Israelite farmer when he sows. He remembers the many failed hopes that every member of the community had surely experienced. How often had the Israelite farmer, affected by failed crops and family, felt himself to be the object of God's wrath! But how often had he not also experienced a rich harvest and the blessing of God? Everything stands before him in a flash. In the light of clear hope for the coming year, what was, the year past, stands before him as a shadow. The future may glitter in gold, but fear lingers in the background.

---

47. *Psalm Studies* 2, part 1, 254–57.

Now we also understand the attitude in Ps 85. The New Year's Festival is simultaneously the conclusion and thanksgiving festival for the old year and the beginning festival for the new. The blessing, which must be evident and proven initially in rain, then in successful planting, then in protection from all dangers in the course of the summer—sirocco, locusts, bedouin raids, and so on—and finally in a rich harvest, should now be obtained through the cult, through the renewed coming of YHWH, through the renewal of the covenant, through the determination of a new sequence of fate ("turn of fate"). Thus the whole change in the attitude of agricultural life, compressed in a brief moment, trembles in the proceedings, experiences, and prayers of the New Year's Festival. The community stands there as those in the greatest degree of need for help—the new foundation of the common life is involved, after all. It portrays itself as needy, "poor," "afflicted," affected by the wrath of the deity because all of this lives as a possibility in the soul of the people. Thus the cultic song, the prayer liturgy, appropriates the forms and motifs of the lament psalm and, in keeping with religious and stylistic practice, depicts the "distress" in the most vibrant colors. There was also the memory of the many "turns of fate" that were so beautiful that the members of the people "stand there like dreamers," their "mouths filled with laughter" (Ps 126:1–2).

The prayer liturgy begins with these beautiful memories as a "motive for confidence" for the subsequent prayer:

> You favored your land, YHWH; you have (often) changed Jacob's fate,
> removed the guilt of your people and pardoned all their sins;
> all your anger you have sent away, withdrawn from your burning wrath.

Then follows the request, in connection with the style of the lament psalm, in words that reveal the tension between the anxious foreboding and the memory of the many failed hopes as an apparently profound distress—which, from a psychic perspective, they were:

> Reestablish us, God our help, "relent"[48] from your wrath against us!
> Will you be angry forever, still be cross with the children's children?
> Are you not the one who can revive us,
> so that your people can again rejoice in you?
> Let us see, O YHWH, your goodness; may your help not fail us!

---

48. Read *wĕhāsēr*, BHK.

This first part of the psalm, consisting of seven lines of verse, was probably performed by the choir of singers representing the congregation. What will God's answer to this ardent prayer say? As in Pss 81 and 95, an individual steps forward now, a prophet from the host of the people in the temple, and proclaims the divine response to the listening congregation, also in a strophe of seven lines. Already in the first words he announces himself as an inspired person through whom (actually: "in whom") YHWH speaks to his people:[49]

> I will listen to what God says [through me]—truly, YHWH speaks salvation
> to his people, to all his pious ones, to "those who turn their hearts to him"![50]
> Indeed, his help is near to his worshipers, so that glory may dwell in our land,
> so that mercy and faithfulness may unite, so that right and salvation embrace.
> Fidelity sprouts forth from the earth, right looks down from heaven,
> and YHWH gives everything good; our land gives (us) its produce:
> right enters ahead of him, and "salvation"[51] follows the path he walks.

Like lovely angels, the hypostases of good fortune descend from heaven and follow YHWH, who comes now to dwell in the land. Like the fruit of the earth, they will sprout and bloom everywhere. The divine *kābôd*, the wonder-working, glorious power of God[52] that his people also share as their driving psychic power; *ḥesed*, the reciprocal love between the parties to the covenant, the members of the people;[53] *'emet*, truthfulness and trustworthiness, the capability to make good, firm, and reliable plans and to act, mutual truthfulness and fidelity within the community;[54] *ṣedeq*, the psychic health that practices right actions and leads to external good fortune, the self-assertion and capacity to maintain the covenant that is the condition of "salvation";[55] and *šālôm*, complete harmony, health, and "wholeness," the "completion" of the individual and the popular soul, which comprehends all good fortune in

---

49. Add *bî* in v. 9 with LXX.
50. Read *wĕ'el yāšîbû 'ēlāw libbām*, BHK.
51. Read *wĕšālôm*, BHK.
52. See *Psalm Studies* 2, part 1, 333–36; and Pedersen, *Israel*, 234–37.
53. Pedersen, *Israel*, 304–10, 525.
54. Ibid., 338–41.
55. Ibid., 338, 351.

itself and whose core is "blessing"[56]—all these "hypostases of good fortune" meet in the land of Israel and constitute the content of the new fate. This can all be summarized—and in so doing, it becomes evident what aspect of "help" and good fortune receives the greater weight—in terms of the fact that YHWH will give everything good and the earth its rich produce. The "salvation" and the "help" prayed for here is roughly equivalent to when the old Nordic Germans sacrificed in the winter festival "for peace and a good year."[57] If one comprehends the essence of ancient Israelite religion, one simply must postulate that liturgies of this kind must have been conducted in the cult. Indeed, we find this psalm in the collection of temple songs.

*

The prayer liturgies of the grand annual festival probably also included Ps 14 = 53. The psalm contains a divine oracle and a request for help against the *pô'ălê 'āwen*, whose wicked hearts and disgraceful behavior is described in verse 1. As I have shown in *Psalm Studies* 1, this expression denotes sorcerers. Usually psalms against sorcerers are psalms of individual lament, placed in the mouth of the sick and the unclean who believe themselves to persecuted by sorcerers. Our psalm differs from these individual songs in two respects: the usual laments about bodily and psychic suffering as a result of the sorcerer are lacking, and the sorcerers are represented here as tormentors of the people, not of an individual. Almost even more than in the individual songs, the psalm lacks specifics. It seems thus to be directed against sorcerers in general. Now, since it is connected with the New Year's Festival by the concept of the "turn of fate," there are only two likely explanations. The widespread sin of sorcery and the fear of these mysterious, unknown oppressors alive among the people led to the inclusion of a prayer for protection from sorcerers in general to the liturgies of the annual festival. Alternatively, "sorcerer" here may be merely an "insult,"[58] a "graphic" description of Israel's national enemies, as, for example, when, in their inscriptions, the Assyrian kings sometimes characterized their enemies as "evil devils," sons of an "evil devil," or the like.[59] The psalm, then, is a prayer liturgy addressed either against a historical enemy or against Israel's enemies in general; in the latter case, it was well-suited to the major festival when YHWH's protection against all dangers was obtained. The enemies are depicted in the form of sorcerers, then. As non-Israelites, they are unclean

---

56. Ibid., 311–35.
57. The old Nordic *fred* was originally as comprehensive as the Hebrew *šālôm*.
58. See *Psalm Studies* 1:40.
59. Sigmund Mowinckel, *Statholderen Nehemia* (Kristiania: Olaf Norlis, 1916), 141.

for Israel; as enemies, they are also evil and thus *rĕšāʿîm*. The purest type of the *rāšāʿ*, however, is the sorcerer.⁶⁰ They also worship other gods, however. A foreign cult is often condemned as magic.⁶¹ Thus both the religious and national hatred and the poetic picturesque language suggest the choice of the attested portrayal.

However the magicians should be understood here—whether literally or "metaphorically"—the structure of the psalm and the relationship between the structure and cultic use are nonetheless clear. The psalm begins with a description of the *rĕšāʿîm*. They are presented in all their wickedness. The depiction offers the reason for YHWH's intervention and, thus, in terms of style, represents the invocation and the request with complaint in the usual lament psalms. As an introduction, there is a description of how YHWH looks down from heaven to determine that all these *rĕšāʿîm* are so evil that his powerful and punitive intervention is necessary (v. 2):

> YHWH looks down from heaven on the children of men,
> to see whether there are any insightful who seek YHWH.

YHWH must determine, however, that the matter is ripe for intervention. He speaks (vv. 3–4):

> All of them "are apostate,"⁶² all are ruined;
> there is no one who does good, not a single one.
> Should the sorcerers not notice, those who eat my people,
> who consume [its] bread … [and] do not "fear"⁶³ YHWH?

The "sorcerers" will surely come to feel the evil they have done. With fearsome wrath, YHWH will intervene against them. Concerning the introduction of the oracle, our psalm exhibits the same form as Pss 82 and 87. YHWH's statement is not introduced and designated directly as an oracle. The poet (singer) has YHWH seize the word in the course of his speech and introduces him as the speaker with the strophe, "YHWH looks down from heaven." Thus, the possibility exists here, too, that the whole first part of the psalm (vv. 1–6) is not to be assigned to the choir and the prophet but that the whole section is to be imagined as spoken by the prophet. According to the analogy of the prophetic punitive oracle, then, the justification for the threat

---

60. *Psalm Studies* 1:5–9, 39–41.
61. *Psalm Studies* 1:42–43.
62. In v. 3, read *nāsôg ʾaḥôr* instead of *sār* (cf. *sāg*, Ps 53:4).
63. In v. 4, read *laḥmô*; a word is missing; read also *wĕyhwh* and *yārēʾû*; cf. BHK.

of judgment is communicated here: the sorcerers have behaved so horribly that YHWH must now punish them (v. 1). Following the divine speech, the prophet discloses the consequences of YHWH's intervention in vv. 5–6:

> Then they were gripped with horror, for God is on the side of the righteous; the council of the godless will become disgrace, for YHWH "rejects them."[64]

The words of the prophet end. A brief pause ensues. YHWH has spoken majestic, comforting words to his people. The reality is still harsh, the might of enemies still great. The soul of the community is wrenched back and forth as though between fear and hope, between belief and despair. The community makes its request that God soon redeem his promise almost timidly. May he shine forth from Zion, where his throne is now established, turn fate and bring a new, better fate! How Jacob would then rejoice and exult aloud! The choir sings:

> O, would that Israel's salvation come from Zion!
> If YHWH turns the fate of his people (now),
> Jacob will rejoice; Israel will celebrate.[65]

Otherwise, the psalm is characteristic of the hyperbolic style of Hebrew poetry. Paul expressed the impression that the wording reflects a more dogmatic than poetic thinker when he understood the psalm as evidence for the doctrine of the universal sinfulness of all humanity (Rom 3:10–12). That is by no means the poet's meaning, however. Even if the sorcerers are to be understood literally here as a reference to the secret evildoers among the people, Israel is still "the righteous," as the relationship between verses 5–6 and 7 demonstrates, who are to be established as "just" by YHWH's intervention even though they are "made unjust" by hostilities. The absolute-sounding statements in verses 1–3 refer to the totality of the enemies, the sorcerers. All of them are apostate; they are *rĕšāʿîm*; they have become *ḥānēp*. In an extreme exaggeration, however, the poet says—as do, furthermore, the prophets of judgment and even the poet of Ps 12—that only evildoers can be found under the whole heavens. Israel, or if the magicians are to be taken literally, the righteous majority of the people, stands as the sole exception. This is how a people

---

64. In verse 6 read *ḥānēp* instead of *ānî* (cf. *ḥônak* 53:6), *tābôš* and, following 53:6, *meʾāsām*.

65. The word *śimḥâ* refers to festival joy.

passionate in feeling and thought experiences the knowledge or suspicion that it is surrounded by many secret or public enemies.

*

It may be that Ps 12 should also be interpreted in a fashion similar to Ps 14.[66] The enemies about whom the psalm complains are also depicted as sorcerers here. The *šaw*-sayings, the flattering lips and the divided heart, the cordial words to the neighbor but harmful words behind his back, the haughty tongue, the mighty lips through which their owners are able to play master over the people and treat them harshly as they have done the singer—all of this characterizes the sorcerer even though the word *'āwen* happens not to be mentioned.[67] Verse 6 implies that the enemies have pushed the supplicant into misfortune by "blowing on" him; this, too, is a characteristic sorcerer's technique.[68]

It is unclear, however, who the speaker is. Balla and Staerk understand the psalm as a public lament song and the speaker as the community.[69] They rely on the readings *tišmĕrenû* (a few manuscripts, LXX, Jerome) and *tiṣṣĕrenû* (eleven manuscripts) in verse 8. The reading is uncertain, however. MT has *tišmĕrem* and *tiṣṣĕrennû*, although the suffix of the first word must be corrected according to the second.[70] Syriac read *tiṣṣĕrenî*. Since, therefore, MT must be corrected in any case, nothing per se prohibits one from following the indication of the Syriac and reading *tišmĕrenî* and *tiṣṣĕrenî*.

If the plural was the original form, the psalm is a communal psalm.[71] Then we would confront the same questions as in Ps 14: Are the "sorcerers" to be taken literally or figuratively, and, in the final analysis, do we have before us an occasional or a regularly recurring liturgy? However these questions may be answered, the psalm resembles Ps 14, in any case. Both the exaggerated description of the enemies, as though the whole world—or the whole country—was full of sorcerers, and the response to the petition through a divine oracle agrees with Ps 14. On the other hand, the psalm resembles the usual psalms of individual lament to the degree that we have in it a direct

---

66. See above, n. 35.
67. *Psalm Studies* 1:18–20, 20–25, 25–28.
68. *Psalm Studies* 1:31–32.
69. Balla, *Das Ich*, 66, 67, 69; Staerk, "Lyrik," 139.
70. The reverse is hardly conceivable.
71. Which would otherwise have been possible even if the singular were the correct text because, undoubtedly, there are cultic psalms in which the congregation, in accordance with ancient Israelite thought, appears to speak as a unity in the singular (e.g., Ps 118).

complaint about the evil behavior of the enemies and a request for help and deliverance, not as in Ps 14 a description of the evil. This is a feature that could be significant for the individual interpretation of the psalm and could support the reading *tiṣṣĕrenî*.

Be that as it may, the complaint of the community—or of the sick person[72]—is answered, in any event, by a divine oracle spoken in the liturgy by a cultic prophet—if an individual psalm, by the priest administering the purification rites (v. 6):

> "Because of the need of the oppressed, because of the sighing of the poor, I now arise"—oracle of YHWH—"I will set free [the oppressed poor], him [on whom the evildoer] has blown."[73]

Full of confident joy and satisfaction, the community—or the sick person—receives this comforting promise and, in the final strophe of the psalm, verses 7–8 (the text of which is, however, very damaged), declares its thanks in the assurance of having been fully heard and of the imminent fulfillment of the promise.

2.2. Prophetic Oracles in Occasional Worship Services

I mentioned the possibility above that Pss 75, 14, and 12 may have had their setting in occasional cultic celebrations. In terms of style, that would mean that these psalms were not congregational prayers but public psalms of lament,[74] a stylistic classification that does not suit Ps 75, however. If this psalm was meant for a public day of prayer, then the section of the liturgy containing the complaint and request will have preceded it. In this case, it contains only the divine response to the request and the thanksgiving.

With regard to the cultic situation of the "public lament psalms," reference will simply be made here to Gunkel's presentation in "Psalmen" (*RGG*) and Balla's *Das Ich* (65–75). If the people are in distress and affected by YHWH's wrath, if drought or pestilence occurs, if it is smitten by the enemies and suffers defeat, and so on, then one calls a public penitential ceremony. The congregation assembles in the temple, fasts and "pours out water before YHWH" (1 Sam 7:6), investigates, perhaps by casting lots (see 1 Sam 14:38–42) or examining witnesses (see 1 Kgs 21:13) who or by what sins it may have awakened YHWH's wrath, confesses its sin (1 Sam 7:6) or attests its innocence

---

72. Such a person would be involved, if the psalm is to be interpreted individually.
73. Regarding the reconstruction of the text in v. 6, see *Psalm Studies* 1:32.
74. See above, n. 37.

(see Ps 44), and prays for the forgiveness of sin and assistance. There is no explicit reference to the sacrifice of sin offerings,[75] although they can probably be assumed. The public psalms of lament are also elements of these penitence ceremonies (Pss 44; 60; 74; 77;[76] 79; 80; 83; 89;[77] 108; and, further, 20; 21 [see below]; Lam 5; Jer 14; Joel 1–2;[78] Dan 3:26–45 LXX;[79] Pss. Sol. 7; stylistically related, but not in terms of cultic content, are the nonoccasional prayer psalms, Pss 90; 102; 137; and Pss. Sol. 9).[80] They contain the sacred words that belong with the sacred procedure whose chief content is indicated in 1 Sam 7:6: confession of sin or attestation of innocence, complaint, request for help. Closely related to the complaint psalms and probably also meant for similar cultic purposes are the "confession of sin psalms." We have only late imitations of them in the Psalter that were probably meant for regularly recurring days of penitence (Ps 106).[81]

With respect to content and structure, the public lament psalms closely resemble the individual. They consist of an invocation, a complaint concerning the crisis, a description of the misfortune suffered and the actions of the enemies, a request with all manner of "motives" (the penitence motive, the innocence motive, the confidence motive, the reputation motive, the compassion motive, etc.), and the certainty of being heard. As Gunkel has correctly seen, the explicit emphasis on the certainty of being heard assumes another, "liturgical" form of this psalm. Judging from the prophetic imitations of this genre (see Jer 14; Joel 1–2), we must assume that, after the complaint and request (the lament psalm proper), a presiding minister of the cult stepped forward and promised in YHWH's name that the prayer would be heard. This means, however, that the divine oracle was also a component of the public lament ceremony, an oracle that responds to the request and promises assis-

---

75. Cf., however, Joel 2:14.
76. In contrast to the current misery, the poet introduces here past saving acts on behalf of the whole people. The interest concentrates chiefly around YHWH's relationship with the people. We hear nothing in these psalms of illness and physical suffering or of private "enemies" and sorcerers. This silence indicates that the praying subject is the people or a representative of the people, probably the king (see Ps 89). Otherwise, the psalm is a fragment; the conclusion is missing.
77. See 528–29 above.
78. The latter two are not, in the usual but incorrect view, true liturgies for days of repentance but prophetic imitations.
79. Probably not a prophetic imitation but composed for the same situation as Lam 5, perhaps for cultic purposes. In any case, it was not originally composed in reference to the situation of the three men in the burning oven (cf. Balla, *Das Ich*, 66).
80. On the last four psalms mentioned, see 547–48 above.
81. See 547 above.

The Individual Psalms 559

tance. Naturally, this oracle was not pronounced by the same choir that sang the psalm proper but by a minister of the cult equipped with a prophetic gift, a priest-prophet.

Both possibilities mentioned above under §2.1 are conceivable. The form and the details of the oracle can be left to the independent talent of the prophet. The only expectation of him is that he give a comforting oracle. Alternatively, the oracle may have been fixed by the liturgical order of worship, both in form and content. The two pertinent psalms that we have in the Psalter, Pss 60 and 108, give us an example each of two cases mentioned.

Psalms 60; 108; 20; and 21 will be treated here.

*

Psalm 60 is difficult to interpret. From a formal perspective, the question arises as to whether a true (cultic) oracle is transmitted in verses 8–10 (so Kittel, *Psalmen*) or the poet offered a free summary of old promises in order to appeal to God on this basis (so Staerk, Buhl, and the older commentators). This question is relatively easy to answer. Were the latter view correct, one would expect another introductory formula and especially an address to God, as in Ps 89:20, where the supplicant actually appeals to older prophecies: "then you spoke in a revelation and said to your faithful," or "in ancient days [*mē'ôlām*], you spoke to your faithful," or the like. If, however, one has discovered the liturgical form and use of many psalms, such as is attested, for example, in Pss 81 and 85, there can be no doubt that Kittel's view is correct. Thus the psalm is a liturgy with a lament psalm, an oracle, a repeated request, and assurance of being heard and of ultimate victory.

The problem of content and history is more difficult. Clearly the psalm was composed for a day of penitence after a defeat, and the oracle refers to the contemporary historical and political situation. The only question is what this situation may have been. The answer depends on the interpretation of verses 8–10. This issue ultimately culminates, as Paul Haupt has correctly perceived,[82] in a text-critical question. The meter of the psalm is 3 + 3. In verses 8–10, however, we have an apparent 3 + 3 + 3. Verse 8a could stand outside the meter, however, as an introductory formula, and verse 9c is not a good tri-meter. Text-critical and exegetical problems are very closely intertwined here. What is the significance of the oracle? It is usually related to the Maccabean struggles with

---

82. Paul Haupt, "A Maccabean Talisman," in *Florilegium ou recueil de traveaux d'érudition dédiés à M. le Marquis Melchior de Vogüé à l'occasion du quatre-vingtième anniversaire de sa naissance* (ed. G. C. C. Maspero; Paris: Geuthner, 1909), 276–82 (cited following Buhl, *Psalmerne*).

the neighboring tribes (Theodore of Mopsuestia, Rudinger, Hitzig, Olshausen, Wellhausen, Duhm, Buhl, Staerk). Usually the actual promise is thought to begin already in verse 8 and the imperfect in verse 8 is interpreted in relation to the future: I will conquer and distribute Shechem and the Succoth Valley. Accordingly, the land of Ephraim is no longer in the possession of the Jews. This parcel of land under the leadership of the tribe of Judah is the object of conflict. Several matters contradict this view, however. As verse 11 demonstrates, it involves the possession of Edom and perhaps also of Moab, if *'îr māṣôr* (in Ps 108:11, *mibṣār*) is to be interpreted in relation to *'ar mô'ab* or to be emended as this name (Buhl, provisionally). It refers to a campaign of conquest against Edom (and Moab). These verses say nothing of the lands of the Philistines or of Ephraim. Furthermore, the expression "Ephraim is my chief power" cannot be interpreted in relation to the fact that Ephraim is an object of reconquest here. To the contrary, Ephraim is one of the most important weapons by which YHWH intends to gain his objective. Ephraim is the royal emblem of YHWH (gods and kings wear the horned helmet as a symbol of power), which is most likely an indication that Ephraim here is a leading tribe alongside Judah. Verse 9 actually contradicts verse 10: I already have Gilead, Manasseh and Ephraim, and Judah as possession, defense, and might—the "vessels of honor," Moab, Edom, and Philistia, however, are "the vessels of dishonor" (Rom 9:21). In this case, however, the future interpretation of the imperfect in verse 8 becomes invalid. Verse 8 would then belong together with verse 9 as a list of YHWH's means of power. Verse 8 must then, as Briggs has seen, refer to Joshua's conquest of the land and the imperfect must be actualizing and descriptive—unless one wishes to assume with H. Winckler that Shechem and Succoth were cities in the (Moabite and Edomite) territories to be conquered, in which case, verse 8 could be understood as the summary theme of promise.[83]

If the references to Judah in verse 9 and to Philistia in verse 10 are original,[84] then, given what was said above, it does not seem overly difficult to find the situation of the psalm. Ephraim stands alongside Judah here as a ruling tribe,

---

83. H. Winckler, *Geschichte Israels in Einzeldarstellungen* II (Leipzig: Pfeiffer, 1900), 204ff.

84. With regard to what was said above concerning Ephraim as the leading tribe and Edom (and Moab) as objects of campaigns of conquest, one could think that vv. 9c and 10c were later additions, the first alluding to Gen 49:10 from a later Judean perspective, and the latter from an eschatological viewpoint interested in the destruction of the whole circle of neighboring peoples. Thereby, the meter of the whole psalm becomes regular (3 + 3; v. 8a lies outside the meter). I do not know whether there are similar grounds that motivated Haupt to strike an element in each of the three verses, 8–10—I have not had access to his arguments. This deletion is unnecessary, however (see text above), and remains a somewhat precarious matter.

indeed, in a fashion indicating that Ephraim, along with Manasseh and Gilead, represents the entire people of Israel in a more traditional manner, while Judah was added to a traditional scheme as the new, actual ruling tribe. Those YHWH has destined to serve Israel include Edom, Moab, and the Philistines. They are, therefore, a danger in Israel's current situation or are, at least, neighboring peoples who signify competitors that should not be underestimated, one or two of whom are supposed to be conquered now, according to verse 11. This situation points to the time of David or Solomon. Since then, Judah has never stood alongside Ephraim as the leading tribe and the Philistines were no longer a danger. In reality, there was no longer a danger under Solomon. Thus, the time of David remains. Even though the superscription seems heavily influenced by 2 Sam 8, it also seems to be correct on some points. The fact that we hear nothing of defeats or setbacks in David's wars is insignificant. Historical reports about him are idealized and retouched, of course. David's defeats would be easily forgotten. The defeats suffered need not have been great, either. In accordance with statements above concerning Ps 85, we understand that even minor setbacks could have given sufficient impetus for days of penitence and vehement prayers. Even the most minor misfortune was sufficient evidence that YHWH had not gone out with the lords of Israel and, that, consequently, he must be put in a gracious mood once again. In addition to the composition under David, another possibility seems worth mentioning. The psalm could refer to Edom's separation from Judah under Jehoram (2 Kgs 8:20–22). Jehoram and his son, Ahaziah, were most likely vassals to the Omrides in Ephraim. If we may assume that Jehoram had the assistance of his overlord in the failed attempt to resubjugate Edom, just as his father Jehoshaphat had to contribute troops to Jehoram of Ephraim when Jehoram attempted to resubjugate Mesha of Moab (2 Kgs 3:7–27), we would have another instance in which Ephraim stood alongside Judah as a ruling tribe. We learn nothing about Moab on this occasion; the report in 2 Kgs 8 is garbled.[85]

We will now glance at the religious content and the liturgical structure of the psalm. As has been said, Israel underwent war with Edom, perhaps also with Moab, and surely suffered a major or minor defeat. The people concluded from this that YHWH must be angry about something and, consequently, did not accompany Israel's armies. A day of repentance with fasting and the

---

85. If vv. 9c and 10c are additions, the psalm was originally northern Israelite. Then, of all the historical situations known to us, the most suitable would be either the time of Omri, who conquered Moab, or the time of Mesha, who freed Moab again. The fact that Edom, which, as a vassal of Judah, must march in the beginning of the war against Moab, attempted later, after the defeat, to throw off the Judean yoke would be very likely per se; 2 Kgs 3:27 implies something to this effect.

assembly of the whole people in the sanctuary (Joel 2:15) was called. Sacrifices were offered to appease YHWH, and then the choir or the leader of the people, the king (note "me" in v. 7, *qere*, versions, Ps 108:7), sang the lament psalm *lmnṣḥ*, "in order to make (YHWH's countenance) shine (again)" (*Psalm Studies* 4:620–24):

> God, you have rejected and broken us; you have turned from us in wrath;
> you have shaken and divided the land—O, heal its breach, for it wavers!
> You have caused your people to endure harsh (days),
> have made us to drink the wine of reeling.
> You cause your faithful to wave like a flag,
> in order to flee before the bow (of the enemy).
> For the sake of the deliverance of those who know you,
> bring help, your righteousness, hear us!

Those are well-known complaints and objections. Israel is not aware that it is guilty of any great sin. It is the people of the God-fearers and "knowers," the covenant partners and relatives of YHWH. Nonetheless, YHWH has smitten the land and people with a severe "breach," severely damaging their "integrity" and "soundness," their "peace" and "justice," making them unhealthy, sick, and unjust. He has dealt with Israel as he otherwise deals with the enemies in the enthronement (judgment) myth. He has caused them to empty the intoxicating cup of poison (v. 5; cf. Ps 75, see above). With bitter irony, the psalm says that, instead of erecting a victory standard for the people, behind which it could assemble—military standards were efficacious symbols of the deity—YHWH has erected a signal staff as a sign of ignominious retreat. YHWH's honor is not served by this situation, however. It is to his own disgrace when those who know him, the members of his clan, of his covenant, are abandoned. May he intervene for the sake of their deliverance, therefore, and transform defeat into victory.

Meanwhile, an oracle priest, a temple official who was prophetically gifted or skilled in the technique or obtaining oracles, communicated YHWH's response. Apparently, the designation ‘*al šûšan ‘ēdût* in the superscription refers to the manner in which the oracle is obtained (see *Psalm Studies* 4:631–35). He stepped forward and, in the unusual form of three lines of 3 + 3 strophes, proclaimed the result, YHWH's response:

In his sanctuary,[86] YHWH has spoken:

---

86. Thus all the old versions. Ferdinand Hitzig's translation (*Die Psalmen übersetzt*

> "Victoriously rejoicing, I divided Shechem
> and measured out the Valley of Succoth.
> Mine is Gilead and mine is Manasseh
> and Ephraim the strength of my head;
> my scepter is Judah.
> My foot basin is Moab;
> I put my shoe on Edom.
> 'I rejoice over the land of the Philistines.'"[87]

YHWH first recalled the fact that had already successfully assisted Israel to the land due it when he conquered Canaan—represented here by the "city of Jacob," Shechem, west of the Jordan, and the Succoth Valley region east of the Jordan—and divided it among the tribes of Israel. He also possessed the powerful means through which he could also procure for his people the land that belongs to them by right: he was the Lord of the majestic tribes of Israel that were his weapons and his royal insignia: Gilead, Manasseh, Ephraim, the old ruling tribe, and Judah, the new scepter-bearer in Israel. In contrast, the hostile environment, Moab, Edom, and the Philistines, also belonged to him, to be sure, but as "vessels of dishonor," as servants of YHWH and his people destined to servitude. He can also celebrate victory over them. The national religion of the conquering people still filled with a sense of its power speaks in this oracle.

The liturgies always prefer to sound the various voices of religion together. It is not rare, then, that a renewed request characterized by the attitudes of prayer follows the oracle (see Pss 82:8; 20:10; 21:14). It is as though the promise is so incredibly wonderful that faith can only appropriate it slowly and tentatively. The request is renewed and even associated with the motives of complaint. Suddenly, however, it is as though the full content of the promise dawns on faith and it finally shifts, rejoicing, to full confidence in having been heard, to jubilant thanksgiving. Old Testament liturgies are often able skillfully to render these impulses of the soul, as in this case. After the oracle, the spokesman of the people, probably the military leader, the king himself,[88]

---

und ausgelegt [Leipzig: Winter, 1863]), "in his holiness," i.e., fidelity and reliability, must be rejected because it is based on a presumption that "prophetic" and "priestly" oracles are principally distinct and because in the Old Testament God's holiness never signifies his reliability and fidelity.

87. Read *'ălê pĕlešet 'etrô'a'*; see Ps 108:10.

88. As I indicated in *Kongesalmerne*, 92, I also consider it possible to understand Ps 60:11 not as (complaining) words of the king (as representative of the people) but as the concluding words of the divine oracle. The sense of the question, then, is: "I, YHWH, have

advanced (in my palladium) to enter as leader of a victorious army into 'the fortification' (and) into Edom. Who of the kings and nobles of the world will lead me there?" The presupposition is that, at least in certain cases, the divine palladium was taken into war. God is then, of course, conceived ideally as the leader of the army. The God present in his palladium needs a representative *in praxi*, however, who as the one commissioned to a degree as minister, chief of court, and field marshal of God executes his plans and "brings" his palladium, and thus God himself, where he wishes to go. God is, indeed, the great king who does not go on foot but has servants who can carry him and his "travel director" who takes care of all practical matters and can, thus, also be designated as the one who "brings" or "leads" (*yôbîl, nāḥâ*) God to this place or that. Since, *in praxi* God also went here or there in and with his image or palladium, he was actually "brought," even though, ideally and in the belief of his worshipers, he was the true leader. A further presupposition of this oracle—assuming the accuracy of this interpretation—is that God depicts himself as though he does not know exactly at first whom he should commission to execute his wish. Consequently, he surveys the people in question, i.e., the kings of the earth, of course, in order to discover the right man whom he can commission with world dominion after the "godless" Nabonidus. Among all the kings and princes of the world, the choice fell on Cyrus, the king of Anšan. In Ps 60:11, this probative survey acquired the form of a question in which YHWH deliberates the matter with himself, as it were, and at the same time also wants to learn who among those in question are willing. This form of divine speech may be compared to the quite analogous question in Isa 6:8: "Whom shall I send, and who will be our messenger?" (cf. further the question in 1 Kgs 22:20). Of course, the poet assumes, and, in reality, so does YHWH in Ps 60:11, that the king of Israel will declare himself willing and that he will be chosen. Thus the question is meant more rhetorically than seriously, but it has, as in Isa 6:8, the purpose of allowing the pious willingness of the Israelite king to be clearly prominent. In response to the divine question, then, the quasi-diffident and somewhat reproachful question initially follows in Ps 60: "But have you rejected us and not gone out now with our armies?" This is followed immediately, however, by the prayer in v. 13: "Help us, etc." The prayer contains something like a condition, then: "Yes, if you will help us, then we are willing to bring you there." In conclusion, the full assurance follows: "in your might, we will surely be able to accomplish it." Several analogies are known for such oracles that express a deity's decision to "go" or be "led" somewhere. I mention two here. First is a letter of Tusratta of Mitanni to Amenophis III of Egypt dealing with the transfer of the healing statue of the goddess Ishtar of Nineveh to Egypt to heal the sick king. It says: "'To Egypt, the land that I love, will I go, will I repeat it (?).' See, now I (i.e., Tusratta) have sent (her), and she is gone" (Amarna tablet, no. 23 in J. A. Knudtzon, *Die El-Amarna-Tafeln* [VAB 2; Leipzig: Hinrichs, 1915], 179). Here, too, we have the same duality presupposed in Ps 60:11. The goddess "goes" *sua sponte*, and the king "conveys" her. In the inscription to his annals (Rassam Cylinder VI, 107ff.), Asshurbanapal discusses the return of the statue of the goddess Nania of Uruk that had been taken to Elam 1635 years before. In this connection he reports, as so often is the case, an oracle given him: "Asshurbanapal should bring me from evil Elam and bring me into Eanna [the major temple in Uruk]" (M. Streck, *Assurbanipal und die letzten assyrischen Konige bis zum Untergang Ninevehs* [VAB 7; Leipzig: Hinrichs, 1916], 50). Streck thinks here of "words spoken to Ashurbanipal by the goddess in a dream" (50 n. 5). In fact, dream oracles play a significant role for Ashurba-

joined in with the question, which while somewhat tentative was supported by a blossoming faith:

> Who, then, will bring me to the fortification?
> Who, then, will "lead"[89] me to Edom?

This is followed by the statement, meant both as a motivation and excuse for the doubt and lack of courage that have not yet been fully overcome:

But, "YHWH," you have rejected us and do not go forth[90] with our armies!

Only YHWH can lead the victorious army of Israel into the capital city of the enemy. O, that he would want to do so! Thus, the renewed request of a faith that would like to attain total confidence follows:

> O give us help with the enemy; human assistance amounts to nothing!

Deal with your glorious promise as only you can! Now, however, the full assurance of faith finally breaks through:

> In YHWH, we do mighty deeds; he tramples our enemy in the dust!
> Thus he will also surely lead Israel's hosts to victory this time.

*

The fact that the form of the oracle on this occasion was improvised ad hoc is clearly evident from the accommodation to the historical situation. This oracle underwent a history of development, however, as is evident from Ps 108.

If Ps 60 belongs to the time of David, as assumed above, then we know from the historical accounts that the oracle was fulfilled this time. David conquered both Edom and Moab. This circumstance, in connection with the fact—or the view of the Jerusalem priesthood—that it was given to King David, the great and beloved of God, led to its preservation with particular esteem. Quickly enough the opinion would have arisen that this promise constituted a promise, valid for all subsequent times, graciously to support

---

nipal. It is less likely, however, that an actual dream of Ashurbanipal is involved. The oracle was probably more likely communicated by a professional oracle priest (perhaps a "dream seer"). I do not know presently any oracles similar in content from Babylonia and Assyria that exhibit the question form.

89. Read an imperfect, BHK.
90. Strike 'ĕlōhîm in v. 12b, Sym. Syr.

the house of David and the people of Israel. We know well enough that there was a proclivity to appeal to the promises made to David (see Pss 89:20–38; 132:11–12).[91] Thus it came about that later, in a situation that may also have been similar from a historical and political perspective, one adopted the old oracle as the divine response to the needy people. This is the case in Ps 108. Thus, the oracle became a fixed element in a fixed liturgy.

In many respects, Ps 108 characterizes the development of later liturgies. It consists of sections of individual lament psalms directed against the evil sorcerers[92] (probably psalms of the sick), namely, the sections of Ps 57 and Ps 60:7–14 that contain the request, oracle, reprised request, and assurance of being heard. The suffering supplicant in Ps 57 has been reinterpreted in terms of a people suffering the attack of some enemy and the poison-spewing sorcerers in terms of this enemy.[93] The fact that in the last section of Ps 57, where the supplicant expresses his confidence in having been heard and then makes a vow, he says, in a rather common exaggeration, that he would "praise YHWH among the peoples and sing his praises among the nations" (v. 10). Thus the psalm was understood as a national psalm of lament, and this very passage, as anticipatory confidence in being heard and vow, has been made the introduction to the new liturgy.

Of course, it is impossible to determine the occasion for this occurrence. We may only attribute so much to measures taken by the redactor. It is not entirely certain that the enemies of the time are to be sought among the nations named in verse 10 (= 60:10). If Ps 60:9c, 10c are later additions, we may surmise that they are associated with the redaction and entered the text

---

91. A similar concern will have been grounds for the fact that the later tradition preserved so many psalms for "David's use"—for that is the original sense of the formula *lĕdāwîd* (see Ps 102:1)—and supplied them with related comments. A lament psalm, for example, that assisted the great David must be particularly beautiful, pleasing to God, effective, and particularly suited "for persuasion," *lmnṣḥ*. Consequently, the cultic psalms are frequently provided with this stamp. These stamps may be historical to the extent that, apart from the actual royal psalms, not a few psalms were composed for use by the king, perhaps even David (see Pss 28:8; 63:12; 84:10; 1 Sam 2:10). This was also the case in Babylonia and Assyria (see Morris Jastrow, *Die Religion Babyloniens und Assyriens* [2 vols. in 3; Giessen: Töpelmann, 1905], 2:106), and, since the majority of Old Testament psalms stem from the royal temple in Jerusalem, the assumption above is actually inherent in this regard in the nature of the matter. The beautiful and artful songs and liturgies were not originally for the common person. This view later gave rise to the theory that David was also the author of the songs in question. This assumption, too, was gradually extended to more and more songs.

92. See *Psalm Studies* 1:25.

93. Cf. *Psalm Studies* 1, ch. 6.

of Ps 60 from Ps 108. In this case, the redaction of Ps 108 could belong to the time of Jehoram (see above on Ps 60). Of course, we cannot know how often the oracle was employed in this new context.

*

These occasional public liturgies for days of repentance probably also include Pss 20 and 21, which, as royal psalms, constitute the transition to the group to be treated below, the royal oracles. In both the king is regarded to such a significant degree as the representative of the people that I prefer to treat these psalms here in order more clearly to assign them to the occasional penitential liturgies in terms of content.

Although Ps 20 does not contain a "lament" and is not a psalm of lament in style, it still belongs to the public "lament psalms" to the extent that it was composed for an occasion and, thus, is not to be assigned to the true community prayers (545–48). It cannot be denied, however, that it may have been performed repeatedly in similar situations that may have arisen.

We can deal with regard to this psalm quite briefly. Its character has been correctly determined by most recent and many older exegetes (see especially Gunkel and Staerk). It is penitential liturgy before the departure of the king to battle, for I consider it proven that "the anointed one" (v. 7) and "the king" (v. 10) is a true, that is, preexilic, Israelite or Judahite king.[94] Likewise, I agree with most of the more recent exegetes (Budde constitutes an exception) that the psalm accompanied or followed immediately after a sacrificial procedure, this not only because of verse 4, which could well refer to all the sacrifices brought by the king in the course of time as so many proofs of his piety, but simply because it is inherent in the nature of the matter and the essence of ancient Near Eastern religions. A day of prayer without some type of sacrifice is simply inconceivable in the preexilic period and under circumstances that were normal to some degree. The fact that the prophecy of the prophet associated with the sanctuary was connected to the sacrificial procedure is also to be regarded as assured and inherent in the nature of the matter (see above, 510–11). Thus, the oracle given in verses 7–9 should be regarded as the result of hieroscopy or a similar interpretation of signs or as more or less ecstatic

---

94. Hermann Gunkel, "Die Königspsalmen," *Preussische Jahrbücher* 158 (1914). Apart from Isa 45:1, where the title has been applied in the "messianic" sense to Cyrus, the fixed term "the anointed of YHWH" in the singular otherwise signifies in the Old Testament nothing other than the historical king of Israel. In Dan 9:25, 26, the word is not a fixed term. Here it means *an* anointed one. In Ps 105:15 = 1 Chr 16:22 ("my anointed ones," i.e., the patriarchs), the concept of the prophet as anointed lies in the background.

inspiration received in conjunction with the sacrifice, although the content and even the wording may also have been established in the order of worship. An element of the liturgy will have been the communication of a favorable oracle with the content offered at this point.

As has been said, the liturgy in Ps 20 lacks the actual lament psalm. It may have taken place in an early phase of the cultic procedure of the day of prayer. The absence may be because no actual need was present and thus no true reason for lamenting and complaining. At any rate, verse 2 speaks of a *yôm ṣarâ*, a reference, as Buhl correctly states, not to the coming danger in battle, but to the current moment. Even the prospect of war is described as "distress," that is, neediness. One cannot feasibly derive any clues as to the magnitude of the danger and the possible historical situation. In religious poetry, the danger and the need are the greatest possible. The psalm contains nothing whatsoever that could not refer to any day of prayer before war. It is an authentic cultic liturgy.

The first part consists of the community's blessing for the king. May YHWH, the strong God, now hear and protect you, send you help from the temple, reckon your piety and your plentiful sacrifice to your account, give you your heart's desire, and make all your "counsels" reality, so that we may rejoice in your victorious power and in the name of our God! This blessing is supposed to put the assurance of victory, victorious power, in brief, "victory," in the king's soul and thus to actualize it. Thus the community helps to create reality, victory, through the efficacious blessing in the cult. The power of the blessing is rooted in God's power to bless, God with whom the community has a covenant that it strengthens in the cult.[95]

Then, however, an individual steps forward, the priest-prophet, and shares the result of the oracle inquiry. If the psalm alludes to the sacrificial procedure (v. 4), it is likely that the oracle was acquired through hieroscopy. The oracle is not communicated literally this time. It is only said that the result of the oracle inquiry was favorable. This, too, is best explained if we think not of an ecstatic-*nābî'*-istic oracle but of a purely technical one. The prophet says:

Now I [truly][96] know that YHWH grants victory to his anointed one,
hears him from holy heaven with the helping power of his hand.

The community follows this communication with the thankful expression of its assurance of confidence in victory. YHWH and his wonder-working name

---

95. Cf. *Psalm Studies* 2, part 1, §1.4.2.
96. *Yādōʻa, metri causi.*

is with them, he, who is the sole true God. What the others, the enemies, are able to offer is not true divine power but only human work, flesh and not spirit, as Isaiah puts it, or horse and wagon, as this psalm does. Consequently, the enemies must also fall. We will remain standing, however, and even though we falter, we will immediately stand up again in the power of our God. The whole concludes with a request that the promise be actualized:

YHWH, give the king victory and hear today[97] our pleading!

The question as to the occasion and the king for which and whom, respectively, this psalm was probably sung for the first time is moot. In keeping with its purely liturgical nature, it will probably have been utilized often on similar occasions.

In literary and formal terms, it occupies a unique position within psalmody. It does not consist, as do most such liturgies (e.g., Ps 85), of a request (lament psalm) and an oracle but of a blessing (see *Psalm Studies* 5) and an oracle with a confident concluding prayer.

*

Psalm 21 very likely had a similar impetus as Ps 20. Usually exegetes understand this psalm as a thanksgiving psalm but disagree as to which blessing the thanksgiving pertains: a long and happy reign in general,[98] a victory won,[99] the coronation anniversary,[100] and so on. It is illuminating that it is not a lament psalm in style. The question of the purpose of the psalm depends, in part, on other questions: Does verse 14 belong to the original psalm? Many doubt that it does.[101] These interpreters understand the verse as a liturgical or eschatological addition, but they offer no real reasons for this understanding. The fact that a verse seems "liturgical" is not grounds for striking it if the psalms were meant for the cult. Psalms 82 and 20 demonstrate that a prayer can, indeed, follow the oracle. The symmetrical structure of the psalm speaks

---

97. "The day of our pleading" is the current day of prayer.

98. Buhl, *Psalmerne*; Staerk, "Lyrik"; and others.

99. E.g., Charles Briggs, *Psalms: A Critical and Exegetical Commentary* (ICC; Edinburgh: T&T Clark, 1906); Franz Delitzsch, *Biblische Commentar über die Psalmen* (4th ed.; BCAT 4.1; Leipzig: Dörfling & Franke, 1883); Thomas Kelly Cheyne, *The Book of Psalms* (London: Kegan Paul, Trench, 1888).

100. Duhm, *Psalmen*.

101. Karl Budde, *Die schönsten Psalmen: Übertragen und erläutert* (Leipzig: Amelang, 1915), Buhl, Staerk, and others.

for the authenticity of the verse.[102] Consideration of the psalm as a whole reveals that the oracle promises what the conclusion requests. The request shows that the oracle refers to a specific situation involving YHWH's might (*'ōz*) and heroism (*gĕbûrâ*). Thus the promise does not pertain to valorous deeds in general but to victory in a certain specific situation. Thus we have an assumption similar to that in Ps 20. Our psalm is, like Ps 20, a liturgy for a day of prayer before the king's departure to war.

I have already mentioned that, from a formal perspective, the psalm exhibits a symmetrical structure similar to Ps 20. The first major strophe of seven lines is not, however, a blessing, as it is in Ps 20, but a thanksgiving psalm. However, that does not mean, as the exegetes contend, that the psalm as a whole is a thanksgiving liturgy. The central point is not the thanksgiving but the oracle. The thanksgiving is to be regarded here as a "motivation" within the prayer liturgy. The thanksgiving is meant to express the confidence of the king and the community. The God who has already given such majestic gifts will, so the community may expect, also help the king now and, as before, grant him the fulfillment of his desire. Consequently, the strophe climaxes in verse 8, which is clearly aimed at the receipt of new blessings:

> For the king trusts in YHWH, in the never-wavering goodness of Elyon.

Otherwise, the strophe is very characteristic of the religious assessment of the monarchy. King and people appear to be identical here. If the king enjoys God's mercy, then the people are assured good fortune. He lives, reigns, and rejoices "in YHWH's might." YHWH will keep nothing from the pious king. YHWH gives him whatever his heart desires. YHWH even anticipates him with blessings, adorns him with the symbol, the "sacramental" carriers of divine power and righteousness, the core of "blessing," and of the royal good fortune that supports the entire people: the golden tiara. At his request, YHWH gives him eternal life. In full possession of the "glory," *kābôd*, of the content of the soul, of the psychic power that produces great and glorious deeds, he stands there with "majesty" and "glory" (*hôd* and *hādār*, two expressions of the same concept): he is "adorned" like a god. Such a superhuman—one could say of him just as well as one did of Gilgamesh that "two-thirds of him is God, one-third of him is human"—may also surely trust in divine assistance and victory in the current "crisis" when he will soon appear in sight of the enemy.

---

102. Two major sections of seven 3 + 3 strophes: (1) thanksgiving; (2) oracle and prayer. Cf. Ps 20, with two major sections of five 3 + 3 strophes: (1) blessing; (2) oracle and prayer.

Nothing hinders the assumption that this part of the psalm was sung by the king himself. Just as the supplicant in the lament and thanksgiving psalms often designates himself not in the first person but as "your servant" (Pss 19:12, 14; 116:16) or the king in similar psalms as "the king," "the anointed one," "your anointed one" (Pss 18:51; 61:7–8; 63:12), he refers to himself here not in the first person but as "the king." This involves a confidence motive: YHWH must be gracious to his king and help him.

After the king has so declared his confidence in divine assistance in the form of a thanksgiving psalm, the prophet raises his voice. Here, too, we may assume that some sacrifice and technical oracular rite preceded the psalm. However, the oracle here has the form of an authentic *nābî'* saying. It is possible, therefore, that, in this case—or on certain occasions—the giving of the oracle was left to the free inspiration, perhaps the dreams and dream interpretations, of a nabi. The content of the oracle is victory over the enemy. The promise itself is kept quite general. As has been said, the context, however, reveals that it refers to the respective imminent war. It says:

> May your hand seize all your enemies, your right hand "smash"[103] your opponents;
> may you "scorch"[104] them as in a burning oven,
> as soon as you show your "countenance";
> may "you" destroy them in "your" anger;
> may the glow [of your wrath] consume them;[105]
> may you remove their fruit from the earth, their seed from the sons of men!
> When they plan evil against you and intend evil—for naught!
> For you make them to show their backs when you aim your bow at them.[106]

Much as in Pss 20 and 82, the choir joins in at the end with the request that the promise may soon be realized and that the people will soon be able to celebrate the glorious victory:

> Arise, YHWH, in your might, so that we may sing and play of your mighty act!

---

103. Read *timḥāṣ*, BHK.
104. Read *taṣṣitemô*, BHK.
105. Strike *yhwh* in v. 10, read *bĕappĕkā tĕballĕēm* and *ēš ḥarônĕkā*.
106. One may not translate "at your countenance"; *pĕnêhem* stands quite apart here.

2.3. Royal Oracles

When one speaks of the royal psalms in the Old Testament, one does not understand this name as the designation for a separate literary genre.[107] Instead, the pertinent psalms include almost all the literary genres of psalmody: individual lament psalms (illness psalms, Pss 28; 61; 63); thanksgiving psalms (Ps 18; 1 Sam 2:1–10); public lament psalms (Ps 89); oracular psalms (Pss 2; 45; 72; 110; 132); liturgies for days of prayer and festivals (Pss 20; 21; 84; 132); vow psalms (Ps 101); and blessing psalms (Ps 72). The common theme in all of them is some treatment of the kings of Israel. Here we deal with the psalms as cultic genres and in terms of the various cultic usages. The royal psalms must, consequently, be treated in terms of their cultic genres in their respective places. Above we have met both regularly recurring and occasional psalms and liturgies for festivals and days of prayer in which the king appears as the representative of the religion and the cult and thus stands at the center of the cultic proceedings (Pss 132; 20; 21). We will also meet him later as sick and in need of cleansing in the individual lament psalms (Ps 28).

There are a few, especially among the oracular psalms, in which the king stands at the center to a very unusual degree in that they involve his becoming king or some event that is significant for his status as king. Given these psalms' overall configuration, we may surmise that they were written not for a unique event but for utilization on certain recurrent occasions, sometimes at long, sometimes at short intervals. Above all, we are dealing with psalms for a king's ascension to the throne. Consequently, they constitute to a certain degree an interim stage between regular and occasional cultic procedures and psalms and will, if oracular psalms, be treated here as a special group. Psalms 2; 110; 72; and 45 will be discussed here. They are public songs in that they view the king as the representative of the community and they belonged to public worship.

I have briefly indicated elsewhere what the king meant to ancient Israel in social and religious respects.[108] I refer here to my previous portrayal. The royal psalms find their explanation in the ideal image of the king outlined there. These psalms, as Gunkel has already quite correctly emphasized, do not deal with this or that historical king but with the king of Israel as he should be according to the fundamental social psychological view and the popular ideal, an ideal that one expected each historical king, the "king after YHWH's heart," to actualize. The question as to which king was probably meant in this or that

---

107. Gunkel, "Königspsalmen"; Sigmund Mowinckel, *Kongesalmerne i det Gàmle Testamente* (Kristiania: Aschehoug [Nygaard], 1916).

108. *Psalm Studies* 2, part 2, 467–72.

psalm is therefore mistaken in principle. The pertinent ruling king is meant, and the question of which king reigned when the individual psalms were first composed simply cannot be answered, since neither specific individuals were depicted nor any historical conditions referenced, at least not in a fashion that is transparent to us. The historical background that sometimes seems to be outlined also usually refers not to reality but to theory. This is best exhibited in Ps 2. The situation outlined in the song is as follows: the king on Zion is the emperor of the world by right; the subjugated vassals, the kings and nations of the whole earth, utilize the occasion of a change on the throne to attempt to throw off the yoke; the king opposes this attempt with his divine legal claim. This is a situation that was never reality in Israel. It may have possessed a certain reality in the oriental empires and may have been applied, along with the oriental royal ideal, to Israelite circumstances. In addition, the influence of the enthronement of God myth, namely, the "battle against the nations myth,"[109] may also have played a role. The myth of the attack by the nations of the world against the new king has been applied by YHWH to his "son," the new earthly king. The explicit emphasis on the priestly status of the king in Ps 110 may, for example, be a barb against the claims of the Jerusalemite hierarchy.[110] This may be a quite isolated case, however. Nonetheless, compare below concerning Ps 45.

It is not entirely clear to me whether Gunkel wants to maintain the cultic character of the royal psalms. He finds their *Sitz im Leben* in the court feasts, the festivities of the royal house. Whether, however, he conceived of these festivities as cultic festivals and would have included the psalms in the rites of the day cannot be clearly perceived. In any case, he says nothing explicit on the point. Staerk assigns at least most of the royal psalms to the "spiritual songs in the more restricted sense,"[111] that is, to the songs that are not only "separate from the cult" but in which "the characteristic styles of the human and prayer are absent or have shrunk to a residue that continues to have mostly rhetorical importance." We have seen above, however, that he often conceives of the forms of cultic poetry much too restrictively. Furthermore, he did not recognize clearly enough the place of the prophetic oracle in the cult.

It seems incontrovertible to me that the royal psalms must have actually been cultic songs. Many reasons support this view: (1) the analogy of the other oracular psalms already discussed; (2) the religious character of the ancient Israelite monarchy; (3) the indissoluble connection between popular

---

109. *Psalm Studies* 2, part 1, 236–44.
110. So Gunkel, "Königspsalmen."
111. Staerk, "Lyrik," 228.

and political life, on the one hand, and religion, on the other—religion was cult then, however; and (4) the clearly attested religio-cultic character of the situation presupposed in many of these psalms: the anointing of the new king and his ascension to the throne.

*

Of the psalms that refer to the enthronement of a king,[112] Ps 2 is the clearest in many respects. Earlier (*Psalm Studies* 2:185–87) I offered a sketch of the proceedings for the anointing and ascension of an Israelite king. I will refer to it here.

From Ps 2:6–9, the explicit accentuation of the divine call of the king who speaks and the subsequent oracle, it becomes clear enough that this case concerns the religio-legal legitimization of the aspirant.

We know well enough that in Israel inheritance alone was not considered the legitimization for the kingship but also internal psychic and spiritual qualities (see 1 Sam 13:13–15; 15; 16:1; 1 Kgs 19:16; cf. Isa 11:1–5). The passages cited also demonstrate that internal legitimacy came to expression and became evident in that YHWH chose the "man after his heart." The divine election was the visible legitimization for the people. This election occurred through one called to proclaim the will of YHWH, a prophet, which does not necessarily mean a *nābî'* in the restricted sense. The one involved could also be a priest provided with the gift of giving oracles, or, as I have designated it here, a cultic prophet, a temple prophet or a priest-prophet (*kōhēn* and *rō'eh*). The story of Saul's election by means of the lot by the priest-prophet, Samuel, demonstrates this process (1 Sam 10:17–21). Even clearer is 1 Kgs 1:32–40, where the priest Zadok, the administrator of the lot, the bearer of the ephod, anoints Solomon king.[113] Here, however, one must recall that in ancient Israel the boundaries between priest and prophet were fluid.

Inheritance as legitimization came under consideration only to the extent that a person was always identical with his clan and house and that the sons normally inherit the "soul," the character traits of the father and the patriarch. In the ancient Israelite view, the soul and character are not the possession

---

112. Pss 2; 110; 72; in addition, probably Ps 101, too. It is not an oracular psalm, however, and thus does not come under consideration here.

113. In view of v. 39, the prophet Nathan in v. 32 is clearly a later insertion. The fact that it now elicits the impression that the pronouncement of election and the anointing were usually performed by independent *nĕbî'îm* depends on the later layering and treatment of the sources in terms of later theories.

of an individual but of a "totality," a supra-ego, a clan, a people.[114] Thus the royal soul normally belongs also to the sons, thus the charisma of being the elect, too. According to common presuppositions, legitimization pertains to the whole household (see 1 Sam 9:20). A person cannot "be honored," cannot ascend, without bringing his whole household along with him.[115] If, however, the unusual case should arise that the sons do not prove to have the "righteousness" of the father, elect status is immediately forfeited. Sonship per se means nothing then. Only under this condition is election linked to the house of David (Ps 132:12).[116]

Election found its most visible and supreme expression in the anointing of the elect by the prophet who proclaims the will of the deity (see the passages mentioned above). This leads us to the relationship between the election of the king and the cult.

Election by the priest-prophet is already a religious act connected to cultic procedures (1 Sam 9–10; 10:17;[117] 11:14–15; 16:5–13). The same is also true, as these passages demonstrate, of the anointing (see 1 Kgs 1:5–9, 32–40; 2 Kgs 11:12). It was performed at the sacred site and was linked to sacrifice and other cultic procedures.[118] It was a sacrament bringing with it the possession of the "spirit" that transforms the soul of the apparently normal person into a royal soul, or, perhaps better, that causes the predisposition to rule slumbering in the soul to unfold to full bloom (see 1 Sam 10:1, 6–7; 16:13; cf. Isa 11:1–5).[119] Briefly put, anointing is a cultic procedure that consummates the transfer of kingship. This cultic procedure, like every other, must have had its own liturgical forms.

It is inherent in the nature of the matter and is also explicitly attested that this sacred procedure was accompanied by sacred words (1 Sam 10:1; 2 Kgs 9:3). These words take the form of YHWH sayings, of prophetic oracles, that

---

114. See the blessings and curses in Gen 49 and Deut 33, which seek to explain the character traits of the various Israelite tribes in terms of the character traits of the patriarchs.

115. See the excellent treatment of clan and individual in Pedersen, *Israel*, 269–75.

116. This is also the presupposition in 2 Sam 7. This passage does not speak of grave, conscious sins that spring from an "unjust" soul and make a person "unjust" to the core of his personality. Nathan speaks only of those sins that can be "atoned."

117. Mizpah is a cultic center.

118. Jehu's anointing by Elisha is a revolutionary and irregular procedure that, as the exception, confirms the rule (2 Kgs 9:1–10).

119. The Old Testament admittedly does not speak explicitly of an "anointing with the spirit." The passages cited suggest clearly enough, however, that the transfer of the spirit depends on the anointing and anointing brings the spirit with it. The Old Testament is sufficiently acquainted with the reality underlying the spiritualized expression.

authenticate possession of kingship. Their content and form is: "Thus says YHWH: 'I anoint you (today) as king over Israel.'" Naturally the words were not as succinct in the solemn liturgy of the day as in the narrative account in 2 Kgs 9. Extensive charges and promises would also have been added in accordance with the prophetic oracle (see 1 Sam 10:1).

If we find psalms in the collection of the Jerusalemite cultic songs that offer prophetic oracles to a king on his enthronement day, we are unquestionably justified in understanding these psalms as the oracles belonging to the liturgy of the day of anointing and to maintain this as the only natural understanding until it is refuted with positive grounds.

Gunkel, Buhl, and others have recognized that the situation presupposed in Ps 2 is the ascent of a new king to the throne. The traditional, but false, messianic interpretation has not yet been universally rejected, however. Even Staerk, who is otherwise markedly influenced by Gunkel with regard to the interpretation of the psalms, still understands the psalm to be "messianic," not only in the sense that originally "messianic" concepts were applied to an earthly king (so, for example, Hugo Gressmann and Ernst Sellin[120]), but in the purely technical sense of messiah: the psalm deals with the eschatological king who already exists but is yet invisible to human eyes. However, as Gunkel has correctly emphasized, the requirement of a uniform explanation for the royal psalms speaks against this understanding. If the king, the anointed one, is the earthly king of Israel in some of these psalms, analogy requires the same exegesis of the other related psalms, and one must demand positive evidence for a divergent interpretation of the figure mentioned in individual psalms. It should be enlightening that the anointed one, who expresses his thanks for wondrous deliverance in battle, whose victory is the subject of prayer and whose already-offered sacrifice is referenced in Pss 20 and 21, who appears in Ps 45 as newly married, who prays for healing for an illness in Pss 61 and 63, who in deep distress refers to an oracle given his ancestor David in Ps 89, to whom an oracle promising good fortune and power is pronounced and who is addressed standing or sitting in the sight of the prophet in Ps 110—that this anointed one is a contemporary figure, not one in the future. Then, however, he will also be so in Ps 2. The assumption that the psalm is a speech placed in the mouth of a figure who has not yet appeared, without having been indi-

---

120. Hugo Gressmann, *Der Ursprung der israelitisch-jüdischen Eschatologie* (FRLANT 6; Göttingen: Vandenhoeck & Ruprecht, 1905), 252–54; Ernst Sellin, *Der alttestamentlich Prophetismus: Drei Studien* (Leipzig: Deichertsche, 1912). I have shown elsewhere that this notion of originally messianic concepts to the earthly king is absolutely false (*Psalm Studies* 2, part 2, §2.14, 469–72). Already before there was an eschatological "messiah," the earthly king was understood in mythological forms as a divine being.

cated as such by an introductory statement, that a mysterious figure speaks here whoever it may be, is very unlikely on its face.

The situation presupposed in the psalm is as follows: The throne on Zion has become empty. The vassals who owe tribute, all the kings and princes, all the nations and tribes of the earth, want to exploit the favorable moment to cast off the hated yoke. The world of nations has become violently agitated; the kings assemble and craft plans. Now the hour of liberation may have been sounded.

Zion is conceived here as a world-class metropolis, the king there as the ruler of the world, and the situation is one often described in Assyria in relation to a change in government such as a monarch like Sennacherib or Sargon amply experienced (see above). The question arises, then, who may be the legitimate ruler called by the God of heaven to rule the world, who should hold the world, calm again, in his hand, to whom the peoples have been given as his property and the nations as a possession. Will the nations, the pagans, succeed in realizing their evil plans against Israel and the ruler on Zion? Will the pagans triumph or Israel? Will the new king, just anointed on Zion and in the process of ascending to the throne, be able to maintain his inherited possessions? Will he truly be all that a king on Zion is supposed to be? By right and by religion, after all, the king on Zion is due worldwide rule. Indeed, his "father" is YHWH, the God of the world, who as such sits on his throne in heaven. His "son," the king of Israel, is his regent on earth. The Israelite kings' claim to worldwide dominion, like Jerusalem's claim to be a world-class metropolis (Pss 48:2–3; 87) and the claims of the regents of Christ of the medieval "Roman" emperors, is not political and historical reality but a religious and idealistic claim. We are dealing here with a common ancient Near Eastern religio-political theory, one that was held by the rulers on the Nile or the Euphrates and Tigris and was also adopted by the Israelite kings and incorporated into their overall religious views. It is more than "courtly style," as Gressmann and others term it.[121] It has become organically connected with both ancient Israel's worldview and God concept and its chief myth. The theory is authentically Israelite to the extent that, for the Israelites, Israel was always the people (see Ps 36:8) and Canaan the "land," the earth. Israel's God is the God of the "land," the earth inhabited by "people." He is the creator of the world and, consequently, the king of Israel and the world. Every New Year's Festival he returns as creator of the world, as king, and reestablishes Israel as the focal point, as the people who rule the world (*Psalm Studies* 2). Therefore, the fact that the earthly king of Israel, the "son" of the God of

---

121. Gressmann, *Ursprung*, 250–59.

the world, must actually be king of the world by right is also an enlightening religious and moral truth for the Israelites.

Israel, however, lives—both in myth[122] and reality—surrounded by a hostile world. These "evildoers" (*rĕšāʿîm*) will exploit any opportunity to debase Israel's grandeur, to cast off its oppressive bonds. The opportunity offered is succession to the throne—such was the case even in political reality. If the ruling king, the "son" who represents YHWH on earth, has died, the "vassals" rebel. Israel cannot imagine anything else than that the "pagans" perceive the "ideal" claim to dominion asserted by Israel and its royal house just as realistically as did Israel itself. But in contrast to Israel, they perceive it as an oppressive reality from which they must always seek freedom. Consequently, ancient Israel also believed, quite naïvely, that the succession on Zion was an event observed by the whole world with heightened attention. Who will be the king of the world now? Another Israelite, a worshiper of YHWH, or do we pagans have a turn this time? Will we succeed this time in gaining our freedom?

Israel responds: "empty, foolish, impudent plans!" He who is enthroned in heaven only laughs at them. Wait a moment, and he will give you a "speech" that will lack nothing in clarity. With the heat of his burning wrath, he will destroy you. For here on Zion already stands the king, who has become YHWH's son today through the anointing and the other initiation rites, who has been equipped today with royal righteousness and good fortune, has received a royal soul, has become a new man, was born today as YHWH's son. All the power on earth has been conveyed to him; all the nations and tribes have been given him as an inheritance. Only one option is open to you: profess your submission as quickly as possible, prostrate yourselves before YHWH, the mighty, in homage to kiss[123] his feet and to bow to the scepter of his son who rules here. If you do not do this, you will surely experience the most fearsome destruction, for his divine wrath erupts quickly, very quickly.

Psalm 2 has the king himself proclaim this firm belief. In form, the psalm appears to be a proclamation by the new king to his subjects, the nations of the world, as an inaugural address of sorts.[124] In the first strophe, the king sarcastically outlines the situation envisioned:

---

122. *Psalm Studies* 2, part 1, §2.1, esp. 230–60.

123. Alfred Bertholet's ingenious suggestion to move the completely meaningless *nšqw br* in v. 12 before *gylw* in v. 11 and to read *wĕnāššĕqû bĕraglāw* is obviously correct (*Das Buch der Psalmen* [HSAT 2; Tübingen: Mohr, 1923).

124. In the current text, there is a difficult and extremely opaque alternation of speaking subjects: vv. 1–5, king or prophet; v. 6, YHWH; v. 7a, king; vv. 7b–9, YHWH; vv. 10–12, king or prophet. If one substitutes in v. 6 the original text attested by LXX and, in part, by

Why do the nations of the world clamor so, the tribes contemplate vanity,
the kings of the earth assemble, princes craft plans together:[125]
"Let us tear your bonds and cast off your fetters!"

Then in the second strophe, the announcement of the harsh reality, encouraging and comforting for Israel and the king, by which the "empty" plans must fail:

The one enthroned in heaven only laughs, the LORD scoffs at you;
then he speaks to them in wrath and terrifies them with his anger.
I, however, "have been anointed" as his king on Zion, his holy mountain.

What is the basis of the certainty of the king who speaks? YHWH's election that has been announced to him—via the prophet or directly—and that has given him legitimacy and power that no worldly power can topple. In the third strophe, he shares YHWH's saying that revealed all this to him:

I will announce YHWH's decision:
He said to me: "You are my son; today I have begotten you!
Only ask me, and I will give you the nations as an inheritance,
the world as a possession;
smash with an iron cudgel, trample them like pottery!"

YHWH announced to the king his "adoption" as YHWH's son and with it the right to worldwide dominion. Thereby he has become king. As king, he is "YHWH's son." The legitimizing word of God is clearly the reference here. It is rendered at least in substance, if not verbatim.

In the fourth strophe the king returns to the beginning, draws the sole necessary conclusion for the hostile world of nations and gives them the appropriate advice:

Now, then, you kings, be clever; take warning, you regents of the earth:
serve YHWH with fear and "kiss his feet" with trembling,
so that he does not become angry and you perish—for quickly his wrath erupts!

Jerome, as well (*nissaktî malkô* and *qadšô*), the king is the speaker of the whole psalm. In vv. 7b–9, he reports what YHWH said to him.

125. Verse 2b is correct, but it is a gloss outside the meter.

What are we to think of as the *Sitz im Leben* of a psalm such as this? After the discussion above, it cannot be doubted that it was associated with the enthronement rites, with the anointing. It presupposes the enthronement of the new king in the background; he communicates a related oracle as indicated for this situation. It is, we see, to be regarded as a proclamation by the new king to his subjects. We need not doubt that his words evoked a storm of enthusiasm among the Israelites who heard this glorious proclamation. Accordingly, it may be considered rather certain that, if it belonged to the cultic celebrations of the day in any way—and I can see no reason it should not have—it must have had its place when the new king appeared for the first time as such in the view of the people, the assembled mass of celebrants. According to 2 Kgs 11:12–13, however, he did so when he exited some room in the temple where the final preparations[126] were completed into the temple court, "took his place on the '*ammûd*,"[127] clothed with the royal insignia and anointed. Then all the people greeted him as king with shouts of joy: "Long live the king!" It is difficult to imagine that the king remained silent throughout this scene. He must have been presented to the people as king in some manner and with some statement. Psalm 2 contains a statement such as could have been made on this occasion. Here the new king presents himself as king, with all the solemnity and legitimacy that the situation might require. We can imagine that the adulation would have been all the more boisterous after such a proclamation.

We may be able to infer something more from the psalm. As we saw, the king reports the divine calling on which is kingship is founded in verses 7b–9. We have seen above that prophetically gifted persons made such statements at the anointing. Now it is very possible that the king reports the words here that some cultic prophet spoke to him immediately before, during the actual act of anointing. "He said to me" would then mean, "he spoke to me through the prophet." It seems to be portrayed here such that the king himself received the divine words. Was it that, at least occasionally, the king himself stepped forward as the one who was "inspired" at the anointing and who received the divine oracle himself? Was it an element, as it were, of the ritual that the king, on certain occasions, should also appear as an inspired person and proclaim sayings entrusted to him in the ecstasy of the sacred hour? We know that it was not a rare belief in ancient Israel that the king also received the prophetic spirit, the gift of prophecy, along with the anointing and the conveyance of

---

126. One could envision ritual washings or something similar, for example.
127. Uncertain; an elevated stand of some sort; hardly "column."

the Spirit (see 2 Sam 23:1–3; 1 Kgs 3:5–14; cf. also the "messianic" passages in Isa 9:1–7; 11:1–9). We can state the supposition; we certainly cannot affirm it.

Was Ps 2 one of the liturgically prescribed elements of the anointing liturgy, or was the formulation of the oracle to be spoken left each time to the independent inspiration and imagination of the—or one of the—cultic prophet(s)? I do not know but consider the latter assumption the more likely. It corresponds best to the often-attested independent forms of Israelite prophecy. We must also not necessarily think that the one who proclaimed the oracle and the one who performed the anointing were always the same person. The chief priest probably usually performed the anointing. Another prophetic minister of the cult could have been grasped by inspiration and proclaimed the fortune-promising oracle to be spoken. It probably was determined in advance who of the many prophets would report God's decision this time.

*

In Ps 110 we have another example of an oracle spoken at the anointing of a king. Here, too, the content of the promise is the transfer of the kingship and the legitimization of the king as king through divine election proclaimed by a prophet. It does not involve an already-ruling king being promised the priesthood in addition nor the monarchy being conveyed to a priest. Instead, kingship and priesthood were simultaneously promised to someone. Verses 1–2 speak of the conveyance of the kingship, verse 4 of the priesthood. The long-preferred interpretation of the psalm in reference to the Maccabean, Simon, is already to be rejected on these grounds—quite apart from the fact that one should not seek "Maccabean" psalms in the Psalter at all, in my view.[128]

The focal point in the psalm is on the legitimization of the new king through a saying of YHWH. The seat of honor at the right hand of God,[129] the extension of the ruler's mighty staff, and the subjugation of the enemies from Zion[130] all signify royal dignity and power. The new candidate is called on here to ascend the throne due him for the first time and from there to exercise dominion in the power of YHWH and with his assistance. The election expressed in this manner is motivated in verse 3 with the reference to the internal dignity and the divine "birth" of the election (cf. Ps 2):

---

128. So also Gunkel. See further *Psalm Studies* 1:166.
129. See 1 Chr 29:23. Gunkel ("Königspsalmen") cites Egyptian parallels.
130. For metrical reasons, *miṣṣiyôn* belongs to v. 2b.

"With you"[131] is "majesty"[132] on the day of your might,
"on the holy mountain" I have begotten you from the lap of the dawn.[133]

Through the "majesty" of his soul, through his noble, generous attitude,[134] the new king has shown that a royal soul dwells in him, that he has the "righteousness" and "blessing" of a king, and, thus, will be in a position to "vindicate" and to "bless" his people, to provide it with internal and external good fortune and salvation. This royal virtue becomes especially evident today, "on the day of his power," when he stands there adorned with the royal psychic power, with *kābôd*, *hôd*, and *hādār* (see Ps 21:6). YHWH wanted to acknowledge this virtue and, for its sake, "honor" him even more and "adorn" him to an even greater degree. It is quite natural that he possesses the royal virtues: he was begotten, after all, by YHWH himself as a new god of light on the sacred mountains of the east, and the lovely goddess of the dawn[135] was his mother. The idea of the divine "begetting" of the king on his day of enthronement, conceived in Ps 2 as an adoption, is expressed here by applying an older, per-

---

131. Pronounce ʿimmĕkā, LXX, Aquila, Quinta.

132. Pronounce *nĕdîbat* (an old absolute state); Bernhard Duhm, *Die Psalmen* (KHAT 14; Tübingen: Mohr, 1899).

133. Read *bĕharĕrê qōdeš mērehem šahar yĕlidtîkā* (see *Psalm Studies* 2, part 2, §2.14, 472). The plural *hadĕrê* does not occur elsewhere. In contrast, the reading *bĕharĕrê* is attested in many manuscripts and old translations. *Mišhar* does not occur otherwise, and the pointing *miššahar* does not help. The initial *mem* is, as has long been suspected, dittography of the preceding final *mem*. The traditional translation, "your young men come to you in sacred adornment like dew from the lap of the dawn" (literally, "the dew of your young men is for you"), yields no meaning, since the warriors do not appear in priestly garments and since the dew, and not as it stands, the young manhood, can come from the lap of the dawn. In addition, *yaldût* does not mean "youth" in the sense of "young people" but only "juvenescent" (Eccl 11:9–10). The statement *yĕlidtîkā* is attested in the Hexapla and is confirmed by Ps 2:7; *lekā tal* is absent in LXX. One should read *kĕtal* and understand it as the exegetical gloss to the one born from the lap of the dawn.

134. In ancient Israel, while it was still governed to a degree by the bedouin virtues, as with the old Germans, generosity (*nĕdîbâ*) was the true, noble, royal virtue. Miserliness, pettiness, in contrast, was the most contemptible vice.

135. The objection that the appellative *šāhār* is otherwise masculine gender amounts to little. The fact that divine beings change genders in the course of time is not unheard of, e.g., Ishtar = southern Arabic ʾattar, who was male, and the old Nordic god Njord, who arose from the old Germanic goddess Nerthus (the *u*-endings, which were originally feminine, became masculine in old Nordic). In Ps 139:8, the dawn is presented as a living, winged being that was surely divine originally. In Isa 14:12, Helal, perhaps the morning star, perhaps the crescent of the waning moon (see Gesenius–Buhl), is a son of the dawn portrayed as a divine being. Whether it is conceived as mother or father cannot be determined.

haps originally Egyptian, myth of the birth to the king of the new sun-god on the mountains of the east.[136]

As Gunkel has very correctly emphasized, the oriental monarchy had two major facets: the judicial office, that is, ruling, triumphing, and protecting; and the priestly office.[137] As in Egypt and Babylonia-Assyria since antiquity, royal and priestly authority were also combined in the person of the king in Canaan. The Israelites adopted the same view. This was all the easier since the ancient Israelite, "pre-Canaanite" chieftains also united the two functions as leader and judge, on the one hand, and seer and priest, on the other (e.g., Moses). Thus we see that Gideon was both chieftain-king and priest (Judg 8:22–28). Both David and Solomon were priests (2 Sam 6:5, 13–14, 18; 7:18–29; 8:18; 1 Kgs 8:14–15, 54–55, 62–66). The history of Judah shows us that it must have even seemed necessary to emphasize this ancient royal right against the "theocratic" claims to power of the Jerusalemite hierarchy.[138] Psalm 110 shows us how the Judahite kings justified their priestly claims "constitutionally": just as the Holy Roman emperors regarded themselves as the legal successors of the Caesars, so the Judahite kings viewed themselves as the legal successors of the old Jerusalemite king, Melchizedek—and so YHWH was identified with the "Jebusite" god of Jerusalem, El Elyon. Admittedly, we have only saga-like and legendary reports concerning this Melchizedek (Gen

---

136. We probably have the same application in Assyria when Ashurnasirpal II describes himself in a lament psalm as follows: "I was born on an unknown mountain" (Jastrow, *Religion Babyloniens*, 2:112). It is unacceptable to assume that he meant to allude to humble origins or to describe himself with this expression as "ignorant and foolish" (so Jastrow). The context demonstrates that the lamenting and praying king wants to introduce a "merit motive" here. He points to something that is supposed to make him especially pleasing to the goddess. He recalls something that serves his fame and honor. Ultimately, this is probably the same myth that was applied to Sargon, Cyrus, Romulus, and Moses in the form of a humanized "birth saga." In Assyria and Babylonia, the idea of the divine birth of the king was frequently expressed by the notion that he was born "in the sanctuary" (so Gudea, Cylinder A 3:6–8; François Thureau-Dangin, *Die sumerischen und akkadischen Königsinschriften* [VAB 1; Leipzig: Hinrichs, 1907], 93) or was nursed by a goddess (as in a prayer liturgy of Ashurbanipal; Heinrich Zimmern, *Babylonische Hymnen und Gebete* [Alte Orient 13.1; Leipzig: Hinrichs, 1911], 20–21; Peter Jensen, *Texte zur assyrisch-babylonischen Religion* [Keilinschriftliche Bibliothek 6.2; Berlin : Reuther & Reichard, 1915], 136–39). The same notion also appears in Egypt (Gressmann, *Texte und Bilder*, fig. 232; cf. Gunkel, "Königspsalmen").

137. Gunkel, "Königspsalmen."

138. Both the revolution against Athaliah (2 Kgs 11) and the introduction of Deuteronomy are to be understood in part as expressions of these efforts (see Deut 17:8–13, 14–20). See als Deutero-Ezekiel's legal drafts (Ezek 40–48) that signify a major restriction of the royal rights (see Ezek 43:7–9; 44:1–3; 45:7–12; 47:1–2, 9–10, 12, 16–18).

14). By no means, however, does this rule out his historicity. This is beside the point here, however. The main issue is the fact that in Jerusalem Melchizedek was considered a king of the holy city who exercised both royal and priestly rights and functions, who as priest had the right to appear before YHWH and to offer sacrifice, to bless the people with his blessing, and to receive the tithe as a due from all the inhabitants of the land—even from Abraham himself. Inherent in this combination of royal and priestly power, according to a primitive view, was the guarantee of the good fortune and the welfare of the people. It is a simple consequence of the divine character, the divine sonship, of oriental kings.

Consequently, priestly status as the legal successor of Melchizedek is also promised the king in the oracle in Ps 110—perhaps in express reaction against the hierarchical claims of the professional priests, the authorized representatives of the priest-king:

> YHWH has sworn and he will not regret it:
> You are a priest forever for Melchizedek's sake.[139]

Because the king is the legal successor of Melchizedek, who also acquired an eternal priesthood in addition to the monarchy, he is promised the same right here "for Melchizedek's sake."

The rest of the psalm is somewhat corrupt. It depicts the mighty appearance of the ideal king after the heart of the old, still-bellicose Israel, as he strides victoriously over the broad earth striking down princes and filling the valleys with corpses.

If prophecy has any place in the cult whatsoever, then there is no reason to doubt the relationship of this psalm to the anointing of a Jerusalemite king. The oracle was spoken in conjunction with the anointing or immediately thereafter.

If one has become acquainted with the religious and constitutional theories of the ancient Near East and has comprehended the weight that was always placed there on legitimacy in the sense discussed above, then it will seem remarkable that several exegetes understand the appeal to Melchizedek as evidence for a particularly late origin of the psalm (e.g., Buhl, *Psalmerne*). The fact that the legend in Gen 14, the only passage besides our psalm to mention Melchizedek, is a very late and unreliable product from a literary

---

139. The phrase *'al dibrātî* does not mean "after the manner of" but always only "because of, for the sake of." Duhm (*Psalmen*) is correct to this extent. To strike Melchizedek, however, would be to rob the words of the true content.

perspective is insignificant on this point, since the passage also knows the names of ancient Babylonian kings. If one considers, for example, that the dynasty-founder Cyrus immediately portrayed himself as called by Marduk to be the legal successor of the Chaldean kings,[140] that the dynasty-founder Sargon, who, along with the Assyrian throne, also assumed the recently renewed Assyrian claims to Babylon, took the programmatic name Sargon, after the old, legendary king of Akkad, and how the dynasty-founder and first German emperor over Rome, Charlemagne, regarded himself the successor of the Caesars, and so on, then—as we may presume with significant certainty—David, the dynasty-founder and first "Israelite" ruler in Jerusalem, would already have had himself proclaimed the legal successor to Melchizedek, called to kingship by El Elyon YHWH. Solomon was already greeted on his ascent to the throne as Melchizedek's successor. The earlier we date the psalm, the more likely that it will appeal to Melchizedek rather than David. If verse 4 refers to the hierarchical power struggles of the priests, then one should recall that these struggles are already attested under Uzziah (2 Chr 26:16–20). We do not know how much earlier they began. The naïve application of the originally polytheistic myth to the king in verse 3 also speaks for its antiquity.

*

Psalm 72 also has affinity with these royal oracles. Here, too, the content speaks with some probability for its relationship either to anointing or to the New Year's Festival.

Formally, the psalm appears to be a blessing for the king. Accordingly, it also begins as an intercession with the imperative: "Give the king your justice, God!" The power of blessing has its ultimate source in the deity and, in the realm of a personal concept of God, is thus ultimately dependent on the will and work of the deity. The imperative transitions immediately into imperfects, however, that depict the good fortune desired for the king and the bountiful consequences for the land and the people that flow from it. In keeping with the peculiarity of the Hebrew verb forms, it can never be said with certainty whether the intent was indicative or jussive. This question rests on modern conceptualization and thought. In reality, there is no distinction whatsoever here between blessing and promise. These two types of efficacious sayings interfuse with one another, just as the ability to speak effective blessings is

---

140. Cyrus Cylinder, see Franz H. Weissbach, *Die Keilinschriften der Achämeniden* (VAB 3; Leipzig: Hinrichs, 1911).

actually identical with the ability to speak effective promises. It is primarily a matter for the prophets to be able to speak effective blessings (and curses). The efficacy of both types of saying rests on the ability of the speaker to incorporate into a saying the psychic power that indwells him, to concentrate, as it were, the content of his soul in the saying and to place it, with the saying, in the soul of the addressee. Words are deeds. All words have their effect, just as the deed must always have effect—assuming that the actor and the speaker do not have a soul that is "empty," weak, "unjust," at the core, a soul that cannot affect or produce anything at all. In this case, neither his deeds nor his words are actually deeds and words but only "illusion" (*šeqer*), "lies" (*kāzāb*), void (*tōhû*), smoke (*hebel*), and wind (*rûaḥ*). One who can pronounce a true blessing does not merely express a wish but forms a reality. He pronounces what will be. He is, to this degree, a prophet. The blessing is prophecy. To this extent, Ps 72 is also to be regarded as a prophetic psalm, even though, as a psalm of blessing, it also belongs in another context to be treated in *Psalm Studies 5*. There the close relationship between blessing and cult will also be discussed.

In accordance with the previous discussion, the psalm does not proceed as an intercession, "may God give the king this and that," but as a description of royal good fortune, of royal righteousness, that agrees both formally and substantively with the descriptions of the future in prophetic promises of good fortune. The only distinction that meets the eye is that this "blessing" employs the imperfect throughout and thus emphasizes the aspect of the not-yet-realized, to be created in the moment of speaking, and thus to be understood as the object of desire. True prophecies, in contrast, frequently prefer the perfect, thereby emphasizing the aspect of the already-real in the eyes of the speaker, the already-existent in the souls of both the speaker and the addressee, the emergent although not yet visible to the masses. The degree to which the former or the latter was the case depends, in the first instance, on the psychic apparatus of the speaker. If his gift was what we would call more "priestly" and he placed his major focus on the creative capacity that has indwelt him since his call and "ordination," his indelible character, then he would prefer the form and the concept of the blessing. If, by contrast, he was disposed more "prophetically," toward the ecstatic and the visionary, and was therefore of a more receptive than creative nature, he would prefer the concept of the oracle, the prediction of the reality seen as already existent, and the form of its description—proceeding in perfects.

In terms of content, the psalm is, as has already been indicated, a description of the desired and promised good fortune of the king. He is promised divine characteristics, especially divine "righteousness" (*ṣĕdāqâ*) and the aptitude for ruling (*mišpāṭ*), that is, the divine capacity to sustain the covenant, to support the parties to the covenant, to supply them with psychic health and the capability to sustain themselves with foreign and domestic good fortune from his own, all-encompassing *ṣedeq*, *ṣĕdāqâ*, or *mišpāṭ*, in a word, the capacity to "judge" (*dîn*) the people, the humble, and the pious. This *ṣĕdāqâ* and *mišpāṭ* are evident, above all, in the fact that the king establishes justice for the oppressed, whether this involves standing with the members of the people oppressed by sorcerers or violent enemies (v. 4) or whether, as was occasionally the case, delivering the people oppressed and endangered by external enemies (v. 2). If the king has this "righteousness," he also has the quality of soul that assures him eternal life (v. 5). Then "righteousness," health of soul, and external good fortune will also blossom for the whole people. The king is compared to the rain that entices forth fertility and plenty from the ground (vv. 6, 3).[141] He can also be assured of worldwide dominion (v. 8); all enemies should fall before him and lick the dust (v. 9); all kings and nations should fall before him in homage (v. 11).[142] They will do so because they must acknowledge that he alone is the "just" (*ṣaddîq*) and "delivering" (*môšiaʿ*) king who delivers the poor, the oppressed, and the suffering and takes fearsome revenge for their blood, because "their blood is dear in his eyes" (vv. 11–14). He sustains their life; consequently, they will also praise his name and give him something more valuable than the gold of Sheba. They will always pray for him, daily bless him, and thereby infuse him with new psychic powers, new good fortune, new ruling capability (v. 15;[143] see also Job 31:19–20). Then a paradisiacal state will govern the land. The grain will sprout like the grass of the field and grow as tall as the cedars of Lebanon (v. 16).[144] The name of such a king should be praised eternally. Blessing for all the other nations of the earth will flow (v. 17) from his "blessing," from the superabundance of

---

141. Verses 6 and 3 should apparently be transposed after v. 7. A semi-verse is lacking in v. 4.

142. Verse 10, with the divergent meter (5 instead of 3 + 3), is probably a later insertion.

143. The subject in v. 11b is the poor and oppressed. Since, however, he is not explicitly mentioned here and since there is no new subject in v. 15a, he will also be the subject in v. 15a. Then, however, *min* must be explained as indicated above (as Buhl suggests). Verse 15a is too brief. Something is missing. Supply, perhaps, *wĕyôdeh ʾet šĕmô*. Of course, the verb can be read as plural with LXX. Cf. the suffix in v. 14.

144. Cf. the words of Asshurbanapal: "In my days, the grain grew 5 elles tall and the ears 5/6 elles" (Rassam Cylinder I:41–51). See also the communication reported in Friedrich Delitzsch, "Zur Erklärung der babylonisch-assyrischen Brieflitteratur," *Beiträge zur Assyrologie* 1 (1890): 620.

the power of his "just" soul[145]—presuming, of course, that they show him the proper submission (see v. 11).

There are no good grounds for disputing that this blessing psalm that transforms into a promise was meant for a recurring cultic celebration. It remains the most likely assumption as long as one holds that the majority of the psalms are cultic psalms. Similarly, it must be admitted that it is best suited to either the enthronement of the king or to the New Year's Festival. Nothing more precise can be said.

*

Psalm 45 must also be mentioned in this context. Two erroneous assumptions in more recent exegesis are to be confronted here. The first is that the psalm only found acceptance in the Psalter by virtue of an (erroneous) allegorical interpretation. A much simpler and more likely explanation of the situation is that the psalm was included because it was one of the temple songs utilized on some occasion in the temple. The technical expressions in the superscription point to this original use (see *Psalm Studies* 4). The second error is related to the first: this psalm is now generally spoken of as a "secular song" and is categorized as profane poetry.[146] The psalm is written in prophetic style; it seeks a religious justification of the facts and proclaims YHWH's blessing on the just king. This is indeed religion. If our first assumption is valid, it also follows that the psalm cannot be a purely secular song. It is, rather, a cultic song, a religious song. Even among us, a cantata written for the church's celebration of a royal marriage can never be called "a purely secular song," nor could it be delivered in a purely secular tone.

It is a prophetic psalm. Already in the introduction the singer portrays himself as inspired. His heart seethes, it overflows with the "good," glorious and promising "word," that now fills it—the word of YHWH, of course, that has come to him and must now go forth in order to appear as a life-creating reality and to have effect. He finds himself in the inspired state in which he allows the word to effervesce. He depicts this sustained, quasi-passive effervescence with the participial construction, *'ōmēr 'ănî*, instead of with a finite verb form. This ecstatic state could almost be compared to glossolalia: his tongue

---

145. The meaning of the formula *hitbārēk bipĕlônî* is not just declarative (e.g., "wish for someone's good fortune"). Words of blessing are effective words. Thus the formula means "to obtain blessing for oneself from the blessing of another by citing the name of the one concerned as a blessing formula, to procure blessing thereby."

146. E.g., Hermann Gunkel, "Dichtung, profane, im AT," *RGG* 2:47–59; and Staerk, "Lyrik."

works now almost like the pen of a skilled stenographer. The word he speaks for the king in this state is simultaneously "deed" (*ma'ăśay*). It translates into a blessing-rich reality. It is an efficacious, prophetic word. The prophetic style is also clearly evident in what follows. Taken strictly, the first section (vv. 3–10) depicts the king's glorious psychic and physical characteristics. In actuality, the singer wants to depict a contemporary situation. He does so, however, in the form of prophetic speech: "because you are such and so, YHWH has done thus and so for you." Prophetic speech also says "has done" when we would render with a present or a future. In the Israelite understanding, YHWH has just done his will in the moment the word becomes alive on the tongue of the prophet—word is deed.

The statement "You are the most beautiful among the children of men" is meant not only aesthetically but also morally. "And grace is poured on your lips" refers to the royal characteristic that has its source in the grace of God and makes the one who possesses it good to and beloved by all people. "Therefore, YHWH has blessed you forever!"

The continuation does not describe the mighty deeds the king once did. No, in prophetic manner, as the representative of the deity, the singer challenges the king to perform mighty acts on earth:

> Gird your sword on your thigh, O hero;
> [in] your majesty and glory, journey forth successfully,
> for the sake of the truth, for the cause of justice![147]

"Truth" (*'emet*) and "right" (*ṣedeq*) are the supporting, positive, fundamental forces of ordered existence, the psychic qualities of the king and people whose source is God. They must be manifest in external good fortune. It is the king's concern to assert them and thus to support the entire "covenant," the entire existence of the society, the nation. The power to do so is promised him here. The king's justice will teach him wonders; the nations will fall at his feet; all his enemies will be destroyed! Once more, the singer repeats the scheme:

> It is firmly established, O divine, your throne is eternal;
> your royal scepter is a scepter of justice;
> you love what is just and hate the evil.
> Therefore, "YHWH," your God, anointed you
> with the oil of joy before all your brothers.

---

147. A *bĕ* has been omitted in v. 4. Strike *wĕhădārĕkā* in v. 5. As Wellhausen (*Bemerkungen*) has seen, *'nwh* must conceal an expression parallel to *'al dĕbar*.

Myrrh and aloe scents your garment.

This section clearly alludes to the anointing and election of the king. Among all the kings and princes of the world, "the comrades" of the king, YHWH has, to use the words of the Cyrus Cylinder, looked around and chosen just this one to be king, the anointed of YHWH, to whom world dominion is due, to ascend to the eternal throne of the legitimate royal house. Since then, his whole person is fragrant with the lovely scent of the precious anointing oil that brings with it the joys of kingship, the oil that was poured over his head, that flowed down through his beard and imparted its scent down to the hem of his garment (see Ps 133:2). Following this allusion to the glory of the king, the next strophe (of three lines) depicts it with particular attention to the actual occasion for the song.

The second part of the psalm (vv. 11–16) also proceeds in the forms of prophetic speech. As an inspired and wise person, the singer gives the queen good advice for this future life: do what ancient practice and piety bids a wife! He adds a promise:

"Then Tyre will kneel before you with gifts;"[148]
the wealthiest "of the nations"[149] will seek your favor.

Naturally, a depiction of the queen's glory follows, also with particular reference to the solemnities of the day and the situation of the moment.

Finally, the third section (vv. 17–18) is a promise in the form of a blessing (see above on Ps 72):

Your sons will take the places of your fathers;
make them princes of the whole earth.
I will proclaim your name to the coming generations;
therefore, nations will praise you forever!

A royal marriage is almost unanimously and, indeed, correctly regarded as the occasion for the psalm. The depiction in both verses 9b–10 and 14–16 refers to the solemnities of the wedding. The psalm concludes with the blessing regarding the continuation of the king's family. The allusion in verse 14 demonstrates that it was composed for a specific king. As usual, however, the exegetes stumble around in the dark seeking the pertinent king. Yet just as

---

148. Read *wĕtištaḥăweh lĕkā* in v. 12 and connect it to v. 13.
149. Read *ʿammîm*.

Gunkel has correctly emphasized with respect to the other royal psalms, this is a rather hopeless process simply because no specific king is depicted here, but *the* king, the ideal Israelite king. All the elements cited here are only rather stereotypical features of the king image. If the psalm was one of the temple songs in Jerusalem, a reference to an Ephraimite king may be rather confidently excluded. Of course, the plural "your fathers" (v. 17) does not suffice to exclude thinking of Solomon, as Buhl thinks. The plural could be poetic. Of the Judahite kings, besides Solomon, only Jehoram, who was married to Ahab's daughter (2 Kgs 8:18), married a foreign princess, as far as we know.

"The hour of the solemn entry of the royal bride into the palace of the ruler" (Staerk) is usually assumed to be the more precise situation of the psalm. Verse 10b speaks against this, however. The king seems to be sitting on his throne, the queen beside him. We must thus think more of a point in the wedding festivities when the king and the queen, seated on the throne, receive the homage of the community. We know almost nothing about how a royal wedding was performed in ancient Israel. It is rather unlikely, however, that the procedure for the "marriage ceremony" was a purely profane act. If anything, the beginning of the marriage must have been blessed with the consecration and added power of religion. In marriage, two families make a covenant, and a covenant is always something religious. The deities of the parties to the covenant always stand behind the covenant as patrons, "witnesses," and participants (see Gen 31:44–54). In the basic overall view of the ancient Israelites, the marital festivities and ceremonies must have had the purpose of acquiring the "blessing" necessary for the continuation of the (husband's) family, the blessing of fertility, the "blessing of the womb." The blessing on the two families—and blessing is primarily a common possession of the family—was solemnly bestowed on the young people so that they might propagate and multiply the blessing. The conveyance of the blessing is a religious act, however, and was linked to cultic rites, as Gen 27 teaches us. In the close circle of the family, the pertinent cultic action has the character of a sacramental communion. Eating enables the concentration of the capacity of the one blessing to bless and the effective infusion of his psychic force into the blessing. This infusion is supposed to transfer the power into the words of blessing that mediate it to the recipient and infuse it into him. Procedures that concern a larger circle, that are significant for an entire people, for example, involve larger institutions, sacrifices, and the like in the cultic procedures for blessing and for cursing (see Num 22:36–24:25). Genesis 24:60 attests that such cultic proceedings for transferring the blessing were components of marriages. When Rebekah was given to Isaac as a bride, the whole clan assembled, the whole family, and gave her the blessing that assured her fertility:

Our sister—may you become ten thousand times thousands;
may your seed conquer the gates of their enemies!

We can assume with certainty that some type of rites belonged with this act of blessing. Despite its extreme simplicity, the entirety is a religious act. Such was the old "cultic religion" of the tribal alliances.

The marriage of a king is a significant matter. The continuation of the house is essentially the assurance of the continuation of Israel. The cultic proceedings that accompanied such an event were undoubtedly more festive and more developed, from a ritual perspective, than those for a common person. We can assume it quite likely, if not certain, that the act of blessing was performed by the one who seemed to offer the greatest guarantee for imparting a powerful blessing, by one of the professional men of blessing, by a prophet or a priest. In view of the whole community, the "household of the king," the one called for that purpose standing before the sitting, standing, or kneeling bridal couple pronounced the blessing on them. Inherently, the cultic procedure must have been connected somehow with the temple, the royal chapel. In all likelihood, "the one called" to pronounce the blessing is to be sought among the sacred persons in the temple. Inherently, the style and forms of speech of the prophetically gifted ministers of the cult may therefore have influenced the blessing. The marriage psalm offers us a mixture of prophecy and blessing that is also evident in Ps 72. It offers us both formally and substantively what we would expect for the situation it presupposes. We have here a "prophetic cultic song."

2.4. Oracles in Private Cultic Procedures

We understand private cultic procedures here to be those cultic procedures not attended by the whole community and not arranged by the community as such but by one or more individuals in certain cases significant for the individuals. The individual sin and thanksgiving offerings are to be considered here. "The individual lament (sin offering) psalms" and "the individual thanksgiving psalms" are components of these respective cultic procedures. None of the latter psalms transmitted to us contains an oracle, however. Thus we will deal only with the individual lament psalms in this section.

I have already discussed the individual lament psalms in *Psalm Studies* 1, so I need only to recapitulate briefly here. I have shown there that, not only in accordance with its origin but also with the exemplars transmitted to us, this genre belongs with the sin sacrifice and the associated rites of purification. Almost without exception, as far was we are able to see, we are dealing with purifications and healings from illness and with illness psalms.

As Gunkel has already shown, and as was explicated further in *Psalm Studies* 1,[150] an element of the rites of healing was the priest's communication of the deity's response in the form of an oracle after the sacrifice and the recitation of the lament psalms. Several psalms exhibit traces of this response. The "anticipatory thanksgiving" that occurs in several psalms relates to it. We have also encountered this situation above in the public lament psalms. As shown in *Psalm Studies* 1:150–59, there are several individual lament psalms whose actual form, especially the subdivision into lament and thanksgiving sections, can only be satisfactorily explained by the assumption that the atonement procedure with the promise of divine assistance was performed between the sections. Psalms 6 and 28 are particularly clear, while Pss 31; 57; and 62 deserve mention.[151]

This divine answer probably consisted in most cases of a fixed, "programmatic" formula (cf. the promise of the forgiveness of sins in our cultic absolution procedure). This is also probably the reason that the response is reported in so few psalms. It is often assumed, however, in the last section of the psalm, as we will see below in a particularly clear example.

Even when the response consisted of a fixed formula, however, the justification to respond in a specific fashion in each individual case will have been derived from certain signs obtained technically, perhaps from the favorable outcome of the hieroscopy or the lot. We can hardly go wrong to assume that there were means for favorably configuring the response in most cases. One might ask what one did if, for example, the sick person nonetheless died after cleansing and hearing the promising oracle. One did nothing. One soothed oneself, as usual, with the idea that the unfortunate must have

---

150. Chapter 5, esp. 149–61.

151. Beside the psalms mentioned here that were already examined in *Psalm Studies* 1:153–58 for traces of oracles, Küchler ("Orakel") mentions Pss 13; 30; 54; and 115 in his essay cited above. He is hardly correct. Ps 13:6 is not a thanksgiving but a confidence motive expressing assurance of being heard: "I will surely be able to sing one day." Ps 30 is nothing other than the thanksgiving psalm of one healed who only cites the earlier complaint. Ps 54:6–9 is not a thanksgiving but a confidence motive and vow. The perfects in v. 9 correspond to a *futurum exactum*. Ps 115 has an entirely different relationship, as I will demonstrate in a later volume, *Psalm Studies* 5. Furthermore, Küchler is hardly correct to understand, in contrast to Gunkel, Ps 22:23–32; 69:31–37; and 109:30–31 as thanksgivings for an oracle already obtained that promised salvation. In Ps 109:30, the situation is quite similar to that in 13:6. Pss 22:23–32 and 69:31–37 are best understood as vows that mention future circumstances. If salvation is depicted as already experienced, the thanksgiving sacrifice meal to which Ps 22:27 refers will have been a present reality. The thanksgiving sacrifice would surely not be offered immediately after the sin offering and the rites of purification but only after the actual healing of the sick person.

sinned severely in some manner after the cleansing and was therefore justly smitten. Alternatively, one may well have also silently bowed on occasion to the incomprehensible dispensation of YHWH whose ways are not our ways and whose thoughts are not our thoughts, who kills whom he will and heals whom he will.

Whether in certain cases the precise formulation of the oracle was left to the pertinent cultic minister or whether one had several oracle formulas to choose from we cannot say here with certainty. In any case, as it happens, we have an oracle containing the divine response transmitted to us in Ps 91.

This psalm is a fragment from a longer liturgy.[152] Later Jews wore it as an amulet against demons. An authentic reminiscence underlies this practice, to the extent that it actually promises God's protection against demons—and the illnesses they cause. Thus it seems to presuppose that it was meant for use by someone beset by need or illness. YHWH's response in verses 14–16 suggests that an individual in distress addressed as "you" (singular) has asked YHWH for help and is now comforted with the promise of liberation from distress and a long life. He had been "emptied," "made unjust," as we may surmise from v. 15b. Now, however, YHWH will once again "make (him) honored," restore him to psychic and physical health, and make his soul "heavy" instead of "light." Since he is promised "life," we may conjecture that the crisis consisted of illness. This conjecture also best explains why so much is said about protection against demons and demonic animals (lion, lindworm [šaḥal],[153] poisonous snake, dragon).

As has been said, the psalm has the form of a liturgy. Lament and petition are missing. The remaining piece consists of two parts: a blessing (vv. 1–13) and an oracle (vv. 14–16). Both contain the divine response to the request. We

---

152. Most of the more recent exegetes admit that v. 1 cannot be the subject of 'mr in v. 2. Then, however, v. 1 has no reference. Additionally, 'mr elicits the definite impression that it is meant as a participle 'ōmēr, coordinated with yōšēb in v. 1. Furthermore, one should note that beginning in v. 3 the intended strophic structure seems to be four 3 + 3 meters. The first strophe, however, has only two. Several exegetes resolve the difficulty by inserting an 'ašrê before v. 1. Thereby, however, v. 1 becomes too long and the defect in the strophe is not remedied. The right idea underlies the suggestion, however. The words yōšēb and 'ōmēr must be understood as the continuation of a description of the just, and, in accordance with the blessing character of the subsequent passage, it would be very suitable for this depiction to be introduced by the blessing formula 'ašrê or bārûk. But more than this word is missing, at least two 3 + 3 units. Since, however, the psalm seems to refer to a specific need, one may well suppose that a lament and a request section have also been lost.

153. So Mowinckel in "Gamle spor og nye veier," in *Festschrift für Lyder Brun* (Kristiania: Grøndahl & Søn, 1922), 7–16.

may conjecture, with good grounds, that both were spoken on the pertinent cultic procedure by one or perhaps two officiating priest(s).

Initially, the first section responds more indirectly. With clear reference to the supplicant, portrayed as inwardly just, the priest responds with a blessing on any who "sit under the protection of the Most High and sojourn in the shadow of the Almighty," who have made YHWH their refuge and trust in him. Such a one will surely be delivered from all distress, including the current one. Nothing can harm him. YHWH's angels always protect him. He need fear neither demons nor wild animals nor any other danger. The supplicant should now apply this blessing cast in general terms to himself and draw from it comfort and new strength. If he is really just, receptive to the power of the blessing, these words have already become salvation for him. The reference to the supplicant is indicated by the fact that the blessing already addresses the supplicant directly with "you" (singular) in verse 3 and thus in clear language pronounces God's protection on him. Be comforted; YHWH will protect you from all dangers and deliver you from all distress—including this one.

The divine response, in the form of a justification,[154] follows in the second part as an authoritative confirmation that the divine blessing relates to the supplicant. Now, however, it is not addressed directly to him but apparently to the officiating priest portrayed as a mediator and intercessor. Consequently, it mentions the supplicant in the third person and in general terms, eliciting the impression that it means to suit all possible cases:

> Because he clings to me, I bring him deliverance,
> protect him, for he knows my name;
> because he calls to me, I hear him;
> in his distress, I am with him.
> I free him and glorify him [...];
> I satisfy him with long life and let him see my deliverance.

The supplicant is acknowledged as a just person, as a "knower of the divine name," as a "true" member of the covenant who, in his intimacy with YHWH and his mighty name based on his membership in the covenant and the covenant religion, has an effective means, as it were, to motivate YHWH to intervene. Consequently, the lord and patron of the covenant, YHWH, as the more powerful, is obligated, as it were, to maintain the weaker and "weakened" covenant partner, cannot neglect to give him assistance. Even when, as

---

154. The *kî* may be a doublet for *bî*.

now, his life is threatened by enemies and dangers, YHWH wants to deliver him and ensure him a long, fortunate life.

The oracle reported here involves nothing that points to a specific individual case. It clearly bears the imprint of a formula, namely, a cultic formula. The knowledge of the divine name relates to membership in the cultic community; the address to YHWH relates to the cultic cleansing procedures and the associated prayers. Even if, with the most recent exegetes whom I consider incorrect, one wanted to understand the psalm as noncultic and as a "didactic poem,"[155] the most obvious assumption would be that the author adapted a cultic oracular formula in verses 14–16 as the justification for the orthodoxy of his "doctrine" and introduced it as divine authority in quotation marks, as it were. The somewhat unprepared and conspicuous "then" in verse 14a, evidently connecting two heterogeneous components, can be adduced in support of this understanding.

We have another oracular formula that belongs here in Ps 12:6, if this psalm is to be understood as an individual lament psalm—which is uncertain, however, as we have seen.

Psalm 62 clearly refers to an oracle to be given in response to the sufferer's petition. I discussed this in *Psalm Studies* 1, §5.3.4. Compare the discussion above concerning Pss 6 and 28.

If it is correct that the divine response to the complaint and petition consisted of a firmly fixed formula, we may presuppose in reality that this was also the answer in purification rites. To this extent, we quite naturally find the oracle only rather isolated and coincidental in the text of our psalm. Naturally, the priest knew the point in the cultic procedure at which the promise should come. It did not belong to the actual lament psalm itself, which was to be sung with the purification.

---

155. See *Psalm Studies* 5 concerning the psalm of blessing and didactic poem.

Psalm Studies 4

The Technical Terms in the Psalm Superscriptions

Preface

This volume will present a collection of both relatively assured and entirely hypothetical and uncertain suggestions. Even if most of them should prove invalid, my submission will still have shined a beam of light on a few Israelite and Judean cultic practices that may be useful to the study of the Old Testament.

The treatment of individual passages took place at quite different times. The manuscript was completed in November 1921. The long period both between the treatments of the individual passages and between completion and publication may excuse a certain unevenness that may result, especially in comparison with the earlier volumes of my *Psalm Studies*, some of which were written *after* this volume. The addenda call attention to some of these cases.

Introduction

Previous attempts to interpret the technical expressions in the psalm superscriptions have led to few results worthy of mention. The most important reason may be the lack of firm guidelines in psalm interpretation. Smend's theory of the "collective ego" could have been such a firm guideline—had Smend and his adherents not failed to draw the sole consequence of the theory that could have provided it with its appropriate justification, namely, an understanding of the cultic purpose and use of the psalms.

Meanwhile, Gunkel's definition of the genres of the psalms offers a starting point. The insights gained must, however, be supplemented by another: not only are the prototypes of our ancestors and psalms in the Psalter, but also they are themselves actual cultic songs that can only be understood in terms of their relationships with specific cultic situations and proceedings.

The fact that this is truly the case has become ever clearer to me. I have attempted to demonstrate this in all the preceding volumes of *Psalm Studies*.

The following explanatory efforts start from this presupposition.

A second presupposition should also be mentioned here. Undoubtedly, the use of the psalms as cultic songs in the latter period of Jewish temple worship, traces of which can be found in the Mishnah and the synagogue tradition, does not correspond in many cases with the original meaning of the respective psalms.[1] The explanations I offer here proceed from the assumption that the psalm superscriptions generally relate to the original meaning and use. I must admit that they do not do so in all cases (see no. 27, below). It seems to me, however, that these cases are exceptions. Indeed, I believe that the great majority of the superscriptions from the last days of the last temple reflect the practices of that time. It would be remarkable were the majority of them to be incorrect. It would be equally remarkable if occasional comments were not found among them that stem from an earlier time and were preserved, even though the respective rite was no longer practiced in the latest period. The difficulties involved in aligning all the psalms bearing similarly

---

1. See *Psalm Studies* 1:165–72.

worded superscriptions under the explanation of the superscription that is most likely or even enlightening for most of the pertinent songs may indicate that this or that psalm has been reinterpreted in accordance with a cultic use originally foreign to it and, accordingly, been gathered with other psalms agreeing with the respective superscription. The pertinent superscription will then suit the original meaning and use of most of the songs that bear it, but for some, only to the extent that they have been reinterpreted and employed accordingly.

For the sake of completeness, I do not deal below with the many terms about which I have nothing new to say or where nothing can be said.

I will not deal with the supposed or actual identifications of authorship and the rabbinic information concerning the occasion for certain psalms.

1

GENERAL AND SPECIFIC DESIGNATIONS FOR PSALMS AND CULTIC SONGS

(1) מִזְמוֹר and (2) שִׁיר will be treated together here. The usual understanding of these two terms is correct from an etymological perspective insofar as *šîr* denotes the song as sung and *mizmôr*, in contrast, the song as performed to instrumental music. *Zmr* II (see Gesenius–Buhl) "to play, to sing, to praise," Assyrian "to play, to sing," is surely identical with *zmr* I, "to pinch off, to pluck, to cut off." The basic meaning, therefore, was "to pick" or something similar.[1] It may be quite possible to discover some internal or external characteristics that may distinguish the psalms designated *mizmôr* from those with the *šîr* superscription. Meanwhile, *šîr* alone occurs only in Ps 46:1 and the synonymous *šîrâ* in Ps 18:1. Otherwise, it always appears alongside *mizmôr* (*šîr mizmôr*, Pss 48; 66; 83; 88; 108; *mizmôr šîr*, Pss 65; 67; 68; 75; 76; 87; 92). The explanation could be that our manuscripts combine two different forms of the text, each with its own terminology. If this is correct, then there was no practical difference between *šîr* and *mizmôr*. In this case, the words are synonymous designations for religious songs. This "text-critical" explanation can rely on the fact that the two terms are separated in Pss 65; 75; and 76 by a reference to authorship (*lĕdāwīd* and *lĕʾāsāp*).

It is also possible to elaborate this explanation somewhat and extend it further. The word *šîr* occurs only in Hebrew. The root *zmr* is the sole designation in Assyrian for both singing and instrumental music. The first word is employed in the Old Testament of both profane and cultic songs, the latter in the Old Testament solely of cultic (or religious) songs and instrumental music. It first occurs in reference to drinking songs in Sir 49:1. One may conclude that *zmr*, a loanword in Arabic, Aramaic, and Ethiopic, is also an Assyrian loan root in Hebrew (Canaanite) and, from the outset, designated only cultic

---

1. Generally following Hermann Hupfeld and Wilhelm Nowack, *Die Psalmen übersetzt und ausgelegt* (3rd ed.; Gotha: Perthes, 1888).

music in Hebrew, while *šîr* was the corresponding native word with a somewhat more expansive use. This explanation would conform with the fact that one may confidently assume that Canaanite-Hebrew temple music, like even the religious poetic style, which is demonstrably so, was of Assyrian-Babylonian origins. If this is the case, the juxtaposition of the two words can be easily explained: *šîr* is then a manuscript variant for *mizmôr*, whether it stems from another textual recension or is a gloss.

(3) שִׁיר הַמַּעֲלוֹת (Pss 120–134; Ps 121, שִׁיר לַמַּעֲלוֹת) refers to psalms for a particular use but not to psalms of a particular kind. Linguistically, it may be noted that the expression may be the plural of a composite *šîr maʿălâ*, "song of ascent," and that "the songs of ascent," as Cheyne (*The Book of Psalms*) recognized, was the original title of the whole collection, Pss 120–134. It was later made the superscription for the individual psalms.

In these psalms, *maʿălâ* denotes neither a staircase (so the Danish Bible translation) nor a (more or less improvised and unceremonial) pilgrimage (so the new Swedish Bible translation) or festival journey (so the Norwegian Bible translation), but, as I have shown in *Psalm Studies* 2, part 1, the solemn festival procession that took place very year on YHWH's enthronement during the New Year's Festival in the month of Tishri.

Several of the *maʿălâ* psalms seem, however, not to have been sung during the ascent but in the temple itself.

Thus Ps 132 was probably sung during the nocturnal celebration in the temple court. The same is true of Pss 124 and 129, which are liturgical antiphonal songs and thus temple songs. So also was Ps 128, a priestly blessing, and Ps 121, a liturgical antiphonal song with priestly blessing. The fact that the cultic and liturgical character of these songs has been only tentatively recognized by isolated individuals demonstrates clearly enough the half-heartedness with which the very promising impetuses to the true understanding of the psalms given by Gunkel have been carried out.

If this understanding of the psalms cited is correct, then מעלה here has a somewhat broader meaning than merely ascent. It would then denote the festivities of the New Year's and enthronement festival, in general, both those that took place on the way up to the temple and those that took place in the temple. The transfer of meaning would then be explicable by the fact that all these festivities revolved around the grand ascent with the ark.

One cannot object against this interpretation that certain actual ascent psalms, such as Ps 24, for example, do not bear this superscription. We do not know the largely accidental causes that determined the selection of psalms in the small volume, Pss 120–134. No law requires that such collections be complete.

(4) מִכְתָּם (Pss 16; 56–60; and Isa 38:9, where *miktāb* is a scribal error for *miktām*). With respect to the old translations and earlier interpretations, see Friedrich Baethgen.[2] The only suggestion worthy of mention would be LXX's στηλογραφια. Excavations in Babylonia and Egypt demonstrate that nothing prohibits the assumption that certain prayers—all the psalms mentioned above are lament psalms or petitions—were written on stelae and erected "before the gods" as an everlasting memorial to the author or patron.[3] The etymological foundation for this interpretation (*miktām* = *miktāb*) is too weak, however.

The following derivation is more in agreement with the content of the pertinent psalms and is fully satisfactory from an etymological perspective:

The word is related to the Assyrian *katâmu* (= "to cover"), from the same root that had most likely acquired the meaning "to stain (especially with blood)" in Hebrew and Syriac (see Gesenius–Buhl, s.v.). The word *miktām* thus indicates a song whose purpose is to cover, that is, to atone for, the sins or the impurity, the illness, the guilt—all of these are synonymous terms. One may compare *kippēr*, "to atone," literally "to cover." Since the penitential psalm mitigates YHWH's wrath, it brings about the "covering" and "atoning" of the sin, just as the other atoning cultic presentations do. The word can thus be translated "atoning psalm" or the like. This interpretation also conforms with the content of the respective psalms. They are all laments and petitions by an individual, or of the people (Ps 60), in distress. The same is also true of Isa 38:9–20.[4] In addition, it may be noted here that the psalm dealt with ill-

---

2. *Die Psalmen* (HKAT 2; Göttingen: Vandenhoeck & Ruprecht, 1892), xxxvii.

3. See, e.g., Hugo Gressmann, Arthur Ungnad, and Hermann Ranke, eds., *Altorientalische Texte und Bilder* (Tübingen: Mohr, 1909), 1:88; see also my *Statholderen Nehemia* (Kristiania: Olaf Norlis, 1916), 149–51.

4. Isa 38:9–20 is not a psalm of lament in distress but a thanksgiving psalm for the thanksgiving offering festival after deliverance, i.e., the healing of illness. (The contention of Buhl, Duhm, Marti, etc. that v. 20 is a liturgical addition is entirely unjustified. The psalm was indeed composed for an individual's thanksgiving sacrifice in the temple, and the others present, relatives and friends, joined with the one healed and thanked God for the deliverance, which was also significant, pleasing, and faith-strengthening for them.) The psalm extensively cites the complaints and petitions that the delivered one spoke earlier, when he was still sick, namely, during the purification rites in the temple, at the sin offering. This is naturally not a verbatim citation but a universally valid summary. This is how one spoke in the lament psalm that was meant to cover all possible cases of illness and impurity. The citation of the earlier complaints in the psalm of lament is a favorite artistic device of the thanksgiving psalms for setting in particularly sharp relief the contrast between now and then. In this manner, the deliverance experience is portrayed all the more gloriously. If the interpretation of *miktām* offered above is correct, the word is employed here in an expanded and somewhat imprecise fashion. It would then denote not only the psalm used with the rites of atonement but (occasionally) also the thanksgiving

ness. Illness is the consequence of sin and is per se impurity. At any rate, the psalms mentioned here are not "penitential psalms" in our specialized sense of the word, since they do not reveal any particularly well-formed consciousness of sin. As a rule, however, it was obvious to the ancient Hebrew that distress or illness was a consequence of sin or impurity. He was not aware of our conceptual distinction between "lament psalm of an innocent" and "penitential lament psalm"[5] (see Ps 69, where the attestations of innocence in vv. 5 and 8 stand quite abruptly alongside the confession of sin in v. 6). "Sin," that is, God-despised impurity, is also on hand when the sick person attests to his innocence. Otherwise, how would he have become sick? Sin is something objective that becomes evident in distress and illness.

(5) מַשְׂכִּיל (Pss 32; 42; 44; 45; 52–55; 74; 78; 88; 89; 142).[6] The word obviously denotes a poem of some kind or for some pupose. Psalm 47:8 demonstrates that it was performed as a song to music. The same is true of 2 Chr 30:22, where the participle *maśkîlîm* is used of the Levites who sang (and played) songs of praise before YHWH (v. 21). Thus it is a cultic song. In Ps 47:8, it is a cultic song of praise. Meanwhile, *maśkîl* appears as a superscript to psalms with the most divergent content: a didactic admonition (Ps 78), individual (Pss 42; 142) and public (Pss 44; 74; 89) songs of lament, a thanksgiving psalm (Ps 32), and a royal hymn (Ps 45). With the exception of Pss 45 and 32, meanwhile, all of these bear the imprint of the lament psalm or the petition to some degree.

This circumstance already absolutely prohibits the meaning "didactic poem." A didactic poem is called a *māšāl* in Hebrew. Delitzsch's "meditation" is not much better.[7] Stormy laments such as Pss 44 and 74 are not meditations.

There is no other possibility than to derive the word from *śkl* (hiphil *hiśkîl*, "to pay attention, to be sensible, clever, insightful"). The participle *maśkîl* usually refers to the person who is insightful from a religious and moral perspective, who knows the proper prescriptions and travels the proper "paths," the pious (see the lexica).

This "insight," however, is—the Hebrews considered this to be obvious—not a theoretical insight. The Hebrews did not differentiate between knowledge and ability. Whoever had the insight also had the capability, the

---

psalm (that contains important elements of the lament psalm) for the thanksgiving offering feast, which can be understood as the all-crowning conclusion of the whole series of atonement procedures.

5. According to Gunkel.
6. See Baethgen, *Die Psalmen*, xxxvii–xxxviii.
7. *Biblischer Commentar über die Psalmen*.

psychic power, that leads to the success of plans and actions. The word *hiśkîl* very clearly reflects this unity of insight and ability, both of which trace back to the psychic power that also comes to expression as blessedness.[8] Every normal "righteous one" has this "wisdom"; only "the fool" does not. It cannot be found in the same degree in everyone, however. One has more power, one more righteousness, one more wisdom, one more honor (*kābôd*, soul-substance) than the other. Just as there are people who have "power" in a special sense, so there are also people who have more *śekel* than others. This is obvious to the Israelite, for all the expressions just mentioned are essentially identical. Those who have "insight" in a special sense include people such as seers, prophets, priests, temple poets, and temple singers. This is inherent in the nature of the matter. With regard to the latter classes, it can be assumed as self-evident that their unique possession of professional traditions that are more or-less secret, particularly sacred, and substantially incomprehensible to the laity, at least, are understood to be effects of their extraordinary *śekel*. Their practice of the cult depends on this possession. The knowledge involved here is significant, efficacious, blessing-producing, sometimes even mysterious, and stems from divine revelation. These people knew what the lay person did not understand, namely, how to treat the divine, how one must deal with the deity. They knew the procedures appropriate for making an impression on the deity. Like the procedures, they also knew the associated holy words, the cultic formulas and the cultic songs. They knew how the songs were to be performed effectively, and they could also produce new songs of the same kind from their insight.

I called attention in *Psalm Studies* 3:517–21) to the fact that there was a close connection between psalm writing and prophecy in the Israelite understanding. Both were regarded as expressions of a particular endowment of power that was understood in later times, in fact, as spirit possession, as inspiration. Passages such as Ps 49:2–5 and 1 Chr 25:1, 2, 3 demonstrate that both psalm writers and cultic singers were generally aware that they composed and sang based on prophetic endowment and insight. Thus we can observe in various passages that the cultic songs themselves assume a prominent position among the sacred, inspired books of the later periods (Gatas, Vedas, Psalter).

Given all this, *maśkîl* must designate the cultic song performed to music insofar as it is the product of a special "insight," of a particular empowerment and inspiration, and, consequently, conveys something of this power and skill and is thus also particularly suited to affect the deity and thereby to procure blessing, good fortune, and liberation from distress and suffering

---

8. See Johannes Pedersen, *Israel: Its Life and Culture* (2 vols.; Atlanta: Scholars Press, 1991), 1:198–99.

for the cultic community. Thus it becomes obvious that the word can denote both the charming hymn that gladdens the heart of God (47:8) and especially the song of lament with its many traditional "motives" for propitiating the deity.

We cannot say why only certain psalms were designated as *maśkîl*. It could be coincidental, related to the collection's history of development. It is also possible that the word attained a special meaning in the course of time, perhaps in reference to a psalm performed to a certain kind of music or for certain sacrifices or times.

(6) שִׁגָּיוֹן (Ps 7) cannot be satisfactorily explained either as a derivative of *šgy*, "to err," or of the related roots *šgg* and *šwg*. Most likely, as has already been asserted (see Gesenius–Buhl), the word has something to do with the Assyrian *šegû*, "lament psalm." This word is formed from the verb *šegû* = Hebrew *šgʿ*, "to rage, rant." A form *šiggayôn* cannot be directly derived from the Hebrew *šgʿ*, however. It points to a third-*yod* root. At the same time, the Assyrian verb *šegû* means "to howl, to raise a lament, to complain" and was employed as a term for the cultic lament in the form of the plaintiff penitential psalm. One must assume, then, that this term came to Canaan in ancient times and thus found entry into Canaanite-Hebrew cultic terminology. Here, of course, a verb *šegû* was understood as a third *he* verb (i.e., third *yod*), and from this a noun *šiggayôn* = lament psalm was formed on the analogy of the Hebrew rules of word formation. Psalm 7 is, indeed, a lament psalm (of a sick person).

If the text of Hab 3:1, *ʿal šigyônôt*, is correct and our understanding of the meaning of the *ʿal* in the psalm superscriptions (see ch. 3, below) is sound, the plural form here must have been used of the cultic procedure at which such songs were sung. Yet, one may perhaps better read *ʿal nĕgînôt* with LXX (see no. 9, below).

(7) תְּהִלָּה (Ps 145) = hymn. Since the word is apparently quite general, it is only an accident that it was employed only once as a superscription. Every hymn was probably called *tĕhillâ*.

(8) תְּפִלָּה (Pss 90; 102; 142; Hab 3) is the general term for a prayer, especially a petition, but apparently in particular for a prayer in poetic form, the "lament psalm." Thus it encompasses the *miktām*, *maśkîl*, and the *šiggayôn* mentioned above. Nonetheless, the subscript to the second book (Ps 72:20) shows that *tĕpillâ* could include, at least occasionally, all cultic and religious psalms and rhythmic praises, both plaintiff petitions and laudatory prayers of thanksgiving.

2

Musical Terms

Comments concerning the instruments used in performing the psalms will be considered first.

The instrument one plays or which accompanies singing is indicated in Hebrew by the prepositions *bĕ* (Ps 150:3, 5) and *ʿal* (Ps 92:4).

The only term that appears with *bĕ* in the superscriptions to the psalms is:

(9) בִּנְגִינוֹת (Pss 3; 6; 54; 55; 67; Hab 3:19 LXX) and the variant עַל־נְגִינַת (read נְגִינֹת with the versions; Ps 61; Hab 3:1 LXX). It always belongs with a subsequent לַמְנַצֵּחַ, as indicated by 1 Chr 15:21. This passage demonstrates that the action denoted by the verb *nṣḥ* is performed to *kinnôrôt*, "zithers," and perhaps also to *nĕbālîm*, "harps," that is, if the infinitive *lĕnaṣṣēaḥ* (v. 21) goes with both verses 20 and 21 and indicates the purpose of the musical presentation of all the Levites-singers mentioned in verses 19–21. One would then translate, "for appeasement [see no. 17] by playing stringed instruments."

Other possible instrumental information must be sought among the terms introduced by עַל.

In the meanwhile, it is worth noting that none of the musical instruments mentioned elsewhere in the Old Testament are named in the superscriptions. It would be more than noteworthy, however, if temple music had entirely different instruments than profane music or instruments with entirely different names than those for daily use. Both assumptions are probably already excluded by the fact that the instruments known otherwise are repeatedly mentioned in the texts of the psalms. This circumstance already gives us an indication that we cannot expect to find instruments among the terms indicated with *ʿal*.

It is also evident that in all the cases in which one may dare a somewhat plausible interpretation, *ʿal* introduces cultic procedures, not instruments.

In contrast, two other terms occur—although not in the superscriptions—that must be categorized as "musical terms."

(10) הִגָּיוֹן appears as a liturgical and musical marking in Ps 9:17 (before סלה) and as an element of the text in Ps 92:4. The root *hgy* means "to produce (dull) sounds" (of the snarling of the lion, Isa 31:4; of the cooing dove, Isa 38:14; 59:11; of a person's moaning, Isa 16:7; Jer 48:31).[1] In addition, the verb also occurs in the meaning "to reflect, to think about something"; the discussion agrees with ancient psychology that thinking is what is muttered in the heart. Accordingly, "*higgāyôn* of my heart" (Ps 19:15) is even used with the meaning "this poem," "this psalm." *Hegyôn libbî*, literally "what my heart has muttered and thus thought out," parallels *'imrê-pî*. The poet of Ps 19B understands both expressions as references to the pertinent psalm itself. He prays in the concluding verse that YHWH may "receive [it] as a sacrifice"—this is, in fact, the meaning of the expression *yihyû lĕrāṣôn 'imrê-pî*.... The phrase *hāyâ lĕrāṣôn* is used of the sacrifice meant to evoke a "benevolent attitude" from YHWH (see Isa 56:7; 60:7; Lev 1:2; 22:20–21; 19:5; 22:19, 29; 23:11; Exod 26:38). Therefore, *higgāyôn* must actually mean "muttering, moaning," and, in connection with singing and music, "noise, sound," or the like (cf. *hāmôn* both of the dull din of a crowd and of the noise of song in Amos 5:23). From this start, the meaning "poem, psalm" is comprehensible. The rendition in LXX, ᾠδή is a possibility, therefore. The meaning "noise, sound," paralleling the ten-stringed lyres and harps is evident in Ps 92:4. Here *higgāyôn* is the sound that resounds *bĕkinnôr*. The only uncertainty here is whether the sounds are produced by the zither or whether the word may denote the sound of the cultic cry (such as hallelujah) accompanied by zither music. In the first case, one would be more inclined to think that an expression such as *hegyôn kinnôr* would be more natural.

Accordingly, *higgāyôn* denotes either the noise of (certain) instruments or certain cultic cries (such as hallelujah) or, finally, the common noise of cultic cries and music. The latter is also the most likely. Cultic cries were most likely accompanied by instrumental music, and the lay community's participation in singing consisted of such intermittent cries.

As is usually assumed, the word in Ps 9:17 is thus a musical notation: at this point, the psalm should be interrupted by music of some kind with the accompanying cultic cry of the congregation.

Undoubtedly, this provides a starting point for the interpretation of:

(11) סֶלָה. If *higgāyôn* has the meaning conjectured here, then it is extremely odd that the word should occur only this once as a musical and liturgical term. We can surmise, with confidence that such an "interlude," with or without cultic cry, was not singular in the performance of the psalms. Why only

---

1. See Baethgen, *Psalmen*, xxxv, where he also deals with earlier interpretations.

here, then? It seems to me that only two answers can be considered: (1) either *higgāyôn slh* is the complete expression (which should then probably best be vocalized *hegyôn slh*; cf. the ᾠδὴ διαψάλματος of LXX); the simple *selâ* would have been the common abbreviation; or (2) *higgāyôn* was a variant or a gloss for *slh*. In the latter case, in terms of meaning, the two words are either identical or at least "parallel" and synonymous in certain cases. Option (1) seems rather unlikely to me. An abbreviation with the result that the genitive survives while the main word has fallen away would be extremely odd. In contrast, no objection with any weight can be raised against the second alternative.

The only interpretation of the word worthy of discussion that has been offered to this point, namely, Wellhausen's association of it with the verb *sll* that occurs in Ps 68:5, also agrees. As Wellhausen saw, this word, which occurs only here (and perhaps in v. 33; see BHK, cf. LXX), parallels *šîr* and *zāmar*.

If *sll* is simply a synonym for *šîr* and *zmr*, then all these verbs, in accordance with Old Testament usage, denote not just playing or singing alone but always the combination of singing and music. Ancient Israelite music and singing had not yet developed into independent arts that could exist separately. They were still combined as elements of the same "musical" art. The same would then also apply to the verb *sll*. Meanwhile, the fact that the etymology would then be unknown and that the word would not occur elsewhere in the Semitic languages speaks against the assumption that *sll* is a simple synonym for *zmr*. A loanword from the Greek ψάλλειν, which seems to have been a purely Indo-Germanic etymon, has even been considered. In my view, the circumstance that Ps 68 is a very old psalm speaks against this, however. Since the derivation of the Greek ψάλλειν from the Hebrew *sll* is inconceivable, the assumed relationship is invalid. Further, the circumstance that there is a root *sll* in the Semitic languages from which the word can be derived without difficulty also speaks against the absolute synonymity of *sll* and *zrm*. The meaning of the root *sll* known otherwise is "to raise." The verb can also have this meaning in Ps 68. We need only to supply a *qôl* or something similar as the object, and the parallelism between *sll* and *šîr* (Ps 68:5) is explained: singing and crying (obeisant cultic cries and words) are both equivalent ways to honor the deity and to do obeisance (see Pss 147:2, 7; 81:2–3; etc.). Thus *sll* here means "to do obeisance to YHWH with cultic cries." It is self-evident that music would be involved and is implied by the collocation with *zmr* (see above, no. 10).

Now, if *selâ* is related to this verb *sll*, it must be a musical notation, like *higgāyôn*. At the pertinent point, the cultic cry of the choir or the whole congregation accompanied by powerful music interrupted the performance. Obviously, this interruption was to be understood as an underscoring, an emphasis on certain points in the psalm. It must, therefore, stand in a certain relationship with the passage immediately preceding the word in the text (see below). We know words such as *'āmēn, hallĕlûyâ, lāneṣaḥ,* and *qādôš hû'* as such cultic cries.

LXX with its διάψαλμα cannot have thought of anything other than that such "interjections" were "interludes" (cf. the ὑπόψαλμα = "a cry by the congregation in agreement with the individual strophes of the psalms performed by the singers" reported by Baethgen [*Psalmen*, xxxix], following Fleischer).

This interpretation receives yet unrecognized confirmation from the other ancient translations. Aquila renders ἀεί, Jerome *simper*, Targum sometimes לעלמין = "eternally" and sometimes תדירא = "forever," Theodotion ἀεί (9:17), Quinta εἰς τοὺς αἰῶνας and Sexta διαπαντός (20:7 εἰς τέλος). Baethgen offers the explanation in antiquity itself of this ἀεί and the like according to Jacob of Edessa "in Bar Hebraeus regarding [Ps] 10:1": "In some exemplars, [ἀεί] is written instead of διάψαλμα בכל זבן." That is, whenever the singers who praise God with songs of praise interrupt their words, the listeners must "always" intone after them as if to say, "may God always be lauded and praised by these songs of praise," much as with us in the church, after the "now and evermore in all eternity," the people affirm by saying "Amen."[2] Baethgen remarks, "This explanation is totally satisfactory in substance. It is not explained, however, and cannot be, how סֶלָה is supposed to have come to mean ἀεί." Baethgen is both correct and incorrect. He mistakenly concludes from Jacob of Edessa that סלה per se must mean "always" in the given case. The matter is entirely clear as soon as one assumes that "forever" or "eternally" is the cultic cry that constitutes the "interlude" along with the sounds of the harp and other instruments and that is indicated by *selâ*—if not originally and always, then at least when the old translations and the Masoretic pointing were undertaken. The word *selâ* per se means only "raising," that is, crying out in the cult with the related music.

Indeed, we have yet another confirmation of this interpretation in the Masoretic Text. In terms of its form, סֶלָה is known to be without analogy and to contradict the rules of word formation. The most likely conclusion to be drawn from this is that the consonants have been provided with the vowels of another word. Which? Naturally נצח = ἀεί (*qamaṣ* instead of *pataḥ* because of the open final syllable)! The reader will understand that it is only for substantive reasons that I call attention here to the fact that, only after I had come to this result did I first read Benno Jacob's study, where I saw that he understands the vocalization the same way I do and, simultaneously—and more impor-

---

2. Baethgen, *Psalmen*, xxxvii.

tantly—that the Jewish tradition still knew that סֶלָה, that is, the pronunciation of the word, is equal to נֶצַח עוֹלָם וָעֶד.[3]

One can make a test based on the example. Does the word always—or usually, see below—appear after passages in which such an "interlude" can be explained in its place, or otherwise? Here one must recognize that our texts provide an uncertain foundation for such statistical investigations. First, it may be considered certain that the word does not now appear everywhere that the "interlude" actually occurred. The reason the word does not occur in all of book 4 and only four times in book 5 (in Pss 140 and 143) is clearly not that these books do not contain cultic psalms or psalms in which such cries took place but, quite simply, because some of the older psalm collections had these musical notations and others did not. Furthermore, one must consider the fact that LXX has the word in many places where it is lacking in MT and vice versa. Such a word, unrelated to the content and meaning of the respective passage, easily falls out in copying. One should probably anticipate copyist errors especially in those psalms that have the word after every strophe but the last. Finally, one must also account for the fact that the copyists often placed the incomprehensible and substantially irrelevant word after the incorrect line, either a line too high or too low in the column, which would be very easy to do in copying stichometry. Thus in Ps 57 סלה stands after verse 4 in MT and after verse 3 in LXX and, similarly, after 61:5 in MT and after verse 4 in LXX. Consequently, we cannot expect to give a reason for the appearance of סלה in all cases. It suffices if the statistical result conforms in the main with the interpretation given. Such is actually the case.

Seen from a purely formal perspective, סלה coincides with the strophe division in several passages, such as 3:3, 5, 9 (strophes of two lines in hexameter;[4] apparently סלה has fallen out after 3:7); 46:4, 7, 6 (quadrameter, strophes of eight lines); 62:5, 9 (three sections each with three strophes of four lines of alternating verses three and two feet;[5] סלה has apparently fallen out at the end); and 76:4, 10 (strophes of three lines of hexameter; סלה has probably fallen out after vv. 7 and 13). Psalm 24, where סלה stands after the first two of

---

3. Benno Jacob, "Beiträge zu einer Einleitung in die Psalmen," *ZAW* 16 (1896): 129–81.

4. 3 + 3s and 6s. Since the period, not the line, is the unit in these cases, I prefer to speak of hexametric verses. They should also be printed as such; then one would be rid of the despicable layout that produces tri-partite hexameter (see, e.g., Staerk, *Lyrik*; Gunkel, *Ausgewählte Psalmen*).

5. With regard to so-called pentameter, the caesura is so sharp rhythmically that the unity of the period is actually dissolved. The line constitutes the unity. Thus pentameter would be best printed as two lines.

the three major sections of the psalm (vv. 6 and 10), or Ps 32:4, where it stands before the turn in the psalmist's fate, also belong here.

סלה coincides with the logical division in a whole series of passages besides those mentioned here. The placement of the word may also just as often fail to coincide with the logical and strophic division. Most often, other considerations will have been determinative. Of course, these considerations also often exert themselves in the cases mentioned above. The passages can be sorted into several groups.

(1) First, the word stands after passages that challenge the singers to offer praise, that declare the intention to play and sing before YHWH, or that promise or presuppose such an attestation of veneration: 44:9; 66:4, 15 (in the offer of praise that constitutes the thanksgiving sacrifice); 68:20, 33; 84:5; 68:4 LXX. One must concede that an affirmation of the call through music and the congregation's unison call of "forever" would certainly have a place here.

(2) The word also comes after statements of triumph or confidence concerning the mighty, benevolent, and gracious or the vengeful and punitive intervention of YHWH in the world to help his worshipers, or after reference to particular manifestations of his majestic characteristics, of his justice, goodness, and so on. In the acclamation, the congregation expresses in part the certainty that these divine attributes will always be exercised to save the pious, in part the wish that it should be so. Frequently the pertinent passage refers to the eternal significance of the activity or manifestation mentioned: 3:5, 9; 21:3; 24:5, 6, 10; 32:5, 7; 44:9; 46:4, 8, 12; 47:5; 48:9; 49:16; 50:6; 55:20a;[6] 57:7; 59:14; 60:6; 61:5; 62:9; 66:7; 67:5; 75:4; 76:4, 10; 77:16; 81:8; 84:5; 85:3; 87:3; 89:5, 38; 50:15 LXX. This group also includes passages that express assurance of eternal reward for the pious and eternal destruction for the evil: 9:17; 32:3-4 ("I" in these verses is the type of those unwilling to confess their sins and who are therefore punished as godless); 49:14, 16; 57:7; 34:11 LXX; 94:15 LXX.

(3) סלה also appears after an acute request for help or revenge. In the acclamation, the congregation takes up the prayer of the singer and adds heightened emphasis: 9:21; 20:4; 52:7; 57:4; 59:6; 67:2; 84:9 (perhaps originally after v. 10); 140:9; 143:6; 80:8 LXX. The conditional self-execration in 7:6 also belongs here.

(4) The word comes after complaints concerning the evil and the persecution of the enemies, especially often concerning "the evil tongue" that

---

6. According to the Masoretic reading of the consonants ("God hears and answer them, he who has ruled since the beginning"). Ehrlich's vocalization deserves attention, however: "Ishmael and Ya'lam and the sons of the East." Of course, the סלה is no longer fitting.

deals in "lies":[7] 3:3; 52:5; 54:5; 55:8; 62:5; 77:4, 10; 82:2; 83:9; 88:8; 89:46, 49; 140:4, 6; 2:2 LXX. Here one could imagine that the "interlude" was meant to underscore the petition and make YHWH aware of the complaint and that the "forever" was meant to intensify the complaint in the hyperbolic fashion well-known in the lament psalms: they plague and oppress me (us) forever. In any case, this would be a significant reinterpretation of the cultic cry "forever." It is therefore more likely that the complaints should be understood as indirect petitions. The transition between petition and complaint is fluid in the psalms. The purpose of the cry would then be to intensify the petition inherent in the lament.

(5) In a few remaining passages, the purpose of the סלה is not evident, and the most likely assumption is that the word has been incorrectly placed: 66:8 (v. 9 would be better suited, see [2]); and 88:11 (v. 10 would suit, see [3]).

Thus, it seems to me that the test has turned out quite well.

---

7. For an explanation of this expression, see *Psalm Studies* 1, §§1.7 and 2.6.

3
Indications of the Purpose of the Respective Psalm

A series of terms consist of the preposition *lĕ* and a subsequent infinitive or verbal abstract. According to normal usage, they indicate the purpose of the procedure, or of the psalm, in this case.

(12) לְתוֹדָה (Ps 100) probably should not be translated "for the thanksgiving sacrifice," since, according to normal usage in the psalm superscriptions, this would be expressed with *'al* (see no. 4, above), but "for a thanksgiving or offering of praise." Naturally one thinks first here of the thanksgiving associated with the thanksgiving sacrifice. Otherwise, this psalm demonstrates the randomness of the psalm superscriptions: Ps 100 is not a particularly distinctive thanksgiving psalm, while the very clear thanksgiving sacrifice psalms, such as Pss 66 and 116, do not have this superscription.

In terms of style and cultic purpose, Ps 100 probably belongs to the group including Pss 93 and 95–99, and is thus related to the enthronement and fall festival. Obviously, community thanksgiving offerings—for the psalm is a communal, not an individual, psalm—were also offered during this festival. Psalm 124 is another communal psalm of thanksgiving associated with the same festival. The superscription could refer to the thanksgiving and praise associated with this communal thanksgiving sacrifice. The expression "I enter his gates and courts with songs of praise," or "with sacrifice," seems to have been employed especially in connection with thanksgiving offering observance (see Ps 66:13; cf. 116:17–10). The psalm may have been reinterpreted in a later time and employed as an individual psalm of thanksgiving. The superscription may refers to this use.

(13) לְעַנּוֹת (Ps 88) should probably be vocalized לַעֲנוֹת instead. It is relatively insignificant, however, whether one understands the word as a verbal abstract or as an infinitive. In any case, it derives from *'ānâ* II, which means "to humble

oneself" in the *niphal*. The substantive *'ănût* occurs in 22:25. One usually translates it "distress, suffering," and the like. This transition is tautological (the suffering of the sufferer). It surely has the same meaning here as *ta'ănît* does elsewhere, "(self-)abasement, penitence." This meaning also fits in the superscription of the distinctive lament Ps 88. When the suffering Israelite brought his concerns to YHWH, he did not endeavor to appear before him in an upright virile posture—in the Israelite view, that would be *gē'ût*, "arrogance, iniquity"—but to assume a posture as small, abject, and sympathetic as possible, to lie down in the dust and to abase oneself, regardless of whether one was aware of his sins. Only Jeremiah has occasionally offered us truly virile notes in the lament song. Consequently, *lĕ'ănût* can probably best be translated: "for self-abasement." This superscription probably also refers to the penitential practices and atonement rites that presumably accompanied the performance of the lament psalm. I consider it a certainty that this lament psalm was composed for cultic use until proof to the contrary is produced.

(14) Benno Jacob has interpreted לְהַזְכִּיר (Pss 38; 70) along the right lines.[1] He understands it to mean "to bring (sins) to memory," that is, "to confess." The text 1 Chr 16:4, where it accompanies *lĕhôdôt* and *lĕhallēl*, demonstrates that *lĕhazkîr* denotes the purpose of a certain kind of Levitical song. Since Ps 70 is not a confessional psalm, however, the sins of the supplicant can hardly be supplied as the object, but the whole matter and occasion that bring him in supplication before YHWH: the distress or illness from which he is now to be cleansed. Under certain circumstances, this distress can be the "sins" of the one involved. It can also be the "sins" of his enemies who have made him unclean and sick through sorcery and secret arts.[2] Numbers 5:15 is comparable (see below).

Jacob did not notice, however, that this interpretation coincides, in reality, with that of the Targums and other ancient witnesses. The Targum associates the word with the *'azkārâ* sacrifice in Lev 2:2 (see Baethgen, *Psalmen*, xxxvi). As Num 5:15 shows, the purpose of this sacrifice—whether originally or in the understanding of a later period makes no difference here—was through the rising smoke to "remind" YHWH of the matter placed before him with the sacrifice.

This combination with the *'azkārâ* sacrifice confirms the supplementation of the ellipsis offered above. In Num 5:15, the *'azkārâ* is supposed to remind YHWH of the *'awôn* done by his unfaithful wife to the one offering sacrifice.

---

1. "Beiträge zu einer Einleitung in die Psalmen," *ZAW* 17 [1897]: 52, 63–68.
2. See *Psalm Studies* 1, esp. 83–85.

In Lev 5:12, in contrast, the *'azkārâ* is supposed to remind YHWH of the sins of the one sacrificing. Frequently the distinction will not have been drawn so precisely. One's own sin and the guilt of the enemies have both caused the misfortune. One's own sin alienated YHWH's protection and thus enabled the enemies' attacks (so in Ps 38; see v. 13).

We can therefore translate "as a reminder" or the like.

(15) לידותון (Ps 39) or על־לידותון (Pss 62; 77) is usually understood as the proper name of a supposed ancestor of the temple singers. Reference is made to 1 Chr 25:1–8; 2 Chr 5:12; 29:14; 35:13. In these passages the three leaders of the singers in David's time are called Asaph, Heman, and Jeduthun, instead of the usual Asaph, Heman, and Etan. In the psalm superscriptions, however, the word can hardly be meant as a proper name because: (1) it always appears with a second proper name (David, Pss 39 and 62; Asaph, Ps 77), and even the rabbis did not think that the pertinent psalms were composed by two authors; and (2) the proper names are otherwise introduced by *lĕ*, not *'al*.

I propose for discussion another interpretation that seems possible to me. The word *yĕdûtûn* could be understood as a verbal abstract, derived from *yadâ* II *hiphil*, "to praise, thank." In the *hithpael*, the verb also means "to confess, make confession, lay one's concern before YHWH." Thus *yĕdûtûn* would mean something like "confession." A psalm "for confession" would be a psalm with confession and petition content performed on some cultic occasion. This agrees with the fact that all of the three psalms mentioned are lament psalms including a confession. Sins are confessed in Ps 39. The central issue in all three is the confession of human insignificance, weakness, and dependence on God; in Israelite terms, confession also turns out to be praise and glory, *lĕtôdâ*, to YHWH.

This result, if correct, is significant in relation to the age of the psalm superscriptions. The transcriptions do not depend on Chronicles, as is often assumed, but the Chronicler (or his later copyists and interpolators) will have misunderstood the psalm superscriptions and construed them as the work of a levitical singer, Jeduthun, alongside Asaph, Heman, and Etan, and identified him, usually, with the latter.

(16) לְלַמֵּד (Ps 60) certainly has nothing to do with religious military training given to Israelite youth, following an erroneous interpretation of 2 Sam 1:18,[3] and hardly anything to do with the *lammēd* that the rabbinic literature uses of

---

3. Franz Delitzsch, *Commentar über dem Psalter* (2 vols.; Leipzig: Dörfling & Franke, 1859), 1:450.

learning the professional secrets of the Levites. The sole useful starting point for an interpretation seems to me to be the expression *limmûdê yhwh* as a designation for the prophets (Isa 54:13; cf. 50:4). One could deduce from this that the verb *limmēd* was used as a term for YHWH's revelation to the prophets. The bulk of Ps 60 is a cultic oracle (vv. 8–11) in which YHWH (through a prophetically inspired minister of the cult) responds positively to the people's petition for help and victory in the imminent war against Edom. If this combination is correct, this superscription says that the psalm is meant to be the divine "instruction" (cf. *tôrâ* as priestly instruction on YHWH's authority) incorporated in the liturgy concerning the outcome of the campaign to be prepared for and consecrated on the day of prayer presupposed in the psalm.[4]

(17) לַמְנַצֵּחַ. I have offered my interpretation of this expression elsewhere.[5]

(1) One can best begin with 1 Chr 15:20–22, which speaks of the Levites and other ministers of the cult commissioned by David. Among them were the singers Heman, Asaph, and Etan with bronze cymbals (לְהַשְׁמִיעַ), Zechariah, Aziel, and so on with harps (עַל־עֲלָמוֹת), and Mattitiah, Eliphelehu, and so on with zithers (עַל־הַשְּׁמִינִית לְנַצֵּחַ). It may be clear here that the two infinitives denote different kinds or acts of cultic music in terms of their different purposes. That is, *lĕnaṣṣēaḥ* here indicates the purpose both of the harps and the zithers. Although there are three kinds of instruments, in terms of purpose there are only two kinds of temple music, that which serves *lĕhašmîaʿ* and that which serves *lĕnaṣṣēaḥ*. The music made with bronze cymbals has another purpose than that made on harps and zithers. The first is said to be "for making heard." Since it is the first mentioned and is made with the loudest instruments, this expression can hardly mean anything other than "to make YHWH hear," to attract his attention.[6] We might say, "as a signal." The striking of the cymbals constitutes the introduction, as it were, to the cultic procedures with their praises, prayers, and atonements. When playing on harps and zithers (with the accompanying singing; see no. 11) is said to happen *lĕnaṣṣēaḥ*, one may assert with quite a degree of certainty that this expression denotes the true chief purpose of the whole cultic procedure and the related music and singing.

Further, 2 Chr 34:12 also attests that music and singing were components of the procedure whose purpose is indicated by *naṣṣēaḥ*. A copyist has mis-

---

4. See *Psalm Studies* 3:558–59.
5. See my "לסנעה I salmeoverskriftene," *Bibelforskaren* 35 (1918): 218–23.
6. The objection cannot be made that this idea is too lowly for Israelite religion (see 1 Kgs 18:26–27). Such cultic terms are ancient and stem from a mode of thought that is entirely different from the prophet's concepts of God. The terms could be pre-Israelite, traditional, and no longer comprehensible to later generations.

understood the *měnaṣṣěḥîm* in verse 13, which refers to an overseer of some kind, and interpreted it as Levites who perform the cult (see below) and therefore added *lěnaṣṣēaḥ*. The glossator attests that, in order to come to the result indicated by the final infinitive, *lěnaṣṣēaḥ*, one must be skilled *kělê-šîr* and simultaneously that the respective procedure must be performed by Levites; it is thus cultic. Thus the word indicates a cultic purpose (*lě* with infinitive) attained through singing and music.

(2) This already implies that the verb does not mean "to direct a choir." We will take up the passages and demonstrate that this meaning does not occur at all. The *piel* participle *měnaṣṣěḥîm* (always in plural) is employed, or so at least it seems, to designate those who lead a work, head it up, or oversee it—thus, perhaps "foreman," "overseer," and the like (see Gesenius–Buhl). This applies rather surely to 2 Chr 2:1, 17. This passage discusses the preparations for the construction of the temple. Solomon employed 70,000 bearers, 80,000 stonecutters, and 3,600 *měnaṣṣěḥîm ʿălêhem*. Verse 17 says that the latter were *lěhaʿăbîd ʾet hāʿām*, which probably means, "to put the people to work" or "to keep at work." The meaning "to lead" also seems to be present in 2 Chr 34:13, where the *piel* plural participle stands in conjunction with *sabbālîm*, "bearers." Admittedly, the word is absent in LXX, and the whole verse has become disordered and heavily glossed. Verse 12b, "all who know how to play instruments for singing and instrumental music," is certainly a gloss, however, since the context does not speak of the regular cultic service but of restoration work in the temple.[7] Since the names of the *měnaṣṣěḥîm* mentioned are absent in verse 13, and since "and Zechariah and Meshullam from the clan of the Kahatides" in verse 12 gives the impression that it was meant to be the subject of a new sentence, the ו both before the *ʿal* and the *měnaṣṣěḥîm* in verse 13, should most likely be stricken and the participle mentioned seen as the predicate of "Zechariah and Meshullam" in verse 12—thus: "placed over them (i.e., *haʿănāšîm*) as overseers (*mupqādîm*) were the Levites Yahat and Obadiah from the clan of Merari, and the Levites Zechariah and Meshuallm were *měnaṣṣěḥîm* over the bearers...." Thus it is clear that, along with the gloss in verse 12b, the *lěnaṣṣēaḥ* in verse 12a must be stricken (concerning the meaning of this gloss, see above). Verse 13's *měnaṣṣěḥîm* thus parallels *mupqādîm* and also means a kind of overseer.[8] In the three passages treated here, the expression *naṣṣēaḥ ʿal* or *lě* has a personal object.

---

7. So also Gerhard Kittel, *Die Psalmen* (KAT 13; Leipzig: Werner Scholl, 1914).

8. The absence of the word in v. 13 of the LXX may depend on a text-critical attempt to bring order to the confused text. The word may be implied, however, in ἐπί, which is linked to ἐπισκοπεῖν in v. 12 of the LXX.

From this meaning, "to have oversight or authority over certain persons, especially laborers," a more comprehensive meaning, "to be placed over a task, to administer or execute a task," seems to have developed—regardless of whether the respective labor administrator had other workers under him. In these cases the verb has as its object a word that means task or work. This is the case in 1 Chr 23:4 and Ezra 3:8, 9. Clearly the word in 1 Chr 23:4 cannot refer to overseeing other workers, for the 24,000 overseers, 6,000 scribes and bookkeepers, 4,000 doorkeepers, and 4,000 singers must not have been among the 38,000 Levites that David appointed to temple service, because the sum of these four posts is precisely 38,000—where were the common laborers who were to be led by the 24,000 overseers? The word can hardly mean "to lead," "to head up" in Ezra 3:8, 9 either, for verse 10 shows that the role of the Levites in the construction work here was the *hallēl ʾet šem yhwh bĕtôdâ*. Admittedly, an *ʿōśēh* (in several manuscripts, *ʿōśeh*) now precedes the object *hammĕlākā* in Ezra 3:9, and, in accordance with the passages discussed above, the discussion must involve oversight over the workers. In reality, however, the whole context does not speak of construction work but of the work of the cult in which the Levites were not foremen but workers. Verse 9 is actually a doublet for verse 8, and it has no *ʿōśēh*. The phrase *mĕleket bêt yhwh* always means cultic ministry in the temple wherever some addition or context does not give it another sense—which is usually based on misunderstanding. The same is true of Ezra 3:8, 9. The first work that they attend to after the return, before laying the foundation stone of the new altar and temple, is to appoint Levites and ministers of the cult (see Ezra 8:15–36). This was quite natural because the placement of the sacred foundation stone is a religious act requiring a minister of the cult. The Levites appointed on this occasion are these very ministers of the cult, not labor foremen. Thus we have grounds for assuming that *ʿōśê* (v. 9) is a gloss for *lĕnaṣṣēaḥ*, perhaps in a corrupt form. The glossator may have written *laʿăśôt*. Thus in these latter passages, *naṣṣēaḥ* means "to perform a task" or some such.

Besides the passages mentioned here, all *piel* infinitives with *lĕ* or *piel* plural participles, only one *niphal* feminine participle occurs in Jer 8:5, with the meaning "enduring."

Whether the meanings "to direct a work" and "to perform a task" can be derived directly from the root *nṣḥ*, "to radiate," "to light," is rather irrelevant here. These meanings can easily be explained in relation to a meaning "to be chief, leader" and these, in turn, to the basic meaning "to radiate." Radiance is, after all, a sign of the might, the psychic power that indwells the chieftain in particular. Consequently, radiance is the specifically royal and divine emblem (cf. the *hvarena* of the Persians and the divine—and royal, see Ps 21:6—*kābôd* among the Hebrews).

(3) The result is that the meaning established here does not help us to understand the למנצח in the superscriptions. The meaning "to direct a choir" is not demonstrable here and is not useful in the two passages that come under consideration for the superscriptions, 1 Chr 15:21 and the gloss in 2 Chr 34:12–13, as we have seen.

There is, therefore, no reason to translate the expression "to the choirmaster" or the like. This translation is virtually meaningless. A cult song was not composed "for the choirmaster" but for the cult, for cultic use. Delitzsch attempts a couple of transpositions here: "to the one practicing = for practice." This equation is entirely capricious, however. It is more than self-evident that a cultic song must be practiced.[9] Moreover, the cultic song is not meant as an etude but for performance.

The translation "for performance in the cult," or the like,[10] is, of course, only an admission of ignorance of the precise meaning. It can by no means be justified etymologically.

With regard to the meaning of the infinitive *lĕnaṣṣēaḥ*, we must proceed from the known root *nṣḥ* ("to radiate," "to shine"), which occurs in Arabic as "to be pure" and in Ethiopic as "to be innocent." What is the cultic and liturgical purpose that can be expressed by a derivative of a verb with the basic meaning "to be brilliant"? If the *piel* vocalization is correct—and we need not doubt it—then without question it is most likely that the *piel* should be taken as a causative (Kautzsch, §52g) in the meaning "to cause to shine," "to make brilliant." The expression must then be an abbreviation. An object must be supplied. Which? One must think of "the countenance of YHWH" as the object, thus נַצֵּחַ אֶת־פְּנֵי יהוה. "To cause the countenance of YHWH to shine" is a cultic term, then, and like so many of the old cultic terms, a strongly anthropomorphic term for the propitiation of the deity. One may compare cultic terms such as the Babylonian "to bring the heart of the god to rest" (*nûḫ libbi ša ili*, "to propitiate"), and further, the Israelite "to pacify the countenance of YHWH" (*ḥillâ ʿet pĕnê yhwh*, "to put YHWH in a gracious mood," "to propitiate") and the Aaronite blessing "May YHWH cause his countenance to shine upon you" (i.e., "May YHWH be gracious to you"). Thus *naṣṣēaḥ* means "to undertake those cultic and liturgical procedures that make YHWH's countenance shine with clemency and grace so that he hears prayers and bestows blessing."

---

9. Justus Olshausen, *Die Psalmen* (KEH 14; Leipzig: Hirzel, 1853).

10. E.g., Frants Buhl, *Psalmerne: Oversatte og Fortolkede* (Copenhagen: Gyldenhal, 1900).

In itself, a term such as this can denote many different kinds of cultic procedures. In Israel, however, as can be seen from 1 Chr 15:21, it attained the special meaning "to put YHWH in a gracious mood through cultic singing performed to zither music." This is quite natural, for singing and music were elements of every cultic procedure. One could say that both the hymn and the lament psalm had the same purpose: to please YHWH and to put him in a gracious mood. The ellipsis in the expression can be explained by its technical use. It seems that the term ultimately became quite abridged and denoted only the performance of certain cultic songs to zither accompaniment.

(4) למנצח must also be explained similarly. Little weight should be given to the vocalization. It only manifests the Masoretic understanding. As all the old translations (see Gesenius–Buhl) and later Ewald and many others thought, the word must be a *nomen actionis*. It denotes the procedure for putting the deity in a gracious mood through cultic singing and music. The superscription indicates that the respective psalm was composed or was to be used for this purpose. Since, as mentioned, both the hymn and the lament psalm, each in its fashion, had the initial purpose of putting the deity in a gracious mood, the term obviously appears above both individual and collective hymns and individual and collective songs of complaint. The formula may properly refer only to collective worship services, however. Consequently, it may have only been placed above individual songs as the result of a collective reinterpretation.[11] The expression could thus be rendered "for putting in a gracious mood" or "for paying homage." The translation of the Targum, לשבחא, is thus the same as the old translations that best render the sense. It is not entirely precise, since it overemphasizes praise. In the main, however, it is correct. It should be apparent that the Targum knew the meaning of the word and did not merely speculate.

We can no longer say whether all cultic songs were considered to be meant למנצח or only those that were performed to a specific kind of music (zither music?) at specific times along with certain cultic procedures or at a specific point in the related cultic procedure, which had many sections, of course.

Thus the two final infinitives, *lĕhašmîaʿ* and *lĕnaṣṣēaḥ* indicate the two main purposes to be attained by temple music. First, the sounding cymbals were to awaken YHWH's attention, then the finer and more artful instruments, harps and zithers, were to please him and put him in a gracious mood.

---

11. See *Psalm Studies* 1:165–71.

4
INDICATIONS OF THE CULTIC PROCEDURES AND SITUATIONS

(18) עַל־יוֹנַת אֵלֶם רְחֹקִים (Ps 56). Probably all interpreters recognize that the vocalization אֵלֶם ("silence") is meaningless, just as they do that the LXX pronunciation (אֵלִם) must be correct. Here, however, unanimity ceases. Most reject the LXX interpretation (gods, divine beings [τῶν ἁγίων]) and translate "terebinth," "oak." They are unable, however, to find any meaning in this translation. What a dove sitting in the distant oak has to do with a cultic psalm is beyond understanding. One often thinks, here as with many of the subsequent terms, of data concerning melodies in the manner of the superscriptions in our hymnals. I consider this a totally impossible resort of desperation. Before choosing, one should consider whether melodies in the style of modern church music or church music stemming from classical antiquity are attested in the ancient Near East or were even possible. If one translates, however, "the doves of the distant gods," the dove meant for these beings, and the whole formula "concerning (or with) the dove meant for the distant deity," then one has a chance, at least, to come to an understanding that corresponds to the content of the psalm.

The starting point for interpretation is the role that the dove plays as a sacrificial animal in certain rites of atonement for sin and impurity according to the law (Lev 1:14–17; 5:6–10). Furthermore, one should consider that not all the animals that were employed in the atonement rites were meant for YHWH but that many were meant as substitutes for the person whose impurity was supposed to be atoned, to "carry" his "guilt" and impurity to the evil demons. The evil demons that have plagued the sick must be satisfied with the animal substitute.

Best known is the ram for Azazel on the grand Day of Atonement (Lev 16). The sins of the community were conveyed upon the ram, which was then abandoned to the demon of the steppe. Now the demon can no longer plague the community after it has received the community's representative in this matter, that is, who is mystically the community itself.

Leviticus 14:2–7 indicates that a bird was employed analogously in relation to the "purification" of the leper. The fact that "purification" here actually took place after the sick had become "clean," that is, after it was already evident that he was in the process of becoming well, means nothing here. The whole content of the ceremony was clearly the same in nature as those whose purpose was to evoke healing and "purification." The fact that even with leprosy the rites followed only after the healing was derived quite simply and naturally from experiences of the incurability of leprosy, almost without exception, and from the aversion one quite naturally nurtured against performing sacred procedures that were notoriously ineffective. Long and sad experience had taught the priest to undertake the cleansing of the leprosy only after the healing.[1] The content of the ceremony remained the same.

For the purification, the priest was to take two live birds along with cedar wood, red wool, and a bunch of hyssop. One bird was slaughtered over a clay basin with "living," that is, pure and running, water. In the bloody water, the priest dripped the cedar wood, the wool, and the hyssop and the second, still-living bird, then sprinkled some of this holy water on the one to be purified. Then he allowed the bird to fly away over the field.

Several series of ideas have clearly been amalgamated here. Obviously, the blood of the slaughtered bird, like all sacrificial blood, has atoning power. It "cleanses" when it is sprinkled on the unclean. We need not go into the basics of this idea. Meanwhile, the idea of representation also seems to be associated with the slaughter of the bird. The fact that the second bird, unquestionably thought of as a substitute for the unclean person (see below), was made to bear the impurity through the dipping in the blood of the slaughtered bird presupposes that it was also understood as a representative substitute. The soul is in the blood, the essence of the person. If the bird was slaughtered as a representative of the person, we understand that his whole being, as it was in the moment, and thus, his impurity, too, was transferred to the living bird through the dipping in the blood. The bird was now supposed to be his further representative. This interpretation is confirmed by the circumstance that another explicit application of the impurity to the living bird took place. This must have been conceived as taking place through the immersion in blood.

Clearly the idea involved in finally releasing the bird to fly away "over the field" is that it should carry the impurity far away from the one purified. The

---

1. Obviously the healed leprosy was, in fact, not leprosy at all but some less severe skin disease.

bird is thus a substitute for the one purified and, from now on, "carries his guilt ['awôn]." The person becomes free and "pure."[2] The concept underlying Zechariah's seventh night vision may be compared here: in the figure of a woman enclosed in an ephah, guilt (read 'ăwônam, Zech 5:6 LXX) is carried away by two flying women with stork wings. The wings may represent a reminiscence of cultic procedures such as those described in Lev 14.

Leviticus 14 does not say where the guilt is supposed to be carried or that the bird is relinquished to the demons. The expression "away over the field" seems, however, to represent a remnant of such an idea. Why not simply "away"? Perhaps because one once thought that the bird flew away to the demons of the field?

Now, obviously we may not imagine that no cultic procedures other than those mentioned in the Torah were known in ancient Israel or in Judaism. The factors that determined the acceptance of this or that ritual in the Priestly Code were entirely accidental. It is sufficient here to recall that P does not mention temple music at all, although we know precisely from the royal psalms, for example, that the preexilic period also had temple singing and music. In the many cleansings that unquestionably accompanied the biblical lament psalms when they were employed in the temple, ceremonies similar to those reported in Lev 14 or 16 may very well have been performed.

The superscription of Psalm 56 must be understood in accordance with this presentation. It clearly presupposes a similar rite. The psalm is meant to be sung "over the dove that is supposed to carry away to the distant divine beings the guilt of the one to be cleansed."

I have shown in *Psalm Studies* 1 that Ps 56, like most of the individual lament psalms, was associated with the cultic cleansings and healings of illness.

Obviously, no more than a rite such as Lev 14 could have been conducted without words could this cultic psalm have been performed without proce-

---

2. Regarding the illumination of this rite in terms of the history of religion, it may be mentioned that in the Babylonian purification rites it was often said that the illness or the demon that had caused it was to disappear "like a bird." Thus an amulet with the image of the demon Labartu says: "May you fly away with the birds of heaven!" (see Morris Jastrow, *Die Religion Babyloniens und Assyriens* [2 vols. in 3; Giessen: Töpelmann, 1905], 2:335). In the series *Muruṣ kakkadi*, the illness is banished with the following words: "Fly like a dove that seeks its nest, like a raven that ascends toward heaven, that flies far away!" (346). Jastrow calls attention to the fact that in many of these "parallels" a corresponding procedure accompanied the words (see, e.g., 312). Thus one can also imagine that the birds mentioned here, or one of them (the others are attributable to poetical parallelism), were released while these words were spoken. Of interest for our topic may be the fact that one of the birds mentioned was, indeed, a dove.

dures.³ The fact that such sacred procedures accompanied the performance of Ps 56 is precisely what the superscript confirms for us. The psalm was sung "over" the dove that was supposed to carry away the impurity evoked by ʾāwen, that is, magic (v. 8).

It is unnecessary to say a few words about the expression "the distant gods." It must refer to beings similar to Azazel, the distant demon of the steppes who lived out in the wilderness far from culture and YHWH's blessing. It is evident from Ps 82:1 (cf. 58:2; vocalize ʾēlîm instead of ʾēlem; cf. 1 Sam 28:13) that in the Old Testament ʾēlîm and ʾĕlōhîm can both be used to designate evil, or at least not good, supernatural beings.

There is little reason to doubt that in ancient Israel and in Judaism illness and impurity were often thought to be transmitted by evil spirits.⁴ Whether the same was true of these distant ʾēlîm cannot be said with certainty. It may be supposed that the distant divine beings were thought of as the causes of the impurity and that, like the guilt in Zech 5:11, they were supposed to be taken "back to their place" by the dove. It is also conceivable, however, that the unclean person has somehow been fallen upon by the evil gods, if they were not deluded by a representative. The former is probably most likely. This interpretation conforms with the fact we have found in *Psalm Studies* 1 that the ʿazzîm—as should be read in verse 8, following 59:4, instead of ʿammîm—originally probably denoted the demons. In both cases the dove is a "sacrificial animal" substituted for the impure person.

(19) עַל in עַל־אַיֶּלֶת הַשַּׁחַר (Ps 22) must be understood on this analogy. Here, too, it seems likely that from the outset a cultic atonement procedure was involved: the psalms are cultic psalms.

In the given case, it is likely, however, that ʾayyelet should not be understood as a feminine form of ʾayyal ("stag"), since, as far as we know, neither the stag nor the doe were used as sacrificial animals in Israel, at least not in the time when our legal texts originated (see Deut 12:15), but as an otherwise unattested feminine of ʾayil ("female sheep").

The reference to a sacrificial animal suits well the content of the psalm. Psalm 22 is a distinct lament psalm. The supplicant finds himself in great distress, which he describes in the well-known hyperbole of Hebrew poetry as a mortal circumstance. According to the hyperbole in the psalms, he is sick,

---

3. See Gunkel, "Psalmen" (*RGG* 4).

4. See Anton Jirku, *Dämonen und ihre Abwehr im Alten Testament* (Leipzig: Deichert, 1912); and *Psalm Studies* 1, §§3.2.1–3.2.2.

that is, impacted by some "blow from YHWH," impure and in need of purification (see *Psalm Studies* 1:77–79).

We can go a step further, however. According to Israelite thought, one stricken by YHWH is, has become, or has been revealed as a sinner. He is oppressed by *ʿāwôn*, by guilt. Psalm 22 is not a "psalm of innocence." To be sure, the supplicant does not explicitly declare himself to be a sinner. That he is so is the obvious presupposition, however (see the closely related Ps 69, in which the awareness of guilt is explicitly stated). We know from the law that the normal sacrificial animal was male. A female animal, a female sheep or goat (Lev 5:6), was sacrificed only for the "sin offering" (*ḥaṭṭāt*). Psalm 22 is thus a prayer for the sin offering, a prayer to be used by those who have committed one of the unintentional sins listed in Lev 5:1–4.

The notion that the supplicant in Ps 22 committed an unintentional sin and thus must bring a *ḥaṭṭāt*, agrees best with what was said above, that he has met with a "blow from YHWH." As emerges from Lev 5:1–4, the sin offering exists precisely for those people who have committed an unintentional sin and consequently have met with a blow from YHWH, with an illness (see *Psalm Studies* 1:83–85).

Thus, in accordance with Lev 5:1–4, it is likely a priori that most of the illness psalms of the Psalter were composed as prayers for the sin offering. They are the psalms for a sick person who needs purification. The superscript in Ps 22 comes as a welcome, but not strictly necessary, confirmation of this fact.

Why, however, is the "sheep (or the doe) of the dawn" mentioned as the pertinent sacrificial animal?

One could interpret the expression on the analogy of the preceding formula (no. 18, above): the sheep to be offered to Dawn. Dawn is understood as a female divine being (see Isa 14:12; cf. Ps 110:3 LXX, where YHWH says to the divine king, "I have begotten you from the womb of Dawn").[5] Now, since the dawn was thought to dwell beyond the ocean (Ps 139:9), one could think that the expression "(sacrificial) sheep for Dawn" contained a reference to the fact that the animal was meant to carry away the guilt of the one offering sacrifice to the extreme boundaries of the world, where Dawn dwells. In this case, one must also assume that Dawn was understood to be a hostile being—otherwise, the analogy would be incomplete—but this is neither attested nor likely per se. Alternatively, one must think that the sacrifice was made to Dawn with a request for assistance, which would be even less likely in a YHWH psalm.

---

5. See Ps 2:7; see also my *Kongesalmerne I det gamle testamente* (Kristiania: Aschehoug [Nygaard], 1916), 30–31.

Thus there is no other alternative than to understand *haššaḥar* as an indication of time: "over the female sheep offered at the break of dawn."

Admittedly, the law says nothing about the time when the private sacrifice, including the atonement and purification sacrifices (sin offering), were offered. In the entire ancient Near East, however, the time before the appearance of the sun was the proper time for sacrifice. The main sacrifice of the Jerusalem temple, "the morning burnt offering," was offered then. In addition to the morning sacrifice, the Musaf sacrifice of the festival was also offered (see, e.g., m. Yoma). The evening sacrifice was less significant. In an earlier time, it is known to have consisted only of a *minḥâ* and may have been secondary in relation to the morning sacrifice. We also know from the Mishnah that the private sacrifice was offered in the morning, after the main sacrifice.[6] Job's atonement sacrifice for his children's possible transgressions was offered early in the morning (Job 1:5). Other sacrificial procedures, such as Abraham's covenant sacrifice (Gen 15:9–12, 17), began at dusk. If the accompanying ceremony was long and complicated, the sacrifice may well have continued until dawn or sunrise. This was the case, at any rate, for the atonement ritual for an Assyrian king.[7] The procedure apparently began at the beginning of dusk and continued through the night until sunrise. The sacrifice, which was prepared shortly before sunrise—thus, while the dawn illuminated the eastern skies—and placed in the fire at the moment the sun rose, was a very important component of the ritual.

Thus the most likely explanation of the superscription in Ps 22 remains this, that it refers to an atoning and purifying sacrificial procedure, *ḥaṭṭāt*, to which sick persons submit themselves in the temple. At a certain point in these purifications, a female sheep was sacrificed just as the dawn illuminated the east. Psalm 22 was sung, then, "over" this sheep, while it was slaughtered or offered, either by the sick person himself or by the priest in his name. Thus the explanation in the Targum, "at the daily morning sacrifice," indicates the correct path. It is correct, in any case, that על in the superscriptions indicates the cultic act or object "over" which the respective psalm was recited.

It is very likely per se that both the rite and the name are older than Israel and Yahwism and were only subsequently reinterpreted and harmonized with it. If this is the case, the interpretation of the dawn as a mythical being rejected above could have been the original meaning no longer understood in Israel.

---

6. See Paul Volz, *Die biblischen Altertümer* (Cologne: Komet, 1914), 79.

7. Published by Hugo Zimmern and cited by Otto Weber, *Dämonenbeschwörung bei den Babyloniern: Eine Skizze* (Der alte Orient 7; Leipzig: Hinrichs, 1906), 17ff.

Indications of the Cultic Procedures and Situations

(20) עַל־שֹׁשַׁנִּים (Pss 45; 69), עַל־שׁוּשַׁן עֵדוּת (Ps 60), and אֶל־שֹׁשַׁנִּים עֵדוּת (Ps 80). Clearly there is some relationship between these three formulas. First, as is often the case, אל is a scribal error for על. In Ps 60, the Masorah connects *ʿēdût* with the preceding word, but in Ps 80 it separates them. If the two words belong together, *ʿēdût* can only be the genitive of the preceding construct state. Understanding the words as an abbreviated clause of some kind (*ʿal* would then be "in the singing style of") only means foregoing comprehension. It only makes room for any caprice.[8] If *ʿēdût* is a genitive, however, it is beyond question most likely that *ʿal šôšannîm* (Pss 45; 69) should be understood as an abbreviation of the complete expression in Ps 60, where, meanwhile, it may be better to vocalize [י]שֻׁשַׁנֵּ. Then, however, the expression in Ps 80 must have been miscopied under the influence of Pss 45 and 69, whether *šôšannîm* is a simple scribal error for *šôšannê* or *šôšan* or originally only the abbreviated *šôšannîm* stood there, to which a later copyist following Ps 60 quite mechanically added the *ʿēdût*.

But what does "the liles or flowers of testimony," "of proclamation," or "of revelation" mean?

In accord with the discussion of *ʿal* above, one must also examine whether it could refer to a cultic act or object "over" which the psalm was sung, for the fact that it does not refer to a musical instruction may well be clear, despite Rashi.[9] Whether *šôšannîm* means lilies, lotus, or flowers in general is relatively insignificant in this context. It is more important that it refers to the use of certain kinds of flowers in cultic and sacrificial procedures. Occasionally we hear something about this in P. Best known is the use of certain fruits and green branches of palms, poplars and *ʿābōt* trees in the Feast of Booths (Lev 23:40; cf. Ps 118:27). According to the Mishnah, the celebrants of the festival carried bundles of palm, myrtle, and ethrog branches in the festal procession to the temple and around the altar. After the procession, the branches were placed around the altar "to bless the altar" (see Yoma). The branches originally served as carriers and conveyors of divine power and fertility. It is also well known that the hyssop plant found use in many purification and atonement rites, indeed as "holy water sprinkler" with which one sprinkled water or blood on the person or thing to be cleansed (see, e.g., 1 Kgs 5:13; Exod 12:22; Lev 14:4, 6, 49, 51–52; Ps 51:9).

The use of flowers in the cult is not unique to Israel. We find them used, although in a less distinct manner, in Egypt. Here they seem not to have been

---

8. See Heinrich Ewald, *Die Dichter des Alten Bundes*, vol. 1/2 (3rd ed.; Göttingen: Vandenhoeck & Ruprecht, 1866): "the law is (like) lilies, i.e., pure, clean"; Delitzsch, *Psalmen*: "A lily is the witness," etc.

9. See Baethgen, *Psalmen*, xlii.

so much a means of power and cleansing as sacrificial gifts.[10] The lotus in particular is often depicted in sacrifice scenes. Here the flowers are among the gifts placed on the table of the god in order to please his eyes and senses. There was hardly any awareness remaining of another, possibly more original, meaning of the rite. We also recall here that flowers along with incense constituted a component of almost every sacrifice among the Buddhists of the East and have usually almost entirely replaced the sacrifice of flesh and foods.

So much for the flowers. Now as to ʿēdût.

The word ʿēdût occurs very often in P as a term for the two tablets of the law (see Gesenius–Buhl). This meaning per se does not come under consideration here, for it is not clear how the tablets of the law can have given occasion for a cultic act, at least not to one with which psalms with the content of those in question here would have been associated. P invested the word with the same meaning, however, when he designated the ark as ʾărôn haʿēdût. P explains this name in relation to the fact that the ark was supposed to contain the two tablets of the law (lûḥôt haʿēdût, Exod 25:16). This explanation only indicates, however, that P was unaware of the origin of the term, for certainly no tablets were contained in the ark. This also further indicates, however, that the expression was older than P. P's explanation is deduced from the name ʾărôn haʿēdût and not vice versa. P had even forgotten that ʿēdût did not even originally denote the written law. Another and more original meaning of the word echoes in P. In a few passages ʿēdût denotes the ark itself (Exod 30:26; Num 17:25). If this expression is also an abbreviation of ʾărôn haʿēdût, it demonstrates that the designation "proclamation," or however it should be translated, was linked with the ark itself, not with the tablets that were supposed to be contained in it. Thus P calls the tent of the ark ʾōhel haʿēdût (Num 17:22, etc.). It is extremely unlikely that the tent was named for the tablets. The meaning of the ʾōhel haʿēdût is indicated, however, by the name ʾōhel môʿēd, which was itself associated with the tent and is common in the older sources and narratives. It has recently been recognized that the name ʾōhel môʿēd results from the fact that the tent was the place where YHWH revealed his plans and responded to questions.[11] This recognition also applies to the designation ʾōhel or ʾărôn haʿēdût. The two words, then, are also apparently etymologically related. Thus, ʿēdût originally denoted the divine "revelation" given orally in the tent. The name ʾărôn haʿēdût itself indicates that the ark

---

10. See Adolf Erman *Die ägyptische Religion* (2nd ed.; Berlin: Reimer, 1909), 58: "On an Egyptian sacrificial table, flowers could no more be wanting than on the dinner table of a noble."

11. See, e.g., Hugo Gressmann, *Mose und seine Zeit* (Göttingen: Vandenhoeck & Ruprecht, 1913), 451–52.

also played a role in the revelation of the *tôrôt* and *ʿēdĕwôt*. We do not know the manner. One may assume that YHWH revealed himself in the incense above the ark. It is more likely, however, that the giving of oracles once took place in front of the ark—according to the more likely explanation the ark is, indeed, either the throne of the deity upon which he sits invisibly,[12] or the divine shrine containing the deity's image.[13] The best translation would be "the ark of revelation."

As far as I can see, based on this analysis, there are two possible explanations of the superscription ʿal-šašan ʿēdût and variants.

(1) The word ʿēdût is a term for the ark itself here. Then we must think of flowers that were placed on or before the ark for some purpose, perhaps only as a tribute, at a certain point in the cultic procedure with its long ritual consisting of sacrifices, prayers, and psalms. We can imagine that the flowers were placed on the table of the bread of presence that stood "before YHWH," at the same time the incense was thrown on the sacrificial fire in the holy of holies (see what was said above concerning flowers and incense in the Buddhist cult).

(2) Alternatively, ʿēdût still stands here in the more original meaning of "revelation." "The lilies of revelation" must have been flowers, then, that were employed in some fashion in the acquisition of the divine response to a question put to him.

---

12. E.g., Martin Dibelius, *Die Lade Jahwäs: Eine religionsgeschichtliche Untersuchung* (FRLANT 7; Göttingen: Vandenhoeck & Ruprecht, 1906); Gressmann, *Mose und seine Zeit*.

13. Hugo Gressmann, *Die Lade Jahwes und das Allerheiligste des Salomonischen Tempels* (Forschungsinstitut für Religionsgeschichte. Israelitisch-jüdische Abteilung 5; Berlin: Kohlhammer, 1920). Previously (see the preface) I entertained the throne theory but have been converted by Gressmann's piece on the ark. Now I see that both Gressmann (*Die Lade Jahwes*; see also Hugo Gressmann et al., eds., *Die Schriften des Alten Testaments in Auswahl* [2nd ed.; Göttingen: Vandenhoeck & Ruprecht, 1921–1925], 2.1:57) and William R. Arnold, *Ephod and Ark: A Study in the Records and Religion of the Ancient Hebrews* (HTS 3; Cambridge: Harvard University Press, 1917; known to me only through Karl Budde's essay "Ephod und Lade," ZAW 42 [1922]: 1–42), have also conjectured the relationship I suspected between ark and oracle giving, although in ways that differ significantly from one another. My opinion coincides precisely with Gressmann's. The oracle giving—which involves casting the lots stored in the ephod—is performed before the ark. I agree with Budde in his criticism of Arnold's thesis (the oracle is the container for the oracle lots) but cannot agree with him that the ark and the ephod had nothing to do with one another. With Gressmann, I consider it entirely likely that there may have been several arks. It is certain that several arks were produced in chronological sequence (see *Psalm Studies* 2:289 n. 117). Regarding oracles in connection with the ark, see Rudolf Kittel, *Geschichte des Volkes Israel* (2nd ed.; Gotha: Koltz, 1925), 1:512 n. 3.

As we can conclude from the use of the sacred lots (Urim and Thummim), the actual divine revelation often consisted of signs that the priestly oracle must translate into words. A similar circumstance must have pertained to the "lilies of revelation."[14] The account of Aaron's staff gives us a hint as to how we can further envision this. Numbers 17:16–22 (Eng. 1–7) recounts that, in order to give visible, divine evidence of Aaron's divine right to the priesthood, YHWH had the twelve tribal chieftains each lay a staff inscribed with his name before the "revelation," that is, the ark. Flowers and fruits were to sprout in the course of the night on the staff of the one chosen by YHWH. On the next morning, Aaron's staff bore blossoms, blooms, and ripe almonds. As with so many legends that deal with cultic matters and regulations, this motif also traces back to a cultic practice actually exercised. It permits us a glance into a form of oracle giving that must have been practiced in Israel. The intention here was to obtain YHWH's response to the practical and important question as to who of the twelve was to be chosen to serve as priest. In order to ascertain this, the twelve staffs were laid in the sanctuary. The one to whose staff a wonder occurred in the course of the night is the chosen. YHWH gave his response in the form of a sign. Surely the same and similar measures were taken in other unreported cases. To be sure, dry staffs would have been employed as in the legend. This element is part of the legendary exaggeration of the miracle. Fresh, budding branches may well have been employed as means of revelation, however. If one wanted YHWH's response to some important question—such as Will we win the battle, or not? Which of the king's sons is the one chosen to rule? Or, will the sick king recover or not?—then one laid budding branches before the ark in the temple—so we may imagine. If the buds had blossomed in the morning, the answer was yes. If they were withered, the answer was no. We can have no doubt that the priest knew certain technical means to manipulate such oracles and to acquire the desired response. It suffices to recall the arts that the Indian fakirs perform with grains and plants or the carrying of the glowing iron in the medieval church.

---

14. As I have subsequently learned from Friedrich Küchler's essay in the Baudissin Festschrift ("Das priesterliche Orakel in Israel und Juda," in Abhandlungen zur semitischen Religionskunde und Sprachwissenschaft: Wolf Wilhelm Grafen von Baudissin zum 26. September 1917 [ed. Wilhelm Frankenberg and Friedrich Küchler; Giessen: Töpelmann, 1918], 293 [285–301]), the conclusion that it was employed for oracles had already been reached earlier and used to explain Hos 4:12. As can be seen in my interpretation of Num 17, I cannot consider Küchler's objection against such an interpretation of $'\bar{e}\s$ and $maqq\bar{e}l$ in Hos 4:12 successful.

Obviously, all of this was performed according to a specific ritual in which prayer, that is, the psalm, also had its place. This psalm, then, was sung "over the lilies of revelation."

I have shown in *Psalm Studies* 3 that oracles were given in connection with the performance of the psalms. Of these two possibilities, I consider the latter the most likely and most reasonable.

Finally, we should ask whether the content of the four psalms conforms to this interpretation. Psalm 60 does so quite well, in fact. It contains both the prayer for victory in the imminent war and the divine response to the prayer (see above, no. 16). Similar circumstances pertain to Pss 80 and 69, the first a prayer for help after a defeat, the latter the prayer of a sick person for healing. Both may have been sung to accompany the placement of the lilies of revelation.[15] The situation seems more difficult in Ps 45, yet I believe that I can also demonstrate the connection between psalm and superscription here. Naturally, Ps 45 is not, as is so often thoughtlessly maintained, a purely secular song that has made its way into the Psalter by error. The marriage of a king is not a purely secular matter.[16] YHWH's advice would surely have been sought on such a weighty matter. It is likely a priori that one sought to obtain a salvation oracle at a festival of this nature. Psalm 45 confirms this assumption. It represents itself as the inspired word of a prophetically gifted poet (v. 2). In the name of YHWH, he promises salvation, good fortune, and every benefit (vv. 7, 17). Thus, nothing hinders the assumption that Ps 45 contains the free formulation of the divine response that the cultic prophet had obtained through the "lilies of revelation" in the form of a sign.

(21) עַל־מַחֲלַת (Pss 53; 88) means "concerning illness"[17] (see Exod 15:26, where there is no reason, in any case, to think of a מחלה ["infertility, lack"] derived from a root מחל [so Socin in Gesenius–Buhl]). The feminine-form

---

15. I do no believe that one may conclude from 69:32 that the psalm is not cultic, even less that it opposes cultic religion. The expression is somewhat hyperbolic, as is almost always the case in oriental poetry. The verse contains little more, however, than the ego of the singer and poet (i.e., probably of the Levitical cultic singer) and his pride in his craft in contrast to the sacrificial priest. We know the strong ego and the growing social significance of the singers, who ultimately threatened to outstrip the priests, from the later Second Temple period (see *Psalm Studies* 1:148; see also *Psalm Studies* 3:534–39 [regarding Ps 50]).

16. See *Psalm Studies* 3:588–89.

17. Delitzsch (*Psalmen*) thinks, alternatively, of illness. Since, however, he is tied to the notions of the evangelical hymnbook or of student drinking books, he thinks of a melody title and conjectures a song with the beginning words *maḥălat lēb*. All of this is nicely modern and nonoriental.

ending ה suggests that the formula is relatively old. Psalm 88 is evidently a psalm of illness. Initially it remains unclear only whether the superscript designates the psalm as addressed "against" the illness or as meant to be read "over" the affected area. For Ps 53 = 14, the most evident assumption is that it was originally composed as a prayer liturgy against the magicians (*pōʿălê ʾāwen*) in general. The subject of the prayer is the community that petitions for protection against those enemies who, through secret arts, bring all manner of misfortune, especially illness, on the people and individuals.[18] The most common effect of the sorcerers, however, is illness.[19] Naturally, individuals feel this effect of the magicians most severely and not so much the people as such. Thus it is entirely possible that, even though Ps 14 = 53 may have originally been meant as an apotropaic psalm against magicians in general, or against evil enemies, for the New Year's Festival, it was later employed as a psalm for rites of cleansing for sick individuals or for the sin-offering procedure.[20]

Even if we hold the collective interpretation of Ps 14 = 53, however, the superscription can be related to the content of the psalm without difficulty. As has been said, the most important effect of the sorcerer was illness. A prayer liturgy directed against magicians as such could, consequently, very easily be regarded as directed against illness in general.

As the expression "to change the fate" in Ps 53:7 and the agreement with Pss 85 and 126 demonstrate, the psalm most likely belonged to the grand New Year's Festival in the fall.[21] Thus it joins all the rites and prayers with the purpose of assuring the blessing, good fortune, and security of the coming year.[22] We may assume rather confidently, therefore, that it was connected with certain rites in the cult that were to be understood as apotropaic rites against the *pōʿălê ʾāwen* and thus also against their most dangerous effect, illness. In this case, the most likely translation of *ʿal* is "against" or "versus." Consequently, the whole expression means "(directed) against illness," that is, "to be read for use against illness" (see, e.g., Isa 15:1).

If, however, we hold an individual interpretation and assume an individual use of Ps 14 = 53, the translation "over the illness," that is, "to be recited over the affected area," is also possible and worthy of consideration. The superscript would then refer to an individual act in the ritual for purifying the

---

18. See *Psalm Studies* 1:13–16, 2:349–53, 3:554–57.
19. *Psalm Studies* 1:13–16, 44–51, 104–10.
20. See *Psalm Studies* 1:139–42.
21. See *Psalm Studies* 2:349–53.
22. See *Psalm Studies* 2:275–76.

sick, namely, to the manipulations to be performed on the affected area.[23] This act would have also included, then, the recitation of the psalm as a prayer and an efficacious ("magical") instrument.

(22) אֶל־הַנְּחִילוֹת (Ps 5) may also have had the same meaning, whether it was a word with the same root and meaning or we are dealing with a scribal error. In either case, one is justified in disregarding the vocalization. With respect to the *yod*, both LXX (ὑπὲρ τῆς κληρονομούσης) and Jerome (*pro hereditatibus*) presume a defectively written text.[24] One can either think of a secondary form נחלה = מחלה or assume a scribal error (נ for מ). The ὑπὲρ of the LXX demonstrates that אל is an error for על. Psalm 5 is also a distinct illness psalm (see v. 6) and is simultaneously also clearly meant for a cultic procedure (see v. 4 with the reference to the "omen sacrifice," *bōqer*).[25] The fact that the Targum renders the formula *ʿal-mĕḥōlôt*, that is, "for the round dances," deserves mention. This points to a reading with מ instead of נ (see above).

(23) עַל־עֲלָמוֹת occurs as the superscription to Ps 46. It originally stood as a superscription to Ps 48:15, where it is now miswritten עַל־מוּת.[26] As the passage treated above (1 Chr 15:20–22) suggests, the formula certainly does not contain a reference to instrumentation,[27] nor does it refer to "virginal, that is, high-pitched instruments" (Gesenius–Buhl, s.v. עלמה). Rather, 1 Chr 15:20–22 demonstrates that the expression most likely refers to a cultic and liturgical act that included playing on the harp (*bannĕbālîm*) and singing.

עַל־עֲלָמוֹת here corresponds somehow to the עַל־הַשְּׁמִינִית in the following verse. The former denotes the cultic occasion, or a particularly prominent cultic occasion, on which harps were employed, the latter an occasion on which zithers came into use. The passage does not suggest whether the two formulas denote two aspects of the same cultic procedure or two different procedures or occasions. The commonality between the two corresponding expressions need only be that both belong to cultic situations involving music

---

23. See 2 Kgs 5:11 and my treatment of it in "Om nebiisme og profeti," *NTT* (1909): 349. The designation *hammāqôm* is hardly, as Kittel (*Psalmen*) and others think, the pertinent sanctuary but the area where the illness has broken out or is located. "To swipe the hand against the area" is a threatening gesture meant to banish the illness demon or the substance of the illness (see Mark 11:25).
24. See Baethgen, *Psalmen*, xxxv.
25. See *Psalm Studies* 1:150–51.
26. See Baethgen, *Psalmen*, on the passage; cf. LXX: εἰς τοὺς αἰῶνας = עַל־עֲלָמוֹת.
27. So Rashi; see Baethgen, *Psalmen*, xlii; "Elamite instruments," according to Heinrich Grätz, *Kritischer Commentar zu den Psalmen nebst Text und Übersetzung* (Breslau: Schottländer, 1883); see Buhl, *Psalmerne*, xlvi.

and singing of certain kinds. One may paraphrase the passage as follows: Levites A and B (were positioned) with harps (in order to play) at the—or (in order to play, among other opportunities) at the—עלמות; X and Y, with zithers (in order to play) at the—or (in order to play, among other opportunities) at the—שמינית, both for the purpose לנצח (i.e., in order to put the deity in a gracious mood; see no. 17, above).

The usual interpretation calls for the two expressions to denote two voices: the soprano and the harmony an octave lower. This interpretation fails due to (1) the fact that we know nothing as to whether our octave scale, which stems from Byzantine music, was the foundation for ancient Israelite music, and (2) the unlikelihood that playing and singing in a certain register would have been expressed by ʿal.

At the moment, only conjectures are possible as to what it truly meant. Neither עולם in the meaning "eternity" nor a derivation from the root עלם, "to be powerful," seems to render a useful meaning. If, however, one understands the word with LXX (ὑπερ τῶν κρυφίων) as עֲלָמוֹת, "secrets," and combines this with the observations that can be made concerning the content of the two Pss 46 and 48, then one may be able to arrive at an interpretive proposal that is at least better than those offered so far.

In my *Psalm Studies* 2 I attempted to demonstrate that Pss 46 and 48 belonged to the fall and New Year's Festival celebrated as YHWH's enthronement festival (see esp. part 1, §§1.1.2; 2.1.4; 2.3.4). Psalm 48, at any rate, presumes a sacred procession, and the major content of the festival was, indeed, the dramatic procession that alluded, in various ways, through minor processionals such as in Ps 132, or through mimic and symbolic gestures and objects, in songs and hymns, to the event that laid the foundation for YHWH's rule, the myth of the creation or the battle with dragon or the myth of the exodus or the battle against the nations (see *Psalm Studies* 2, part 1, §2.1). In the symbolic and mimic actions, these very saving realities that constitute the foundation for community's life and existence are repeated and revitalized in the festival, newly experienced by the festival participants and celebrated in related hymns.

What do "the secrets" have to do with this festival, however? This may become clearer if attention is paid to an additional, particularly important, feature. Revitalization is understood in the festival as participation in a new creation. The new creation accomplished in the cult lays the foundations of a new—and naturally better—communal existence. New life, the future, always arises out of the cult. The cult dips down into the past, as it were, and repeats it as a present event. Thereby, it creates anew all of life and thus also the future. This new existence appears as a—transfigured—repetition of what was. The enthronement of YHWH experienced in the cultic procession, the cultic drama visible to the eyes, simultaneously grants and guarantees the repetition of all YHWH's saving acts that sustain the people. Now the community knows what is supposed to happen. From now on, it may expect a glorious repetition of all the mighty deeds celebrated in the enthronement myths as its future fate. The deity revealed to the community his entire activity, both what was and what is now repeated, as what is supposed to happen henceforth. The deity has appeared and has revealed to the community the secrets of his acts and activity.

Above all, the secrets of the future are revealed to the participants in the cultic drama. It quite literally unfolds before the spiritual eyes of the festival participants. Something has long been expected of God's enthronement. The expectation of the one to come is the dominant mood of the festival. Now one interprets the future in the light of YHWH's primordial victory and ascent to the throne. From this grows the community's joyous certainty that great good fortune has been bestowed upon it. The festival hymns and psalms sing of this certainty. The song of praise hurries forth on the wings of faith and experience into the future. The world drama, mirrored in the cultic drama, now lies open before the eyes of the participants. Its secret is revealed; Israel knows what is to come. It already knows and has already comprehended the wondrous good fortune that lies before it. Thus the prophetic words that promise and interpret what is to come are also a fixed component of the festival liturgies.[28] There the voices of the cultic prophets resound and, in fixed, established forms, promise Israel a radiant future. Such festival oracles are the promises included in Pss 81, 85, and 132, for example.

Several circumstances indicate that this activity of the deity revealed in the festival drama was understood as a revelation of profound secrets. First, it should be noted that, in Israel as in many other places, the appearance and activity of the deity in general was regarded as surrounded by profound mystery. Normally human eyes may not see it (see Gen 2:21; 15:12–21; 32:27). Deuteronomy 29:28 states this as a principle: "the secrets belong to YHWH, your God." In certain cases, only permitted individuals may know them (Amos 3:7).

In the cultic drama, however, these secrets, both the mystery of YHWH's first activity on earth, the chaos battle, and so on, in brief especially the deeds that were mirrored in the cultic myth, and also the mysteries of the future were revealed to the participants. In addition, as has been said, there were also revelations by the cultic prophets. Some of the festival psalms, especially Pss 46 and 48, indicate that the participants in the festival have now seen with

---

28. See *Psalm Studies* 3:523–24.

their eyes wondrous, almost incredible things. What they had merely suspected from hearsay before, they have now seen with their own eyes in the city of God. In the midst of the temple, they have been able prayerfully to contemplate YHWH's gracious acts (48:9–10). The poet of Ps 46 challenges the community to consider YHWH's deeds with their own eyes. I have attempted to demonstrate in *Psalm Studies* 2 that these passages most likely refer to certain rites in the cultic drama that perceptibly depict YHWH's wondrous deeds (see the portrayal of their consequences in 46:9–10 and 48:9–10). Psalm 48:4 (YHWH has since "become known and identified," *nôdaʿ*) indicates that all of this was understood as a revelation of previously unknown facts and unsuspected aspects of the divine being. Reference should be made here to Ps 7:2, which also belongs to the same festival: YHWH has now been revealed, *nôdaʿ*, in Judah and Jerusalem.

Further reference should be made to the fact that, for many peoples and religions, the great cultic celebrations are considered secret, if not in the specific sense of the actual mystery religions, then nonetheless in the sense that only the called or sanctified should be present. It is known that this understanding was also held in ancient Israel. Thus, for example, an uncircumcised male could never enter Israel's cultic assembly. Two psalms belonging to this festival explicitly emphasize the idea that only those who are pure of heart and hands may participate in the cultic procession ascending to the sanctuary (Ps 24:3–6; 15).[29] Only the just and pure may view what was taking place.

All of this justifies, I believe, drawing the conclusion that *ʿălûmôt* was a technical designation for certain elements of the festival rites and dramas for the grand fall and enthronement festival and that Pss 46 and 48 were related to this cultic proceedings. They were sung "over (or with) the secrets."

I find confirmation for this association of the expression with the fall festival in the fact that the comment in 1 Chr 15:19–21 discussed above refers in its current context, in fact, to a special occasion, the transfer of the ark to Zion (see 2 Sam 6), and, moreover, that this festival was already understood in the sources as YHWH's enthronement festival. Both the author of the account in 2 Sam 6 and the Chronicler of 1 Chr 16 depict it on the model of the enthronement festival and the latter linked to the enthronement psalms (see *Psalm Studies* 2:285–87).

The expression *ʿal-ʿălûmôt* may have contained a special reference to the promises of the cultic prophets mentioned above that belonged to the festival procession and interpreted the things seen in relation to the future and thus disclosed the secrets of the future. Two circumstances may support this

---

29. See *Psalm Studies* 2:295–97.

assumption. First, the LXX translation, ὑπέρ τῶν κρυφίων, agrees with the translation of סָתֻם in Ps 51:8: τὰ κρύφια. The paraphrase ἰδοὺ γὰρ ἀλήθειαν ἠγάπησας, τὰ ἄδηλα καὶ τὰ κρύφια τῆς σοφίας σου ἐδήλωσάς μοι is syntactically imprecise but correct in terms of substance. The passage apparently deals with cultic means of revelation through which the sick learns either the cause of his suffering or the promise that it will be healed. The interpretation of the depths and hidden things of the heart contradicts the context. In Job 38:36, טֻחוֹת parallels the clouds of heaven, conceived as a means of revelation (soothsaying by the course of the clouds is sufficiently known), and must thus refer to some secret means (or site?) of revelation. The same must be true in Ps 51:8 of *sātûm*. The verse contains a "motivation of confidence": you, who love (to reveal) truth through "the secret (?)" and who teaches me the wisdom (of your saving revelation), cleanse me now with the hyssop. The psalm is virtually a "cultic song," despite verses 18–19, like most of the other individual lament psalms (see further in *Psalm Studies* 1:146–49).

A second confirmation is offered by 1 Kgs 3:15 and 1 Sam 10:5 (see also 16:16, 23). When the prophet is supposed to soothsay, that is, to invoke the Spirit, he resorts to stringed music; he sends for the troubadour. Thus one comprehends why 1 Chr 15:21 explicitly emphasizes that the Levites stroked the harps "over the secrets," that is, to accompany the disclosures of the cultic prophets.

It may be considered certain that such cultic oracles did not have their only place in the festival under discussion.

(24) I have nothing to say about עַל־מוּת לַבֵּן (Ps 9). Psalm 9–10 is, like so many other psalms in the Psalter, a lament psalm directed against the *pōʿălê ʾāwen*, the magicians, and perhaps also against their assistants and counterparts, the demons,[30] with a petition for deliverance from their power. It is introduced by a thanksgiving hymn for YHWH's acts of deliverance experienced earlier in similar situations, which is intended as a confidence motive (see Ps 27, perhaps also 40). Accordingly, it cannot have anything to do with the enthronement festival, unless the first-person speaker of the psalm is to be interpreted collectively and the psalm understood like Ps 14. Even then,

---

30. Following Bernhard Duhm (*Die Psalmen* [KHAT 14; Tübingen: Mohr, 1899]), *gôyim* should be consistently replaced with *gēʾim* (contra *Psalm Studies* 1:75; the psalm is a unity and the disruption of the alphabetic scheme in the central section probably depends only on accident). *Gēʾim* is a synonym for *pōʿălê ʾāwen*, although it originally denoted the demons and still may frequently do so. See *Psalm Studies* 1:74–75. In 9:7, *ʿārîṣîm* should be read instead of *ʿārîm*. It, too, was originally a designation for demons (see *Psalm Studies* 1:75).

it would probably have nothing to do with the grand festival procession and the cultic drama. The often-suggested understanding that sees a scribal error for ʿal ʿălûmôt in the first two words (see Gesenius–Buhl) cannot be correct, therefore, unless the expression belongs to Ps 8 as a subscript (see Ps 48), for this psalm also belongs to the fall festival (see no. 26, below). I would not entirely rule out the possibility that the superscription of Ps 9 might be a historical comment regarding the first (or occasional) use of the psalm as an illness purification psalm and that, accordingly, it should be translated as follows: "against the death threatening the son (of some king)." This interpretation might explain the undeniable nationalistic tone that clings to certain sections of the psalm despite the emendation of gēʾîm for gôyîm. In the ancient Israelite view, the concern of the royal house is a national affair. The misfortune of this house is the misfortune of the people. It is very likely per se that the psalms of the royal temple were initially meant for use by the king and his family.[31] I only mention this possibility; I do not consider it very likely.

(25) עַל־הַשְּׁמִינִית (Pss 6; 12; 2 Chr 15:21) is, as we have seen above regarding number 23, an expression that corresponds to ʿal-ʿălûmôt in certain cases. It seems to denote one of the characteristic cultic procedures in which zithers were played. If the vocalization is correct, it means "over the eight" or "over the eighth." What, however, is "the eight" or "the eighth"? Certainly not a musical instrument and most likely not a register either (see no. 23). The content of Ps 6 and 12 offers the only positive clue.[32] They belong to the same genre, the individual psalm of lament that complains of persecutions by the evil enemies, the "magicians" (6:9), or of "those with the smooth lips and the magniloquent tongues"[33] (12:4). Both psalms conclude with an expression of triumphant certainty that YHWH has heard the petition of the supplicant (6:9–10; 12:6–12). The latter even reports YHWH's response verbatim. In Ps

---

31. So it was also in Babylonia and Assyria; see Jastrow, *Religion Babyloniens*, 2:106.

32. Regarding Ps 12, I have long vacillated between the individual and the collective interpretations. The individual seemed more likely to me in *Psalm Studies* 1 (see 57), the collective, in contrast, in *Psalm Studies* 2 (see 348–49), while I expressed myself more cautiously in *Psalm Studies* 3 (see 556 and 546). One thing is certain, in any case: that the psalm belongs to the individual lament psalms in terms of style and that it is most likely that the magicians ("lip men") should be taken literally under any circumstance (see *Psalm Studies* 2:556). Now, however, the correspondence between ʿal ʿălûmôt and ʿal haššĕmînît seems to point to the fact that the latter expression also refers to the rites of the fall festival (see 637–41, above). The situation is, then, that Pss 6 and 12 have been interpreted in relation to the community and that they do not involve rites for healing illness but purification rites for the whole community.

33. *Psalm Studies* 1, §§1.7 and 2.6.

6, the words fall with a certainty that seems to require the presupposition that the supplicant has received a response just as direct as that in Ps 12 through the words of a cultic prophet, a response whose wording is not reported, however.[34] If both psalms are cultic psalms, then it cannot be doubted that we are dealing here with liturgies consisting of several elements. Psalm 12 is particularly clear: verses 2–5 are the complaint and petition of the sufferer; in verse 6 a priest (cultic prophet) responds in YHWH's name and promises a hearing; verses 7–8 express the jubilant thanksgiving of the supplicant for the divine promise that includes forgiveness of sin, purification, and healing. Psalm 6 contains only the first and third of these elements: complaint and petition (vv. 2–8), thanksgiving and assurance (vv. 9–11). We may assume here, however, as mentioned, that something intervened between verses 8 and 9 that can explain the jubilant tone in verses 9–11. This "something" is, indeed, the priest's warrant that promised YHWH's gracious assistance.

To the extent that the psalms are liturgies, the superscription can, naturally, refer to one part or the other. It may be that it must be explained in terms of the prayer character of the two psalms. It may also be, however, that the superscription related somehow to the oracular character of the psalm.

In both Ps 6 and Ps 12 we may imagine that, alongside the promise, purification and atonement rites were performed meant to remove the sin, the impurity, and the sickness materially, as it were. In any case, both psalms belong to the somewhat decisive point in the atonement ritual. It may be assumed that the cultic absolution has already taken place by the third (second) part of the two psalms. This explains the laudatory thanksgiving at the conclusion.

The number eight is known to play a significant role in many purification rites. Thus, for example, the eighth day is the decisive moment in many of them. The unclean person remains in his impurity for seven days. On the eighth day, he can be cleansed. So it is with the newborn: on the eighth day he is cleansed from the impurity of uncircumcision (Lev 12:3). The same is true of the one afflicted with "discharge" (*zôb*, Lev 15:13–14), the menstruant (Lev 15:19, 28, 30) and the one who has slept with her (15:24), and the Nazirite who has become unclean through contact with a corpse (Num 6:9–11). The law concerning the purification of lepers is particularly instructive (Lev 14). After the one to be cleansed has been sprinkled seven times with bloody water, the preparation of which is described in verses 4–6 (see above, no. 18), he should wash his clothing, shave his hair, bathe, and then remain for seven days "within the camp," although outside his "tent." On the seventh day, he should

---

34. See *Psalm Studies* 1:57–58, 153–54, 2:348–49, 3:556–57.

shave all hair from his body, wash his clothes, and bathe. "Then he is clean" (v. 9). What follows is probably, for the most part, a reduplication of the cleansing for the purpose of a sure affect, for he was already clean. The sprinklings of verses 17 and 18 parallel those in verses 7 and 14. On the eighth day, the one to be cleansed should appear, along with the recommended sacrifice, before the sanctuary in order to be readmitted to the community. The "sin," therefore, is not yet "atoned." One of the two male sacrificial lambs brought along is now sacrificed as an 'āšām. The blood is smeared on the right ear, the right thumb, and the right big toe of the one to be cleansed. This smearing with the blood of the sacrificial animal can be regarded as the eighth sprinkling with blood after the seven sprinklings with the blood of the sacrificed bird mixed in the water (v. 7). A series of additional cleansing sprinklings follows, this time with oil. "The priest fills his left hand" with the oil that has been brought and sprinkles it "before YHWH" seven times. Then he smears the rest of the oil on the aforementioned three body parts of the one to be cleansed and pours the last drops on his head: "thus [*waw* consecutive] the priest makes atonement for him before YHWH" (v. 18). This smearing of the body with oil is to be regarded as the eighth smearing with oil after the seven "before YHWH." According to the wording, it is this eighth sprinkling that, as the last and most important member of the long series of atonement rites, "makes atonement" for the sick person. Finally, a female lamb is sacrificed as a *ḥaṭṭāt* sacrifice and the second goat kid as a burnt offering, "and so shall the priest make atonement for him; then he is clean" (v. 20). This clause apparently refers to the whole ritual.

One is undoubtedly justified in assuming that similarly complex rituals were also employed for other purifications. The law is silent regarding how these other atonements were performed. It is an accident, indeed, that we know so much about the purification of lepers.

Thus it seems even to have been a rule that the final cleansing—and thus also the priestly proclamation of the same—was only attained after seven "attempts." Only the eighth time was decisive: whether sprinkling with oil or blood, the preparations for sacrifice, or something similar, depending on the various cases, only the eighth was regarded as the actual cleansing. The divine oracle had its place in the announcement of complete purification after this eighth iteration. Naturally, however, all the various acts, and especially the last, were accompanied by prayers and psalms.

Since, as we have seen, Pss 6 and 12 were undoubtedly meant for the climax of the purification of a sick person, it is very likely that they should be linked with the concluding "eighth act of purification." The missing noun is difficult to identify. Since, however, we need not necessarily think of cleansings for leprosy and since the number eight seems to have played a rather large role in all cleansings, it may be most likely that a very general term, perhaps טָהֳרָה, "purification," or perhaps simply פַּעַם, "time," should be supplied.

"The eighth (time)" or "the eighth (cleansing procedure)" would then be regarded quite simply as a cultic term for the last and decisive purification act of the long ritual for healing the sick. We may certainly presume that purification rites also took place during the fall and enthronement festival presupposed by the Chronicler in 1 Chr 16 (see no. 21 above).

(26) עַל־הַגִּתִּית (Pss 8; 81; 84) surely does not mean "on Gattite instruments" (so the Targum) or "according to the Gattite scale" (Ewald and others). First, ʻal demonstrably does not have this meaning elsewhere in the superscriptions. Second, there is nothing at all—in theory—of foreign origin in the cult, nothing that the deity had not already commanded domestically and in the primordium. Even if a cultic practice was actually foreign in origin, no admission was made of the fact. In ancient Israel, all the cultic practices, and thus indeed also the modes of singing, were "Mosaic" in origin. The fact that Ahaz had a copy of a Damascene altar produced for the Jerusalem cult was not accredited to him for the good in the priestly tradition (2 Kgs 16:10–16). In any case, naming after the Philistine city of Gath would be inconceivable in this sense. The understanding represented by LXX, Symmachus, Jerome, Aquila, and the Midrash and affirmed by Baethgen (*Psalmen*, xl) and others, which calls for reading הַגִּתּוֹת, translating it "among the winepresses," and relating it to the Festival of Booths, is also untenable, at least in this form.

First, the religious portion of the Festival of Booths was certainly not celebrated "among the winepresses." Second, it is not clear how "the winepresses" could become a designation for the religious portion of the Festival of Booths, even if the festival had been a wine harvest festival in the first instance, for the central component of the religious harvest portion of the festival was the offering of the firstlings and the festive eating and drinking "before YHWH," not the winepresses.

Admittedly, the LXX pronunciation may be correct (see below). The reference to the fall festival is also indeed correct in substance.

Psalm 81 clearly refers to the New Year's and enthronement character of the festival, defined more precisely, to the renewal of the covenant that follows YHWH's entry.[35] Since it mentions the blowing of the shofar and *tĕrûʻâ* cries as a major practice of the festival and this practice was regarded as a particularly sacred commandment, it is possible to conclude that it stood in rather direct connection with the major rite of the festival, the grand entry

---

35. *Psalm Studies* 2:328–33.

procession of YHWH, the new king. The entry was accompanied by trumpet sounds and cries of jubilation ("obeisance to the king," *tĕrûʿat melek*, Num 23:21; cf. Ps 89:16; see Ps 47:5). Psalm 8, the hymn to creation, also belonged with this festival. The day of enthronement was simultaneously the day of new creation.[36] The same is true of Ps 84, which, like Ps 132, presupposes a solemn procession, celebrates YHWH as king, and contains an intercession for the anointed one.[37] The reference to the fall and enthronement festival common to all three of these psalms must constitute the starting point for interpreting the superscription.

Psalms 132 and 24 demonstrate that the ark played a prominent role in the festival procession.[38] The ark is YHWH's palladium; sitting on (or in) it, YHWH "ascends." The superscription על־הגתית must stand, it seems to me, in some relation to the ark. The following considerations lead me to his conclusion.

On the first ascent of the ark, it is known to have spent three months in the house of Obed-edom *haggittî*—supposedly because of the accident involving Uzzah (2 Sam 6:10–11). The designation of the man as *haggittî* is certainly not accidental. It is most unlikely, however, that it rests on "historical" memory and refers to Obed-edom's place of origin. The author of the source probably had no authentic reports and no detailed contemporary accounts concerning how the festival was celebrated under David. The whole report is, in my view, the historical—or legendary—projection of the festival, to the extent that it was celebrated in the time of the author, back into the Davidic era. The cult is prototypical. History, myth, and eschatology were projected backward and forward from the cult. We know nothing about whether there was even a man by the name of Obed-edom in David's time. The comment does suggest, however, that before the procession the ark customarily spent a certain period of time somewhere outside the temple, "in the house of Obed-edom"—quite naturally, for if the ark was to be ceremoniously brought up to the temple annually, it must be brought out each time in advance somewhere outside the temple where it then spent, let us say, three days. This point of departure for the procession was thus the house of Obed-edom. Now we know from other passages that Obed-edom was the name of a Levitical clan and that this clan was tasked to be "gatekeepers of the ark" (*šōʿĕrê lāʾārôn*, 1 Chr 15:24; 16:38). The theological criticism, which has, for the most part, no understanding of the significance of the cult for living religion, judges these passages to be pure

---

36. *Psalm Studies* 2:224–30.
37. *Psalm Studies* 2:294.
38. *Psalm Studies* 2:283–303.

inventions by the Chronicler from the "historical" comment in 2 Sam 6:10, while in reality the situation is vice versa.

Reference to a supposed ancestor of Obed-edom in David's time as *haggittî* probably expresses this relationship of the clan of Obed-edom to the ark.

At the moment I cannot say very much, however, as to the meaning of the words *haggittî* and *haggittît* (or *haggittôt* LXX) and as to how all of this is to be explained more precisely. In any case, "the Gattite" is hardly to be explained as an epithet for the ark. The word *'ārôn* is otherwise masculine gender, although feminine in Ps 132:6. Thus it is difficult to raise any cogent linguistic objection against this assumption. A reference to the ark as "the Gattite," however, is unlikely prima faciae (see above). Admittedly, according to the saga, it spent a period in Philistine Gath (1 Sam 5:8–9). That was only one episode, however. It also spent time in Ashdod and in Ekron. Might the LXX pronunciation and translation "the winepresses" be correct? Was there a winepress in the "house" of Obed-edom, in which the ark was hidden before the festival and then "found" by festival participants playing the role of David's men (see Ps 132:6)? Were the gatekeepers called "the wine-pressers," *haggittî*, for this reason? Were the three psalms 8, 81, and 84 sung "over the winepressers," perhaps before the beginning of the procession (132:7)? Or, does the name (and the ark?) stand in some connection to a place name, Gath? These are questions that I cannot answer.

(27) אַל־תַּשְׁחֵת (Pss 57; 58; 59; 75) remains. It apparently belongs to none of the groups treated above. Here, too, one often thinks (following Ibn Ezra; see Baethgen, *Psalmen*) of the initial words of a song to whose melody the words of a psalm were sung. Meanwhile, since there are no ancient Near Eastern analogies to such melody indications, it is much more likely, on the Babylonian analogy, that one should think of the words as the title of a "series" of psalms from which these four were taken. Then one may best understand the "Do Not Destroy" as the initial words of the first psalm in the series. Thus, in the Babylonian creation epic Enuma Elish, all the tablets of the series are designated in a subscription as belonging to the series Enuma Elish—according to the first words of the first tablet ("when above"; cf. the rabbinic names for the first five books of the Pentateuch).

By "series," as the Assyriologists employ the word, one need not understand a coherent, organic unity, such as the Babylonian creation epic. Babylonian series also include more accidental collections of rituals that were employed at the same or similar cultic procedures. Such is the case with the incantation series *maqlu* ("burning"), which consists of cultic purification and healing rituals in which the "burning" of some objects played a role (cf. the series Šurpû, i.e., "burning").

Psalms 57–59 are designated *miktām*, that is, atonement psalms (see no. 4, above), in the superscription, and all belong to the genre of individual songs of lament: complaints and prayers against evil and deceitful enemies portrayed as magicians. The occasion is most likely any illness.

"Do Not Destroy" as the title of the collection could stem, then, either from the initial words of the first psalm (perhaps: "Do not Destroy, O YHWH, your servant in your wrath!" see Deut 9:26), or it could have been employed to designate certain atonement psalms indicating their contents and purpose—perhaps because it was once a frequent expression in the lament songs.

I believe, however, that the explanation presented here as a possibility requires modification in terms of one of the alternatives just mentioned. I believe that we are dealing with a "series superscription" but that it was derived from the keyword for the procedure connected with "psalm series," or, more correctly, with the liturgy constituted by these psalms. My explanation also presupposes the cultic cohesion of the four psalms, whether original or not. A circumstance that initially seems to contradict this cohesion provides the starting point.

One could object with some justification against the assumption of at least a somewhat cohesive "series" of these psalms that Ps 75 differs entirely in nature from the other three. Psalm 75 contains a divine oracle and an adjoined communal psalm of thanksgiving and most likely belongs, in terms of content and conceptual world, to the enthronement festival.[39] Thus it apparently has nothing per se to do with the individual psalms of lament. It is possible, however, to find a relationship. One could assume that Ps 75 was reinterpreted individually at some point and correspondingly found inclusion in an atonement ritual for a ceremony for healing an individual's illness. The reverse explanation is much more likely, however. The three originally individual songs were subsequently reinterpreted collectively and applied to the congregation and, accordingly, made, along with Ps 75, into components of a prayer liturgy (associated with the fall festival) with complaints, petitions, divine oracle, and thanksgiving. This prayer liturgy was then addressed against the oppressors of the people in general and was concluded with the proclamation of divine attention and the promise of the protection sought (for such a prayer liturgy, see, e.g., Ps 14; see no. 21, above). The collection of the *ma'alôt* songs related to the fall festival, of which Pss 120, 130, and 131 were originally meant to be individual,[40] manifests to us that originally individual songs were reinterpreted in this manner. Indeed, traces of such a reinterpretation also appear

---

39. *Psalm Studies* 2:246.
40. *Psalm Studies* 1:170–71.

in the Pss 57–59. In Ps 58 the "collective" sense might even have been original. The psalm constitutes a substantive parallel to Ps 82, which was directed against the evil "gods." In this case, the great similarity with the individual songs would depend on the fact that the "gods" are portrayed through the image of the demons and magicians[41] and were battled with the same weapons of curse. The emendation *gôyîm* instead of the original *gē'îm*[42] in Ps 59 evidences that such a reinterpretation occurred.[43] Thus *'al tašḥēt* would have then been the characteristic keyword for this prayer liturgy and the associated rites.

I believe this explanation can be corroborated. In Isa 65:8 we read, "As when one finds juice in a grape and (consequently) says: 'Do not destroy, for there is a blessing in it,' thus I (i.e., YHWH) will do for the sake of my servant (i.e., Israel), so that I do not completely destroy it." The context speaks of the pardon and restoration of the degenerate people. The pertinent passage, however, has not yet been satisfactorily explained. Usually one finds the statement a comparison to everyday life. The statement actually suggests that the comparison refers to a common situation frequent in the addressee's world of experience, not to a singular case. If it were taken from a freely imagined situation, the metaphor would be difficult to explain and unclear. Where in everyday life does one deal with grapes in this fashion? Could such a thing occur when eating? Then the situation must have been indicated. Or perhaps with vintners? I do not think that when dumping the grapes into the winepress to tread them one examined the individual grapes so precisely that there was room for discussion and intercession. One expects that the image would stand in some substantive connection with the topic, the pardon of the people. One may recall what was said above (no. 18 [627 n. 2]) concerning the "symbolic" procedures that accompanied the words in rites of atonement or prayer liturgies. If one assumes that the comparison in Isa 65:8 was borrowed from a commonly known cultic rite that accompanied a communal prayer liturgy in which prayer was offered for protection and assistance against all enemies and for the pardon and restoration of the degenerate community—or of the community portrayed in the prayer as degenerate and suffering[44]—then the significance of the passages is clearer, at any rate. We may imagine that during the recitation of the prayer someone manipulated a grape that was interpreted "symbolically" in relation to the community. One may imagine the matter as follows: something was done to the grape. If there should subsequently be

---

41. See *Psalm Studies* 1:79.
42. See *Psalm Studies* 1:74–75.
43. See *Psalm Studies* 1:171.
44. See *Psalm Studies* 3, ad Ps 85.

proof that it still contained juice—and this should normally prove to be so, since the community gathered for the festival was, despite everything, "just" at the core and thought that it had a claim to divine grace—then this omen was related to the fate of the people. This "grape" should not be destroyed, for there is blessing in it. In these or similar words the matter was then placed before YHWH: Do not destroy! Thereupon, finally, pardon and protection was promised the community.

The words of Trito-Isaiah were probably spoken in connection with such a cultic practice. Just as in the New Year's Festival one sought to determine that there was still "blessing" in the grape and then petitioned YHWH, "Do not destroy it," to which he received a promise of grace, so should it be now with the people. YHWH would never again destroy it. One must admit that the choice of the grape as a "symbol" for the community in a rite that occurred in the fall festival was very obvious. Israel is, after all, otherwise known as the vine, YHWH's planting (Isa 5:1–10; Ps 80:9–17).

If this is so, then we have in Pss 57–59 (originally independent) elements of a liturgy that was once associated with the rite deduced here, a rite whose refrain was indeed "Do not destroy." If this interpretation is correct, this expression also supports the information treated here concerning cultic procedures.

PSALM STUDIES 5

BLESSING AND CURSE IN ISRAEL'S CULT AND PSALMODY

Preface

The following investigation was presented in significantly shorter form in the 6 December 1918 session of the Gesellschaft der Wissenschaften in Kristiana (Videnskapseelelskapet I Kristiania) under the title "Salmestudier. I. Velsignelsen og forbanneisen I israelistsk-jødisk kultus og sameldiktning. En religions- og literaturehistorisk studie." Shortly thereafter I withdrew the essay and now present it in revised form in the German language to the society and the public.

Introduction

Among the psalms in the Psalter, we find psalms of blessing (e.g., Ps 128), psalms of curse (e.g., Pss 109; 137), as well as psalms that exhibit the dual scheme of blessing and curse, even though in diminished form (namely, Pss 1 and 112).

Some of these psalms (i.e., Pss 1; 112; 128; Pss. Sol. 6; 10) already purport to be psalms of blessing, or of blessing and curse, through their initial words, *'ašrê hā'îš*. To be sure, at first glance this seems to be a somewhat exaggerated claim. First, in the general view, the expression does not have the significance of a wish formula in Hebrew but states a fact: "Fortunate are those who...." Second, there is no corresponding formula introducing the second section of the bipartite psalms. In fact, even psalms such as Pss 1 and 112 bear greater similarity to didactic poems than to blessing and curse formulas. A description of the fate of the just and of the evildoer (the godless) constitutes the content of these psalms, and to this extent they bear a rather broad similarity with other more or less "didactic" psalms that deal with the topic of "the two paths" (i.e., Pss 37; 49; 73)—psalms, however, that are also not meant as didactic poems in the proper sense of the word but as instructive thanksgiving psalms.[1] In Pss 1 and 112 we would expect after the introductory formula that the second section dealing with the fate of the godless would be structured similarly to the first and introduced with a "woe to the person who" or something similar. The absence of the second introductory formula, however, is surely to be judged a departure from an originally balanced scheme. In Ps 112, the reason for the irregularity is even clearly perceptible. The psalm is an acrostic, and after the author had utilized the letters from *aleph* to *qoph* for the depiction of the righteous, he could use neither *'ôy, hôy* ("woe"), nor *'ārûr* ("accursed") as the first word of the second part. He had to place the word *rāšaʿ* for the letter *resh* as the first word if he wanted to create his bipartite scheme at all. The fact, however, that a formula corresponding to the *'ašrê* belonged as an introduction to the second section of the original scheme is

---

1. *Psalm Studies* 1:132–33, 136–37. See further below, §3.2.3.

evident through comparison with Jer 17:5–8, a passage that constitutes a precise parallel to Ps in form and content, although with a peculiarly "prophetic" application.

The saying in Jer 17:5–8 just mentioned demonstrates, however, that the scheme ’ašrê–hôy (or vice versa) we have deduced from Pss 1 and 112 is only a weaker variant of the more forceful ’ārûr–bārûk (accursed–blessed). As our treatment of the blessing and curse in ancient Israel below will show, ’ašrê or hôy is just as good a blessing or curse formula, respectively, as bārûk or ’ārûr, respectively. The situation is not such that one must draw a sharp distinction between ’ašrê as the supposed indicative and bārûk as the supposed optative expression. This distinction depends on modern conceptualization. Both formulas constitute a fact: this or that person has inherent good fortune or blessing. At the same time, the establishment of the fact per se is already an increase of the good fortune and blessing of the one concerned and creates new blessings.[2] Both schemata establish a situation but are simultaneously true curse and blessing sayings. These formulas mean both "PN is accursed or blessed" as well as "may he be so and may hereby become even more accursed or blessed." To this degree, psalms that begin with ’ašrê or hôy are also true blessing and curses.

Now, since the psalms mentioned above all bear a more or less clear didactic stamp, and since, furthermore, the formulas mentioned occur rather frequently in the wisdom literature,[3] the assumption seems likely that this scheme originated in wisdom literature and was adopted by the psalmists. This also seems to be the view of Balla and Staerk.[4] The latter indicates, however, that he finds the model "in the prophetic blessing in Jer 17:7–8."

---

2. It is a matter unto itself that, in each individual case, the focus rests on one or the other of these two aspects, depending on the context. The usual understanding that ’ašrê has an "indicative" meaning while bārûk usually appears as an "optative" is correct. The Hebrew, however, did not perceive a fundamental difference.

3. See ’ašrê—Prov 3:13; 8:32, 34; 14:21; 16:20; 28:14; 29:18; Job 5:17; Eccl 10:16–17; Sir 14:1–2, 20–27; 25:7–9; 28:19; 31:8–9 (34:8–9). Of these passages, Prov 14:21; 29:18; Eccl 10:16–17; and Sir 28:13–19 have the bipartite scheme with reference to both the righteous and the godless. In the latter passage, the discussion of the godless is introduced by a καταρασθη ("accursed"; 28:13). In Eccl 10:16, which does not, however, discuss the righteous and the godless per se but the land that has a bad or a good government, the first saying is introduced with the weaker ’îy lĕkā ’ereṣ. This diminution is a necessity given the particular topic to which the scheme is applied. In both of these passages, the curse or the woe appears in first position, as in Jer 17:5–8.

4. Emil Balla, *Das Ich der Psalmen* (FRLANT 16; Göttingen: Vandenhoeck & Ruprecht, 1912), 41–44; Willy Staerk, *Lyrik (Psalmen, Hoheslied und Verwandtes)* (vol. 3.1 of *Die*

In my view, however, there can be no doubt that Gunkel correctly points to a relationship with certain cultic formulas. In his article "Psalmen," he remarks in regard to the discussion of cultic procedures with which the psalm genres may have originally been connected that "blessing and curse were also once pronounced in sacred procedures."[5] It is unclear, however, how he conceived of the relationship of this style to the composition of the sayings. His brief suggestions say nothing about this relationship.[6] In any case, he seems on the whole to derive the "didactic or wisdom psalms," as they are called by most exegetes (e.g., Staerk), from the *māšāl* (see, in contrast, *Psalm Studies* 1:130–33).

Now if the general thesis recognized by Gunkel that the psalms stem from the cult is correct—and I doubt it not a moment—then one must also first examine the individual psalms, in my view, as to whether they can be explained as actual cultic psalms. After all, the established certainty of psalm research is that the psalms came to us as the cultic hymnal of the Second Temple. Therefore, one must consistently maintain that, if the cultic explanation of a psalm is possible, it deserves preference over others. The cultic explanation means that the pertinent psalm not only relates to a cultic situation in form and genre but also that the individual specific psalms were composed for a cultic procedure. Thus we must also investigate the psalms of blessing and curse in reference to their relationship to the cult. If it can be satisfactorily explained as a cultic psalm, nothing in principle can then be objected against this explanation.

Thus the examination of the stylistic form mentioned leads to an investigation of blessing and curse in the cult of Israel and Judaism. What we can say, however, is very fragmentary. We have more than a few of the fragments of the original image. We cannot, however, join them together seamlessly. Nonetheless, we can obtain an impression of the character of the ancient cult.

Schriften des Alten Testaments in Auswahl; ed. H. Gressmann et al.; Göttingen: Vandenhoeck & Ruprecht, 1911), 246–57.

5. *RGG* 4:1939.

6. See Gunkel, "Psalmen, 16," *RGG* 4:1948; and idem, "Weisheitsdichtung im AT," *RGG* 5:1869–73.

1
The Blessing in Cult and Psalmody

1.1. Blessing

In the ancient Israelite view, blessing and curse are the two fundamental forces of life, the positive and the negative, the good, beneficial and the evil, harmful.

Blessing, *běrākâ*, is, in a few words, the soul's life force and capacity, the expressions of this force in good fortune and prosperity and in the extension of good fortune to the surroundings.[1] The Hebrew *běrākâ* signifies not only the blessing or the pronouncement of blessing but also "blessedness," the state of being filled with blessing, as well as specific "blessings" that result, good fortune, might, and so on. It is both an internal and an external matter; the ancient Israelite did not distinguish between these two aspects of reality. Everything that has life force has blessing (see Isa 65:8). The blessing can be greater or lesser depending on the variety of the souls of the individual living beings and things in the world. Every "species" received its particular "blessing" in creation (Gen 1:22), and it is the blessing of humanity to be able to multiply on the earth and to rule over the other creatures (Gen 1:28; 5:2). The fact that one always has good fortune (*ṣālaḥ, hiṣlîaḥ hiśkîl*) and another, by contrast, can accomplish nothing depends, in Israelite terms, not on external and inexplicable coincidences but on the internal force of the soul, on the fact that the first "can" (*yākôl*) but the latter cannot. This "ability," itself, is the blessing (see 1 Sam 26:25). Both the state of blessedness and the ability to bless depend on the strength of the soul. Blessing is soul power. The Israelite can also express this situation in terms of the "competent" as the one who is skillful and who has "wisdom" or "insight." Insight is the ability to carry out one's will and plans (see Job 12:13–16). Blessing expresses itself in the per-

---

1. The subsequent paragraph substantially follows Johannes Pedersen, *Israel: Its Life and Culture* (2 vols.; Atlanta: Scholars Press, 1991), 1:182–212. See also Hans Schmidt, "Gebet und Gebetssitten in Israel und im Judentum," *RGG* 2:1150–57.

son's decisions. Council is not just deciding or advising but simultaneously the execution of plans. The two go together.

Every species and every being has its particular blessing that can express itself in the most manifold ways. Certain constitutive fundamentals consistently recur, however. First and foremost, blessing is the capacity to multiply, the power to reproduce, fertility.[2] Genesis 1 states this clearly. Repeatedly many descendants are promised as an expression of blessing.[3] In addition, however, the fertility of field and cattle and increased possessions are also promised.[4] Finally, military might that can vanquish the foes and subjugate the nations[5] is also mentioned as the third major aspect of blessing. The blessings on Judah and Joseph comprise all three of these elements (Gen 49:8–12, 22–26).

In the final analysis, blessing is not the property of the individual. From Abraham and Isaac, it is transferred to Jacob, and he bequeaths it further to Joseph and his other sons. The blessing goes from father to son, and the father's blessing traces back to the psychic power of the ancestors. The whole household lives and prospers in the blessing of the *paterfamilias*, the whole tribe in the blessing of the chieftain, and the whole people in the blessing of the king (see Ps 72). When Israel becomes chief and king of all the nations, they will be blessed in it or in its name.[6] This understanding depends simply on the fact that, in the ancient Israelite view, the soul was conceived not as purely individual but as collective. Everything constituting the substance of his life, and thus above all his tribe and his "house," belongs to a person's soul. To a certain degree, the individual's soul manifests the soul of the greater community, the "super-ego," to which he belongs. The individual exists only in connection and identity with the greater ego of the community (the family, the clan, the tribe, the people). Thus psychic power is also a common possession to a degree. Blessing transfers from one to the other because, in the final analysis, it is a common possession, the common source of power for the whole community. It can also be conveyed through external means.[7] Thus on

---

2. This may even be the basic meaning of the root *brk* and the word *bĕrākâ*. See Pedersen, *Israel*, 1:199; and Friedrich Delitzsch, *Assyrisches Wörterbuch zur gesamten bisher veröffentlichten Keilschriftliteratur unter Berücksichtigung zahlreicher unveröffentlichter Texte* (Leipzig: Hinrichs, 1896), s.v. *birkū*.

3. Gen 12:2; 13:16; 24:60; 26:24; 48:19; 2 Sam 7:11–16; Ruth 4:11–12; Tob 10:11–12.

4. Gen 24:35; 26:12–14; 27:27–28; Exod 23:25–26; Lev 25:21; Deut 7:12–14; 28:1–13; Job 21:8–13; 29:6; 42:12; Joel 2:14; Zech 8:12–13; Mal 3:10–11.

5. Gen 27:29; Num 24:17–18.

6. Gen 12:3; 18:18; 22:18; 26:4; 28:14.

7. See below.

all of the more important occasions the great gives some of his blessing to the small (see 1 Kgs 8:66). Conversely, even the small give blessing to the great, the chieftain. They "bless" him and thereby actually confirm and increase his share of blessing.[8]

Behind the whole sequence of fathers, behind the whole community that constitutes a "covenant," however, stands the deity, the lord, protector, and psychic source of power for the covenant. In every transfer of blessing, ancient Israel felt something of the sacred. To this extent, blessing is always a sacred procedure when the Holy One, the deity, is perceived as present in the background and is usually named directly as the author of blessing. Consequently, YHWH or God is repeatedly said to be with the blessed.[9] God blesses Jacob and gives him wealth; that is, he gives Jacob the strength and the ability to become wealthy. The divine power of the blessed is simultaneously his own power. "YHWH is with you, you mighty hero," says God's angel to Gideon. Shortly thereafter he says, in the same sense, "Go in this your might and deliver Israel from the power of Midian" (Judg 6:12–14). Indeed, being blessed originally meant having a part in the mysterious, salvation-producing, good forces of life. This possession was originally gained and given through mysteriously effective procedures and words. Later, when gods and cults of the gods originated, the mysterious power was linked to the gods. To a certain degree, deified and deity figures developed from the concepts of power. Thus a connection between the power active in the blessing and the deities developed. Through the procedures that evoked the blessing, one was placed in a mysterious connection with the deity. This psychic connection with the deity, originally conceived in quite mystical terms, was loosened somewhat in the course of the development of religion in Israel. The energetic understanding of YHWH as a benevolent personality and the gradual shift toward the transcendent in the understanding of God brought to the foreground the more rational idea that YHWH is the giver of blessing. This development is also evident in the fact that, in a somewhat later time, the transfer of blessing from one person to another was not always quite clearly regarded as inherent in the nature of the self-activating force of blessing force, as it were, but as the expression of a particular divine benevolence. This is evident in the Joseph narrative, for example (Gen 39:2–5). Joseph is a "fortunate man," an *'îš maṣlîaḥ* one in whom there is blessing, good fortune, and "ability." Consequently, proximity to him automatically brings blessing on the whole house of Egypt; that is clearly the original meaning of the verses cited. In the course of

---

8. 2 Sam 14:22; Job 31:20; Ruth 2:19–20.
9. Gen 26:2, 28; 1 Sam 16:18; 18:12, 14; 20:13.

time, however, the account here was revised. Now it says that YHWH blessed the house of Egypt "for Joseph's sake," an idea that contradicts the expression mentioned above. The many repetitions in the verses cited betray how it was originally conceived.[10]

Since blessing is a psychic force—and this idea was always preserved in the background of consciousness—blessing signifies a transfer of this power from the one blessing to the one blessed. Within a covenant, this transfer actually occurs continually. If the lesser finds himself in the protection of one who is mightier and blessed, the latter always and automatically gives to the former of his blessing, as though automatically, and thereby creates a new, effective blessing (see above concerning Joseph). The transfer can also take place, however, in a special manner and through special measures, and it must be done so in particularly important cases, on particularly solemn and significant occasions. Extraordinary circumstances require extraordinary measures. In general, physical proximity is a precondition for an effective transfer of blessing (see Isaac and Jacob). The transfer of power is mediated through bodily contact. This usually takes place through the rite of the laying on of hands, such as when Jacob blessed his grandchildren (Gen 48:14-20) and when Moses installed Joshua as his successor and transferred to him something of his "glory," that is, blessed him (Num 27:18-20). In a diminished form, the laying on of hands became an extension of the hands toward or over the one involved, as was the case in later times with the Aaronic blessing.[11] Thus, the effective transfer of blessing involves a solemn procedure with certain objects considered carriers of the blessing. Ancient Israel understood every power and effect of power, and thus blessing, too, objectively and materially. Consequently, blessing can also be contained and embodied in a material object. The grape has "blessing," in the sense of juice, in it (Isa 65:8); it possess a power that, as anyone can see, brings with it an increased sense of life and power. Rainfall bears YHWH's blessing down to the earth (Ezek 34:26). When Elisha sent his servant to Shunem with the prophet's staff in order to awaken

---

10. We have a precise parallel to this revision in 2 Sam 6:6-7, the account concerning Uzzah, who died because he touched the ark with the best intentions. The "holiness" of the ark has a spontaneously fatal effect because it is imbued with power, is "taboo." It may only be touched by those who have submitted themselves to the whole purification ritual and are called to carry it. Thus it was originally the holiness of the ark that killed. In the "Yahwistic" revision, however, the death of Uzzah was based in the fact that "YHWH's wrath" was kindled against him. This late Israelite-Jewish manner of thought introduced the personal God without regard for the fact that thereby the account was made doubly as offensive, from a religious perspective, as it had been before.

11. See below.

the dead son of the widow by means of the staff, the man of God's power of blessing was contained in the staff. This is evident from the command that the servant took along on the way: bless no one and accept no blessing from anyone on the way (2 Kgs 4:29). He may not diminish the power of the blessing embodied in the staff by blessing someone nor alter the prophetic blessing by accepting the blessing of other people.[12] The gift that one might give a friend on parting also carries a part of the soul, of the blessing, of the giver and is often even called a blessing, *běrākâ*.[13] A blessing can also imbue certain days and times with a particular quality. YHWH blessed the Sabbath.[14] It has thereby become "taboo" and may not be "profaned" by any sort of work. The same situation pertains to the curse (see below).

Blessing can be embodied in a word just as it can be in an object. Any word that expresses something good for someone is, ultimately, a word of blessing, the "beatitude" (*'ašrê*) no less than the solemn formula of blessing, just as the woe or the swear word is a curse (see below). The greeting is already the establishment or the confirmation of a psychic connection and mediates blessing. "To greet" is even *bērēk* in Hebrew.[15] All explicit, solemn transfers of blessing involve the words of blessing that contribute to the proceedings and increase their efficacy: before a wedding (Gen 24:60), before a journey (Gen 28:1), when friends part (Gen 31:28; 32:1; 47:10; 2 Sam 13:25; 19:40), when a father on his death bed transfers his blessing to his sons or to the leader of his people (Gen 27; 48:14–20; 49; Deut 33), and at the dismissal of a cultic assembly (Josh 22:7; 2 Sam 6:18; 1 Kgs 8:55, 66). Thereby, those who are departing carry with them abroad or back home the power of the community as an effective source of power and might. All such procedures and words transfer blessing and create new blessing.

In accordance with everything said above, the efficacy of the blessing depends on the psychic power of the one blessing. The "direct" influence of other souls through blessing and curse procedures and words did not become purely mechanical, that is, effective *ex opera operato*.[16] The spoken word is not

---

12. Pedersen, *Israel*, 1:201.
13. Gen 33:11; Josh 14:13; 15:19; Judg 1:15; 1 Sam 25:18, 27; cf. 30:26; 2 Kgs 5:15.
14. Gen 2:3; Exod 20:11.
15. 1 Sam 13:10; 25:14.
16. It may be that the frequent distinction between "direct," i.e., understood in a more psychic fashion, and "mechanical," or as it is usually put "magical," i.e., effective *ex opere operato*, influence and efficacy (so, e.g., Gustav Hölscher in *Geschichte der israelitisch-jüdischen Religion* [Giessen: Töpelmann, 1922], 19) should, consequently, be avoided as too theoretical and based on an abstraction, just as the still-customary distinction between religion or cult and "magic" is entirely false. Even though a procedure or a word is thought to be effective *ex opere operato*, the concept of the significant psychic capacity of the one

efficacious in itself, for there are also "empty" words. The word of the psychically powerful, however, is an effective blessing.[17] If one is fortunate and full of blessing, he can share with others out of his excess. Naturally, the most effective blessings are pronounced by the deity himself.[18] Effective blessings (and curses) are also spoken by the representatives of the deity: by kings (2 Sam 6:18; 1 Kgs 8:55); by the "men of God," the priest (Gen 14:19; 1 Sam 1:17), the *nābî'*, the seer, and the prophet (Num 23:7–10, 18–19; 24:3–9, 15–10; 2 Kgs 2:24; 4:16–17); or by the ancient progenitors and patriarchs who, as progenitors, on the one hand, contain all the power of the people, and, on the other, are considered *něbî'îm* who stand in a closer relationship to the deity than do normal people.[19] The words and the procedures do not mean very much in themselves. Whether the one blessing begins with an *'ašrê* or a *bārûk* is, in itself, quite beside the point. Behind and in the words stand the souls of those who pronounce the words. They are what lend the words their effective force. Whoever has a powerless soul, "who himself is not possessed of the blessing can create nothing in others."[20] Even the worthless, the accursed, can curse and thereby cause disaster,[21] because their whole nature is an infectious cursedness (see below), but they cannot bless. The very latest development of illegitimate magic regards this effectiveness as dependent only on the words and procedures.[22] If a blessed person containing blessing has spoken the blessing, then an effective reality has been produced that cannot be reversed, not even if the blessing person should have had the misfortune of blessing the wrong person. The Isaac narrative illustrates this. The blessing, with its inherent power, must have effect. "That which at one time has been real cannot be undone, but it can of course be counteracted."[23]

The Isaac narrative also shows us, however, that not everyone can be blessed, although, seen superficially, it seems to contend the contrary. The whole story presupposes, indeed, that the blessing actually comes to its proper place here. The violent fool Esau does not have a soul receptive to the blessing.

---

active, on whom the outcome depends at least in part, is very rarely completely excluded. Indeed, this exclusion takes place mostly when the procedures have degenerated into illegitimate "magic," and even then rarely indeed. Not every person is suited to be a magician. Even magic involves a certain "power." See the excursus in n. 25, below.

17. See Pedersen, *Israel*, 1:167–68.
18. Gen 1:28; 3:14–19; 12:2, 7; 25:23, etc.
19. See Gen 20:7, 17; Exod 15:20; Num 11 and 12; Gen 48:14–20; 49; Deut 33.
20. Pedersen, *Israel*, 1:200.
21. The lament psalms, which complain about the curses of the worthless "liars" and the illness they cause, demonstrate this (see *Psalm Studies* 1).
22. See n. 16 above.
23. Pedersen, *Israel*, 1:200.

He is empty and filled only with folly. Consequently, only the lot of the fool, of the godless, namely, the curse, can be placed on him. If the one to be blessed is not receptive, no blessing can be placed on him. Only someone who has something of the good force of the blessing, of "blessedness," can be effectively blessed. The Balaam narrative demonstrates this for us. Balaam had a special gift for blessing. Balak knew that whomever Balaam blessed was blessed and whomever he cursed was cursed. Nonetheless, he could not put a curse on Israel, could not automatically create blessing or curse. Israel had a fortunate soul that was receptive only to blessing. It was blessed by YHWH; consequently the seer must also bless it. Balaam "could only work in harmony with reality."[24] This fundamental view continues to be active in the New Testament: "If the house in question is not worthy of your greeting of peace [greeting is blessing, however; see above], then your greeting of peace will return to you" (Matt 10:13). In the Balaam legend we encounter this fundamental view in an already somewhat diminished form. The seer declares, so it says, that he can say only what YHWH has placed in his mouth (Num 23:12 and parallels). The original concept appears in the clear light of day when it is said that YHWH gave him blessing because Israel was already blessed. The curse accomplishes nothing against the one who is truly blessed in the full sense of the word, and, vice versa, blessing is useless to the truly accursed in the full sense of the word.

Thus, every true, not "empty," word of blessing presupposes that the one to be blessed already has internal blessing, that his soul has authentic content, that he is "a son of blessing," as the Israelites could say (see Luke 10:6, υἱὸς εἰρήνης = ben šālôm). In certain contexts šālôm is a synonym for bĕrākâ. To this extent, the word of blessing confirms an already-existent circumstance. On the other hand, it increases the blessedness of the one to be blessed; it creates new blessing. The same is also true of the curse (see §2.1, below).

In the diction of historical Israel, when YHWH became the one wishing and working personally, on whom everything that occurred depended, this idea was understood and expressed as follows: only the righteous receives blessing from YHWH. Whereas blessing was formerly the natural "fruit" of righteousness, it now became the divine reward to which the righteous was due. This idea often comes to expression in the Old Testament (see, e.g., Ps 24:4–5). The old fundamental view that the excess of blessing must actually from come of itself if the person is just and has internal "blessing" was never abandoned in the Old Testament. It was only shaped and expressed in the spirit of historical Yahwism.

---

24. Ibid.

1.2. The Blessing in the Cult

1.2.1. We saw above that the blessing, the power expressed in the words of blessing, is essentially a common possession of the whole community and that it has its original source in the deity heading the covenant. Israel's blessing is the blessing of Abraham, Isaac, Jacob, and the twelve patriarchs passed on from them to all the true, normal members of the people. It ultimately stems from YHWH, the God of Abraham and Israel, from his own great store of blessing, from his mighty "majesty."

Simultaneously, the situation is such, however, that it is repeatedly necessary to gain new blessing as protection and defense against all the evil influences in the world. As shown elsewhere (*Psalm Studies* 2:199), one of the fundamental convictions of primitive people is that nothing has eternal effects. Even the greatest and most enduring infusions of power must be repeated from time to time so that they do not ultimately fail. This notion rests, furthermore, on good psychology and is also obvious in the religious realm: return ever to the foundational experience of God, acquire new power repeatedly in communion with God, whether through the emotional reliving of the moment of breakthrough, through new mystical immersions into the fundamental ground of all being, through the repeated consumption of the sacrament, or through self-reflection and reflection on the will of God for me and through prayer. Thus, blessing must ever be re-created and occurs by ever reconnecting with the ultimate source of blessing, whether with the mysterious power or with God, and by some means enabling an infusion of blessing in the most concentrated form possible from the source into the community and individuals.

The means that ancient Israel had for reconnecting with the deity for the purpose of obtaining the divine blessing was the cult.

By cult, I understand not only those procedures and words meant to effect gods and divine beings but absolutely all those procedures undertaken by self-understood or professional representatives of a community (a clan, a tribe, a people, etc.) and the related words intended to procure and assure for the pertinent community and thereby for all its individual members what they need for life, prosperity, and security. The procurement and assurance of these things requires, however, extraordinary, "holy" means that differ from everyday "profane" things.[25] Thus the ceremonies and dances of the

---

25. Excursus: I note here expressly to hinder misunderstanding that I reject the distinction between religion (cult) and magic in the customary sense of this distinction as entirely preposterous. Usually this distinction is accepted as self-evident, and despite all the variety in the determination of the individual criteria, there seems to be unanimity that

they are to be sought in the realm of concepts (religion presupposes personal gods, magic impersonal powers; religion prayer and influence of the will, magic mechanical control of the "natural circumstances," etc.). It can be widely demonstrated that this demarcation is entirely capricious and does not correspond to the facts. One works here with abstractions that do violence to reality. Gillis P. Wetter has offered a quite incontrovertible and demolishing critique of the theories offered to date in his essay, "Religion och Magi," in *Bibelforskaren* 34 (1917): 289–342. Almost the entire discussion on this question has been confused by the fact that two different questions have been intermixed. The first question concerns a suitable scientific, and thus appropriate to our modern thought, principle of order that will bring order to our knowledge of those phenomena that concern the relationship of human beings to the "supernatural." Here, as Wetter shows, a remarkable conceptual realism has held sway as though the terms and the realities they are supposed to reflect were extant as established facts with identifiable external and internal criteria, while in reality the only issue involves finding a suitable principle of order that could illuminate our intellectual appropriation of matters. The word "magic" was adopted from the popular, casual, and arbitrary diction of antiquity and the Middle Ages. It has been assumed that behind the word stands a concept and that this concept coincides with an established reality that can now be comprehended and defined in modern scientific terms. The (normally perhaps unconscious) quasi-scientific distinction between "black" and "white" magic has had an extremely unfortunate effect. An entirely different question is confused with the first: the question, which deals purely with the history of culture, of the content of the concept of "magic" that belongs to a past culture, surviving only in the nooks of the intellect. The modern scientific term "magic," yet to be defined, and the primitive concept of magic, which we can ascertain only historically, have simply been combined. This commingling of different things often proves to be destructive in studies of the history of religions. As an admonitory example, reference can be made to Morris Jastrow's *Die Religion Babyloniens und Assyriens* (2 vols. in 3; Giessen: Töpelmann, 1905), where the word *magic* acquired a usage that has caused a hopeless confusion, both with respect to the terminology and the composition of the book and to the assessment and understanding of the cultic phenomena. Priest and magician, cult and sin, good and evil are placed in line with one another. Sharp distinctions must first be made here, however. With regard to the first question, it should first be established that the previous theories are erroneous. In this regard, I point to Wetter's essay. There is no perceptible primary contrast between what has been called religion and what has been called magic, either in relation to procedures and forms or in relation to the object and concepts associated with the procedures, i.e., concepts of the relationship between the phenomenon and the essence and nature of matters. There has never been a "prereligious," "magical" phase in the development of the human spirit, no more than there have been significant areas within this or that religion that are only "magic." Wetter is also correct in the positive statement that, if one is to distinguish between religion and magic at all, the distinction must relate to the internal relationship of the human being to religious procedures and concepts. Whether Wetter's elaboration of this idea (in religious devotion, the supernatural is the subject for people; in magic, it is the object) is entirely fortunate is somewhat more dubious to me. It seems to me that the second question has become entangled in Wetter's definition, and it seems entirely dubious to me whether an investigation between religion and magic in this sense has any practical

Australians are no less cultic procedures than is, for example, the mass of

---

or scientific value. Naturally, the study of religions must examine in each individual case the person's psychic attitude toward traditional religion and its procedures and rites. This investigation is, indeed, of central importance. Whether the word "magic" is suited, however, to designate a more impious attitude toward religion is very doubtful to me. An entirely different question concerns the content of the term sorcery (Norwegian, *trolldom*), witchcraft, or whatever one wishes to call it. This question results simply from the fact that much of what we would call magic in the above sense would be regarded by the people in question as good and legitimate, thus as religion (Semitic "fear of God"), while the same people also know something else that they call "sorcery" and regard as evil, proscribed, forbidden. This other thing is a reality and a concept that belongs to a culture that is no longer ours, even though it may survive in the sublevels and corners of intellectual life, a culture that has been called "prelogical" but that could, at any rate, be called "prescientific." For those people, sorcery was as certain a reality as chemistry is for us. In the life of primitive peoples, including Jews no less than ancient Israel, the concept of sorcery plays a very significant role as the sum of evil, sinister, and pernicious in the world. The determination of what this or that primitive people—and, in principle, all primitives—understood by this "sorcery" is a purely historical task that can only be accomplished by interrogating the primitives as witnesses. What we think is entirely immaterial here. The question is only and solely this: What did the ancient Norwegians understand by *seid*, the Israelites by *'āwen*, the Christian Middle Ages by "witchcraft," and so on? How did they assess it, and what is common to all these primitive cultures and peoples? Here it is now clear to me that there is often no difference between the procedures, forms, and concepts with which sorcery works and those of religion. An act of sorcery can so resemble a cultic procedure as to be confused for one. The difference lies in another realm and is more fundamental in nature, but it can hardly be reduced to a formula. Sorcery is the use of the mysterious power but for evil and illegitimate purposes or in an illegitimately selfish manner. Sometimes it is understood as the use of a particularly evil variety of the "power." Sorcery is almost always regarded as something evil, illegitimate, practiced in secret, ruinous to the normal, decent person, harmful to the interests of the community, that pursues the self-interests of the practitioner in an inconsiderate manner that violates the rights of the neighbor, is practiced especially by women or strangers, and competes with, and thus runs contrary to, the sacral orders of the community. It is often practiced with a bad conscience, which is aware that it involves evil and danger. Otherwise, I call attention to my suggestions in *Psalm Studies* 1:63–77. Thus, for example, among the ancient Semites, all orderly people understood any curse or execration that proceeds from an evil person, an "enemy," and causes harm to a good and orderly person, "weakening" or sickening a person, leaving behind a wound in his soul that debilitates his capacity to act, as the effect of the power of sorcery. In both the Babylonian and the biblical psalms, "the evil curse" stands in line with the sorcerer's spells and gestures (see §2.1 below on the curse and sorcery). The attitude toward and the relationship with public religion, from which the sorcerer acts, is usually, if not always, impious—here my understanding coincides with that of Wetter. Whoever resorts to the evil arts believes that he can thereby better serve his own interest and come to his objective more quickly, more surely, and, above all, more cheaply, than through the means of legitimate religion. He does not have the virtues, perhaps, that religion requires as the condition for success, or he does

the Roman Church. On the other hand, it is obviously not a cultic procedure when the men of the tribe take their weapons and slay game or when the woman gather plants meant for food. If at certain times, however, the tribe performs certain nonprofane procedures, often regarded as mysteries inaccessible to the unauthorized, and speaks words whose purpose is to influence and assure the prosperity and the plentiful availability of the animals desirable as prey or of plants used for food, these are undoubtedly cultic procedures and cultic words, regardless of whether "gods" or "demons" are invoked in the process. Through the cult, the true foundations for the life of the pertinent community are created or renewed; whether they are understood as solely "material" goods or "spiritual" goods, they are also included. We can also identify this fundamental view that the cult creates and renews reality in the higher stages of cultic religion. Even though the

---

not want to make the required effort. The power of the deity does not reach as far as the power of his arts. Consequently, orderly and pious people maintain that the sorcerer is a godless denier, an "atheist." "The evildoer—i.e., in context, the sorcerer—says in his heart, 'There is no god'" (Pss 14:1; 36:2–5). Consequently, he sometimes resorts to procedures and concepts that were once religion (cult) but that have been overcome or suppressed by another religion and only survive in the corners or in the lowest and most despised layers of the people, in the remnants of the earlier population or of the adherents of the suppressed religion. Thus the ancient Norwegians learned sorcery chiefly among the Finns. Even Job depicted the pariahs in the land as sorcerers (see *Psalm Studies* 1:115–16). Relatedly, the religion and the cult of the enemies or of the neighbors is very often regarded as sorcery. What is sacred to one is sorcery to the other. Idolatry and sorcerer always stand in line with one another in the Old Testament. They are correlates if not identical terms (see Deut 18:10–11; 2 Kgs 9:22, etc.; see also *Psalm Studies* 1:42–43). Thus the boundaries are fluid. In the primitive judgment of what is sorcery and what not, the subjective aspect always proves to be significant. One always condemns what one calls sorcery as something evil and illegitimate. Not just the Old Testament, but even Gudea of Lagash and Hammurabi of Babel promulgated strict laws against sorcery. Here and there may be certain phases of culture or certain epochs—in this case, usually epochs of decline—in certain primitive cultures in which one did not distinguish strictly between the good and the evil arts and effects of the ones gifted with power. The medicine man or the shaman, to whom the community and individuals turn in distress and difficulty for healing, is also credited with being able occasionally to appear as a "man of harm" and to bring harm capriciously upon this or that private opponent. Consequently, he was feared more than he was honored. Then, however, we are dealing with a community that either has not yet advanced to fixed moral concepts and practices or where the whole established culture, built on custom, is in the process of dissolution. Whether this state was ever a universal transitional phase in the development of all primitive cults seems very doubtful to me. I do not want to have explicitly denied the possibility that there was ever a time in which one did not yet distinguish between cult and sorcery. It seems to me to be definite that priority is due to the cult and that here, too, "sin is called forth by the law." I cannot go further into these matters here.

supporting realities of life are regarded as gifts of the gods or of the deity, the presupposition is still that the cultic procedures are indispensable conditions without which the gods will not prove to be gracious. An extremely common, if not universal, principle, especially at the older stages of development, is that the reality in the cult is created, renewed, or influenced by the fact that one imitates it in drama. Through this imitation, which is sometimes not realistic but symbolic, and through the alternation of procedures and sayings performed or spoken, respectively, by different persons, the cult almost universally takes the shape of a creative drama. But we need not go into this facet of the matter here.[26]

The procedures and words intended to create, increase, and transfer blessings are, indeed, cultic procedures in the sense of the word presented above. The goods involved in the cult of Israel are the very same that constitute the content of the blessing. Thus, the very purpose of the Israelite cult, both the more comprehensive state cult and the more limited clan and family cult, which included a plethora of sacred "technical" customs, such as harvest customs, can be regarded as producing the influx of divine blessing to the covenant and the members of the covenant. Whoever ascends the mountain of YHWH comes to gain blessing (Ps 24:3–5). Celebrating a cultic festival is called "blessing" (Exod 12:32). The whole cult with all its proceedings can thus be regarded as a means to convey and to increase the concentrated blessing. Thus it is inherent in the nature of the matter that the word of blessing must have been associated with procedures long part of the cult of ancient Israel that more or less clearly symbolized and mediated the transfer of the blessing.

The blessing is always a sacred procedure. It is always interwoven with the typical religious feelings of solemnity, holiness, and the presence of the overwhelming and the divine. Not every transfer of blessing is equally solemn and holy. As we have seen, there is also an everyday grant of blessing to the blessed that takes place almost of itself. Life has its highpoints, however, when the solemn becomes festival and the feeling of the proximity of the divine becomes cult. Thus there are solemn and more significant transfers of blessing in the simple life of the household, the family, and the clan that are simply to be regarded as cultic procedures. One can distinguish between folk and community cult, on the one hand, and family and clan cult, on the other, and label the former public and the latter private cult. The difference is not qualitative, however, but more quantitative and formal.

---

26. See *Psalm Studies* 2:197–211.

Undoubtedly, when, in certain solemn ceremonies the dying father conveys his blessing to his sons or his oldest son, as we read about in Gen 27, it should be regarded as such a family cultic procedure. The fact that Isaac must eat a meal here before he can bless is, as has long been recognized, an allusion, easily understood by the Israelites, to a sacred cultic procedure meant to transfer and increase blessing. The meal is to be regarded as a communion through which Isaac establishes a connection with the deity. Originally, the divine power was inherent in the animal that was to be eaten: the animal embodied the divine, the deity. It may be that one can hear a remnant of this understanding in Jacob's (admittedly deceitful) words: "God sent it (the animal) to me." The fact that the animal must be personally hunted by the son to be the blessed heir of his father reminds us of the widely known practice, common especially among North American tribes, in which the youth who wants to be accepted into the circle of adult men and thus as a participant in the blessings and goods of the tribe must first spend a period in the wilderness. There he must hunt, fell, and bring to the dedication ceremonies an example of the first type of animal he sees in a dream or encounters in reality. Thenceforth, the pertinent species of animal is a personal totem—or "guardian spirit," as some researchers term it.[27] Thenceforth he wears the skin or the feathers of the slain animal as an amulet and source of power and fortune, especially on hunts and raids.[28] When the departing daughter is solemnly blessed before the wedding by her paternal family for the purpose of gaining the desired fertility (Gen 24:60), this is also, without doubt, to be regarded as an allusion to a customary procedure in the family cult, even though the religious background is much clearer in the first case. In both cases, the ceremony climaxes in a word of blessing.

We may deduce from the Balaam legends, however, that the public cult also knew sacred procedures whose purpose was the transfer of blessing and whose chief component was the explicit word of blessing. Admittedly, this involved a curse. The conclusion from analogy is all the more certain here, however, since the curse procedure is transformed into a blessing procedure

---

27. See James G. Frazer, *Totemism and Exogamy: A Treatise on Certain Early Forms of Superstition and Society* (4 vols.; London: Macmillan, 1910), 1:50.

28. When Jacob dons the pelt of the animal prepared for the meal, one may see in it a quite diluted and now quite humorous memory of the practice mentioned above. It was also not unknown among the Semites that one thereby interiorized the "divine" power that one wrapped about oneself in the pelt of the sacrificial animal that embodied the "divine." The wonder-working hair mantel of the prophets may thus best be explained as the pelt of the initiation sacrifice. Contemporary Dervishes offer parallels (see my "Om nebiisme og profeti," *NTT* 10 [1909]: 225–27).

in the legend. Before Balaam can curse (or bless), a sacrifice must first be brought (Num 23:4–6, etc.): he must make connection with the deity. Thereby he is filled with the divine power that enables him to speak effective words of curse (and blessing), just as, indeed, it was originally the divine power obtained through the cultic procedure that enabled the seer to speak effective words that influence and predict the future.[29] The deity is the source of life (Ps 36:10) from which also stream the life sources of all those participating in festive inspiration in the deity's cult (Ps 87:7). The one bestowing and mediating blessing must make connection with this source of power through cultic procedures and rites. He draws from the source and gives the other members of the covenant to drink. Through him streams sacred power. The vocational mediator of blessing is, consequently, the vocational administrator of the folk and community cult, the administrator of public affairs, in general, the chief, the king, the priest, the seer, who was originally always a priest at the same time, in brief, the one equipped with power, who already embodies extraordinary power.[30]

We encounter the cultic word of blessing, which, in a sense, expressed the whole meaning of the cultic procedure and bears the whole purpose of the cult in concentrated form, both as a regular and an occasional cultic practice. Unquestionably, already in very ancient times, every worship assembly in Israel, that is, every festival, concluded with the leader's explicit blessing, and in solemn cases, with the king's, who was actually the supreme leader of the cult in ancient times.[31] Just as synagogue worship ends with the blessing (m. Ber. 5:4), the daily cult in temple worship probably ended with the Aaronic blessing (Num 6:23–26). We understand this precisely because we have adopted this cultic practice from the synagogue cult and thus indirectly from the temple cult. Both the Catholic and the Greek Orthodox churches know cultic blessing.[32] Even Protestant orders of worship have it in every worship procedure, both in regular Sunday worship services and at baptisms, confirmations, weddings, burials, and communions.

The transfer of the blessing through the cultic procedure can occur directly or indirectly. The blessing, the "holy" power, can be transferred through rites of various kinds to all manner of cultic objects and devices. Thus they become useful in various ways to fellow members of the cult, the members of the com-

---

29. Ibid., 223, 224–25, 335–36.

30. Num 23:6–24:25; Deut 10:8; 21:5; 2 Sam 6:18; 1 Kgs 8:55; 1 Chr 23:13.

31. 2 Sam 6:18; 1 Kgs 8:55. The solemnities mentioned here are depicted on the model of the annual New Year's Festival (see *Psalm Studies* 2:285–88).

32. On the former, see *Ordo Missae* XLI. On the latter, see, e.g., Hugo Gressmann, "Liturgie, religionsgeschichtlich," *RGG* 3:2324–30.

munity. The central purpose of the many complicated cultic procedures is to connect the community at all points and in every way with the holy, with the powers of blessing. Thus the temple, the altar, and so on are blessed so that they may surely fulfill their purpose for the salvation of people. We will see examples of this below (§1.2.3).

Blessing can also be placed directly on the parties to the cult, not just through the medium of the word and the accompanying laying on of hands or stretching out of hands. This is the most common.

Just as often as the Old Testament says that this or that person, the priest, the king, the *paterfamilias*, or the like blessed those assembled at the conclusion of this or that cultic celebration, so rarely does it communicate to us the wording of the cultic blessing. I think here, in the first instance, of the popular and the community cults. We may probably assume with certainty that, in the course of time, and probably rather early, fixed forms for the regular cultic word of blessing developed. At least one such has been transmitted to us, namely, the one with which the priest blessed the people at the end of festival, and later probably daily, worship, the so-called Aaronic blessing in Num 6:24–26. This formula is structured simply and nobly. The poetic form, the fortunate circumstance that any temporally bound specification is missing, and, finally, the noble imprint that the prayer bears have resulted in the fact that to this day it is one of the most sublime and poignant elements in our worship. Verse 23 presupposes that blessing with this formula was one of the priests' regular tasks and that, consequently, it is to be regarded as a fixed element in worship. Both Lev 9:22 and Jewish tradition tell us where it belonged. After the sacrifice ended, the priest stepped before the altar, turned to the assembly, spread his hands, and blessed the congregation with these words:

May YHWH bless and keep you.
May YHWH look graciously upon you and be gracious to you.
May YHWH direct "his eyes"[33] toward you (for good)
and give you good fortune and well-being!

P transmits the blessing that is unquestionably older.[34] No specific date can be given, however. The fall festival thanksgiving psalm, Ps 67, presupposes

---

33. *Pānāw* in v. 26 is probably a scribal error for *ʿēnāw*. The repetition of the same word in two lines is noteworthy since the saying is otherwise careful to vary the vocabulary as much as possible. For the meaning, cf. Gen 39:7: "to direct the eyes toward someone" means "to become fond of someone."

34. See, for example, Bruno Baentsch, *Exodus–Leviticus–Numeri* (HKAT I/3; Göttingen: Vandenhoeck & Ruprecht, 1903).

and imitates the saying. The age of the psalm cannot be determined, however, although nothing prohibits the assumption that it originated in the preexilic period. The practice of the liturgist blessing the congregation from the altar is much older than P, as 1 Kgs 8:14 shows us. In the dedication of the temple, Solomon acts as priest, sacrifices and finally blesses from the altar (see also 2 Sam 6:18, where David performs these same functions). We see in 1 Kgs 8:14 that the people, who probably sat or reclined during the long sacrifices, at least during the subsequent meals, arose for the blessing and received the word standing (see Neh 8:5, where the people arose when the text of the law was read). We do not know the wording of the Solomonic blessing. Verses 15–21 is a prayer and a thanksgiving by the Deuteronomistic redactor in agreement with the later understanding that the "blessing," that is, the praise of YHWH, was a major component of worship (see also Neh 8:6).

The Mishnah, which mentions the eight concluding blessings for the Day of Atonement, shows that later Jewish worship also knew other cultic blessings. Among these is one for Israel, one for the priests, and one for "absolutely everything else that is an object of blessing," šĕʾār hattĕpillâ (m. Yoma 7:1).

1.2.2. The cult is not just the procedure through which blessing is applied to individuals but also the means for increasing the blessing and creating new powers of blessing. The cult was originally a creative act that produced and created the primary forces of reality.[35] Through the sacred procedures and words, the community's whole treasure of blessing was concentrated in a center, so to speak, and intensified in order to radiate out from this center to all the participants.

The cult creates blessing, or, put differently, through the cult, those practicing the cult create blessing and produce new powers of blessing by virtue of their connection with the divine and the holy. This primal and genuinely primitive understanding still echoes in the diction of a significantly later time. For example, when, after suffering many blows, Pharaoh, according to the Yahwist, was finally comfortable with releasing the Israelites, he did so with the following words: "Go and bless me, too" (Exod 12:32). Admittedly, this is always translated, "go and pray for blessing on me." This translation depends, however, on flawed knowledge of the primitive mindset. The text quite clearly reads ûbēraktem gam-ʾōtî. The narrator presupposes that, after their exodus, the Israelites were supposed to celebrate a cultic festival in the wilderness for which they will also need their cattle and sheep. Pharaoh's words include the obvious presupposition that the celebrants of the cult will thereby "bless," that

---

35. *Psalm Studies* 2:197–211.

is, produce blessing, namely, for themselves. Pharaoh would like to participate in this blessing so that his land and people may recover after the harsh blows of fate. Naturally, the later period and perhaps the Yahwist himself understood this "blessing" as a request for blessing. No doubt the practice of the community celebrating the cult speaking through its representative (*in casu Mose*) effective words thought to produce blessing still existed in his time.

This blessing-generating nature of the creative cult is even clearer if one considers certain procedures and rites by which one "blesses" certain sacred objects and loads them, so to speak, with blessing force so that the community that becomes associated with them receives the largest possible portion of the blessing. This "indirect" manner of transmitting the blessing to members of the community may be more original than the direct means through the word of blessing spoken to the community.

Traces of this ancient mindset also appear in the Old Testament, sometimes still in full vitality.

The women's words to Saul when he asked about "the seer" lead us directly into the heart of the primitive mindset (1 Sam 9:12–13). "The seer has just come into the city, because the people are celebrating a sacrificial festival on the high place today. If you go into the city you will meet him, for he goes to the high place to eat because the people will not eat (of the sacrificial flesh) until he comes and blesses the sacrifice. Only then will the guests eat." Here "to bless the sacrificial flesh" is, of course, something quite different from saying a Lutheran table prayer. The sacrificial meal is a sacramental meal. By consuming the sacrificial flesh, the participants receive mysterious, divine powers that unite them in a covenant with one another and with the deity. They all share the same power, the same "soul." The sacrificial flesh and the sacrificial animals are themselves "holy," filled with holy, mysterious, extraordinary power. Yesterday or the day before, however, it may have been a quite ordinary, profane animal. Some "holy" and sanctifying procedure must have been performed on it before it became a sacrificial animal suited for sacramental consumption. In what manner did the animal become a bearer of sacred power? It became so through certain procedures performed on it and certain words spoken to it, just as in the Roman Catholic Mass, the words of institution transform the normal, profane bread into the sacred, power-producing, soul cleansing, and healing body of Christ. Such words of blessing are envisioned in 1 Sam 9:13. Samuel does not appear here as a *nābî'*—the later, altered tradition transformed him into one—but as "seer," that is, as sanctuary guard and oracle-giver, precisely what ancient Israel understood priests to be.[36] Samuel

---

36. See *Psalm Studies* 3:501–7.

is a priest at the *bāmâ* of the pertinent city. If the guests were to eat before he had "blessed" the sacrificial flesh, the communal meal would have become only a normal meal, not a sacrificial feast. Then the community would not have received sanctifying power for use in the battles and against the difficulties of daily life; the whole thing would have then become purposeless.

This was the original primitive mindset. The sacrificial animal becomes a bearer of the divine power infused into it. The blessing is a power-producing word that infuses these powers into the sacrificial animal. In primitive Christianity, this mindset turns up again to rise again in full force in Catholicism. In the Catholic Church, the εὐχαριστία of the Lord's Supper became the power-producing word that makes the sacrament the sacrament. One can hardly doubt with good reason whether the early church understood its eucharistic prayer quite as "spiritually" as Protestant theologians would like to have it.

Thoughts like these were not foreign to later Judaism either. The rite and the word concluded the festal procession on the eighth day of the Festival of Booths, according to m. Sukkah 4:5. After the priests placed fresh willow and poplar branches around the altar, the participants in the procession circumambulated the altar seven times and garlanded it with their green branches while bidding it "farewell" with the cry *yôpî lĕkā mizbeaḥ* "beauty for you, O altar."[37] The general meaning of the ceremony is quite clear.[38] The green branches are the ubiquitous "mayflowers," symbols and media of fertility and power. The vitality inherent in the branches is transferred through contact to persons, animals, and objects.[39] It is also generally known that cultic objects participate in the mediation of power in this fashion so that they become suited for their use and can mediate the power further. Every "dedication" of cultic houses, objects, and implements traces back to this fundamental idea.[40] The "greeting" is actually a cultic word that, together with the procedure, produces a certain effect. In this case it was meant to mediate the transfer of "power" and holiness. It is thus a word of blessing. The quality transferred here to the altar is expressed by the word *yôpî*. Of course, it does not designate a purely aesthetic quality. To "wish" aesthetic beauty for the altar would make no sense, nor should the interjection be taken as an indicative and understood as a judgment of taste. The word must have a meaning here similar to the

---

37. According to Rabbi Eliezer, the words were: "for YHWH and for you, o altar" (m. Suk. 4:5).

38. See *Psalm Studies* 2:280–81.

39. See, e.g., Martin P. N. Nilsson, *Årets folkliga fester* (Stockholm: Hugo Gebers, 1914).

40. Naturally, catharsis also plays a significant role here, but it is not solely dominant.

meaning in "the beauty of your wisdom,"[41] that is, your beauty gained through wisdom. Here it denotes a characteristic, a quality, from which proceed good and useful, blessed effects and which, consequently, also has an aesthetically beautiful effect: for the primitive, the good and useful are beautiful and vice versa; for the primitive, beauty is always καλλοκαγατία. Self-evidently, the acquisition of this quality, among others, is also a fruit of "wisdom," that is, insight into powers and nature, the ability to assert oneself, and having good fortune, as in Ezek 28:7. The interjection "wishes" for the altar and infuses into it substantially the same as the power and holiness that can contribute to making the sacrifices of the community appropriate, making them reach their target, namely, that it is able to assure the divine goods of the cult. Clearly this idea is un-Jewish, ancient Israelite, and primitive; consequently, the rite and the word did not originate in late Jewish times. The Mishnah tradition certainly preserved an ancient element of the Israelite cult here.

We have a parallel to this rite and blessing in the Day of Atonement. Among the eight "blessings" that the high priest was supposed to pronounce at the conclusion of the worship service, is also a blessing on the temple, *hammiqdāš* (m. Yoma 7:1).

A similar "wish for blessing" or a reference to such seems to me to be present in Ps 93:5bc, even though this psalm does not relate to Atonement Day but to enthronement day, the fall festival in the proper sense. It is usually translated "holiness is due your house" or "holiness suits your house." But what does that mean? What would the naked statement of the religious claim that the sanctuary must be holy have to say in the context of this enthronement and creation psalm? No one knows. I have been unable, at least, to find anything on the matter in any commentary. Since *qādôš* is otherwise a masculine genitive, one cannot vocalize *na'ăwâ* (perfect third-person singular) as does MT. The adjective *nāweh*, which is often suggested as a reading (Delitzsch, Buhl, etc.), helps little, since the meaning remains the same. Apparently the author meant *něweh*, as a construct state related to the subsequent *qôdeš*. The word would appear here, then, as a substantive, "beauty, comeliness." The clause can then be translated either as an indicative ("your house has the beauty of holiness") or an optative ("the beauty of holiness for [i.e., be upon] your house!"). In the first case, supported by the indicative in verse 5a, the lines express the reason for the community's confidence: the house now, after being cleansed for the festival and the entry of YHWH, has the holy loveliness

---

41. "To be wise," "to have insight," "to be able, have the power," "to be able to prevail and assert one's self," and "to be just" are almost synonymous concepts for the ancient Israelites (see Pedersen, *Israel*, 1:196–99).

and beauty that guarantees the fulfillment of our prayers. In the second case, this holy beauty was "wished down upon" the house. In both cases, "comeliness," "beauty" is not a purely aesthetic but a religious quality.

1.2.3. The passage discussed above, 1 Sam 9:13, permits us, however, to look even more deeply into the religious ideas of a primitive culture.

I noted above that the task of the mediator of blessing was to preserve and increase, to elevate, the community's shared treasury of power through the cult. Behind this treasury of blessing stands the deity, however. The blessing has its origin in the deity. Thus in the earliest times it was also the task of the cultic administrator, of the mediator of blessing, just as it ultimately was the very purpose of the cult, to increase and elevate the power of the deity. The cult creates reality, keeps the gods alive, infuses new power into them, and permits them to arise again to new life. This is, indeed, the original meaning of the mysteries and all primitive religions of the mystery type. Examples can be found everywhere in abundance. One of the nicest is the old Mexican religion.[42] We are permitted a glance into this thought process via 1 Sam 9:13. The sacrificial animal has been filled with the sacred powers. The sacred, however, is the divine. Good grounds can be found for the assumption that the sacramental sacrifice often originally represented the deity himself. In mystical fashion, the deity is in the sacrificial animal, the sacrificial animal is the deity.[43] The cultic blessing of the sacrificial animal is thus a means for increasing the power of the deity for the community's use. The cult, and thus also the cultic blessing, gives the gods "well-being" ("wholeness," full vigor, good fortune) so that they can, in turn, give the community "well-being."

The Old Testament also contains many traces of this ancient understanding, such as when it says that cultic praise "gives honor" (Pss 29:1–2; 96:7) to YHWH. Thereby, one gives YHWH actual "honor," *kābôd*, that is, not just renown, praise, but *gravitas*, psychic substance, psychic force.[44] In parallel, it also says explicitly, therefore, that one thereby "gives" him "might," power (*'ōz*)—not in the modern sense, however, of attaching or attributing. Instead, one elevates his might in the world and therewith his capacity to bless and protect Israel and to give it "salvation." Consequently, the psalm mentioned concludes with the assurance that, for his part, YHWH will now "bless his people with strength (*'ōz*) and well-being (*šālôm*)" (Ps 29:11).

---

42. See *Psalm Studies* 2:205; for the whole question, see 197–211.
43. This is particularly clear in the cult of the Thracian Dionysos.
44. See Pederson, *Israel*, 1:213–33, esp. 224 and 228–31.

The frequent expression "bless YHWH" (*bērak 'et yhwh*) and "blessed be YHWH" (*bārûk yhwh*) are especially important in this context. In our texts, these expressions mean nothing more than "to praise, laud, thank YHWH" and "YHWH be praised, envied." This is obviously an abatement, for *bērak* does not "mean" to praise or thank. It means "to bless," and blessing is an effective procedure through rite and word. The fact that the expression was originally cultic still shines through in Isa 66:3. "To bless something" sometimes means, in effect, "to believe in this God and to trust in him."[45] The expression presupposes that the cult was once responsible for "blessing" YHWH in the literal sense of the word, that is, to increase his power so that he may "bless" the community again. The cult is the very creative principle of life. Thus it also creates divine power. The expression *bārûk yhwh* is a precise parallel to the old Norwegian cultic saying "heilir aesir, heilar ásynjur, "good fortune ('wholeness,' 'well-being'; cf. Hebrew *šālôm*) to the gods, good fortune to the goddesses."[46] Vilhelm Grønbech remarks concerning this expression that it was the phrase "by which the gods were given good fortune and with which they were simultaneously praised for good fortune."[47] The words *bārûk yhwh* intensify YHWH's power, increase his "glory." This meaning of the word is preserved in the "blessing" of the sacrificial flesh and the other cultic elements and objects.[48] YHWH is praised for his blessing, however, with the same word and at the same time. The meaning is unilaterally emphasized in historical Yahwism. This duality—one blessing the deity so that the deity can, in turn, bless with greater effect—is clearly expressed in the formula of blessing in Gen 14:19–20:

> Blessed be Abram by El Elyon, the creator of the heavens and the earth, and blessed be El Elyon, who has given your enemies into your hand!

---

45. See Pss 10:3; 52:3. As an object for *bērēk* in Ps 10:3, a term parallel to *ta'ăwat napšô* should be supplied here, perhaps *hawwātô*. The terms *hillēl* and *hithallēl* that parallel "blessing" are terms for cultic "boasting" in God. The meaning of the passage is that the robber regards his appetite as his god whom he must satisfy above all else.

46. Edda song, Sigrdrifumál, strophe 4. Regarding this formula as a cultic formula that endows the gods, for example, the earth deity, with power, see Magnus Olsen and Theodor Petersen, *En runeamulet fra Utgaard, Stod* (Det Kgl. Norsek Videnskabers Salskabs Skrifter 2, 1919; Trondhjem: Aktietrykkeriet i Trondhjem, 1920), 19–22. See further, Andreas Heusler, "Dichtung," *Reallexikon der germanischen Altertumskunde*, 1:448. We should not be misled by the fact that we now encounter the traces of the use of the formula essentially in the lower, more popular ("magical") cultic procedures.

47. Vilhelm Grønbech, *Vor Folkeæt I Oldtiden IV: Menneskelivet og Guderne* (Copenhagen: Pio, 1912), 108.

48. See 675–78, above.

It is not unlikely at all that, expect for the name Abram, we have a very old cultic blessing formula here, which, in the given case, probably stems from Jerusalem's pre-Yahwist period. This is how the Jebusite priests of El Elyon blessed their victorious king and their god on festive occasions.

According to the discussion above, it is probably not too bold to express the suspicion that the cultic cry "beauty for you, O altar" discussed above originally referred to the deity and, accordingly, was *yôpî lĕkā yhwh* or *yôpî lĕyhwh*. We have direct confirmation for this supposition in the statement by Rabbi Eliezer mentioned above.[49] If this is so, this cultic formula will once have wished and given YHWH the "beauty," which is simultaneously the power for the benefit and wellbeing of the community, quite analogously to the *bārûk yhwh* or the old Nordic *heiler aesir* (see above).

1.2.4. We can see now that I have established in our sources two major types in the understanding of the blessing—and also of the curse—over the course of time. According to the presentation above, we understand that originally the cultic blessing procedure, like every cultic procedure, was understood as self-efficacious[50] to a degree. The blessing is the community's great common possession of power that is intensified, increased, and applied to individuals through cultic acts and words of blessing. The leader of the cult establishes a connection with the source of blessing, the "force," the deity, and thus the forces of blessing flow through him to the community.

This original nature of blessing is also expressed in the form of the pronouncement of blessing. The pronouncement of blessing was not originally a prayer. It was a power-filled word that exerted an extraordinary effect. Correspondingly, it has the form in Hebrew that otherwise expresses an orientation of the will, a person's effort to attain something: may such and so happen, such and so should be! The usual form in Hebrew is the jussive. It may not be understood as a mere wish, however. It is more; it expresses a conscious effort of the will; it is an act. The one blessing infuses the word with the force of his soul. Thus we also see that the imperative, the form of command, quite often appears alongside the jussive: "Be!" (Gen 12:2). Indeed, the purely indicative imperfect even occurs: such and so occurs now, in and with the spoken words (Num 24:20 LXX). Thus the person of the one blessing is sometimes more prominent in the consciousness of the one receiving the blessing than the person of the deity who constitutes the source of the blessing. The effect of the blessing depends on the psychic force of the one blessing.

---

49. See n. 37, above.
50. Most scholars of religion call it "magical" (see n. 25, above).

Obviously, this understanding changed in the course of the development of Yahwism with its transcendent and personal concept of God. YHWH became more and more the sole author of all effects, the personal God characterized by a will according to which he acts, the giver of all gifts and all blessings. This development began quite early. We have no sources in the Old Testament that were not influenced by it. In the service of this personal God, every word of blessing and curse received, as though of itself, something of the quality of prayer. Thus, for example, in the lament psalms a precise distinction between the curses against the enemies and the prayer that they be taught a lesson is impossible, just as the presentation in Ps 72 oscillates between blessing and intercession. The blessing and cursing priest is not only the cultic person endowed with power who produces certain effects *ex opere operato* but simultaneously the community's intercessor who petitions YHWH to bless it (1 Sam 1:17).

This new, higher idea is never carried out, however. One always perceives a difference between the professional blessing (and curse) of the priest and the actual petition for divine blessing. We still see this in synagogue worship. One may employ the actual blessing formula in Num 6:24–26 only when a priest is on hand. If a layperson functions as liturgist, he must formulate the words as a prayer.[51] The cultic words of blessing in the Old Testament were never pure prayers.

These two understandings—the "blessing" is a self-acting and physically forceful word of the one endowed with power, and the "blessing" is a prayer to YHWH for blessing—also corresponds to the dual form of the statement of blessing. The original form, with no mention of the source of blessing, was "blessed be you" or "blessed be whoever …" (thus, e.g., Num 24:9). In this form, the idea actually stops with the "mediator," the conveyor of the blessing; to a certain degree, it sees the basis of the blessing in the one bestowing it without asking about the foundation and ultimate source of the blessing. Naturally, the consciousness lies in the background here, too, that the one blessing is not himself the ultimate source of the blessing. The other form, which, even though old, is the later form shaped by historical Yahwism, is the most common. It names God as the author of the blessing and contains an element of petition: "may YHWH bless you and give you good fortune."[52] An intermediate form is present in statements such as "may you be blessed by YHWH" (*lĕyhwh*; 1 Sam 15:13; Ruth 2:20; or *mēʾet yhwh*; Ps 24:5) or "in the

---

51. See m. Ber. 5:4 (O. Holzmann, *Berakoth* [Die Mischna II/1; ed. G. Beer and O. Holzmann; Giessen: Töpelmann, 1912]).

52. This form is present, e.g., in Gen 27:28–29, 28:3–4, and 48:15–16 and many other passages.

name of YHWH" (*bešēm yhwh*; Deut 10:8; 21:5; Ps 129:8), that is, with the power inherent in the name of the deity.

1.2.5. We have represented to some extent all of the various stages and forms of the development sketched above in the "blessing" of the wine and food in the ritual of the Passover celebration from late Jewish times (m. Pes. 10:2, 7). In the Mishnah, Ber. 6:1–3 instructs us concerning the form of this "blessing": "Blessed be he who created the fruit of the trees; blessed be he who created the fruit of the vine; blessed by he who created the fruit of the field (or fruits of the earth and vegetables); blessed be he who raises up bread from the earth." This oldest version still echoes in the form "blessed be he, God, who does such and so." The other, which is surely of equal age but, by contrast, less in need of paraphrasing according to the demands of Yahwism, which we have in 1 Sam 9:13, is distinguished by the fact that these formulas were designated as "blessings of the wine, the fruit, the bread," and so on, but simultaneously also in the fact that they were also actually regarded as consecrations of the pertinent sacramental elements. Still in the latest period, Passover was surely understood as a sacramental, covenant-founding meal.[53] Passover was certainly a sacramental meal from the outset.[54] It is the Jewish festival that best preserved its original Israelite character and still manifests a connection with the culture and religion of the nomadic period. There was never a proper agrarian festival in the Canaanite spirit, even though the wine festival found acceptance.[55] The "holy" quality of the elements eaten and drunk gained through special consecration—namely, the "blessing"—also belongs to the sacramental character of the festival. The third and final stage is finally evident in the main interpretation that the words of blessing received in Judaism: *bĕrākâ* in the Mishnah often means simply a thanksgiving prayer (εὐχαριστία). Thus here also the word is understood as thankful praise. It had become a prayer whose content is thanksgiving to God who has given all the good gifts that "gladden people's hearts" (see Ps 104:15) and that exert their sacramental and mystical power in the holy Passover meal.

The original "blessings" and consecrations of food have been preserved in their diminished and Judaized character in Judaism's *bĕrākôt* before and after every meal, even the daily, profane meals. Yet here also something proto-

---

53. See Georg Beer in the introduction to his edition of Tractate Pesachim in Beer and Oskar Holzmann's *Die Mischna: Text, Übersetzung und ausführliche Erklärung* (Giessen: Töpelmann, 1912–).

54. See *Psalm Studies* 2:213.

55. See Beer, Tractate Pesachim, 7. Significantly, the Samaritans until this day reject the use of wine in the celebration of Passover (48 n. 3, 91).

Semitic and primitive is at work to a degree, namely, that no meal is actually profane. A shared meal always has something "sacred" about it. One with whom I have eaten is my "brother" (see Ps 101:5 LXX).

1.3. Psalms of Blessing

The proper form of the cultic word is rhythmic/metrical and poetic. Thus since antiquity the cultic prayer, the cultic praise, and the cultic thanksgiving in Israel have been "psalms." Our biblical psalms originated in the cult. Gunkel recognized this fundamentally, and in my earlier *Psalm Studies* 1 endeavored to extend this understanding. Thus we should expect from the outset that the cultic blessing will have also assumed poetic form as soon as the cult came to a somewhat more richly developed liturgy. The facts confirm this expectation for us. The Aaronic blessing (Num 6:24–26) is already a song, even though a brief one. It bears all the signs of Hebrew poetry. It is unmistakably driven by a solemn rhythm. This rhythm fits into the usual scheme of Hebrew poetry. The first series is a quatrameter, the second a pentameter (3 + 2), the third a heptameter (4 + 3). The three series constitute a threefold parallelism: bless and protect you || look graciously upon you || graciously give you well-being. Each individual element constitutes its own parallelism: bless you || protect you, let his countenance shine (graciously) on you || be gracious to you, and direct his eyes (benevolently) toward you || give you well-being and good fortune.

A combination of blessing and psalm (cultic song) is thus within the realm not only of possibility but of likelihood. One needs only to think of the Aaronic blessing spoken in a solemn tone suitable to the rhythm as a kind of recitative, that is sung and, further, performed by a choir of priests instead of an individual, and we already have a song of blessing, a psalm of blessing. The first of these two presuppositions, which is inherent in the nature of matters, is certainly true. The second, however, is explicitly attested as an occasional practice at least.[56]

1.3.1. Thus we also find the priestly blessing in the procession liturgy for the Festival of Booths in Ps 118[57] as a part of the worship sung or recited in connection with the thanksgiving psalm. When the procession reaches the gates of the temple, the leader of the community (perhaps the choir director) calls on the gatekeepers to open the gates for those coming (v. 19). The gatekeepers answer and invite the procession to enter (v. 20). When the procession

---

56. Ps 118:25: "we bless you." See further Ps 134:1–2: the "servants" of YHWH (*'abdê yhwh*) who stand (*'ābad*) in his temple are the priests.

57. *Psalm Studies* 2:297–303. For the supposed age of the psalm, see 2:270–71, 368.

enters through the gate, a classical thanksgiving hymn is sung (vv. 21–24). It is followed by a prayer that YHWH may bless the day with help and good fortune so that the festival and everything associated with it may turn to the well-being of the community (v. 25):

> Ah, YHWH, give (your) help!
> Ah, YHWH, give success and good fortune!

The choir of priests responds with the solemn blessing (v. 26):

> May he who comes in the name of YHWH be blessed;
> we bless you (here) from YHWH's house.

The community responds to this blessing in verse 27 with the confession of YHWH's name and thereby appropriates the blessing. In the sacred power of the blessing acquired in this fashion, the festival participants can now call upon each other to perform the most celebratory act of the procession, the circumambulation of the altar:

> YHWH is the God [of our salvation];[58]
> he makes light for us [in the darkness]![59]
> (Now) close the round with branches,
> up to the horns of the altar!

The first period in the strophe probably contains an allusion to the lights of the festival. In addition, the notion in the Aaronic blessing of the illuminating, gracious countenance of YHWH probably exerted influence. The act indicated in the second period was concluded with the blessing on the altar treated above. The whole liturgy concludes with the brief thanksgiving song in verses 28–29 that summarizes the attitude of the whole.

We find another cultic formula of blessing that stands in a unique connection with the lyrical formation of the attitudes of the cultic experience in the beautiful Ps 122, a *ma'ălâ* psalm, that is, a song associated with the fall

---

58. The meter of the psalm is 3 + 3 almost throughout, linked in strophes of two each (vv. 7 is a variant of v. 6). In addition, there are isolated pentameters to be understood as brachycatalectic 3 + 3 meters. The formula of blessing in v. 26 is a 4 + 4. The quite isolated quatrameter in v. 27a stands out. According to the strophic structure, one would expect a 3 + 3. A couple of words have most likely fallen out, perhaps *yîšēnû* and *baḥōšek*.

59. See previous note.

festival.⁶⁰ In my opinion, we are not dealing here with a private poem in which an individual dwells on a memory of a previous pilgrimage to Jerusalem⁶¹ but with an actual cultic communal song.⁶² The antiphony form and the apparently—or almost—literal adoption of a cultic formula of blessing speak for a cultic purpose. On the other hand, it must be admitted that the psalm is markedly influenced by the style of the individual songs, especially the thanksgiving song, such as Ps 84, for example.⁶³ The poet has included his own personal experiences and attitudes in the poem. He speaks entirely as the representative of the community, however. His experiences and attitudes are typical and, to this extent we have here one of the few cases in which one can correctly speak of a "collective ego." An individual can also appear in the communal songs and speak as the representative, the voice of the community.⁶⁴

---

60. See *Psalm Studies* 2:184–85. The word actually denotes the grand festival procession up to the temple, then, however in an expanded sense, the whole festival characterized by the grand procession, the fall, New Year's, enthronement festival.

61. So, e.g., Frants Buhl, *Psalmerne: Oversatte og Fortolkede* (Copenhagen: Gyldenhal, 1900); Gerhard Kittel, *Die Psalmen* (KAT 13; Leipzig: Scholl, 1914).

62. For the interpretation of this psalm, see *Psalm Studies* 2:318 and 367–68. Consult further the index of biblical passages. Gunnar Hylmö, "Gamla testamentets: litteraturhistoria," in *Studier tillägnade Magnus Pfannenstill: Den 10 Januari 1923* (Lund: Gleerup, 1923), 76ff. may be consulted on the text, meter, etc.

63. See *Psalm Studies* 2:294. The idea of the joy of being about to enter the holy city probably stemmed originally from the thanksgiving song in which a formerly unclean (sick) person speaks, a person once excluded from the public cult but who can and now may visit the sacred mountain as one who has been healed.

64. Excursus. Regarding the theory of the "collective ego in the psalms," I would like to make the following remarks. In the form represented particularly by Rudolf Smend ("Über das Ich der Psalmen," ZAW 8 [1888]: 49–147), I consider it generally false and ultimately refuted by Emil Balla's work, *Das Ich der Psalmen* (FRLANT 16; Göttingen: Vandenhoeck & Ruprecht, 1912. Nonetheless, the theory contains a kernel of truth. Its chief error was that it predominantly related to the psalms Gunkel and others termed "individual lament psalms," with which it had virtually nothing to do. As Gunkel ("Die israelitische Literatur," in *Die orientalischen literaturen* (vol. 1.7 of *Kultur der Gegenwart: Ihre Entwicklung und ihre Ziele* [ed. P. Hinneberg; Berlin: Teubner, 1906] = Gunkel, *Die israelitische Literatur* [Darmstadt: Wissenschaftliche Buchgesellschaft, 1963]), followed by others (Balla, *Das Ich*; Staerk, *Lyrik*; Kittel, *Psalmen*; Walter Baumgartner, *Die Klagegedichte des Jeremia* [BZAW 32; Giessen: Töpelmann, 1917]) has already suggested and more or less consistently substantiated, and as I believe I have ultimately demonstrated in my *Psalm Studies* 1, these psalms are related to the cultic (ritual) cleansings and healings of an individual suffering sickness and distress. The I speaking in them is a not a collective entity but the sick individual who submits to the rites of purification in the temple and prays for assistance with illness, distress, magic, and magicians.

A second and equally fateful error in Smend's theory, however, was the fact that it was not connected with a thorough understanding of the essence of the primitive cult and the primitive psychology expressed in it and did not thereby receive a corrective. According to primitive and thus Israelite psychology, the individual per se is insignificant. He exists only in identity with his family and his community. A person's soul extends back to the first ancestor and extends to all those with whom he feels to be of one blood. All of this is a person's ego. In his soul, he comprises his whole community. The soul of Israel is manifest in the individual Israelite. In him Israel exists and lives and, in certain cases and under special circumstances, the great ego of the people is totally concentrated in the person of the individual. This is particularly true of the king, the chieftain, the agent of the community, and quite especially when he appears for the people at the highpoints of life, such as the cult. Then he is not only a representative in the modern sense of the word, but the whole people is in him and he is the people, just as the Letter to the Hebrews can still maintain that all the later Levites were in Abraham's loins when he made the covenant with Melchizedek (Heb 7:9–10). Through the chosen representative, the community becomes conscious of itself in such moments and he is aware of himself, not as an individual in the modern sense, but as a "super-ego." He expresses the feelings and thoughts of the community and it becomes as though the whole community acts in him and is tied to him. As I suggested in *Psalm Studies* 2:197–211, the primitive cult is actually, in essence, a drama in which reality is created. Actually, only two persons act in this drama: the deity (or the divine) and the people, the tribe, etc., in brief, the community. Occasionally "the enemy" also appears as a third person. The people are represented in every moment only by an individual person. It can be a priest, a shaman, or the like. It can be the chieftain, however. In Israel, in ancient times, at least in the most important cultic procedures, it was the tribal chief or head of the family. Later it was the king. Depending on the circumstances, however, he can be represented by another, by a priest, by the song leader, etc. Ideally, only the consciousness of this community should come to light in the representatives of the community. The super-ego, not the individual, appears and acts. More precisely, no distinction whatsoever is perceived then between the greater and the lesser egos. The "representative" speaks and says "I." He does not mean "I, the king, the priest, etc." but, "I, Israel." Since the cult seeks to retain the ancient as long as possible, this manner of speech and thought, grounded not in the external circumstance of representation by an individual but in primal psychology, was preserved in this cult with great tenacity, especially in the communal festival cult that bore the most significant dramatic contours. Now, however, a more individualistic—or pluralistic, which means the same in this context—mindset gradually permeated. It no longer saw the community so clearly as a super-ego but regarded it as a collection of individuals. The individual began to live his own life. This also gave rise to a new diction that gradually also found its way into the cult. The "representative" of the community began to feel like more than what we would call a "representative," like one of many, whose wishes he expressed and on whose commission he was to act. When he appeared as representative of the community, he now generally said "we." The old form and sometimes the old mindset, too, persisted for a long time alongside the new. Thus we also see that in the truly "collective" cultic psalms, such as the national lament psalm, an "I" alternates with the more regular "we" (e.g., Pss 44:5, 7, 16; 74:12; cf. also Pss 118; 122; 123). The oldest form, which, as we may surmise, had "I" throughout, is very rare in the preserved texts (as in Pss 120; 129; in

The superscription and the similarity to Pss 46 and 48 in attitude and tone, and the allusions to the pilgrimage in verse 1 and to the promise to David in verse 5 (see Ps 132:11–18), point to the relationship with the fall festival.

The psalm consists of two parts. The first part (the first three strophes), verses 1–5, is a personally felt and originally expressed hymn to Jerusalem, the glorious city of God. The sacred city is the place where the community has religious experiences, where the source of life's power and the center of reality are. Its external character also corresponds to this spiritual character: the firmly established fortification, the spiritual and political focus of the tribes of YHWH bound by the unity of the true religion, which YHWH himself defined as the proper place for pilgrimages and worship pleasing to him, the seat of the house of David, who reigns there as representative of the deity and of the people and mediator between the two. The reference to the fact that Jerusalem is the royal seat suffices as a justification for the emphasis on the religious significance of the city as the divine seat precisely because one presumes it to be self-evident that the king, who has this role, dwells in the shadow of his God.[65] Because Jerusalem has this all-overarching significance, the poet speaking here in the name of the whole community rejoices each time the words proclaim that the time has come to make pilgrimage to the house of YHWH. The plethora of experiences of a folk religion that has arisen from the peoples' experiences of reality echoes in these words of the poet. Moreover, as Gunkel has correctly emphasized, the Deuteronomic idea shines through here.[66] At the same time, however, we simultaneously gaze into the religious experiences, feelings, and value judgments that, in addition to the interests of the priesthood, produced this idea. As in Ps 48, the first part of the psalm is an indirect hymn to YHWH himself, who dwells in this glorious city. This idea is not expressed directly, however, perhaps because for the poet YHWH dwells primarily in heaven. We cannot definitely say whether this part of the psalm was sung by an individual or by a choir representing the community. The latter is the more likely.

In the second part (vv. 6–9), consisting of two strophes, this hymn to Jerusalem transforms into a call to declare blessing on Jerusalem. It is unique liturgically and, at the same time, characteristic of the distinction between

---

Pss 129 and 130, perhaps also in 131; the matter differs somewhat, since we probably have original psalms of the individual here that were reinterpreted as communal psalms; see *Psalm Studies* 2:307, 351, 355.

65. In v. 5, I strike *lĕmišpāṭ* as a gloss, perhaps also the second *kisôt* (see *Psalm Studies* 2:367 n. 6).

66. Hermann Gunkel, *Ausgewählte Psalmen* (4th ed.; Göttingen: Vandenhoeck & Ruprecht, 1917), 170–71.

laity and priesthood that the priest apparently does not perform the cultic procedure or pronounce the cultic word *sua sponte* but acts in response to the community's request. This has analogies, for example, in the requirement that the father of the household read the festival legend aloud during the Jewish Passover Feast, a practice presupposed in Exod 12:26–27 and 13:3–16.[67] Here the call that Ezra read aloud the sacred text from the book of the law on New Year's Day, which does not represent a singular event but mirrors a cultic practice,[68] should be mentioned. In order to understand the stage of religion for which the cultic word spoken by the correct mediator was a powerful reality, it is no less significant that we do not have in the psalm a direct prayer to YHWH for blessing on the city but a call to some group that it should invoke blessing on the city through certain words. It is actually obvious that the communal psalms of petition should request "grace and blessing" (Ps 67:2). The purpose of the cult, after all, is to mediate to the community the divine blessing in the most comprehensive sense of the word. Here the request to the minister of the cult is that he should pronounce the word of blessing in the technical sense:

> So, wish salvation for Jerusalem
> and "peace"[69] for her "tents."[70]
> May salvation dominate in her walls
> and joy in her fortifications!

There can be no doubt here that we should see in this strophe the community's call to the professional mediators of blessing, the priests, all the more so since verse 7 provides the words with which the priest is supposed to bless, if not precisely verbatim, still substantially. This understanding is confirmed in the continuation, in which an individual as representative of those addressed repeats the blessing formula in verse 7 in substance, although not verbatim. Significantly, we do not have a request that YHWH bless either in verse 7 or

---

67. See my *Ezra den skriftlaerde* (Kristiania: Universitets Forlaget, 1916), 83.

68. Neh 8:1–2. I have tried to show in my *Ezra den skriftlaerde* (72–91) that Neh 8 does not deal with the promulgation of a new law, as has been thought since Graf and Wellhausen, but with the regular celebration of a New Year's Festival with an equally regularly public reading from the law. Gustav Hölscher (*Die Bücher Esra und Nehemiah* [Tübingen: Mohr, 1923]) has joined me in his treatment of the books of Ezra–Nehemiah for the 4th edition of Kautzsch's translation of the Old Testament. Hölscher graciously made the page proofs available to me.

69. Actually, sure invincibility, "salvation" in the original sense of the word, which is sometimes still preserved in the Nordic languages (*hel* = whole, complete, incorrupt, etc.).

70. Read *wĕšalwâ lĕohālêkā* in v. 6 (LXX).

in verses 8–9 but the pronouncement of a blessing formula in the usual form of the self-efficacious words of blessing. The expression *šāʾal šĕlôm pĕlōnî* does not per se indicate that the blessing is sought as a gift of YHWH. It means to wish and desire the blessing with all the force of one's soul and to mediate the power of blessing through words that embody the same full force of the soul and thereby to create blessing. In other words, it means "to provide for someone's well-being." The priest had this power because, as priest, he stood in connection with YHWH and was filled with the supramundane and sacred. He was "clothed in salvation (or righteousness)" (Ps 132:9, 16). The content of the expression cited must be interpreted in terms of the explication in verses 8–9. There, too, nothing is said of soliciting blessing.[71] The ancient Israelite, in contrast to Judaism, knows a wish that is only wish and not simultaneously the deed and expression of the soul's might only in psychically broken people who have become "unjust" and "perverse." Cult and liturgy tend to preserve the ancient.

Therefore, we may also surmise that the last strophe of the psalm, in which one of those addressed responds and complies with the call, is an authentic blessing formula that was actually in use and that the psalm is not a "spiritual"[72] imitation of an originally cultic form but an actual liturgy portrayed for us in the psalm. Thus, the spokesman of the priestly chorus says:

For the sake of my brothers and companions,[73]
I "pronounce"[74] salvation on you;
for the sake of the house of our God
I wish you good fortune.

---

71. See also the expression that occurs in Assyrian and Aramaic (Elephantine), שלם ישאלו אלהיא "פ. From whom should the gods—let alone YHWH! (cf. Pap. Sachau 13495 [Arthur Ungnad, *Aramäische Papyrus aus Elephantine* [Leipzig: Hinrichs, 1911], no. 1, ll. 1–2)—"request" someone's salvation? The expression is not a transfer of concepts from the human sphere to the gods that empties the words (= "to greet" or the like, as they are often translated). It suits the original concept of blessing too well for this (see above; so also Pedersen, *Israel*, 304 and the note on 524).

72. As Gunkel, and following him, many others, term it.

73. So must *lĕmaʿan* be interpreted here and in v. 9. The exegetes who translate it as such have not satifisfactorily explained what it should mean that one wishes for salvation "for the temple's sake" (best is Buhl, *Psalmerne*). The "brothers and companions" are fellow officials, then, who mediate the blessing. I add explicitly that the cultic and liturgical interpretation of the psalm is independent of this understanding of *lĕmaʿan*.

74. Strike *na*.

Good fortune and blessing have their visible seat in the house of God. They can be found there, concentrated, as it were. As the guardians and ministers of the temple, the priests cause blessing to stream forth from there to Jerusalem, the embodiment of the community. This blessing wish has no trace of prayer. It does not even say, "May YHWH bless you." It has the customary form of efficacious words. Literally, it says, "I infuse you with salvation through my words," "I wish forth good for you."

The time of this psalm can be determined with approximate certainty. As we saw, to a degree the ideals of Deuteronomy echo through it. On the other hand, it assumes the existence of the monarchy.[75] Thus it originated in the latest preexilic period. It shows us very clearly what the festival continued to be for religious people at the time.

In all appearance, Ps 115 also seems to be a cultic liturgy.[76] More precisely, it probably involves a segment of a sacrifice liturgy, as Heinrich Ewald has already conjectured.[77] The conjecture expressed by Staerk (*Lyrik*) is very promising. He suggests that it involved the ʾazkārâ offering and that the zōkĕrēnû in verse 12 alludes to this. We have seen above that blessing and sacrifice are closely related. After the completion of the sacrifice, the priest-king David blessed the community (1 Sam 6:18; 1 Kgs 8:14, 55). Through the sacrifice, the liturgist makes a connection with the holy. Originally, one conceived matters such that the sacred, efficacious actions intensified the power of the soul and the force of blessing of the one offering sacrifices. Through them, the divine power flowed into him, perhaps through the consumption of part of the divine sacrificial animal. Later it was probably envisioned generally such that the pleasant odor of the sacrifice and the pious attitude of the one sacrificing attracted the deity's attention so that he could successfully invoke the divine blessing. The normal sequence was probably sacrifice–blessing. Deuteronomy 10:8 summarizes the work of the priest in these two procedures. We said above that the Aaronic blessing was the conclusion to the cultic procedure. Thus the liturgy in Ps 115, which culminates in the priestly blessing, also probably belongs after the actual sacrificial procedure.

The psalm consists of a petition expended with hymnic motifs (vv. 1–11; four strophes, three trimeter duplets each), a blessing wish (vv. 12–15; one

---

75. One cannot follow Gunkel (*Ausgewählte Psalmen*, 171) in deducing from v. 5 that the poet knew the Davidites merely as the supreme judges and no longer as kings.

76. Regarding the understanding of the psalm, see esp. Staerk, *Lyrik*, 41. His characterization of the psalm as a hymn is inaccurate, however. It is a complete liturgy, instead, and an authentic one, not a "learned" imitation.

77. Vol. 1.2 of *Die Dichter des Alten Bundes* (3rd ed.; Göttingen: Vandenhoeck & Ruprecht, 1866).

strophe also with three periods), and a hymnic concluding strophe (three periods) with a vow to praise YHWH forever (vv. 16–18).[78]

The prayer is explicitly liturgical and general in nature and rather insignificant both in terms of ideas and poetry. Although it is not to be interpreted in relation to a specific crisis but is cast rather generally, it has the form of the lament song with hymnic motifs. This reflects the religious practice and character of the ancient Semites. One who wants to request something always portrays himself as sorrowful, suffering, and needy as extremely as possible in order to inspire sympathy. He always comes *in toga sordida*, as it were, crying relatively authentic tears. He is the poor, the humbled, the oppressed, "a worm and no longer a human being" (see Ps 22:7). Consequently, almost every religious prayer in the Old Testament essentially acquires the imprint of the lament psalm and makes the impression that it was always spoken in a specific, concrete, frightful crisis and that deliverance from this crisis was the sole focus of the prayer. This has mostly misled the exegetes who believed that it should be taken into account that the praying Israelite would always observe European standards of manliness and enticed them, for example, with psalms such as Ps 85 to ask about the specific difficult historical background of the plaintiff's request in the first segment. Both cases involve only whether the New Year is imminent. Now the community requests that its fears concerning the harvest and fate in the coming year may not come to pass but be transformed into their opposites.[79]

The very same is true of the petition in Ps 115. The "crisis" consists only of the desire to attain something. The prayer begins like the psalm of lament with the invocation and follows it with the request, now closely intertwined with an honor motif in antithetical form for greater effect: "not for our sake but for the sake of your own reputation, may you help us." Obviously, the repeated "not us, YHWH, not us," is not to be taken seriously but is to be attributed to the calculating and creeping humility of the oriental.[80]

Nothing is said explicitly concerning the actual content of the request. How should YHWH glorify his name? Given the whole context, he will doubtlessly do so by proving to be Israel's aid and shield and by making an end to all the pagans' mocking questions. He does just this by "blessing" his people and

---

78. Verse 1b is an insertion. In v. 5, the second, in v. 6, both *lāhem* are superfluous and to be stricken, thereby improving the meter. After v. 7, *'ap 'ên-yeš rûaḥ bĕpihem*, should be supplemented based on Ps 135:17. Verses 12aβb and 13a are later expansions (see below).

79. See *Psalm Studies* 3:549–50.

80. The "confession of sin, the quiet, humble acknowledgement of one's own unworthiness in submission to God's rod," which Staerk (*Lyrik*) wants to hear in the words of the prayer, is, in fact, mute. I do not find in this psalm the prophetic spirit but a youthful spirit.

granting it power and good fortune. The first part of the liturgy is to be understood, indeed, as a petition for divine blessing. In the details, it is executed as follows: the honor motif intertwined with the petition is extended with the remark, in words borrowed from Ps 79:10, that YHWH's failure to hear would give the pagans an occasion to mock the impotence of Israel's God. Thus YHWH's honor requires Israel's good fortune. Such a derisive claim by the pagans would, however, be a lie contrary to the facts, for our God dwells in heaven, indeed, and does whatever he wishes. This claim is extended polemically. In reality, the gods of the pagans can do nothing because they are not gods, only idols. In expressions that echo Deutero-Isaiah and were probably borrowed from Ps 13:15–18, the poet shows how they are only lifeless material, silver and gold, made by human hands, who can help neither themselves nor their worshipers. These arguments continue the hymnic motif, already adumbrated in verse 3, in a more indirect fashion. The situation with Israel is quite different from that with the worshipers of the dead idols. The whole sacred and pious people, both laypersons and priests,[81] trust in YHWH, who is not like those idols. He is their help and shield. The hymnic motif and the whole prayer sounds a markedly emphasized confidence motif, and the whole prayer ends in a strongly emphasized confidence motif constructed of three highly parallel periods, the second member of which is always the same and names in a proudly triumphant tone the actual reason for the unconditional confidence in the first section: the fact that YHWH has always proven to be help and shield.[82] It has long been suspected, it seems with great likelihood, that these three periods were sung antiphonally by two choirs or by the choir and the whole community.

The pronouncement of blessing (vv. 12–15) follows as the priests' response to the congregation's petition:

May YHWH, who remembers us, bless (you) [],
both the small and the great!
May YHWH multiply you, you and your children!
May you be blessed by YHWH, the creator of heaven and earth![83]

---

81. I find the usual understanding that "God-fearers" (v. 11) refers to proselytes no more correct here than in Ps 118:4. The sequence speaks against it. The phrase *yir'ê yhwh* is a combination of the first two groups (Israel = laypersons and priests = the whole sacred and pious people). See *Psalm Studies* 2:368.

82. In vv. 9–11, one should read the perfect *bāṭaḥ* instead of the imperfect, along with twenty-one manuscripts of the LXX and Syr. The *qere* in the second section presupposes either a second-person pronominal suffix or, responsively, a first-person.

83. If we may start from the notion that a certain regularity must be attributed to Isra-

In terms of content, we encounter the ancient and persistent concept of blessing here: the fertility, the increase of the people. This is indeed the good fortune requested in the first portion of the psalm. The increase of the people presupposes everything else: peace, good harvests, health, prosperity of the children, protection against enemies, and so on.

When a God like YHWH (who created heaven and earth and does whatever he wants) blesses, it becomes a blessing. A people who trusts in him must become a grand and fortunate people. It can never perish or "become ashamed." The world belongs to such a people. This is the attitude that the solemn blessing of the priests evokes as an echo in the soul of the community. Out of this attitude comes the response by which the community appropriates the blessing, as it were, and gives thanks to the one who gives the blessing in the form of a vow. They want to laud and praise their God, YHWH, as long as they exist on earth, for the honor and fame due to such a God can only be given him as long as Israel exists on the earth. The dead, "who are cut off by his hand" (Ps 88:6), can no longer praise him:

> Heaven is YHWH's heaven; he gave the earth to the children of men.
> The dead do not praise YH, nor does the one who has gone to silence.
> We, however, want to praise YHWH from now onward and forevermore.

The poet speaks of the human race. In contrast to the deity in heaven, it received the earth as an inheritance. Why? For what purpose? So that it may praise and give honor to the deity. Only those alive among the children of men come under consideration as those who can praise the deity. At the center of the historical stage stands only Israel, however. If Israel should no longer belong among the living—this is the obvious presupposition—then YHWH's fame on earth is done. As long as Israel exists, however, YHWH may be assured of the praise due him.

Nothing more precise may be said concerning the date of this psalm. If one abandons the historical interpretation disputed by Ferdinand Hitzig, Edouard Reuss, and Julius Wellhausen, the point of departure supposed in

---

elite poetry, the form of the text in these verses cannot be original. The tripartite v. 12 (3 + 3 + 3) is intolerable alongside the duple triplets in vv. 13–15. Verse 12b or 13a, therefore, is suspect as a later interpolation. Thereby, however, the originality of the specialization (Israel, Aaronites, God-fearers) becomes dubious. Since the psalm otherwise clearly falls into strophes of three doubled triplets, I believe that neither v. 12a nor 12aα, 13b were original to vv. 12–13.

verse 2 falls aside.[84] According to Buhl (*Psalmerne*), who does not substantially follow the exegetes mentioned, the role of the Aaronic priests, first, and the reference to the proselytes, second, support a composition "in the later postexilic period." The second argument, however, is, as stated above, at least very uncertain, if not totally invalid. Nor is the first unconditionally cogent, for the priesthood did not create the Aaronite theory. According to E, too, the priests are Aaron's descendants.[85] The leading role of the Aaronite priests in the cult and in the religious consciousness, in clear contrast to the laity, was clearly established at least since Ezekiel and the Deuteronomists. One should remember that we are dealing here with a psalm from the circle of the temple personnel. The early postexilic period or the latest preexilic period would suit just as well as "the late postexilic period."

We have a small liturgy of a similar nature in Ps 134. According to the superscription, it belongs to the great fall festival (*ma'ălâ*),[86] and since, according to verse 1, it was composed for a nocturnal celebration, it also belongs to the first night of the festival, the night of full moon during the fall festival,[87] as the concluding liturgy. Such vigils are explicitly attested.[88] For the vigil of the fall festival,

> the whole festival congregation assembles in the grand court of the temple. Boys from priestly families light the large lamps standing in the court at nightfall. Torches are lit so that all Jerusalem is illuminated by the bright light around the temple. The temple singers stand on the great stairs that lead to the court of the temple building and sing psalms. Later, people pass the time until morning with torch dances and all manner of pastimes. Early, at the first cockcrow, priests encourage the end of the celebration with horn calls, and the congregation, uplifted by the festival, is sent home.[89]

---

84. Ferdinand Hitzig, *Die Psalmen übersetzt und ausgelegt* (Leipzig: Winter, 1863); Edouard Reuss, *Le Psautier ou le Libre de Cantiques de la Synagogue* (Paris: Sandoz & Fischbacher, 1879); Julius Wellhausen, *Bemerkungen zu den Psalmen* (Skizzen und Vorarbeiten 6; Berlin: Reimer, 1899).

85. See Deut 10:6-9 (?); Exod 4:14-16; see also Rudolf Kittel, *Geschichte des Volkes Israels* (3rd ed.; Gotha: Klotz, 1927), 348 n. 6, 349 n. 3, 483 n. 4.

86. Beer (Pesachim, 46) relates the psalm to the Passover Festival. This is contrary both to the superscription and to the testimony in m. Suk. 4:1 and Mid. 2:5.

87. So also Kittel, *Psalmen*, 408. See also my *Psalm Studies* 2:269–70.

88. See m. Suk. 5:1–4, Josephus, *C. Ap.* 1.22; and Isa 30:29 already refer to such vigils.

89. Kittel on the psalm, with reference to Paul Volz, *Das Neujahrsfest Jahwes (Laubhüttenfest)* (Tübingen: Mohr, 1912), 4–7, where there is a more extensive description of the details; and to Heinrich Graetz, "Die Halleluja- und Hallel-Psalmen," *MGWJ* 28 (1879): 246.

The dismissal occurs in the form of the priestly blessing, and our psalm represents the (or a) liturgy for this proclamation of blessing. It shares with Ps 122 the congregation's call to the priests, a call replaced in Ps 115 by a prayer to YHWH. Notably, however, the response in verse 3 apparently does not correspond to the call. The congregation, probably represented by the choir of singers, calls for blessing YHWH:

> Now, then, bless YHWH, all you servants of YHWH!
> [Now then, bless YHWH], all who stand in YHWH's house!
> In the depths of night, raise your hands in holiness and bless YHWH![90]

If the MT of verse 3 is correct and *bārĕkû 'et* should not simply be read instead of *yĕbārekĕkā* and the whole understood as a call to blessing, the response of the priests follows in verse 3 in the form of a blessing on the congregation (addressed as "you [masculine singular]," as in the Aaronic blessing):

> YHWH bless you from Zion, YHWH who made heaven and earth!

Then, however, the "blessing of YHWH" in verses 1–12 must be understood in substance on the analogy of Ps 115: by blessing the people of YHWH and thereby creating good fortune for it, the priests glorify YHWH and bless him to the extent that they increase his reputation, his honor, and thereby his power to bless. "YHWH's blessing" in verses 1–2 then means: to praise and glorify him by blessing in his name. There is also another possibility, however, for harmonizing the apparent contradiction between the call and the response: the congregation calls upon priests to "bless" YHWH, naturally with the intention that he would in turn bless the community with his much greater blessing. The priests respond: "YHWH on Zion, the creator of the heavens

---

90. Verse 3b demonstrates that the meter of the psalms must be not a pentameter but the duple triplet (perhaps some isolated sextameters). In 1aβ, *kol* is one beat; *qōdeš* in v. 2 must be assigned, then, to the second series and *ballêlôt* in v. 1 tied to v. 2 (so LXX). The placement of the *athnach* in v. 2 is also supported by the fact that the customary translation, "raise your hands to the sanctuary," would actually be senseless if it were indeed to involve a blessing of the congregation. Then one would extend one's hands toward the congregation. In v. 1b, a sequence parallel and perhaps identical to 1aα must have been lost. The translation above has been emended accordingly. If a specific subsequent celebration is intended, *ballêlôt* must be an amplificative plural and denote the depth of night. The time of the first cockcrow is the time of deepest sleep. According to Kautzsch §118n, *qōdeš* is to be understood as an adverbial accusative. It refers to the psychic *habitus* of the blessing priests, analogous in substance with "clothed in salvation (or righteousness)" in Ps 132:9, 16.

and the earth, is mighty enough to bless you with no further consideration, he does not need our prior blessing. Now he blesses all of you through us."

Roughly the same is true regarding the age of this psalm as of Ps 122. The circumstance that we have in the *ma'ălôt* song booklet two notoriously pre-exilic psalms, 122 and 132, does not argue for a particularly late dating of the others (see further on the matter, *Psalm Studies* 2:368).

I believe that Ps 121 must also be understood as an actual cultic antiphonal liturgy with a priestly blessing in the technical sense of the word. While the older critical exegetes do not raise the question of the form and purpose of the psalm at all, Gunkel, Staerk, and Kittel believe that it must be seen as a "spiritual" imitation of the cultic antiphonal liturgy. The poet speaks with his own soul and is his own priest. This understanding depends on a very questionable interpretation of verse 1. "The mountains" are supposed to be the mountains of Jerusalem—but why the plural, then?—and the poet is supposed to be situated outside the Holy Land, toward whose mountains he is now only able to raise his eyes longingly from afar. All of this is neither necessary nor likely. It is correct, to be sure, that the song is felt very personally. The poet regarded his feelings and attitudes as typical for the whole community. It is also correct that the form of the individual songs has been influential. The psalm is to be understood, however, similarly to Ps 122. The poet speaks in the name of the community; in this sense, the actual speaker is the community, just as it is addressed mostly with "you" (masculine singular) in the blessings.

I have indicated elsewhere how I understand verse 1 and thus the whole psalm (*Psalm Studies* 2:346). The psalm, a *ma'ălâ* song (v. 1), belongs to the fall festival and, like Ps 122, also refers to the grand festival procession. The singer presents himself as one seeking help who is on the way to salvation but does not really know where to find its true locus. A contrast between "the mountains" in verse 1 and YHWH in verse 2 is clearly intended, and the sense of verse 1 is: "Where should I seek salvation and assistance? There are, after all, so many mountains, all of which have sanctuaries, and every religion or school claims that its 'mountain' is the real 'rock,' the true dwelling place of God where help is to be sought." But no true Israelite (v. 2) asks such questions. The question is thus actually rhetorical. It is raised only to repudiate every false response *a limine*. Confidence erupts suddenly. Only one, YHWH, the creator of the heavens and the earth, is the true helper in all crises. We have nothing to do with the (many) mountains, only with YHWH. It could have added, with Zion, the sole true mountain of God (see Ps 48:2).

> I look high to the mountains—whence comes my salvation?
> Salvation will come to me from YHWH, the creation of the heavens and the earth!

He will not permit [my] foot to slip; [my]⁹¹ guardian does not slumber!
Indeed, the guardian of Israel neither sleeps nor slumbers!

As in Ps 115, this first part of the liturgy is a prayer, specifically for the blessing that assures all well-being, and is to be understood as the confidence motive. The symmetrical structure of the strophe is noteworthy. In both sections the petition (vv. 1 and 3) appears first, although in a somewhat tentative, almost indirect, form: in verse 1 in the almost reluctant question, in verse 3 in the wish. Then, however, confidence erupts immediately in both instances (vv. 2 and 4): I now know for certain that the salvation of YHWH comes, that the guardian of Israel never sleeps!⁹² To the extent that the prayer was spontaneously answered by faith and the promise of assistance was anticipated, one may say with Gunkel and others that the poet appears here as his own priest. This by no means excludes, however, the possibility of a confirming statement by the true priest and the explicit reception of the words that bestow blessing. Thus, in the second part (vv. 5–8), the priest (or priests) speak(s) and respond(s) to the prayer with a cultic blessing that takes up and affirms the last words of the congregation:

> YHWH is your guardian, YHWH is your patron,
> he goes at your right hand,
> the sun will not smite you by day [nor] will the moon (harm you) by night.
> May YHWH guard you from all evil, may YHWH guard your life,
> Guard you going and coming from now on and into eternity.

With objective certainty, the congregation is promised YHWH's gracious protection in all dangers, against the harmful powers of nature,⁹³ against all demons, against every evil. The pious Israelite may go to his work secure and comforted; he will return unharmed back to his house in the evening. He is

---

91. The whole structure of the psalm makes it obvious that one sees in the first part (vv. 1–4) the community's petition and in the second (vv. 5–8) the priests' response. However, *raglî* and *šōmĕrî* must then be read in v. 3. The psalm consists, then, of two strophes with four periods each. Each pair of the four periods forms a section. The periods are not, as is usually assumed, pentameters but duple trimeters and hexamaters (as in vv. 4 and 5). Further, *wĕ'al* should be read in v. 3b, *wĕlō yārēḥ* in v. 6. The *yhwh* in v. 8 should be connected to v. 7.

92. In *Psalm Studies* 2:346, I still attributed vv. 3–4 in the traditional manner to the one speaking in vv. 5–8.

93. Regarding "moonstruck" in v. 6, see Kittel (*Psalmen*) on the passage.

always in YHWH's protection. The blessing he now receives accompanies him when he goes out and flows out to him when he returns. Thus the fact that the concluding words of the psalm are still a cultic formula of blessing among us is not just an adaptation in the more original manner, as Gunkel and others think, but a thoroughly correct adherence to the meaning of the psalm.

If my interpretation of verses 1–2 is correct, the psalm may have originated at roughly the same time as Ps 122. For the pious, Jerusalem is the only place where divine help can be found. On the other hand, one must still take into account the possibility that the other sacred "mountains" may exert a certain attraction.[94]

1.3.2. Given what was said above (§1.1), we understand that in the Israelite conception intercession is also a blessing. With the growing comprehension of YHWH as a volitional and active personality and the giver of all blessings and good fortune, the prayer for divine blessing and the cultic ministers' intercession for the community and individuals must necessarily somewhat suppress the old self-efficacious blessing formula, or, in any case, rather significantly influence its style and form. Thus there arose cultic psalms of prayer that bear substantially the imprint of the old blessing.

Psalm 72 and the first part of Ps 20[95] stand at the boundary between intercession and blessing. While in the psalms treated in §1.3.1 priests were to be understood as the speakers of the blessing pronounced on the whole community as such, Ps 72 and 20:2–6 are meant as the community's blessing-producing intercessions for an individual at its head, for the king who sustains the people. Whether we imagine that the prayer was spoken or sung by the choir of singers representing the community or by an individual minister of the cult, perhaps a priestly prophet (or prophetic priest) is of subordinate importance. Ideally, the one involved appeared as the representative and spokesman of the community.

This is particularly clear in Ps 20, where, after the intercession for the king in the first-person plural, an individual, apparently a cultic prophet, appears and proclaims the deity's response to the petition, speaking in the first-person singular ("Now I truly know that YHWH stands with his anointed"). Unquestionably, the prayer in verse 2–6 is to be explicated cultically and literarily in relation to the prayers for assistance (or lament psalms) of the people on spe-

---

94. This is in line with Ps 87, at any rate. It also polemicizes lightly against the other "dwellings" [of YHWH] in Jacob, and I consider it, too, to be preexilic (see *Psalm Studies* 2:360–62).

95. For more on the cultic and literary context of these psalms, see *Psalm Studies* 3:567–69, 585–88.

cial days of prayer organized for particularly unfortunate occasions (defeat, pestilence, hunger, drought, etc.).[96] Psalm 20 involves such a particular occasion. War is imminent; the people are threatened by enemies and seek now to ensure YHWH's assistance.

The intercession in Ps 20 reads:

> May YHWH hear you in distress; may Jacob's God protect [] you![97]
> May he send you help from the sanctuary, succor from Zion!
> May he remember all your offerings and find your burnt offering fat!
> May he give you what you desire and fulfill all your plans!
> May we rejoice over your victory, "elevate"[98] ourselves
> by the name of our God!

The influence of the occasional cultic psalm of prayer is evident in the reference to a specific historical situation in verse 2 and in the appeal to the king's previously active cultic piety (v. 4; the "piety or righteousness motif"). On the other hand, the address to the king instead of to the deity and the form "May YHWH do this and that good for you" betray the influence of the cultic pronouncement of blessing.

Since the king is both the leader in battle and the representative of the people in general, in whom it has its life and security,[99] he obviously plays an outstanding role in the cultic celebrations preceding a military campaign. In keeping both with the ancient Near Eastern and the ancient Israelite understandings, the whole affair is considered the king's concern in such cases. On the other hand, the clear distinction otherwise made between the king and the people involving the latter's appearance as an intercessor for the former is a clear sign of the dissolution of the old mindset that was unaware of any contrast between the community and individuals. The old period would have had the "super-ego" of the people, manifest in the person of the chieftain, appear in prayer semi-independently in the words of the natural representative. To this extent, the psalm attests to a later period and probably also to the influence of the autocratic despot ideal of Canaanite culture and the major states. For them, the direct psychic unity of king and people was no longer

---

96. See Gunkel, "Psalmen," *RGG* 4:1934–35.
97. Strike *šēm*, *metri causa*.
98. One should probably read *migdōl*. Verse 6b is probably a doublet of v. 5.
99. See *Psalm Studies* 2:468–72.

self-evident. In this understanding, the good was first for the king and only derivatively and secondarily for the people.[100]

The fact that the king, or the chieftain, received the people's blessing before particularly important actions such as war is entirely consistent with the ancient, original viewpoint. Just as the people "blesses" even the deity, so it quite naturally blesses its superior and elevates its power along with his by subjugating its soul and power to him, that is, by being absorbed into him. In the covenant, the mightier party has a just claim to this support from the lesser parties. It is the only thing that they can contribute.[101] Secondarily, this phenomenon is associated with the cultic prayer for assistance in crisis when the people appear in the cult, not as subjects, but as quasi-cultic figures. A dilution of the original sense of the pronouncement of blessing is evident especially in the fact that the whole is conceived as a prayer to the deity. A cultic prophet subsequently communicates the divine response probably obtained through some technical means (Urim and Thummim, hieroscopy, or the like).

The same admixture of prayer and blessing is also evident in Ps 72. After Gunkel's "Die Königspsalmen,"[102] I consider it established that the king mentioned in the psalm was not the messiah but the historical king of Israel. The psalm begins as a regular prayer with the invocation of the deity and an address to him in the second person (vv. 1–2). The king is also mentioned subsequently in the third person. Already in verse 3 the prayer shifts into the form of the blessing. The psalm also concludes with the regular pronouncement of blessing:

"May he be blessed"[103] eternally, as long as the sun shines.
May his name flourish (?).
May all nations be blessed in him; may [all the families of the earth][104] praise him.

The blessing is extended so broadly and the author evaluates the traditional promises so copiously that the psalm awakens the impression of a prophetic promise. Since, as has been demonstrated elsewhere (*Psalm Studies* 3), the promising oracular responses of the prophets played a major role in the Isra-

---

100. Regarding this later ideal of the ruler in contrast to the original, see Pedersen, *Israel*, 1:224–26.
101. Ibid., 1:234–36.
102. Herman Gunkel, "Die Königspsalmen," *Preussische Jahrbücher* 158 (1914): 42–68; see also Kittel in his commentary.
103. Read *bārûk* instead of *šĕmô*, following LXX.
104. Supplied following LXX.

elite cult, one might be tempted to see in the psalm not an actual intercession by the community but an oracle by a cultic prophet. The psalm would then take its place alongside Pss 89:20–38 and 132:11–18. However, the beginning of the psalm and the circumstance that YHWH is not mentioned as the giver of the gifts, nor does he appear in the first person, as was almost always the custom in the cultic oracle, speaks against this. It is probably correct to see the psalm as an intercession for the king on the day of his ascension to the throne. It is so strongly influenced by the cultic blessing and the prophetic promise in terms of content and form that it hardly bears the imprint of the intercession any longer. The psalm expresses the wish and the promise to the king of all the paradisiacal happiness one normally wishes the new king on his ascension and that one otherwise actually and originally expected from the annual enthronement of God[105]—the king was, after all, YHWH's son, in Israel's view.[106]

I need not demonstrate that Pss 20 and 72, as royal psalms, are preexilic. A more precise determination of the time may be impossible, since there are no clear allusions to contemporary history. They are, as Gunkel correctly observes, "not comparable to occasional poems in the strict sense but rather to formularies" that are meant to suit any king in similar conditions.[107] Thus they do not depict the individual king as he actually was but the royal ideal.[108]

1.3.3. Psalm 128 represents a further development of the poetic priestly blessing inserted into the context of a "psalm" ("liturgy") sung by the choir of singers that was discussed above under §1.3.1. The psalm ends in a pronouncement of blessing (vv. 5–6) that, in manner and style, is quite similar to those treated above. Psalm 128 differs from the psalms discussed there, however, first in terms of form, in that we cannot discover any trace of an antiphonal liturgy here. It seems to have been sung by a choir *uno tenore* in a cultic performance. It differs, second, in content, in that the pronouncement of blessing is preceded by a lengthier description of the expected content of the blessing. It explicitly states that the God-fearing person will be blessed in this manner.

If I am correct in the cultic interpretation of the psalms above, then here, too, there should be no objection against the assumption of an original cultic purpose for Ps 128. In any case, the understanding that Gunkel and Kittel, for example, seem to propose that we are dealing here with a purely private poem

---

105. See *Psalm Studies* 2:323–53.
106. Pss 2:7; 89:27–28; 110:3.
107. Gunkel, *Psalmen*, 26.
108. See my *Kongesalmerne*, 20ff., 117–18.

intended only to express the wishes of some private individual is likely.[109] One would then not expect a formal pronouncement of blessing as the conclusion. If the poet expresses his own wishes, then why "you" (masculine singular) and why not the conclusion one would then expect, "May it be so with me"? If he offers his wishes for others, then one would expect a conclusion such as, "May you also be pious and fear YHWH so that it may be so with you." No more satisfactory is Staerk's understanding of the psalm as a "didactic" song. The "instruction" is meant here, however, only as the substructure, as the "motive," for the pronouncement of blessing. Otherwise, instructions concerning the lot of the pious, such as we so often read in the book of Job, for example, do not end with a formal pronouncement of blessing.

Staerk has correctly emphasized one thing, however, that the psalm is influenced quite markedly by the style and topic of "wisdom poetry." The lot of the pious and of the godless was a favored topic of Israelite proverbs from antiquity. From the outset there was a certain connection between the style of this poetry and the blessing and curse formulas. One needed only to configure these formulas a little more extensively and one would have immediately had the description of the lot of the pious and the godless discussed above. It is possible, even probable, that this topic of proverbial poetry actually arose from the formulas of cursing and blessing. The rather frequent use of the introductory formulas "blessed" and "cursed," now mostly attenuated into "beatitudes" and "cries of woe," points to this development. In Ps 128, we can make the converse observation: the proverbs have in turn influenced the cultic blessing.

The question arises, however, as to whether the psalm is really meant as a priestly blessing formula. This is not likely. It is also rather long for this purpose. Another possibility is the sung liturgy that includes the blessing "sung" by one or several priests as an organic element. Yet another is the completely "unison" psalm, sung by priests—and not, for example, by the singers—that deals with the blessing as a theme. I, for one, cannot quite imagine a cultic act such as the one just mentioned.

I understand the matter instead such that our psalm is conceived as a greeting to the festive crowd performed by the usual choir of singers and that this practice developed from the priestly blessing. As the liturgical locus of this psalm I think, then, of the arrival of the festival procession in the temple court as in Ps 118:19–26, for example, where the entry of the procession is greeted by the blessing of the priest. It seems to me a rather likely possibility that this pronouncement of blessing was replaced on certain occasions by a

---

109. Indeed, earlier exegesis also understood the matter similarly, although it never raised the principal question.

psalm depicting the blessing somewhat more extensively. This would also be well-suited to the fact that the superscription connects the psalm to the fall festival, which is also undoubtedly true of Ps 118.

In a manner not unlike the admonitions for the festival procession in Pss 24 and 15, the occasion was utilized, then, to impress upon the community the conditions of blessing, the fear of God, and through the most charming description of the good fortune of the one blessed by YHWH to stimulate the religious zeal of the community by placing the beautiful promise before their eyes. Thus the address "you" (masculine singular), which is also characteristic of the pronouncement of blessing, can be explained in the simplest fashion. This explanation also accounts for the gradual transition of the description of the blessing into a formal pronouncement of blessing in the fashion of the priestly blessing while the whole retains the imprint of a conditional promise: if you fear YHWH, you can expect this reward and can bring it home from this place.[110] With reference to this moment of promise, the psalm has affinities with the cultic oracles that promise the same blessing and good fortune in response to the community's prayer (thus, perhaps, Ps 85).[111]

In accordance with both the ancient Israelite viewpoint and the content of the fall fertility festival, the fertility of the family and the undisturbed enjoyment of the produce of the field were portrayed as the actual content of the blessing:[112]

> Blessed by the one who fears YHWH,
> who walks in his ways.
> You will eat the produce of your hands—
> blessed be you, and it shall be well with you!
>
> Your wife is like a fertile vine
> within the house;
> your sons like olive shoots
> around your table.

Gunkel has correctly emphasized that both an unmistakable individualization of the awaited good fortune of the pious and the simple conditions of the life of the small farmer shine through in this description. As Gunkel demonstrates, this description reflects the uncertain conditions in the life of the

---

110. I would also like to understand Ps 133, and perhaps Ps 127, as such a "festival greeting" by the temple personnel to the surging crowd.
111. See *Psalm Studies* 2:336–37.
112. See *Psalm Studies* 2:343–45.

oriental minor state, perhaps under foreign dominion, in any case under the pressure of heavy tribute, exposed to thieving attacks by the sons of the desert and Palestine's uncertain climate, along with the fearful suspicions and the touching hopes of the insignificant person. All the more remarkable alongside those individual hopes for good fortune is the collective shape of the ideal expressed in the second part of the psalm:

> So []113 will the person be blessed,
> the one who fears YHWH.
> May YHWH bless you from Zion,
> [the creator of the heavens].114
>
> You will see Jerusalem's good fortune
> all the days of your life,
> and grandchildren will see you!
>   Salvation for Israel!

First, it is established here that this good fortune is available to the one who fears God. The following promise contains an admonition at the same time: "May it go the same way with you! May YHWH bless you now from Zion!" Here the poet adopts the cursory style of the old blessing formulas, including the imperfect verb that we found above to be the formal style of the pronouncement of blessing. By transforming the promise into a regular pronouncement of blessing, the old collective ideals appear immediately. Despite everything, the psalm intends to be a communal psalm. The supreme good fortune of the Israelite is Israel's good fortune. The two are inextricably interdependent. When the individual has children, Israel prospers, and the holy city of Jerusalem, the center of the community and the visible sign of YHWH's grace, rejoices and exults. Conversely, the peaceful existence and well-being of Jerusalem is the source of the highest joy for the pious person. As long as Jerusalem stands along with the temple and the cult, Israel has hope. Consequently, the psalm concludes with the wish that actually represents its overall objective: salvation for Israel! Be pious so salvation will be actualized!

    The psalm may be somewhat younger than Ps 122. The religious assessment of Jerusalem, which was both the origin and the consequence of Deuteronomic thought and which the restoration after the exile will have sig-

---

113. Strike *kî*.
114. A short element is missing. It has been supplied above based on Ps 124:8, etc.

nificantly increased,[115] is apparent here even more markedly than in Ps 122. As Gunkel has emphasized, the explicit ideal of the quiet life better suits the period of foreign domination than of the existence of the national state.

In literary terms, Ps 128 denotes a transitional phase from the cultic liturgies of blessing to the "psalms of blessing" such as Pss 1 and 112 mentioned earlier and to be discussed further below.

We can already deduce from Ps 72 that similar descriptions of the blessing of the pious also played a role otherwise in the cult. The mixture of intercession, wished-for blessing, and prophecy present here has its most essential content, in fact, in the portrayal of the expected blessing. The same conclusion can be also drawn from Ps 91, in which I see the fragment of a liturgy for the purification of a sick person.[116] The first part of the preserved piece consists of a description of the good fortune of the pious that has close affinities in many respects with similar depictions in the book of Job and with Pss 1 and 112. It is difficult to be more precise concerning the more immediate purpose of the piece and its place in the liturgy, since, as has been said, the psalm is only a fragment. It apparently contains a comforting and promising address by the priest to the sick person to be cleansed and is continued by a direct divine oracle promising full restoration.

1.3.4. We saw above that a condition was associated with the blessing in Ps 128: the condition of piety and righteousness. This is, indeed, always the obvious precondition. Significantly, however, it is stated explicitly. The natural form of the pronouncement of a conditional blessing meant to have general validity in the cult and to relate to all those present, in the event that they were receptive to the blessing at all, is: "blessed be the one who does thus and so." Thereby, the cultic pronouncement of blessing explicitly became a carrier of the ethicizing and, under certain circumstances, ethical ideas of religion. The fact that this happens is a matter of great importance. Nothing was perceived as more sacred in a religion at the level of Israel's than that such cultic words encompass the whole fullness of reality, as it were, as the efficacious word of blessing does. By becoming carriers of the moral ideas of religion, such words also lend morality some of their own unconditional, compulsory holiness. This meant an intensification of the moral ideas of religion. This intensification led automatically to expansions and specializations of the blessings that expressed ethical demands. One can no longer be satisfied, then, with the quite general formulation "Blessed be the one who is righteous or who fears

---

115. Cf. my book *Ezra*, 140.
116. See further in *Psalm Studies* 3:593–96.

God." Instead, one expanded and specialized the formulas: "Blessed be the one who does thus and so, and who does thus and so, and who does thus and so," and so on.

Such multipartite blessing formulas are no longer preserved for us in the Old Testament. We may, however, conclude with rather significant certainty that they were once present. We will offer evidence of the probability for this below in chapter 3. Here attention will be drawn to a further indication that can be deduced from the cultic psalms. I think of Pss 24 and 15.[117]

It may be regarded a certainty that Ps 24 is a festival procession song[118] specifically for the procession of the grand fall and YHWH-enthronement festival.[119] There can be no discussion of "spiritual imitation" here. The central section of the psalm, a dramatic scene set before the temple gates,[120] is meant to see that no unauthorized person enters the sanctuary, that all the participants in the festival are pure and worthy so that the presence of an evildoer or one who is internally unclean does not awaken divine wrath and evoke disaster on Israel. At this festival, the holy YHWH is in the midst of the community in a special sense. Represented by the ark, he enters into his palace at the head of his people as a victorious king. Consequently, before the temple gates, a serious, admonitory γνῶθι σεαυτόν is addressed to those entering.

It will almost always be the case that, among the conditions of purity and holiness established for participation in the cult, some will also be found that could not be monitored externally. This must necessarily be the case when the religion exhibits a strong ethical element, as was always the case in Israel in the historical period. Often no one can know what the individual has done far from the sanctuary or in secret. How, then, can one separate the unworthy from the cultically competent? The individual must be confronted with the seriousness of unworthy entry. It must be said to every individual before entry that only those who meet the requirements may enter. Whoever does not meet them attracts the burning wrath of the deity and will be destroyed by its punishment. One can do this in two ways: either, as in Delphi, through a general, comprehensive appeal to the conscience: Examine yourself! Or—and this suits the less-developed Semitic intellect better—one can support the conscience through a casuistic examination: Have you done, or failed to do, this or that? In both cases, the presupposition is that the deity is involved and will immediately punish the liar. According to Ps 24, the practice during the enthronement festival procession in Israel was for those ascending to the

---

117. For additional comments on Pss 24 and 15, see addendum 1, p. 777, below.
118. Gunkel, "Psalmen," *RGG*; idem, *Psalmen*; Staerk, *Lyrik*.
119. *Psalm Studies* 2:294–303.
120. For an analysis of the psalm, see ibid.

temple to ask, "Who may ascend to the mountain of YHWH? Who may stand in his holy place?" The priests' answer then came from the temple, "Whoever has done thus and so and refrained from thus and so." This was rather certainly ancient cultic practice in Israel. Psalm 24 is surely preexilic in origin, just as the prophetic and eschatological imitation of the practice in Isa 33:14–16 most likely is.[121]

In the context treated here it is significant, as Kittel correctly accentuated regarding Ps 15, that the answer does not correspond formally to the question. The question was, "Who may ascend to YHWH's mountain and spend time in his sanctuary?" However, the answer was,

> Whoever has clean hands and heart, who does not meditate on vanity,[122]
> will receive blessing from YHWH and (his) vindication
> from the God of his salvation.

"He will receive blessing," it says, not, "he may ascend." Kittel also suggested the correct explanation of this circumstance. The answer follows a customary priestly formula of blessing. Accordingly, there were cultic formulas of blessing that stated, "Blessed be the one who walks blamelessly and does justice; blessed be the one who speaks the truth in his heart; blessed be the one who does not cause harm with the tongue," and so on,[123] based on the individual

---

121. On Ps 24, see *Psalm Studies* 2:366; on Isa 33, see ibid., 409 n. 6. I see no reason to deny the cultic purpose of Ps 15. It is often said that this psalm lacks the cultic and ritual requirements. This claim is only conditionally correct. Ps 24 also requires "clean hands," an expression that probably also includes Levitical purity. The same may be the case, furthermore, for "walking blamelessly" (Ps 15:2), which Kittel limits, without justification, to "strict moral behavior." If, however, the ritual is so significantly mitigated, it should not be explained in terms of the poet's possible distancing from such requirements, as, for example, Staerk seems to think when he describes Ps 24 as "born of the prophetic spirit." The priests could easily control whether the participants performed the external purifications necessary for the festival. The ritual is presupposed as obvious (so Kittel, *Psalmen*, correctly). The concern here, however, is to determine through an appeal to individuals made in YHWH's sight that the uncontrollable requirements have also been sufficiently met. Quite naturally, the chief emphasis will then be placed on ethos and observance. I find the expression "prophetic" very misleading in this connection, since the "prophets" did not create the ethical trend in Israelite religion. In reality, the prophets are only comprehensible if one presupposes that the religion already had a strong ethical component before them. Incidentally, Kittel correctly emphasizes this point.

122. Verse 4b is probably a metrically redundant expansion based on Ps 15. Or is something missing?

123. The phrase "to cause the tongue to run around" refers to speaking magical incantations that cause the neighbor's ruin (see *Psalm Studies* 1:20–25).

clauses in Pss 15 or 24. We cannot say anything certain about the locus in the cult where such pronouncements of blessing, which correspond precisely to the curses in Deut 27:14–26 to be discussed below, will have been spoken, nor whether they were regularly recurring or occasional cultic sayings. We will return to such blessing below in chapter 2. The fact that Ps 24 presupposes them suggests that they are rather old, however. This psalm, which belongs to a festival procession with the ark,[124] is surely preexilic because it presupposes the existence of the ark.

---

124. See *Psalm Studies* 2:294–97, and compare regarding Ps 132, ibid., 283–95.

2
The Curse in Cult and Psalmody

2.1. Curse

If the blessing is the positive force of life (see §1.1), then the curse *'ālâ, qĕlālâ, ta'ălâ* is the negative.[1] The word *'ālâ* appears in Ps 10:7 as a synonym for *mirmôt*, "deceit," and in Ps 59:13 as a synonym for *kāḥas*, "lie." "Lie" and "deceit" do not come under consideration here as designations for the untrue or nonexistent, however, but designate the negative in the sense of the destructive, harmful, and unhealthful.[2] To this extent, *'ālâ* is a synonym for *'āwen*, "magic," "evil, disaster-producing power" (see below).

The Hebrew *'ālâ* signifies not only the word or act of cursing and its effects in misfortune and failures but also and at the same time the state of being cursed, of being filled with curse, the evil and unfortunate nature that such effects produce, and the power that is evil, "negative," or applicable for evil, that produces such effects.[3]

The curse is like a poisonous substance that fills the soul. It consumes and empties so that the soul loses its power and becomes "flaccid," "light," and thus "unjust." It is above all a devastating power that destroys everything it touches. The earth loses its power, the plants wilt, cities collapse, the inhabitants mourn and perish (Isa 24:6–12), and the land wilts and the eyes wither (Jer 23:10). If the curse enters an adulterous wife, her belly swells, her loins atrophy, she can bear no children and becomes "a curse among her relatives" (Num 5:21–27).

---

1. On the following, see Pedersen, *Israel*, 1:437–52; and idem, *Der Eid bei den Semiten in seinem Verhältnis zu verwandten Erscheinungen sowie die Stellung des Eides im Islam* (Studien zur Geschichte und Kultur des islamischen Orients 3; Strassburg: Trübner, 1914), esp. 64–102.

2. See *Psalm Studies* 1:43–62; Pedersen, *Israel*, 1:411–14.

3. Cf. the definition of the curse among the Semites: "The curse denotes everything that is harmful, everything that does not conform to normal conditions, the negation of life" (Pedersen, *Der Eid*, 64).

The sinner and evildoer is already full of curse, by definition. Just as blessing is the psychic power of the just, so is curse the evil power effective in the soul of the sinner and evildoer, whether the whole being of the one concerned is "lie," "magic," and "curse" or some enemy has put the curse and the corruption in him and "made [him] a sinner" or pushed him deeper into sinfulness, that is, into the state of misfortune (see below).

The curse in Deut 28, with the parallel in Lev 26, shows us in drastic manner what ultimately happens to him. The accursed is a person for whom nothing succeeds. His soul is confused, flaccid, and powerless. It wavers and staggers like a blind person. Misfortune clings to everything he does and plans. From him, the curse is transmitted to his house, his wife, his children, his family, and his people. It touches upon and destroys everything he has: house, land, garden, vineyard. The curse empties him, robs his soul of content, substance, and honor (*kābôd*), takes his blessing and peace. He becomes empty and "light." The usual words for cursing, *qillēl* and *hēqal*, actually mean "to make light." This is the "normal" existence, indeed, for the great sinner. The *rāšaʿ* is empty; he is a "lie" and a "deceit"; his being is "nothingness." But the originally just person can also be emptied by the curse and "made into a sinner" (Isa 29:20–21). One with no *kābôd*, no psychic content, no blessing, and no justice must by necessity perish. The cursed one is certain plunder for death.

The curse, accursedness, is thus identical with sinfulness, perversion, "nothingness." There are people who are always such, one might say, who are "unjust" and accursed at the core of their souls. The *rāšaʿ* is "alienated" from his mother's womb, standing outside the covenant, peace, and justice (Ps 58:4). This is true of beings such as magicians, demons, apostates, idolaters, major sinners, murderers, blasphemers, and the like. There are also people, however, who are healthy and just at the core of their souls, who were not strong enough and "blessed" enough to be able to successfully resist the evil influence of the curse. They become sinners and accursed people by unwittingly coming into connection with something unclean and accursed, by committing some unwitting sin and thereby exciting God's wrath, so that he has withheld his mercy from them, withdrawn his protection and permitted the seed of impurity, of the curse, to have its effects on them. Like the demons in the New Testament (Matt 12:43–45), the curse is animated, as it were, by a true *horror vacui*. Where righteousness, psychic power, and health have evacuated, where God's assistance has been withdrawn, the curse enters and fills the person with "nothingness," with misfortune, with evil nature, and thereby destroys them completely. The misfortunate can also be filled with misfortune by others, for example, by demons or magicians, and be made into sinners. Evil people have spoken an effective curse against them and thereby pushed them into misfortune.[4] Indeed, it suffices for them to have been in contact with an accursed person, one filled with curse.

An explicit manifestation of the curse on the part of its author is not necessary. The evil, accursed person already acts like a source of contagion in his environment. "The power of the curse is not *per se* implied in the wish or the word. It lies in the mysterious power of the souls to react upon each other. He whose soul creates something evil for another—be it in thought, in word or in deed—he puts the evil into the soul of his neighbour, where it exercises its influence."[5] If one is filled with curse, it spreads and attacks like an infection those who come into contact with the accursed. "A cursed man becomes a curse for his surroundings,[6] ... and therefore it is to be preferred that the cursed should be entirely removed."[7] Just as the effect of blessing is increased through incorporation in explicit words and acts of blessing,[8] so also is the efficacy of the curse. The curse can also be embodied in procedures, things, and words and, through them, be inserted into the soul of another person. The rite of laying on of hands can also transfer the evil force, sinfulness and its consequences, misfortune, and curse (accursedness). We infer this from the regulation concerning the goat for Azazel: when the priest stretches has hands over the goat, he transfers the *'ăwônôt* of the people, that is, its sinfulness together with its consequences such as misfortune, illness, pestilence, to the goat, which then bears the misfortune away into the wilderness (Lev 16:22). Zechariah 5:1–4 very likely presupposes another curse ritual. The prophet sees here a scroll flying away over the land and is told that it is the curse *ha'ālâ* that "goes out" over all thieves and perjurers. The vision probably presupposes the practice of writing a curse formula on a piece of paper and allowing it to be blown by the wind over the pertinent area.[9] We have an analogy in Num 5 (see below). The fact that Shimei underscored his curse by throwing stones and clods of dirt at David and his men (2 Sam 16:5–13) should probably also be understood as a means for intensifying the power of the curse, the efficacy of the evil created in Shimei's soul against David. The power of the curse is embodied, to an extent, in the stones. The power of the curse and misfortune can be infused into certain times and days, just as blessing can. There were people in Israel who had the power to ban certain days and to make them days

---

4. Pss 10:7; 59:13; see further, *Psalm Studies* 1.

5. Pedersen, *Israel*, 1:441.

6. Num 5:21, 27; Deut 28:37; 29:18; Jer 43:18; 44:12.

7. Ibid., 1:442–43.

8. See above, 662–63.

9. Rudolf Smend, *Lehrbuch der Alttestamentlichen Religionsgeschichte* (Tübingen: Mohr, 1899), 311 n. 1.

of misfortune (Job 3:8). One sees in these examples how closely related curse and magic are.

The most common and effective concentration of the power of curse, however, is created in the words and formulas of curse. Words effect what they say, that is, if the one involved has the required psychic character (see below). The insult is already a curse (2 Sam 16:5). If the villain calls a just man a blood hound and a scoundrel (*'îš bĕliyā'al*), the evil power of the evil words intrude into his soul and exert their ravaging and destructive effect. The one involved can never feel entirely secure before he has broken the power of the curse by striking at its root. The source of the evil must be stopped, its roots eradicated by blood vengeance, which, in ancient times, was the only means for self-preservation, for the preservation of the honor and psychic power of a person and his family (1 Kgs 2:8–9). The threat is also an effective word, a curse. The prophetic threat was understood as an effective word of judgment.[10] The "one who has evoked vigorous wrath" (*za'ûm*) is cursed thereby (Num 23:7–8; Prov 24:24). Furthermore, there is the direct curse formula in the jussive. Such a statement cannot be understood as a mere wish. It is more than a wish; it is an effective word. The question arises as to whether the customary translation, "may this or that occur," is actually too weak and whether one would not better translate, "this and that should (hereby) take place." The words have real power for evil. Thus, the saga also explains the actual circumstances in the present by the effective curses of the psychically powerful men of the primordial period (Gen 49:3–27). One attempts to smite an unknown thief by sending a curse out against him.[11] One may infer from Lev 5:1–6 that the curse was often actually effective. One day the perpetrator will be met by some misfortune and will see in it the effect of his sin and the powerful curse; he "bears his guilt," *nāśā' 'ăwônô*. He may have heard the curse, and the general belief in the power of the words and a bad conscience collaborate to break his capacity for resistance, empty his soul of power, rob him of his self-confidence and his capacity for self-preservation, and make him weak, perhaps soon even sick. He sees in this the impact of the curse. The hypothetical, prohibitive curse (see below) simultaneously lays a mine under the one who heard it. In the very moment he touches it, he commits an act that is covered with curse; the mine explodes under those who heard it. Consequently, as a rule, no one dares to act contrary to a prohibition accompanied by a curse (1 Sam 11:7; 14:26).

---

10. See below, §2.2.3.
11. Judg 17:2; Lev 5:1; 1 Kgs 8:31; Prov 29:24; cf. Zech 5:1–4.

The curse is always a great danger for the one involved. The magnitude depends on the character of the one involved. If he is just, has a strong, healthy soul, if he has a great blessing, he can meet the danger. He must only take care that he is able to oppose it with as much blessing as possible. When possible, even should it take a long time, he must render the author harmless.[12] If the curse has already begun to work in him, if he has become ill, for example, and believes that the illness was caused by the sorcery curses of some enemies, he must cleanse himself of the impurity as quickly as possible through cultic measures that remove "guilt," procure God's blessed assistance against the unknown perpetrator, and thus stop the source of evil by destroying the agent. The lament psalms of the sick always request this destruction. In and with the destruction of the enemies, the power of the ban is broken.[13] This is true of the people no less than of the individual (2 Sam 21:3). If the one in whom the curse sits is himself unjust, if "curse" (in the sense of sin and injustice) is his nature, then he must sink deeper into misfortune, and the curse (in the sense of execration) intruding from outside will only hasten the end. Consequently, the curse spoken against the criminal, the violent, the sorcerer, and the like is particularly effective (see Num 5:23–24). Thus the curses against unknown sorcerers and enemies are among the fixed components of the atonement psalms (lament psalms).

We may now ask: Who can pronounce (send forth) the effective curse? Given all this, it is clear that the curse can proceed both from evil, "inane" people who have the curse in themselves ("accursed") and from the sound, just person. The evildoer, *rāšāʿ*, is full of curse, and from him curse streams forth automatically. He can, however, consciously and intentionally concentrate the negative power of his soul in word and deed and pronounce disastrous curses. The just, the patriarch (Isaac, Jacob, Moses; Gen 27; 49; Deut 33), the prophet (Balaam, Elisha; Num 22–24; 2 Kgs 2:24; 4:16–17), the priest (1 Kgs 8:31), and the righteous sufferer in the atonement psalms can also speak the curse against the evildoers, however. The curse is to a certain extent the nature of the evildoer, the blessing to a degree that of the just. While the evildoer cannot effectively bless, the just can effectively curse.

This is explained by the fact that the content of the curse presented here as the evil force of existence constituting the nature of the evildoer and expressing the same in disaster-producing deeds and words points to an older, more neutral understanding of this power that expresses itself in disaster. The secondary concept of the morally evil and objectionable, associated with the

---

12. As David did Shimei (1 Kgs 2:8–9).
13. *Psalm Studies* 1:104–10.

concept of the curse especially in the Psalms, did not originally belong to it. The older, morally indifferent meaning is still generally valid, especially when the curse is viewed in the sense of the pronouncement of curse as a means of defense for the just and, under certain circumstances, also as a cultic means of defense (see below). Psalms 10:7 and 59:13 suggest—and the overall perspective of the atonement psalms and similar Babylonian psalms confirm—that *'ālâ* is a synonym of *'āwen* in certain circumstances. As I have shown in *Psalm Studies* 1, this word designates the evil power used for evil purposes, in addition to the actions and means that serve these purposes—in brief, what, according to a purely historical determination of the content of the concept, primitive thought considered to be sorcery. Doing *'āwen* in the Old Testament includes all the special circumstances and secret magical practices that were universally considered to belong to the evil sorcerer (night and darkness, intercourse with demons and the spirits of the dead, mysterious formulas, rites and gestures, etc.). The fundamental meaning of the word, however, is power (*'āwen* > *'aun* < *'ôn*), the mysterious power that can be found everywhere but that is particularly at home in individual persons and objects and that can be employed by particularly skilled individuals to achieve all their objectives and to fulfill all their wishes, regardless of whether these objectives and wishes are beneficial or harmful, "good" or "evil" for other people. The original content of the curse concept should also be conceived accordingly. The curse is actually the procedure and means (words) through which the "power" is set into motion with the intention of making another harmless, of breaking his power, of destroying him, as well as that power released for this purpose; the two belong together, since the Hebrew always thinks in totalities. The curse falls under the heading of good or evil depending on whether that "other" is an enemy of the righteous, of the community, or of the individual "just" person. The one cursing appears, accordingly, as the sustainer and defender of legitimate rights and good. Alternatively, the one to be cursed is a good, just person and the one cursing a person who, in a self-serving manner, breaches the rights of the other. In the latter case, it is sorcery, in the former *fas* or *jus*, under certain circumstances, even cultic rite, religion. Hence, it is a short path to the understanding presented above that the curse is evil power, in general, the destructive, the "void," that constitutes the essence of the villain, an understanding we encounter especially in the Psalms. The older understanding survived alongside it, however.

2.2. The Curse in the Cult

2.2.1. Given what we have said above, one can easily understand that the curse also constituted a part of the cult, both private and public. The curse is the use of the mysterious power for harm, or specifically, the evil, harmful might in addition to its use for harm. It does not matter with respect to the use, to the person of the originator, to the nature of the object, or to the purpose of the curse whether the curse is to be assessed as legitimate defense, as a good, beneficial act, as a religious procedure, or as a prohibited, secretive, evil activity, that is, as sorcery.[14] If some arbitrary person wants to bring harm to his "brother" or gain advantage over him in a prohibited and illicit fashion and does so with the aid of the secret powers and arts through "an evil curse," religion and cult have nothing to do with it. It is sorcery. Thus we are not concerned here with this kind of "curse." We saw above, however, that the just person can and may also use the curse as protection and defense against and as punishment of the evil and disastrous powers and beings of life. Originally and essentially, curse was only a particular use of the psychic power accessible to him; later it was the evil power to be pitted against evil—just as one must meet sword with sword, fire with fire, repay evil for evil (see Ps 18:26–27). When the just person resorts to the curse to sustain his just cause and to defend against evil attacks that seek to "pervert justice" for him and thereby continues to maintain himself and to gain advantage, he does so precisely because he is just, because he has the capacity for self-preservation that belongs to the just, because, in the final analysis, he stands in covenant with the deity. The rites and solemnities related to the "sending forth" of the curse belong, however, in the sphere of the religious, cultic procedures. This becomes completely clear when it involves not the cause of an individual but that of the community, the tribe, the people, the congregation. When the people or the congregation, threatened by some danger, by overwhelming enemies, or by corruption and profanation through some unknown evildoer carrying out his insolent game in its midst, resorts to the curse as a means of protection, defense, and punishment, it does so, of course, in solemn forms, through certain representatives of the community called for that purpose, and in alliance with the community's deity. This means, however, that we are dealing with a cultic procedure. Whether that occurs in the interests of the whole community or in the interests of the individual whose justice has been particularly perverted or threatened is essentially insignificant. Behind the individual stands the community that has a particular interest in the "vindication" of its "brother" and supports his efforts with all the powers at its disposal, with its whole power for blessing and curse. Just as we have worship procedures such as baptism, marriage, burial that pertain, in the first instance, to an individual but that are nonetheless experienced and evaluated as congregational proceedings, so did

---

14. See the excursus in ch. 1, n. 25.

ancient Israel. We see this when, for example, the purification of a leper (Lev 14)—and, we may add, undoubtedly all other healings and purifications of the sick[15]—takes place in the temple or at the holy place, the appropriate sanctuary. In every case the sacred rites and words infuse the whole psychic power inhabiting the community and administrated, as it were, by the cultic priest into the enemy of the community and of the individual as a power destructive to the enemy and, consequently, evil for it. This takes places through the cultic curse.

We can point to a plethora of analogies to such cultic curses. Only a pair of the best-known will be mentioned here. The declaration of the major ban in the Roman Church is an occasional cultic curse. Words and "symbolic" actions accompany one another here in the old, primitive manner. Lamps are thrown to the floor and extinguished. Thus the lights of the accursed are removed from their place.[16] In ancient times the reading of a curse formulary against various categories of sinners belonged to the regular Maundy Thursday worship.[17] The synagogue also knew the major ban. Here, too, the curse was involved. It transitioned into the New Testament as the ἀνάθημα.[18] The curse against the Minim, or all manner of heretics, including Christians, introduced in later times was in fact a regularly pronounced curse.[19]

2.2.2. The more a priori observations above are now fully confirmed by our texts. We find the cultic curse both as occasional and regularly repeated components of the Israelite-Jewish cult.

We turn first to the curse against the specific perpetrator of a specific misdeed and then meet, first of all, the ban. We read in Josh 7 what took place when someone committed a severe crime. As perilous guilt, as a sin that sought to have effect, it burdened the community with a curse that sought to translate into misfortune. It then became necessary to render the one concerned harmless with all the means available to the community and radically to stop the source of curse flowing from him. The procedure reported here is a cultic procedure. Achan had stolen goods that belonged to the deity. Consequently, YHWH's wrath weighed heavily on Israel. It must be appeased, YHWH propitiated; stated more primitively, the misfortune streaming from

---

15. *Psalm Studies* 1:139–63.
16. See, for example, "Exkommunikation," *RGG* 2:787–89.
17. See, "Bulla in coena domini," in (the Catholic) *Kirchenlexikon* (2nd ed.).
18. See the brief summary in Paul Volz, *Die biblische Altertümer* (Cologne: Komet, 1914), 241–42.
19. See Emil Schürer, *Geschichte des jüdischen Volkes im Zeitalter Jesu Christi* (4th ed.; Leipzig: Hinrichs, 1909), 2:543–44.

the black soul and the evil deed of Achan must be banned by bringing the stated black soul to nonexistence. For this important affair, the entire people assembled. It sanctified itself, tht is, it put itself in a cultic state, cleansed itself from everything profane and from all "constraints" so that the force of its soul might concentrate as energetically as possible on the imminent sacred procedure, so that it might put as much force as possible into its sacred act. It must now "remove the evil from its midst" by means of a "curse" that would shatter all resistance. For this, it required concentration, the intensification of psychic power. Consequently, everything profane must be removed from it and from the body—body and soul belong together. Through the lot, the guilty party will be identified. Thereby YHWH himself will have pointed him out. Now, the chieftain and priest—in this case, Joshua—steps forward and, as representative of the community and holder and administrator of the community's sacred powers, pronounces the powerful curse meant to hit Achan at the core of his being and destroy him, cutting off the source of his life: "Just as you have brought us into misfortune, may YHWH bring you into misfortune today."[20] Thereafter the community stoned him along with his whole household. Finally, his curse-filled soul was rendered harmless and bound forever to the dead body by the erection of a large pile of stone over the corpses. The stones with which the execution was performed were probably originally understood, not just as a physical means to kill in our sense but as material bearers of the curse's power.

In this case it was possible to discover the guilty party. The community could, therefore, assist the power of the curse somewhat with their own vigorous actions. This is not always possible, however. One cannot always discover the criminal. One must leave the execution of the death penalty contained in the curse entirely to the power of the curse formula or, more precisely, to the power of the psychically powerful representative of the people infused into the formula through the cultic proceedings. If something has been stolen or if some other secret crime has been committed, one has a curse pronounced against the perpetrator so that he will be stricken by the power of the curse (Judg 17:2; Lev 5:1; Prov 29:24). If items of lesser value are involved, it may be that the one robbed may suffice with his own curse power. In more important cases, one turns to a person with particularly strong psychic power so that, by observing certain rites considered legitimate and sacral by the whole community, he may send forth the curse. One sees from 1 Kgs 8:31 that cultic procedures are involved. The curse is spoken from the altar, probably before

---

20. The wordplay between the verb ʿākar and the place name ʿākōr makes it doubtful that we have the original wording of the curse formula here.

the gathered congregation (see Lev 5:1; Prov 29:24), so that, with its "Amen" it may infuse its whole psychic force into the curse and probably also so that as many as possible may hear it and it will be that much easier to find its person. If one had no other means to affect a criminal, this was certainly the customary way. The one cursing was, of course, the priest, in earlier times, the "seer," who, as guardian of the temple, was simultaneously the "priest" in that time[21] and who as "man of God" had a particularly powerful soul and could, consequently, exert a powerful curse effect. The seer or the priest played precisely the same role here as the medicine man of the primitive peoples or the privately practicing, charlatan master of witchcraft in progressive cultures.[22] We are dealing here with quite primitive orders. The historical period probably understood this curse, for the most part, as an appeal for YHWH to intervene.

In other cases, the curse was addressed to future or potential perpetrators of some evil. The purpose of the curse, then, is prohibitive, apotropaic, not, as in the previous cases, directly punitive.[23] The curse is placed on the practice of this or that act. It is comparable, then, to a loaded but unexploded mine. Examples include the curse that Joshua placed on any who would rescind the eternal ban extended over Jericho (Josh 6:26) or Saul's curse against those who would take something to eat on the day of the battle before the enemy was completely destroyed (1 Sam 14:24). Here, too, we are dealing with procedures surrounded by sacral rites and measures to be considered cultic procedures. In Josh 6:26, Joshua, the leader of the people, pronounced the words. Like Moses, he was originally thought of as both priest (guardian of the sanctuary, "seer") and chieftain. In a later time, when priesthood and chieftainship became distinct,[24] a priest (see Neh 5:12) assisted or entirely replaced the respective leader of the people in the curse procedure. In analogy to Deut 27:14–26 (see below), the formula was something like, "Cursed be the person who eats bread before the evening" (1 Sam 14:24). We have occasional reports of an accompanying "symbolic," that is,

---

21. See *Psalm Studies* 3:501–7.

22. The last comparison clearly shows us the difference between cult (the original) and sorcery (the degeneration).

23. See Pedersen, *Der Eid*, 103–7.

24. This "later" time arrived for Israel as early as the immigration and the first occupation of Canaanite cultic sites. Canaan probably already had a professional priesthood. If we may trust the Mosaic legends, however, during the wilderness period the chieftain was originally considered the priest, just as, for example, in ancient Norway and Iceland. He may also occasionally employ a servant as guardian of the sanctuary, like Moses employed Joshua. Still, in later times the king also retained priestly status and occasionally also priestly functions.

efficacious, procedure (Neh 5:13). The process in these cases was as follows: the priests administered an oath to the whole people, causing every individual to swear that he or she would respect Nehemiah's measures. Thereafter, Nehemiah placed a curse on acting contrary to the obligations. While doing so, he shook his cloak and said, "So may (or, better, should) God shake from his house and possession any who does not observe this legislation; so may he be shaken out and empty." To this, the whole people responded, "Amen! So be it!"

The cultic procedure described in Num 5:11–31 is also one of the conditional cultic procedures. It is explicitly stated here that the curse will only be effective in the event that the one concerned has actually committed the evil of which he is suspected. In this case, the cultic curse has the full character of an ordeal. If a man suspects his wife of adultery, he is to bring her to the priest and as well as a sacrifice in the form of a cereal *minḥâ*. This sacrifice is described as a jealousy offering, *minḥat haqqin'â*. In terms of purpose, it is a "remembrance offering, meant to bring to memory the guilt (of the wife)," *minḥat zikkārôn mazkaret 'āwōn*. After the wife has been presented before the deity with her hair let down, and thus in the state of mourning of the accused, that is, of one who is no longer just and is thus placed in the accursed state, and the "curse water" has been prepared, the priest puts the *minḥâ* in her hands. It alone should bring her guilt or innocence to mind. Then the priest adjures, *hišbîaʿ*, her, declaring that the curse water will not harm her if she is innocent. By contrast, if she has sinned against her husband, she will be affected by the following "curse oath," *šĕbûʿat haʾālâ*. He then imposes the curse by having her "take an oath," that is, by having her say "Amen" to an adjuration. The curse formula was: "May YHWH make you a curse (i.e., one filled with curse, who acts as a curse that causes misfortune) and an 'adjuration'[25] in your people by causing your loins to atrophy and your belly to swell; may this curse water enter your bowels to cause your loins to atrophy and your belly to swell." To this, the woman was to respond "Amen, Amen" and thus assume the curse. The actual procedure follows, actually a duplication of the curse for purposes of intensifying the effect. The curse formula was written on a *šēper*, probably a piece of papyrus, and the writing was washed off in the "curse water" (*mê hamĕʾārûrîm*). The priest had previously prepared this water from "holy water" (*mayîm qĕdōšîm*), consecrated water, which contained hyper-physical forces, by mixing dust from the floor of the

---

25. One sees here how fluid the transition between "oath" and "curse" is. The oath is often a hypothetically imposed curse (Pedersen).

sanctuary[26] into the water. Curse clung to the dust. The "accursed," the unfortunate, and the impure sat in the dust. Dust belonged to the realm of curse, to the underworld, where, according to the Gilgamesh Epic, "dust lay on all the crossbars." Dust is the food of the accursed serpent, which was originally an underworld deity. The mixture of the dust into the water already makes the water the bearer of curse. Now the curse power inherent in the formula is also infused into the water. The woman must now drink this water. Thus the curse enters her and exerts its effect. At the conclusion, some of the cereal offering is burned *lĕ'azkārâ*, to remind YHWH of the matter, so that he may bring the power of the curse to actualization. The effect of the curse and the water—in the event that she is guilty—is that the woman's stomach swells up and her loins atrophy so that, as verse 28 suggests, she is no longer in a condition to bear children. Then she has truly become a "curse" and can no longer exercise a woman's normal occupation. Thus she becomes "for her people," that is, her clan, not only a scandal and a shame but a curse, a misfortune-producing thing that causes misfortune to cling to her whole clan. The curse spreads to the whole family of the sinner, the "curse-possessed."[27] This also explains the second name assigned to the curse water: "the waters of bitterness," that is, "woe and misfortune activating water" (*mê hammārîm*).

Quite clearly this procedure originally had nothing whatsoever to do with the personal concept of God and the related religion of Yahwism. The curse worked entirely *ex opere operato* of its own. There is not even an appeal to YHWH, as J. Pedersen has correctly observed. Only one element of YHWH religion is linked with this ritual, the *'azkārâ* sacrifice, which was supposed to "remind" YHWH of the matter and motivate him to intervene and punish the guilty party. This entirely secondary matter intersects with original idea. If the redactors of the Priestly Document ever adopted ancient material, they did so here. This *torah* would certainly not have been included in P if it had not long since been documented in writing and did not have the air of ancient holiness.

We may certainly assume that every Israelite was convinced that the truth of the matter would come to light through these procedures, and this universal belief in the effectiveness of the curse also surely made it effective in most cases by virtue of the power of the suggestion of the eerie words and rites.[28]

In Num 5:11–12 we are dealing with an occasional cultic procedure. We also have several regularly recurring cultic curses, however, such as the

---

26. It does not matter where the dust came from (Heinrich Holzinger, *Exodus Erklärt* [KHCAT 2; Tübingen: Mohr, 1900]; Pedersen, *Der Eid*, 104 n. 5).

27. See Pedersen, *Der Eid*, 73–74.

28. For the literature on Num 5:11–31, see Bruno Baentsch, *Exodus–Leviticus–Numeri* (HKAT 1.2; Göttingen: Vandenhoeck & Ruprecht, 1903).

document in Deut 27:14–26, which is very interesting from the perspective of the history of religions and which one sometimes refers to as the sexual dodecalogue.[29] This designation is incorrect to the extent that we are certainly not dealing here, as Ernst Sellin thinks, for example, with "an offshoot of the Decalogue."[30] The situation is rather the reverse. The brief collections of cultic and ethical commandments that we have[31] as the conditions of the covenant in J, E, and the Decalogue[32] are to be explained in relation to the combinations of such casuistic, cultic curses and blessings. In its current context, this passage looks like the execution of Moses' prescription in Deut 27:11–13 concerning a solemn imposition of blessing and curse on a specific occasion (see below). The completely different role of the Levites in verse 12 and in verses 14–26 indicates, however, that this connection is secondary, as most of the older critical commentators have seen. Sellin contends, however,

---

29. Thus, e.g., Hugo Gressmann, *Die älteste Geschichtsschreibung und Prophetie Israels* (vol. 2.1 of Die Schriften des Alten Testaments in Auswahl; ed. H. Gressmann et al.; Göttingen: Vandenhoeck & Ruprecht, 1910), 253ff. For additional comments on Deut 27:14–26, see addendum 2, p. 777, below.

30. Ernst Sellin, *Einleitung in das Alte Testament* (3rd ed.; Heidelberg: Quelle & Meyer, 1920), 31.

31. Originally one wanted to assure the "commandments," the primary principles of the community, both cultic-ritually and morally, through the cult. Consequently, their transgression was backed by the curse, their observance supported by the blessing. At cultic celebrations, in fact, the Australian tribes, for example, communicate the principles of the tribe to youths and instruct them in their observance. Later the commandments gain their own life, as it were, can appear without cultic supports, and stand as God's commandments that require precise observation as such. Of course, this does not mean that they were not formerly divine commandments, too. Even the divine commandments are inculcated through the cult, however, and their observance ensured because the cult intends to ensure absolutely everything that is fundamental for the society. More below.

32. The Decalogue was not the original covenant document in E. It has clearly been interpolated in its current position, as Carl Steuernagel (*Das Deuteronomium* [2nd ed.; HKAT 3.1; Göttingen: Vandenhoeck & Ruprecht, 1923]) maintained, for example. The "Covenant Code" (the name "Mishpat Collection" and the sigla M^1 would be more accurate) in Exod 21:1–22:16 along with later additions (M^2) in Exod 22:17–27; 23:1–9 was interpolated later in E, perhaps by R^{JED}, and certainly later than R^{JE}, since otherwise this redactor could not have understood the covenant conditions of J in Exod 34:14–26 (dodecalogue) as a repetition of those in E (Steuernagel). We have E's covenant conditions in Exod 20:23–26; 23:10–19, which, in the main, parallel those of J and from which it is possible, without doing violence, to extract a Dodecalogue by removing later expansions and doublets. The designation "Covenant Code" in E (Exod 24:7) refers to these covenant conditions. Unfortunately, I cannot give a more precise justification here. Despite the efforts of many recent scholars to show otherwise, the Decalogue in Exod 20:2–17 cannot be older than the exile.

that the connection is "original" and stems from E, that Deut 27 originally followed Deut 11:29–30, and that our passage is "a section of the liturgy customary for the celebration of covenant-making in Shechem (after the reading of the Covenant Code)."[33] In verse 14, "the Levites" is an insertion, and the circumstance that the Levites in verses 11–13 appear as a tribe like the others indicates the antiquity of these verses. In my view, these are largely unproven and indemonstrable claims. As I try to show elsewhere,[34] Deut 6–11 is entirely secondary and stems from an exilic edition of Deuteronomy, while the original introduction of proto-Deuteronomy is found in Deut 1:1–3:20; 4:1–2. In its current form, Deut 11:29–30 is only a secondary redactional preparation for chapter 27, although it traces back to a comment in E. This comment may have once stood in connection with Deut 27, but this chapter grew up out of many layers[35] and the connection of verses 14–26 with the other content of the chapter is secondary.[36] It is not impossible per se that an annual covenant festival was celebrated in Shechem. As an enthronement festival, the annual fall festival was simultaneously a festival of covenant renewal.[37] This festival, however, was not celebrated in Shechem only. It attained its apex in Jerusalem. The old claim by Kuenen that the Covenant Code[38] "originally," that is, in the work of E, had the place that Deuteronomy now occupies is not impossible; it is even quite likely. In the given case, however, the original E did not create this circumstance, but a later elaborator, an E^2 or E^3 did. M originally existed independently and was later inserted into the Elohist's covenant conditions.[39] J and E wanted to be narrators, not legislators. Each brought legislative material restricted to a dodecalogue and a set of covenant conditions. If it was not P^g, as is now generally recognized, who brought an extensive Mosaic legislation, then it was certainly not E. H and D were the first to do so. With regard to verses 11–13, I see in the circumstance that Levi is a tribe alongside the others here no evidence of particular antiquity but, to the contrary, evidence of a later, but still rather old, construction. There was certainly never a "secular" tribe of Levi.[40]

---

33. Sellin, *Einleitung*, 31.
34. See my *Ezra*, 104–5.
35. So Gressmann, *Die älteste Geschichtsschreibung*, 156ff.
36. See below, chapter 3.
37. See *Psalm Studies* 2:294, 326–33.
38. More accurately, the Mishpat Collection (M), see n. 32, above.
39. See n. 32, above.
40. The word *lēwî* originally mention nothing other than priest. There was no more a tribe with the name "priest" than there was a "family" with the name "Valley of the Craftsmen" (1 Chr 4:14).

No trace of a reason can be given for striking the Levites in verse 14. In addition to the argument derived from the differing significance of the Levites in verses 13 and 14, the disagreement between the two sections in terms of content also contradicts the original literary unity of the sections Deut 27:11–13 and 14:26. Verses 14–26 do not offer the blessings that we may and must expect after verses 11–13.[41] We will see below that Sellin may still have been correct in that a substantive relationship between verses 11–13 and 14–26 may once have existed, namely, in the liturgy.

Sellin is surely correct, however, that we have in Deut 27:14–26 a section from a liturgy. Considered alone, the section does not narrate a unique event in connection with the immigration but gives the words of a regularly repeated cultic procedure. Unfortunately, nothing is said about the occasion on which the passage was used. It seems most likely to think, with Sellin, of one of the great annual festivals and then, most likely, of the grand annual festival, the fall festival in the month of Tishri. The passage contains, in brief summary, the most important principle commandments of the society, the transgression of which is a "breech" of the "covenant" that makes the land and the people unclean and must therefore be assigned a curse. This summary has not been connected with the supposedly Mosaic Book of the Covenant, Deuteronomy. As mentioned above, the grand fall festival, however, was simultaneously a festival of covenant renewal. The circumstance that the passage has not been connected redactionally with the immigration into Canaan speaks further for an original relationship to this festival. In ancient times the fall festival was simultaneously the festival of the exodus from Egypt, which only achieved its objective with the immigration into Canaan.[42] One may compare the combination of these two facts in the festival psalm, Exod 15, which is linked to the fall festival, YHWH's royal festival, through the reference to YHWH's kingship.[43] If R connected the piece with a postimmigration celebration mentioned in E, namely, in Deut 27:1–3*, then it could represent a reminiscence of the original cultic context of our passage.

In its current form, the passage is post-Deuteronomic; that is, it is presupposed that YHWH's *tôrâ* mentioned in the twelfth curse refers to Deuteronomy (v. 26). The current recension cannot be significantly younger than Deuteron-

---

41. This observation also contradicts Gressmann's assumption (*Die älteste Geschichtsschreibung*, 156ff.) that Deut 27:14–26 continues Deut 11:26–31 and that the whole is a variant of Deut 27:1–13 (and Josh 8:30–35 and Josh 24). The continuation of the cultic rites presupposed here must have been a bipartite liturgy of blessing and curse (see below, ch. 3).

42. See *Psalm Studies* 2:233–36.

43. Regarding the fall festival as an enthronement festival, see *Psalm Studies* 2, part 1. On Exod 15, see ibid., 2:236.

omy either, because it does not understand the "Levites" to be the subordinate temple servants that developed from the former rural priests rather quickly after the introduction of Deuteronomy but from the priests. It was the priests' responsibility, not that of the lower temple servants, to pronounce the cultic curses and blessing. "Levites" here still has the old pre-Deuteronomic meaning. This connection of the passage with Deuteronomy is clearly secondary, however, because the first eleven curses are addressed to transgression of both commandments that appear in Deuteronomy and those that are not codified there.[44] Since the twelfth saying speaks of those "who transgress the words of this law," the eleven preceding prohibitions cannot be understood either as an excerpt from "this law" in the sense of "Deuteronomy"—why, then, commandments that do not appear in Deuteronomy?—nor as an addition to it—why repeat something that is already present? On the other hand, the number twelve is surely original. The original twelfth curse has thus been replaced by another. Originally, verse 26 may have had *'et hattôrâ* or *'et tôrōt yhwh* in the sense of "everything (else) Israel considers commandments of God." The expression does not envision a closed, documentary law code but other divine commandments the violation of which was covered by a curse. Thus, the passage is pre-Deuteronomic and contains material regarded as a kind of liturgical, religio-moral catechism, an interesting thematic parallel to the dodecalogues in J and E and to the Decalogue, but, as noted above, a preliminary stage from a formal perspective.

The time when the piece originated cannot be determined. It is only certain that it is younger than the dodecalogues in J and E, for it prohibits both carved and cast images, while they only proscribe cast images.[45] The marked prominent interest in sexual sins also points to a somewhat later time, when the old tribal ethics and the natural sexual morality of a still self-contained tribal culture were dissolving. On the other hand, it is surely older than the Decalogue, since the Sabbath, which was a major commandment in later times, is not even mentioned here. This also points to postexilic origins.

From a formal and liturgical perspective, the twelve curses constitute a striking parallel to the Roman *Bulla in coena Domini*, which are not to be understood as an imitation of Deut 27:14–26 but as having arisen independently from entirely different historical preconditions.[46]

We cannot say where the curses belonged in the worship service. At some point, however, the priests stepped forward and pronounced the solemn

---

44. Verse 18 = Lev 19:14; v. 21 = Exod 22:28; Lev 18:23; 20:15; v. 22 = Lev 18:9; 20:17; v. 23 = Lev 18:17; 20:14.

45. Exod 20:23 (E); 34:17 (J).

46. See the reference in n. 17, above.

curse on those who were stained by some mortal sin and who thus by their mere existence constituted a danger to the community. The curse here had both a punitive and an apotropaic character. It was supposed to find both those who had already committed such sins and those who may do so in the future with its deadly power. In particular, mention was made of those sins that are otherwise difficult to trace, such as secret sexual sins, in addition to those considered the most serious crimes: idolatry, manslaughter or murder, perversion of justice, and displacement of boundary stones, a crime the ancient Semites considered as base and detestable as did the ancient Nordic Germans and contemporary farmers. The form of the words is brief and lapidary; every clause falls like a merciless blow of the axe: "Cursed be the one (*'ārûr hā'îš*) who curses father or mother! Cursed be the one who displaces the neighbor's marker! Cursed the one who assassinates the neighbor!" The congregation and, thus, each individual, assumed each of the twelve curses with a unanimous, threatening, "Amen! So be it!" Thus each individual called down upon himself the whole disaster of cursedness if he should be guilty. May evil be far from Israel! One may suppose, perhaps, that the whole ceremony belonged at the beginning of the worship service, analogous to the τὸ ἅγιον τοῖς ἁγίοις at the beginning of the Eucharist in the early Christian community and the positive statements at the beginning of the procession ceremony in the temple courts in Pss 24 and 15. The apotropaic character of the rite became even more prominent in this way. Who among those present who was guilty of one of these sins and thus signified an imminent danger to the community and who was now preparing to view God in its midst would dare to assume the curse on himself with his "Amen"? Must he not expect immediately to be met with the divine wrath, on the spot? The "fear of God" would surely be visible on his face in the same instant! Who can stand before the ravaging flame of the God appearing to the community in the cultic festival?[47] Thus the cultic community could feel assured that, after these repulsive words, no "curse-bearer" hid in its midst.

2.2.3. All the cases treated above in §2.2.2 involve curses against domestic enemies and evildoers in the midst of the community. We may assume with certainty, however, that the curse was also employed as a powerful means of protection and defense against external enemies in the hour of crisis or danger. It was, indeed, the task of the community's cult leader to obtain blessing and to render the community's enemies powerless, to put them in the

---

47. See Isa 33:14 and *Psalm Studies* 2:307. We have an eschatological echo in Isa 33:14 of the very attitudes associated with the questions in Pss 24 and 15.

state of cursedness, to smite them with the curse. Thus the curse must have also been solemnly cast in the cult against the people's enemy, perhaps at the occasional lament ceremony because of the threat of attack or defeat in war.

Direct examples of such curses have not been transmitted to us, although the Balak-Balaam legends clearly presuppose the practice itself (Num 22–24). It may not be objected that the Israelites are not involved here, but the Moabites. The legend quite obviously has the Moabites behave—undoubtedly for good historical reasons—just as Israel tended to behave in similar cases. Balak of Moab felt threatened by the approach of the Israelites. Since he did not feel up to open battle with them, he favored weakening the enemy through cultic measures, hitting them with a powerful curse at the core of their soul and power so that it would be easier to overpower them with this military might and to expel them from the land. So that the curse might be as powerful as possible, he sends for a famed man of God, the seer Balaam, from a distant country. As man of God and seer, Balaam is a man of great psychic power, a man who stands in continuous and direct connection with the sacred power, with the source of power, or, as they would later say, with the deity, and thereby can always fill his soul with new power. Balaam came, and the sacred cultic procedure took place. Through cultic procedures at the sacred place, especially through sacrifice, that place the "seer" in even more intimate connection with the deity and powerfully increases the force of his soul, the necessary psychic preconditions for the cursing should be created. These sacrifices are described as sacrificial meals (see Num 22:40). Originally it was surely the power inherent in the sacrificial flesh that was thought to increase power. The "covenant" enacted in the sacrificial meal, in which the others infuse their wills and souls into those of the leader so that they gather all their wishes with his around the purpose of the procedure, increases the power of the one cursing even more. Quite literally, he feels his soul swelling with power. Now he can pronounce the powerful curse.

In the current form, the original meaning of the account has been obscured. Later generations forgot the original, generally cultic, and priestly vocation of the seer and saw him almost exclusively in the image of the later *nābî'*, whose calling was above all else to communicate predictions of the future. These *nĕbî'îm* could only communicate what God had showed them or what the spirit spoke through them. Accordingly, the subsequent words of Balaam were also understood more as predictions than as effective blessings. Originally, it involved effective words that the "seer" was supposed to speak from the "power" of his soul, words that did not depend on what God showed him or said to him, but were always supposed to correspond to the demands of the historical and political situation. If the community and the king required it, the one gifted with power, who was originally always primarily a servant of society, had to pronounce the words that strengthened his own community but weakened the enemy. In a much later time the *nĕbî'îm* in Israel were also asked to do so.

If the king in particular repeatedly required the prophets not only to predict the outcome before a military campaign but also the king's victory and the defeat of the enemies, and if hesitation to do so was understood as high treason,[48] the related presupposition, as ever more scholars have recognized, is that the word of the prophets not only predicted the future but as an efficacious word influenced and created it. Through his word he actually put victory in the king's soul and defeat and "shame" in the souls of the enemy.[49] The prophetic words that pronounce the defeat of the enemies amid solemn cultic procedures[50] were, by nature, a curse meant to break the power of the enemies. Indeed, they actually did break it, or at least restricted and threatened it.[51]

Thus, we understand not only that prayers to YHWH prayed at similar cultic celebrations for vengeance on the enemy and for its destruction are essentially curses,[52] but also that they exhibit in form as much of the curse as of the prayer. We will find examples in subsequent paragraphs.

2.3. Curse Psalms

Like the cultic blessing, the cultic curse also left traces in cultic psalmody. We encounter it as a component of the cultic song both in the congregational cultic celebrations and in the cultic procedures performed for individuals. We begin with the congregational psalm.

2.3.1. Given what was said above (§2.2.3), I find it quite natural that the national lament psalms against the enemy of the people or of the community are the locus of the cultic curse. Prayer for assistance and revenge and curses against the enemy go hand in hand here. The communal lament psalms are to be understood, beyond question, as cultic psalms for public days of

---

48. See 1 Kgs 22 and the Jeremiah narratives, esp. chs. 27–28 and 38:1–13; note v. 4.
49. See Sigmund Mowinckel, "Om mebiisme og prefeti," *NTT* 10 (1909): 335–42.
50. See Jer 28:1, "in the temple of YHWH before the priests and the whole people."
51. See Pedersen, *Der Eid*, 86–87.
52. "In the Muslim understanding, the curse is a prayer to God. The same word that means 'prayer,' *dū'a*, also denotes the pronouncement of the curse" (ibid., 86). Of course, as Pedersen observes, this is not original. He points out the same transition from curse to prayer, although always with the preservation of the essential elements of the old understanding of the curse, among other Semitic peoples.

repentance and prayer. In Ps 83, the lament concerning the attacks of united neighboring peoples precedes the prayer:

> Do to them what you once did to [ ]⁵³ Sisera, to Jabin at Kishon Brook,
> who were exterminated there at En-dor and became dung on the field.
> Make [ ]⁵⁴ their nobles like Oreb and all their princes like Zeʾeb [ ].⁵⁵
> Those who said, "Arise, we will take for ourselves the pastures of [YHWH]."
> Make them, O my God, like chaff, like stubble in the wind,
> as when fire consumes the forest, as when blazes scorch the mountains;
> hunt them with your storm and terrify them with your gale;
> fill their countenance with shame[ ]⁵⁶ so that they perish in ignominy.⁵⁷

This is a true curse. Formally it is a prayer, however. If one wishes to know how an old cultic curse formula went, one need only change the imperative with YHWH as subject into a jussive, as verse 18 has. The self-acting curse is original. In earliest times, one resorted to it at cultic celebrations before war. With the development of the religion and the prominence of the concept of a personal God in Yahwism, the curse became a prayer that called on YHWH himself to intervene with his destructive power. We also hear similar tones, although not as clearly as here, in the other songs of communal lament.

We find cultic curses not only in the occasional national lament psalms but also in the more regularly recurring congregational prayers and laments. Psalm 137 is a genuine cultic curse psalm. The tradition recounts that it was sung⁵⁸ at the annual lamentation on the 9th of Ab instituted after the restoration as a commemoration of the destruction of Jerusalem in 586.⁵⁹ According to Jacob, the account may refer to synagogue worship.⁶⁰ Of course, this does not rule out the possibility that the synagogue has adopted a custom already practiced in the temple. In fact, it must be maintained that, if Ps 137 was composed for the cult, it must have been intended for such a celebration. Furthermore, it is difficult to understand why it should not have been composed for the cult. This assumption is always the most likely for an ancient book of

---

53. "Like Midian" is an insertion.
54. Strike the suffix in *šītēmô*.
55. "And like Zebach and Salmunna" is an insertion.
56. Strike v. 17b as a gloss on, and the first two words in v. 18 as a doublet of, v. 18.
57. Move *ʿădê ʿad* after *wĕyōʾbēdû*. Verse 19 is a later insertion.
58. Sopherim 18 (according to Benno Jacob, "Beiträge zu einer Einleitung in die Psalmen," *ZAW* 16 [1896]: 145).
59. See Zech 7:3 and 2 Kgs 25:8.
60. Jacob, "Beiträge."

cultic songs. It will be difficult to produce evidence that our psalm was not composed as a cultic psalm. Thus we will be well-advised to stick with the information in the tradition.

In terms of style and content, the psalm is a communal lament song, not occasional, like Pss 44, 74, 79, 80, 83, and 89, but a regularly repeated song requesting liberation from permanent distress such as Ps 90. It ends with a severe curse on the people that, more than all others, made it difficult for the Jews to abide the memory of the great catastrophe; the Edomites more than any other people were the object of their burning hatred. The current text speaks, however, of Babylon (v. 8) despite the quite clear beginning in verse 7, and most exegetes correctly permit this nonsense to stand. Paul Joüon wants at least to change "Babylon" to "Edom," while Briggs has suggested the only correct solution, namely, to strike *bat bābel haššědûdâ*.[61] It is clear from verse 7 that the prayer for revenge is directed against Edom. Quite remarkably, the poet drops the Edomites subsequently and directs his entire hatred against Babylon in verses 8–9. One absolutely expects a treatment of how God should remember the Edomites' atrocities against Israel. Evidently, however, as Briggs and Buhl have already noted, verse 9 does not actually have Babylon in mind, as it absolutely should, given its current context. The word *hassāla'* unquestionably constitutes a clear allusion to the capital city of the Edomites by the same name. In addition, there is the witness of the meter, which, in any case, has little significance for the defenders of the "mixed meter" they call the macarism meter. The entire central section of the psalm (vv. 4–7) clearly manifests pentameter, as does verse 9a (the *'et* in verses 4 and 6b is entirely superfluous and is to be attributed to the copyist). The same meter can also be restored without difficulty in verses 1–3. In verse 1, *bězākrēnû 'et ṣîyōn* is a materially correct but entirely superfluous gloss. In verse 3 *śimḥâ* is missing in the LXX but could also be placed after *dibrê šîr*. The fact that, in terms of meaning, an *'āměrû*, perhaps, should be supplied after *wětōlālênû* causes neither substantive nor stylistic difficulties. Thus it should be clear that the pentameter was also the original intention in verse 8, and as soon as one decides with Briggs to strike the thematically objectionable words *bat bābel haššědûdâ*, which are also related to the superfluous *lāk*, then the meter is in order. The fact that we attain a song with such a thoroughly regular structure confirms these text-critical operations: three strophes of four five-beat periods that correspond precisely to the logical arrangement.

---

61. Joüon cited according to Buhl, *Psalmerne*; Charles A. Briggs, *Psalms: Critical and Exegetical Commentary* (ICC; Edinburgh: T&T Clark, 1906).

Because Edom, the former brother, exploited the opportunity in 586 to make common cause with the Chaldeans and to plunder Judah and, long after the return of the exiles, controlled great sections of ancient Judean land claimed by the reestablished community, they were regarded as the true hereditary enemy of the Jews and hated as a type of the outrageous and God-despised secular power that would meet with eschatological judgment before all others.[62] The desired vengeance on Edom became almost synonymous in eschatological expectations with the last judgment and the complete restoration of Israel. We see in Ps 137 how this attitude found expression in public worship.

The purpose of the ceremony of lament and penitence was to do penance and thereby to awaken God's sympathy and motivate him to forgive sins and to restore. We see here, however, that one was not satisfied with the simple prayer for the punishment of the oppressors but also wanted to hasten it, in quite ancient fashion, through the powerful word. The cultic curse was meant to prepare the way for restoration by smiting the enemy with misfortune. Whether in this late period this ancient meaning of the curse was consciously in mind may be doubted. The concluding strophe of the psalm is probably to be understood more as a direct expression of welling hatred and the thirst for revenge. In the depths of the soul, however, lay still half-slumbering the old idea of the effective word that is sent out against the enemies. Here, too, the curse has adopted the prayer form,[63] although only in part. The second half still has the direct form of the self-acting word (see below).

The psalm, which expresses the attitude of the returning exiles, begins poignantly by recalling the dull despair of those once captive when they were surrounded in a foreign land by the arrogance and the poorly concealed triumphalism of the enemy:

By the rivers of Babylon we once sat and cried [];
on poplars there we hung our harps.
For there our captors desired "songs,
our plunderers" (said), "Sing us some Zion songs!"

In the land of many rivers and streams where willows and poplars grew on every bank, in the fat and fertile land of Sinar, there they sat on the ground crying and in despair, as mourners do. Joy and jubilation were stilled. The

---

62. See Isa 34 and Sigmund Mowinckel, "Zu Deuteronomium 23:2–9," *Acta Orientalia* 1 (1923): 86–90.

63. See above, §2.2.3 (725–27).

harps hung silent on the branches of the trees. So the poet paints the picture before us with wondrously vivid clarity.[64] There they also experienced the greatest ordeal known to ancient Israel: the harsh lack of comprehension and willful, arrogant derision. There their "plunderers" demanded of them joy and gaiety: "Sing us some Zion songs." The songs of Zion are the old cultic songs, the festival songs that once resounded at the joyous processions when YHWH visited his people. Singing and festival belong together; singing and joy belong together. The song of Zion resounds where YHWH lives and sojourns, personally, in the midst of his people. Then these foreigners came and desired songs of them—immediately! The poet laid out this picture because most of the Jews of the postexilic period still lived under the same dull oppression. They knew this feeling all too well. All of life in the ancient Holy Land was, after all, only a puny reflection of what they had once hoped for when Deutero-Isaiah raised his lovely voice and boomed out his inspired songs. Everything turned out quite differently. The community lived in a state of permanent oppression. The fulfillment of the "messianic" hopes was not yet to be seen. This is the dreary attitude that also expressed in Ps 90. How could they, then—and, actually, how could they even now—sing the old triumphant songs of Zion? That is the content of the second strophe:

> How could we sing YHWH songs in a strange land!
> O Jerusalem, if I forget you, may my right hand [wither],[65]
> my tongue cling to my gums if I do not remember you,
> if I do not place Jerusalem above all my joys!

To sing Zion and YHWH songs abroad while Jerusalem lay in ruins smitten by YHWH's wrath would be mockery, indeed, blasphemy. It would be infidelity to one's city, one's people, and one's religion. May I be cursed if I were ever faithless! Those are not just sounds from the past. All of this has quite current significance. How could we forget the shame in which Jerusalem still sits, without king, without Urim and Thummim (see Ezra 2:63), while her lord, the booth of David, has fallen to the pagan king in a foreign land? Israel is not even sovereign in its own land—indeed, the accursed Edomites sit in the whole south, even in Hebron where the monarchy of David was once established! Before the eyes of the poet rises the image of the faithless brother. His behavior in the Holy Land and the not-yet avenged atrocity that he fell like an

---

64. Obviously, this may not all be taken as a literal description of the historical reality. Poetry is poetry.

65. Read *tikḥaš* (BHK).

assassin on the back of the mortally wounded Israel, made common cause with Israel's enemies, became for the poet, as it did probably for most of the poet's countrymen, the symbol of foreign dominion, the humiliation of Israel, the daily visible expression of the fact that Jerusalem still lies as though in bonds and looks in vain for the promised salvation. The desired vengeance on these hereditary enemies became the symbol of the great "messianic" judgment that will one day destroy the pagans and restore Israel to full glory. The poet does not think of Babylon. The majesty of the Babylonian Empire had long since ceased. Furthermore, it is noteworthy how little we feel of the hatred toward Babylon in the actual postexilic period. This is probably related to the fact that the mighty and influential Jewish colony, whose help at the royal court the Palestinian Jews could not do without,[66] now lives there. All hatred gathers on Edom's head. As long as Edom has not been humiliated, Israel's honor has not been restored; it has received no "vindication." Thus the psalm has come to the main point, the prayer for revenge, the curse on the enemy:

> Remember against the Edomites, O YHWH,
> the day of Jerusalem's sorrow,
> when they said, "Tear down, tear down, level it to the ground!"
> [¹]Blessed be the one who requites you for what you did to us;
> blessed be the one who grasps your children
> and smashes then against the "rock"!

The third strophe is the climax and focal point of the psalm. The emotional reminder of past attitudes is not the main point, to which the prayer for vengeance is appended, as it were, as the result of a mood that suddenly appeared in association with the main attitude. Rather, the whole poem aims at the curse and exists for its sake. The song seeks Jerusalem's well-being; it intends to evoke this well-being. The means to well-being, however, is the destruction of the enemy, of whom Edom is the type. In accordance with the religion of both Judaism and the historical period of ancient Israel, the psalm seeks to obtain vengeance and well-being through a prayer to YHWH. In accordance also with the earliest views of the people, however, views that survived and exerted influence far down into the historical period, the prayer changes back to the curse form in the second half of the concluding strophe. The form of the curse is unique, however. It is the form of the blessing! It is, one might say, an indirect curse. Through the beatitude, which is only a form of blessing,

---

66. See the intervention and the sending of Nehemiah and Ezra and of the Jew Hananiah in the Sachau Papryus 13464 (no. 6 in Ungnad, *Aramäische Papyrus*).

power and good fortune is infused into the soul of the one who will destroy Edom and make the hated people into a "curse" among the nations. By giving its future opponents blessing and power, Edom is weakened and covered with a curse.

We have in Ps 129 a psalm with a liturgical curse, although in rather dampened form. The liturgical call in verse 1 and the repetition in verse 2 (see the equally certain liturgical psalm Ps 118:1–4, where the same form of call occurs) already suggests that the psalm was composed for liturgical use. According to the superscript, the psalm is one of the *ma'alôt* songs used in the celebration of the fall festival. It is one of those psalms of the annual festival that pray for help against all conceivable enemies of the community.[67] The prayer, however, has the original form of the curse. In contrast to the truly occasional national lament psalms, it is not directed against a specific enemy but requests, as a regularly repeated congregational prayer, protection and defense against the enemy in general, whoever it may be. Clearly the psalm originated in the later period of the people's history. Israel looks back here on a longer, sorrowful history, although it need not be postexilic. A more precise dating is impossible, however.

The psalm begins with a confidence motif in the form of the psalm of thanksgiving.[68] Confident of YHWH's saving acts experienced in the past, the people may hope that he will also henceforth smite their pertinent enemies with a curse. The confident thanksgiving for past saving acts is supposed to put YHWH in a gracious mood and motivate him to intervene further. In addition, of course, one should also note that this introduction intends to express the confident attitude that gave rise to the psalm. Israel feels confident in defense against all enemies. If the form of the antiphonal song, with call and response, is more than an ancient literary form, it is most likely that the choir leader sings the first semi-strophe in verse 1. The choir of singers representing the people takes up the word and extends the idea. Interestingly, this psalm, which exhibits the old form of the curse instead of that of a direct prayer, also has an archaic contour, since Israel appears in the first-person singular. This is an original and accessible form for the old cultic song in particular. In the cult, the professional leader represents the people.[69] The choir leader begins:

"They have oppressed me harshly since my youth,"

---

67. *Psalm Studies* 2:307, 312–13.

68. Meanwhile, Balla (*Das Ich*, 73) is unjustified in assigning the psalm to the public songs of thanksgiving. The central point is the curse, not thanksgiving. It comes under consideration only as the confidence motive for the petition inherent in the curse.

69. See the excursus in ch. 1, n. 64.

Israel will say!

As stated, the choir joins in and adds the actual point of this retrospective:

> They have oppressed me harshly since my youth,
> yet they did not prevail over me.

The congregation reflects on all the humiliations, all the misfortunes that have repeatedly bent it to the ground throughout many centuries. As tenaciously and elastically as a steel spring that can be bent but not broken, Israel always looked to the heights, remained standing, hoping for the grand restoration, waiting on the turn of fate while empire after empire fulfilled its mission and crumbled to dust. Israel has YHWH, he who is "just," ṣaddîq, who has a covenant with the people and who also has the power to maintain himself, his covenant, and his people. He manifests his ṣĕdāqâ when had aids Israel to victory:

> The plowers plowed long furrows on my back.
> Yet YHWH is just; he shattered the yoke of the godless.

In the manner of Israelite poetry, the images change abruptly and suddenly. Israel was both plowed land and plow animal, servant to all and suffering severely.

In the second half, the last two strophes, the real focus of the psalm follows: the curse in the untranslatable form of the Hebrew jussive, which expresses both the powerful, creative wish and also the faithful certainty that the words will be fulfilled. One must always vacillate as to whether to translate "may it happen" or "it should happen":

> All Zion's enemies should be ashamed and give ground,
> become like the grass on the roofs that withers before it [shoots],[70]
> with which the reaper does not fill his hand, nor the binder his bosom,
> and about which by-passers do not cry out,
> "YHWH's blessing be upon you!" [][71]

Here, too, we have the abrupt transition from one image to another characteristic of Israelite poetry. The poet speaks of the singed, rootless grass on the roof in expressions that suit only the grain in the field. He does not think of the fact that no one could expect that the grass on the roof should "fill" the

---

70. Read ḥălōf, BHK.
71. Verse 8b is a variant of v. 8aβ.

hand of the reaper or the bosom of the binder who follows him selecting the cut ears and binding them into sheaves and that no one would be likely to pronounce a harvest blessing on these withered plants. Unnoted, he shifts from the grass to the image of the grain harvest. It is equally characteristic for him independently to elaborate and lovingly color an individual element, a detail in the context, in this case the metaphor with the grass or the grain, as though it were a major element in the structure of the song.[72]

This psalm is characteristic of the terseness of the old religious concepts. The poet wants to write a congregational prayer, a prayer for God's defense against all enemies. Precisely because he wants to say a prayer, he begins with the motif of thankful confidence. Instead of a true prayer, however, there follows a curse with the ancient conception of the self-effective cultic word. Here explicit thought about YHWH and his help recede into the background entirely.

2.3.2. The fact that the cultic curse also had its place in the individual psalms of lament, the psalms for sin offerings, is simply self-evident according to §2.2.3. These psalms are, almost without exception, written for the use of a sick person or a person otherwise unclean at the sin offering and the associated purification rites in the temple.[73] In the view of ancient Israel, illness and impurity were very often caused, however, not by a sinful deed on the part of the sick person but by the evil arts of some secret enemy. The lament psalms repeatedly complain about these unknown enemies who have produced illness and distress. The means by which these evil people—demons are also occasionally in mind—have made the pious and just person sick are those encompassed throughout the world in the concept of black magic, as it was in Israel. Sick persons complain about the sorcery (*'āwen*) of their enemies and the evil *pōʿălê 'āwen* almost as a rule in the lament psalms. With these terms, the ancient Israelite designated all secret and illegitimate powers and arts through which an evil being can cause a person harm. Naturally, these powers and means also include the power and the harm-producing curse word and act if they are employed by an evil person for evil purposes. We have seen above in §2.1 that curse and sorcery are related to one another. If the curse is employed as the weapon of an evil person for evil purposes, it is sorcery. Thus

---

72. Particularly representative in this respect is the lament psalm of the innocent, Ps 139, in which an individual motif, the "innocence motif," with the reference to the omnipotence of God, who also knows the supplicant and knows that he is innocent, is expanded into a consideration of God's omnipotence in general, quantitatively occupying the largest part of the psalm and laying claim to the focus of our interest.

73. On the following, see *Psalm Studies* 1.

'āwen and 'ālâ are sometimes treated as synonyms.[74] Just as "the evil curse" is a designation for sorcery in the Babylonian and Assyrian lament psalms, so is the curse in the Psalter. The sorcerer employs the evil, destructive power which the curse per se is, secretly to harm a just person—this is his sorcery.

The enchanted and cursed, those who have become sick and unclean, must break this harmful influence. They can do so in one of two ways. First, they can create purity and blessing through cultic purification rites and thus drive out the evil from body and heart. Second, they can stop up the source of evil, rendering harmless the author of the evil curse, exterminating him from the surface of the earth. One does this, however, by sending out against the sorcerer an even more powerful, but now beneficial and thus good and legitimate, curse. In order to do so, one must, of course, strengthen oneself with psychic power, with "righteousness" and with "blessing." One acquires these, in fact, through cultic purification, with YHWH's aid through the mediation of the priest. The harm-producing power and the state of misfortune produced thereby, which the Israelite designates with the word "curse," were, as we have seen, originally ethically indifferent, neutral. The art of cursing ultimately depends on the capacity to control the secret powers of existence or to be connected to them. Thus, as we have seen, the just can also curse by virtue of his psychic power. Through connection with the deity, he intensifies this capacity. If, therefore, the sick person, cleansed once again in the cult, sends out a powerful countercurse in the context of cultic purifications, or if the sacred representative of the deity, the priest, joins in such a curse, it contains so much sacred and harm-producing[75] power that it can surely break the power of evil. The sacred power that stems from the deity, is in itself neutral. It is available to the priest to strengthen and intensify his psychic power and is made available, as it were, to the sick person through the sacred purification procedures. It now acts as a harm-bringing curse for the evil sorcerer. Evil is used against evil; evil is cast out by evil. The legitimate curse that serves the well-being of the community and belongs to the sacral system breaks the evil, harmful, secret curse, which, as such, belongs to the realm of sorcery.[76]

---

74. So in Pss 10:7; 59:13 (cf. vv. 3, 6). The terms *qĕlālâ* and the verb *qillēl* occur in the same meaning in Pss 37:22; 62:5; 109:17, 18, 28. See *Psalm Studies* 1:20.

75. The sacred can also be harm-producing, especially for the evil person or for the one who makes unauthorized contact with it (see 2 Sam 6:7; Isa 8:12-15, where, of course, *taqdîšû* should not be amended to *taqšîrû* in v. 13 but, conversely, *qešer* should be changed to *qōdeš* in v. 12).

76. Regarding this understanding of sorcery as an illegitimate, private use of "power," neutral in itself, for evil and selfish purposes, see Nathan Söderblom, *Gudstrons uppkomst*

Thus we must assume that curses and rites originally probably pronounced or performed, respectively, by the officiating priest constituted a fixed component of purification procedures and words accompanying the sin offering for the sick and suffering.[77] Rites such as those described in Num 5:11–31 support this assumption, as does the analogy of the Babylonian cultic lament psalms that often mention the related curse rites and formulas and as does, finally, the circumstance that the curse and prayer for vengeance occupy such a prominent place in the individual lament psalms in the Bible.[78]

When we find these curses in the psalms as components of prayers to be spoken by the sick or, more likely, in his name by the priest, they should probably actually be viewed as the stylistic influence of the priests' curse formulas. Originally, the sick probably cited the prayer or a priest recited it in his name, but the priest performed the procedures that banned and destroyed the sorcery and the sorcerer and pronounced the appropriate curse. Since, on the one hand, however, in the Semitic understanding there was a close relationship between prayer, especially prayer for help, and vengeance directed against someone,[79] and since, on the other, it often, perhaps always, happened that the priest also spoke the prayer in the name of the sick person, it was natural to combine the two kinds of effective sayings and to furnish the prayer with more or less stylistically authentic curses. Thus the old cultic curses quite clearly influenced the individual lament psalms, and one can infer from the latter how the former must have been worded.

We may still have in Ps 109 an example of a once-independent cultic curse formula pronounced during the purification and sickness-banishing rites. First, the original form of the self-acting word is clearly preserved. Formally, the words exhibit no trace of a prayer and also clearly differ to this extent from the otherwise closely related words in Ps 69:23–29. Second, there is also a clear difference between the concept of the enemies who cause the illness in the curses and in the other parts of the psalm. In the song of lament proper (vv. 1–5, 21–31), the supplicant portrays his enemies as a great host that "surrounds" him and "wars against him" (v. 3); they stand around him and derisively shake their heads (v. 25). Verses 6–19, in contrast, consistently

---

(2nd ed.; Stockholm: Gebers, 1914), 181ff. See also *Psalm Studies* 1:63–76; see also the excursus in ch. 1, n. 25).

77. So already Gunkel, "Psalmen," *RGG* 4:1946.

78. See Pss 5:11; 10:15; 28:4; 35:4–8; 40:14–15; 55:16; 63:10–11; 69:23–29; 70:3–4; 109:6–20; 140:9–12; 141:10; 143:12. Cf. the prophetic imitations in Jer 12:3; 15:16; 17:13; 18:21–23; 20:11.

79. See above, 727.

discuss only an individual who has caused the supplicant's misfortune.[80] All of this may indicate that a fixed curse formula has been incorporated into the psalm. Verses 23–24 imply that the psalm is meant as the prayer of one, that is, any, sick person offering a sin offering for purposes of restoration. As a sick and unclean person, the supplicant is despised and taunted by his neighbors because he has thereby been situated as a sinner (vv. 25, 31). The cause of his misfortune is his (secret) enemy's evil, misfortune-producing words of sorcery. With an "evildoer's mouth," "deceitful words," and a "lying tongue,"[81] they have made him sick, although he has no guilt in the matter (vv. 2–3). He states explicitly that they employed curses against him (*qillēl*, v. 28). Now their magical curse will be broken by a powerful, legitimate countercurse. By all appearances, the poet adapted the words of this countercurse from an existing formulary. Since, in any case, it is characteristic of the curses in the Psalms and the cultic healing rites, I will reproduce it here:

Appoint an [enemy][82] against him; let an accuser stand at his right hand;
let him go out of the court guilty; let his prayer be counted to him as sin!
May his days be few; may another take what was meant for him.[83]
May his children be orphans; may his wife sit as a widow;
may they[84] wander about as vagrants and beg, [driven][85] out of their ruins.
May the creditor take everything that is his
and strangers plunder his belongings.
Let no one show him kindness, no one pity his orphans;
may his fate be to be eradicated, [his][86] name
extinguished in [one][87] generation!

---

80. The childish explanation of many exegetes that, in similar cases, a particularly prominent person among the many (pagan or nonbelieving) enemies is involved, is to be rejected. This varying form of portrayal also occurs in the sin-offering psalms and depends ultimately on the fact that the enemy is unknown. He does not know whether one sorcerer (demon) or many have caused the sickness. See *Psalm Studies* 1:98 and esp. 103 n. 76.

81. The word *šeqer* and its synonyms are quite often synonyms for *'āwen* = sorcery (see *Psalm Studies* 1:43–62).

82. The *rāšā'* in v. 6 is incorrect, of course, and arose through an error of the eye regarding the *r* in v. 7. Originally, it read *'ōyeb* or something similar.

83. That is, in days of life.

84. I.e., the children and wife; *bānāw* is a gloss to be stricken, *metri causa*.

85. Read *yĕgōrĕšû*, LXX; "ruins" is proleptic.

86. Read *šĕmô* instead of *šĕmām*; see BHK.

87. Read *'eḥād* instead of *'āḥēr*, LXX.

May his fathers' iniquity be remembered [],[88]
and let not his mother's sin be blotted out!
Let them be before YHWH's eyes; may he obliterate
[his][89] memory from the earth!
For he did think to exercise love …
but pursued the miserable and poor and the ones [smitten][90]
at heart [to death.][91]
Because he loved the curse, let [it come on him!][92]
Because he did not like blessing, [may it remain distant].[93]
Let him[94] clothe himself with the curse
[like a belt that he wears daily].[95]
Let it [press][96] like water in his insides,
like oil in his bones.[][97]
May this be the reward [][98] of my enemy
who pronounced misfortune on my life.[99]

With respect to specific explanations concerning the person of the "enemy" and the more precise circumstances of his appearance, this curse formulary is just as general and bland as a formulary meant to fit all specific cases should be. The authors of such formularies did not even think of a specific individual or situation. They only wanted to lame "the" typical sorcerer in all cases with an effective course. Nor did sick persons who utilized these psalms and formularies in purifications think of a specific person. Mostly they did not even know who the enemies were who "watched for their lives in secret" and who pushed them into misfortune.

---

88. Strike *el yhwh*, *metri causa* (gloss).
89. Read *zikrô*, LXX.
90. Read *ûnĕkē*; see BHK.
91. Read *lamāwet*, Syriac.
92. Read *ûtĕbō'ēhû*.
93. Read *wĕtirḥaq*, strike *mimmennû*, *metri causa*.
94. Read *wĕyilbaš*.
95. Verse 19b belongs after v. 18aα.
96. Read *wĕtābō'*.
97. Verse 19a is a variant of v. 18aα.
98. Strike "from YHWH," *metri causa*.
99. Kittel's translation (*Psalmen*), "who plan my misfortune," is too dilute. "To speak" is meant literally. The author thinks of words of sorcery and curse.

3
The Bipartite Blessing and Curse Formula in Cult and Psalmody

3.1. The Bipartite Blessing and Curse Formula

The cultic sayings included not just independent blessing or curse formulas. The two kinds of efficacious sayings were combined into a two-sided cultic procedure, blessing and curse, or vice versa.

3.1.1. The passage already mentioned above, Deut 27:1*, 4*, 5*, 6, 7, 11–13, points to such a cultic practice.

Before we can consider the content of the passage, we must burden the reader with a source-critical analysis, however.[1] We read in verses 11–13 that before his death Moses prescribed that, when Israel entered into Canaan, six tribes were to position themselves on Gerizim for blessing (*lĕbārēk*) and six on Ebal for cursing (*'al haqqĕlālâ*). Now, as indicated above, verses 11–13 apparently stand in some relationship to what is reported in verses 1–8. These verses, however, discuss both an altar on Gerizim,[2] which apparently was supposed to be used in the ceremony mentioned above, and also the erection of a great stone (where?) on which the law was to be inscribed (i.e., accord-

---

1. For additional comments on Deut 27:1–13, see addendum 3, p. 778. below.
2. The original text in 27:4 must, unquestionably, have read so originally, as it still does in the Samaritan Pentateuch (see my *Statholderen Nehemia* [Kristiania: Olaf Norles, 1916], 209). Subsequently, Gerizim is the mountain of blessing, and the altar would have doubtless stood on the mount of blessing. Obviously, in fact, the Samaritans would have chosen a previously sacred mountain and not a locus of curse as a sacred site (so also Gressmann, *Die älteste Geschichtsschreibung*, 157). The Masoretic reading "Ebal" is a tendentious emendation meant to rob the Samaritan temple of any appearance of legitimacy. The Jewish accusation against the Samaritans that they falsified the sacred text falls back on their own head.

ing to the current state of Deuteronomy). Joshua 8:30–35, which relates altar, stone, law, and blessing–curse to one another, reports the execution of the prescription. It has long been contended that we have before us here an interweaving of two reports about quite different matters, one of which spoke of stones and the law, the other of an altar. With respect to the sources and age of the two passages, however, opinions differ. Often the whole passage is considered Deuteronomistic or even post-Deuteronomistic. It may be clear that the Deuteronomist,[3] or at least the Deuteronomistic redactor of the "pre-Priestly" historical work,[4] R^{JEDtn}, had a hand in the matter. The copying of the Deuteronomic Code and the solemn public reading of it according to Josh 8:34 are acknowledged "Deuteronomistic" concepts. The observation that we have two pairs of ideas here offers the key: (1) the stones and the law and (2) Gerizim–Ebal and blessing–curse. The altar is only the necessary apparatus for the cultic act of blessing and cursing. Of these pairs of ideas, the stones and the law in their current form belong, of course, to the Deuteronomist; the other stems from one of the historical sources of the Pentateuch, J or E. From which, it cannot be said at the moment.

Meanwhile, as has been correctly noted, the possibility that the Deuteronomist would have independently arrived at the notion of exhibiting the law in one of the rural sanctuaries he proscribed is rather excluded unless he were tied to something similar in his original. The relationship of the whole passage to Deuteronomy depends on the later editing of an extant original. It is unlikely, however, that the Deuteronomistic editor himself would have simultaneously combined the two motifs (blessing-curse, on the one hand, and the erection of great stones, on the other) and reinterpreted the stones as memorials of the law, thus creating a connection that is almost incomprehensible. One must therefore assume that the contamination of two reports and motifs from two different sources was already available to the Deuteronomist or, in other words, was already extant in the work of the Yahwist, JE. One may further conclude that one motif originated with J and the other with E and that they were combined with one another by R^{JE}. If the Deuteronomist, apparently R^{JEDt}, included the complex in Deuteronomy, the

---

3. I.e., the exilic/postexilic redactor of the expanded Josianic law code, who may have also expanded the book with brief "historical" comments concerning Moses' final prescriptions and death. I use the word "Deuteronomic" to designate what was present in proto-Deuteronomy and "Deuteronomistic," in contrast, to denote the later redactional additions both to the version of Deuteronomy not yet linked with JE and to the whole historical work.

4. I.e., the Hexateuch, or, more precisely, the "Deuteronomistic" History—before the inclusion of the Priestly Document (P).

reason was probably that he found the blessing and curse mentioned in the work of JE to be those blessings and curses imposed on those who observed or did not observe Deuteronomy (Deut 28). The next question is: What is the reason for the redactional combination of these apparently disparate motifs? The question is raised here already because its response will give us the clue to finding the end of the string. The reason was probably the fact that both reports spoke of great stones: in one, stones for building an altar; in the other, stones that were meant to serve another purpose. Thus, verses 5a, 6, 7[5] belong to the first report and verses 1*–3, 8 to the second. Verse 4 is a doublet for verse 2 and therefore belongs, in essence, to the first report, but it has been edited and harmonized with verse 2 by R^{JEDtn}. The words *ha'ēlleh 'ăšer 'ānōkî měṣawweh 'etkem hayyôm* and *wěśadtā 'ōtām baśśîd* belong to this redactor. The location information (originally *běhar gěrizzîm*, see above) belong to the original report. Verse 5's *šām* 5 refers back to it, as do the first five words of the verse, "when you have crossed the Jordan, you should take stones." The verse originally read something like: "when you have crossed the Jordan [and have entered the land that I give you], then you shall stand on Mount Gerizim and take [great] stones." After a lacuna (now supplied by the Deuteronomistic verses 9–10) verses 4*, 5a, 6, 7 were followed by verses 12–13, provided with a redactional introductory formula (v. 11); they are not extant in their original wording (more at 745). Originally, a comment parallel to verse 1, of which *wěziqnê yiśrā'ēl* is a remnant, introduced the whole.

The Deuteronomistic redaction of the report affected verse 1*–3, 8 much more significantly. Clearly a reinterpretation of the older report is present here. Indubitably, given the overall situation of the verses, the twelve stones of the law were envisioned as standing on the Jordan. No Deuteronomist on his own, however, would have placed them either there or on Gerizim. Thus it may be considered rather certain that the original narrator, as Hölscher assumes, thought of the erection of twelve memorial stones in Gilgal on the Jordan (Josh 4:3–9).[6] Consequently, we are dealing with the preparation for the report in Josh 4:3–9, indeed, with the Yahwistic strand of the Joshua report,[7] since the twelve stones in Deut 27 are surely envisioned as standing on the bank, not in the riverbed. As stated, R^{JE} combined with this Yahwis-

---

5. Verse 5b is probably a gloss based on Exod 20:25–26.

6. Gustav Hölscher, "Komposition und Ursprung des Deuteronomiums," *ZAW* 40 (1922): 218. Hölscher's source analysis is entirely different from the one assumed here, which follows the more traditional analysis. With regard to Josh 4:3–9, I do not accept Sellin's Gilgal near Shechem.

7. See the source analysis in Gressmann, *Die älteste Geschichtsschreibung*, 139–40.

tic report about the memorial stones in Gilgal on the Jordan the report, to be considered Elohistic, concerning the stones for the construction of the altar on Gerizim. This assumption suddenly explains the whole meaningless geographical gloss in Deut 11:30, according to which Gerizim and Ebal "are situated in the Jordan Valley near Gilgal." This gloss depends on a combination of the two reports in Deut 27:1–13 and represents the desperate attempt by R^{JE} to harmonize. He took the comment in 11:29–30 from the Deuteronomistic compiler of Deut 6–11.

The same Deuteronomistic redactor who edited Deut 27:1–13 also intervened in Josh 8:30–35. We are dealing here, that is, neither with a purely redactional addition based on Deut 27:1–13, as many exegetes seem to think, nor with the relatively original Deuteronomistic model according to which Deut 27:11–13 was inserted by a later redactor to prepare for the Joshua passage. Here, too, source material has been revised by the Deuteronomist. In verse 34, the law is clearly a secondary doublet for blessing and curse. If we excise the redactional additions, the Elohistic report in verses 30, 31aβb, 33 (*hallewîyîm nōśʾeh ʾărōn bĕrît yhwh*), 34a (*kol-dibrê hattôrâ*) remains.

Deuteronomy 11:29, a section of the core stemming from an older source of the pericope, 11:26–30, which is now in Deuteronomistic form, confirms our analysis. The redactor probably thought of the sayings of blessing and curse in Deut 28. The fact that he moved the procedure to Gerizim and Ebal shows, however, that here, as so often in the introductory speeches in Deuteronomy, he has excerpted from older historical sources and that the comment stems materially from E, as is also universally acknowledged. Evidently it cannot depend in its current form on Josh 8:30–35 or Deut 27:1–13. It knows only one motif: blessing–curse, Gerizim–Ebal. The redactor says nothing about the stones and the law. In fact, only the geographical gloss by R^{JE}, which places Gerizim and Ebal in the Jordan Valley, suggests awareness of the second motif, the twelve memorial stones.

After this literary analysis, we turn to the substance: the E account.

Notably, in Deut 27 blessing and curse are pronounced by people who stand on the two mountains (*ʿal*, v. 12; *bĕ*, v. 13), with half the people standing on Gerizim and the other on Ebal, while in Josh 8:30–35 the two groups apparently stand on either side of the altar, one toward (*ʿal-mûl*) Gerizim and the other toward Ebal. Now, since the altar here stands on (*bĕ*) Gerizim—for so Josh 8:30 should be read instead of "Ebal"; see above—both groups stand on Mount Gerizim. It is not entirely clear how we are to envision the situation. If the congregation stands "on" Gerizim, it cannot pronounce blessing and curse "toward" (*ʿal-mûl*) Gerizim and Ebal. In reality, it is very unlikely both that one would enter the mount of curses, Ebal, and that a cultic celebration was ever held in which the two halves of the congregation stood each on a mountain separated from one another by the whole valley, calling to one another. Therefore, the reading 'al-mûl in Josh 8:33 is surely more correct and original than 'al in Deut 27:11–13. We do not have the original wording in Deut 27:11–13. The ceremony will probably have taken place between the two mountains, in the valley below. The altar flanked by the divided congregation was situated there. The variant in Deut 11:26–30 mentioned above, which stems ultimately from E, confirms this assumption. It states that the blessing should be "placed on" (wĕnātattâ) Gerizim and the curse on Ebal. This indicates that the blessing or the curse should be placed on the pertinent mountain so that the power inherent in the words was deposited on the mountain. Thence, blessing or curse would stream forth on the land depending on the circumstances. Deuteronomy 11:30 explicitly says, moreover, that the two mountains were situated "near the oracle terebinth."[8] This terebinth was certainly an ancient sanctuary. The altar near which the words were pronounced will also have stood near it. The comment actually only has a purpose if it is assumed that the cultic procedure took place near the terebinth mentioned. This sanctuary with an oracle terebinth is most likely identical with the sacred site with a massebah and terebinth in Shechem (Josh 24:26). One may assume with certainty that there was an altar there. Accordingly, this sanctuary lay in the valley between Gerizim and Ebal and was not identical with the temple of Baal-berith on the mountain in Shechem (Judg 9:4, 46)—one may not press the expression "in Shechem" in Josh 24:1. In contrast to the Baal-berith sanctuary, which was a building, the sanctuary assumed here was probably an open-air bāmâ, which the whole situation in Deut 11; 27 and Josh 8 requires. How, then, can it be explained that both Deut 27:4 and Josh 8:30 speak of the erection of an altar on Gerizim in connection with this cultic celebration and that Deut 27:11–13 has six tribes each climb the mountains of Gerizim and Ebal for the celebration? It seems to me that Gressmann has given the solution to this difficulty that I could not explain before.[9] In fact, there was also a sanctuary with an altar on Gerizim, and some editor of the Elohistic account confused this altar with the altar in the valley and created the current confusion. Deu-

---

8. Read the singular ʾēlōn (Sam, LXX, Aq, Sym, Theod, V) instead of the plural ʾēlōnê. Judg 9:6 and probably also Gen 35:4 and 12:6 mention this oracle terebinth. Verse 11 is also mentioned in Gen 35:8 and Judg 4:5. Regarding sacred trees, see further Gen 13:18; 18:1; Judg 6:11; 1 Sam 10:2; Friedrich Lundgreen, *Die Pflanzenwelt in der alttestamentlichen Religion* (BZAW 14; Gießen: Töpelmann, 1908), 11–12, 17–25; James G. Frazer, *Folklore in the Old Testament: Studies in Comparative Religion, Legend and Law* (3 vols.; New York: Macmillan, 1923), 3:54–61.

9. Gressmann, *Die älteste Geschichtsschreibung*, 160ff.

teronomy 27:11–13 is not, in fact, the original continuation of verses 4–7* but originates from a later level in E.[10]

E portrayed the cultic celebration assumed here as a unique event performed after the conquest of the land. Through this procedure the land was both taken into possession and provided with blessing for the just and with the threat of curse on everything evil. The fact that according to JE this took place in the YHWH sanctuary of Shechem on Gerizim can be explained by the overarching importance of this sanctuary, both during the period of the northern kingdom and in the "period of the judges." Shechem is the city of Jacob and Joseph (Gen 48:22), the site of Abimelech's monarchy and of Baalberith (Judg 9). At the same time, we have in this report of E a foundational stage for the sanctuary in Shechem.

Now it is inherent in the nature of the matter that the old narrators did not invent the picture of such a cultic celebration. They relied on the customs actually practiced in their time. Thus we can conclude from our passage that a cultic celebration of the kind E described took place in Shechem at certain times in the monarchical period. It is very likely that one should think of a regular repetition during an annual festival, most likely during the fall festival, that truly grand annual festival at which, as we have seen above (723–24), both blessing and curse were imposed. This assumption corresponds to the fact that, according to E, YHWH himself, represented by the ark borne by the priests, is present in the midst of his people (Josh 8:33). As shown elsewhere, the ark played a central role in the great Jerusalem fall festival.[11] The presence of the ark in Josh 8:33 could, indeed, be the free invention of E derived from the circumstances of the recently completed entry. It is difficult to imagine, however, that E could have come to this if it did not correspond to any reality. Indeed, the presence of the ark in the situation he described was by no means necessary.[12]

---

10. It is unlikely that something was inscribed on the stones of this altar in the E account. The motif of the inscription of the words of the law stems from the Deuteronomist, R^{JEDtn}, who reinterpreted J's memorial stones erected on the Jordan in this manner and related them to Deuteronomy. The transfer of the inscription to the altar stems from an even later redactor.

11. *Psalm Studies* 2:283–303 Since the (Jerusalemite) ark was never located in Shechem, according to our sources, we must come to the very likely conjecture that each major sanctuary had its processional ark, an assumption to which Hugo Gressmann has already come by another path (see *Die Lade Jahwes und das Allerheiligste des Solomonischen Tempels* [BZAW 1; Berlin: Kohlhammer, 1920]). With Gressmann, I consider it certain that the ark is a processional vessel, not a "migratory sanctuary."

12. This consideration is not compelling. It is indeed possible that Ernst Sellin (*Gilgal: Ein Beitrag zur Geschichte der Einwanderung Israels in Palästina* [Leipzig: Deichert, 1917],

Accordingly, we can envision the presumptive cultic procedure as follows. The people assemble at the sacred site, slaughter, sacrifice, celebrate a sacrificial meal, and "rejoice before YHWH." After the sacrifice, perhaps as the conclusion of the whole celebration, the priests take up position with the ark in the vicinity of the altar—perhaps the ark was even placed on the altar[13]—the people take positions on either side of the ark, one half in the direction toward Gerizim, the other toward Ebal. At the head of the people stand all its elders and chieftains.[14] Then the leading liturgist—for E, Joshua—steps forward. In the earlier period, he was probably not a priest but a chieftain, perhaps the king of the people.[15] Turning alternately toward Gerizim and Ebal, he pronounces blessing and curse with a loud voice.[16] The statement in Deut 27:11–13 that the tribes arise to bless and curse is to be understood in terms of the two divisions of the people responding with an "Amen" after each element of the multipartite blessing or curse formula (see Deut 27:14–26). We cannot say how the sayings were worded since, as mentioned above, verses 14–26 do not constitute the original literary continuation of verses 11–13. The continuation of the procedure must have taken a course analogous to Deut 27:14–26, however.[17]

One can imagine that the first objects of the blessing or the curse were probably those who observed or transgressed a certain commandment. The blessing was supposed to be deposited as an effective power on Gerizim and thence to stream forth on all those who are "the sons of blessing," as the ancient Israelite might have said, and on those who act in agreement with ancient custom and divine commandment. The curse was deposited as a potentially threatening power, as a personified demon in a certain sense, on Ebal to meet

---

57) and Gressmann (*Die älteste Geschichtsschreibung*, 157; cf. Georg Hoffman and Hugo Gressmann, "Teraphim, Masken und Winkorakel in Ägypten und Vorderasien," *ZAW* 40 [1922]: 88) are correct that the ark was secondarily inserted in Josh 8:33 and 7:6. One must then also assume an Elohistic foundation in v. 3, however. The *ziqnê yiśrā'ēl* speak for E. Now, since *mizzeh ûmizzeh* seems to require a continuation, one must probably assume that *lammizbēaḥ* originally stood there instead of *lā'ārôn*, etc., as in v. 30–31. Even then, however, the insertion of the ark could have been borrowed from a common cultic practice, especially if, as seems inevitable to me, one may assume that every large cultic site had its "ark"; see previous note.

13. 1 Sam 6:15 supports this assumption.

14. The *šōṭĕrîm* who, according to Josh 8:33, were also present, have probably been inserted based on Deut 16:18.

15. See 2 Sam 6:18; 1 Kgs 8:14, 55.

16. Josh 8:34: *qārā'*.

17. Despite the different understanding of the literary question, my understanding here has very close substantive affinities with Sellin's (see above, 721–25).

all those who do what YHWH hates. The blessing should be shared with all those who are just and walk in YHWH's paths and, along with them, with the whole land if the people per se is just. The curse should befall all enemies of the people, all the evil powers of the land, all the godless and evildoers, all the "fools" among the people, criminals and sorcerers, and so on, and along with them the whole land if such are tolerated in the midst of the people. In other words and with a religious motivation, blessing is for the one who keeps YHWH's commandments, and curse is for the one who transgresses the commandments.

Formally we should probably imagine the sayings on the analogy of the curses in Deut 27:14–26: Blessed be the one who does thus and so! Amen! Cursed be the one who does thus and so! Amen!

Thus salvation and blessing are created annually for just people or for the nation and individuals to the extent that they are just, but misfortune for all evildoers and everything evil in the land. Under the protection of this dual power, the pious Israelite may enjoy the fruit of his righteousness.

If this procedure belonged to the fall festival, it involved a covenant. The passage speaks, then, of the blessing that follows if the people have observed the covenant and kept its provisions. The curse concerns the violators of the covenant conditions. The great fall festival was the festival of covenant renewal.[18] This still shines through in Deuteronomy when it relates the rite to the Deuteronomic commandments. To this extent, it correctly interpreted its original. E certainly discussed the making of a covenant.[19]

Consequently, this observation also leads to the conclusion that there may have been a substantive relationship, despite literary disparity, between the celebration reported in Deut 27:1–13 and the liturgical passage in 27:14–26. A corresponding blessing may, in fact, have once belonged with 27:14–26, and this liturgy may have had the form deduced from 27:1–13. It must only be emphasized that the curse in the form transmitted in 27:14–26 must have belonged, then, to the most recent liturgical forms of the pertinent festival.[20] The festival and the related practice of blessing and cursing are much older than the form of the liturgy we have in Deut 27:14–26.

A peculiarity of the ritual deduced from Deut 27:1–13 is that both the blessing and the curse were localized in this place. Since then, the blessing has dwelt, so to speak, on Gerizim, the curse on Ebal. The fact that the blessing is at home at sacred places in concentrated form, as it were, also has parallels in

---

18. *Psalm Studies* 2:294, 327–29.

19. Gressmann also interprets the passage in this way (see *Die älteste Geschichtsschreibung*, 156ff.) and is correct to parallel it with Josh 24.

20. See above, 724.

the Old Testament (thus, e.g., in Ps 133:3: "for there [on Zion[21]] YHWH has offered the blessing"). In ancient Israel this idea was absolutely self-evident. Blessing is present in its strongest form at the sacred sites. From there, it flows forth on the land. Remarkably, however, a curse-originating site located in the midst of the land is discussed here as a counterpart. Otherwise, the wilderness is the proper locus of the curse.[22] Admittedly, it is true, as Pedersen says, that there is no objective demarcation between the land of human beings and blessing, on the one hand, and the land of wilderness and curse, on the other. The land of curse surfaces here and there in the midst of the land and lives of human beings, especially where blessing is absent or has disappeared. Ebal is regarded as such a place here. We may surmise that the mountain was already regarded as a mountain of demons and evil powers before the rise of the cultic site discussed here, somewhat like the Hinnom Valley was later. There are such places in the popular belief of almost every people at every time. We can offer only vague suspicions[23] concerning whether the basis for this belief was analogous in this case to the basis for the reinterpretation of the Hinnom Valley, that is, whether a cult proscribed early on by the Israelites was once practiced on Ebal, perhaps a cult of the underworld, a Nergal cult,[24] or a cult of the dead.

Now, the redactional combination of Deut 27:1–13 and 14–26 is substantially established to the degree that we must imagine the sayings spoken in the rite presupposed in 27:1–13 on the analogy of the curses in verses 14–26. They may have been worded as follows: "Blessed be the one who does or does not do thus and so," and "Cursed be the one who does or does not do thus and so." Although blessing and curse were imposed on the land and each was localized at a specific site, blessing and curse were, in fact, imposed directly on the

---

21. Thus according to MT. It may be, however, that one should read ṣiyyâ. Then, šām points to the concept to be derived from the preceding: where brothers, i.e., compatriots, dwell together, where they have their "spiritual"—we would say—focus, i.e., given the overall attitude of the psalm, where they assemble for the cult and receive blessing (see *Psalm Studies* 2:344).

22. See Pedersen, *Israel*, 1:455–56.

23. An understanding of the processes presupposed in this passage similar to mine, already recorded in a first version in 1918, appears in Gressmann, *Die älteste Geschichtsschreibung*, 159–60. He views the passage as a variant of Josh 24 and links the cultic procedure with a "covenant-making," which I have also indicated by relating it to the fall festival. The fall and enthronement festival is a covenant festival (see *Psalm Studies* 2:294, 327–29.

24. The cylinder seal of "Atanaḥili, the son of Habsi, the servant of Nergal," found in Taanach, suggests a Nergal cult in pre-Israelite Palestine (Ernst Sellin, *Tell Taanek: Arbeit un Sitte in Palästina* [Denkschrift der Akademie der Wissenschaften, Philosophisch-historische Klass 50; Gutersloh: Vienna, 1904], 27–28).

individual perpetrators of this or that good or evil deed. Given this, it is very reasonable to assume that there was once a counterpart to the curse formulas in Deut 27:14–26 whereby blessing was imposed on the just. As mentioned above (705–8), we would then have echoes of such blessing formulas in Pss 15 and 24 and perhaps also in the "moral catechisms" of Ezek 18. Indeed, ultimately the combinations of the most important religious and moral commandments into brief "decalogues" or "dodecalogues" will trace back to such morally hued cultic sayings of blessing and curse. We will outline this latter relationship somewhat more extensively here.

3.1.2. It should be rather clear that a stylistic relationship exists between the cultic words of blessing and curse and the brief commandments in the "catechisms." This relationship is also usually assumed in one form or another such that priority is to be sought either in the commandments or in the curse formulas. Thus Gressmann and many others call the curses in Deut 27:14–26 "the sexual dodecalogue," while Seillin views the same as "an auxiliary of the Decalogue." The relationship, however, is not just stylistic but substantive and genetic. I dare to assert that the (do)decalogues developed from the cultic blessing and curse sayings and, as a genre, were originally connected to the cult. The presupposition here is obvious, in my view: the Decalogue in Exod 20 and Deut 5 is not the creation of a Moses who founded a cult-less religion but is, instead, much younger than the (do)decalogues of J and E.[25]

It must be established, first, that brief compositions of divine commandments and prohibitions unquestionably originated from cultic blessing formulas. As we have seen above (705–8), Pss 24 and 15, along with their eschatological imitation in Isa 33:14–16 and the prophetic allusion in Mic 6:6–8, demonstrate this. These commandments stand, as certain formulas of blessing and curse already did,[26] in relation to the cult of the fall and New Year's, that is, the covenant-renewal festival, and were publicly read there. As we have seen, both the curse formula in Deut 27:14–26 and the prototype of the celebration described in Deut 27:1–13 also point to the same festival (723, 746–50).

This situation already makes it seem possible that the solemn reading of such brief "catechisms" as the (do)decalogue stood in some connection with cultic celebrations. Another circumstance also points to this. These brief legal collections are transmitted in the tradition as "covenant codes," as YHWH's conditions for the covenant. We know from other clear indices that the fall and New Year's Festival was celebrated as the festival of covenant renewal, as

---

25. See ch. 2, n. 32, above.
26. See 674, 676–78, 683–86, 694–96, 706–7, 723, 733, 746.

an exodus and Sinai festival,[27] and that psalms and liturgies that belonged to this festival inculcate YHWH's conditions and laws for the covenant (Pss 81; 95; 132; 50). It thus becomes very likely that, at one time in some cultic context in relation to this festival, brief summaries of the divine commandments were proclaimed and inculcated. A few additional features of the tradition should be mentioned in this context. In Exod 24 E offers a depiction of the covenant ceremony at Sinai. On this occasion, "the Covenant Code," that is, the covenant conditions now dispersed in Exod 21–23, the "dodecalogue" of the Elohist,[28] were proclaimed, and then the covenant was made. It is likely from the outset that E did not freely invent the details of this festival but depicted it on the model of a festival celebrated in his time. The public reading of the Covenant Code[29] may also have been one of these details. The public reading of Deuteronomy at Josiah's covenant renewal would not have, therefore, been an absolute novelty. Further, attention should be directed to Deut 31:10–13. It prescribes that Deuteronomy should be read publicly every seventh year to the whole community during the fall festival. This is an innovation to the extent that it refers to the "Josianic" book of Deuteronomy. It is certainly based, however, on an older practice. If this should represent only an entirely secondary repetition of the public reading at Josiah's covenant renewal, it is incomprehensible why the ceremony was not shifted to the Passover Festival (see 2 Kgs 23:21–23) and, instead, that the fall festival in particular was chosen. Otherwise, several traces are evident in the latest period of a preference for Passover as the major annual festival.[30] Apart from the replacement of the older brief dodecalogue with Deuteronomy, the innovation in Deut 31:10–13 may consist in the establishment of the time: "after every seventh year, during the Sabbath Year." It is possible that divine commandments were originally read publicly during the fall festival every year but that a change to "every seventh year" was based in the fact that the large book of Deuteronomy was no longer to be read in entirety. That would generally have been too much for the patience of the audience.

This assumption also explains the change of the original "the laws of YHWH" in Deut 27:26 into "the words of this law," that is, of Deuteronomy, discussed above (724). The curse formulas in Deut 27:14–16, which were apparently associated with the great annual festival in the fall, always referred, then, to a public reading of the divine commandments undertaken during this

---

27. *Psalm Studies* 2:233–36, 326–33.

28. See ch. 2, n. 32, above.

29. Not to be confused with "M," Exod 21:1–22:15! For additional comments on the Covenant Code, see addendum 4, p. 779, below.

30. See *Psalm Studies* 2:380–85.

festival. After 622, however, the explicit mention of the great legal corpus valid henceforth was interwoven into the formulas.

Another circumstance, namely, the formula introducing the materials transmitted, also points to a—quite specific—cultic origin for the (do)decalogue. The introductory formula of the original E-(do)decalogue has now been lost as the result of the activity of R^{JEDtP} and has been replaced by the corresponding P (and Dtn) Decalogue, Exod 20:1–17. The introduction to the J-dodecalogue has been significantly altered by later revisions and by combination with E but is contained, beyond doubt, in Exod 34:6b–7. The words are absolutely not suitable in the mouth of Moses, as the current context suggests. The subject of *wayyiqrā'* in verse 6 is, without question, to be sought in the first "YHWH" and *'ănōkî* should be inserted before the second "YHWH." Further, *nōśē' 'āwōn wāpeša' wĕḥaṭṭā'â* is a gloss on *nōṣēr ḥesed* and *wĕnaqqēh lō yĕnaqqeh* is a transition to what follows made necessary by the aforementioned gloss. The phrase *wĕ'al bĕnê bānîm* (= *'al šillēšîm*) is also a gloss. As the original introduction remains: "I am YHWH, a merciful and gracious God, patient and rich in mercy and fidelity, who maintains mercy for thousands and visits the guilt of the fathers on their descendants to the grandchildren and great-grandchildren." This formula is not very old and seems to have been composed from two different formulas. The beginning, "I am YHWH," is significant, however. This formula, widespread throughout the ancient Near Eastern world, is the standing expression for the introduction and self-presentation of the self-revealing God, the deity coming for the epiphany. The fact that the concept of the epiphany of the deity was, from the outset, cultic and that, accordingly, the relevant formula was a customary cultic formula may not be lightly doubted. In ancient Israel, however, the cultic epiphany of God was, without question, linked with the fall festival. Thus the "I am YHWH" formula of the J (do)decalogue also points to a relationship with the fall, enthronement, covenant-renewal Festival.

The introduction to the P (and Dtn) decalogue (Exod 20:1–17; Deut 5:6–21) speaks even more clearly on this point. Its wording was: "I am YHWH your God, who brought you out of Egypt."[31] This formula is generally regarded as "Deuteronomistic," and correctly so, to the extent that the Deuter-

---

31. The phrase *mibbêt 'ăbādîm* is probably a later Deuteronomic gloss. In the Gunkel Festschrift, Hans Schmidt ("Mose und der Dakalog," in Ευχαριστηριον: *Studien der Religion und Literatur des Alten und Neuen Testaments* [ed. Hans Schmidt et al.; FLRANT 36.1; Göttingen: Vandenhoeck & Ruprecht, 1923], 90–91) has attempted to demonstrate that the words above could not be the original introduction to the Decalogue. Instead, they are to be found in Exod 20:5b–6. I cannot consider his reasons convincing but must reserve the opportunity to go into the details for another place.

onomists preferred it very much. They did not invent it, however. Rather, the diction of the Deuteronomists often echoes old cultic language. This formula is clearly a cultic epiphany formula that points to the fall festival as much as do those in the J-(do)decalogue. Significantly, it is explicitly attested in connection with the fall festival as the festival epiphany and covenant renewal. We find it as the introduction to the self-revelation of King YHWH coming for the covenant renewal in Ps 81:11, a psalm that is shown by the parallel Ps 95 and by the testimony of the tradition to belong to the New Year's and enthronement festival (epiphany festival).[32] The same is true in Ps 50:7, where the now-lacking second series of the verse must certainly be supplied with "who brought you out of Egypt." I have shown elsewhere that this psalm is also related both stylistically and thematically to the concepts and rites linked to YHWH's enthronement festival.[33] The cultic and mythical situation presupposed by these psalms is as follows: YHWH comes again to assume kingship over his people and the earth. He reveals himself to renew the covenant with Israel. Related are both the communication of his name and the reference to the liberation from Egypt, as well as the presentation of his requirements and the conditions for the covenant. In the psalms cited, the formula mentioned introduces, in fact, a reference to the commandments that pertain as the foundation of the covenant. The Deuteronomists depend on this style, which is also related to the introduction of the Decalogue.

Thus, so many traces point to a relationship between commandment collections, fall festival, and words of blessing and curse that one cannot avoid maintaining a genetic connection. Sellin also found this to be true when he characterized the curses in Deut 27:14–26 as an "auxiliary of the Decalogue."[34] The matter is obviously not such, however, as Sellin thinks, that the cultic curses and blessings developed out of the cultic reading of the commandments but the reverse. Whoever has the slightest idea of the natural course of development of religion will know, indeed, that the original situation is that the "just" person is strengthened in the cult through blessing and the villain and violator of the fundamental commandments of society is destroyed by curse. The original cult does not teach; it acts. The cultic inculcation of the fundamental laws underlying the society and the cult, which coincide for the most part with the fundamental laws of human society, develops, however, from the words of blessing and curse. Thus the connection of the cultic blessing with certain conditions develops ("the one who does such and so will be

---

32. *Psalm Studies* 2:329–33.
33. *Psalm Studies* 2:253–54, 333, 3:534–38.
34. Sellin, *Einleitung* (2nd ed.), 31.

blessed" [the preliminary stage of Pss 15 and 24]), as does, further, the admonition ("the one who comes to this place and desires blessing will behave thus and so" [Ps 15; 24]) and the direct instruction ("these are the commandments that YHWH requires of his covenant partners" [dodecalogue; Decalogue; Ps 81; 95; 50]).

The explicit commandments that developed from the formulas of blessing and curse, which were collected in brief "catechisms," bear the full imprint of priestly provenance. Their style is that of the priestly *tôrôt*. At some point they came to be proclaimed by priests at the festival worship services. How and under what circumstances, we do not know. This may have occurred relatively early on. Among the lesser-developed Australian tribes, certain fundamental societal commandments are communicated to youths during the initiation rites for the acceptance of the youth into the covenant of adults.[35] Both J and E probably presuppose the practice. As indicated above, we must assume that the depiction of the institution of the covenant in Exod 34 and Exod 20–24 is patterned on an actually observed cultic practice. J was probably written in the early monarchical period. It is doubtful, however, whether the pertinent passage in Exod 34 belonged to the original state of the book. Apparently we must also take into account later revisions in J. In any case, as indicated above, the introduction of the Deuteronomist in 2 Kgs 23:2 presupposes the practice of reading aloud fundamental religious laws at cultic celebrations. The Decalogue in Exod 20:1–17 and Deut 5:6–21 was also written in connection with this practice, even though it seems doubtful to me whether it was ever meant for a cultic use. In the case assumed here, it probably involved the edification of the exiles in the synagogue, for the exilic origin of the Decalogue still seems to me to be the sole plausible assumption.

The emphasis of the temple *nābî'* on the divine commandments valid as conditions of the covenant in connection with the promises of God's appearance in epiphany (enthronement, etc.) and for covenant renewal, which I have inferred elsewhere from the psalms mentioned above,[36] also links with the priestly reading of the brief legal collections. We may confidently presuppose this practice in the second half of the monarchical period.[37] Thus, finally, the most valuable witness of the moral nature of Israelite religion, the Decalogue, also stems from much-maligned cultic religion, even though here, in contrast to the covenant conditions of J and E, the influence of the great prophets of reform exerted itself.

---

35. Söderblom, *Gudstrons*, 141.
36. *Psalm Studies* 2:208–24.
37. *Psalm Studies* 2:366–80.

3.1.3. In addition to the character of the bipartite blessing and curse formulas treated here, which divides the procedures meant for blessing or curse into several parts ("blessed or cursed be the one who does thus and so"), there was also another type of bipartite blessing and curse formula that did not specify the procedure in terms of the one to be blessed or cursed but, in brief clauses, the effects of the blessing and the curse.

The blessing and curse sayings that conclude the legal collections should be mentioned first. We find the concluding blessing and curse sayings both in Deuteronomy (ch. 28) and in the Holiness Code (Lev 26). This practice is not strictly Israelite per se. We find the same blessings and threats in the law code of Hammurabi, for example. It should be clear that there is a stylistic relationship between Hammurabi and the Israelite laws. A substantive and material relationship between Hammurabi and "Moses" is out of the question. It is unclear, meanwhile, whether pre-Israelite Canaan was directly influenced by Babylonia or whether some common, ancient Amorite cultural material is present here. Still, a stylistic difference is present: Hammurabi, the king himself, is the speaker. Consequently, he is also the one blessing and cursing. In the "optative" blessing and curse clauses, he invokes the intervention of the gods against lawbreakers and petitions for their blessing on those who do not alter or violate the law. In the Holiness Code, YHWH is the lawgiver and the one speaking. Consequently, YHWH speaks in the first-person singular even in the concluding section and explains in indicative clauses what he will do, how he will distribute blessing and curse depending on the individual's relationship to the law. The verbs are, therefore, imperfects or perfect consecutives. It should be clear that this form is secondary. It was most certainly influenced by the style of prophetic promises or threats. Deuteronomy contains a mixed form. Moses speaks and predicts what YHWH will do in imperfect clauses. This form is closer to the actual blessing and curse style than that of the Holiness Code. If this style does not stem directly and exclusively from the cultic formulas of blessing and curse, it very likely still stands in some relationship to it. As we have seen, many indices suggest that there was an old relationship between the promulgation of law and the cult in Israel.

We mentioned above the likely relationship between the cultic blessing and curse sayings and the brief dodecalogues and decalogues. The observations made there lead to the assumption that the brief collections of divine commandments or laws trace back in some fashion not only to the cultic blessing and curse formulas but also that the public reading of such collections and the formulas mentioned had a place in the cultic festivals and that the blessing and curse formulas referred in some fashion to Debarim (Deuteronomy; see Deut 27:26).

Indeed, this partially explains the fixed practice in Israel of concluding the collections of divine laws with sayings of blessing and curse. Thus the Holiness Code and Deuteronomy become indices for the early existence of bipartite blessing and curse formulas in the cult. Uniquely, these formulas place the main emphasis on the description of the effects of the blessing and the curse, as Ps 128 also does.

It seems to me that we have not just the traces and imitations of such formulas but also a direct example of this genre embedded in Deut 28. I mentioned above the form of the words of blessing and curse in Deut 28: "if you keep or transgress the law, then YHWH will (shall) do thus and so to you." Among these clauses influenced by prophetic style, we encounter one blessing and curse formula each that have the fully original form of the self-acting sayings: *bārûk 'attâ—'ārûr 'attâ*. These clauses stand out from their contexts by virtue of the fact that they have a clear poetic and metrical form. If we juxtapose Deut 28:3–6 and 16–19, passages that unquestionably correspond to one another, we obtain a bipartite blessing and curse formulary such as one may have been worded at celebrations of the kind mentioned above, or such as should or may have been used at other occasions when blessing on the just and curse on evildoers was to be pronounced, whether deeds committed should be rewarded or punished or the pronouncement of conditional blessings and curses were involved. The sayings were as follows:

Blessed be you in the city,
blessed be you in the field,
blessed be the fruit of your body,
[blessed] be the fruit of your field []38
[blessed] be the offspring of you cattle,
[blessed] be the young of your sheep,
blessed be your basket and your kneading trough,
[blessed be your oil and your must],39
blessed be you when your come in,
blessed be you when you go out!

Cursed be you in the city,

---

38. "And the fruit of your cattle" is absent in LXX (Luc) and in v. 18. It is a gloss based on v. 11.

39. The isolated three-beat lines parallel one another in pairs, and the combination into pairs was certainly originally intentional. In this case, however, an element is missing in v. 5. Our formula is clearly imitated in 7:12–13. The lacking element can thus be supplied on the basis of 7:13.

cursed be you in the field,
cursed be your basket and your kneading trough,
[cursed be your oil and your must],[40]
cursed be the fruit of your body,
[cursed] be the fruit of your field,
[cursed] be the offspring of you cattle,
[cursed] be the young of your sheep,
cursed be you when your come in,
cursed be you when you go out!

This formula, and the whole chapter, for that matter, is characteristic of the ancient understanding of the content of blessing and curse. Blessing is, in a word, the gift of success; curse is failure. For the one who has blessing (*habbārûk*), everything succeeds, and that is particularly evident in fertility. For the one who has curse (*ha'ārûr*), nothing succeeds. It can be considered a certainty that the author of Deut 28 adopted an older formula and incorporated it into his text. Given everything said above, we may also assume that an old cultic formula is present here. The Deuteronomic author also manifests elsewhere his preference for such cultic formulas.[41]

Apparently the formula also betrays a hint of its former, although probably not its most original, cultic use. I have supplied above a "blessed" or "cursed" before every element. The supplied words are marked by square brackets, the "cursed" and "blessed" in the text by normal font. Without question, the repetition of the "blessed" or "cursed" before every element is also what was originally intended. Just as "city" and "field," "entry" and "exit" have each received a "blessed" and are thereby emphasized as independent concepts, one would expect that "the fruit of the field" would receive the same independence in relation to "the fruit of the body." One would certainly think that the new pair of concepts, "offspring of cattle" and "young of the sheep," must be emphasized by its own introductory formula. The meter also demonstrates that the supplementation above suits the original. Thus we obtain ten regular trimeters, linked in pairs of trimeters containing a pair of concepts each. Thus the whole blessing and curse formula achieves two times five, or ten, symmetrically structured paired trimeters, an otherwise preferred and symbolic number (e.g., the Decalogue), with ten *bārûk* and ten *'ārûr*. The currently transmitted text omitted the introductory word *bārûk* or *'ārûr* in several cases and replaced it with *wĕ*. The result was six *bārûk* and six *'ārûr*.

---

40. See previous note.
41. Deut 21:7–9; 26:3–10, 13–15.

Two times six, or twelve, is the traditional number of the tribes of Israel. This number automatically reminds us of the situation presumed in Deut 27:11–13: six tribes position themselves in the direction of Gerizim to bless, six tribes in the direction of Ebal to curse. Thus the current state of the text seems to presuppose a rectification of the formula for a cultic situation that was analogous or similar to the one just mentioned. Accordingly, we may envision the use of the formula as follows. The community was positioned on either side of the liturgist—who probably stood before the altar—each section divided into six subsections corresponding to the twelve tribes. Six times the liturgist raises a *bārûk* and each time one of the six groups of the congregation, probably standing on the right, responds with an "Amen!" Six times he raises an *'ārûr*, and each time one of the other six groups responds with an "Amen!" This rite probably constituted the conclusion of a longer ceremony. We may imagine that theses blessings and curses were connected with the public reading of divine commandments. If this is so, the two parts of the formula were probably preceded by a general blessing and curse saying, perhaps: "blessed (or cursed) be the one who keeps (or breaks) these commandments (or YHWH's commandments)." Anything further must remain pure speculation.

3.2. Poetic Imitations and Echoes of the Scheme

3.2.1. The bipartite blessing and curse liturgy, which must have once belonged to the rite presupposed in Deut 27:11–13 and to which we have found a parallel in Deut 28:3–6, 16–19, had a varied impact on Hebrew literature. We have already seen that the cultic formulas were at least one influence on the rise of the brief collections of YHWH's religious and moral commandments in the dodecalogues and decalogues, even though we need not think here of the bipartite formula itself. Such a formula seems to have been on the mind of the priest Ezekiel when he formulated his religious and moral "catechism."[42] He enumerates here the actions and omissions that make a person just, a *ṣaddîq*, but disregard for which makes one a godless evildoer, a *rāšāʿ*, and adds the promise of divine reward or the threat of divine punishment. If one inserts here a *bārûk hāʾîš* or an *'ārûr hāʾîš* before the individual members of the list, one immediately has a blessing and curse liturgy that exhibits significant similarity, both formally and substantively, with Deut 27:14–26: "Blessed be

---

42. Ezek 18:1–13. Whether the author of the ritualistic and moral/nomistic prose passages in the book of Ezekiel was really the exilic *nābîʾ* Ezekiel may be set aside here. I am aware that in the near future a very necessary literary critique of the book of Ezekiel will be presented by Hölscher in which the transmitted text will be cleaned up significantly—and surely with good reason.

the one who (1) is just and does justice, (2) does not eat on the mountains, (3) who does not lift his eyes to the idols of the house of Israel, (4) does not defile his neighbor's wife, (5) who does not go in to a woman when she is unclean, (6) does not oppress anyone and returns what he has distrained, (7) acquires nothing by force, (8) gives his bread to the hungry and clothes the naked with his garment, (9) gives nothing at interest and receives no interest, (10) keeps his hand far from impropriety, (11) renders an honest judgment between people, and (12) walks in my commandments and observes my laws to fulfill them faithfully!" So also the reverse: "Cursed be the one who eats on the mountains, raises his eyes to the idols of the house of Israel," and so on. Is it only an accident that we find twelve commandments listed here? Do we not have a relationship here both to the dodecalogues in J and E and with the twelve-part curse formula in Deut 27:14–26?

3.2.2. We find the clearest echoes of the dual blessing and curse formulas, however, in poetry, particularly in the proverbs and related genres.

We already have this inclination to the didactic, which characterizes proverbs, in the true blessing psalms, especially in Ps 128. It actually becomes evident immediately if one attempts to depict the content of the blessings and curses in detail. The blessing and curse sayings underwent such a development in the proverbs.

The content of the proverbs is practical wisdom for life. The proverbialist, and sometimes also the popular proverb from which literary proverbs developed, originally offered observations and experiences from life and the results of reflections concerning what he observed and experienced in the form of the brief gnomic statement, later also in the larger more coherent discussions of a theme. This took place for a specific purpose: to admonish and instruct people. This pedagogical purpose is also present when the form merely states the objective as fact. Proverbs intend to offer practical wisdom for living.

It is self-evident that, at the foundation of Israelite culture, this wisdom for living was always colored by religion. Religion was the spirit of popular life. There was no distinction between a religious and a profane sphere of life. Wisdom is piety; godlessness is folly. If one is wise and wants to see good days, one also makes use of the best means to obtain good fortune, namely, divine assistance available through piety. The one who does not do so is stupid. This circumstance was obvious for the Israelites, who always regarded godlessness as the sign of a rotten, sick, useless, perverse soul. For them, religion is primarily a means to an end, a means to obtain external good fortune and internal liberation. Why should one be pious if piety did not bring its reward? But it most assuredly brings its earthly reward, and whoever does not make use of it is just as stupid as the one who finds a precious pearl in the path and leaves it lying. Wisdom is piety. This understanding is grounded so profoundly in the soul of the Israelite that it finds expression everywhere in his speech. Righteousness, ṣĕdāqâ, includes both an internal quality, which is also religious and moral in nature, and the external effects of this quality in success and good fortune. Further, ṣĕdāqâ sometimes even means good fortune, success, well-being, and hiṣlîaḥ is a synonym for ṣedeq. Another synonym, however, is hiśkîl, with the meaning "to have good fortune, to succeed, to attain the goal" (e.g., Isa 52:13), from the root śkl, "to have insight, to be wise." From this viewpoint, verbs that denote capacity, capability, execution, performance, prevailing, or victory can become synonyms of ṣedeq. A word such as yākôl, "to be able," encompasses all of the concepts just mentioned. One who is just also has insight, counsel, wisdom, and "ability." Righteousness also encompasses piety, however. The just person also stands in the correct relationship to the divine powers of life. His righteousness has its ultimate source in the righteousness of God, with whom he is covenanted. Thus wisdom and piety are also practically synonymous terms, seen from this psychological perspective. One who is wise is pious and one who is not pious cannot possibly be wise. The words that denote the fool, the intellectually and morally incompetent, are employed in the psalms especially as designations for the greatest sinners, such as sorcerers and blasphemers.[43]

Proverbs also want to inculcate practical wisdom for life and piety by impressively portraying the—actual or hypothetical—experiences of many generations. The poets want to ground their admonitions in experiences of reality. It is inherent in the nature of the matter, however, that the description of experience and observation—sometimes also dogmatic inference (cf. Job's friends)—of the good fortune of the wise, pious, and righteous is a preferred theme of proverbs. Good fortune is portrayed as an example worthy of imitation in order to spur people on to "wisdom." The illumination of a matter through antitheses is a greatly favored technique of Israelite poetry. Thus it came about—and is furthermore inherent in universal human nature—that a depiction of the misfortune of the fool, the godless, and the evildoer was established as the opposite of the good fortune of the righteous. One of the main themes of proverbs is the depiction of the reward of the "righteous," of the ṣaddîq, and the bitter fruit of the "godless" (rāšāʿ). Regarded from a somewhat different viewpoint, the same theme can also be formulated as a response to the question: How does one avoid misfortune and obtain good fortune? Then the proverbialist confronts the task of depicting the conditions of good fortune, that is, the nature and content of piety and, as the opposite,

---

43. E.g., Ps 14:1, see *Psalm Studies* 1:6.

the nature and essence of godlessness. Both of these viewpoints and literary elements appear in wisdom literature in the somewhat common treatments of the theme of the two paths: the way of righteousness and good fortune and the way of godlessness and misfortune, the way of life and the way of death.

For the sake of greater emphasis and more impressive admonition, proverbial literature turned quite early to the livelier and more passionate form of the beatitude (*'ašrê hā'îš 'ăšer*) and the cry of woe (*hôy hā'îš 'ăšer*) or of the blessing and curse.[44] It seems especially likely that they appealed to the solemn form of the cultic formulas of blessing and curse and linked it with the theme and the purpose of proverbial literature. If a proverbialist meant to portray two ways, the lot of both the godless and the righteous, in a coherent passage, the option of borrowing from the bipartite formulas of blessing and curse must have suggested itself. Thus a kind of didactic poem developed in the form of the cultic blessing and curse. Both of the major types of blessing and curse formulas mentioned above were influential here, the one that places major emphasis on the listing of the conditions of blessing or curse ("blessed or cursed be the one who does this and who does this and who does this") and the one whose focus was on the description of the consequences of blessing or curse (as in Ps 128). In connection with the first type, one could offer a description in the form of participial or relative clauses describing *hā'îš* in the introductory formula both of the ideal of the righteous and the type of the godless, that is, portray the virtues and just deeds of the first as worthy of emulation and warn against the vices of the latter. In connection with the form employed in Ps 128, one could thoroughly depict both the reward, the blessings of righteousness, and the consequences of godlessness. By adopting these venerable forms, the *māšāl* poet could infuse all the force of his soul into his words and nurture the power and good fortune of the righteous and, in contrast, smite the evil with the words of his mouth and hasten even more their sure demise. This was a practical and pedagogical aid of the admonition that was not to be undervalued.

On the other hand, the main point in didactic literature is the depiction of reality. If the teacher was satisfied with blessing those who agreed with him and pronouncing the curse on those who think and act differently, didactic literature was not particularly suitable for convincing his audience of the truth of his views. This is, however, what the wisdom teacher wanted. Through reference to experience of reality, he wanted to show young people that his wisdom is the path of life, that it actually goes this well for the righteous who do thus and so but that it goes this poorly for the godless who commit this and

---

44. See 656 n. 3.

that evil act. The fact that the proverbial literature prefers the weaker forms *ašrê* and *hôy* over the stronger *bārûk* and *'ārûr* is probably related to this purpose.⁴⁵ Although these two pairs of words originally included both the indicative and the optative, the first pair were nonetheless understood, at least in later times, primarily as the statement of a fact, while the latter were heard as the intervention of the psychic one blessing or cursing with the intent of producing an effect. At least in later times, *bārûk-'ārûr* was more emotion-laden than *ašrê-hôy*, more, perhaps, than was appropriate for the calm dignity of the wisdom teacher.

The transmitted proverb collections have only Sir 28:13–26 as an example of a larger, coherent passage that emulates the bipartite blessing and curse formulas. It actually represents only a quite superficial emulation of the bipartite scheme. The passage contains no depiction of the righteous and the godless or of their reward and punishment but a depiction of the disastrous consequences of the evil tongue and a warning not to pursue this vice. The appearance of the dual scheme is achieved by the statement, approximately at the middle of the poem, that "blessed is the one who is protected from it [i.e., the evil tongue]" (v. 19). In verse 20 the depiction of its disastrous effects begins again. To this extent a passage such as Job 11:13–19 is in greater agreement with the scheme treated here, although the form of the blessing and curse saying is absent there. Both of these passages demonstrate, however, that there was once a style that, in connection with the cultic formula, offered a depiction of the righteous and their reward introduced by "blessed is the one" and a description of the godless introduced by "cursed is the one." The existence of such a form explains the structure of the passage in Job and the style of the passage in Sirach.

This genre created by the wisdom teachers with depictions of both the character and the fate of the righteous and the evildoer was, in turn, emulated by the prophets and utilized for their purposes. Such a case is present in Jer 17:5–8. The adoption of this form by the prophets is easily understood. Like the word of blessing and curse, the prophetic word is an effective, creative word. Like the wisdom teachers, the great writing prophets wanted to admonish and warn the people. By portraying the fate threatening the evil, they wanted to motivate people to adopt the correct attitude toward YHWH. They wanted to predict what was to come but also to justify it morally. Consequently, for them the description of the evildoer and the depiction of his fate also belonged together.

---

45. See above 656 n. 3.

Jeremiah's intent in 17:5–8 was to warn, as forcefully as possible, against all plans for rebellion and political calculations of the wise who steered the rudder of state: help can be found only with YHWH; "flesh" cannot help anyone. This purpose influenced the form and content of the blessing and curse poem. It offers a list of the individual virtues or vices that are the conditions for blessing or curse. For the prophet, blessing and curse depend on a single condition: the person's basic attitude toward God. Where there is unconditional trust in YHWH, there is blessing; the one, however, who "makes flesh his arm" perishes—the new content is poured into the old form:

Cursed be the one who depends on people, who makes flesh his arm, whose heart turns away from YHWH [...]![46]
He is like a shrub[47] in the steppe; he never sees good;
he lives in the drought of the wilderness, in a salty, inhospitable land.

Blessed by the one who depends on YHWH, whose refuge is YHWH!
He is like a tree planted by the waters who stretches his roots to the brook;
he sees no scorching heat; his leaves remain green;
in dry years, he has no distress; he produces fruit without ceasing.

Formally, it should be noted here that the curse occupies first place. Elsewhere blessing is mentioned first.[48] In terms of content, the poem is not a true blessing or curse but an admonitory didactic poem. The major point is the admonitory and cautionary depiction of the lot of the evildoer and of the righteous. If the poem stems from Jeremiah, however, the focus does not, in fact, lie on this depiction. Jeremiah wanted to emphasize that confidence in human means of power is apostasy from YHWH, who demands unconditional trust even in political matters, and that, consequently, trusting in "flesh" will bitterly haunt one. The more precise portrayal of the punishment, and even more the depiction of the reward for fidelity, is of subordinate importance here. The fact that the poem nonetheless offers a depiction of the fate of the righteous and of the evildoer as a direct admonition demonstrates that this didactic depiction belongs to the genre adopted by the prophet and that his original contribution consists of the unique motivation: trust in YHWH, on the one

---

46. One phrase is missing.
47. The variety of plant to which ʿarʿār refers is not known.
48. Pss 1; 112; Deut 27:12–13; 28; Lev 26.

hand, and trust in "flesh," on the other. In other words, a didactic poem had already arisen from the blessing and curse saying long before Jeremiah.[49]

3.2.3. Products of this didactic genre in the form of the blessing and curse saying have also entered the Psalter and partially influenced authentic psalmody.

Psalms 1 and 112 should be mentioned first here. By doing so, we have returned to our point of departure, and the circle of our investigations is closed. Neither Ps 1 nor Ps 112 is a psalm in the strict sense of the word. They are not, indeed, cultic songs and have only one detail in external form in common with them. They represent the genre of didactic literature in the Psalter.[50] The topic in both is the lot of the righteous and of the godless; the

---

49. The statement above pertains under the assumption that the poem was truly composed by Jeremiah. It must be admitted, however, that this assumption is not certain. Assuming prophetic authorship, the idea in the poem also corresponds to Isaiah better than Jeremiah (cf., however, Jer 27).

50. [Excursus]. Strictly speaking, only these two psalms do so. One may also include Pss 127A and B, perhaps also Ps 133 and, in a certain sense, Ps 15. The word "didactic psalm" has been very misleading. Besides, the word is a *contradiction in adjecto*. Staerk (*Lyrik*) has extended this concept furthest. I permit myself a few words on the subject here. In addition to Ps 15, the hymn Ps 146, the thanksgiving Ps 34, the alphabetical hymn Ps 111, the "didactic petition" Ps 25, and the "song of praise on the law" Ps 19:8–11, he also assigns to the "didactic" psalms, a genre to which he also gives the name "lyrical wisdom literature" (246), the following psalms: 1; 32; 37; 49; 50; 78; 91; 101; 105; 112; 119; 127; 128; 133. Inherent in the concept of "didactic poem" is, first, the notion that the purpose of the pertinent poem is didactic. Apart from Pss 1 and 112 and, in a certain sense, 15; 127; 133, however, this is not the case with any of these psalms. Ps 15 is didactic to the degree that it offers an instructive response to a direct question. The question, however, as Ps 24 demonstrates, is part of a cultic liturgy. The psalm instructs the participant in the cult concerning who may participate in the cult and thereby obtain blessing (see *Psalm Studies* 2:295). It is not, however, a didactic poem in the true sense of the word. The purpose of the hymn is to praise God. Whoever has the serious intention of praising God does not think of instructing people. His poem cannot have any didactic imprint even though the description of divine activity can be somewhat extensive and prosaic. This, however, is simply a lack of poetic talent. His poem does not thereby become an intentionally didactic piece. Praise is never, ever instruction. Thus, Pss 111 and 146 can be immediately excluded from Staerk's collection. Ps 105 is also a hymn, not a didactic poem in hymnic style. The fact that, in listing YHWH's *těhillôt*, the author places the major emphasis on his mighty historical acts and lists them rather prosaically cannot make his hymn a didactic poem. He speaks to God, not his fellow human beings. It is equally clear that a "petition," if truly a religious prayer and not the outflow of pharisaical dissimulation, is not a didactic poem. Thus one can also exclude Ps 25. The didactic impression is due to the many confidence motifs that mention the divine activity rather extensively. Ps 19B is also to be understood

form is that of the bipartite blessing and curse. They have nothing of psalm style. Regarded as poetry, both are rather inferior. Psalm 1 would be the better if it were not so horribly unoriginal. If it is not, in fact, plagiarized from Jer 17:5–8, then it is at least a rather faithful copy of an established genre and does not have even a single original phrase. Psalm 112 suffers from all the weaknesses that tend to pertain to the "alphabetic" poems. They are not poetry at all but only metrical prose, vain handicraft. The alphabetic scheme usu-

---

as a prayer. The focus is the petition for protection from the *zēdîm*, i.e., the demons that seduce one to "great sins" (*Psalm Studies* 1:75–77). The statements of praise for YHWH's Torah that preserve people from sin are to be understood as confidence motifs. The same is also true of Ps 119. This psalm, too, does not intend to be a didactic poem but the prayer of one plagued by the *zēdîm*, that is, by a sick and unclean person. The statements concerning the excellence of the Torah are meant partly as confidence motifs and partly as innocence motifs (cf. *Psalm Studies* 1:77). Ps 101 is a vow containing a king's promise to walk in YHWH's paths. Its cultic locus was in the celebration of the first or the annually observed enthronement of the king (see *Psalm Studies* 2:217–18 n. 75, 353, 471). I believe that I have shown elsewhere (*Psalm Studies* 2:253–54, 333, 3:533–38) that Ps 50 is to be understood as the admonition and warning of the God appearing to renew the covenant during the enthronement festival, pronounced by a cultic prophet. Here, however, one may speak with a degree of justification of a didactic tendency. The last foreigner to this genre to be considered is Ps 78. The prophetic admonition to be true to the covenant this time, with reference to the former transgressions of its obligations, has become a survey of the history of the faithless people. Here, too, the purpose is to warn the people, and thus a didactic imprint is unmistakable. Even this psalm, however, betrays something of the prophetic consciousness that is the major point in Ps 50. Neither of the two is a didactic poem in the true sense. The similarity between Pss 78 and 106 relates only to the material, not the cultic purpose; Ps 106 is a prayer with extraordinarily prominent penitential motifs, a "psalm of confession," a subspecies of the "lament psalms" or of the "communal prayer" (see *Psalm Studies* 3:558). We saw above (705; see *Psalm Studies* 3:593–96) that Ps 91 is not a didactic poem but a fragment from a healing liturgy with a blessing and an oracle. The blessing has affinities, however, with the depictions of the reward of the righteous in proverbial literature. We have also seen the situation pertaining to Ps 128 above. Pss 32, 34, 37, and 49 are all to be understood as thanksgiving (offering) psalms of a sick person who was delivered and healed (see *Psalm Studies* 1:129–37). It is correct, however, that the psalms of thanksgiving address not only God but also the assembled congregation and that, in terms of style and content, they belong to proverbial literature. They are, as Staerk says, "lyrical wisdom literature." We are probably dealing here with sayings that were related to the fall festival because of their content and that, consequently, found their way into the booklet of *ma'alot* songs. Whether something similar was the case with Ps 133 seems doubtful to me. The psalm seems to have its actual point in v. 3b and may very well have been composed for the cult. It has more the tone of the hymn than of the wisdom saying and should probably be understood as a hymn to the sacred place that is the center of "the religious and cultic community of compatriots" (Staerk). Several such Zion hymns occur among the *ma'alot* songs. As a Zion hymn, it is indirectly a hymn to God.

ally weighs so heavily on the crafters that they can almost never afford such luxuries as orderly arrangement and sequence of thought. As I have already shown in the introduction, the author of Ps 112 did not succeed in achieving a balanced relationship between the two parts of the poem. The first part goes from *aleph* to *qoph*, the second from *resh* to *taw*. The alphabetic form forced the author to omit the *hôy* or the *'ārûr* as the introduction to the second part. He had only the letters *resh*, *shin*, and *taw* available to him. Psalm 1 suffers from a breech of the scheme. The author wanted to produce three strophes of three trimeter bicola (and hexameters)[51] each. The first two strophes of each deal with the righteous. Contrary to all the rules of Hebrew prosody, he placed the new section in the midst of the last period of the second strophe (vv. 3b + 4a); in other words, he concluded the section on the fate of the righteous with a phrase that already anticipates that the results will not be the same for the godless, "not so the evildoers, not so." In the third strophe, then, the positive depiction of the evildoers begins. The superficial scheme of the bipartite blessing and curse has been abandoned. No *hôy* in the second section follows the *'ašrê* in the first.

The criterion of the righteous or the godless established by the author is what gives Ps 1 its particular interest in this context, however. The ideal righteous person is the scribe who meditates day and night on the problems of the law and walks according to all its provisions. Accordingly, the evildoer is, conversely, the one who does not precisely observe the thousand commandments and who is thus a "scoffer" and a "sinner." The one who meticulously observes the law is blessed; cursed, however, is the one who does not know the law! The interesting aspect here, from the standpoint of the history of religions, is the fact that this understanding, as we have seen above, already had its roots in the old cultic blessing and curse formulas. Here, too, as in the exemplar of Deut 27:14–26, one's relationship to the law was a cause of blessing or of curse, although only alongside many others. The fundamental view had not yet become nomistic. The pertinent saying may have already been related to the literarily fixed and demarcated Deuteronomy at the covenant renewal under Josiah, just as both Deuteronomy and the Holiness Code already made blessing and curse dependent on the relationship to this very legal code. The older wisdom literature usually portrayed piety in general as the condition of blessing, without meticulously circumscribing the concept of piety. In fact, for

---

51. In v. 2, *kî 'im* should probably be pronounced as a contraction, *kim*. Instead of *yômām* one can read *yôm* and understand it with *wālaylâ* as a metrical foot. In v. 3, perhaps *ranān* should be inserted after *kĕ'ēṣ*. In v. 4a, *lō'-kēn* should be inserted following LXX, in v. 4bα *yihyeh* is missing, and in v. 4bβ *mippĕnê 'āreṣ* should be inserted with LXX (*'ăšer* can stay). In v. 5 *'al-kēn* is superfluous; in v. 6 the first *derek* is probably only a doublet.

the wisdom teachers piety was precisely what was considered piety at the time. In its strict nomism, Ps 1, in contrast, denotes the final result of the "Deuteronomization" of the old cultic formula.

3.2.4. The scheme treated here also influenced the cultic thanksgiving psalm in one instance. The case is found in Ps 32. The psalm is not, as Staerk thinks, for example, "a didactic poem on the blessing of penitence" but first of all the thanksgiving song of a healed sick person. The depiction of the former misfortune in verses 3–4 points to illness. "Inertness" (*rĕmiyyâ*) housed in his soul and took his natural psychic force ("righteousness") and also his physical health from him. His "bones rotted" while he moaned all day long (in pain); his "heart,"[52] that is, his whole person, including his body, "was transformed," ruined, "like a field under the heat of summer." He summarized that "YHWH had placed his hand on him heavily," an expression that also describes both physical and spiritual deterioration elsewhere. He expressed the same notion in other words, saying that he had to bear an *ʿāwōn* (v. 2). In the Old Testament, however, guilt almost always comes to awareness in and with a misfortune. One can hardly infer from his words that he had become aware of some specific sin. Misfortune had shown him that some guilt—God alone knew which—laid on him. It may also have been that he had not asked about the reason and later found something in himself that could have awakened God's wrath. He then decided to admit his sins and not to conceal his guilt; he confessed them to YHWH. Thereupon YHWH forgave his guilt. We cannot know whether he found specific sins in himself or whether he only acknowledged his sinfulness in general terms. The latter assumptions finds support both in the Old Testament understanding of sins and suffering and in the penitential psalms in the Psalter, which never name a specific sin. This silence is quite natural on its face, since they are ritual prayers meant to suit all possible cases. How and under what circumstances did he confess his sins? There is nothing in the psalm on this question. On the analogy of the other thanksgiving psalms, which were undoubtedly written for the thanksgiving offering feast, it cannot be doubted that he thinks of the ritual procedures, confessions, and prayers that, together with the "sin offering," were prescribed when it had come to awareness—namely, through some misfortune—that a "guilt" burdened him.[53] One may hardly infer from the words of the psalm that he struggled against this admission for a long time in stubborn defiance and only made it when the hand of YHWH lay upon him even more harshly or that

---

52. So v. 4 should be supplemented following one manuscript, *metri causa*.
53. See Lev 4:2, 13, 28; 5:1–4; see *Psalm Studies* 1:140–41.

he had decided to confess after he had suffered several pangs of conscience. The words in verses 3–5 are probably only a particularly strong expression of the belief, and of the poet's experience, that things would go better for him only after he submitted himself to the ritual purifications and confessions. Just as people today usually call the doctor only when the illness becomes acute or chronic, people then decided to make a sin-offering and ritual penance only when they were suffering acute and chronic illness. Human nature is always the same. In this case, complete healing took place after the ritual penance with its sin offering, cleansings, and confessions. Through it, the psalmist experienced God's gracious assistance; he experienced the blessing of humility and remorseful penance. He became certain that he would have not been healed had he not come to the temple and appeased YHWH with repentant words and the unconditional admission of all his sinfulness, perhaps including specific sins that may have come to his knowledge. So must all pious people do if they want to be freed from sin and sickness. In the light of this experience, any hesitancy seems to him to be stupid defiance, such as might be expected of irrational animals, but not of an insightful person. His heart overflows with joy and gratitude.

Now he has come to the celebration of the thanksgiving offering and is to sing the thanksgiving song of the healed before the assembled community. As the style of the thanksgiving song requires, he recounts to the community what he experienced, reporting his former distress and the great grace that God has shown him. He bears witness before the community by speaking of his experiences, just as any authentic religious witness does even today. It was also customary for this witness to be concluded with a call to those present, should they come into distress, to do the same as he has done, to turn to YHWH for help.[54] YHWH helps the pious who humbly turn to him in distress and confess their sins. He is hostile, in contrast, to the proud and obdurate; they must die in their guilt. This is, indeed, instruction. The didactic element characterizes this part of the thanksgiving song from the outset. When this instruction assumes a somewhat more general form, its content automatically constitutes the traditional doctrine concerning the fate of the righteous, the pious, and the humble and, as the occasional contrast, also the frightful end of the godless and defiant. The psalm of thanksgiving has always had affinity with wisdom literature on this point. The authors of songs of thanksgiving may maintain on the basis of their own experiences that they have newly solved, in a positive sense, the real problem of life in ancient Israel, the problem of the relationship between piety and good fortune, to the extent that they

---

54. See Pss 34:12–19; 40:5.

have verified the old solution in their own persons. If the evil seem to triumph for a period—and they do so precisely when the pious person is sick, for evil people have usually evoked the illness through magical curses—this is only appearance. They now know by experience that the pious ultimately triumph and, with God's help, "can look upon their enemies with satisfaction." Thus a rather didactic tone becomes evident in the thanksgiving psalm. They are far from being problem literature or didactic literature because of it, however.[55]

This admonitory interest becomes especially evident in Ps 32. The whole account is configured as a testimony, and the testimony is meant as a call to follow his—the poet's—example. Do not be defiant and unreasonable like a horse or a mule. Go to YHWH in distress, confess your sins, and do penance, for that alone brings healing, good fortune and well-being. The illnesses and strokes of fate (*makōbîm*) of the godless, who do not want to submit to YHWH's discipline, are many. Thus, in terms of content, the whole song is configured as a depiction of the fate of the pious and of the godless attested by a personal example, with the restriction that piety is portrayed in reference to the occasion of the psalm as willingness to repent and to confess sins and godlessness as defiance and unwillingness to repent under YHWH's hand.

Here the bipartite scheme of the blessing and curse has had a superficial effect. The psalm begins with the testimony and employs the beatitude form: "Blessed be the one whose guilt is forgiven, whose sins are atoned." A true bipartite division of the psalm never came about, however. The style of the thanksgiving psalm prohibited it. This style concluded with an apostrophe to the other devout persons present, usually with a call for them to praise God along with the poet or something similar. So is it here, too. Consequently, the poet could not end with a depiction of the godless. After mentioning them, he returns to the righteous. Thus the godless are mentioned only in passing, as it were. Furthermore, the testimony in the thanksgiving psalm Ps 40A (see v. 5) is also in the form of the beatitude.[56]

---

55. See the discussions above (*Psalm Studies* 1:131–32).

56. The beatitude form (*'ašrê hā'îš* ...) also occurs in psalmody in various meanings. In 41:2 and 119:1—both are individual psalms of lament—the formula introduces a confidence motif. In this form, the supplicant attested that he had belonged to those who have practiced the pertinent virtue and, consequently, may trust in the appropriate reward (similarly, Ps 84:5–6, 13; 94:12; 106:3; 144:15; 146:5). In Ps 137:9, the beatitude encompasses the curse and the prayer for vengeance: "blessed be the one who destroys our hereditary enemies." Ps 127:5 probably contains a regular *māšāl* (see above, 764 n. 50).

Conclusion:
A Summary from the Perspective
of the History of Religions

I will summarize the results in a picture of the history of religion. The result will not be a unified or complete picture, only a sketch.

We have found both blessing and curse in the cult, both regularly repeated and as occasional sayings. The wish for blessing greets the festival procession before the gates of the temple or on the temple site (Pss 24:4–6; 118:26). Blessing as greeting is entwined into the songs of the festival procession (Ps 122:6–7). These songs also raise the request for blessing that finds response in the solemn tones of the priest (Pss 122:8–9; 115:12–15). The priest's full-toned blessing from the altar (Num 6:24–26) summarizes the overall content of the festival, and the blessing returns in the song of thanksgiving as praise for YHWH magnifying the power and glory of the deity (Ps 124:6).

From all the liturgical elements mentioned above, religious art constructed impressive and gripping liturgies for worship, liturgies in which greeting, prayer, intercession, blessing, and thanksgiving flowed together with the assistance of various voices, choirs, and soloists, through antiphonals and responsorials, into mighty religious harmonies. How sad that the Priestly document reports to us nothing of this aspect of worship and the festival! What an opportunity, however, the academic theologian has here to develop the two characteristics without which the Psalter would be "taboo" to him: understanding of the stirrings of religious sentiment and artistic imagination!

The blessing contains everything that the people and the individual expect from cult and religion. The purpose of the cult is to obtain blessing. Consequently, the blessings are voiced for the whole people and each individual during every solemn cultic procedure, especially at the great festivals that were the cult in earlier times, but later even at the daily cult in the temple. Audible, visible, and comprehensible to all, the blessing applies the divine gifts and goods to people. Little is said in the cultic formulas and cultic psalms concerning the content of the blessing. Everyone knew what "blessing" meant.

In a word, it was "everything people desire." The vast majority related it to external good fortune. Even if it were occasionally described more precisely, external good fortune was still the major focus. Fertility, in particular, was depicted as the true fruit of blessing (Ps 128)—in harmony with ancient Semitic thought. In a liturgy dealing with the healing of a sick person and defense against all manner of demonic powers, the major focus lies on protection against all evil (Ps 91). Individuals will also have thought of what we call spiritual goods: peace of mind, internal calm, immunity against the demons who tempt one to mortal sins, and the like. Here, however, one should note that ancient Israel did not know our distinction between secular and spiritual goods. For the Israelite, external good fortune was the logically and morally necessary outcome of a "beautiful," "just," and sound soul and the effect of the internal quality of a person, a quality the Israelites called ṣĕdāqâ.

Belief in individual good fortune became widespread and evolved into belief in the eternal, fortunate, glorious future of Israel and Jerusalem as the final, great, blessed objective (Ps 128:5). The blessing of the individual has both its roots and its ultimate objective in Israel's blessing.

The objects of blessing were manifold. The people, the land, and all the individuals in it will be blessed. Above all, the righteous who have a soul receptive to blessing will be blessed, or, as it would be put later, the pious who do YHWH's will, who keep his commandments. Everything that is good and useful for the people will be blessed and thereby increased: male potency and the womb, cattle and field, grain and must, basket and kneading trough. The deity is also blessed and thereby given "glory and might."

The liturgical passages that belong here permit us insight into a very significant development in the history of religion. At the beginning of the process stands the power-laden, self-efficacious formula, or, more correctly, the formula effective by virtue of the psychic power of the one pronouncing it. Blessing and curse are inherent in word and deed. Things and persons are blessed or cursed and thereby infused with salvation or catastrophe. On one hand, in the course of time, something of the original psychological foundation of these ideas disappeared. Occasionally it was forgotten that the effect of the pronouncements of blessing and curse depended on the psychic preconditions of the speaker. Therefore the words sometimes became diminished to formulas that worked purely *ex opere operato*. The original basic idea was never entirely forgotten, however. These pronouncements of blessing and the related cultic acts were so powerful that one was even convinced that the covenant of blessing between deity and people that constitutes the precondition for any blessing was reciprocal in every respect. In the cult, the people also blessed YHWH and thereby actually gave him increased might, blessedness, and "honor" (psychic content). On the other hand, there was something new. The deity, who had stood in the background from the beginning and who was the true ultimate ground and source of blessing and also of the salvific curse that breaks evil, moves increasingly into the foreground. The personal YHWH governed the religious thought and gradually also the cultic forms of ancient Israel. Blessing and curse were regarded as the direct effects of his intervention in matters. It thus became the priest's task to invoke God's blessing. The formula received something of the imprint of the prayer. It was often worded not "blessed be you!" but "may YHWH bless you!" YHWH is the one truly blessing and cursing. The person is only the means that he utilizes, the mediator of his blessing. YHWH blesses whom he will and curses whom he will. This effects the old concept of the blessing of the deity and, thereby, ultimately also the whole meaning of the word "blessing." A person cannot give God anything (see Ps 50:9–13). In relation to God, a person must only bow and accept what he offers. A person can only request, thank, and praise. A person should thank and praise even when God has not blessed, even when one is cursed with severe blows. A person should thank him for the grace that he offers. If God is angry, a person should thank him that the punishment is not even harsher. Even then one says, *yĕhî šēm yhwh mĕbôrāk*, "blessed be the name of YHWH" (see Job 1:21). Blessing the deity now attains the exclusive meaning "to thank and praise God" (cf. the *bĕrākôt* in the Mishnah tractate by the same name).

The cultic curse stands as the dark counterpart to the cultic blessing, everything that stands in the way of the good fortune, blessing, and unhindered self-maintenance of the people, that could impair, "pervert," and diminish their "righteousness." Thus, and in relation to the development toward a personal and transcendent concept of God mentioned above, everything is also cursed that can impair the good relationship between YHWH and his people and makes the people unjust in the eyes of YHWH, so that his countenance becomes dark instead of graciously glowing, everything that can somehow keep the divine gifts at a distance from the people and individuals. Consequently, in the cult one cursed those who have transgressed against consecrated goods, the secret thief, the unknown murderer, the faithless who has made the heart of her husband bitter and a dwelling for a demon of jealousy so that he can rejoice neither over grain nor wine, and, further, the sorcerer and the witch who make the land monstrous and God-forsaken through their mysterious arts. In brief, accursed was everything harmful and evil to both the people and individuals, the upstanding, "calm" people who are not like the chaotic opponents of God, the demons and the "raucous" people in the land. The curse resounded at a cultic occasion, not just every time violations such as those mentioned here were committed. A general curse against all the enemies of YHWH and Israel, both internal and external, was also proclaimed at certain regularly recurring cultic celebrations. Before war or when the people must suffer under their lasting oppression, national enemies were met with a powerful curse (Pss 83:10–18; 129:5–8; 137:7–9). One sought especially, however, to destroy through a regular curse the enemies among the people, who did not appear in public, who practiced their evil arts in the dark, all secret sinners, especially the sorcerers. The curse was directed against them in defense at certain regularly repeated occasions (Pss 14; 53; 120:3–5; 125:5). Thus the twelve-part cultic formula enumerates all those who are supposed to be eradicated from the land through the power of the curse, all those who harm the people, both directly through evil deeds such as murder, theft, adultery, sorcery and indirectly by rendering the land unclean through such acts as provoking YHWH's wrath on the land. The frightful, stony words were proclaimed with grave and eerie solemnity. The unison repetition of "cursed be the one who…" on these occasions surely evoked a growing eeriness of frightful effect on those present. The presumed sinner in the circle of the cultic participants was also supposed to be driven out of the community with such words. This offers a truly psychological glance behind this cultic practice. They certainly must have also occasionally had the effect that some secret sinner, crippled psychically, collapsed and "gave God the glory" through his horrifying end.

Here we encounter blessing and curse again. From the outset both are supposed to guarantee the good fortune and security of the people. Placing them both in relation to the moral and religious state of the individual and to his relationship with the divine commandments enabled them to contribute, on the one hand, to maintaining the moral consciousness of the people and the ethnical impulse of the religion and, on the other, to creating a pure cultic community. Passages such as the curse formula in Deut 27:14–26 and echoes of corresponding blessing formulas in Pss 24 and 15 cast light on another important development from the perspective of the history of religion involving the conditions for blessing and curse. We could sketch it briefly as follows.

In the beginning, the formulas essentially meant "Blessing for Israel, curse for all Israel's enemies!" This materialistic and nationalist tone resonated for a long time; indeed, in essence it was never fully overcome. Rather, one must say that later nomistic Judaism signifies to a degree a relapse to this amoral view: the Israelites are due the blessing because they are Israelites and observe the law. Alternatively, we can also clearly observe a relationship between the ethical strands in the religion and the cultic formulas mentioned. Religion and morality were always interrelated in Israel. Popular morality, the ethos, always adhered to YHWH's sacred commandments.[1] In the course of the

---

1. That is, as far back as our sources reach.

development of Israelite culture and religion, a deepening of morality and a closer connection between morality and religion took place. This also left behind traces in the cult, which stands to reason already because the cultic blessing and curse depended on the relationship to the divine commandments even though these commandments, as the (do)decalogues in J and E show, were originally understood chiefly as cultic and ritual commandments. There came a time when one was not satisfied in the cult with pronouncing blessing and curse but also indicated in some form the divine reasons for this act. The conditions of blessing were also emphasized, and the curse was provided a religious and moral motivation. This actually began to take place from the moment when the blessing and curse formulas specified "blessed be the one who does thus and so, and cursed be the one who does thus and so." Thus blessings and curses became a means, not only for differentiating between Israel and pagans, but also between the righteous and sinners within the people. It is very significant that this distinction also finds expression in the cult. The moral distinction thereby obtains a powerful religious sanction. Only this moral element in the official cultic religion makes the appearance and the ideas of the great major prophets fully comprehensible to us. One can imagine what a factor for popular edification these cult formulas must have been. With firmly fixed, brief, solid words, a series of specific, easily understood examples of pious and godless behavior must have been hammered into the consciousness of the Israelites already in rather early preexilic times at the major festivals at which all the people assembled. The inherent requirements were impressed upon them as YHWH's requirements, as the indispensable conditions for any blessing and good fortune, and also for inner communion with God, an idea that was in the process of becoming vital for some, at least (see Jeremiah). Year after year, one heard these words at the festivals. The chill that the curses brought upon dispositions would have made the requirements all the more holy in people's hearts. Obviously, the vast majority would have understood all of this very, very superficially. Such cultic words must, nonetheless, have been a strong factor in religious and moral training, as attested to us above all by the fact that such words actually gave rise to the Decalogue.

Addenda: Some of the Texts Discussed

Addendum 1: The blessing formula to be inferred from Ps 24:4–6 may have been worded as follows:

1. Blessed be the one whose hands are clean.
2. Blessed be the one who is pure of heart.
3. Blessed be the one who has not incited his soul to some mischief.

Verse 4b is probably an insertion based on 15:4b.
The blessing to be inferred from Ps 15 is more extensive:

1. Blessed be the one who walks innocently and does justice.
2. Blessed be the one who speaks truth in his heart.
3. Blessed be the one who does not let his tongue run (with disaster-producing words).
4. Blessed be the one who does no evil to his neighbor.
5. Blessed be the one who does not burden his relatives with shame.
6. Blessed be the one to whom the one rejected (by YHWH) is contemptible.
7. Blessed be the one who honors those who fear YHWH.
8. Blessed be the one who swears [] and does not break (the oath).
9. Blessed be the one who does not lend his money at interest.
10. Blessed be the one who does not take bribes from the innocent.

The number ten is surely no accident. Kittel's conjecture (in his commentary) that a semi-verse may have fallen out of verse 3 is, therefore, unjustified.

Addendum 2: After a few later glosses and extrapolations have been removed, the relevant twelve-part curse formula was worded as follows:

1. Cursed be the one who prepares a carved or a molten image [] and erects it in secret!—Amen!
2. Cursed be the one who curses his father or his mother!—Amen!

3. Cursed be the one who displaces his neighbor's boundary!—Amen!
4. Cursed be the one who leads a blind person astray on the way!—Amen!
5. Cursed be the one who perverts the justice of foreigners, orphans, and widows!—Amen!
6. Cursed be the one who sleeps with his father's wife![]—Amen!
7. Cursed be the one who sleeps with any animal!—Amen!
8. Cursed be the one who sleeps with his sister![]—Amen!
9. Cursed be the one who sleeps with his sister-in-law!—Amen!
10. Cursed be the one who "smites" his neighbor in secret!—Amen!
11. Cursed be the one accepts a bribe when the spilling of innocent blood is involved!—Amen!
12. Cursed be the one who does not keep "YHWH's commandments"!—Amen!

Addendum 3: As far as is possible, a translation of the original narratives in J and E is to be offered here. The Yahwistic account read as follows:

> [1a]Moses gave the people the following command: [2a]When you cross the Jordan, you should take the [twelve] great stones.... [R[Dt] omitted the rest of the account and replaced it with vv. 2b–3, 8. The execution follows in Josh 4:3–9.]

The E account would have been something like the following:

> [1a]Moses gave the elders of Israel the following command: [4a]"When you have crossed the Jordan [[2b] and have entered the land that I give you], [4b]you shall 'take' [] [great] stones ... on (?) Mount 'Gerizim' []. [5a] And there you shall build an altar for YHWH, your God []; [6]from unhewn stones you shall build the altar of YHWH, your God; and on it you shall offer burnt offerings to YHWH, your God, [7] and slaughter shelamim offerings, and there you shall hold the sacrificial meal and rejoice between YHWH, your God....[12] And one (half) shall take position 'in the direction of' Gerizim for blessing [], (namely) Simeon, Levi, Judah, Issachar, Joseph, and Benjamin; [13] the other (half) should take position 'in the direction of' Ebal for cursing, (namely) Reuben, Gad, Asher, Zebulun, Dan, and Naphtali."

According to E, the execution of the command comes in Josh 8:30–33.

> [30]Then Joshua built an altar to YHWH, the God of Israel, on (?) Mount "Gerizim," [31] [] an altar of unhewn stone over which no iron has been swung, and they sacrificed burnt sacrifices and slaughtered shelamim offerings, [],

³³ meanwhile, all Israel and its elders, [] the priests [] having returned, stood on either side of the ark, one half in the direction of Gerizim, the other in the direction of Ebal, as Moses [] had commanded []; ³⁴ª and then he (i.e., Joshua) recited with a loud voice (*qārāʾ*) [] the blessing and the curse.

Instead of "on" (*ʿal*) in Deut 27:1 and Josh 8:30, "beside" or "at the foot of" was probably original (see 744).

Addendum 4: I would like to remark explicitly here that I find the "Covenant Code" of J, following older criticism, in Exod 34:14–26. I must reject the view advocated by Sellin, Kittel, and others that J also had an additional parallel to Exod 21–24 and even to the Decalogue in Exod 20:1–17 as entirely unfounded and as a *petition principii*. In any case, they are correct that Exod 34:14–26 are not an equivalent to the Decalogue in Exod 20:1–17. The Decalogue is not the foundation for the covenant in E but in P (so also Carl Steuernagel, *Einleitung in das Alte Testament* [Tübingen: Mohr Siebeck, 1912]; and Johannes Meinhold, *Einführung in das Alte Testament: Geschichte, Literatur und Religion Israels* [Giessen: Töpelmann, 1919]). In the text above, I did not address whether Exod 34 was originally meant to be a decalogue or a dodecalogue. Renewed study has made it clear to me that there were originally ten words there. They can be very easily obtained from the thirteen in MT if one understands the three specific festival commandments as later, although correct, expansions of the general festival commandment in verse 23. The original introduction is concealed, as shown on 752, in verses 6b–7. In order for one to be able easily to compare the Decalogue with the transmitted curse and blessing formulas, I print them here. The Covenant Code of J was:

⁶ᵇ"I am" YHWH, a merciful and gracious God, patient and rich in grace and fidelity, ⁷ who keeps grace for thousands [] and visits the guilt of the fathers on the descendants [] to the grandchildren and great grandchildren.
1. ¹⁴ You should bow to no other gods.
2. ¹⁷ You should make no molten images for yourself.
3. ¹⁹ª All the firstborn belong to me.
4. ²⁰ᵇ You should not come with empty hands to view my countenance.
5. ²¹ Six days you may labor. On the seventh day you should refrain (from it; or: rest). You should refrain (from it; or: rest) even in plowing and harvest time.
6. ²³ Three times a year, all the males among you shall view the countenance of YHWH your God.
7. ²⁵ª You should not offer the blood of "my" sacrifice together with leaven.

8. ²⁵ᵇ You shall not leave the fat offered at "my festivals" until the morning (read *ḥgy* following Exod 23:18 and pronounce *ḥaggay*; strike *happesaḥ*; Passover is not a *ḥag*).
9. ²⁶ᵃ You shall bring the best of the first-ripened fruits of your field to the house of YHWH your God.
10. ²⁶ᵇ You shall not boil the kid in its mother's milk.

The "Covenant Code" according to E was a significantly expanded recension of this Decalogue that no longer clearly reflected the original number ten. It occurs in Exod 20:23–26; 23:10–19. R^JEDtn inserted M (Exod 21:1–22:16), which may have once occupied the place of the current Deuteronomy—but not from the outset! Whether Exod 22:17–27 and 23:1–9 are later additions to M or to the E Covenant Code may be left aside. In contrast to 721 n. 31, I now consider the latter the more likely.

The exilic Decalogue was both included in Deuteronomy and used by R^P as a Covenant Code after the Priestly document. In its relatively original version, it went as follows:

I am YHWH, your God, who brought you out of Egypt.
1. You shall have no other gods beside me.
2. You shall make no idol image.
3. You shall not pronounce the name of YHWH your God for (anyone's) harm.
4. Remember to "sanctify" the Sabbath day.
5. Honor your father and your mother.
6. You shall not kill.
7. You shall not commit adultery.
8. You shall not steal.
9. You shall not appear as a false witness against your neighbor.
10. You shall not "covet" your neighbor's house.

The Psalmists

1
INTRODUCTION

1.1 (1).[1] The rabbinic tradition cites the following as authors of the biblical Psalms: Moses (Ps 90), David (Pss 3–9; 11–32; 34–41; 51–63; 68–70; 86; 101; 103; 108–110; 122; 124; 131; 133; 138–145, altogether, seventy-three psalms), Solomon (Pss 72; 127), Asaph (Pss 50; 73–83; altogether twelve psalms), "the Korahites (Pss 42–43; 44–49; 84–85; 87–88; altogether, eleven psalms)," Heman the Ezrahite (Ps 88, along with the Korahites), and Etan the Ezrahite (Ps 89). In contrast, the expression *lîdûtûn* (= *lĕyĕdûtûn*; Ps 39 along with David) which appears along with the more frequent *ʿal yĕdûtûn* (Ps 62 along with David and Ps 77 with Asaph) is not to be understood as an indication of authorship, as I have demonstrated elsewhere.[2]

1.2 (2). The fact that this information already transmitted in the biblical tradition does not reflect actual circumstances has long been recognized. This recognition is the common property of the psalm exegesis of all the academic schools of all Protestant denominations. Only laypersons, who do not know better, and perhaps a few Catholic theologians, who are bound by the church's scripture dogma, can treat this information as historical realities today. As is generally true of the superscriptions to the psalms, the indications of authorship do not stem from the original authors and do not belong to the original text of the psalms but were added later by the copyists, collectors, and scribes (*sôpĕrîm*) and represent a tradition of Jewish scholarship or of the temple administration.[3] Both the circumstance that, with the aid of the LXX, we can

---

1. [Note: In the German edition Mowinckel numbered the sections consecutively through all of volume 6. His original numeration has been retained in parentheses after this translation's chapter-specific numbering.]
2. *Psalm Studies* 4:619.
3. The scholarly class in late Judaism, *sôpĕrîm*, on the whole, probably arose from the circles of the temple personnel, especially, perhaps, from the lower ranks. The priest Ezra was a *sôpēr*, the "learned" author of Chronicles beyond doubt a temple singer.

establish the gradual expansion of these comments[4] and the information concerning the "historical" situations that often accompany the superscriptions[5] speak for the "redactional" nature of the superscriptions.

In itself, the redactional nature of the authorship information does not demonstrate their nonhistoricity. They could, nonetheless, contain accurate tradition. On the other hand, it has been known long enough what should often be thought of a "tradition" of the Jewish schools of learning. Such a tradition is very often not a historical tradition at all in the true sense of the term but simply merely a theory, a "hypothesis" based on learned inference and speculation, as we would say today, that became "traditional" over a shorter or longer period.

1.3 (3). We need not waste many words on the fact that most of the psalms could not have stemmed from the "authors" named in the superscriptions. That has long since been demonstrated and acknowledged, even though not a few of the arguments employed overshoot the mark and proceed from false assumptions. This is true, for example, of the theory of the "Maccabean" psalms. I definitely believe, and have good grounds for doing so, that there is not a single Maccabean psalm in the Psalter.[6] This is also true of the emphasis, common until most recently, on the postexilic origins of most or almost all of the psalms. In reality, there are very many preexilic psalms, some very ancient.[7] This is particularly true of the assumption that most psalms, especially the individual lament psalms (sin-offering psalms), presume the religious partisanship of later postexilic Judaism. I have demonstrated elsewhere[8] that this assumption is false.[9]

On the other hand, the social tensions among the people that gradually developed in the course of the monarchical period have undeniably asserted themselves in a few psalms and partially influenced the image of the "enemy" in them. We will deal with this further below.[10] As a consequence of this development, terms such as "rich," "mighty," and the like became synonyms for terms such as "oppressor," "evildoer," "sinner," and "sorcerer." This is the case, for example, in Pss 49, 73, 34, 37, 52, and 62. This understanding is possible, however, as has been said, only in the middle and late monarchical

---

4. See below, §4.4 (no. 24).
5. See below, §4.5 (no. 25).
6. See *Psalm Studies* 1:166. So also Gunkel.
7. E.g., the royal psalms. See further, *Psalm Studies* 2:366–78.
8. *Psalm Studies* 1, see esp. 81–137.
9. See below, §§2.4 and 3.7 (nos. 8 and 19).
10. See §3.7 (no. 19), below.

period. The ancient period regarded wealth and power as the logical effluence of a good, strong, and just soul. The simultaneous result, however, is that the psalms just mentioned could not have been composed by David or his presumed contemporary Asaph.

Other psalms contain clear historical allusions that exclude the traditional indications of authorship. Both "Asaphite" psalms, Pss 74 and 79, speak of a conquest of Jerusalem and a plundering of the temple. Thus they could have been composed, at the earliest, under Rehoboam (1 Kgs 14:25–26). The Etan psalm, Ps 89, looks back on the time of David as the time of the old, long-since diminished, glory. Many David psalms also give occasion to similar reservations. Psalms 51 and 69 presuppose the conquest of Jerusalem. Others mention the temple on Zion, not the Davidic tabernacle (*hêkal*, Pss 5:8; 27:4; 134:2; *bêt yhwh*, Pss 27:4; 122:1; etc). Psalm 24 even mentions the temple on Zion as an ancient sanctuary ("the ancient gates").

Grounds based in the history of religions also point in the same direction. It is impossible to harmonize the devaluation of the bloody sacrifice in psalms such as 40, 50, and 69 with the type of piety represented by David and his contemporaries.[11]

Arguments from the history of language also deserve consideration. An Aramaizing diction such as that in Pss 139 or 145 cannot stem from the time of David. Even if the Israelites spoke an Aramaic dialect before or at the time of immigration, it was not the Aramaic of these psalms, and it would have been completely assimilated to Hebrew in the course of the centuries between Moses and David. Aramaisms first intruded into the language once again in the last Assyrian period.

In some cases, the information concerning authorship quite obviously rests on false historical connections, that is, on midrash. This is true, first, quite clearly of the name Moses given as the author in Ps 90. A congregation that feels that it is under the enduring pressure of divine wrath speaks here, a weary people that deserved punishment for its sins, that no longer asks for political greatness, only for moderate good fortune, that requests the undisturbed enjoyment of the work of its hands. The petition for the turn of fate is not motivated by the promises to the people, not with regard to the existence of the people, but is purely individualized. "Because we, the generation living now, can count on a lifespan of, at most, seventy to eighty years, and have as of yet seen only misfortune, may the good fortune, the reward for our suffering, come soon!" Whoever has the least knowledge of the spirit and thought of ancient Israel knows that Moses could never have spoken in such

---

11. See 2 Sam 6:13, 18; 21:9; 24:18–25.

a fashion. For the ancient period, the people was everything; individuals did not matter. In contrast, individual persons with their personal requirements become very prominent in Ps 90, so that the community almost recedes into the background. The fact that the psalm is understood to be Mosaic rests on the fact that the supplicants, whose days and years disappeared under divine wrath, were seen as the people of the wilderness wandering,[12] whose members left Egypt in the bloom of adulthood but now, after an almost forty-year wandering in the wilderness, stand at the end of their lives: circa 30 + 40 = 40–80 years! The statement in verse 16, "May your activity appear to your servants, your glory to your sons," offers confirmation to the interpretation: only the sons of the migrants may see the promised land.

The name Solomon in Pss 72 and 127 depends on a similar midrash. A psalm such as Ps 72 that parallels the people of Israel with "your (i.e., YHWH's) oppressed" (Ps 72:2) obviously cannot stem from Solomon's time. It assumes a period in which Israel repeatedly suffered, as it were, from the attacks of mightier neighbors. The superscription depends on a rabbinic exegesis of verse 1: the "king" who is simultaneously "the king's son" must be Solomon, although more so since the psalm speaks of the tribute of the kings of Saba.[13] Psalm 127 consists of one or two wisdom sayings that speak quite generally about that fact that one who builds a house without YHWH builds in vain, for all good fortune depends on the divine blessing. These sayings were reinterpreted later and related to the fall festival, which was simultaneously the temple dedication festival.[14] Later scribes extrapolated this interpretation further and regarded Solomon, the builder of the temple, as the author of the saying. The fact that the LXX omits it already demonstrates the secondary nature of the superscription.

We will see below that a whole series of passages that cite David as author also depend solely on midrash and are later additions to the text of the already-edited Psalter.[15] The fact that most of the psalms attributed to him could not be so old is indicated by the statements made in the beginning of this section.

With regard to the other "authors," Asaph, Heman, Etan, and the Korahites, it can be shown that, in reality, they were not historical individuals[16] and thus could not have composed the psalms even though, as will be shown

---

12. This explanation of the authorship information has also been indicated by Benno Jacob, "Beiträge zu einer Einleitung in die Psalmen," *ZAW* 16 (1896): 160.

13. Verse 10; see also 1 Kgs 10.

14. See below, §2.8 (no. 12).

15. See §§4.4–5 (nos. 24 and 25), below.

16. See §§3.2–3 (nos. 14 and 15), below.

below, the superscriptions conceive of them as individuals.[17] We will see, nonetheless, that these names contain something of a tradition.

Thus the traditional indications of authorship, in general, stand in a very dubious light. Consequently, one is correct to disregard them completely at first when investigating the psalms. As we will see below, the information concerning the historical situation prefacing the psalms in many cases is not to be judged as support for the historicity of the authorship information. They rest solely on midrash, on untenable exegetical connections and speculations, and presuppose the authorship information.[18]

1.4 (4) Thus we are presented with the task of discovering the true authors of the psalms. This cannot involve discovering the historical individuals who may have composed this or that psalm. The older critics did so often. Individuals speculated quite wildly concerning individuals in the Old Testament.[19] For a period, the prophet Jeremiah in particular enjoyed great popularity. This, however, is nothing other than an empty game of the imagination. The psalms are anonymous and will always remain so. The older method depends on the false assumption that the individual psalms were to be understood as historically contingent occasional poems by individual personalities who composed the on specific occasions of their individual lives and peppered their poems with references to purely personal experiences. It has been increasingly acknowledged, however, that the poets of the psalms, even when they speak in the first person, do not depict purely individual but typical experiences, attitudes, and feelings of the members of a larger circle and that individual allusions almost never come clearly to light. This circumstance is related, in part, to the poet's captivity to a fixed traditional style that was developed from the outset as an expression not of individual experiences but of the typical attitudes and feelings of a larger circle—or, put otherwise, of the normal Israelites participating in the cult or in certain cultic procedures. Gunkel recognized this in essence and thereby simultaneously rectified the former onesidedness that saw in the first-person speech of the psalms that also employed first-person style, not the typical Israelite individual, but the very personification of the congregation, an understanding that led to extremely skewed results, especially for the "individual psalms of lament."[20]

---

17. See §3.2 (no. 14), below.
18. Further in §4.5 (no. 25), below.
19. Ferdinand Hitzig (*Die Psalmen übersetzt und ausgelegt* [Leipzig: Winter, 1863]) distinguished himself particularly in this fashion.
20. Hermann Gunkel, "Die israelitische Literatur," in vol. 7.1 of *Die Kultur der Geg-*

Because we do not have in the psalms the words and experiences of this or that individual composer, but those of typical normal Israelites in certain life situations, our search can only involve discovering the circles in which the psalms originated. Here Gunkel's view, and probably, at the moment, that of the majority of recent exegetes,[21] that the various genres of the psalms were originally meant for the cult but that the old styles were later imitated by private poets and reinterpreted "spiritually," goes astray. These private poets were supposed to have composed songs that were not originally meant for the cult. One can infer from this that Gunkel wants to seek the poets of the oldest psalms, and probably also of a few of those still preserved, among the cultic personnel, the officials at the major sanctuaries.[22] He assumes—and as far as I can see, most of the others with him—that the vast majority of the preserved songs originated in private circles, indeed, in the pious conventicles of the Jewish community, in part still in the later preexilic but mostly in the postexilic period. They mirror the opposition between the pious, who were simultaneously the poor and insignificant, and the "godless," the apostate or the secularly minded, who were concurrently the powerful, the social oppressors, and the mockers of the poor pious. Most psalms were composed by "simple men of the people."[23] Later these songs, originally meant to give expression only to the religious attitudes and emotions of those "simple men," were used as songs in the temple cult and were included in the remnants of the cultic literature still extant. They were comparable to our "spiritual songs" in the *Missionsharfe* (Missionary Harp) or similar collections, which in terms of style and genre arose in part in the cult but were then "spiritualized" in the private circles of the little people and finally "returned to the cult," that is, were

---

enwart: Ihre Entwicklung und ihre Ziele (ed. P. Hinneberg; Berlin: Teubner, 1906); idem, "Psalmen," *RGG* 4:1927–49.

21. The introductions to the Old Testament and to the Psalms have remarkably little to say about this and almost never offer a principal treatment of the question. Willy Staerk (*Lyrik [Psalmen, Hoheslied und Verwandtes]* [vol. 3.1 of *Die Schriften des Alten Testaments in Auswahl*; ed. H. Gressmann et al.; 2nd ed.; Göttingen: Vandenhoeck & Ruprecht, 1920]), Gerhard Kittel (*Die Psalmen* [KAT 13; Leipzig: Scholl, 1914]), Walter Baumgartner (*Die Klagegedichte des Jeremia* [BZAW 32; Giessen: Töpelmann, 1917]), Emil Balla (*Das Ich der Psalmen* [Göttingen: Vandenhoeck & Ruprecht, 1912]), and others stand in Gunkel's tracks.

22. Gunkel even speaks of a "priestly poetry." See "Psalmen," *RGG* 4:1940.

23. Hermann Gunkel, *Ausgewählte Psalmen* (4th ed.; Göttingen: Vandenhoeck & Ruprecht, 1917), s.v.

included in the church hymnals.²⁴ The question of the poets of the psalms is thus related to that of their original purpose.

---

24. Gunkel, "Psalmen," *RGG* 4:1942. Antonin Causse, *Les "Pauvres" d'Israël: Prophètes, Psalmistes, Messianistes* (Paris: Istra, 1922), 81–82, envisioned the origin of the psalms similarly. He says of the poets: "They were farmers, laborers and shepherds like their fathers. By day they worked, cultivating the rocky ground beneath the burning sun. In the evening they returned to their homes and during the Eastern night sighed the complaints of their souls." I cite Causse's words because they clearly express the now still-customary understanding graphically and beautifully—in contrast to the unclear concepts of most psalm exegetes.

2

The Purpose of the Psalms:
Private or Cultic Songs

2.1 (5). Given the discussion above, the first question to be clarified is whether the majority of the psalms in the Psalter are private compositions, the outpourings of the hearts of more or less beautiful souls intended only to express what they felt themselves, or whether they are really cultic psalms composed from the outset for cultic and liturgical purposes.

I must say, first of all, that it is entirely puzzling to me, in view of the fact that the Psalter has been transmitted to us as the cultic hymnal of the Second Temple, how Gunkel, Causse (*Les "Pauvres" d'Israël*), and the other earlier scholars who also considered the psalms, with only a few exceptions, to be private compositions, envisioned the inclusion of the presumably private compositions in the cult. The analogy with the originally private church songs of Protestantism, especially since the time of the Pietistic and post-Pietistic movements, to which Gunkel refers does not fit. With respect to the early Protestant era, the Reformers acknowledged very early that congregational singing was a chief component of worship. Therefore, it was necessary to create appropriate songs, and one took them where they could be found. People also sat down to write their own cultic songs that bore the stamp of their worship purpose. Thus a revision of the biblical Psalter was a major component in Calvinist church song, and among us the original "cultic" purpose of the songs of Thomas Kingo is betrayed in the fact that the majority of them were written for the major feasts of the church or followed very closely the prescribed sermon text for the individual Sundays and were quite often only versified paraphrases of the same. When the *ecclesiolae* arose later, it was already an axiom for these circles that the song was a major component of every assembly for worship or edification. The fact that they created such songs reflecting the attitudes, views, and religious experiences of these circles, for their more private devotional gatherings intended more or less to replace the church, was both a historical and a psychological necessity. When these circles gained influence on the official churches in many places and, as was true among us, influenced them to some depth, the revision of the old church hymnals in the sense of the newer, more subjective piety oriented toward individual experience became a logical and historical necessity. Then church officials, influenced by the new movements and gradually including persons sympathetic toward the new spirit, officially commissioned revisions of church hymnals to include the devotional songs of the circles influenced by Pietism, Methodism, and the like and ultimately also the purely private compositions of individuals that had, partly, become popular religious literature.

Can one truly believe that the bureaucracy of aristocratic officials of the Second Jewish Temple, who were profoundly convinced of the divine provenance of all their institutions,[1] to the degree, in fact, that regular temple song and music appeared to them to be divinely inspired, would have been willing to admit the equality of purely private and obscure lay poetry with the venerable temple songs or, indeed, would have officially prescribed the inclusion of such poems in the temple hymnal? If not, how, then, does one envision their inclusion? Did the simple, devout people smuggle them in under the name of David? Why did they not then also succeed in smuggling in the "Solomonic" psalms that bore the name of an equally honorable author? What became, then, of the truly old cultic songs, which must indeed have been extant in quantity since the preexilic period? Can one truly believe that the views of certain private circles, remote from the temple cult, so massively permeated the ranks of the temple authorities that the "spiritually minded" succeeded in ejecting those old songs and replacing them with newer "spiritual" products. Believe that if you can.

One can envision this problem vividly: the Psalter was transmitted as the temple hymnal; there was once an authentic cultic literature associated with the temple; at one point—how and when goes unstated—the temple officials are supposed to have thrown this old cultic literature onto the rubbish heap and for some reason accepted an entirely anonymous collection of private (i.e., in the view of the cultic personnel, profane) songs, composed and collected by unnamed private individuals. How do scholars envision this? They have not even perceived or raised the question! Before it is to be answered even unsatisfactorily, the contention of the private origin of most psalms must be definitively rejected. Thus the question cannot be positively answered. Once posed, it must be denied: such a thing is not possible.[2]

---

1. Cf. the Priestly Document.

2. Thus, the correctness of my interpretation of the individual psalms of lament as cultic prayers for the healing of illness, directed against the illness-producing sorcerers and demons (*Psalm Studies* 1; see also below 799 n. 24), is already demonstrated negatively.

One might object here that the presence of "anticultic" compositions such as Pss 40, 50, 51, and 69 demonstrates, indeed, that some such process actually took place. As I have occasionally indicated elsewhere and will demonstrate more precisely below (§3.3 [no. 15]), there is nothing to the asserted "anticultic" view of these psalms. The understanding rests on a much too restricted concept of the cultic.

2.2 (6). What becomes of the assumption of the theory treated here, namely, the assumption that there were "social circles" in Judaism in which the composition and singing of devotional "spiritual" songs was a major occupation?[3] There were certainly private, self-contained circles of the devout in the latest period (see below). Undeniably, poems were also composed in them. The existence of the Psalms of Solomon, which sometimes imitate the style of the old cultic songs but were not composed for the cult, demonstrates this for us. These circles certainly did not extend back into the preexilic period, however.[4] The circles of disciples that may have gathered around the prophets and maintained their predictions and eschatological expectations may also have observed a simple and moral life as a precondition;[5] they are not identical with the later religious conventicles but are to be regarded as a continuation of the prophetic guilds. For them, the chief concern was ecstaticism and the preservation and extension of the sayings of the master.[6] The conventicles of the kind that Gunkel, for example, apparently envisions were something else.

In a review of my book in *ThLBl* 43 (1922): 244ff., Gerhard Kittel thinks it necessary to reject my interpretation, in part, with the justification that I "elevate as reality what is possible, but not more." This admission satisfies me, for the acultic interpretation that Kittel proposes is, in fact, not possible. The individual psalms of lament must be cultic psalms; one may postulate this a priori, given the discussion above, as simply the most likely. It is necessary, then, to interpret them as cultic psalms and to understand the complaints about enemies, illness, and 'āwen on this assumption. Then, however, my explanation is the sole possibility. Conversely, even the fact that those psalms can be so explained becomes a demonstration of the correctness of my postulate: they can be explained as cultic psalms, i.e., as what we must consider them a priori, and only as cultic psalms.

3. This, not the existence per se of conventicle-like circles of pious persons, is the true issue here.

4. The evidence for the preexilic existence of such social and religious circles that Gunkel ("Psalmen," *RGG* 4:1945) finds in the use of the term 'ebyôn in Jer 20:13, is entirely invalid, as will be demonstrated further below.

5. We may first learn of them under Isaiah (see Isa 8:16–17, possibly an authentic Isaianic saying).

6. Cf. the relationship of the "Trito-Isaianic" prophecies to Deutero-Isaiah.

We first find the beginning of such groups in the second century,[7] namely, in apocalyptic circles, unrelated to the old prophetic guilds, that arose from the ranks of scripture scholars.[8] If we may judge based on the literary legacy that is clearly the product of conventicles, the later conventicles chiefly cultivated eschatological and messianic expectations and writings, speculative and mystical theology, and a strict observance of the law. We know nothing, however, as to whether they also held their own worship and devotional assemblies where psalmody was a major concern—and this is the main point.

Gunkel sees the frequent expressions "the assembly of the pious," "of the righteous," and so on (Pss 1:5; 111:1; 149:1) in the vows of the lament psalms to thank God "in the (great) assembly" after deliverance (Pss 9:15; 22:23, 26; 26:12; 30:5; 40:10–11; 109:30–31) as evidence for the existence of such psalm-writing conventicles.[9] In all these passages, however, the expressions mentioned do not denote the conventicles but either the cultic community assembled for a thanksgiving feast, whether major or minor,[10] or the majority of the people pictured as righteous.[11]

There is good reason to doubt that there were purely private devotional gatherings at all in the Judaism of the time, disregarding purely sectarian groups who do not come under consideration here, however, since the Psalms are not sectarian in the least. What we know is that the religious need that temple worship simply could not satisfy for geographical reasons found adequate expression in synagogue worship. I doubt very much that there were ever "cult-like" devotional assemblies of the pious other than attendance at the temple and synagogue worship. We hear nothing or very little, however, concerning the singing of psalms in the synagogue.[12] There is good reason

---

7. See Gustav Hölscher, *Geschichte der israelitische und jüdischen Religion* (Giessen: Töpelmann, 1922), 207.

8. Ibid., 187–93.

9. *Psalmen*, 37. Causse, *Les "Pauvres" d'Israël*, 104–14, follows him.

10. Even Gunkel seems to want to admit this. Note the reference to the thanksgiving sacrifice in his *Psalmen*, 37. It was not offered in the conventicle. It is all the more remarkable when, with appeal to the passages mentioned above (Pss 9:15; 22:23, 26; 26:12; 30:5; 40:10–11; 109:30–31), he says: "We must understand these sayings such that the believers have assembled in small circles where they suffered and triumphed with one another."

11. Such as the passages mentioned above: Pss 1:5; 111:1; 149:1.

12. According to the talmudic sources, the major elements were: the Shema, the prayer pronounced by the worship leader in the direction of Jerusalem, to which the congregation responded, the reading from the Torah and the Prophets, an exegetical sermon by some member of the congregation, and, finally, the blessing (if a priest were present, otherwise a prayer for blessing; see Hölscher, *Geschichte*, 178 n. 12). I cannot admit that the passage in Soph. 18 refers, as is usually assumed, to synagogue worship (so also Jacob, "Beiträge," 145).

to doubt that these circles ever played a role in the ancient period, at least before the fall of the temple. Psalm singing belonged to the temple cult and had its place there since ancient times. The only case that can be considered psalm singing outside the temple is the celebration of the Passover in homes, during which the great Hallel (Ps 113–118) was indeed sung, at least in the first century of the Common Era (Mark 14:26). The matter was such here, however, that, on the one side, despite Deuteronomy, the Passover celebration was indeed understood as a sacrificial procedure, and singing belongs with sacrifice, and, on the other, singing from a book long regarded as canonical was involved here, not the performance of freely composed *Missionsharfen* songs. The practice was surely borrowed directly from temple worship.[13]

2.3 (7). According to Gunkel, the "individual lament psalms" in particular were supposed to have originated in these private circles and to have been composed and sung by them for private devotion. They were indeed the songs "that the sick person composed on his sickbed or with which the suffering comforted himself."[14] Is it likely per se, however, that all of these psalms were composed by sick people? Indeed, they are mostly sickness psalms, but were they composed by the sick persons involved? Were not all these sick persons who complain so miserably in these psalms too sick to write? May one assume offhand that these "simple men of the people" were familiar with the traditional style of the cultic psalms to such a degree that they could all compose psalms that resemble one another very closely and agree with the old cultic lament psalms in all the stylistic details? Why, then, do unique details of their illness or allusions to specific personal circumstances of any kind never appear? This is puzzling indeed.[15] Furthermore, is the sickbed usually the appropriate place for writing? Did these sick persons have nothing else to do?

The statement of the mishnaic and talmudic literature concerning the use of the Psalms in the synagogue cult demonstrates, in fact, that it did not involve psalm singing but the use of the words of psalms as prayers. Psalm singing was understood as belonging to the temple cult. Compare the assessment of the outstanding connoisseur of this literature, Jacob, in "Beiträge," 172: "Nothing of the temple music was transferred to the synagogue. It maintained worship without music that it had always had apart from the temple."

13. Most of the Hallel Psalms belong to the Feast of Booths, and thus this group of psalms within the Psalter was probably originally chosen for this feast, and the practice later transferred to temple worship on Passover (or on Mazzoth), and only thence transferred to domestic celebration.

14. "Psalmen," *RGG* 4:1943.

15. The supposed personal allusions, for example, in Ps 42, all resolve on closer examination into more or less original realizations of traditional images: for example, the supposed Jordan cataract in Ps 42 and the tents of Kedar in Ps 120.

If they were not too sick to write at all, then the depictions of the illness and the suffering that they sometimes offer were overstated beyond measure. Was the sick person in Ps 22, who portrayed himself as already dead, whose bones could be counted, whose "gums were as dry as a sherd, and whose tongue cleaved to his jaws" from fever, not too sick, indeed, to have composed not only the lament (vv. 2–22) but also, in anticipation, the thanksgiving song (vv. 23–32) that he wanted to sing one day at the thanksgiving feast "in the great assembly," to say nothing of the unfortunate person who is supposed to have written Ps 119 with its eight times twenty-two alphabetic verses?

Finally, were all these simple men of the people really literate? Whence does one have the right to envision conditions in pre-Christian Palestinian Judaism on the analogy of our time with public schools and obligatory education? Even the priest Jeremiah had to go to a professional scribe when he wanted to record his oracles (Jer 36), this undoubtedly because he could not write, and even during Jesus' time the vast majority of the people did not know the law and were thus not literate.[16] I agree with Gunkel that most of the "individual psalms of lament" are sickness psalms. I cannot imagine, however, that they were composed by the sick persons themselves, and I believe that I can also offer a better explanation of the circumstances (see below).

2.4 (8). What are the actual reasons that Gunkel, who was, after all, the first to recognize the cultic origin of the psalms as genres and the very typical character of the experiences and attitudes depicted in them, nonetheless maintained, in agreement with earlier exegetes, the acultic, purely private character of the psalms?[17]

Above all, it seems that the understanding inherited from older criticism has thus become "traditional," namely, that most of the psalms, especially the individual psalms of lament, reflect the social and religious tensions in Judaism. Proceeding from the fact that certain evil enemies appear *en masse* in these psalms and are described as evildoers (*rĕšāʿîm*), fools (*nĕbālîm*), and so on in opposition to the pious (*ḥăsîdîm*), the righteous (*ṣaddîqîm*), the humble (*ʿănāwîm*) and those oppressed by their enemies (*ʿăniyîm*), the "poor" (*ʾebyônîm, dallîm*), and so on, the conclusion was that two social and religious

---

16. John 7:49. If there had been common schooling, the Torah would obviously have served as the textbook. One who does not even know the Law cannot read.

17. This discussion pertains only to Gunkel and the scholars he has inspired (Gressmann, Balla, Staerk, Baumgartner, Kittel, etc.). The older scholars gave no reasons whatsoever but simply took the private, noncultic origin of the Psalms to be self-evident. In praxis, they seem to have entirely forgotten that the Psalter was once the hymnal of the temple and that this fact yields certain consequences with regard to the scholar's tasks.

parties confronted one another here, a pious but socially oppressed minority and a wealthy, secular, "apostate" majority. These parties were then identified with the religious parties of the pious and the Hellenists known from the Maccabean period. In this respect, Gunkel went further than the older exegetes only in that, with a certain degree of justification, he pointed to the precursors of those tensions and parties in the earliest postexilic period and even in the social tensions of the later preexilic period.[18]

Such movements undeniably existed in the postexilic period and sharply opposed parties arose from them in the "Maccabean era."[19] I believe only that the significance of the social aspect for the late period has been significantly overemphasized and misdirected by the expressions ʿānî, ʿānāw, and ʾebyôn. The Pharisees in the New Testament period, at any rate, were often wealthy, respected people. Nothing suggests that the "pious" of the Maccabean period, who opposed Hellenistic innovations, arose from the socially oppressed. The occasional reference to them as "poor" or "oppressed" is a political and religious designation that they borrowed from the scriptures, especially from the Psalter, and that sometimes acquired contemporary religious and political significance when they were persecuted by the Syrians and later, sometimes even by the politically intolerant and intractable Hasmoneans. If we return to the older postexilic period, there were no such sharply distinguished parties (the Syrian religious persecution first created them), but only the two schools that we know from Nehemiah's time: the school of the "exilic" circle zealous for the law and the more lax "Palestinian" circle.[20] Here, of course, social contrasts also played a role but did not coincide with the religious. The "Palestinians" included, above all, the temple aristocracy but also the common folk, on the whole, for whom the legal rigor of a Nehemiah was simply incomprehensible (see Neh 13:10–27). The "exiles" included primarily those circles that actually returned from the exile and expanded as the result of continuing immigration, especially middle-class commercial circles in Jerusalem. There is evidence that on certain occasions the debt-laden rural population took their side or were played against the aristocrats by the leaders of the exiles (see Neh 5:1–13). Neither Nehemiah nor Ezra says anything about the poor at that time being more pious than the wealthy. Finally, with regard to the late preexilic period, sharp social tensions were certainly already evident. We know that, for religious reasons, the prophets of judgment protected the oppressed at that time. The prophets never say, however, that the socially lower-ranked,

---

18. "Psalmen," *RGG* 4:1945.
19. Pharisees, Sadducees, Zealots. See Hölscher, *Geschichte*, 218–23.
20. See my *Statholderen Nehemia* (Kristiania: Olaf Norls, 1916), 164–82.

rural population was more pious than the leaders of the nation. There was no religious party of the poor and pious at that time. As mentioned above, Gunkel refers to the expression *'ebyôn* in Jer 20:13. The word *'ebyôn* here does not appear, however, in a social or economic meaning. As a synonym for *'ānî*, in certain contexts it acquired the more comprehensive meaning "finding oneself in some situation of distress and need," "oppressed," and "miserable" and does not permit economic conclusions. Furthermore, the word already had this meaning at the beginning, as did *'ānî*. Every sufferer, for example, every sick person, was always able to describe himself as *'ebyôn* or *'ānî*.[21] Jeremiah's use of the word rests on a purely mechanical adoption and, to this degree, on a reinterpretation of concepts and expressions that actually signify and state something entirely different than what he infused into them. He describes himself as *'ebyôn* and his opponents who challenge his prophetic vocation and want to kill him as an annoying prophet as *mĕrē'îm*. We will see straightaway what the expressions actually mean. It must be emphasized that, even if the pious and the evildoers designate two parties in the Psalms, it would be impermissible to draw any social or economic conclusions from the designation of the former as *'ănāwîm*, *'ănîyîm*, or *'ebyônîm*.[22]

The preceding survey has shown that two sharply divided religious parties existed only after the exile. The preexilic prophets of reform had no party. The Maccabean period first created the fully delineated parties. If the individual psalms of lament reflect the antagonisms between two parties, they opposed each other with such asperity that one can hardly avoid relocating, with Duhm, the majority of the Psalms to the Maccabeean period. Gunkel wants to avoid just this. It may be impossible for many reasons.

In reality, however, as I have shown elsewhere,[23] the whole interpretation of the individual psalms of lament based on supposed religious and social party relations is unjustified. In addition to these terms, the frequent expression *pō'ălê 'āwen*, to be translated "sorcerers" or the like, demonstrates the proper understanding of the enemies in these psalms. The enemies are the

---

21. See *Psalm Studies* 1:120–24; cf. 3:549–50. Derived from *'bh*, *'ebyôn* actually means: "desirous of something, needing something, to be in need of something." What one needs, of course, need not be money, goods, and earthly possessions. It can also be help, health, assistance in all manner of need and hardship. Both the meaning "poor" (*pauper*) and the meaning "miserable," "suffering" derive from this basic meaning. The latter is not derived from the former. In the Psalms, and also in the "confessions" ("monologues") of Jeremiah, *'ebyôn* is almost always to be translated "miserable," not "poor."

22. This would be just as impermissible as drawing, *mutatis mutandis*, such conclusions from the [Dutch] party name "Geusen" [beggars].

23. All of *Psalm Studies* 1 deals with this question.

innumerable evil sorcerers and demons who have made those complaining and petitioning in these psalms sick and are characterized as a violent person (*'îš ḥāmās*), "evildoer," harmful person (*'îš bĕlîya'al*), liars (*'ōyĕbê šeqer*), or the like.²⁴ The pious and righteous characterize themselves as "oppressed,"

---

24. The objections against my interpretation brought by several of my honored colleagues in discussions of my *Psalm Studies* 1 give me no cause to change it. They have not been able to shake my position in the main, I think. I have not even expected that an entirely new viewpoint would immediately find universal agreement. At any rate, the expectation that my central thesis would not be rejected with such frivolous arguments as those brought to the market by H. Duhm (in *TLZ* 13 [1922]) seemed justified to me. The response to Duhm's rejection of my interpretation of the enemies in Ps 6 with a reference to v. 2, which I supposedly "ignored completely," in Ps 38 with a reference to vv. 2–3, and in Ps 41 with a reference to v. 5, is already included in my book (84, ll. 1–4 from the top). I gladly admit that my interpretation of this passage or that where the word *'āwen* occurs may not be tenable (see the arguments by Paul Humbert in *RTP* 46 [1922]). This is not the main point, which is that I recognized the previously unrecognized basic meaning of the word *'āwen* and have explained the previously unexplained relationship between enemies and sickness in many psalms (see Ernst Sellin in *Das Alte Testament und die evangelische Kirche der Gegenwart* [Leipzig: Deichert, 1921], 134; even Kittel had to admit this in his bittersweet treatment in *ThLBl* 16 [1922]; cf. his remarks in *Psalmen*, 21, 100–101). Many of my critics seem, however, first, to have forgotten that I have explicitly emphasized in my book that, indeed, the word now often appears in a much faded, general sense, as a disparaging designation for the evil and harmful act and attitude, and that often only still-extant idioms that may not have been understood by the pertinent authors betray the original meaning. In any case, I must insist that the evidence that this is always the case in the Psalms will be difficult to produce and that the spiritualizing interpreters bear the burden of proof. The evidence, however, has not been offered in Kittel's observations concerning Ps 6 (*Psalmen* [4th ed.], 21 bottom). He thinks that the fact that the prayer does not call for the destruction of the enemies but for their humiliation demonstrates that the religious understandings in this psalm are "significantly spiritualized." Under certain circumstances in Hebrew, however, "humiliation" is nothing other than "destruction" (see Ps 83:14–18). This entirely unsubstantiated and more than dubious assertion of a "spiritual" reinterpretation of the original ideas and expressions constitutes the central precondition of Kittel's exegesis of the Psalms, which, consequently, is not exegesis in many cases but eisegesis. Second, my critics understand the term "sorcery," it seems, much more restrictedly than the ancient Israelites and I with them have done. It may be that I have not expressed myself clearly enough on this point. I call attention here to what I said in *Psalm Studies* 5 (709–14) concerning curse and sorcery and to the discussion of sin and curse by Johannes Pedersen (*Israel: Its Life and Culture* [2 vols.; Atlanta: Scholars Press, 1991], 1:411–52), who agrees on the whole with my views. For the ancient Israelites, any insult, any defamation, any evil wish directed against a "righteous person" came under the heading of the "evil curse" or of "sorcery" because they believed that inherent in these things was a real, misfortune-producing power, originating in an evil soul and related to the demonic and evil "futile" powers of life, that eats its way into the soul of the one impacted and "weakens" it, "per-

"suffering," "miserable" to the extent that the enemies have pushed them into misfortune.[25] With a particular religious nuance, in the sense of a "piety motif," they also occasionally characterize themselves as the "humble" (*'ăwānîm*). When, especially in the vows of the lament psalms that anticipate the thanksgiving psalm, they include themselves with others under this name, they think of other people who may have once found themselves in similar misfortune and whom they refer to their own example. There is nothing remarkable about the fact that they characterize themselves as just and pious and include themselves in prayer among likewise just people whom YHWH is obligated to aid in times of crisis; it is, rather, self-evident. Thus, nothing can be concluded concerning the private and coventicular origin of

---

verting [its] honor." The concept of *'āwen* is, beyond question, broader than our "sorcery," precisely because our modern scholars have formed a concept of sorcery that is too narrow and thus false. They no longer know as a matter of experience what sorcery is and usually disdain determining the meaning of the concept from a purely historical perspective by interrogating the primitive witnesses. The error of my book is that I did not yet know Pedersen's *Israel* when I wrote and thus based the discussions of *'āwen*, *šāw*, and the like on a somewhat too narrow psychological foundation and, as a consequence, did not make it clear enough to my critics what I—or, more precisely, the ancient Israelites—understand by "sorcery." Thus, if I were an ancient Israelite, I would call the somewhat spiteful suspicion of my intellectual property rights to my book, which does not agree with the facts, at the conclusion of Kittel's treatment mentioned above, both *'āwen* and *dibrê šāw* that produced (or were meant to produce) *rĕmîyâ* in my "soul" or that "poured" *dĕbar bĕlîya'al* in it—if such a claim to priority did not seem rather secondary to me. Thus I can also quite easily admit that sometimes in the Old Testament, indeed, especially in Proverbs and the Prophets, *pō'ălê 'āwen* designates, for example, slanderers and false accusers or especially clever extortioners or creators of latifundia. If such "unjust" people had success, the ancient Israelites surely thought that they did not do so by just means. They had "made a covenant with Sheol" and "the throne of perdition in order to do injustice contrary to the law" (see Isa 28:15; Ps 94:20). I place no weight whatsoever on the word "sorcery." The main issue is that one comprehend the correct content of the Hebrew term *'āwen* and finally stop treating the psalms as modern individualistic lyric. If one should wish to say "the evil, illness-producing curse," with the ancient Babylonians, instead of "sorcery," and to see in the enemies of the lament psalms the usually unknown evildoers who have made the ill sick "by unjust means," then I have nothing whatsoever to object against it. (I have explicitly noted myself that the anxious or malicious although innocent friends and neighbors of the sick person are sometimes reckoned among the enemies because their behavior intensifies the suffering of the sick person. Kittel's discussion of Ps 41 or Humbert's remark [*RTP* 46 [1922]: 76] do not pertain to my theory.)

25. The expression in Jer 20:13 also depends on this terminology (see above). Conclusions regarding social conditions before Jeremiah may not be built on this expression. See further §2.6 (no. 10), below.

these psalms.[26] I have indicated above and will return below[27] to the fact that, in a certain sense, the social tensions influenced those psalms, nonetheless.

2.5 (9). Gunkel's second argument for the noncultic origin of most of the psalms seems to be that they "do not presuppose a specific procedure" (namely, of a cultic nature). "They are not to be sung on specific occasions but can be sung or prayed at any time."[28] "They belong neither to a specific procedure nor are they conceived for performance in worship."[29] In the first instance, the claim that noncultic psalms exist relates primarily to individual lament psalms.

It must be said that Gunkel actually did not offer positive reasons for the assertions printed above. He seems, however, to want to justify them based on the fact that these psalms do not mention cultic procedures and he interprets the occasional allusion metaphorically.[30] It should be asked, however, where it stands written anywhere in the world that a cultic song absolutely must mention or refer to those rites and procedures with which it is somehow connected. Indeed, the cult does not consist solely of rites and precisely corresponding words in reference to them. Rather, the cult also includes, for example, invocations, songs of praise, and prayers that are, in fact, parts of the whole that also includes rites and procedures, but that can, nonetheless, constitute relatively independent units within the whole. A prayer need not necessarily accompany a procedure. The pertinent part of the cultic ritual can consist, in fact, of the prayer itself. The same is true, of course, for songs of praise, invocations, and so on. Admittedly, a hymn is usually sung before or after a sacrifice, yet there is no absolute necessity to mention the sacrifice every time. Admittedly, more or less formulaic prayers are associated with the rites of cleansing and healing, yet it is not necessary to remark explicitly in the prayer that we are now going to perform a couple of purification rites! The purpose of the prayer is not, after all, to call attention to the ritual procedures but to the distress, the need, and to help worthy piety or penitence of the one to be cleansed. Thus there are also undoubtedly Babylonian cultic prayers that do not mention the related cultic procedures in the text.

It must further be said that a strict proof of the "spiritual" and metaphorical interpretation of the references to the cult that actually occur will be sought

---

26. See §2.2, above, concerning "the great assembly" as a designation for the cultic community.
27. See §3.7 (no. 19), below; see also above, 784–85.
28. "Psalmen," *RGG* 4:1941.
29. Ibid., 4:1943.
30. Such as Pss 26:6; 51:9; see ibid., 4:1943.

to no avail. In reality, there are actually significantly more such references in the Psalter, even in the individual psalms of lament, than Gunkel and others want us to believe. I have elsewhere pointed extensively to such traces of cultic purpose.[31] Even if some of what was mentioned there should be uncertain, a rather goodly series nonetheless remains. Between the psalms that contain such references and the other individual psalms of lament, however, there is otherwise no stylistic or substantive difference.

On the other hand, it would indeed be remarkable if the illness psalms were to have been sung privately, outside the cult, in the circle of friends or alone "on the sickbed," while the thanksgiving psalms, very frequently vowed in them,[32] were performed in the cult and in the temple, indeed, in connection with the likewise often-vowed (Pss 22:26–27; 54:8–9; 56:13) thanksgiving sacrifices.[33] What in the whole world could have motivated those pious persons among the people to reject one part of the cultic procedures (rites of purification, atonement sacrifices, psalms for sin offerings) but to retain the other that did not differ substantially (thanksgiving sacrifice and psalm for the thanksgiving sacrifice)? There is not a single passage in the whole literature that indicates that the usually "orthodox" pious person rejected the sacrifice for atonement and the related rites[34] but retained thanksgiving sacrifice and other types of sacrifice. If, however, in sickness and other cases of impurity, they submitted themselves to the purification rites and sin offerings prescribed in the law (Lev 5; 12–15), they also recited individual psalms of lament in the cult. Undoubtedly this psalm genre originally accompanied purification rites and sin offerings.[35] Moreover, one cannot assume that the priests, who accepted the sin offering *torah* into the Priestly Document during the postexilic period, would have omitted the sin-offering psalm and, in contrast, retained the thanksgiving-offering psalm. If, however, sick persons came

---

31. *Psalm Studies* 1:144–61.

32. Pss 7:18; 13:6; 22:23, 26; 26:12; 28:7; 31:8; 35:18, 28; 42:6, 12; 43:4–5; 51:17; 52:11; 54:8; 58:8–11; 59:17; 61:9; 69:31–37; 71:14–16, 22–24; 109:30–31; 119:171–172, 175; 142:8; 144:9–10.

33. Gunkel also seems to admit that the thanksgiving songs presuppose the thanksgiving sacrifice and are thus cultic songs (see "Psalmen," *RGG* 4:1944; *Psalmen*, 37). Nonetheless, he calls them "private" songs, in part because he thinks of the private sacrifice in contrast to the congregational sacrifice and in part because he assumes—or so it seems, at least—that the one healed composed the thanksgiving song. He cannot have any knowledge of this, however (see, nonetheless, §3.8 [no. 20], below). I always use the word "private" here in contrast to cultic (meant for cultic and liturgical purposes).

34. Not even the sectarian Essenes rejected sacrifice; see Hölscher, *Geschichte*, 210–11 n. 4.

35. Gunkel demonstrated this once and for all.

to the temple and also recited sin-offering psalms, why did they then need to sing psalms at home and on their sickbeds? One must indeed assume with confidence that they regarded the long sacred cultic psalm as more powerful and effective than the more formless domestic prayer, if the temple cult meant anything at all—and the temple certainly meant a great deal to the psalmists. We will deal with this in greater detail below.[36] One may say that there were many sick persons who could not come to Jerusalem. For good or ill, they had to be satisfied with composing and singing a psalm at home. I readily admit that such could have occurred and probably did. But are the priests and temple officials in Jerusalem supposed to have thrown all of their old temple sin-sacrifice songs on the trash heap and adopted "private" poets in the temple hymnal? Believe that, if you can! The theory of the noncultic lament psalm that later "returned to the cult" becomes entangled in a series of irresolvable contradictions.

2.6 (10). Gunkel also adduces the "confessions," that is, the personal complaints of Jeremiah, as evidence of the noncultic character of the individual lament psalms.[37] Without question, Jeremiah employed the style of the individual complaint song in a metaphorical sense and reinterpreted the expressions spiritually. He spoke metaphorically of "pain" and "healing" (Jer 15:18; 17:14) but understood this to refer to his suffering under the persecutions and ridicule of his neighbors and to his vindication through the intervention of a prophetic prediction. Jeremiah, however, certainly did not invent this genre of the "metaphorical complaint song."[38]

The first part of this argument is undoubtedly correct: Jeremiah used the style of the lament psalm metaphorically. He spoke of "healing" and meant vindication as a prophet and deliverance from his personal enemies.[39] It is not known whether he followed older models in this reinterpretation; nothing in his words indicates so. It seems more likely to me that this essentially

---

36. See §3.4 (no. 16), below.
37. On this, see Baumgartner, *Klagegedichte*.
38. "Psalmen," *RGG* 4:1942.
39. The use of the traditional expressions *'ebyôn* (in the style of the lament psalms in the meaning "sick") and *mĕrē'îm* (in the style of the lament psalms as a synonym for *pō'ălê 'āwen* in reference to sorcerers, demons, etc.) is also based on this reinterpretation. If Jer 20:13 stems from Jeremiah (see 2.4, above), which is rather dubious, it represents a rather typical expression in cultic, sin-offering psalms that has been rather mechanically adopted and applied to quite different circumstances. No argument can be made against my interpretation of the enemies and the "suffering" in the Psalms offered in §2.4 based on the meaning of these expressions in Jeremiah (contra Humbert in his review of *Psalm Studies* 1 in *RTP* [1923]: 78).

absurd literary adaptation of the old style and its literary expressions argues, indeed, that it represents a novel reinterpretation. There was no distinct style for purely personal, independent complaint prayers concerning needs not foreseen in the cultic rites. Consequently, the prophet had to resort to the cultic sin-offering psalms but was still so dependent on his models that he employed expressions that were actually useless for what he wanted to say.

What Jeremiah did for the first time, here, however, the psalmists could well have done after him. It must be said in this regard that there was a difference between the prophet and the "simple men of the people." At any rate, they differed in that Jeremiah's poems quite clearly state that he means something other than his literary models, while the supposed noncultic lament psalms in the Psalter would not differ at any point from the cultic. Thus, Jeremiah said clearly that he meant the men of Anathoth and and the like when he spoke of the "enemies," the "oppressors," the *mĕrē'îm*, the *rĕšā'îm*, and so on. Not a single word suggests, however, that the individual lament psalms understand the *pō'ălê 'āwen* to refer to anyone other than the sorcerers that the old cultic psalms undoubtedly had in mind.

Thus the "confessions" of Jeremiah produce no evidence that the lament psalms of the Psalter were meant in a metaphorical, noncultic sense. Such approaches cannot yield more than a possibility. This possibility fails, however, for the reasons presented above.

2.7 (11). Gunkel's actual, most profound, and yet psychologically most effective basis for his theory is probably that he *greatly undervalues cultic religion* in the manner of the ancient prophets and liberal Protestant theologians. Unconscious or semi-conscious motives that one cannot always identify literarily but can, nonetheless, suspect with good reason are involved here. It seems very likely to me that this unconscious motive has influenced Gunkel. This is the only way I can understand his justification of his contention of the originally noncultic nature of such poems as Pss 28; 61; 63; 84; and 1 Sam 2:1–10 on the grounds of their "subjective" character.[40] This argumentation seems to presuppose that "subject nature"—and this should probably be understood

---

40. "Psalmen," *RGG* 4:1942. Gunkel apparently misunderstood these psalms. He regards them as originally purely private songs that later found acceptance in the cult of the royal temple in Jerusalem and, on this occasion, were therefore provided with a secondarily appended intercession for the king (cf. also *Psalmen*, 208). In many cases, the strophic structure of these psalms, which does not permit the excision of the lines that deal with the king, speaks against this assumption. Excision has no substantive basis. Instead, these psalms are prayers written in the name of the king. The first person supplicant is the king himself. This alone already speaks for an originally cultic purpose.

here to mean personal feelings and perceptions based on personal experiences—may not be found in a cultic song. Gunkel seems to presuppose here that actual cultic songs reveal nothing personal. He apparently wants to view them as pure "formularies."[41] This may be an unjustified assessment, however. Even cultic songs were composed by living people, indeed by people whose hearts were in cultic religion and who had, or at least could have had, religious experiences during festive cultic occasions at the religious festivals. Why should they, too, not express, if capable, their experiences and perceptions in their poems? The experiences and perceptions expressed in these psalms are not "personal" in the sense that they differ from those of other devout people at the time. They are, indeed, only typical attitudes, normal for and pervasive in the religiosity of the time.

I have tried to show elsewhere (*Psalm Studies* 2:306–21) what Israelite cultic religion at its apexes was able to offer to its adherents and how its professional officials expressed the experiences they had at the festivals and the related feelings, sometimes in a truly "subjective," that is, authentic and deeply felt, manner. One who has recognized the cultic context of the experiences and feelings depicted there will not be so easily inclined to dismiss the cultic songs that are "subjective" in nature, even if this "priestly poetry" was created by cultic personnel. Now I will say a few words about the cultic interpretation of the Psalms in order to present the positive section of this chapter.

2.8 (12). In addition to the understanding of the psalms as private poetry, one occasionally finds a cultic explanation, but it was not employed as a general principle of interpretation previously. The older critical scholars also assumed that several individual psalms were composed from the outset as liturgical compositions. Thus one quite often finds a corresponding interpretation of this or that psalm, for example, in Frants Buhl's commentary.[42] It has often been noted and argued that a psalm such as Ps 118, for example, was composed for cultic purposes. Bernhard Duhm in particular turned his attention to the liturgical character of many psalms.[43] Thus, for example, he clearly recognized the purely liturgical character of most of the "enthronement psalms" in the more restricted sense (Pss 47; 93; 95–100), and already in 1897 he drew the fully correct conclusion from a passage such as Job 33:26–28 when he said, "Passages such as this, with parallels in the Psalms, should lead one to the conclusion that, when offering a thanksgiving sacrificed in the temple, the laity

---

41. See "Psalmen," *RGG* 4:1944, §13.
42. *Psalmerne: Oversatte og Fortolkede* (2nd ed.; Copenhagen: Gyldenhal, 1918).
43. *Die Psalmen* (KHAT 14; Tübingen: Mohr, 1899).

sang an appropriate song or had one sung by the temple singers."[44] Bertholet, like Stade before him, also exhibited a clear view of the purely cultic and liturgical nature of many psalms.[45] Benno Jacob should be mentioned as the sole true exception before Gunkel.[46] He concluded from some of the superscriptions and from many biblical, mishnaic, and talmudic references "that there was a close internal connection between the Psalter and the legitimate temple cult" and that "both communal and private sacrifice (i.e., sacrifices, such as sin and thanksgiving sacrifices, offered in the temple by private individuals) were accompanied by psalms."[47] For him, it is not just an obvious assumption but an axiom that he was also willing to subject to proof that our psalms were indeed composed for this purpose.[48] He explicitly asserted that the relationship between the Psalter and the temple cult "is an internal and original relationship, that the psalms were composed from the outset in unity and harmony with the sacrificial cult, indeed, that it was the lifeblood of psalmody, one of its strongest impulses and most abundant sources." He demonstrated this assertion by reference (1) to the general attitude of the psalmists toward the cult and (2) to the open and concealed allusions to the temple, the service, value, and ideal quality of the cult, and so on. Finally, he also treated the supposedly antisacrificial passages in the Psalter. Even though a few clear overstatements have crept in,[49] it is still undeniable that he presented material that psalm interpreters have overlooked only to the detriment of their profession. I have mentioned Jacob here to this extent because, unaware of his work, I later came by a quite different path to very similar results and see in this circumstance a very significant confirmation of the basic view we share.[50] The shortcomings in Jacob's investigation are, first, that he is oriented too unilaterally toward the cult of the latest temple period and, second, that he lacks insight into the ancient relationship between cult and psalmody inherent in the nature of the matter that can only be gained by a methodical investigation

---

44. Bernhard Duhm, *Das Buch Hiob* (KHCAT 16; Freiburg: Mohr, 1897), 162.

45. Bernhard Stade and Alfred Bertholet, *Biblische Theologie des Alten Testaments* (Tübingen: Mohr, 1911), 2:66–73; see also 1:328. Remarkably, Bertholet seems to have assumed a certain contrast between "processional songs" and liturgical and cultic powers. Were religious processions not cultic procedures? Or did he think, perhaps, of formless, quasi-accidental processions of ascending pilgrims? The latter is false, however.

46. See Jacob, "Beiträge," *ZAW* (1896): 129–81, 265–91; (1897): 48–80, 263–79; (1898): 99–119.

47. *ZAW* (1897): 263.

48. Esp. in *ZAW* (1897): 263–79.

49. See esp. ibid., 267–70.

50. See my investigation of the psalms for traces of cultic procedures in *Psalm Studies* 1:144–63, and see 4:612, 617–18.

of genre. Consequently, his argumentation must remain unconvincing as long as that relationship is unrecognized. Gunkel's unforgettable merit is his recognition of this relationship. Thereby he was the first to bring an actual method to psalm exegesis and to offer the cultic explanation of the psalms through his fundamental recognition that the various psalm genres and their styles can only be explained by their definitive cultic situations, that the original psalms were cultic songs, and that not a few cultic psalms can still be found in the Psalter.

Gunkel did not deduce the necessary consequences of this fundamental recognition. The most influential, but probably unconscious, psychological factors for this seems to me, as indicated above, to have been (1) dependence on the traditional explanation of the lament psalms in terms of "contemporary history" in relation to the party circumstances of Judaism and (2) a certain underappreciation of cultic religion and its inherent possibilities in relation to personal experiences and feelings, in other words, a significant overestimation of the distance between the piety of the cult and of prayer, the establishment of a contrast that does not consist of such exclusivity. In relation to the background of the psalms transmitted to us, therefore, Gunkel's exegesis of the psalms signifies a certain retreat in contrast to Jacob's recognition, while Gunkel's own assumptions should have led to a thorough appreciation for it.

If one proceeds from Gunkel's fundamental perception and, on the other hand, gives sufficient attention to the fact that the Psalter was transmitted to us as the hymnal of the cult of the Second Temple and was undoubtedly used as such, the result for scholars is simply the obligation to examine whether the majority of the psalms can best be explained as actual cultic songs, composed from the outset for the cult. Therefore, I propose as a principle: *if the Psalms can be satisfactorily explained as cultic psalms, there is simply no reason to draw on any other explanation, let alone to prefer it.* I have indicated above the difficulties to which other explanations lead.

By cultic and liturgical compositions, I understand not only those psalms that were sung for a specific cultic procedure but any psalms *that were used as essentially independent liturgical pieces in temple worship and that were also composed as such from the outset*—regardless of whether the cultic act in question was performed for the whole congregation or only for an individual member of it.

In contrast to the views of Gunkel and earlier scholars, I have sought to show in several individual studies that *the majority of the psalms are not private, originally noncultic compositions but actual, authentic cultic songs*. I will not repeat my reasons for this view here but will only refer to the studies mentioned.

The results to which I have come—following Gunkel, I want to emphasize that explicitly once again—are as follows:

The "individual psalms of lament" are prayers related somehow to the rites of purification and healing performed for a sick and unclean person in the temple and to the sin offering he presented. Consequently, they are best termed "individual sin-offering psalms."[51] The enemies about whom the supplicants in these psalms complain and from whom they plea for deliverance are not some private opponents of this or that individual but the sorcerers (*pōʿălê ʾāwen*) and demons who have made the one come to be cleansed in the temple sick and unclean.[52] As has often been assumed,[53] they correspond to the individual psalms of thanksgiving as "thanksgiving offering psalms."[54]

When we come to the "collective" psalms or the psalms of the people or the community, it is generally accepted that many hymns in the Psalter were composed for the temple cult. The criteria according to which Gunkel,

---

51. See *Psalm Studies* 1, esp. 81–161. The following psalms come under consideration here: 3; 4; 5; 6; 7; 9–10; 11; 12 (?); 13; 16; 17; 22; 25; 26; 27; 28; 31; 35; 38; 39; 40B; 41; 42–43; 51; 52; 54; 55; 56; 57; 58; 59; 61; 62; 63; 64; 69; 70; 71; 86; 88; 102:1–12, 34–38; 109; 119 (the praise of the Torah is not the central purpose, but a confidence and justice motif); 120 (in its original meaning); 130 (likewise); 131 (likewise); 139; 140; 141; 142; and 143. Of these, Ps 131 is more a motif than a request. The attestation of humility and confidence is an indirect petition. Ps 19B may also have been intended as a petition (see above on Ps 119; see *Psalm Studies* 1:75–77, 5:764–65 n. 50). How Humbert (see above 799 n. 24) can adhere to the now-traditional interpretation of the enemies of the sufferer and nonetheless accept my explanation of the pertinent psalms as cultic psalms is incomprehensible to me.

52. See 798.

53. See Gunkel, "Psalmen," *RGG* 4:1944.

54. See *Psalm Studies* 1:129–37. The group includes the following psalms: Ps 18 (a king's thanksgiving song after deliverance in battle and thus substantially a public song of thanksgiving); 23; 30; 32; 34; 37; 40A; 49; 66B; 73; 92; 103; 116; 138; 1 Sam 2:1–10 (a king's thanksgiving); Isa 38:9–20 (likewise?); Jonah 2:3–10; and perhaps also Pss 145 and 146. Some of these have been influenced by the style of the congregational hymn, but they are in first-person singular (e.g., Pss 103; 145; 146). Ps 23 bears the stamp of a pure psalm of confidence, a motif that otherwise characterizes the lament and petition psalms (see, e.g., Pss 3; 4; 16; and esp. 131), but that also occurs in hymns. Just as the thanksgiving psalms often cite the previous complaints and prayers and do so in the style of the sin-offering psalms, so also the sin-offering psalms quite often offer an anticipatory thanksgiving psalm that originally referred to the divine promise given after the lustrations and the prayer of complaint (so Pss 6:9–11; 22:23–32; 26:6–9; 31:22–25; 57:8–12; 62:7–12; and 69:31–37). Occasionally the thanksgiving psalm is shifted forward as a confidence motif and is to be understood, then, as the psalm of thanksgiving for previous benevolent acts (so in Pss 9:1–19; 21:1–8; 27:1–6). Ps 107 is a thanksgiving psalm for use by several individuals who simultaneously pay their vows and celebrate a thanksgiving feast. All of this is essentially according to Gunkel, but see *Psalm Studies* 1:130–33.

for example, assigned many hymns to the noncultic, "spiritual" songs[55] are extremely puzzling to me.[56]

The hymn had its primary liturgical locus in the grand festivals, especially in sacrificial procedures, even though it ultimately found use in every cultic procedure in some fashion. Thus, a hymnic motif is very often interwoven into prayers of petition and complaint. In reference to most of the hymns transmitted to us, the cultic occasions for which they were composed or at which they were employed cannot be determined. In general, every hymn will probably have had its specific cultic purpose. Nonetheless, we can say with all certainty concerning a few that they belong to a specific festival. I think here of the so-called enthronement hymns[57] and other epic and lyrical hymns and somewhat hymn-like psalms and polyphonic liturgies (see below) in which the idea of YHWH's kingship and other associated ideas, such as creation, the battle with the gods and nations, judgment, renewal of the covenant, the turn of fate, and the like, take center place. Occasionally someone attempts to explain these as "eschatological" hymns, understood as hymns "that celebrate the end time" and that praise God's mighty acts that are supposed to have once occurred and thus raise the song of jubilation "that one day the final generation is supposed to sing."[58] Sometimes explicitly[59] but usually implicitly, Gunkel and his adherents assign most of these hymns to noncultic, "spiritual" literature.[60] Following the suggestions

---

55. Gunkel, "Psalmen," *RGG* 4:1943). Surely not because of the occasional appearances of first-person speech? Of course, it would not exclude a cultic purpose (see above, §2.7; see also the preceding note).

56. Cultic hymns and predominantly hymnic "polyphonic liturgies" are: Pss 8; 19A; 24 (liturgy); 29; 33; 46; 47; 48; 66A; 76 (liturgy); 81:1–6; 84; 87; 89:2–3, 6–19; 93; 95:1–7; 96; 97; 98; 99; 100; 104; 105; 107:33–43; 111; 113; 114; 117; 118 (liturgy); 135; 136; 147; 148; 149; 150. Ps 133, in wisdom style, should probably also be categorized with the psalms conceived as hymns. It sings of the blessing of the shared cultic "community life" of "brothers" and is to be understood as a hymn to the cultic site, Zion (cf. the Zion songs, Pss 46; 48; 87 and the prayer liturgies Pss 122; 125).

57. In the more restricted sense, this group includes Pss 47; 93; and 95–100.

58. Gunkel, "Psalmen, *RGG* 4:1944.

59. Thus, e.g., Staerk, *Lyrik*.

60. However, the context in which Gunkel discusses these hymns (*RGG* 4:1943) seems not to exclude an original cultic use of some of them (see the beginning lines of §12 of his article). On the other hand, in §§2–8, where he deals with cultic songs, he does not mention eschatological hymns, nor does he suggest specific cultic occasions to which they may have belonged. His statements in *Psalmen* (135) can hardly be interpreted otherwise: "the psalms adopted enthronement songs [that is, to the earthly king] and applied them to YHWH and his enthronement in the end time." An allusion to a cultic use of such hymns may be present in *Psalmen*, 80, where he speaks of a "communal" song of jubilation in

by Duhm[61] and Gressmann,[62] I have attempted to show that they are to be understood as festival psalms for a festival of YHWH's enthronement and that this festival was none other than the old fall and New Year's festival in the month of Tishri.[63]

Some of the hymnic songs bear the stamp of public psalms of thanksgiving and evidence some degree of affinity with the individual psalms of thanksgiving. Communal thanksgiving sacrifices were surely offered. Some of these psalms express thanks for God's benevolent acts in general,[64] some for a particular act of grace such as a victory.[65] The former belong to the major festivals, especially probably to the fall and New Year's festival; the latter were performed at occasional thanksgiving celebrations.

In addition to the communal hymns and psalms of thanksgiving, there were the communal prayers, prayer psalms, repeated with some degree of regularity, especially at the major festivals.[66] Here prayers were offered for victory, fertility, salvation, and all manner of benefits and for protection against enemies, sorcerers, and all the evil powers. Most of these communal prayers seem to be connected to the fall festival;[67] others, in contrast, refer to regularly repeated repentance ceremonies held by the Judahite community[68] and

---

relation to Ps 46. Hugo Gressmann differs. In a letter to me, he interprets his arguments in *Ursprung der israelitische-judischen Eschatologie* (FRLANT 6; Göttingen: Vandenhoeck & Ruprecht), 294–27, as follows: "they are eschatological hymns, i.e., songs with eschatological motifs sung at a not-yet-determined festival in honor of YHWH, which, in the fervor of the festival are experienced and foreshadowed in the present." In contrast to the "hymns" underscored by Gressmann here, Gunkel often says "that these songs" are "prophecies in terms of content" (*Psalmen*, 134) and "YHWH hymns in terms of form" (see *Psalmen*, 80).

61. Regarding Ps 47 in *Psalmen*.
62. Gressmann, *Ursprung der israelitische-judischen Eschatologie*, 294–301.
63. *Psalm Studies* 2:181–305.
64. Pss 65 (harvest thanksgiving psalm); 67 (likewise); 118; 124; 129 (simultaneously an execration psalm; see text below).
65. Pss 18 (because it is a royal song of thanksgiving cast in the style of the individual psalm of thanksgiving) and 68 (the historical event is styled in accordance with the myths of the enthronement festival).
66. See *Psalm Studies* 2:290–92, 294, 302, 306–53 (passim), 3:549–53.
67. Pss 12 (if not an individual sin-offering psalm); 14; 36; 53; 85; 94; 115; 120 (originally probably an individual sin-offering psalm); 121; 122; 123; 125; 126; 129; 130; 131; and 132. See *Psalm Studies* 3:547–48 and 534 n. 15. Ps 72 was probably associated with the accession of the king to the throne (blessing and intercession).
68. Pss 90; 102 (a collectively reinterpreted and expanded sin-offering psalm); 106; and 127. These prayer psalms have some stylistic affinities with communal lament psalms, which are also prayers. This affinity pertains especially to the psalms mentioned in this note.

have very close stylistic affinities with the actual occasional communal lament psalms.

In addition to regularly repeated communal prayers, we have occasional communal lament psalms in which the people or the king as their representative complain about a definite and specific crisis and plea for deliverance from it[69] or ask for assistance in a difficult situation, such as before a battle.[70] These prayers belonged to intermittent, occasional repentance ceremonies, and this cultic character is recognized rather universally.[71]

In the cult, the divine response through the words of a priest or a cultic prophet corresponds to the prayers and complaints of the individual and the people (the congregation).[72] The response can be given as direct divine speech in the first person or be indicated more indirectly. Cast in poetic form and provided with an introductory formula that emphasizes divine provenience, the cultic prophet recites from it the poetic cultic oracle.[73] Such words constituted an established part of the ritual. Linked with prayers and statements of thanksgiving, they formed images with more or less prominent prophetic elements. Such prophetic words, usually linked to the worship agenda, have their place both in congregational worship and in those with cultic procedures to be performed for the individual, such as healings of the sick and the like. Such psalms and liturgies are also transmitted in the Psalter.[74]

---

69. To these I assign: Pss 44; 60; 74; 77; 79; 80; 83; 89 (the king speaks); 108; 144 (like 89). See *Psalm Studies* 3:557–58.

70. Ps 20 and probably also Ps 21 (see *Psalm Studies* 3:567–71).

71. E.g. Gunkel, "Psalmen," *RGG* 4:1944; Balla, *Das Ich*, 63–75.

72. See *Psalm Studies* 3.

73. Examples of the direct type are Pss 50 and 82; of the more paraphrastic type, Pss 14; 53; 87.

74. These include: prophecies for the major annual festival (Pss 132; 89:20–38; 75; 82; 87; 81; 95; 50 [Ps 89 is probably a final literary precursor to the prophetic admonition at the covenant-renewal festival]); prayer liturgies with an oracle (besides Ps 132) are Pss 12; 60; 108, to the king as representative of the people (Pss 20 and 21); other royal oracles (besides 132:11–18 and 89:20–38) are Pss 2; 110; 72; 45; oracles for private cultic proceedings (healing of the sick) include Pss 12 (?) and 91:14–16. The sin-offering psalms contain many allusions to the oracle to be pronounced on this occasion (e.g., Ps 62 et al.; see *Psalm Studies* 1:153–58). Regarding cultic oracles and oracular psalms, see, besides my *Psalm Studies* 2, Friedrich Küchler, "Das priesterliche Orakel in Israel und Juda," in *Abhandlungen zur semitischen Religionskunde und Sprachwissenschaft: Wolf Wilhelm Grafen von Baudissin zum 26. September 1917* (ed. W. Frankenberg and F. Küchler; BZAW 33; Giessen: Töpelmann, 1918), 285–301.

The transmitted procession songs are also cultic.[75] Some have a hymnic character but are also provided with motifs from thanksgiving psalms, petitions, psalms, and oracular psalms and should often be regarded as liturgies (see below). In all likelihood, they belong to the enthronement and fall festival.[76]

Psalm 101, a royal-vow psalm,[77] also belongs to a cultic celebration, mostly likely to the enthronement festival of God that also celebrates the enthronement of the earthly king. Stylistically, it arose from the vows in the individual sin-offering psalms.

Finally, the blessings and curses that belong to the cult are also occasionally transformed into blessing and curse psalms and liturgies.[78] Such psalms have also been preserved in the Psalter,[79] and most of them should be regarded as true cultic psalms.[80]

None of the poetic *torah* inquiries that were once posed by the penitent in connection with the rites of purification and atonement and answered by a priest, and of which we have a prophetic imitation in Mic 6:6–8,[81] have been transmitted in the Psalter.

---

75. Pss 24; 84; 118; 132. Part of the procession liturgy consists of the "entry *torah*"; see Ps 24:3–6. Ps 15 offers an extensive parallel (see *Psalm Studies* 2:295–96).

76. See *Psalm Studies* 2:283–303.

77. With regard to the content of the psalm, it has already long been understood as a "Mirror for Rulers," placed on the lips of the king. In "Psalm CI," *ExpTim* 8 (1897): 202–4, Karl Budde rejected this interpretation, chiefly because "much of the activity and behavior reported in vv. 2–8 cannot be attributed to people at all, not even to a collective concept such as the ideal Israel, while everything is admirably suited to frequent statements concerning YHWH's activity toward human beings and the conditions for their admission into YHWH's presence" (Budde's own words in "Zum Text der Psalmen," *ZAW* 35 [1915]: 191). One can see from *Psalm Studies* 2:468–74 (concerning the Israelite understanding of the person of the king), that I do not think that I can share the precondition for this criticism and thus Budde's rejection of the old interpretation. Nonetheless, the content does support Budde's understanding to a degree. The fact that the beginning of the psalm does not agree with his interpretation and must be emended quite drastically remains a major difficulty.

78. See Gunkel, "Psalmen," *RGG* 4:1939, bottom.

79. Pss 72; 91; 115; 118:26; 121; 122; 128; 129; 132; and 137. In terms of their purpose, most of these should be viewed as psalms of petition. The curse also constitutes a rather essential component in the individual sin-offering and communal lament psalms (see Pss 83 and 109). Pss 1 and 112 are "spiritual" but rather spirit-less imitations influenced by proverbial style, yet nothing prohibits the assumption that Ps 112 was composed for temple worship in imitation of the blessing and curse psalms. The final collector of the Psalter probably composed Ps 1 as a motto in connection with Jer 17:5–8.

80. See *Psalm Studies* 5.

81. See Gunkel, "Psalmen," *RGG* 4:1939.

The delineation of a special genre of "royal psalms" has no cultic-liturgical and stylistic justification.[82] In terms of style, they represent almost all the genres of the Psalter, and, in terms of the cult, they were performed on very diverse occasions. Most likely, many psalms that do not explicitly mention the king were nonetheless composed for the king's use.[83]

In addition to those simple genres, for which the stylistic and the cultic-liturgical assignment coincide, one often finds composite psalms that consist of quite divergent stylistic elements and that, therefore, must be categorized according to cultic and liturgical perspectives. We have also mentioned that the regularly repeated communal prayers usually bear a somewhat different imprint than the occasional communal prayers to be defined as communal lament psalms but that the stylistic distinction is fluid. Regularly repeated prayers also sometimes bear the imprint of the lament psalms, and in the occasional prayers lament can diminish significantly alongside the petition. The hymn and thanksgiving psalm can assume a prominent place as prayer motifs in the psalms of petition and lament,[84] just as, conversely, a hymn can echo in a prayer or can include prayer motifs (e.g., Pss 84; 125). More important than this mixture of style, however, which has aesthetic and religio-psychological foundations to a degree, is that of another composition of various elements based on purely cultic and liturgical grounds, which Gunkel called a "liturgy." It does not involve an actual mixture of styles but compositions consisting of several more or less independent pieces that have been combined into a unit through a common theme and a specific cultic and liturgical situation and which were divided among several voices when performed in the cult. In the remarks above I have repeatedly referred to such liturgies. The procession songs in particular are usually composite liturgies. This circumstance does not mean, however, that the compositions were only combined secondarily out of originally independent pieces, as used to be sometimes supposed.[85] Usually,[86] instead, the liturgies were composed from the outset as polyphonic compositions for specific cultic situations. These situations can vary. Some liturgies are largely communal prayers (Pss 85; 121; 122; 132); others are to be assigned to the communal lament psalms,[87] still others to the hymns or the psalms of

---

82. See Hermann Gunkel, "Die Königspsalmen," *Preussische Jahrbücher* 158 (1914); and my *Kongesalmerne i det Gamle Testamente* (Kristiania: Nygaard, 1916).

83. See below, §4.2 (no. 22).

84. So especially for example, in Ps 21.

85. Thus, for example, Buhl (*Psalmerne*) and Duhm (*Psalmen*) often do in their commentaries. Even Gunkel rejects the original unity of Ps 24.

86. With the exception of Ps 108, for example.

87. Pss 60; 108; 144; see 811 nn. 69 and 74.

public thanksgiving (Pss 24; 76; 118), the sin-offering psalms,[88] or the psalms of blessing or curse.[89] It should be especially noted that the oracle psalms usually do not appear as mere oracles[90] but are liturgical compositions made up of hymn, petition, oracle, and thanksgiving. In the cult, the oracle appears as the response to a prayer and is answered with congregational praise. Most of the congregational liturgies transmitted to us seem to have belonged to the fall and enthronement festival, at which a wide variety of genres of psalms and liturgies were performed.[91]

The cultic use of the psalms did not always remain constant. Especially in later (postexilic) times, it was not rare for the original individual songs composed for use in the cultic procedures involving an individual (lustrations of the sick and thanksgiving sacrifices) to be reinterpreted and used in congregational worship. This was especially true for a few of the fall festival psalms, the *ma'alot* songs.[92] In the latest times of the existence of the temple cult, this reinterpretation may have been the rule.[93]

---

88. Pss 12 (?); 91; see further 811 n. 74.

89. Pss 91; 115; 118; 121; 122; 134; see 812 n. 79.

90. Pss 2; 14; 50; 53; 87 (?); 110; and 45 constitute exceptions.

91. In addition to the true enthronement psalms in the restricted sense (see 809 n. 57), I assign the following psalms (see *Psalm Studies* 2, part 1) to the fall and New Year's festival psalms: Pss 8; 29; 33; 46; 48; 66A; 76; 81; 114; 133; 149; Exod 15:1–18; and, further, the processional liturgies, Pss 24 (predominantly hymnic); 84 (likewise); 118 (likewise); 122 (likewise); and 132 (a petition and oracle liturgy). Furthermore, the harvest thanksgiving hymns, Pss 65 and 67, also belong here, as does the general psalm of thanksgiving, Ps 124 (and the thanksgiving liturgy, Ps 118; see above). In addition, there is a series of congregational prayers and prayer liturgies, such as Pss 14 and 53 (turn of fate); 85 (turn of fate, good harvest); 94 (appears in the midst of a collection of true enthronement songs); 121; 125; 126 (like 85); and 129. A series of oracle psalms and liturgies that refer with greater or lesser clarity to YHWH's enthronement and epiphany also belong to this festival: Pss 50; 75; 81; 82; 87; 95; and 132. Ps 89:20–38 is the same in nature as the oracle in Ps 132. The collection of the *ma'alot* psalms (Pss 120–134), which has been prepared for the later Festival of Booths and which the tradition explicitly associates with this festival, contains a small collection of New Year's and fall festival psalms and liturgies. Since the Festival of Booths is the heir to the older New Year's, fall, and enthronement festival, these psalms also come under consideration. The content of the collection varies widely: hymns, thanksgiving psalms, prayers, blessing and curse psalms, oracle liturgies, etc. Some of them have already been mentioned above. Some of these songs were probably originally individual sin-offering psalms (Pss 120; 130; 131) that have been reinterpreted in relation to the congregation and sometimes provided with an addition indicating this reinterpretation (see *Psalm Studies* 1:168–69; however, see also 3:547 n. 39).

92. See the preceding note and 808 n. 51, 810 nn. 67 and 68.

93. Thus the Maccabean period employed the individual thanksgiving Ps 30 as a con-

The two sayings combined in one psalm[94] and related to the Festival of Booths as the festival celebrating the dedication of the temple (see 1 Kgs 8:2), as the festival of YHWH dwelling in the midst of his people, and as a fertility festival were probably *not* originally composed for cultic purposes. Otherwise, except for Ps 1 and perhaps Ps 112, I know of no psalm that was not, or at least could have been, composed for cultic purposes.

---

gregational psalm in the festival celebrating the dedication of the temple (see *Psalm Studies* 1:166–71).

94. See above, §1.3.

3
The Actual Psalmists

3.1 (13). If the majority of the transmitted psalms are actually cultic psalms, the circle in which they must have originated is easily determined. The conclusion that Gunkel has already reached concerning the earliest psalmody is inevitable: *the psalms originated among the temple personnel.*

However, Gunkel is hardly correct to speak of "priestly poetry." Other scholars have already observed how rarely the psalms speak of the priests and actual priestly functions.[1] The priests in Israel apparently arose from two roots. On the one hand, they stem from the old seers and sanctuary guardians[2] who on occasion also officiated at the community's sacrifices. On the other hand, they are to be understood as technical representatives of the chief, who in Israel's earliest times seem to have been both leader/judges and priest/oracle-givers.[3] As a representative of the king, he was responsible, in particular, for the king's sacrificial duties. In historical times, however, the sanctuary priests were primarily sacrificial priests, administrators and guardians of the cultic, ritual, and sometimes moral *tôrōt*, gradually also the administrators and executors of the legal *mišpāṭîm*. Their role in the cult, however, is primarily to offer sacrifices, to perform the lustrations and consecrations and to speak the pertinent accompanying words. Their role as cultic prophets, as communicators of the divine responses and revelations to be pronounced in connection with the various cultic procedures, was already undertaken rather early by special temple prophets who appeared in the forms of the origi-

---

1. Causse, *Les "Pauvres" d'Israël*, 112 n. 1.
2. Cf. Hebrew *kōhēn* ("priest"), Arabic *kāhin* ("seer, oracle-giver"), as well as the seer and priest Samuel. See *Psalm Studies* 3:495–515; Gustav Hölscher, *Die Profeten* (Leipzig: Hinrichs, 1914), 100–107; idem, *Geschichte*, 82–85.
3. E.g., Moses, who was both chieftain and seer/priest. Regarding the engagement of a professional priest who exercised the religious functions of the owner of a sanctuary or of the king for pay, see Judg 17:5; 2 Sam 8:18; 1 Kgs 12:32.

nally free, non-Israelite, orgiastic and enthusiastic *nābî'*-ism.[4] They were not classed among the priests but were subordinate to them (see Jer 29:26). Later they were classed among the "Levites" and subsumed into the multitude of the lower temple officials.[5]

In addition to the priests, a special class of temple officials seems to have arisen rather early on. Their task was to care for the musical portion of the cult, including the performance of the prayers with musical accompaniment to be pronounced in the name of the congregation and gradually probably also in the name of individuals. They were the singers (*měšōrěrîm*) who were probably classed in earlier times among the temple slaves, or at least among the lower temple servants,[6] and later among the Levites subordinate to the priests.[7] As will be shown in greater detail below, the temple prophets and singers were always very closely related.

A class of temple singers seems to be directly attested first around 400 B.C.E. (in Ezra 2:41). We hear in preexilic times, however, that the women sang cultic funeral songs about Tammuz in the temple (Ezek 8:14). According to the context, they would have been the temple singers. Beyond doubt, the "male and female singers" of Hezekiah, whom he had to hand over to Sennacherib,[8] were used not only at profane royal festivals but also in temple worship; at the time, the temple was, after all, the king's "palace chapel." In reality, the cultic singers are already attested in Ps 68:26, a psalm that, contrary to most exegetes, I consider very old.[9] Singers (*šārîm*) led the cultic procession presumed here, followed by instrumentalists (*nōgěnîm*) surrounded by drumming virgins. Since the institution of the cult in the larger temples in Israel was undoubtedly undertaken by Canaanites influenced in the main by Babylonian and Egyptian culture, and since professional temple singers and musicians seem to have been general practice in both Babylon[10]

---

4. See *Psalm Studies* 3:507–15.

5. In Chronicles, the "Levites" appear as cultic prophets (see 2 Chr 20:14; see further *Psalm Studies* 3:517–21, and §3.5, below).

6. Still so in Ezra 2:41 from the time of Nehemiah or shortly thereafter (ca. 400 B.C.E.).

7. So in Neh 11:17; 12:24 and in Chronicles.

8. Taylor Cylinder III, 38–39 (see Hugo Gressmann, Arthur Ungnad, and Hermann Ranke, eds., *Altorientalische Texte und Bilder* [Tübingen: Mohr, 1909], 1:121). Like the Hebrew *zāmar*, the Assyrian *zamāru* means both "to play" and "to sing."

9. Benjamin leads the tribes and is the ruler of the other *rōdēm*. This statement suits the time of Saul or Ishbaal. "Jerusalem" was interpolated into the text later (v. 30), as was Judah (in v. 28). The Mount of YHWH is in Bashan (vv. 16–17); the defeated enemy may have been Edom, to which *śē'ār* in v. 22 may allude.

10. In Babylonia, there was a special class of priests that bore the name *zammaru* (Morris Jastrow, *Die Religion Babyloniens und Assyriens* [Giessen: Töpelmann, 1905], 1:382).

and Egypt,[11] we may reasonably assume that the chief temple very early, and Jerusalem perhaps from the very outset, had a host of professional singers (male and female).

The task of these singers was to perform the musical element of the cult. This included both singing and instrumental music. The Hebrew words šîr and zāmar included both. The songs were always performed to musical accompaniment, and the purpose of the instrumental music was to accompany the singing.[12] In general, the laity was not able to perform artful singing with music. But every cultic religion places extreme significance on the correct performance of all the details and subtleties of the cult. At atonement procedures and lustrations undertaken for individuals, the priests may have recited the prayers to be said in the name of the penitent. Otherwise, with respect to the relative display of pomp and accoutrements, much probably fell to the person of the penitent. The process for the atonement of the king differed from that for a simple man of the people.[13] At the major festivals, we may consider it a certainty that most of the songs performed in the name of the congregation were performed by the choir, if the ritual did not expressly require that an individual, and then probably usually the king, speak in the name of the congregation.[14] Thus the singers were the performers, the curators, and the transmitters of the cultic songs. They were the "skilled" and the "wise" who knew the songs, what such songs should be like, how to perform them, and how they should be created.

Then we would also have to assume, however, that they were the ones who composed the songs. After all, the traditions were maintained in their circles. As curators of the traditional songs, they were also the copyists, the sōpĕrîm. In Israelite antiquity, there was no difference, however, between copyist and author. Thus the production of such songs will also have been a matter for the singers. It was up to them to create the library of psalms required by the cult.

A few scholars have already recognized that the majority of the psalms originated in the lower ranks of the temple officials, the Levites—which is to say, in this context, the singers, as I, too, have discovered. Heinrich Grätz has already clearly said so, and Ernest Renan also reached this conclusion.[15] These

---

11. See Adolf Erman, *Die ägyptische Religion* (2nd ed.; Berlin: Reimer, 1909), 61, 233.

12. See, indeed, the rather clinical poet of Ps 49 (see v. 5).

13. If in earlier times he did not have to be satisfied with the relatively primitive manipulations of the local priest. The royal temple was for the king!

14. See *Psalm Studies* 2, 289 and 217–18 n. 75.

15. Heinrich Grätz, *Kritischer Kommentar zu den Psalmen* (Breslau: Schottlaender, 1882), 1:35; Ernest Renan, *Histoire du peuple d'Israël* (Paris: Lévy, 1895), 4:26–33. Despite his principal understanding of the Psalms as private compositions by individuals, Causse

scholars deserve to be mentioned as laudable exceptions to the guild of psalm exegesis that operates in the conceptual realm of pietism and conventicles. They did not, however, attempt a demonstration that approaches the matter from all sides, probably because they did not have true insight into the nature of the cult or a specific and colorful picture of it. Jacob should also be mentioned in this context (see above).

The question arises now as to whether we can identify support in the tradition for our initially rather deductive theory.

3.2 (14). The tradition expressly states that many of the psalms, at least, were composed by the temple singers, if only one reads the tradition correctly. I think here, first, of the superscriptions *lĕ'āsāp*, *lĕ'êtān*, and *lĕhêmān*. It should have never been doubted that these superscriptions were meant to indicate authorship and that, accordingly, Asaph, Etan, and Heman are to be understood as actual (whether historical or legendary) personal names and the *lĕ* as *genetivus auctoris*. The analogy *tĕpillâ laḥăbaqqûq hannātî* (Hab 3:1) already speaks for this understanding. Now, who are these men?

We encounter Asaph for the first time around 400 B.C.E.[16] He was considered then to be the ancestor of the temple singers. According to the "tradition" contained in Chronicles, he was supposed to have been a contemporary of David, who installed him in office. The singers called themselves *bĕnê 'āsāp*, the Asaphites. The legend in Chronicles should be viewed as unhistorical. The later period placed all the temple institutions back in the time of David and Solomon. We can no longer know whether this Asaph ever lived at all. For us, he is the *heros eponymos* of the temple singers, indeed, originally, of all the singers (Ezra 2:41), not, as in Chronicles, only a third of them. Nor do we know how early the singers were named for Asaph. If he was a historical person, he apparently would have lived no earlier than the postexilic

---

(*Les "Pauvres" d'Israël*, 96) also had to admit that "the cause of the poor (who were the authors of the psalms, according to Causse) had its most passionate proponents among the temple servants, the *mĕšōrĕrîm*, the *šô'ărîm*, the *nĕtînîm*." He infers this from the many connections between the psalms and the temple cult, especially temple songs. In this case, he should also think that these adherents from the temple environment must have composed some of the psalms. Why in the world, then, did they not try to compose for the cult, which was, after all, their profession? What would the cultic songs composed by the very same temple officials have looked like? Who else would have created the cultic literature? If such views were widespread among the temple workers, why would they not also be widespread in the temple songs? Why not understand the psalms transmitted, then, as temple songs, or at least attempt such an interpretation?

16. Ezra 2:41; Neh 11:22 is somewhat later.

period[17] and was probably the leader of the singers at that time. Obviously, this Asaph—whether a contemporary of David or of Zerubbabel—cannot really have been the author of the psalms attributed to him. In reality, they stem from quite divergent periods. Psalm 80 may have originally been northern Israelite in origin from the period shortly after 722;[18] Ps 83 stems from the Assyrian period (see v. 9); Pss 74 and 79 were probably written under Jehoiachin shortly after the conquest; Ps 50 is probably postexilic,[19] as is Ps 73. In this context, however, all of this information is relatively insignificant. The main point is that the tradition attributed the authorship of these psalms to the eponymous ancestor of the singers.

A similar situation applies to Heman and Etan. In the Chronicler's lists these two, along with Asaph, were supposed contemporaries of David and the ancestors of the two other major clans of singers. Chronicles naturally considers them to be Levites and divides them into the three supposed Levite clans.[20] Jedu(i)tun occurs in a few passages as a variant (1 Chr 25:1–6; 2 Chr 5:12; 29:14; 35:15). It is a by-form that can hardly be based on older tradition but has been elicited from the technical superscription *'al (lĕ) yĕdûtûn* incorrectly understood as an attribution of authorship.[21] These ancestors of singer clans cannot be considered identical with the old wise men Heman and Etan mentioned in 1 Kgs 5:11. Just as the later "wise men" and apocalypticists deduced from the circumstance that Ezekiel mentioned Noah, Daniel, and Job once (Ezek 14:14, 20) as (legendary) types of piety that Daniel was an exilic contemporary of Ezekiel,[22] so later wise men concluded from the comparison of Solomon with the legendary wise men Heman, Etan, Calcol, and Darda that they were contemporaries of David. Since the temple singers, as singers, poets,

---

17. The fact that all the families listed in Ezra 2, who are named for persons descended from men who lived after the exile, supports this conclusion. The first priestly family was named for Jeshua ben Jehozadak (see my "Om den jødiske Menighets og Provinsen Judeas Organisasjon ca. 400 f. Kr.," *NTT* 16 [1915]: 250–66). Eduard Meyer's attempt (*Entstehung des Judentums* [Halle: Niemeyer, 1906]) to demonstrate the preexilic origin of the family name depends (1) on a *petitio principii*, (2) on an entirely inadequate insight into name classifications and naming in the various periods in Israel's history, and (3) on ignorance of the characteristics of the old clan names in relation to later personal and "family" names.

18. "Israel" does not parallel "Joseph," but it does parallel "Ephraim and Benjamin" (vv. 2–3; "Manasseh" is a later addition, as the meter indicates; the allusion in v. 18 assures "Benjamin").

19. See *Psalm Studies* 2:333.

20. Asaph was one of the sons of Gershom, Heman one of the sons of Qahat, and Etan one of the sons of Merari; see 1 Chr 6:18–32, etc.

21. See §1.1, above; *Psalm Studies* 4:619.

22. Cf. the book of Daniel.

and prophets, were tradents of "wisdom,"[23] they saw these traditional wise men as men like themselves and declared them patriarchs. This probably took place relatively late: Ezra 2:41 still knows only Asaph as the patriarch of the singers. Thus Heman and Etan as patriarchs of the singers were not historical persons but legends. Even 1 Kgs 5:11 mentions them, as Ezekiel mentioned Job, not as historical persons but as types of wise men known from literature or legend.[24]

Thus we have the case here, too, that the supposed patriarchs of the singers were regarded as the composers of the psalms. Remarkably, moreover, the "tradition" is older in this case than Chronicles, where Heman and Etan are already regarded as Levites. In the superscriptions to the psalms, they are not yet Levites but "Ezrahites," that is, members of the Judahite (originally Edomite[25]) clan of Zerah, a tradition that is preserved in another list in Chronicles.[26] It agrees with 1 Kgs 5:11, where, however, only Etan is considered an Ezrahite, while Heman (along with others) is mentioned as a son of Mahol. It is easy to understand that later tradition, which named the two together, made them both into Ezrahites.

How is the circumstance that the supposed patriarchs of the singers were cited as authors of the psalms to be explained? Naturally, the explanation involves the fact that the psalms originated among the temple singers. Relatively old, famous, or well-regarded psalms in particular were readily attributed to the patriarchs. This attribution was a particular recommendation of the pertinent compositions, evidence that they were songs (*maśkîl*[27])

---

23. See §3.5, below.

24. Even if we were to declare them historical persons from David's time, the superscriptions in Pss 88 and 89 could not claim historicity. It is evident that Ps 89 viewed the time of David as the distant past.

25. Gen 36:13, 17, 33; see Eduard Meyer, *Die Israeliten und ihre Nachbarstämme: Alttestamentliche Untersuchungen* (Halle: Niemeyer, 1906), 350.

26. 1 Chr 2:6. The Chronicler was probably unaware of the original identity of the Ezrahites Heman and Etan with the "Levites" Heman and Etan.

27. See *Psalm Studies* 4:606–8. Regarding my interpretation there of this term as a designation for a song originating from an extraordinary insight and psychic power and thus effective, or inspired according to a later concept, it should be mentioned further that Levitical singers who play and sing—and I will add, compose—are characterized as *měbînîm* (1 Chr 25:7) and as possessors of a *śēkel ṭôb* (2 Chr 30:22). The Targum's rendition of *maśkîl*, שכלא טבא, is comparable. The fact that the Targum had a notion of the insight involved here is indicated by the rendition given the word in Ps 78, formulated, of course, in terms of a later period: שכלא דרוח קודשא!

pleasing to God, composed by truly "wise" men, and therefore effective in the cult. Indeed, favorite "patriarchal psalms" were designated by this term.[28]

3.3 (15). *Libnê qōraḥ* should also be understood as an actual attribution of authorship. On first sight, this seems remarkable. How could a psalm be composed by several authors, by "the Korahites"? Not even Jewish scribes could have thought so, could they? Nor is it to be so understood. As has long been suspected, the "Korahite" psalms originally constituted an independent collection.[29] The overall title of this collection was the superscription *libnê qōraḥ* in the sense of "the psalms composed by the Korahites." Later in the redaction of the Psalter (or of the collection Pss 42–89 or 2–89) the superscription was placed mechanically over all the psalms in the Korahite collection, giving rise to the appearance that every individual psalm was composed by a group.[30]

According to the report in Chronicles, these Korahites were known as a "clan," in reality, a service division, a choir of temple singers (1 Chr 6:18–23; 2 Chr 20:19), whom the Chronicler categorized as Levites. The order according to which Korah was the name of a choir of singer seems to be somewhat older than the period of the Chronicler. In his list of Levites, Korah is still only the name of one of the ancestors of the Hemanite "clan," to which the Kahatites were assigned. In one passage, which probably stems from the Chronicler's prototype (2 Chr 20:19), the Kahatites and the Korahites were the two clans of singers. On the other hand, this order seems to be later than Ezra 2:41, a passage that mentions only Asaph. This is not certain, however, since at the time the Korahites could have already been a subclan of the Asaphites not mentioned separately in the list. The account in Num 16 suggests the existence of a Levitical clan, Korah,[31] that is, probably a clan of singers, already before the final redaction of the Pentateuch, which, by all appearances, took place before Nehemiah.[32] Since other passages in the Chronicles mention the Korahites as gatekeepers (1 Chr 9:19; 26:1, 19), the name was probably applied to a clan of gatekeepers in the time of the Chronicler, perhaps as the result of a reordering

---

28. See *Psalm Studies* 4:606–8. The "patriarchal psalms" designated as *maśkîl* were Pss 42; 44; 45; 74; 78; 88; and 89. Otherwise, the term appears before Pss 32; 52–55; and 142.

29. See the Old Testament introductions. Pss 84–89 probably also originally belonged to the "Elohistic Psalter" (Pss 42–83), since clear traces of an Elohistic redaction are also evident there.

30. The situation is analogous with the superscription of the *šîr hamma'ălōt*, as Thomas K. Cheyne (*The Book of Psalms* [London: Kegan Paul, Trench, 1888]) has seen.

31. See §3.6, below, 836.

32. See my *Ezra den Skriftlærde* (Kristiania: Olaf Norlis, 1916), 134–38.

of the ministerial classes that "demoted"[33] the Korahites, perhaps, however, only for purely "accidental" reasons that we can no longer detect.

Thus in the superscription *libnê qōraḥ* the tradition has given clear information that, in the fourth century, these psalms were still considered compositions by the Korahite temple singers. The existence of a Korahite clan of singers is, as stated, older than the actual author of Chronicles.[34]

There is no contradiction between the two statements in Ps 88, "by the Korahites" and "by the Ezrahite Heman," since in Chronicles Heman represents the Korahite clan (1 Chr 6:18, 23). Given the discussion above, the existence of a division of singers called "the Korahites" could be much older than the reclassification of the singers as Levites. Nothing, therefore, prohibits the assumption that Ps 88 had already been attributed to the Korahite and Ezrahite Heman in the collection of the Korahite songs. It is rather unlikely, however, since the other Korahite songs are anonymous. Thus, Ps 88 contains two traditions. The psalm was included in several smaller collections. In one of them, it was categorized as a Korahite song; in the other, it was attributed to the Ezrahite Heman. Consequently, we may say that, in a certain sense, the Korahites, Asaph, Heman, and Etan are accurately identified as authors.

3.4 (16). In addition to these, as it were, direct witnesses, a series of indications can be derived from the psalms themselves. The first point to be mentioned here is the close relationship of psalmists to the temple.

As is well known, it is not rare for the psalmists to express their joy in the temple and the celebration of the cult. The temple (see Pss 23:6; 26:8; 27:4; 42:43; 65:6; 84), the Temple Mount,[35] the temple courts, the holy city,[36] the altar (Pss 26:6; 43:4; 51:21; 84:4; 118:27), indeed, even sacrifice[37] are repeatedly mentioned as the most valuable benefits. The poets live in all these things;

---

33. The latest layer in Num 16 recounts this. See Wolf Wilhelm Baudissin, *Die Geschichte des alttestamentlichen Priesterthums Untersucht* (Osnabruck: Zeller, 1889), 153.

34. Accordingly, these psalms must be at least this old; indeed, the collection must have been in one volume. Not a single substantial indicator contradicts this view. Pss 45 and 84 (royal psalms) are certainly preexilic; Pss 87 (see *Psalm Studies* 2:360 n. 64) and 44 (a national lament psalm; Israel still makes war against its enemies; see also the extremely ancient notion in v. 24) are also quite likely preexilic, and Pss 46; 47; and 48 (see *Psalm Studies* 2:367–68) probably are as well. Pss 42–43; 49; 85; and 88 could belong to almost any time between ca. 700 and ca. 200. In any case, the superscription constitutes a new argument against the often-claimed Maccabean origins of Ps 44.

35. See the passages listed in Jacob, "Beiträge," *ZAW* (1897): 265–66.

36. Pss 31:22; 46:5; 48:2, 3, 9; 50:2; 87:3; 97:8; 101:8; 102; 125; 132:13; 135:21; 137.

37. Referred to as: *zebaḥ* (Pss 4:6; 27:6; 66:13, 15; 107:22; 116:17); *ʿōlâ* (20:4; 52:21; parallel to *kālîl*, 66:13, 15); *minḥâ* (20:4; 96:8; 141:2); *neder* (22:26; 50:14; 56:13; 61:9; 65:2;

they mention them with sacred emotion and reverential and joyous words. This is not unusual in cultic psalms but quite natural. The temple and the cult is the very place in which the adherents of a cultic religion have their foundational religious experience. They experience God in the cult at sacred sites. Thence flows everything beneficial to life.[38] In the cult, in the ecstasy of the festival, they experience God's presence that assures them everything they need for a happy life. In the temple, the puzzle of theodicy is resolved for the poet of Ps 73; there the poet of Ps 63 sees God.

We do not want to deal here with those passages that attest a high estimation of joy in the temple and the cult, nor with those that presuppose that the respective psalm was performed in the temple and thus attests to its cultic purpose.[39] Jacob has already called attention to this joy in the temple and the cult on the part of the psalmists and drawn the correct conclusions regarding the psalms as cultic poetry.[40] I find a few statements among those made in the psalms concerning the temple, however, that can best be understood on the assumption that they were composed by people who were at home in the temple, so to speak. First, attention should be turned to the use of the verbs šākan ("to stay, dwell"; Ps 15:1), qûm ("to stay, abide"; Ps 24:3), and yāšab ("to dwell"; Ps 84:5) to designate the cultic visit in the temple. Both the fact that the pertinent psalms were composed from the heart and in the name of the celebrating cultic community and that the verb gûr ("to be a guest") parallels the expressions mentioned (Pss 15:1; 24:3; see also Isa 33:14) demonstrate that a brief visit is involved. Even the most pious of the "simple men of the people"[41] or among the "farmer, laborers and shepherds" in the countryside[42] could not say that they dwelled in the temple, not even when they traveled there as often as possible and remained there as long as possible. Consequently, the reference to Hannah in Luke 2:37 suggested by Kittel (regarding Ps 23:6) is irrelevant, and his dilution of the Lucan expression is unjustified. The addition προφῆτις characterizes this Hannah as a woman who stands in a closer relationship to the temple than normal people. The expressions yāšab

---

66:13; 76:12; 116:14); nĕdābâ (54:8); tôdâ (50:14, 23; 56:13; 116:17); qĕṭoret (66:15; 141:2); following Jacob, "Beiträge."

38. See *Psalm Studies* 2:197–211, 258–60, 306–21, 323–25.

39. See *Psalm Studies* 1:144–61.

40. Jacob, "Beiträge," ZAW (1897): 264–73. Causse is also aware of this characteristic of the psalms (*Les "Pauvres" d'Israël*, 108–14), apparently to a greater degree than Gunkel, for example. It is all the more remarkable that he says so much about the psalmody of the ʿănāwîm in private conventicles and so explicitly underscores the supposed opposition of these conventicles to the sacrificial cult (see 110 n. 3).

41. Gunkel, *Psalmen*.

42. Causse, *Les "Pauvres" d'Israël*, 82.

and the like are actually only justified on the lips of those who remain continuously at the holy sites and dwell there, on the lips of temple personnel.

Passages that characterize the greatest good fortune not as a visit to the temple but as dwelling or remaining there, and sometimes as remaining there "forever," can also be explained in this fashion. Examples include the statements: "May I dwell in YHWH's house the length of days" (*lĕ'ōrek yāmîm*, i.e., forever; Ps 23:6); "I desire only one thing of YHWH: to be able to dwell in YHWH's house all the days of my life" (Ps 27:4); "happy are those who dwell in your house; they may praise you eternally";[43] "better is a day in your courts than a thousand outside; better to lie on the threshold of the house of my God than to dwell in the tents of the godless" (Ps 84:11), and so on. The feelings and attitudes of the temple personnel are infused here into the cultic psalms of the whole community and of individuals within it. The happiness of the "children of men" who dwell in YHWH's shadow in the general description "they are refreshed by the fat of your house" (Ps 36:9) should also be mentioned here. Underlying this expression is probably the notion of the fatty parts of the sacrificial animals that belong to YHWH and the priests and constitute an important component of the income of the temple personnel. Strictly speaking, the expression only suits temple officials, not the congregation or "the children of men" generally. This understanding also sheds light on the statements in the lament and petition psalms that portray a visit to the temple as the sole desire of the petitioner.[44] In part, such statements mean, "as a sick and suffering person, I long for the cleansings in the temple that guarantee healing,"[45] and, in part, "may I soon have the opportunity to enter the temple as a healed person and offer thanksgiving and praise" (Ps 63:2–3). The fact that these ideas are expressed as praise for the temple and for "dwelling" there, however, indicates a closer relationship to the temple than that of simple rural farmers and shepherds—who are, moreover, supposedly emancipated from the cult!

3.5 (17). Furthermore, we may point to the *relationship between singers and temple prophets* treated above (§3.1) as confirmation of our thesis.

This relationship can be demonstrated with certainty.[46] First, it should be regarded as a certainty that there was an organized group of temple *nĕbî'îm*[47]

---

43. Ps 84:5. Read *'ădê* with LXX instead of *'ôd*.
44. E.g., Pss 26:8; 27:4; 42:3; 43:3–4; 61:5; 63:2–3; 84:3; 122:1–2; and Jonah 2:5. Bertholet (Stade and Bertholet, *Biblische Theologie* 2:65–66) has already called attention to this point.
45. This is especially clear in Ps 43:3–4.
46. On the following, see *Psalm Studies* 3:517–21.
47. *Psalm Studies* 3:507–15.

that still existed in Nehemiah's time[48] and that the temple prophets were subordinate to the priests and were counted among the lower ranks of officials.[49] Furthermore, it is certain that in later times all these subordinate temple officials were subsumed under the leading Levites and given the status of these Levites. We see this in Chronicles. Whenever the Chronicler records the appearance on some cultic occasion of an inspired prophet with a statement that was supposed to be pronounced in accordance with festival ritual, it is a Levite.[50] The Chronicler employs the word *nibbā'*, denominated from *nābî'*, for the cultic functions of the singers, or he calls the singers *nĕbî'îm* outright (2 Chr 25:1–3, 5; 35:15).

As the passages from Chronicles just cited indicate, the singers were also characterized as prophets. This circumstance depends on a very old relationship between the two professions. Just as the prophets were inspired and spoke by virtue of their spirit possession, so, according to the primitive Israelite view, also found among the Arabs,[51] did poets and singers. The prophetesses Miriam and Deborah were also singers and poets.[52] Just as the prophet "with closed eyes" (Num 24:3), which are, in reality, the only ones that are "open" (24:4), sees distant things and with opened ears hears secret divine voices (1 Sam 9:15; Isa 22:14), so the poet hears the hymn of heaven, which is "speechless and wordless and inaudible" (for human ears; Ps 19:2–5). Just as the prophet was inspired by music (1 Sam 10:5–6, 10–13; 2 Kgs 3:15), so also was the poet (Ps 49:2–5).

Now, if the temple prophets and the temple singers were so closely interconnected, we may expect to find notable traces of prophetic consciousness and style in the psalms composed by the singers. Such is, indeed, the case. While they were "inspired" by music (Ps 49:5), these poets inclined their ears toward mysterious and wise discourse (*māšāl*, *ḥîdā*) and allowed wisdom and insight (*ḥŏkmâ*, *tĕbûnâ*) "to bubble forth" (*nābaʿ*; Pss 19:3; 78:2) from their mouths as from the prophets' mouths. They listened in on mysterious divine voices (Ps 81:6); the deity, YHWH himself, spoke through them (Ps

---

48. Neh 6:10–11; the *nābî'* was permitted to enter the interior of the temple, but the layperson Nehemiah was not.

49. Jer 26:29–30; see also 20:1–2. The prophetess Huldah (2 Kgs 22:14) is the wife of the keeper of the temple wardrobe (*šōmēr habbĕgādîm*; see 2 Kgs 10:22; Rudolf Kittel, *Die Bücher der Könige* [HAT I/5; Göttingen: Vandenhoeck & Ruprecht, 1900], on the passage). Surely he did not have priestly status.

50. See 2 Chr 20:14–19; *Psalm Studies* 3:514.

51. When rhythmic words first flowed from Muhammad's mouth in ecstasy, he believed that he had been possessed by a jinn.

52. At least according to legend; see Exod 15:20; Judg 5:1. See also Hermann Gunkel, "Poesie und Musik Israels," *RGG* 4:1641.

85:9 LXX). They proclaimed what YHWH had whispered (Ps 110:1), divine revelation (*tôrâ*; Ps 78:1; see also Isa 8:16; 42:4). They saw how in his heavenly council YHWH leafed through the book of nations and heard what he said to himself (Ps 87:6). They saw him look down from heaven in order to inspect humanity and knew the decision he made (Ps 14:2–6). They heard the verdict that he issued in the council of the gods when he ascended to his throne and were able to proclaim it to the congregation (see 2 Kgs 5:26). Just as the prophet's "heart" (*lēb*) reveals distant and mysterious matters, the psalmist's heart also speaks the divine decision to him.[53] Therefore, a psalm is frequently designated a *maśkil*, that is, an especially effective song based on extraordinary expertise, wisdom, and knowledge.[54]

All the "oracle psalms" that introduce a divine revelation reveal this prophetic consciousness.[55] These psalms, as I tried to demonstrate above and elsewhere (*Psalm Studies* 3), involve divine sayings that were supposed to be announced at certain points in the temple liturgy by a cultic official considered divinely authorized. In terms of content and, to a degree, in terms of wording, these sayings were determined by the order of service. Sometimes they seem to involve prophecies that resulted from hieroscopy or were obtained by other technical means.[56] Thus only the precise formulation of the oracle was left to the pertinent prophet. If this was the case, we might expect to find the style of the oracle obtained by technical means, that is, the priestly *torah*-style. Such is not the case, however. All the oracle psalms clearly and distinctly exhibit the style of *nābî'*-like, inspired speech. This can be explained by the very fact that early on there was already a close connection between the temple *nĕbî'îm* and the psalmists. We now know that the profession most closely related to the temple *nĕbî'îm*, and with which they were probably simply identified in the very early period, was the profession of temple singer. This observation points quite definitely to the temple singers and temple prophets as the poets of the psalms.

The markedly psalm-like poetry of the *nābî'*, Habakkuk, who, according to tradition was even a Levite,[57] also suggests the temple prophets (and singers) as the psalmists. He also composed a cultic psalm that is entirely analogous to those in the Psalter.[58] The book of Joel exhibits the same mixture of prophecy and psalmody.

---

53. Ps 27:8; see *Psalm Studies* 1:152.
54. *Psalm Studies* 4:606–8.
55. See above, 811 n. 74.
56. Such is probably the case in Ps 20.
57. As in "Bel and the Dragon," v. 1.
58. Hab 3. See *Psalm Studies* 3:519–21.

3.6 (18). I see a further indication that speaks for the temple singers as the authors of the psalms in a circumstance that is otherwise understood as evidence for the noncultic, indeed, even anticultic character of the psalms. I mean the rather frequent emphasis on psalms, especially psalms of thanksgiving, at the expense of the bloody sacrifice (e.g., Pss 50:8–23; 69:31–32), that occasionally rises to the level of an apparent rejection of sacrifice (Pss 40:7–8; 51:18–19). Related to these are passages that explicitly mention as the object of the vow of the one seeking assistance the thanksgiving song but not sacrifice.[59]

First I will offer a few words concerning the customary noncultic interpretation of these psalms. It should be recalled that the bloody sacrifice is not identical with the cult per se. The temple cult entails much more than animal sacrifice. It also entails many quite varied rites, such as lustrations, symbolic rites, and the like, including prayers, praises, blessings, and so forth.[60] The sacrifice is only one detail among many others. It would be quite false simply to identify the terms "cultic religion" and "sacrificial religion." Both Catholicism and Greek Orthodox Christianity are actually cultic religions in essence, although they know no bloody sacrifice. The failure to mention or even the devaluation of sacrifice is not necessarily the same as rejecting or distancing oneself from cultic religion.

For the most part, these psalms do not involve a rejection of sacrifice but simply a shift in the estimation of the individual elements of the temple cult. While there were other circles that valued sacrifice as the most valuable and important part of the cult—and the sacrificial priests would have certainly done so (see the entire Priestly Document)—the psalmists often accentuated matters differently and placed central importance on another element of the cult, on the song. If one wants to determine how much or how little is inherent in these statements, one usually begins with the harshest passages (Pss 40:7–8; 51:18–19) and interprets the others accordingly and comes to a rather general rejection of sacrifice by the psalmists. In view of the many passages that speak of the temple, the courts, the altar, and sacrifice as valuable goods,[61] it seems commendable to set out on the opposite path and to take as the starting point those passages that take the thanksgiving song instead of sacrifice as the object of the vow or presuppose it as the chief element of the thanksgiving feast to be

---

59. Pss 7:18; 13:6; 22:23–26; 26:12; 28:7; 31:8; 35:18, 28; 42:6, 12; 43:4–5; 51:17; 52:11; 54:8; 57:8–11; 59:17; 61:9; 71:14–16, 22–24; 109:30–31; 119:171–172, 175; 142:8; 144:9–10.
60. See the overview of the rites of the fall and New Year's festival in *Psalm Studies* 2:272–303.
61. See above, 824–25.

celebrated after the healing of the supplicant.[62] Clearly, the thanksgiving psalm is assumed to be the most pleasing and valuable in the eyes of God and the most important part of the festival, in the poet's view. On the other hand, it is equally clear that no principle disinclination toward sacrifice is involved here. This can simply be assumed as a given. At least one passage states directly that this is so (Ps 22:23–27). The thanksgiving psalm with the testimony "before the brothers in the midst of the cultic community (*qāhāl*), before the pious" appears as the actual vow. In addition, however, there is a reference to the thanksgiving sacrifice to be offered on the same occasion: "the humble will see it (i.e., the deliverance given me) and eat to their satisfaction—namely, of the thanksgiving sacrifice; those who seek YHWH should praise him." Thus, the praise envisioned here, the thanksgiving song, is the cultic thanksgiving song that belongs to the thanksgiving sacrifice (*tôdâ* sacrifice) itself, and the "great assembly" (*qāhāl rāb*) is the cultic congregation consisting of the friends and relatives of the "lord of the sacrifice," the poor from the respective locality and other invitees. The psalm is mentioned as the most important element in the whole thanksgiving festival, as its most prominent characteristic that comprehensively and categorically defines the whole festival. The same circumstance will have pertained in the other passages where praise appears as the object of the vow. Both this mode of expression and this religious estimation are easily understood. The thanksgiving sacrifice was a *šelem* sacrifice, a sacrificial meal for the participants. Only a portion of it was presented to the deity as a burnt offering. Since antiquity, it has been called *tôdâ*, a thanksgiving and praise offering. This name expresses the purpose attributed to the sacrifice. Since the majority of the sacrificial animals were eaten by the guests, however, it was quite natural for one to see that purpose most clearly expressed in the thanksgiving psalm that accompanied the sacrifice or belonged to the festival. The psalm was what was actually given to YHWH and presented for his honor. The sacrificial meal was more the celebratory meal of the guests and a welcome gift to the invited "poor" and "humble." Deuteronomy had already most explicitly prescribed that they be invited,[63] undoubtedly reflecting a very old practice.

Passages that explicitly emphasize the deity's preference for the psalm are only a shade sharper (Pss 50:8–23; 69:31–32). They say nothing more than that the thanksgiving psalm is absolutely the most valuable and pleasing part of the sacrificial festival or of the cult. Psalm 50:8–23 quite clearly indicates that no rejection of the cult is intended whatsoever but that the poet's stance

---

62. See 829 n. 59.
63. Deut 12:12; 14:27–29; 16:11, 13; 26:11–13.

can be summarized in the words, "one should do the one and not forsake the other." Sacrifices are good per se and prescribed by YHWH. YHWH need not admonish the people about them. They are more likely to bring an excess of sacrifice. They should remember that YHWH has no need of them. One should not believe, however, that, covered by sacrifices, one can neglect the moral commandments. Instead, if one wants to bring the best sacrifice, "one should sacrifice thanks and praise."[64] The reference here to the "payment of vows" alongside the thanksgiving psalm certainly includes the thanksgiving sacrifice meal to be enjoyed by the "poor." The psalm was the focus, after all, of the cultic thanksgiving sacrifice festival that the poet has in mind. Other passages that depict prayer as sacrifice also demonstrate that these poets' thoughts and ideas were very closely tied to the cult: "My prayer consists of incense before you, my lifted hands an evening sacrifice" (Ps 141:2). Or, "May the words of my mouth and the mediations of my heart [i.e., this psalm] be pleasing (*lĕrāṣōn*) (to you)" (Ps 19:15). The expression *hāyâ lĕrāṣōn* is a term for the gracious acceptance of the sacrifice that was pleasing to God.[65] The sense is, "may this psalm be a pleasing sacrifice for you!" A person who has emancipated himself from cultic religion would not talk this way, think what he may about the bloody sacrificial animal. Both the cases mentioned here involve petition (such as Ps 51:18–19), not thanksgiving.

Seen against this background, one must hesitate to see in the admittedly absolute-sounding passages Pss 40:7–8 and 51:18–19 a categorical rejection of animal sacrifice. They must be viewed as somewhat hyperbolic formulations of the same idea found in the other psalms, formulations that relate to the otherwise apparently passionate temperament of the psalmists that inclines toward exaggerations and absolute-sounding statements. The purpose of these formulations is to express as sharply as possible the positive component of the idea, the high estimation of the pious attitude and of the poetically formulated prayer. One is surely accurate regarding the intention of the author of Ps 40 when one explains his words in this fashion: God is not pleased with sacrifice per se but with congregational poetic praise that springs from the "wisdom" of the heart.[66] Psalm 51:18–19 is similar: You (YHWH) take no pleasure in the

---

64. See *Psalm Studies* 3:536.

65. See Gesenius-Buhl, s.v., no. 1. Regarding the interpretation of Ps 19:15, see Gunkel, *Psalmen*, 23.

66. The expression "but you have drilled ears for me" refers to this. Halevy called attention to the Assyrian *birit-uzna* = opening the ears = clarity of mind, reason. "Ears" is a synonym for "heart," for example, in the Shamshiadad inscription (KB 1:174–75). Anton Fridrichsen offers Hellenistic parallels in "Ps 40, 7 Aures perfecisti mihi," *ZAW* 40 (1922): 315–16.

sacrifice itself, and if I were merely to bring a burnt offering you would not accept it. The proper atoning sacrifice for a penitent is the repentant attitude of the heart, the broken spirit and the shattered heart, expressed particularly in the penitential psalm; it also gives the sacrifice its value. This psalmist also advocates the usual preference of the psalm over other cultic procedures, as is evident from the form of his vow (v. 17): "open my lips so that my mouth can sing your praise"; that is, "heal me and give me the opportunity soon to offer you a thanksgiving psalm in the congregation." God is not satisfied with external sacrifice; sacrifice per se is nothing. It must be offered as the expression of a pious, now broken, now joyously thankful heart. The main concern, the truly valuable thing, is the psalm expressing the piety of the heart. That is what these poets wanted to say. They did not succeed in formulating this idea clearly, however, for the following reasons: (1) because of the Jewish incapacity for clear abstract thought, the conceptual distinction between sacrifices and sacrifice per se was not entirely clear to them; and (2) the Hebrew language lacks the potential for expressing such nuances of thought. One cannot say "sacrifice per se" in Hebrew. The Hebrews must resort to hyperbole instead of abstraction.[67]

Obviously, this relatively low estimation of sacrifice in the psalms should be regarded in terms of a larger context in the history of religions. We are dealing here with the same spiritual trend against which the major preexilic prophets should be explained. In the earlier period, sacrifice, in the broadest sense of the word, was actually the center and focus of the cult. This circumstance is already evident in the massive increase in bloody sacrifice in times of misfortune and distress. The anticultic polemic of the prophets began at this very point. The mere appearance of these prophets demonstrates, however, that the old form of the cultic religion had already begun to lose its firm grip on hearts.[68] More

---

67. In addition, attention can be called to Jacob's argumentation in "Beiträge," *ZAW* (1897): 273, which I first saw after the presentation above was written. Jacob demonstrates, in my view irrefutably, that the customary Protestant interpretation of Pss 40; 50; and 51 is already untenable on linguistic grounds. The phrase *zābaḥ tôdā* cannot mean "to render thanks." The verb *zābaḥ* always means "to slaughter," to "sacrifice" in the literal sense. The *nĕdārîm* are always specific sacrificial vows (we may add: alongside the associated rites and sayings, especially the thanksgiving psalm). The noun *zebaḥ* (Ps 51:18) admittedly appears in a metaphorical sense. Otherwise, he interprets passages as I have above (see also *Psalm Studies* 1:146–49). He remarks concerning Ps 40:7, correctly it seems to me, that *'ōlā wăhaṭā'ă* ... cannot be translated "you do not desire burnt offering and sin offering." Sin offering is always *ḥāāṭṭ'āt*. Otherwise, *ḥaṭā'ă* means both sin and the occasion and opportunity for it. Thus the psalm passage should be translated, "You do not like (making) whole offerings and (simultaneously) sinning"; see also Isa 1:13.

68. See *Psalm Studies* 2:488–89.

profound natures began to seek new paths. This incipient separation from the old cultic experiences is primarily expressed as a distancing from excessive sacrifice. Both the greed and avarice of the priests and the natural emotional reactions of simple, somewhat rationalistic persons, a class that included some prophets (see Amos 7:14-15), may have contributed to the extravagance of sacrificial worship.[69] This internal dissolution of the cult was completed in and after the exile. Judaism is not a cultic religion, but a religion of law and observance. Postexilic Judaism, despite its rich temple cult, actually no longer understood what the authentic, original cult was.[70] It made a commandment of the cult. The temple cult was practiced because YHWH commanded it. It simply no longer understood many of the old forms and procedures. It sometimes associated no clear meaning with them and sometimes reinterpreted and spiritualized them. Above all, the original and logical meaning of the sacrifice was completely lost. Sacrifice was made because the law demanded it and because the priests had an economic interest in it. In accordance with the new form of religion, the cult actually became a cult of prayer and submission to the law, as expressed in the cultic re-creation of Judaism, synagogue worship. Even the temple cult was spiritualized, and only that which had a counterpart in the synagogue cult was emphasized and appropriated: God's word, prayer, praise, blessing, and singing.[71] The description of New Year's worship in the temple court on the 1st of Tishri given by the Ezra source[72] is very representative. The author reports the bringing and opening of the Torah scroll, introductory praise (*běrākâ*), reading from the Torah and Ezra's sermon, the emotions of the congregation, and the concluding joyous feast. Not a single word is said about the many sacrifices of New Year's Day. To the author, they were an obvious but quite secondary matter. Postexilic Judaism relates to sacrifice with a total lack of understanding. Sacrifices are necessary only because they were commanded (Sir 32:6); in itself, the sacrificial service alone is worthless (Sir 7:9; 21:3; Jdt 16:17). On this point, the psalmists have affinities both with the

---

69. Consider the animosity of the simple, rural, and, in the eyes of city folk, of course, extremely uncultured Amos against all cultural accomplishments and any opulence and luxury (Amos 3:12, 15; 4:1; 5:11; 6:4-5). Amos clearly also aimed at the extravagance of sacrificial worship (see 4:4-5; 5:21-25). He was angry when he thought both of a daily roast and of hecatombs of sacrificial animals. The humanists and Luther would employ the same arguments.

70. See *Psalm Studies* 2:212-13.

71. See Hölscher, *Geschichte*, 177. Regarding the discussion above, see the picture of synagogue worship presented above, 794 n. 12.

72. Neh 8. For an interpretation of this chapter, completely misunderstood by criticism in the tradition of Graf and Wellhausen, see my *Ezra den Skriftlærde*, 32-40, 78ff.; and Gustav Hölscher, *Die Bücher Esra und Nehemia* (HSAT; 4th ed.; Tübingen: Mohr, 1923).

prophets and with the usual understanding of exilic and postexilic Judaism, in general, although we cannot therefore speak of a rejection or an avoidance of the cult. Just as Ben Sira or Judith take an entirely positive stance in relation to the temple cult, so also do the psalmists. They merely accentuate and interpret it differently than the ancient period and, in later times, indeed the priests—the professional representatives of sacrificial worship—did.

The issue in this context is the following. In the negative, in the relative devaluation of sacrifice, the prophets, later Judaism, and the psalmists are agreed; in the positive, however, they largely go their own ways.[73] The psalmists' attitude cannot be explained as a product of the preaching of the writing prophets. The prophets juxtapose sacrifice primarily to internal piety, obedience, humility (Mic 6:8; Jer 7:22–23; 1 Sam 15:22–23), and, in terms of specific behaviors, especially righteousness (*ṣedeq, ṣĕdāqâ*) and mercy (*ḥesed*) toward poor neighbors (e.g., Amos 5:24; Isa 1:17; Mic 6:8). In later Judaism the constant counterpart of sacrifice was observance of the commandments, first of all, in addition to benevolence and righteousness.[74] The situation differs in the psalms. As demonstrated above, sometimes the psalmists emphasized the psalm (in distress the psalm of penitence and petition, after deliverance the thanksgiving psalm in the midst of the cultic community) almost exclusively as the alternative for, but mostly as the main element of, the sacrificial procedure. Occasionally the pious and humble attitude they express is also mentioned explicitly (Ps 51:18–19).

The swelling of these streams, which the "writing prophets" did not create but which must, conversely, simply be postulated in order to explain their appearance, was promoted in particular—I consider this a certainty—by the lower temple personnel. We are dealing in part with an "inner-temple" development. It is related in particular both to the religious type of "*nābî'*-ism" and to the evaluations that must have been evident to the cultic singers. Indeed, "*nābî'*-ism" had its locus in temples, especially in the temple in Jerusalem (see *Psalm Studies* 3). It is related to the religious experiences of the "inspired men of God" κατ' ἐξοχήν (i.e., par excellence), the prophets and poets. They were the very men who "have seen God." Many anonymous individuals must have experienced forms of Isaiah's experience in the temple (Isa 6), although sometimes in other shades and in varying intensities (see Pss 63:3; 73:17). For them, God became a "tangible" reality that overpowered them. For them, he became an experience of the reality of the *mysterium tremendum et fascinosum*. There-

---

73. Gunkel also called attention to this occasionally, although only with regard to the prophets and psalmists (see *Psalmen*, 88).

74. See Sir 32:1–5. The author of Neh 8 also accentuates almsgiving on the festival (8:10), while he is silent concerning sacrifice (see above).

fore, they attained and nurtured a form of religion that, despite its bondage to tradition and society, is an explicitly individualistic and emotional and experiential religion. Thus it already differs from the more objective and sacramental type of religion practiced by the sacrificial priests. This experiential religion must sooner or later become manifest as unique and distinct from the sacramental religion of the priests, and this awareness must lead to a depreciation of the material, purely "objective" cultic procedures of the priests, especially of bloody sacrifice, and, accordingly, to a heightened assessment of the elements of the cult that express convictions. The proponents of this "subjective" type of religion primarily experienced God as that which incites emotion; in essence, after all, *nābî'*-ism has many points of contact with the elements of mysticism in all periods. In the emotional reactions of the saints to the numinous, both in the humble prostration and abasement of broken, sinful creatures before the Almighty and in the joyful, exultant submission to the glorious, gracious, and wondrous, this religiosity quite naturally sees the suitable, obvious attitude toward the divine. This attitude is more natural, immediate, and therefore more appropriate than any sacrifice or external rites. They found both of these two major types of emotional religious reactions expressed in the penitential psalm and in the thanksgiving psalm, or hymn, and they also expressed them in new psalms of the same kind. Thus for them the psalm became the major element in the cult beside which sacrifice receded entirely into the shadows. It retained value only to the extent that it could be reinterpreted spiritually and valued as a symbolic expression of emotions, of subjective piety. However, they esteemed the cultic psalm—for, beyond question, the thanksgiving psalms of the Psalter are cultic, as the penitential psalms surely are as well, in my view. These psalms were so highly valued they became the contrast with and corrective norm to sacrifice. This clearly indicates that we should seek the people who composed the psalms in the circles of the cultic personnel, among the singers and temple prophets.

It should be very clear that, in addition to the religious assessment of the spiritually reinterpretable elements of temple worship, these ideas simultaneously express the pride and self-consciousness of the professional psalmist in contrast to the perspectives of the sacrificial priests. This observation excludes the possibility that the poets of the cultic psalms may be found among the priests, while the assumption that the poets are to be found among the singers explains everything aptly. The fact that the psalmists also substantially agree on this point with the prophets, to whom they were more closely related,[75] can also be explained in this fashion. It is only human and very understand-

---

75. See §3.2, above.

able that the various classes of the administrators of temple worship would have had a certain inclination to assess their own particular professions and part in the cultic procedures as the most valuable, necessary, and pleasing to God. We also know otherwise about an antagonism between the priests and the lower clergy represented especially by the singers. The singers claimed priestly rank and respect. They obviously did so with the motivation that the cultic procedures for which they were responsible were at least as valuable and necessary as the priestly procedures. This antagonism is already apparent in the final Priestly redaction of the P narrative in Num 16, where the Korahites appear as the outrageous aspirants to priestly rights. In reality, things did not go according to the pious wishes of the Priestly narrator, since the earth swallowed up the "godless" Korahites. To the contrary, in the first century C.E., the singers asserted their claims and received the right to wear the purple priestly garment as an outward sign. In Josephus's view, however, the destruction of Jerusalem was the well-deserved divine punishment for this transgression of the law (*Ant.* 20.216–218). We see in the assessment of the sacrifice and of singing in the psalms the religious side of these social and economic disputes. They also occupy a place in the larger context in the history of religion, however.

The fact that the psalms speak so relatively infrequently of the priests,[76] but all the more frequently of the implements and activities of the singers,[77] is also related to the extremely relative undervaluation of sacrifice treated here. This circumstance is also evidence that we will find the poets of these psalms not among the priests but among the temple singers.

3.7 (19). The assumption that the psalms were composed by lower temple personnel, more precisely by the singers, also explains another characteristic of the psalms: their rather frequent partisanship on behalf of the poor, the propertyless, the socially oppressed, the "widows and orphans," as the Hebrews put it. Here, too, we must go into greater detail and say a few words explaining the pertinent passages in the Psalter.

---

76. Pss 115:9, 12; 118:3; 132:9, 16; 133:2; see Causse, *Les "Pauvres" d'Israël*, 112 n. 1. Contrast, however, Jacob, "Beiträge," *ZAW* (1897): 272, whose exegesis is to be utilized only with caution.

77. E.g. *šôfār*—47:6; 81:4; 98:6; 150:3; *ḥaṣăṣĕrôt*—98:6; *kinnôr*—33:2; 43:4; 49:5; 57:9; 71:22; 81:3; 92:4; 98:5; 108:3; 137:2; 147:7; 149:3; 150:3; *nēbel*—33:2; 57:9; 71:22; 81:3; 92:4; 108:3; 144:9; 150:3; *ʿāśôr*—33:2; 92:4; 144:9; *zāmar* 43 times; *šîr* 38 times; *nāgan* 4 times; *rnn* 11 times; *hôdâ* is very frequent. Terms for cultic song include *sappēr* (22:23; 26:7; 79:13; 107:22) and *higgîd* (75:10; 92:3). See Jacob, "Beiträge," *ZAW* (1897): 266–67, 273.

Starting from *'ănāwîm*, *'ănîyîm*, *'ebyōnîm*, and *dallîm*, frequent expressions in the psalms, the common assumption has been that the psalms were written by people who belonged to the poor and lowest social classes of the people, even though it has been admitted that these designations acquired a secondary religious meaning and sometimes denoted nothing more than "pious" or the like. The reason was supposed to have been that the upper classes were irreligious and secular in sentiment, while the simple and poor people in the countryside remained true to the patriarchal religion and therefore had to endure even more.[78] I have already indicated above (§2.2) that this theory is false in its form and generality. It rests both on an erroneous interpretation of the "enemies" in the psalms and on false historical assumptions. In reality, "poor" and "pious" are terms that only rarely corresponded to one another, and even though "the poor" may have become the name of a party or a sect,[79] this should be judged simply as claiming the "biblical" terms for one's own party. Any circle may have correctly perceived and deduced from "scriptures" that the *'ănîyîm* mentioned in the psalms were regarded as the pious. Like modern exegetes, they may have concluded from the juxtaposition of the expressions "the oppressed" and "the pious" (righteous, etc.) that "oppressed" was nothing other than another designation for the pious. It would have, indeed, been very convenient to portray oneself as the (unjustly) oppressed. Ever since and even today, the "pious" have favored this portrayal—even when they were the oppressors. In the psalms, the terms cited name neither parties nor schools but denote, in part, the pious generally as the humble (before God), in part, the sick and suffering who complain in the psalms and other people who may be or once have been in the same situation and who, consequently, see in the salvation and deliverance of the sick a comforting confirmation of YHWH's goodness and of the success of the cultic purification of the sick with lament psalm and sin offering. Sometimes they designate the needy in general. Sometimes, however, they also refer to the truly poor, who are also invited to the

---

78. Heinrich Ewald (in vol. 1.2 of *Die Dichter des Alten Bundes* [3rd ed.; Göttingen: Vandenhoeck & Ruprecht, 1866]) already argued for this understanding. Reference here should be made to Alfred Rahlfs, עני und ענו in den Psalmen (Göttingen: Dieterich, 1892); see further Causse, *Les "Pauvres" d'Israël*, 81–135. Rudolf Smend's "Über das Ich der Psalmen," *ZAW* 8 (1888): 49–147, is also built on this assumption. The commentaries by Friedrich Baethgen (*Die Psalmen* [HKAT 2; Göttingen: Vandenhoeck & Ruprecht, 1892]), Buhl (*Psalmerne*), Duhm (*Psalmen*), Kittel (*Psalmen*), and others are also based on it.

79. To our knowledge, such was only the case with reference to the early Christian Ebionites. They may have had late Jewish prototypes, however.

thanksgiving offering feast according to ancient custom and who then join the healed in lauding and praising YHWH.[80]

Undeniably, on the other hand, the documents of the Israelite religion transmitted to us, the prophets and the law as well as the psalms, are explicitly sympathetic toward the lowest social classes, the poor and the oppressed.[81] From a social perspective, this can be explained by the fact that both the priests who wrote the law and the prophets who represented simple patriarchal ideals in the face of the newer culture themselves belonged to the propertyless and, consequently, were poorly situated socially already beginning in the middle monarchial period. In theory, at least at the smaller sanctuaries and in the countryside, the priests had actually always been,[82] even in the earlier period, propertyless and dependent on the gracious gifts of those visiting the cultic sites.[83] Consequently, the law insisted tirelessly that the "Levites" not be forgotten at the feasts and other cultic proceedings. What was true of the priests was certainly true of the lower temple officials subordinate to them, the temple slaves, the singers, and the gatekeepers. They will have been true "proletarians" in somewhat earlier times and were so long after the exile.[84] The same is true of the prophets. They are also assumed to be propertyless and insignificant persons (1 Sam 10:11). They lived chiefly from gifts.[85] This circumstance also explains the fact that, when cultural developments produced a profound cleft in the people and created an economically and socially oppressed underclass, the prophets always had ears open to the complaints and the sighs of the lower classes and translated their unarticulated resentment into clear and powerful words that have survived the millennia. They knew the distress of the common people by personal experience, and their cries echoed in the prophets' souls, thirsty for righteousness, where the old patriarchal ideal of justice lived on.

The psalmists joined this context. Their partisanship on behalf of the propertyless and oppressed is evident in various ways, initially in their indirect emphasis on introducing the poor to the thanksgiving sacrifice meal (Pss

---

80. Such is probably the case in Ps 22:27, where the concept of the humble dominates in parallel to those "who seek YHWH" (see Pss 69:33; 34:3). On the question, see *Psalm Studies* 1:120–23, with a list of passages.

81. Having depicted this in context is the merit of the wonderful book by Causse mentioned above. It also offers the correct social explanation concerning the psalms, although it draws much too wide-reaching conclusions.

82. Disregarding the priestly and Levitical cities in P.

83. See 1 Sam 9:7–8; Judg 17:10.

84. See the difficulty Ezra had in bringing the Levites (in the later sense) to Jerusalem (Ezra 8:15–20; further Neh 13:10–14 where the singers are also mentioned explicitly).

85. 1 Sam 9:7–8; 1 Kgs 14:3; 17:9–16; 2 Kgs 4:8–10, 42; 5:15; 6:5.

22:27; 34:3; 69:33). This partisanship has analogies in Deuteronomy's admonition to invite the Levites, widows, and orphans.

Above all, however, this relationship comes to light in the fact that sometimes the ʿānî and the ʿānāw with social connotations are viewed as the type of the pious, and sometimes the traditional oppressors are depicted with the image of the rich and ruthless upper class. The words ʿānî, ʿānāw, and the like in the psalms neither always nor even predominantly have the meaning "poor" or socially "oppressed." In themselves they denote the state of being oppressed or suffering in general, often also with connotations of being humiliated and humbled. With some degree of clarity, they sometimes also include the religious meanings "humble," "pious,"[86] inherent in the semantic field from the outset. Thus they could designate the people of Israel who were pleasing to God and sometimes also oppressed by enemies (Pss 18:28; 68:11; 72:2; 74:19; 149:4). The term ʿănāwîm appears in at least one passage (Ps 37:11), however, as the very type of the pious who "inherit the land," that is, who are supposed to attain well-being and good fortune. For the most part, this diction has a stylistic foundation. Those who speak in the psalms, actual sufferers, "oppressed" and "bowed" by demons and sorcerers, always represent themselves as pious, sometimes as suffering justly and innocently, sometimes as at least penitent, sound, and just at the core of their souls. This may be inherent in the cultic purpose of those psalms: lustrations and cultic repentance are not provided for the godless but for the suffering pious. Thus it could have come about via purely stylistic means that "oppressed" and "pious" became interchangeable terms in certain contexts in the lament psalms. It demonstrates nothing about the diction of actual life. The psalms' rather frequent emphasis on the fact that YHWH manifests his goodness by delivering and helping the suffering, the oppressed, the needy, and the poor quite generally[87] will have contributed to the same linguistic result. No enduring religious quality is inherent in these words. Instead, the psalmists obviously assumed that the sufferers must be pious in order to be delivered. The more traditional the diction of poetry became, the more easily ʿānî and similar terms could become interchangeable with "pious," "righteous," and the like. Social conclusions would be difficult to draw from this circumstance. Thus it is very unclear whether the concept of humility or of being oppressed is the more prominent in Ps 37:11. It is all the more difficult to draw social conclusions from these terms, since neither ʿānî nor ʿānāw, by far the most common of the terms involved here, means

---

86. Actually "bowed," "bend," "bowing before God," or "bowing" and thus "humble," "pious," because in later times humility was the chief virtue of the pious.

87. Pss 9:13, 19; 10:17; 12:6; 18:28; 25:9; 35:10; 68:11; 69:34; 109:31; 140:13.

propertyless from the outset. Even *'ebyôn* need not designate the propertyless or the socially disadvantaged,[88] nor did it do so originally.[89] Undeniably, however, social and economic conditions resonate in a few passages. In addition to those unjustly sickened by demons,[90] the economically poor and the socially disadvantaged in particular come under consideration as the object of God's willingness to give aid.[91] The propertyless and insignificant enjoy particular sympathy with the psalmists.

This sympathy becomes significant, on the other hand, when, as indicated above, the wealthy and powerful are portrayed as oppressors and evildoers and are depicted with clear antipathy.[92] This situation is not original but a circumstance that contradicts fundamental ideas of the Israelite religion and worldview. For Israel's elders, it was obvious that wealth, might, and so on were the logically, morally, and physically necessary results of being just and pious.[93] This basic idea remained vital and led to Israel's actual life problem, the problem of retribution. In such ancient times, honor, fame, and pride seemed much more appropriate for the righteous and pious than humility and prostration. This fundamental sensibility is still expressed in religious language when God appears as Israel's *tĕhillâ* or *tip'eret* (Deut 10:21; Jer 17:14; Pss 71:6; 109:1), when Israel or the pious has a feeling of strength, power, and majesty (*'ōz*) "in God" (Exod 15:2; Isa 12:2; Pss 29:11; 118:11), or when piety and purity is the "hope" and "confidence" of the righteous (Job 4:6). The self-testimony of Job (chs. 29–31) offers us the best example of the pride and feeling of power of the pious and righteous. This is his true sense of life. The misfortune is that it was unjustly stolen from him.

The obvious assumption of the unified tribal culture of ancient times was, however, that the mighty should bear the lesser members of the tribe or the clan, lend them "blessing" from their own "blessing," and step forward as their patron, protector, and helper (see Job 29–31). The dissolution of the tribal bonds and tribal culture through the political and social developments of the monarchial period gave rise to a new court and municipal upper class that accumulated property and whose concept of honor and ideals of life were despotic and individualistic. In addition, it gave rise to an increasingly propertyless

---

88. See Ps 74:21 concerning the people smitten and subjugated by enemies.
89. See Neh 5:1–13.
90. See n. 87, above.
91. Pss 72:4, 12; 76:10; 82:3–4; 107:41; 113:7; 147:6; cf. 132:15.
92. This is more or less clearly the case in Pss 37; 49; 52; 62; and 73. I admit this with much less reticence that I did in *Psalm Studies* 1:126–27. See also Ps 113:7–8 and 1 Sam 2:4–8.
93. On what follows, see Pedersen, *Israel*, 1:418–19.

lower class that had lost the old support of the tribal bonds. The prophets can be understood in relation to these ruptured relations that had already begun to appear in the middle royal period. They were the defenders of the under class and the unsuccessful sustainers of the old social and cultural ideals. For them, the wealthy upper class consisted of the "men of violence" (*'îš ḥāmās*). In Israel, "violence" was always a typical synonym word for "sin." It designated everything understood as transgression of the bond of brotherhood and the duties of the covenant.[94] At the same time, they were also the "men of lies" (*'îš šeqer*) because they depended on a wealth that did not arise out of the power and blessing of a "just" soul and that was, consequently, only apparent, an illusion, a "lie." "Lie" had also always been a typical designation for "sinfulness" that originates in a "vain" soul.[95] Because the poor can no longer enjoy fair living conditions in the protection of the powerful, to which they have a right as members of the covenant, but have an unfulfilled demand on the powerful, they are the righteous in relation to the powerful and approach God as such. This circumstance is the origin of the quite paradoxical relationship in which righteousness corresponds to misfortune and oppression and of the fact that in the circles of the poor, including the prophets, being oppressed came to be a synonym for righteous. Something else also contributed to this situation. Beyond question, those responsible for the development of religious thought in Israel were adherents of the cult, both priests and prophets. For the most part, however, the people of the cult related to individual worshipers when, in distress, they made requests of God in the temple. They knew the pious chiefly as sufferers and in the prayers that they formulated for these sufferers. In the official religious thesaurus, they dealt with the suffering, distressed, "oppressed" righteous. This circumstance gradually influenced religious concepts and thought in a certain direction (see the statements above, 839–40, concerning the "stylistic" influence on religious concepts).

Another phenomenon comes into view prominently here, namely, the personal religious experiences of the cultic prophets and poets, of the "inspired" mentioned above (834–35). When people encounter God as *mysterium tremendum et fascinosum*, they become quite small and quiet. "Woe is me; I am lost, for I am a man of unclean lips, and I dwell in the midst of a people of unclean lips. And now, my eyes have seen King YHWH Sabaoth." Then, however, humility and prostration is the natural religious attitude. On the day when a person experiences such a thing, when only YHWH is majestic, then everything lofty and towering collapses. Thus humility became piety,

---

94. See ibid.
95. See ibid., 1:411–13.

indeed—and this is the significant point—in the official religion of Israel among those who, as leaders of the cult, established the language of religion, exercised influence on the whole people, and determined the course of "development." This purely religious assessment combined with the traditional cultic language, on the one hand, and with the assessments of things that arose from social conditions, on the other, into a religious estimation of the lowly, suffering, and oppressed that gave new content to both the concepts of prostrate, suffering, and oppressed and to the concepts of pious, just, and God-fearing. The unfortunate and suffering, the humiliated and unjustly deprived of their rights, and the debased became YHWH's most beloved children. Prostration and humility became religious virtues; pride became arrogance and insolence. Righteousness and piety became subjective submission to God; the "sense of creatureliness" consciously assumed a prominent place in the realm of religion. Only "boasting in YHWH" is still justified and valued. Here, if ever, one can see the nature of the cult and the simple cultic prophets (and poets) of Israel's religion.

Some psalmists sided entirely with the prophets also on this point. This is evident in the fact that they sometimes depicted the traditional enemies of the lament and thanksgiving psalms with the image of the new, violent upper class that trusted in "false" wealth. According to the overall situation assumed and the cultic purpose of the psalms under consideration here, those enemies are to be understood entirely otherwise. They were the traditional sorcerers who sickened the sick ones needing purification.[96] These psalms are not meant as manifestos against the wealthy per se or as laments concerning the attacks from some specific rulers; such laments would have had no place in the psalms of the cultic procedures. The poets depicted the traditional enemies as violent members of the upper class and wealthy, however, and thereby betrayed a genuine hatred of them. In this hatred, the unknown and mysterious sorcerers and the fat and well-fed aristocrats became interchangeable. Both were violent, liars, oppressors, sinners who must soon collapse because they trusted in transitory, "lying" and deceitful power and wealth because they did not trust in the appropriate righteousness of their souls.[97] The fact that both "violence" and "lies" were long-favored and characteristic descriptions of the sorcerers undoubtedly contributed to this fusion of the two categories.[98] It is also quite possible that both the ordinary sick person and the poets of the sin offer-

---

96. *Psalm Studies* 1:125, 133–37.

97. If one notes this ambiguity of the terms, the objections that Paul Humbert (*RTP* 55 [1923]: 65) lodged against my interpretation of Ps 52 (*Psalm Studies* 1:26–27; see also 124–25) are met.

98. *Psalm Studies* 1:6, 8–9, 20, 32, 38, 43–62.

ing and thanksgiving psalms were inclined to see a particularly despised rich person as the secret cause of the misfortune.[99]

This somewhat indirect and disguised position that favored the poor and propertyless over against the new upper class, whose entire fortunes could be regarded as a crime against the old popular ideals, can best be explained if one assumes that the psalms arose in circles that belonged to the poor and lower classes. As indicated above, this was not the case, however, with the conventicles of later Judaism. Nothing suggests that they consisted chiefly of poor and insignificant people. Nor does this characterization suit the priests of the late monarchial period. We know that the lower temple officials had long belonged to the propertyless class in the most eminent sense of the term. They lived on meager offerings or on tithes of the tithes to the priests. The social ascent of the lower clergy only began in the time of the Chronicler or even much later, when the Psalter may have already been closed. Gunkel, Causse, and others have been correct to emphasize that the psalms arose among the poor, but they sought these poor in the wrong place. They did not want to see that the poor could be found "in the forecourts of YHWH."

3.8 (20). I believe that it is necessary to establish the thesis proposed and defended as an axiom. Most of the psalms in the Psalter were composed by the temple singers. Other origins are rare exceptions.

However, there is a genre of psalms that occasionally includes exceptions, it seems to me: the individual psalms of thanksgiving. Admittedly, they, too, were probably composed without exception for cultic purposes, for performance at the thanksgiving sacrifice meal. It seems likely to me that this situation included the practice that one who was or wanted to be particularly pious and who wanted to perform the "payment of his vows" with the greatest precision possible, composed the psalm to be sung at the thanksgiving sacrifice feast himself, brought it to the temple, and probably placed it there "before YHWH" as a testimony. Such originally privately composed cultic psalms will have also entered the temple's psalm collection.

It seems to me that this possibility is supported, first, by the fact that the thanksgiving psalms were often written with inferior art, little observation of the traditional rules of style, and often in a diction much inferior to the other psalms. Reference should be made in this context to the mixture of styles in

---

99. It would have been thought that he owed his wealth to secret and evil arts, as when Isaiah accused his political and religious opponents of trusting in a covenant with the powers of hell (Isa 28:15, see *Psalm Studies* 1:69–70). One can find analogies everywhere in folk circles.

Pss 103, 145, and 146,[100] to the entirely irregular meter in Pss 30 and 116, and to the poor diction in Ps 116.

Second, the circumstance that, conversely, we find among these very psalms those most distinguished by the authentic tones of personal experience and perceptions points in the same direction. Reference should be made here in particular to Ps 73 and perhaps also to Ps 23.[101] In Ps 73 personal experience almost totally dissolved the old fixed form and created its own particularly effective form that employs elements of the lament psalm, the thanksgiving psalm, and the proverb and problem poem. The inimitable air of personal agitation and the passions of a soul blessed by its God hovers over all of this.

Third, it can be established in support of my understanding of the situation that we read a regular thanksgiving psalm in Jesus ben Sira that refers in the customary fashion to deliverance from a threat to life (Sir 51:1–12). This threat to life was probably not, as used to be thought on the basis of the LXX, caused by the wrath of a king excited by defamation. The reference to the king is lacking in the Hebrew text.[102] The danger is depicted in the usual imagery: Ben Sira is in the grave, in Sheol, in hell, surrounded by blazing fire, in the womb of *těhôm*. From the depths of the earth and the gates of the underworld he cried to YHWH for assistance. In the psalms this image always, or almost always, depicts dangerous sickness—or sickness conceived as dangerous.[103] Ferocious enemies, his "opponents," "who seek his life" have caused this distress. They have done so insidiously, with "schemes" and "intrigues." They have used "lies" and "deceit" (*kāzab, šeqer, mirmâ*) against him. Their means were the tongue and the "slanderous" word (*dibbâ*). As it says in Job 13:4, they have "pasted him with lies," affixed to him lies that consume the core of his soul, smitten him without such sinful words that they have made him miserable and sick. The words of their tongues have hit and wounded him like "arrows." This is the diction well known in the psalms for depicting the "ʾāwen-doers," the "sorcerers."[104] I see no reason why this description should not be taken in its original and authentic sense. Ben Sira was sick once and then healed—we do not know whether with or without cultic lustrations and provisions. As usual, he saw the sickness as an effect of the evil arts of certain

---

100. See 808 n. 54.

101. See ibid. and the reference to *Psalm Studies* 1 there.

102. I do not know how it found its way into the Greek and Syriac text. מרמה (*mirmâ*) may have been understood as *mārôm* and interpreted to mean "(royal) highness." Or is βασιλεῖ merely an exegetical gloss mirroring contemporary political conditions?

103. See Gunkel, *Psalmen*, 212–15.

104. See *Psalm Studies* 1:20–25, 44–51; see also 133–37.

"tongue-men."[105] In distress, he called to YHWH for help; he saw the healing as God's gracious response. After being healed, as a pious man he naturally offered a thanksgiving offering and sang a thanksgiving song. He composed this thanksgiving song himself at the time and later included it as an addendum in his book.

Fourth and finally, an Egyptian analogy may be adduced for our hypothesis concerning privately composed thanksgiving offering psalms brought to the temple. The Theban thanksgiving songs by the painter Neb-rê to the god Amon published by Adolf Erman and discussed by Gunkel in his *Reden und Aufsätze* were self-composed in grateful memory of the gracious deliverance of his son, Necht-Amon, from a severe illness and were later inscribed on stelae and erected in the necropolis of Thebes.[106] Here, too, thanksgiving songs are involved. We do not know whether private thanksgiving sacrifices in the temple after healings were known in ancient Egypt. At any rate, the sick

---

105. Thus I cannot support Ernst Sellin who, in his review of my *Psalm Studies* 1 in *Theologie der Gegenwart* (1922), saw in this thanksgiving psalm evidence that the "'aundiction" was transformed in the course of time and came to be employed in a quite different meaning. Taking up my hypothesis (*Psalm Studies* 1:172) that the appearance of a purely profane healing art may have been a contributing cause to the discontinuation of the cultic lustrations of the sick, Sellin pled for his notion that there were enough secular physicians in the land during Ben Sira's period. I do not believe, however, that this conclusion is binding. If the cultic illness rites were no longer in use at that time because some people went to exorcists and some to secular physicians, this does not demonstrate, of course, that one no longer believed in demons and sorcerers' curses as the causes of illness. Two centuries later, in the time of Jesus, one sees belief in demons, fear of magic, and exorcism in full bloom among the Jews. Of course, the stated circumstance is even less convincing as evidence that one no longer offered a thanksgiving sacrifice and sang thanksgiving psalms after being healed from illness. Of course, we cannot say whether by the ancient expressions Ben Sira meant people skilled in magical arts following the older Israelite notion or demons in agreement with late Judaism. In the meantime, however, I have begun to doubt whether I was correct to conjecture that the official lustrations and purifications for the sick in connection with private sin offerings fell into total disuse in the later period. At any rate, they were probably not officially abolished. Nonetheless, the private activity of the exorcists, on the one hand, and the appearance of a private healing art, on the other, probably suppressed the lustrations for the sick in the temple except for the cases explicitly mentioned in the law. In any case, the image of a person offering a sin offering included by Paul Volz in his revision of Kinzler's *Die biblischen Altertümer* (Tübingen: Mohr, 1914), 79, has little to do with reality. The law, with its *nāśā' 'ăwōnô*, does not think of a pang of conscience because of some conscious sin but of an actual misfortune understood as divine punishment for a conscious or unconscious evil. It was also surely such a misfortune, i.e., in most cases certainly an illness, that motivated a person to offer a sin offering.

106. Adolf Erman, "Denksteine aus der thebanischen Gräberstadt," *Sb Berl* 49 (1911): 1086–1110.

person also made vows there and made consecrated gifts after being healed, especially, it seems, in the form of memorial stelae.[107] We may conjecture that the offering and the erection of these stelae were performed along with certain solemn and ritually regulated ceremonies. The fact that the priest of the pertinent deity played a role as leader of the proceedings is, nonetheless, entirely likely in the later period. In the case cited above, however, Neb-rê—and surely not he alone—was not satisfied with the ritually established portions of the solemnities. He felt moved to appear as poet and singer of the gracious god's praise to proclaim his fame to the whole world.

One may ask, if one admits this point concerning the private origin of individual songs composed for cultic purposes, why not then for many of the individual lament psalms? I respond: (1) because it is to be assumed a priori that the priest and the ritual determined by the order of worship played a greater role in the sin offering and the lustrations than in the pious family feast of a thanksgiving sacrifice (thus, the considerations against the use of private poems presented in §2.1 become pertinent immediately); and (2) because it seems to me to be an assumption contrary to psychology that sick people who already imagine themselves to be in the jaws of Sheol and are gripped by a shuddering fear of death would have depended in large numbers on art.[108] The lament psalms with their stereotypical phrases are by far in most cases only the poetry of professional poets who are able to imagine themselves in and sympathize with the pertinent situation.

---

107. See Adolf Erman and Hermann Ranke, *Ägypten und Ägytpisches Leben im Altertum* (2nd ed.; Tübingen: Mohr, 1923), 309–10.

108. See §2.3, above.

4
The Origin of the Pseudonyms

4.1 (21). In contrast to the relatively accurate attributions of authorship to Asaph, Heman, Etan, and the Korahites,[1] we have inaccurate and entirely nonhistorical information in the names Moses, David, and Solomon. These names neither denote specific individuals who really composed the pertinent psalms,[2] nor do they have anything to do with circles within the bureaucracy that produced these psalms.

The conclusion is evident both from the data concerning the settings—which are secondary, however, in relation to the information concerning the names[3]—and from the analogous information concerning "a prayer by the prophet Habakkuk" (Hab 3:1).

It has often been speculated that the expression *lĕdāwîd* once had a different meaning in the "temple liturgy."[4] There is, as we will see below, something correct in this speculation, but not in the sense in which it is normally understood. Usually the matter is understood as though the information was on the level of *lĕ'āsāp* and similar terms, as though all this information originally had liturgical significance, designating psalms of a certain kind or songs that were sung on certain occasions or by a certain choir. According to Duhm, "psalms of David" designates religious temple songs in contrast to secular songs, perhaps also those religious songs not employed in the temple, pilgrim songs and the like, for example.[5] Only when *lĕdāwîd* was incorrectly understood as information concerning authorship did the other superscriptions come to

---

1. See §§3.2–3.3, above.
2. See §1.3, above.
3. See §1.3, above, and §4.5, below.
4. E.g. Jacob, "Beiträge," *ZAW* (1896): 161–63 Buhl, *Psalmerne*, xxiii; further, Baethgen, *Psalmen*; W. Robertson Smith, *The Old Testament in the Jewish Church* (Edinburgh: A&C Black, 1881); Samuel Rolles Driver, *An Introduction to the Literature of the Old Testament* (9th ed.; New York: Scribner's, 1899); Karl Budde, *Die schönsten Psalmen: Übertragen und erläutert* (Leipzig: Amelang, 1915); Duhm, *Psalmen*; etc.
5. Duhm, *Psalmen*, xv.

be understood in the same sense. As we saw above, however, this position is untenable because the information treated in §§3.2–3.3 was always meant as attributions of authorship. Even the original meaning of the expression *lĕdāwîd* was different from that conjectured by the scholars cited.

We have already seen above that the attributions of authorship to Moses and Solomon depend solely on later midrash. They are actually only comprehensible if one starts by assuming that other comments understood as statements of authorship were already in the Psalter, statements that awakened the interest of Jewish scholars in the question of the authors of the psalm and that, based on what was given, they "researched" further and formed new midrash. We may justifiably assume that the information concerning Moses and Solomon belongs among the comments added last to the psalm superscriptions.

For a cultic psalm, the question of its author is entirely peripheral. The point of religious interest is solely the utility of the psalm, its ability to please God, its character as a "wise," "inspired" song originating from knowledge of the divine commandments and the requirements of the cultic liturgy. Indeed, much of the technical information in the superscriptions relates to this aspect of the matter,[6] and we must regard this very information as the oldest addenda to the psalms. The interest in the authors is literary and academic, not immediately religious. Reports, whether historical or fictive, concerning the authors of the cultic psalms have religious interest only if such reports guarantee that the pertinent psalm bears the proper sacred character. In the ancient view, this guarantee is offered primarily when it seems certain that the respective cultic psalm was employed as such from antiquity and has been faithfully transmitted since then by those responsible for doing so. The (supposed or actual) fact that they were transmitted by the temple singers and even composed by their patriarchs seems to provide this guarantee. Thus, one may assume that Asaph, Heman, Etan, and the Korahites are the oldest of the "author names."

As stated, however, the interest in such information does not seem to have a direct religious foundation. Accordingly, one must assume that this interest arose only secondarily and that it was associated with certain information that could easily be interpreted as attributions of authorship but were not meant as such from the outset. In other words, the attributions of authorship originated in association with and through the reinterpretation of other comments

---

6. Thus, for example, *maśkil*, "a song produced by (inspired) wisdom" (see *Psalm Studies* 4:606–7); *miktām*, "atonement psalm" (*Psalm Studies* 4:605–6); למנצח, "in order to make [YHWH's countenance] shine" (*Psalm Studies* 4:620–24).

introduced by the preposition *lĕ*. This is the correct component of the usual understanding of the expression *lĕdāwîd* mentioned above (see below).

As Duhm and Buhl have indicated, the superscription in Ps 102 presents itself in an unaffected fashion with this type of specification: *tĕpillâ lĕʿānî...*, "a prayer by a misfortunate when, pining, he pours out his complaint before YHWH." It should be quite clear that *lĕ* here does not introduce an indication of authorship but designates those who were meant to employ the psalm. The whole superscription is to be understood on the analogy of the normal prayers "for," that is, for the use of a "seafarer," "a penitent sinner in physical and spiritual distress," "a healed sick person," " a sick person when he confesses and goes to the table of the Lord," "a dying Christian," and so on included in our (Norwegian) hymnals. Such a normal prayer for the use of a "sufferer" in general, a sick person "when he pours out his complaint before YHWH," that is, when he submits to lustrations in the temple, offers a sin offering, and pronounces the related penitential and lament prayers, is, in fact, the individual lament psalm at hand in Ps 102:2–12, 24–28,[7] just as are the individual lament psalms, the sin-offering psalms, in general. This information agrees precisely with the actual purpose of the individual cultic psalms. They are not the products of individuals A and B written in their specific circumstances but normal prayers, "formularies," if you will, composed for use by any Israelite who has come to the place that he must offer either a sin offering or a thanksgiving offering. This circumstance explains the wholly unspecific nature and formulaic character of these psalms.[8] The fact that this information, which was doubtlessly envisioned as a reference to an individual but was subsequently reinterpreted and revised collectively, appears in Ps 102 demonstrates that such comments were already appended to this or that psalm in a rather ancient period before the collective reinterpretation of many psalms,[9] some, indeed, even before the assembly of the Psalter.[10]

---

7. The supplicant was later reinterpreted as the unfortunate Zion and the psalm expanded with the section, vv. 13–23, 29, that makes this statement.

8. See *Psalm Studies* 1:103–4. Apparently, even Humbert, who rejects my interpretation of the "enemies," admits this (see *RTP* [1923]: 78–80). It is unclear how he then thinks he can establish the cultic purpose of the psalms.

9. Regarding this later reinterpretation, see *Psalm Studies* 1:165–71.

10. The understanding proposed by Julius Wellhausen (*Bemerkungen zu den Psalmen* [Skizzen und Vorarbeiten 6; Berlin: Reimer, 1899]), Baethgen (*Psalmen*), Charles A. Briggs (*Psalms: Critical and Exegetical Commentary* [ICC; Edinburgh: T&T Clark, 1906]) and others that *ʿānî* in the superscription to Ps 102 refers to Israel is without foundation. The question is not, however, as Buhl (*Psalmerne*) thinks (s.v.), "of minor significance." Rather, the superscription in Ps 102 has very major significance for understanding both the superscriptions in general and the use and original purpose of the psalms.

It is thus assured that quite early on individual psalms were already provided with comments designating those for whose use the respective psalm was intended and that these comments were introduced by the preposition *lĕ*.

4.2 (22). Originally, I believe, *lĕdāwîd* also had the same meaning, and an incorrect reinterpretation of this expression gave rise to the view that David was poet and psalmist. This thesis will be further substantiated in this and subsequent sections.

Undoubtedly the type of superscription and the use of the preposition *lĕ* manifest in the formula *lĕʿānî* represent an older type of superscripted comment on the psalms than the indications of authorship. In cultic psalms, the comments concerning the cultic use of the individual songs was significantly more important and necessary than indications of authorship, which in themselves have no practical or liturgical value or purpose. Now if the attributions of authorship are supposed to have arisen from a reinterpretation of such comments introduced by *lĕ*, the assumption is that these comments also included some that contained a proper name. Otherwise, there would be no point of departure for such a reinterpretation. Since, as we have seen, Moses and Solomon were the very last author names based solely on historical conjecture,[11] and since Asaph, Heman, Etan, and the Korahites were also meant as author names from the outset,[12] the starting point for these speculations and conjectures can only be the previously unexplained formula *lĕdāwîd*.

We have already expressed the view that this formula should be interpreted on the analogy of the formula *lĕʿānî*. What is the practical value or purpose for transmitting the information, whether actual or fictive, and to remark at the beginning of the pertinent psalm that it was composed or intended "for David's use"? First, it should be determined that such a comment also includes the idea that the respective psalm was actually employed, cited, sung, or recited by David on a certain or on several similar occasions, obviously when he was in some situation that made the recitation of such a psalm—whether a psalm of petition or a thanksgiving psalm—requisite and necessary. David once "sang [this or that psalm] before YHWH" when he was sick or threatened by enemies; he sang some other psalm as a thanksgiving psalm after being healed or after a victorious war. This information offers the opinion of the scribe, singer, or priest who transmitted this information that the respective psalm also actually benefited David at the time. By means of the lament psalm, David was able to appease YHWH and to obtain his help;

---

11. See §1.3, above.
12. See §§3.2 and 3.3, above.

through the thanksgiving psalm, David praised YHWH so beautifully and magnified YHWH's glory among humankind such that he assured YHWH's benevolence in the future and remained continually in his favor. David was always the great ideal in Judah. The tradition was able to recount loudly that David always had good fortune. Thus, the historical realities proved a psalm that helped the great and ever-fortunate David and assured him the favor of the deity to be a particularly effective, God-pleasing psalm. It was recommended for use in similar situations. It was a particularly appropriate cultic psalm, both in public and private cultic proceedings. Inherent in the superscription *lĕdāwîd*, thus, is a strong recommendation for the psalm and a guarantee of its suitability.

Ancient Assyrian offers us analogies both for this view and for this labeling of the psalms. For example, the attribution of the well-known lament psalm, "I attained a (long) life,"[13] to the legendary king Tabu-utu-Bêl[14] undoubtedly has the objective of portraying the psalm as especially effective. According to the accompanying comments in the Assyrian copy of the psalm, the one who recites it at the cultic procedure for which it was written will surely experience blessed results such as those the old king experienced. It will have had the same meaning when older psalms that were composed for a certain king and even named him in the text were copied in later times and conserved. This procedure was certainly not undertaken for love of the literature. It may also be mentioned here that the sign supposedly given to the ancient king Sargon of Akkad was still recorded in the late Assyrian period, undoubtedly in the belief that such signs that served the famed king as good omens would also presage and bring the then-reigning king good fortune and well-being even later should they appear.[15]

The original labeling of certain psalms with David's name contains a historical core to the extent that many of the Jerusalemite temple psalms were undoubtedly composed for the king and for his use in certain cultic situations. Apart from the royal oracles,[16] which are also occasionally placed on the lips of the king (Ps 2), attention should be called here to Ps 101 (the king's vow); Ps 18; 1 Sam 2:10; Isa 38:9–20 (royal thanksgiving psalms); Pss 89 and 144 (public royal lament psalms); and Pss 28; 61; 63 (individual illness or lament psalms, i.e., sin-offering psalms, of the king). Many other psalms in which the speaker does not identify himself as the king or the anointed may nonetheless be described as prayers for the king's use. In earlier times, indeed throughout

---

13. Translation in Gressmann, *Texte und Bilder*, 1:29–30, for example.
14. See Jastrow, *Religion Babyloniens*, 2:120–37.
15. See ibid., 2:224–33, concerning the Sargon *omina*.
16. Pss 2; 110; 132; 21; 45; 72; see *Psalm Studies* 3.

the preexilic period, the temple in Jerusalem was, in the first instance, the sanctuary of the king,[17] who played an outstanding role in all cultic celebrations. Undoubtedly, he was richly supplied with songs and prayers meant for the king and his household and recited by them or in their name on various occasions, whether in distress or in peace. One may reasonably doubt, for example, whether the solemn and costly purification procedures and rites with psalms and prayers for healing from illness and possession were originally meant for the common man. In most cases he was probably satisfied with much simpler arrangements in the local sanctuary. This also agrees with circumstances in Babylonia and Assyria. The overall style of the psalms still demonstrates that they were originally meant for the king and dignitaries, just as a whole series of psalms, including illness psalms, appear as prayers of the king, often even a named king.[18]

In reality, the superscription *lĕdāwîd* will have, essentially if not formally, meant written for David and used by him and other kings after him. Ultimately, the superscription *lĕšlōmō* could also have originally had this meaning. Solomon was also a fortunate person whose name contained a good omen. He was, after all, the temple builder, the richest of all kings, the wisest of all people.

It is another question, however, as to whether this "tradition" was correct in specific individual cases. One must first reckon with the possibility that we no longer possess the psalms that first received this superscription and from which it was obviously transferred to others in the course of time. We may have only psalms to which it was applied in the reinterpreted sense (see below). Further, it should be noted that a comment produced not by literary and historical but practical and religious interests offers only a rather limited guarantee of historical accuracy. Once the idea of commending a cultic psalm with David's name arose, the theory was quite naturally extended to ever more songs, and a comment to this effect was placed over songs that, in reality, originated in a much later period. Since by far the majority of cultic psalms were anonymous, it was usually not known after a period either who composed them or when. Psalm 72 itself, which was related to Solomon because of the reference to the kings of Sheba, demonstrates that this or that psalm was associated with this or that personality for purely midrash-like reasons.[19]

---

17. See 2 Sam 7:18; 2 Kgs 12:5–16; 16:10–18; 18:15–16; 19:14–19; Ezek 43:7–9.
18. Jastrow, *Religion Babyloniens*, 2:106–7, 117, and the passages mentioned in 106 n. 4.
19. See §1.3, above.

The question as to whether some psalm headed with *lĕdāwîd* was actually used by David can actually never be answered positively with certainty. It should be transformed into the converse: Are there psalms in the Psalter that stem or could stem from David's time? In fact, most of the psalms attributed to him are later.[20] On the other hand, I do not want to deny the possibility of "Davidic" songs in the sense discussed above. Everything suggests that Israel already had religious cultic songs before David's time. The so-called Song of Deborah (Judg 5) was already influenced by the style of the religious hymn. I have mentioned elsewhere that Ps 60 may have originated in the time of David or Solomon;[21] Ps 19A may be the fragment of a psalm older than the YHWH cult.[22] Other psalms are so general in conception and expression that they could have originated in almost any time (e.g., Ps 88). Further discussion does not belong in this context, however. It will suffice here to have established that the presence of the comment "for David's use" is not enough to assure the historicity of David's use of the psalm. To the contrary, one must say that the whole mode of thought expressed here that seeks to commend a psalm as having been used by David points to a time after David that saw in him the grand, never-regained ideal of a fortunate and God-favored king. In any case, this would have been the judgment since the division of the kingdom. Once this notion had arisen, however, it was possible to preface both old and new psalms with this comment. Thus it could have occasionally been given to psalms that actually originated in David's time or even earlier. In principle, the presence of the superscription *lĕdāwîd* has no relevance to the question of the age of individual psalms.

4.3 (23). The fact that a psalm was composed and used by David does not mean, of course, that David himself composed the pertinent psalm, not even that David actually used it. So far, no rational person has asserted that those Babylonian/Assyrian psalms that say "I Nebuchadrezzar, I Ashurnasirpal, I Asshurbanipal, beg you," and so on, for example, were also composed by the kings cited. Some of these are, indeed, older psalms in which, in the copy preserved for us, the often-attested blank space in the text of the psalm where the name of the respective petitioner should be placed has been filled with the name of the person for whom the copy was prepared. Most of them, however, are psalms composed by a "learned" minister of the cult in the name of the respective king for specific purposes. Thus one can reasonably doubt whether

---

20. Ibid.; see also §4.5, below.
21. *Psalm Studies* 3:559–65.
22. YHWH is not mentioned; the psalm sings the glory of El as the creator god.

the Israelite/Judean kings themselves composed the cultic psalms that they recited. Not everyone was supposed to know the forms for composing a cultic song as a *maśkil* or *miktām* that pleases God. Writing had certainly become a proper art. David will surely have usually had other things to do than to write poetry, to say nothing of whether a former shepherd boy and bandit leader was literate.

Inherent in the mode of ancient oriental thought and "tradition" formation, one came to the notion very soon that "David" also composed the psalms that went by his name and, accordingly, understood the *lĕ* as a *lĕ auctoris*. The first collectors of smaller collections underlying the Psalter will have understood the information in this sense, that is, at least in the early postexilic and probably already in the preexilic period.[23] Thus David became the great psalmist. Since he actually was the founder of the Jerusalem Yahwistic cult,[24] the quite unhistorical theory found in Chronicles arose that he arranged the details of temple singing and the Levites' ministerial divisions. In reality, the modest portion of this arrangement that is authentically ancient traces no further back than to Solomon, the builder of the temple.

Usually one thinks that the circumstance that so many psalms are attributed to David rests on the fact that he really composed religious songs, whether any of them are preserved for us or not. If, however, our determination of the original meaning of *lĕdāwîd* above is correct, there is no longer any basis in reality for such an assumption. It must be rejected as unjustified and dependent solely on a false theory and an incorrect interpretation of a term with an entirely different meaning. This expression contains no tradition concerning the author of the psalms. As is so often the case, we are dealing here not with a tradition but with a theory.

Consequently, the effort to choose from the roughly seventy psalms characterized by *lĕdāwîd* some that might be old enough and understand them as compositions of David must be rejected. The hypothesis that speaks of "Davidic material" concealed in later revisions becomes pure speculation.[25] The psalms that Ernst Sellin, for example, characterizes as such "Davidic" compositions, namely, Pss. 3, 4, 7, 8, 19A, 23, 24, 29, and 60, offer no traces whatsoever of revisions such as can be found in so many cultic psalms that were in use throughout the centuries. Why, then, the supposed original form

---

23. The author of the books of Samuel already regarded David as the great poet who produced whenever an opportunity presented itself (see below). He may already have been dependent on the "tradition" represented in the psalm superscriptions.

24. He brought the ark to Jerusalem and erected a tabernacle there (2 Sam 6; 24).

25. See, e.g., Ernst Sellin, *Einleitung in das Alte Testament* (3rd ed.; Leipzig: Quelle & Meyer, 1910), 139–40.

of these psalms should be more likely to be Davidic compositions than the others is not clear. Besides the fact that some of them may be truly old (Pss 8; 19A; 29; 60), the only perceptible reason that Sellin wants to categorize these very psalms as Davidic is probably the fact that he values them especially highly and would, therefore, dearly love to be able to attribute them to his darling David. The situation is no different concerning the Davidic origin of Ps 18 proposed by some scholars. The fact that it is also transmitted in 2 Sam 22 truly constitutes no reason to evaluate it differently than the other "psalms of David." Sellin's reference to the "dual witness of the tradition" here is entirely irrelevant. One of the latest redactors of the book simply either adopted 2 Sam 22, superscription and all, from the Psalter or from the collection containing Pss 2(or 3)–41 or Pss 2(or 3)–89. The reason that this and only this psalm was adopted from the larger collection of "songs of David" is simply that the redactor, who wanted to conclude the book with a psalm of David, could not copy all or half of the Psalter but chose the one that could be employed as the conclusion of the David narrative. According to a quite nonhistorical midrash,[26] this psalm was sung by David "when YHWH had freed him from all his enemies and from Saul." Thus, the psalm stood at the time in a collection of "songs of David" that not only bore the superscription *lĕdāwîd* but was also provided with quite secondary information concerning the situation, that is, in one of the collections known to us mentioned above. The circumstance that it spoke of a "victorious, fortunate king"[27] obviously does not demonstrate that the king was the poet, even when the poem speaks in the first person. Furthermore, we cannot know how many of the pompous words of the psalm correspond to historical reality and how much of it is style and rhetoric. "The ancient language" to which Sellin appeals is no more ancient than that in so many other writings that surely belong to a later period; the "body of ancient concepts" in the theophany (vv. 6–16) is no more ancient than so many later eschatological depictions;[28] Ezekiel also advocates the "naïve concept of vengeance in verses 25–27"; it is not evident why the spirit expressed in verses 30 and 42 is more "reminiscent of the period of the judges" than, for example, Ps 149.[29] All of these arguments *pro et contra* are secondary, however, in relation to the principal recognition that the psalm

---

26. Ibid., 139.
27. Ibid.
28. See, e.g., Isa 42:12–17; 63:1–6; Hab 3:3–14.
29. Sellin's claim that vv. 22–24 are a "later keyword gloss" is completely unjustified and is refuted by the strophic structure of the psalm (strophes with four double trimeters). In contrast, v. 51b (not v. 51, as Sellin claims) is a later insertion because it is metrically superfluous.

superscriptions upon which the redactor of 2 Samuel also depends do not permit any conclusions as to the author. Since Ps 18 is actually very sparse in specific historical allusions, we can hardly say anything more concerning the time of origin other than that it belongs to the preexilic monarchial period.

Some think that the theory of a psalm-writing David can be supported by reference to his talent as a musician (1 Sam 16:18; 2 Sam 6:5) and to statements that portray him as an author of profane poetry (2 Sam 1:17; 3:33–34; 23:1–7). In response, one may observe that playing and performing are not *eo ipso* identical with composing. Further, a poet of secular songs does not necessarily also compose cultic psalms. Indeed, David is said to have participated in the cultic dance for the ascent of the ark (2 Sam 6:5, 14). This dance was accompanied by "songs, zithers, harps, hand-drums, and cymbals," but David is not said to have been among the musicians at the procession (see Ps 68:26–27). It may be that the legend concerning David as a young harpist at Saul's court contains historical information—personally I consider all legends concerning the first encounter between the young David and Saul pure fiction[30]—but this does not make him a poet, not to mention a psalmist.

In contrast, it seems much more likely to me that the "tradition" concerning David as a poet has only been spun out of the viewpoint represented in the psalm superscriptions and that this understanding found secondary support in an incorrect interpretation of the "last words" of David (2 Sam 23:1–7) that the redactor of the books of Samuel had already incorrectly considered to be Davidic. Here David was called *nĕ'îm zĕmîrōt yiśrā'ēl*, "the darling of Israel's songs," the one whom the poets of Israel loved to extol. Already at the time, as even today in the official Norwegian Bible translation, this statement was interpreted to mean "the beloved singer of Israel" and found to be an authoritative confirmation of the theory. I rule out the possibility that the enigmatic prediction concerning an enduring blessed reign of the house of David—which is placed in the mouth of David himself, with an analogy in the supposed prediction placed in the mouth of the legendary seer Balaam (Num 23–24)—was supposed actually to have been composed by David himself.[31] The concept of David as poet does not lie behind this stylistic device, but that

---

30. Naturally, David will have gained prominence in Saul's court as a warrior and not in the idyllic role of a harp-playing minstrel. This fact still shines through in the legends.

31. See also Hugo Gressmann, *Die älteste Geschichtsschreibung und Prophetie Israels* (vol. 2.1 of Die Schriften des Alten Testaments in Auswahl; ed. H. Gressmann et al.; Göttingen: Vandenhoeck & Ruprecht, 1910), 185, who is somewhat more reserved, however. Otto Procksch's essay, "Die letzten Worte Dawids," in *Alttestamentliche Studien: R. Kittel zum 60. Geburtstage dargebracht* (ed. R. Kittel; BZAW 13; Leipzig: Hinrichs, 1913), 112–25, has not dissuaded me from my view above.

of the pious darling of God gifted with prophetic insight in his hour of death.[32] This stylistic device does not authenticate any tradition concerning David as poet no more than one may deduce from the blessing of the dying Jacob (Gen 49) or the dying Moses (Deut 33) that the later period regarded these men as "poets." We first find the notion that David was a great poet in the probably postexilic author or redactor of the books of Samuel. The appeal here is to the elegies over Abner and Saul and Jonathan. The lament over Abner (2 Sam 3:33–34), however, is a professional elegy in the usual popular style. One may infer from the source's report only that this song was sung at Abner's funeral and that the king participated publicly and demonstratively in the lament. It is not stated, however, that he also authored the text. The understanding of the lament over Saul and Jonathan (2 Sam 1:18–28), which was transmitted in the "Book of the Nobles" and was undoubtedly contemporaneous, as a composition of David also depends, I believe, on a midrash-like interpretation of the expression "Jonathan, my brother." Jonathan had, indeed, made a fraternal covenant with David because Jonathan "loved" him (1 Sam 18:3; 20:17). The speaker in the song over Saul and Jonathan also speaks of his "love" for Jonathan. Thus David was deduced to be the author. It is psychologically unlikely, however, that David would have composed this profoundly emotional song over Saul and described him as *neʾĕhāb* and *nāʿîm*, unless the good David was a much greater dissembler than he undoubtedly was on occasion. In reality, the plaintive vocative "my brother" belongs to the fixed style of the professional dirge (see Jer 22:18) and probably has no additional purpose here. According to the customary exegetical principles of the *sōpĕrîm*, the expression was related to the covenant between David and Jonathan. Finally, it should be mentioned that *kĕdāwîd* in Amos 6:5 is no doubt a later gloss,[33] indeed, a rather unsuitable one. It presupposes the theory of David as a musician and poet but belongs to the later *diaskeuasis* of the book.

Thus I believe that I can maintain with good reason that the passages that mention David as a poet depend on rather late, erroneous interpretations not justified in the sources and that they presuppose the nonhistorical theory, based on the expression *lĕdāwîd*, concerning David as a psalmist. The later psalms were attributed to him not because David was known as a poet but because the expression, which originally stated something quite different, was found in old psalm texts; David was made into a poet of both religious and secular songs.

---

32. See Gressmann, *loc. cit.*
33. See, e.g., Ernst Sellin, *Das Zwölfprophetenbuch* (3rd ed.; Leipzig: Deichert, 1929).

4.4 (24). It was this interpretation of *lĕdāwîd* found in certain old psalm texts that awakened the scribal interest in the psalmists. Naturally it was believed that David was also the author of many other psalms that had no superscription to this effect. When a "scribe" (*sōpēr*) set about to collect the volume of psalms extant in Pss 2–41,[34] he characterized them as psalms of David. The collector of the "Elohistic Psalter" (Pss 42–89 [or 83]) or one of his predecessors produced another collection of psalms in Pss 51–72. One of them is categorized as Davidic, even though, according to its superscription, it was written "for Solomon" (Ps 72). The original meaning of the *lĕ* may have still been recognized, and one occasionally interpreted one comment or another accordingly.

Of course, once the interpretation of the *lĕ* as an indicator of authorship was available, and after the collections of the "Davidic" psalms had been brought to a relative conclusion, the question arose in the same scribal circles of poets, singers, and copyists as to who composed the other psalm collections that developed in the course of time. In one case, someone responded very soberly and rationally, it was the Korahites, the clan of singers whose repertoire included the collection in question. The volume was provided with a superscription to that effect that was subsequently transferred to individual psalms in this collection.[35] It is only natural that, in other cases, the supposed patriarchs of the singers, Asaph, Heman, and Etan, were cited as the poets.[36] Indeed, these psalms had been transmitted for ages in the pertinent clans. These four or five authors were present in the first great collection of psalms, Pss 2–89.

By all appearances, the second great collection (Pss 90–150), which was appended to this first, was originally entirely anonymous. The superscriptions present here were all purely technical and liturgical in nature: hallelujah (Pss 105–107; 111–118), "the songs of ascent" (Pss 120–134), and so on. A broad field for the exegetical scholarship of the later *sōpĕrîm* lay open here. Their results are recorded in statements concerning authorship added later. The fact that, through hair-raising exegesis, the first psalm in this new collection could be attributed to Moses, the founder of revelation in Israel,[37] must be characterized as a very intricate accident. The fact that the psalm, which speaks

---

34. Ps 2 surely also belongs to this collection, since the king speaking in it was interpreted to be David. It was placed at the head of the collection as the introduction. The fact that the *lĕdāwîd* presupposed in LXX is lacking here depends on a textual error or on the combination with Ps 1 into one psalm attested later.

35. See §3.3, above.

36. See §3.2, above.

37. See §1.3, above.

of the construction "of the house," must have been composed by Solomon is self-evident.[38] This *diaskeuasis* took place quite haphazardly and without plan. Within the last three "books" of the Psalter, only fifteen psalms are attributed to David (Pss 101; 103; 108–110; 122; 124; 131; 133; 138–145). Something like exegetical and historical deliberation seems to have dominated here in only two of them (Pss 101 and 110), and one could have attributed all the others to David just as well as these fifteen. Thus they seem to involve substantially accidental additions by the copyists who seem to have acted on the analogy of the first two "books" and the theory concerning David as the great psalmist. Of those fifteen, five are lacking in the LXX[39] and (or) other old manuscripts, usually also including several or a few of the Hebrew manuscripts. Thus we have a glimpse into the gradual growth of these statements.

This phenomenon becomes even clearer when we come to the LXX. We find fifteen instances of τῷ Δαυίδ that do not appear in the MT (Pss 2; 33; 67; 71; 91; 93–99; 104; 137). In addition, we also find in the MT[40] "indications of authors" other than "Moses" and "Solomon" that have been obtained by the very same exegetical means, through capricious deduction, and are equally worthless: Jeremiah (Ps 137, along with David), "Haggai and Zechariah" (Pss 138; 146–148), and "the sons of Jonadab and the first exiles" (Ps 71; see also 2 Kgs 10:15; Jer 35). Additionally, we also find a few that only occur in individual manuscripts: "Jeremiah and Ezekiel and the people abroad (τοῦ λαοῦ τῆς παροικίας) when they were supposed to set forth" (Ps 65), "Haggai and Zechariah" (Ps 112), and Zechariah (Ps 139, interpreted in relation to the Diaspora). Most of these additions are probably quite late, some even later than Origen,[41] and some seem to trace back to the exegetical traditions of the Antiochene school. The dual attributions that sometimes occur point in this direction: Jeremiah, the sons of Jonadab, and Zechariah alongside David. According to Theodore's theory, in fact, David composed all the psalms but composed them in the spirit of Jeremiah, the exiles, the Maccabean period, and so on.

4.5 (25). The settings that accompany the attributions of authorship in some psalms are secondary in substance but contemporary with the attributions of authorship. It has long been recognized that they are completely worth-

---

38. Ibid.

39. Pss 122 (omitted in two manuscripts, LXX^A, Jer, Targ); 124 (omitted in three manuscripts, LXX^A, Jer); 131 (omitted in LXX manuscripts, Jer); 133 (omitted in two manuscripts, LXX manuscripts, Jer, Targ); 138 (omitted in Aq, Sexta).

40. See §1.3, above.

41. See Willy Staerk, "Zur Kritik der Psalmenüberschriften," *ZAW* 12 (1892): 91–151; Buhl (*Psalmerne*) in Ps 65.

less from a historical perspective and depend entirely only on midrash-like deductions and speculations.

The universal assumption and starting point for speculation is the theory of the Davidic authorship of the psalms and the presence of the "indications of authorship." From a literary-critical perspective, the settings are additions to an existent *lĕdāwîd*.[42]

Since a glance into the origin of these comments is instructive, both for an understanding of Jewish exegesis and for the assessment of so much of Israelite/Jewish "tradition," I conclude our examination with a survey of these comments. It will become evident that they were obtained by the very same means as the names Moses and Solomon.

The superscription to Ps 3 interprets the psalm in relation to the time "when David fled from his son Absalom." It contains nothing, however, that might point to this particular situation. It contains the usual laments of the "individual sin-offering psalms" concerning the attacks of innumerable enemies, that is, of the sorcerers. The "confidence motif" in verse 5 indicates that the supplicant finds himself on "the sacred mountain" and thus is not a king in flight.[43] The scribal redactors deliberated concerning the situation in David's life to which verse 3 could relate and found Absalom's rebellion. At that time, there actually were "many" who considered the king's situation hopeless (2 Sam 16:3, 8; 17:1–3). They found verses 6–7 to be an allusion to 2 Sam 17:22, which recounts that "in the morning," after a dangerous night in flight, not a single one of David's men was missing.

Psalm 7 should "be sung" before YHWH "because of the Benjaminite, Kush." No Benjaminite named Kush is otherwise known. Karl Budde, however, has attempted to demonstrate—in my view, convincingly—that this is a corrupt text, that no one other than "the Benjaminite Shimei ben Gara" (2 Sam 16:5–14) can be meant, and that the text originally read this way, whether the text originally read as indicated above and was also confused later with the "Benjaminite Shemei ben Kish" in Esth 2:5 or this text was already present in the original text.[44] Consequently, *kîš* should be read for *kûš*, in any case. The fact that Ps 7 was (later!) employed as the festival psalm for the Purim Festival, for which Esther was the festival legend, justifies adducing the

---

42. This also seems to be the general assumption. See further Jacob, "Beiträge," *ZAW* (1896): 160.

43. The psalm could have been composed for a king, nonetheless, as the nationalistic tone in v. 9 suggests (see Kittel, *Psalmen*). Since "the sacred mountain" doubtlessly refers to Zion, this typically post-Davidic expression is probably also evidence against Davidic authorship (Buhl, *Psalmerne*).

44. Karl Budde, "Zum Text der Psalmen," *ZAW* 35 (1915): 179.

Esther passage. The enemies of the supplicant belong to the *pō'ălê 'āwen* (see v. 15), the sorcerers (see *Psalm Studies* 1), the "peoples" (*lĕ'ummîm*), and the "nations" (*gōyîm*) in verse 8. Later "collectivizing" corrections of an original *'ēlîm* ("demons") and *gē'îm* ("the proud") also designate demons and sorcerers.[45] The supplicant is threatened with death and is thus, on the analogy of most of the other individual sin-offering psalms, a sick person. First, the occasional reference to the enemy as an individual[46] contributed to the association of the psalm, understood as authored by David, with Shimei, as did, second, the fact that the supplicant attests his total innocence in relation to his enemy—David certainly did not compose a song for Shimei personally— and, third, verse 17, the allusion seen in "his misfortune comes upon his head and his violence falls back on his crown," to Solomon's words to Shimei in 1 Kgs 2:44 ("now YHWH will bring your evil on your own head").

Psalm 18 is supposed to have been sung by YHWH's servant, David, "who spoke the words of this song to YHWH when YHWH had delivered him from the hand of all his enemies [and from the hand of Saul]." The words in brackets here may be a later addition. In any case, the comment understands the psalm as a thankful reminiscence of the deliverance from many dangers and from "all" enemies. The fact that the psalm was placed as the conclusion of the David narrative in 2 Sam 22 is related to this comment.[47] The content contradicts this understanding of the psalm, however. To be sure, it is a royal thanksgiving psalm, but it refers to a unique episode in a particular battle in which the king was in great danger but from which he was delivered. The enemy, then, is a certain, specific hostile king and his army, not "all his enemies" in general. The words in verse 38–46 gave rise to the understanding in the superscription. Here, on the basis of an immediately preceding experience, the king pronounces the confident belief that YHWH will deliver him from all his enemies and will subjugate peoples and nations to him. These general plurals misled the Jewish scribes.

For the sake of completeness, the "historical" comment in Ps 30 should also be mentioned here: "a song for the dedication of the temple" (Hanukkah Festival). It is certainly correct to the extent that the psalm was later used as a Hanukkah psalm. This was certainly not the original meaning of the psalm,

---

45. See *Psalm Studies* 1:74–75. Regarding the collective reinterpretation of originally individual psalms, see also *Psalm Studies* 1:165–71.

46. This is a stylistic peculiarity that also occurs elsewhere and is based simply on the fact that, naturally, one did not know the enemy who was causing the illness and, consequently, never knew whether an individual or a group was behind the misfortune. Thus, hyperbolic style usually inclines toward a plural depiction. See *Psalm Studies* 1:102–3.

47. Naturally, the psalm entered Samuel from the Psalter and not vice versa. See §4.3.

however. Instead, it depends on a collective reinterpretation of the thanksgiving sacrifice psalm meant for individuals.[48] The delivered worshiper is reinterpreted as the restored Zion. Thus this is also late material based on false exegesis.

The moralizing and didactic individual thanksgiving psalm, Ps 34, is related to the episode mentioned in 1 Sam 21:13–15: by David, "when he feigned insanity before Abimelech and was driven out so that he escaped." The fact that "Abimelech" here is an error for "Achish," influenced by Gen 20, is relatively insignificant. Of greater importance is the fact that any trace of a reference to the situation cited is missing in the song and that the warning against "deceitful speech" (v. 14) in the mouth of the one whose life had just been saved would be at least somewhat naïve.[49] The psalm is a thanksgiving psalm and, furthermore, as always, is to be sung by a sick person who has been healed.[50] It has nothing to do with David's deliverance from the uncomfortable situation in Gath. Presumably, the expressions in verse 19, "YHWH is near to those with broken hearts (*nišběrê lēb*) and those with a shattered spirit (*dakkě'ê rûaḥ*) he helps," gave the scribes reason. When would David have been more broken-hearted and shattered in spirit than when he had to "disguise his sanity" in fear of death? In any case, this exegesis seems almost to be a shattering of spirit and a dislocation of reason and is therefore authentically Jewish.[51]

Psalm 51, with the superscription "by David, when the prophet Nathan came to him when he had gone in to Bathsheba," is a penitential psalm for a sick person[52] and was likely performed (see v. 9) at rites of purification.[53] The illness is understood as the effect of beings who seek the "blood" of the supplicant.[54] This interpretation already demonstrates that it has nothing to do with the Bathsheba–Nathan episode. David was neither sick at the time, nor was anyone seeking his life. Verse 6, "I have sinned against you alone," thoroughly contradicts the accuracy of the comment. David had sinned severely against Uriah. Once Davidic authorship was established, with or without reason, there was no other event in the tradition in relation to which the psalm could

---

48. See *Psalm Studies* 1:166–67.
49. See Buhl, *Psalmerne*, ad loc.
50. *Psalm Studies* 1:135–36.
51. Gustav Redslob and Ferdinand Hitzig have speculated that *ṭa'mû* in v. 9 reminded the scribes of *ṭa'mô* in 1 Sam 21:14 and that, consequently, they linked it with that episode (according to Buhl, *Psalmerne*, 226).
52. See *Psalm Studies* 1:146.
53. *Psalm Studies* 1:146–49.
54. See v. 19 and *Psalm Studies* 1:146.

be interpreted. The words cited in verse 6 were seen as an allusion to David's words in 2 Sam 12:13, "I have sinned against YHWH." Nothing was said there about guilt in relation to people either. The word *dāmîm* (v. 16) may even have been understood as bloodguilt incurred by the supplicant in relation to the murder of Uriah.[55]

The comment in Ps 52, "by David, when the Edomite Doeg came and reported to Saul, saying, 'David has entered the house of Ahimelech,'" refers to the account in 1 Sam 21:8; 22:6–19. The comment is at least imprecise. David, who was absent, could not have known when Doeg recounted the encounter with Ahimelech. It should read, therefore, "when David learned—that is, through Abiathar the sole survivor of the house of Ahimelech (1 Sam 22:21)—that Doeg had reported the incident to the king." The content of the comment is, therefore, as impossible as the others. First, the "violent one" of whom the psalm speaks was not, by all appearances, a specific individual but the type of the violent enemies who push the pious, and thus the supplicant, into misfortune. They may have been as personally unfamiliar to the singer as the enemies were elsewhere in the individual lament psalms.[56] Second, the evil of which he is accused here is lying and deceitful speech. Doeg reported only the truth to the king,[57] however, and the matter becomes no better if the correct ancient Israelite sense of the terms "lies," "deceit," and the like lies in the background. In the context of the lament psalm, they denote disaster-producing words of curse and sorcery.[58] Third, Doeg's words had disastrous consequences, not for David, but for Ahimelech and his house (1 Sam 22:16–19). The psalm does not say a single word, however, about the actual victim of Doeg's betrayal but only discusses the contrast between the evil "tongue-man" and the supplicant himself. The superscription was elaborated from the word *gibbōr* (here, "strong and powerful men"[59]). Doeg was in Saul's entourage, one of his *gibbōrîm*—such was the deduction from the statements in 1 Sam 22:17, 18. David's complaint about a *gibbōr* can only refer to Doeg.

Psalm 54 is associated with the event reported in 1 Sam 23:19: "when the Ziphites came and said to Saul, 'David is in hiding among us.'" The psalm is a common cultic individual lament psalm with complaints about the "insolent" (*zēdîm*), undoubtedly a reference to the demons that cause sickness and impurity (sinfulness).[60] Otherwise, the psalm contains no specific information that

---

55. Compare Buhl, *Psalmerne*.
56. See above, 861 n. 46.
57. Cf. 1 Sam 22:9–10 with 21:7, 9–10.
58. *Psalm Studies* 1:43–62.
59. *Psalm Studies* 1:26–27 and passim.
60. *Psalm Studies* 1:75–77.

would point to the stop in Ziph and the betrayal of the Ziphites, which one would expect if it had such a specific "historical" occasion. As a normal cultic sin-offering psalm, however, it had nothing to do with this event. The comment was probably extrapolated from the agreement of the wording in verse 5, *biqěšû napšî*, with 1 Sam 23:15, *lěbaqqēš 'et napšô*.[61] A clever mind among the Jewish *sōpěrîm* and *dōrěšîm* most likely found in the זֵדִים (*zēdîm*) an allusion to the זִפִים (*zēpîm*).

Psalm 56 offers the following information concerning its setting: "[by David,] when the Philistines had captured him in Gath." It refers to 1 Sam 21:11–16.[62] The psalm hardly has anything to do with this event, however. It contains the usual laments concerning enemies who, through *'āwen* (v. 8), that is, sorcery, have pushed the supplicant into misfortune. These enemies are also described as *'azzîm*,[63] an old term for demons and sorcerers.[64] There should be no doubt, however, that this is an old, cultic sin-offering psalm for a sick person.[65] The Jewish scribes thought that, if David so urgently and tearfully (v. 9) complains here about enemies who press him hard and threaten him with death, then he must have been in their power. Since they deduced from the false reading *'ammîm* in verse 8 that the enemies were pagans, they turned to the account in 1 Sam 21:11–16, the only tradition that speaks of David's capture by foreigners.

Psalm 57 is, in reality, exactly the same in character as Ps 56. The men of the curse and sorcery[66] activated through their tongues are depicted here as fire-spewing and man-eating lions.[67] As is so often the case, it also says

---

61. So Buhl, *Psalmerne*.

62. Kittel (*Psalmen*) would like to see the comment as a "tradition" independent of Samuel, since David "is not captured or imprisoned" in 1 Sam 21:11–16. This is erroneous, however. The words of the king in v. 15 ("Why do you bring him to me?") presuppose that David was produced by the people of Achish and was thus "captured" or "imprisoned." Consequently, there is no reason to assume an "independent" tradition, which of course would then be purely midrash-like.

63. With Duhm (*Psalmen*), one should read v. 8 thus instead of *'ammîm*.

64. *Psalm Studies* 1:73–74; see also 1:25–28.

65. This use of the psalm is supported by the technical information in the superscription, "over the dove meant for the distant demons (*'ēlîm*)," which alludes to a cultic procedure that is to be conceived on analogy with the rite of the goats for Azazel (see *Psalm Studies* 4:625–28).

66. See *Psalm Studies* 1:20–25; regarding Ps 57, see 1:25, 157.

67. The verb *lāhat* with an object (v. 5) does not mean "to flame" but "to consume like flames"; see the Assyrian Taylor Cylinder 1.8–9. Lions who "consumed people like flames" are conceived as fire-spewing.

that they pursue him secretly and insidiously.[68] The Jewish scribes, however, related the psalm to the event narrated in 1 Sam 24: "[by David,] when he fled into the cave before Saul." They probably deduced this information from verse 5. They understood the man-eating lions, whose teeth were spears and arrows and whose tongues were sharp swords, as warriors and interpreted David, "who was among them," as the one in the depths of the cave whose exit was barred by Saul's armed men in the outer part of the same cave. They will have found confirmation for this interpretation in verse 2b: "I had refuge in the shadow of your wings until the ruin had passed by." In the interior of the cave were shadows that, through God's gracious providence, concealed David from Saul's eyes; David could hope to remain concealed there until the "destruction (the destroyer, Saul) had passed by."

Psalm 59 is entirely analogous to the two psalms just mentioned. It, too, is a cultic lament psalm, probably for a sick person, concerning the animosities of the evil demons and sorcerers[69] who, through curses and maledictions ("lies"), have driven the supplicant into misfortune (v. 13). Meanwhile, it bears the superscription: "[by David,] when Saul sent (people) to watch the house in order to kill him." This superscription refers to 1 Sam 19:1–7. If the enemies are the sorcerers and demons, they are not Saul's people. These ambushers sent by Saul certainly did not act like the demons in the psalm: "Every evening they return and howl like gods and prowl throughout the city" (vv. 7, 15). This behavior would have not been very well suited to the objective. The purpose of this prowling stated in verse 16 fits the demons but not Saul's people: "They prowl about for food and snarl when they are not satisfied."[70] Nevertheless, the superscription was inferred from the very verse cited, "every evening...." The term lā'ereb could also be interpreted as a reference to a single evening. Only the account in 1 Sam 19:11–12 narrates the sole danger of death David faced at night.

Psalm 60 has the following addition to the "indication of authorship": "when he fought with Aram Naharaim and with Aram Zobah, and Joab returned and smote the Edomites in the Valley of Salt, twelve thousand men." The comment is taken from 2 Sam 8 (see the wording in 2 Sam 8:13). This is the only explanation for the combination of Edom and the Aramaic states that are not mentioned in the psalm. A rather extensive account of the victory over Moab, Edom, Aram of Damascus, and Aram Zobah is offered in 2 Sam

---

68. Verse 7; see *Psalm Studies* 1:18–20.
69. See *Psalm Studies* 1:70–73.
70. See the devil, the lord of all demons, in 1 Pet 5:8: "he roams about like a roaring lion and seeks whom he may consume." Regarding the canine form of the demons, see the Babylonian parallels cited in *Psalm Studies* 1:72.

8, which also mentions victories over the Philistines. The psalm mentions Moab, Edom, and the Philistines. The combination was easy enough. Instead of Aram of Damascus, the comment in Ps 60 has Aram Naharaim. This comprehensive expression was defined more precisely by the explicit mention of *hannāhār* Euphrates in 2 Sam 8:3. The twelve thousand men in Ps 60 for eighteen thousand in 2 Sam 8 probably depends on a simple scribal error, regardless of whether Ps 60 or 1 Sam 8 has the better text. Only the reference to Joab in Ps 60 is remarkable; 2 Sam 8 does not mention him. David himself "returned and smote Edom in the Valley of Salt." The style in Ps 60:2, however, is very cumbersome. Why is Joab omitted in the first clause if he is to be mentioned as David's general in the lands of the Arameans, as the statement "returned" implies? The best assumption is that יואב is only a miswritten or misread doublet for the preceding וישב. Thus the combination of Ps 60 with 2 Sam 8 rests solely on the reference to Edom, Moab, and the Philistines, who also appear in 2 Sam 8. I admit the possibility that the scholarly association may have *accidentally* been correct. The psalm is a cultic communal lament for a penitential ceremony after defeat in a war with Edom (and Moab)[71] including an oracle promising ultimate victory. At any rate, we hear nothing of David's defeat in a war against Edom. In itself, however, this is not decisive. The tradition can amplify minor setbacks, and the defeat need not have been major; even the most minor military misfortune was also seen as a sign of divine wrath that must be atoned with a penitential ceremony.[72] Elsewhere (*Psalm Studies* 2:245–49) I have dealt with this possibility in greater depth. I mentioned the Omride period as another possibility but inclined toward the first assumption. Now, however, I would like to suggest the time of Solomon instead of David. We know positively concerning Solomon that the Edomites gave him significant difficulties and that finally Hadad, the king's son, succeeded in claiming the throne in Edom (1 Kgs 11:14–22). If the times of David and of Solomon are the choices, the latter may be preferable.

Psalm 63 is said to have been composed by David "when he was in the desert of Judah." The flight from Saul in 1 Sam 23:14–29 is in mind. The fact that the psalm is a cultic illness song for a king, sung in the temple, may be considered a certainty.[73] Verse 12 contradicts the superscription most blatantly: "the king rejoices in God because the mouths of the liars (i.e., the illness-causing sorcerers) have been stopped." "The king" here is the suppli-

---

71. If, for example, *'îr māṣôr* (v. 11; in Ps 108:11, *mibṣār*) were to refer to the capital city in Moab or were simply to be regarded as a scribal error for *'ar mô'ab*.

72. See Josh 7:5–36: men fell. On this basis, the decision was made to investigate the cause of YHWH's wrath.

73. *Psalm Studies* 1:44–46, 144.

cant himself. When David was in the wilderness of Judah, however, Saul was king, and he did not rejoice over David's deliverance.[74] The superscription has been obtained through a false interpretation of verse 2: the supplicant says in picturesque manner here that sojourning in a dry and waterless land is an image for his distress, for the illness. The reading "like a dry and waterless land" is equally well-attested and more obvious. Just as the dry land languishes for rain, the king languishes for YHWH's assistance. The scribes have taken this expression literally and thus came to their exegetical result.[75]

Finally, we come to Ps 142. Like Ps 57, it is situated in the time when David "was in the cave." Here, too, we are dealing with a cultic lament psalm for a sick person who sees the sorcerers as the cause of his illness.[76] Therefore, it is not an occasional poem by David sitting in the cave. In verse 8 the supplicant describes his illness with the common image of being in prison.[77] Furthermore, he says in verses 4–5 that his path has been blocked by snares and every refuge has been denied him. Thus there could be no doubt for the Jewish exegetes that "David" composed the psalm when he was in the cave, while Saul and company blocked his escape.[78]

The fact that all these comments, with the exception of Ps 142, appear in the first two "books" of the Psalter probably demonstrates that they are relatively old and, with the exception mentioned, were added in a time when only the collection Pss 2–89 was extant and the addition, Pss 90–150, still had no attributions of authorship. This kind of scholarship is, therefore, older that Jesus ben Sira, who probably presupposed the current Psalter. In reality, it is even older than Chronicles, which manifests midrashim of the very same kind. When people gradually began to provide Pss 90–150 also with attributions of authorship, information about the settings followed on their heels until the canonization of the biblical text established a dam against further additions.

This *diaskeuasis* is continued in the LXX. Psalms 76 and 80 contain the addition: "in reference to (or concerning) the Assyrians." Undoubtedly, the reference is to Sennacherib. In Ps 76 the comment arose from the same considerations that have led a few modern interpreters to relate Pss 46 and 48 to Sennacherib's attack. It is easy to understand how this interpretation could be applied to the catastrophe presupposed in Ps 80. Psalm 97 is supposed to

---

74. See Buhl, *Psalmerne*, xxii.
75. So also ibid.
76. See *Psalm Studies* 1:101, 109, 111, 129.
77. See Ps 88:9. The image also occurs in the Babylonian and Assyrian illness psalms (see, e.g., Jastrow, *Religion Babyloniens*, 1:431; and *Psalm Studies* 1:96).
78. Similarly, although with doubts, Buhl, *Psalmerne*.

have been sung by David "when his land was established (again)." Like so many of the more recent interpreters, the LXX interpreted this festival hymn historically. It probably thought of the reestablishment of the country as the suppression of Sheba's rebellion (2 Sam 20), perhaps, however, as the attainment of the monarchy over all Israel (2 Sam 4–5), which was followed by the transfer of the ark to Zion in the tradition (2 Sam 6). According to the LXX, David wrote Ps 142 "when his son persecuted him." As in the psalm, David also had the opportunity then to remember YHWH's "former benevolences" and to compare them to the dreary present. It is easy to understand how Ps 144 could acquire the superscription "in relation to Goliath," when one reads that "David" complains here about the "evil sword" of a "foreigner" (vv. 10–11), describes YHWH as his shield (v. 2; see also 1 Sam 17:45), trusts that YHWH will teach him to use weapons,[79] and also attests his familiarity with playing the harp and singing (v. 9; see also 1 Sam 16:18; 18:10). It is hardly profitable to follow this kind of "historical" exegesis further. Its ultimate academic offshoots can be found here and there in the commentaries of a Hengstenberg, Delitzsch, or Hitzig. Just for curiosity's sake, reference may be made to the fact that only twenty-five years ago an "orthodox" Norwegian pastor, J. C. H. Storjohann, the founder of the Norwegian "sailors' mission" and highly respected in the practical and ecclesial fields, undertook with precisely the same means to arrange all the psalms headed *lĕdāwîd* according to the historical or legendary episodes or events in the life of David known to us,[80] which he succeeded in doing without too much effort.

Completed May 1923

---

79. Verse 1; see also 1 Sam 17:38–40. When David is supposed to go to battle, he could neither wear armor nor carry a sword. Shortly thereafter he cut off Goliath's head with his much larger sword.

80. J. C. H. Storjohann, *Kong David: Hans liv og hans psalmer*, trans. as *König David: Sein leben und seine Psalmen* (trans. O. Gleiss; Gütersloh: Bertelsmann, 1900–1901).

Index of Sources

Hebrew Bible

Genesis

Reference	Pages
1	660
1:22	659
1:26	230
1:28	659, 664
2–3	455
2:3	663
2:10–11	340
2:21	639
3:14–19	664
4:4–5	67, 150, 516
5:2	659
6:1–4	19
12:2	660, 664, 680
12:3	660
12:6	745
12:7	664
12:17	83, 141
13:16	660
13:18	745
14	583
14:19	664
14:19–20	679
15:9–12	630
15:10–11	67, 150
15:12–21	639
15:17	630
18:1	745
18:18	660
18:28	440
20	862
20:7	664
20:17	664
22:18	660
24:35	660
24:60	591, 660, 663, 671
25:23	664
26:2	661
26:4	660
26:12–14	660
26:24	159, 660
26:28	661
27	20, 591, 663, 671, 713
27:27–28	660
27:28–29	681
27:29	660
28:1	663
28:3–4	681
28:10–22	159, 289
28:14	660
31:28	663
31:44–54	591
32:1	663
32:27	639
33:11	663
35:4	745
35:8	745
35:18	39
36:13	822
36:17	822
36:33	822
39:2–5	661
39:7	673
45:18	238
47:10	663
48:14–20	662, 663, 664
48:15–16	681
48:19	660

Genesis (cont.)		20:2–17	721
48:22	746	20:5–6	752
49	575, 663, 664, 713, 857	20:7	56
49:3	36	20:11	663
49:3–27	712	20:22–26	262
49:8–12	478, 660	20:23	724
49:22–26	660	20:23–26	721, 780
49:10	476, 478, 560	20:25–26	743
49:25–26	275	21:1–22:15	751
		21:1–22:16	262, 721, 780
Exodus		21–23	751
4:1–17	503	21–24	779
4:14–16	694	22:7–8	505
7:14–25	503	22:17	39
8:12–19	503	22:17–27	721, 780
11:1	83	22:17–23:19	262
12	213, 380	22:24	120
12:11–12	380	22:28	724
12:22	631	23:1	59
12:26–27	688	23:1–9	721, 780
12:27	380	23:10–19	721, 780
12:32	670, 674	23:15	380
13	381	23:16	263
13:3–16	688	23:18	780
13:4	380	23:25–26	660
13:21	414	24	329, 333, 751
14:21	367	24:7	721
15	183, 192, 233, 236, 237, 298, 317, 390, 723	24:8	502
		24:8–10	471
15:1	236, 238, 278	25:16	632
15:1–2	75	26:38	610
15:1–18	184, 236, 367, 814	30:26	632
15:2	278, 335, 840	33:7–11	502
15:2–18	372	33:18	335
15:11	335	33:20	335
15:12	24	34	262, 329, 754
15:17–18	236	34:6–7	752
15:18	183	34:14–26	779
15:20	664, 827	34:17	724
15:26	635	34:18	380
18:14–23	502	34:22	263
18:26	505	34:29–35	471
20	750	35:5	277
20–24	754		
20:1–17	752, 754, 779		

Index of Sources 871

Leviticus		18:17	724
1:2	610	18:23	724
1:14–17	625	19:5	610
2:2	618	19:8	141
4:2	767	19:9–10	273
4:13	767	19:10	120
4:28	767	19:14	724
5	802	19:20	150
5:1	712, 717, 718	19:24–25	263
5:1–4	629, 767	19:26	39
5:1–6	712	20:14	724
5:1–13	140	20:17	724
5:2–3	83	22:19	610
5:6–10	625	22:20–21	610
5:12	619	22:29	610
5:17–19	83	23:11	610
7:18	141	23:22	273
9:22	673	23:39	262
12	141	23:39–43	279
12–15	802	23:40	631
12:3	643	23:42–43	381
14	141, 627, **643–44**, 716	25:9	265, 382
14:2–7	626	25:21	660
14:4	631	26	710, 755, 763
14:6	631		
14:6–7	141, 515	Numbers	
14:12	141	5	247
14:15–18	133	5:11–12	720
14:49	631	5:11–31	719, 720, 737
14:51–52	631	5:15	618
15:1–18	141	5:17–31	65
15:13–14	643	5:21	711
15:15	141	5:21–27	709
15:19	643	5:23–24	30, 713
15:19–24	141	5:27	711
15:28	643	6:9–11	643
15:30	643	6:23	673
16	216, 625, 627	6:23–26	672
16:2	216	6:24–26	302, 673, 681, 683, 771
16:4	216	10:34	525
16:17	216	10:35	291
16:20–22	216	10:36	291
16:22	711	11	664
17:16	141	11:24–30	471
18:9	724	12	664

Numbers (cont.)		Deuteronomy	
12:3	120	1:1–3:20	722
12:6–8	502	4:1–2	722
14:34	141	5	750
15:22–31	140	5:1	56
16	836	5:6–21	752, 754
16:30	24	5:20	59
16:32	24	6–11	722, 744
16:34	24	7	263
17	634	7:12–13	756
17:16–22	634	7:12–14	660
17:22	632	9:26	648
17:25	632	10:6–9	694
22–24	713, 726	10:8	672, 682
22:36–24:25	591	10:21	840
22:40	726	11:6	24
23–24	856	11:26–30	744, 745
23:1–5	510, 516	11:26–31	723
23:4	67	11:29	744
23:4–6	672	11:29–30	722
23:6–24:25	672	11:30	744
23:7–8	712	12:12	830
23:7–10	664	12:15	628
23:12	665	14:26	723
23:14–16	510, 516	14:27–29	830
23:18–19	664	15:11	120
23:21	16, 35, 37, 38, 42, 221, 366, 379, 530, 646	15:19–20	273
		16	262, 264
23:23	16, 35, 39	16:11	830
23:29–30	510, 516	16:13	263, 270, 830
24:3	518, 827	16:14	274
24:3–9	664	16:18	747
24:4	512, 518, 827	16:21	380
24:9	681	17:8–13	583
24:15–10	664	18:9–12	66
24:17	471	18:9–22	17, 502
24:17–18	660	18:10–11	669
24:17–19	476	18:10–14	39
24:20	680	17:14–20	583
26:10	24	18:15	502
27:18–20	662	21:5	672, 682
29:1–11	383	21:6	141
29:12	279	21:7–9	757
		21:17	36
		24:12	120

Index of Sources

24:14	120	24	723, 748, 749
24:15	120	24:1	745
26:1–15	274	24:26	745
26:3–10	757		
26:11–13	830	Judges	
26:13–15	757	1:1	505
27	722	1:15	663
27:1	779	4:5	745
27:1–3	723	5	853
27:1–13	723, **741–50**	5:1	827
27:11–13	721, 723, 758	5:20	357
27:12–13	763	6:11	745
27:14–16	751	6:12–14	661
27:14–26	708, 718, 721, 723, 724, 747, 748, 749, 750, 753, 758, 759, 766, 774	8:22–27	471
		9	746
		9:4	745
27:26	751, 755	9:5	189
28	710, 744, 755, 756, 757, 763	9:27	263, 274
28:1–13	660	9:46	745
28:3–6	756, 758	17:2	712, 717
28:16–19	756, 758	17:5	817
28:37	711	17:10	838
29:18	711	18:6	505
29:28	639	20:18	505
31:10–13	751	20:27–28	505
32:32	6		
33	575, 663, 664, 713, 857	1 Samuel	
33:4	215, 224, 234, 323, 390	1:4	273
33:13–17	476	1:9	274
34:10	502	1:13–14	274
		1:17	664, 681
Joshua		1:18	274
4:3–9	743, 778	2:1–10	130, 134, 572, 804, 808
6:26	718	2:4–8	840
7	716	2:6–10	131
7:5–36	866	2:9	370
7:6	747	2:10	566, 851
8:30	745, 779	2:25	505
8:30–33	778	3:21	502
8:30–35	723, 742, 744	4–6	288
8:33	745, 746, 747	4:1–11	291
8:34	742, 747	4:4	292
14:13	663	5:8–9	647
15:19	663	6	329
22:7	663	6:7–16	314

1 Samuel (cont.)

6:15	747	14:37	503, 505
6:18	690	14:38–42	557
7:1	292	14:41	505
7:6	277, 557, 558	14:41–42	503, 506
8	476	15	502, 574
8:11–18	125	15:13	681
9	502	15:22–23	834
9–10	575	15:23	17, 35, 37, 39, 40, 42, 70
9:7–8	838	15:32–33	508
9:9	502	16:1	574
9:12–13	675	16:3–13	186
9:13	274, 675, 678, 682	16:5–13	575
9:15	518, 827	16:13	472, 575
9:20	575	16:14	7, 83
10:1	186, 575, 576	16:16	641
10:2	745	16:18	661, 856, 868
10:5	510, 511, 513, 514, 641	16:23	641
10:5–6	288, 512, 827	17	329
10:6	186, 473	17:38–40	868
10:6–7	575	17:45	868
10:9	473	18:3	857
10:9–10	471	18:10	868
10:10–13	512, 827	18:12	661
10:11	838	18:14	661
10:17	575	19:1–7	865
10:17–21	574	19:11–12	865
10:24	186	19:18–24	513
11:6–11	471	19:19	510
11:7	712	19:20	502, 513
11:13	187	20:13	661
11:14–15	575	20:17	857
11:15	186	21:7	863
12	215	21:8	516, 863
13:7–15	502	21:9–10	863
13:9–10	471, 472, 503	21:11–16	864
13:10	663	21:13–15	862
13:13–15	574	21:14	862
14:3	503	22:6–19	863
14:18	505	22:9–10	863
14:18–19	503	22:16–19	863
14:24	718	22:17–18	863
14:26	712	22:18	503
14:36	505	22:21	863
14:36–42	505	23:2	505
		23:2–5	505

23:9–12	505	6:17–18			471, 472
23:14–29	866	6:18	583, 663, 664, 672, 674, 747, 785
23:15	864	6:18–19			303
23:19	863	6:19			262
24	865	7		528, 529, 575
24:7	472	7:8–17			529
25:14	663	7:11–16			660
25:18	663	7:18		471, 472, 503, 852
25:27	663	7:18–29			583
26:25	659	8			865, 866
28:6	505, 506	8:3			866
28:13	114	8:13			865
30:7–8	505, 506	8:18		287, 471, 583, 817
30:7–10	505	10:12			291
30:8–9	505	11:11			291
30:26	663	13:25			663
31:4	472	14:17			471
		14:22			661
2 Samuel		15:9–10			186
1:14	472	15:10			186
1:17	856	15:12			186
1:18	619	16:3			860
1:18–28	857	16:5			712
2:1	505	16:5–13			711
3:33–34	856, 857	16:5–14			860
4–5	868	16:8			860
5	525	17:1–3			860
5:19	505	17:22			860
5:23–24	506	19:40			663
5:28	505	20			868
6	220, 261, 285, 287, 289, 292, 305, 366, 379, 389, 471, 524, 525, 640, 854, 868	21:3			713
		21:9			785
		22			855, 861
6–7	459	23:1–3			581
6:3–4	292	23:1–7		471, 503, 856
6:5	288, 292, 583, 856	23:3–4			471
6:6–7	662	24			854
6:7	84, 736	24:11			503
6:10	647	24:16			84
6:10–11	646	24:18–25			785
6:11–12	305				
6:13	292, 785	1 Kings			
6:13–14	287, 471, 583	1			189
6:13–19	503	1:5			186
6:14	292, 856	1:5–9			575

1 Kings (cont.)	
1:8	186
1:9	186
1:11–40	186
1:19	186
1:31	472
1:32–40	574, 575
1:33	186
1:34	186
1:38	186
1:39	186
1:40	186
1:45	186
1:46	186
1:47	186
1:50–53	187
2:8–9	712, 713
2:44	861
3:5	159
3:5–14	581
3:5–15	516
3:15	641
5:11	821, 822
5:13	631
8	220, 261, 285, 366
8:2	261, 262, 263, 815
8:5	503
8:14	674, 690, 747
8:14–15	583
8:14–64	503
8:15–21	674
8:31	712, 713, 717
8:54–55	471, 472, 583
8:55	663, 664, 672, 690, 747
8:62	329
8:62–66	303, 583
8:66	661, 663
9:1–5	459
10	786
11:14–22	866
11:29–40	508
12:32	262, 266, 817
14:3	838
14:25–26	785
17:7–24	503
17:9–16	838
18	513
18:16–40	510
18:16–46	278
18:26–27	620
18:26–29	512
18:28	514
18:41–46	279
19:11–12	422
19:16	574
20:25	513
21:13	557
22	508, 514, 727
22:5–13	500
22:6	513
22:19–22	230
22:20	564

2 Kings	
1:9–16	503
2	513
2:3	510, 513
2:5	510
2:8	503
2:14	503
2:19–25	503
2:24	20, 664, 713
3:7–27	561
3:15	288, 511, 512, 514, 827
3:16–20	503
4–8	503
4:1	513
4:8–10	838
4:16–17	664, 713
4:29	663
4:38	510
4:39	513
4:42	838
5:11	637
5:15	663, 838
5:22	513
5:26	152, 512, 828
6:1	513
6:1–7	513
6:5	838

Index of Sources

8	561	1:10–17	538
8:18	591	1:13	42, 58, 832
8:20–22	561	1:17	834
9	576	1:18–20	442
9:1–10	575	2	438
9:3	575	2:1–4	461, 462
9:13	186	2:2	457
9:22	669	2:4	457, 462
10:15	859	2:10–17	75
10:15–21	507	2:12–17	421
11	472, 583	2:19	419
11:4–12	186	2:21	417
11:8	186, 245	3:13–4:1	442
11:10	186	3:14–17	440
11:11–14	186	4:2–3	451
11:12	186, 575	5:1–10	650
11:12–13	580	5:18	33, 55
11:14	186	5:26–30	438
11:19	186	6	378, 451, 487
11:20	186	6:1–7	319
12:5–16	852	6:1–8	307
13:7	435	6:5	215, 490
13:21	435	6:8	564
13:22	435	7:3	450
14:8–14	435	7:5	451
16:10–16	645	7:13–14	475
16:10–18	852	7:14	477
16:15	150	7:14–15	475
18:13–16	244	7:16	475
18:15–16	852	7:17	475
18:17–19:37	244	8:1–3	453
19:14–19	852	8:5–6	438
19:35	84	8:5–8	419
22:14	827	8:9–10	427
23	381	8:10–11	438
23:2	754	8:12–15	736
23:3	531	8:14	83
23:21	380	8:16	828
23:21–23	751	8:16–17	793
25:8	728	9:1–6	477
25:27–29	187	9:1–7	581
		9:4	462
Isaiah		9:6	476
1–12	213, 278	10:1	30, 37, 38
1–39	450	10:1–2	13

Isaiah (cont.)

10:5–11	439	28:15	69, 800, 843
10:20–23	451	28:16	421
10:22–23	451	28:17	423
10:33–34	477	28:22	421
11:1	476	29:5	76
11:1–5	574, 575	29:20	9, 12, 21, 38, 40, 75, 76, 84, 343
11:1–9	477, 581	29:20–21	21, 33, 55, 710
11:2–5	186, 473	30:7	234, 366
11:6	455	30:28	54
11:6–8	457	30:29	270, 694
11:6–9	455, 461	30:30	335, 417
11:9	444, 455	31:2	39, 40, 41
11:11	451	31:8	6
11:14	462	32:5	33
11:16	451	32:6	21, 37, 40
12	**277–78**	32:6–7	9, 12, 43
12:2	335, 840	32:6–8	8, 19, 39
12:3	213	32:7	43, 54
13:11	75, 76	33	**409–12**, 482
14:12	582, 629	33:9	419
15:1	636	33:14	308, 408, 725, 825
16:7	610	33:14–16	442, 707, 750
17:4–14	438	33:17	215, 405, 417
17:5–6	273	33:20–22	457
17:12–14	427	33:22	215, 405, 476
17:14	437	34:8–10	419
18:2	360	34:9–15	116
22:5	419	37:21–22	487
22:14	518, 827	37:32	450, 451
24–27	232	38:9	605
24:6–12	709	38:9–20	130, 141, 605, 808, 851
24:13	451	38:14	610
24:21–23	232, 390	40–55	463
24:23	405, 408	40:1–2	434
25:3	76	40:2	439, 445, 446
25:4	76	40:3–4	414, 457
25:5	75, 76	40:3–5	414
25:6	467	40:6–8	428, 429
28:2	419	40:9–10	434
28:5	451	40:9–11	374, 414, 415
28:7	510	40:11	414, 466
28:7–8	221, 274	40:12–17	465
28:11	409	40:18–26	430
28:14	421	40:19–20	429
		40:26	36

40:29	36	43:5–7	414
40:31	339, 393	43:8–12	430, 431, 455
41:1–4	430	43:10	429, 455
41:1–5	429, 431	43:14	428
41:2	447, 465	43:15	215, 405, 413
41:2–3	429	43:15–21	371, 372, 454
41:4	454, 455	43:19	454, 455
41:8–6	465	43:19–21	414
41:10	447	43:20	456
41:17–20	454	43:22–28	445
41:18–20	455, 456	44:1–5	434
41:21	215, 405, 413	44:3	456
41:21–24	429	44:5	215, 429, 463, 464
41:21–29	430, 455	44:6	405, 413
41:23	431	44:6–8	429, 430, 455
41:25	429	44:7	431
41:25–27	431	44:21–23	375
41:26–28	431	44:22	445
41:28–29	429	44:23	375
41:29	43, 54, 61	44:24–28	454
42:1–4	447	45:1–3	463
42:1–7	465	45:1–6	463
42:2	447	45:1–7	428, 429, 431
42:3–4	447	45:4	430
42:4	828	45:5–7	430
42:8–9	454	45:8	447
42:9	455	45:10–13	464
42:10	375	45:11	454, 455
42:10–11	375	45:11–13	430
42:10–13	414, 426, 427	45:12–13	431
42:10–17	228, 370, 371, 390	45:13	414, 447, 463, 465
42:11	424	45:14–15	463, 464
42:12–17	855	45:15	458
42:13–17	429, 431, 464	45:16	430, 465
42:15	419, 424	45:16–17	373
42:15–16	414, 456	45:18–25	430, 464
42:16	457	45:19	372
42:16	414	45:20	429
42:17	231, 428, 429, 430, 431, 435, 465	45:20–25	465
		45:21	431, 455
42:18–20	445	45:22	463
42:18–25	445	45:22–23	464
42:19	414	45:24	428, 430, 431, 435
43:3	463	45:24–25	447
43:3–4	429, 463	45:25	434

Isaiah (cont.)		51:4–6	465
46:1–2	429, 432, 435	51:6	424, 425, 428, 447
46:3	446	51:8	447
46:3–13	430	51:9	429
46:5–7	431	51:9–10	234
46:5–9	429	51:9–11	415, 465
46:9–11	431	51:9–13	454
46:10	431	51:9–16	371
46:12–13	447	51:11	414, 434
46:13	447, 465	51:16	338, 455
47	428	51:17	429
47:2	419	51:17–20	445, 446
48	373	51:17–23	445
48:1–15	373	51:21	247, 429
48:3–7	430, 431	51:23	465
48:4	445	51:41–42	463
48:5	429	52:1	445, 458
48:6–7	454	52:7	376, 405, 413, 463
48:6–8	454	52:7–10	374
48:8–9	445	52:7–12	414, 415
48:10	446, 447	52:9	418
48:12	455	52:12	414
48:12–16	371	52:13	760
48:13	465	52:13–53:12	465
48:13–16	430	54:1–3	456
48:14	429	54:1–8	456
48:16–19	460	54:4–5	418
48:17–19	372	54:8–10	459
48:18–19	373	54:9	428, 480
48:20	434	54:10	460
48:20–21	414	54:11–12	457
49:6–7	465	54:12	459
49:8–11	456	54:13	620
49:8–12	414	54:13–14	456
49:11	414, 457	54:14–17	458, 481
49:13	434	54:17	447
49:17–23	414	55	418
49:26	465	55:1	456
50:1	445	55:3	416, 459
50:2–3	419, 454, 465	55:3–4	527
50:4	620	55:3–5	459
51:1	447	55:5	463, 465
51:3	456	55:5–7	429
51:4	447	55:7	18, 39, 40, 41
51:4–5	464	55:12	375

Index of Sources

55:12–13	414	8:5	622
56:7	610	8:14	446
58:9	12, 21, 29, 37, 38, 39	9:14	446
59:4	9, 25, 37, 38, 43, 54, 55, 59	10:10	405, 409
59:4–5	10	12:3	737
59:6	9, 25, 37, 38	14	409, 496, 558
59:11	610	14:2–10	103
59:21	459	14:5–8	127
60:1–3	418	14:18	510
60:1–22	455	15:16	737
60:2	417	15:18	803
60:5–7	462	15:21	76
60:7	610	17:5–8	656, 762, 763, 765, 812
60:19	417	17:7–8	656
61:2	338	17:13	737
61:8	459	17:14	803, 840
62:4–5	418	18:15	58
63:1–6	855	18:18	510
65:8	280, 649, 659, 662	18:21–23	737
65:17	425, 455	20:1–2	827
65:20	457	20:1–6	515
65:25	461	20:7–9	490
66:3	43, 70, 679	20:11	737
66:15	419	20:13	793, 798, 800, 803
66:18–21	461	22:18	857
66:22	455	23:5–6	476, 478
69:19–20	406	23:10	709
		25:15	446
Jeremiah		25:15–29	247
1:1	510	25:15–38	542
1:15	432, 438	26	510
2:30	59	26:1–7	187
4:9	510	26:29–30	827
4:14	18, 39, 40, 41	27	764
4:15	39	27–28	508, 727
4:28–31	420, 421, 423	28	510, 514
4:30	59	28:1	727
5:13	152	29:26	510, 511, 515, 818
5:15–17	438	30–33	459
5:22	232	31:31–34	444
6:6	438	33:14–15	478
6:13	510	35	859
6:22	432, 433, 438	36	510, 796
6:29	59	38:1–13	727
7:22–23	834	41:5	148

Jeremiah (cont.)		13:17–19	68, 83
43:2	76	13:17–23	55
43:18	711	13:23	59
44:12	711	14:14	821
46:11	59	14:19	247
48:15	215, 405, 409	14:20	821
48:31	610	14:21	442
48:45	60	16:38	442
48:47	459	16:60–63	459
49:6	459	18	750
51:7	247, 407	18:1–13	758
51:34	24	20:33	247
		21:13–17	419
Ezekiel		21:19	29, 512
1:3	510	21:22	29, 512
2:2	513	21:26	67
3:12	513	21:28	59
3:12–15	512	21:34	59
3:14	513	22:22	247
3:24	513	22:28	59
5:10	442	23:32–33	446
5:15	442	28:3	76
6:11	29, 512	28:7	677
7:3	442	29–32	426
7:7	419	30:11	76
7:8	442	31:12	76
7:27	442	32:13	76
8:1–3	512	34:23	478
8:2–3	513	34:23–24	476
8:3	513	34:25	459
8:4	417	34:26	662
8:14	818	36:19	442
9:3	417	37:26	459
10:18–22	417	38	426
11:1	513	38–39	427
11:1–2	512	38:1–9	427
11:2	40, 42	38:6	432
11:9–11	442	38:8	439
11:24	513	38:15	427
11:24–25	512	38:16	439
12:24	59	38:18–23	428
13:6	59	38:19–20	419
13:7	59	39:2	432
13:8	59	39:17–20	467
13:9	59	40–48	476, 583

Index of Sources

40:1	264, 382	2:1–11	419		
40:2	457	2:2	433		
43:7–9	583, 852	2:14	660		
44:1–3	583	2:15	562		
45:7–12	583	2:20	432, 456		
45:18	267	3:1–5	444		
45:18–20	382	3:5	453		
47	192, 406, 456	4	428		
47:1–2	583	4:18	455, 457		
47:1–12	455				
47:9–10	583	Amos			
47:12	583	1:3–2:3	441		
47:16–18	583	1:11–12	438		
		1:14	419		
Hosea		2:1	438		
1:9	449, 453	2:4	43		
2:1	449	2:4–5	44		
2:16–23	450	2:7	120		
2:20	457, 459, 461	2:8	221, 245, 274		
3:4	472	2:9–10	436		
4:3	423	2:11	507		
4:12	634	2:12	275		
5:10	247	3:2	442		
6:8	9, 38, 39, 42	3:7	639		
6:11	459	3:12	449, 451, 833		
7:3	61	3:15	833		
7:5	221, 366, 379, 389	4:1	833		
8:7	24	4:4	273		
9:4	274	4:4–5	833		
9:5	262	4:5	274		
9:11	451	4:6–11	436		
9:12	451	4:6–12	418		
9:16	451	4:12	436		
10:4	55	5:2–3	451		
10:5	70	5:5	39, 70		
10:8	40, 42, 70	5:11	833		
10:13	61	5:15	435, 436, 449		
12:1	61	5:18	486		
12:2	58	5:20	421		
12:4	36	5:21–23	538		
12:12	42, 54	5:21–25	833		
12:14	502	5:23	610		
		5:24	834		
Joel		5:26	379		
1–2	558	6:3	435		

Amos (cont.)		5:5–8			451
6:4–5	833	5:6–8			449
6:5	857	6:6–8		750, 812
6:6	435, 436	6:8			834
6:13	436				
6:14	438	Nahum			
7:1–9	418	1:4			427
7:14	508, 513	3:1			61
7:14–15	833				
8:4	120	Habakkuk			
9:1	476	1–2			520
9:3	423	1:2			519
9:8–15	437, 449	1:2–4			441
9:13	455	1:3		9, 25, 38, 39
9:14	459	1:3–4			519
12:9	436	1:12			442
		1:12–13			519
Obadiah		2:1–4			519
15	408	2:3			326
16	247, 408	2:5–15			441
18	409	2:5–20			519
21	405, 408	2:15–16			247
		3		516, **519–21**, 608, 828
Jonah		3:1		608, 609, 820, 847
2:9	33, 55	3:3–14			855
2:3–10	130	3:8			427
2:5	826	3:19			609
2:6	233				
2:9	34, 134	Zephaniah			
		1			420
Micah		1–2			421
2:1	18, **25–26**	1:1–3:20			439
2:1–2	8, 9, 12, 37	1:3			423
2:12–13	414	1:8			467
2:13	405	1:16			439
3:11	510	1:18			422
4	405, 406	2:3			120
4:1–8	461	2:7			453
4:3	462	2:9			453
4:6–7	405, 449	2:11			461
4:7	215, 451, 453	3:8			421
4:11–12	428	3:14		405, 408
5:1–2	476	3:20			459
5:1–9	478	4:28–31			439
5:3	471				

Index of Sources

Haggai
2:10–12   505

Zechariah
1:1   515
1:8   457
3:8   478
5:1–4   711, 712
5:6   627
5:11   628
6:12   478
7:3   510, 548, 728
7:5   548
8:4   457
8:12–13   660
8:19   548
9:9   186
9:10   462
10:2   35, 42, 43, 54, 59
10:10   457
12   244, 426
12–14   406
12:1   408
12:2   407
12:3   407
12:3–4   407
12:6   408
12:9   407, 428
13   407
13:7–9   442
14   221
14:1–2   407
14:1–5   428
14:2   407
14:4–5   408
14:6–7   406
14:8   456
14:8–9   461
14:8–10   406, 455, 461
14:9   405, 408
14:9–11   457
14:10   457
14:12   407, 408
14:12–15   428
14:13   408
14:14–15   408
14:16–19   221, 406, 462

Malachi
3:1   459
3:1–5   442
3:10–11   660
3:14   59
3:15   76
3:18–21   442
3:19   76

Psalms
1   126, 655, 656, 705, 763, 764, 765, 766, 812, 815
1:4   51
1:5   794
2   359, 473, 495, 572, 573, **574–81**, 811, 814, 851, 858, 859
2–41   855, 858
2–89   823, 855, 858, 867
2:2   615
2:7   471, 472, 473, 582, 629, 701
2:8   472
3   128, 609, 808, 854, 860
3–9   783
3:2   103
3:3   613, 615
3:5   613, 614
3:6   159, 161
3:7   103, 613
3:8   108
3:9   613, 614
4   128, **160–61**, 808, 854
4:2   108
4:2–3   109
4:3   49, 50, 52, 101
4:6   824
4:9   159
5   128, 637, 808
5:3   215
5:4   67, 150
5:6   9, 25, 37, 38, 39, 40, 43, 46, 54, 96
5:6–7   10, 21, 43, 135
5:7   50

Psalms (cont.)

5:8	144, 785
5:9	109
5:10	19, 20
5:11	737
6	112, 128, **153–54**, 157, 596, 609, 642, 643, 644, 799, 808
6:3	108, 109
6:3–8	14
6:9	37, 38, 642
6:9–10	642
6:9–11	808
7	74, 103, 112, 128, 608, 808, 854, 860
7:2	109, 640
7:6	614
7:7	108
7:8–9	171
7:9	108, 110
7:13–14	11, 137
7:15	37, 38, 39, 43, 50, 54, 61, 94
7:15–16	39
7:15–17	28
7:18	802, 829
8	184, 225, 317, 367, 645, 646, 647, 809, 814, 854, 855
8:4	343
8:6	57, 335
9	641, 642
9–10	74, 641, 808
9:1–19	808
9:7	76, 641
9:13	121, 839
9:14	108
9:15	794
9:17	610, 612
9:19	121, 839
9:21	614
10	31, 128
10:1	612
10:2	120, 121
10:3	119, 473, 679
10:3–4	135
10:4	119
10:5	32, 33
10:7	9, 20, 37, 38, 43, 46, 50, 54, 135, 709, 711, 714, 736
10:7–11	18, 127
10:8–11	12
10:9	120, 121
10:11	6, 119
10:12	108, 121
10:13	119
10:15	737
10:17	121, 839
11	128, 131, 808
11–32	783
11:2	18, 101
11:2–3	109
12	28, **31–32**, 57, 128, 151, 253, 347, **348–49**, 524, 535, 546, 555, **556–57**, 642, 643, 644, 808, 810, 811, 814
12:2	48
12:3	50
12:3–5	25, 101
12:4	642
12:6	121, 596, 839
12:6–12	642
13	103, 128, 593, 808
13:4	108
13:5	24, 101
13:6	593, 802, 829
13:15–18	692
14	25, 40, 75, 128, 129, 253, 256, 257, 307, 338, 347, **349–50**, 394, 444, 484, 524, 535, 546, **553–56**, 557, 636, 641, 648, 774, 810, 811, 814
14:1	6, 20, 119, 358, 669, 760
14:2–6	828
14:4	12, 25, 38, 40, 41, 47
14:6	121
14:7	393
14:9	360
15	162, 184, 253, 254, 295, **296–97**, 354, 410, 411, 440, 444, 640, 703, **707–8**, 725, 750, 754, 764, 774, 777
15:1	306, 405, 825

Index of Sources

15:2	707	22	**77–79**, 101, **105–6**, 128, 501, 628, 629, 630, 796, 808
16	131, 605, 808		
16:1	109	22:4–6	163
17	103, 112, 128, **159–60**, 808	22:7	6, 691
17:8–9	109	22:8–9	111
17:9	101	22:10–11	163
17:12	101	22:13	103
17:12–13	101	22:13–14	101
17:13	108	22:16	101
18	126, 130, 167, 472, 572, 808, 810, 851, 855, 856, 861	22:17	101, 103
		22:20	108
18:1	603	22:21	103
18:5–6	433	22:21–22	101
18:9	422	22:22	103, 120
18:13	422	22:23	794, 836
18:16–17	433	22:23–26	829
18:21–25	125, 472	22:23–27	830
18:24	22	22:23–32	593, 808
18:26–27	715	22:25	120
18:28	120, 122, 370, 839	22:26	794, 824
18:51	571	22:26–27	802
19A	518, 809, 853, 854, 855	22:27	121, 122, 593, 838, 839
19B	126, 610, 764	22:30	238
19:2	535	23	130, 131, 135, 808, 844, 854
19:2–5	827	23:6	824, 825, 826
19:3	827	24	162, 165, 175, 180, 183, 184, 253, 254, 271, 285, 286, 291, **295–96**, 305, 307, 354, 366, 374, 384, 389, 410, 411, 440, 604, 613, 646, 703, **706–7**, 725, 750, 754, 764, 774, 785, 809, 812, 814, 854
19:8–11	764		
19:12	571		
19:14	76, 77, 109, 571		
19:15	610, 831		
20	86, 558, **567–69**, 570, 571, 572, 576, **698–700**, 701, 811, 828		
		24:1–2	225, 390
20:3	183	24:2	183, 192
20:4	472, 614, 824	24:3	305, 405, 825
20:5–6	472	24:3–5	670
20:10	563	24:3–6	354, 640
21	558, 567, **569–71**, 572, 576, 811, 813, 851	24:4	50, 59
		24:4–5	665
21:1–8	808	24:4–6	771, 777
21:3	614	24:5	333, 447, 614, 681
21:5	472	24:6	614
21:6	582, 622	24:7–10	183
21:12	50	24:10	614
21:14	563	25	101, 128, 764, 808
		25:5	126

Psalms (cont.)

25:6	163
25:9	121, 122, 839
25:16	108, 120
25:18	108
25:19	103
25:20	109
25:22	169
26	128, 808
26:1	110
26:3	126
26:4	18, 50, 54, 58
26:5	125
26:5–10	145
26:6	141, 801, 824
26:6–8	125
26:6–9	808
26:7	836
26:8	824, 826
26:9	109, 134
26:9–10	125
26:11	108
26:12	794, 802, 829
27	32, 47, 128, 131, 152, 641, 808
27:1–6	808
27:2–3	109
27:4	67, 145, 150, 319, 411, 417, 785, 824, 826
27:6	824
27:7	108
27:8	828
27:10	111
27:11	109
27:12	101, 110
28	**13–14**, 86, 117, 128, 134, 153, **155–56**, 572, 596, 804, 808, 851
28:2	108
28:3	19, 25, 37, 39, 40, 109, 125, 128, 145
28:3–4	133
28:3–5	134
28:4	737
28:6–8	156
28:7	802, 829
28:8	566
29	165, 183, 184, **226–28**, 319, 367, 391, 392, 417, 422, 534, 809, 814, 854, 855
29:1	335
29:1–2	356, 678
29:3	192, 391
29:3–4	390
29:4	335
29:6	391
29:7	391
29:8	391
29:10	183, 192, 390, 534
29:11	283, 333, 335, 394, 678, 840
30	130, 166, 168, 593, 808, 814, 844
30:3	109
30:5	122, 794
30:6	131
31	33, 101, 128, 153, 156–57, 593, 808
31:2	6
31:5	101
31:7	34, 50, 55
31:8	802, 829
31:10	108
31:10–25	106
31:12	111
31:14	101, 103
31:19	48, 50, 101
31:21	48
31:22	824
31:22–25	808
31:24	122
32	130, 132, 134, 308, 606, 764, 765, **767–69**, 808, 823
32:2	50
32:4	614
32:5	614
32:6–10	132
32:7	131, 614
32:9	56
33	183, 184, 237, 304, 366, 368, 809, 814, 859
33:2	836
33:4–5	183

Index of Sources

33:5	183	36:12–13	25
33:6–9	183, 225, 243, 390	36:13	37, 38
33:10–19	183, 340, 390	37	8, 124, 125, 126, 130, 132, 133,
33:10–22	243		137, 655, 764, 765, 784, 808, 840
33:16–17	342	37:11	122, 839
34	101, 126, 135, 168, 269, 764, 765,	37:14	121
	784, 808, 862	37:22	20, 736
34–38	808	37:35	76
34–41	783	38	**45–46**, 49, 101, 104, 109, 128,
34:3	121, 838, 839		618, 799, 808
34:7	120	38:7	120
34:8	131	38:12	111
34:11	131, 614	38:12–13	110
34:12–19	132, 768	38:13	50, 101
34:14	49, 50	38:20	50
34:17–22	131	38:23	108
35	47, 101, 103, 104, 109, 112, 128,	39	128, 619, 783, 808
	130, 472, 808	39:2–4	170
35:2	108	39:10	170
35:4	101	40	101, 325, 538, 641, 785, 793, 831,
35:4–8	737		832
35:7	101	40A	130, 134, 769, 808
35:7–8	101	40B	128, 808
35:10	121, 839	40:5	28, 44, 50, 131, 132, 232, 336,
35:11	110		768
35:12–14	125	40:7	832
35:17	60	40:7–8	829, 831
35:18	802, 829	40:10–11	794
35:19	49, 50	40:14–15	737
35:20	50, 101	40:15	101
35:21	24	40:18	120
35:23	108, 110	41	**22–24**, 58, 103, 111, 112, 128,
35:24	110		130, 167, 799, 808
35:28	802, 829	41:6	12
36	128, 546, 810	41:7	37, 46, 48, 50, 54, 55
36:2	6, 20, 119	41:7–8	35
36:2–5	669	41:7–9	56
36:3	19, 21	41:9	12, 58
36:4	37, 38, 43, 46, 50, 135	41:10	111
36:4–5	54	41:14	108
36:5	18, 19, 37, 38	42	606, 795, 823
36:8	577	42–43	**46–47**, 104, 109, 128, 783,
36:9	360, 826		808, 824
36:10	7, 361, 672	42–83	823
36:12	40	42–89	823, 858

Psalms (cont.)

42:3	826
42:4	111
42:5	288
42:6	802, 829
42:7–8	104
42:10–11	111
42:11	6
42:12	802, 829
42:43	824
43:1	50, 103, 110
43:3–4	826
43:4	824, 836
43:4–5	802, 829
44	103, 166, 558, 606, 729, 811, 823, 824
44–49	783
44:5	215, 686
44:7	686
44:9	614
44:10–17	104
44:16	686
44:24	108, 166
44:27	108
45	572, 573, 576, **588–92**, 606, 631, 635, 811, 814, 823, 824, 851
45:1	516
45:4	335
45:4–6	472
45:5	473
45:7–8	472, 473
45:8	373, 472
46	180, 184, 237, **239–41**, 242, 243, 304, 312, 317, 341, 351, 358, 359, 366, 367, 374, 390, 391, 393, 394, 410, 421, 425, 457, 463, 475, 541, 543, 637, 638, 639, 640, 687, 809, 814, 824
46–48	392
46:3–4	392, 425
46:4	244, 613, 614
46:4–5	456
46:5	192, 340, 393, 455, 824
46:6	195, 244, 303, 427, 437, 613
46:7	391, 392, 613
46:8	614
46:9–10	640
46:9–11	225
46:9–12	184, 340
46:10	192
46:11	342, 359, 393
46:12	614
47	165, 175, 179, 180, 183, 184, 190, 191, 193, 221, 262, 358, 366, 371, 375, 462, 534, 805, 809, 810, 824
47:2	187, 355, 357
47:4	394
47:5	614, 646
47:6	175, 183, 184, 187, 221, 260, 285, 305, 367, 374, 389, 836
47:7	355
47:8	606, 608
47:9	183, 187
47:10	188, 192, 294, 342, 357, 359, 393, 394, 463
48	165, 175, 180, 183, 184, 237, **241–43**, 281, 282, 297, 304, 312, 317, 326, 336, 341, 351, 358, 359, 366, 367, 374, 390, 391, 393, 394, 410, 411, 457, 463, 541, 543, 603, 638, 639, 642, 687, 809, 814, 824
48:2	696, 824
48:2–3	312, 340, 393, 577
48:2–4	184
48:3	183, 434, 457, 535, 824
48:4	640
48:5–7	303
48:6	409
48:6–7	192, 410
48:6–8	392
48:6–9	191
48:7	410
48:8	391, 412
48:9	195, 303, 614, 824
48:9–10	640
48:10	297, 305
48:11	358
48:11–12	225, 252, 343
48:12	252, 278, 359, 392, 417, 448
48:13–14	282, 285

Index of Sources

48:15	637
49	124, 125, 126, 130, 132, 133, 136, 326, 655, 764, 765, 784, 808, 819, 824, 840
49:2–5	518, 607, 827
49:2–36	511
49:5	827, 836
49:13	375
49:14	614
49:16	614
50	165, 184, 253, 254, 325, 333, 343, 356, 378, 384, 390, 392, 440, 443, 444, 524, **534–38**, 539, 544, 751, 754, 764, 765, 783, 785, 793, 811, 814, 821, 832
50:2	824
50:3	422
50:6	375, 614
50:7	372, 753
50:8–23	829, 830
50:9–13	773
50:14	824, 825
50:15	614
50:19	49, 50
50:23	825
51	108, **146–48**, 162, 171, 325, 538, 785, 793, 808, 832, 862
51–63	783
51–72	858
51:6	84
51:8	149, 641
51:9	141, 145, 146, 631, 801
51:17	802, 829
51:18	832
51:18–19	829, 831, 834
51:21	824
52	8, 26, 28, 95, 103, 109, 124, 125, 127, 128, 129, 158, 784, 808, 840, 842, 863
52–55	606, 823
52:3	101, 679
52:4	50
52:4–5	47
52:4–6	25
52:5	50, 615
52:6	50
52:7	614
52:9	7, 36
52:11	122, 802, 829
52:21	824
53	128, 256, 338, 347, 350, 394, 444, 546, **553–56**, 636, 774, 810, 811, 814
53:2	6, 119
53:4	554
53:5	12, 38, 40, 350
53:6	555
53:7	393, 636
54	75, 109, 112, 128, 593, 609, 808, 863
54–59	101
54:3	110, 119
54:4	349
54:5	75, 76, 101, 615
54:8	802, 825, 829
54:8–9	802
55	101, 103, 109, 112, 128, **158–59**, 609, 808
55:4	8, 30, 37, 38
55:8	615
55:10	20
55:11	37, 38
55:11–12	38
55:12	46, 50
55:12–13	375
55:13–15	111, 117
55:16	737
55:19	12, 103
55:20	614
55:22	19
55:24	9, 43, 46, 50, 54
56	10, 74, 101, 109, 112, 128, 625, 627, 808, 864
56–59	101
56–60	605
56:3	85, 103
56:3–7	8
56:6	18, 85
56:8	37, 38, 85, 103, 171
56:9	85

Psalms (cont.)
- 56:13 — 802, 824, 825
- 57 — 109, 112, 127, 128, 153, **157–58**, 566, 593, 613, 647, 808, 864, 867
- 57–59 — 648, 649, 650
- 57:4 — 614
- 57:5 — 101
- 57:5–6 — 25
- 57:7 — 101, 614
- 57:8–11 — 829
- 57:8–12 — 808
- 57:9 — 836
- 58 — 109, 112, 127, 128, 129, 230, 248, 647, 649, 808
- 58:2 — 50, 114, 628
- 58:4 — 7, 50, 710
- 58:4–5 — 101
- 58:4–7 — 25
- 58:5 — 27
- 58:5–7 — 25
- 58:8–11 — 802
- 59 — 20, 70, 73, 74, 75, 101, 109, 128, 647, 649, 808, 865
- 59:2–5 — 11, 137
- 59:3 — 9, 37, 38
- 59:4 — 38, 628
- 59:5 — 108
- 59:5–6 — 108
- 59:6 — 19, 37, 38, 96, 103, 171, 614
- 59:7 — 72
- 59:8 — 21, 119
- 59:9 — 103, 171
- 59:13 — 39, 50, 61, 709, 711, 714, 736
- 59:14 — 614
- 59:17 — 802, 829
- 60 — 103, 293, 409, 495, 500, 543, 558, **559–65**, 565, 605, 619, 620, 631, 635, 811, 813, 853, 854, 855, 865, 866
- 60:1 — 516
- 60:2 — 866
- 60:5 — 247, 446
- 60:6 — 614
- 60:10–11 — 104
- 60:11 — 563
- 60:13 — 59
- 61 — 109, 128, 134, 572, 576, 609, 804, 808, 851
- 61:3 — 433
- 61:5 — 613, 614, 826
- 61:7–8 — 571
- 61:9 — 802, 824, 829
- 62 — 109, 112, 124, 125, 127, 128, 153, 158, 593, 596, 619, 783, 784, 808, 811, 840
- 62:4 — 101
- 62:5 — 20, 50, 613, 615, 736
- 62:7–12 — 808
- 62:9 — 613, 614
- 63 — **44–45**, 86, 104, 109, 128, 134, 572, 576, 804, 808, 825, 851, 866
- 63:2–3 — 826
- 63:2–4 — 144
- 63:3 — 834
- 63:10 — 101
- 63:10–11 — 737
- 63:12 — 50, 566, 571
- 64 — 109, 127, 128, 411, 808
- 64:2–5 — 49
- 64:2–6 — 8, 11, 12, 137
- 64:3 — 25, 37, 38, 85
- 64:4–5 — 25, 49
- 64:4–6 — 20
- 64:5 — 18, 101
- 64:6 — 20, 119
- 65 — 130, 165, 167, 185, 229, 239, 273, 276, **314–16**, 340, 367, 394, 534, 603, 810, 814, 859
- 65:2 — 824
- 65:6 — 343, 824
- 65:8 — 60, 391
- 65:9 — 235
- 65:10 — 393
- 65:10–14 — 455
- 65:12 — 338, 392
- 65:18 — 455
- 66 — 603
- 66A — 184, 233, 235, 390, 809, 814
- 66B — 130, 133, 808
- 66:1–12 — 184, 235

Index of Sources

66:4	614	71	101, 106, 109, 808, 859
66:7	614	71:6	163, 840
66:8	615	71:12	108
66:9	615	71:13	101
66:13	617, 824, 825	71:14–16	802, 829
66:13–20	235	71:17–18	163
66:15	614, 824, 825	71:22	836
66:18	39, 125, 128	71:22–24	802, 829
67	185, 273, 314, 359, 361, 362, 367, 464, 465, 603, 609, 673, 810, 814, 859	71:24	22
		72	123, 353, 359, 471, 477, 478, 546, 572, 574, **585–88**, 590, 592, 660, 681, 698, **700–701**, 705, 783, 786, 811, 812, 851, 852, 858
67:2	614, 688		
67:5	614		
67:8	341	72:1	472
68	191, 194, 291, 317, 603, 611, 810	72:1–2	472
		72:2	122, 370, 786, 839
68–70	783	72:4	121, 472, 840
68:2	291	72:5	472
68:4	614	72:6	472
68:5	611	72:8	456
68:11	120, 121, 122, 839	72:8–11	472
68:20	614	72:9	472
68:26	287, 818	72:12–13	121, 472
68:26–27	287, 856	72:12–14	473
68:33	614	72:16	472
69	101, 107, 109, 128, 171, 325, 501, 538, 606, 629, 631, 635, 785, 793, 808	72:20	608
		73	20, 124, 125, 126, 130, 132, 133, 136, 501, 655, 784, 808, 821, 825, 840, 844
69:1	516		
69:5	49, 50, 103, 109, 110	73–83	783
69:9	111	73:11	119
69:13	111	73:17	834
69:14	338	73:19–20	52
69:16	24	73:22	358
69:23–29	737	73:23–26	490
69:30	120	74	103, 123, 558, 606, 729, 785, 811, 821, 823
69:31–32	829, 830		
69:31–37	593, 802, 808	74:1	530
69:32	635	74:3–9	104
69:33	121, 838, 839	74:9	516
69:34	121, 839	74:12	215, 686
70	109, 128, 618, 808	74:14	467
70:2	108	74:19	122, 839
70:3–4	737	74:21	121, 840
70:6	120	74:22	108

Psalms (cont.)

75	184, 194, 245, **246–48**, 317, 321, 341, 343, 358, 367, 390, 392, 410, 484, 495, 524, **540–43**, 557, 562, 603, 647, 648, 811, 814
75:3	252
75:4	614
75:4–5	392
75:7–8	355
75:8	392
75:9	247
75:10	836
76	184, 237, 239, 243, 304, 317, 341, 359, 367, 390, 391, 392, 393, 394, 410, 457, 463, 541, 543, 603, 809, 814, 867
76:2	278
76:2–4	541
76:3	195, 312
76:4	613, 614
76:4–6	412
76:4–10	184, 340
76:7	236
76:9	252
76:9–10	343
76:10	120, 121, 613, 614, 840
76:12	394, 825
77	558, 619, 783, 811
77:4	615
77:10	615
77:16	614
77:19	422
78	606, 764, 765, 822, 823
78:1	828
78:2	827
78:31	238
78:51	36
79	103, 184, 558, 729, 785, 811, 821
79:2	122
79:10	692
79:13	836
80	103, 558, 631, 635, 729, 811, 821, 867
80:8	614
80:9–17	650
80:15	108
81	162, 165, 179, 180, 184, 192, 194, 221, 233, 236, 246, 253, 254, 262, 293, 294, 307, 319, 321, 328, **329–33**, 337, 343, 344, 354, 367, 372, 382, 384, 390, 392, 393, 394, 411, 412, 417, 440, 444, 459, 460, 484, 511, 524, **531–33**, 534, 537, 541, 552, 559, 639, 645, 647, 751, 754, 811, 814
81:1–6	809
81:2–3	611
81:2–6	355
81:3	836
81:4	221, 260, 265, 836
81:5	261
81:6	152, 827
81:7–16	375
81:8	614
81:10	355
81:11	371, 753
81:14–15	358
81:15–16	351, 352, 394
81:16	358
81:17	238, 340, 393, 455
82	50, 165, 184, 245, 246, **248–53**, 320, 326, 341, 349, 350, 355, 356, 390, 391, 392, 421, 430, 441, 495, 524, 534, **539–40**, 541, 554, 569, 571, 649, 811, 814
82:1	628
82:2	615
82:3–4	121, 840
82:5	392
82:8	343, 430, 563
83	103, 558, 603, 728, 729, 811, 821
83:7–9	104
83:9	615
83:10–18	774
83:14–18	799
84	86, 131, 183, 184, 217, 285, **294–95**, 306, 353, 366, 367, 572, 645, 646, 647, 685, 804, 809, 812, 813, 814, 824
84–85	783

Index of Sources

84–89	823		606, 729, 783, 785, 811, 822, 823, 851
84:3	826		
84:4	183, 824	89:2–3	809
84:5	614, 825, 826	89:5	614
84:5–6	769	89:6–19	809
84:6	412	89:16	646
84:8	334, 412, 417	89:19	294
84:9	614	89:20	559
84:9–10	217	89:20–37	359
84:10	566	89:20–38	566, 701, 811, 814
84:10–14	343	89:21	472
84:11	329, 826	89:26–37	472
84:13	769	89:27–28	701
84:14	341	89:29–38	524
85	185, 217, 256, 257, 273, 293, **337–38**, 367, 394, 411, 458, 484, 524, 546, **549–53**, 559, 569, 636, 639, 703, 810, 813, 814, 824	89:31–38	473
		89:38	614
		89:39–46	104
		89:46	615
85:2	344, 393	89:49	59, 615
85:3	614	90	103, 309, 547, 548, 558, 608, 729, 731, 783, 785, 786, 810
85:9	152, 330, 828		
85:10–13	373, 455	90–150	858, 867
86	75, 109, 112, 128, 312, 783, 808	90:10	39, 128
86:1	120	91	**594–96**, 705, 764, 765, 772, 812, 814, 859
86:11	126		
86:14	75, 76, 101, 119	91–100	193
86:17	149, 151, 516	91:14–16	811
87	184, **360–62**, 367, 393, 464, 465, 524, **543–44**, 554, 577, 603, 698, 809, 811, 814, 824	92	130, 133, 165, 166, 168, 603, 808
		92:3	836
		92:4	609, 610, 836
87–88	783	92:7–8	40
87:3	614, 824	92:8	25, 39, 40, 41, 128
87:4	234	92:10	39, 41, 128
87:7	288, 312, 672	92:13–16	131
88	603, 606, 617, 618, 636, 783, 808, 822, 823, 824, 853	93	165, 179, 180, 183, 190, 191, 226, 286, 390, 391, 547, 617, 805, 809
88:6	693	93–99	392, 859
88:8	615	93–100	320, 366, 370, 371, 375, 377, 380, 462
88:9	111		
88:10	615	93:1	183, 187, 278
88:11	615	93:2–3	183
88:16	120	93:2–4	192
88:19	111	93:3	392
89	87, 103, 104, **527–31**, 558, 576,	93:5	281, 677

Psalms (cont.)
94   **9-10**, 68, 74, 109, 128, 165, 166, 534, 535, 546, 810, 814
94:1-7   444
94:2   25
94:4   21, 25, 37, 38, 40, 135
94:7   119
94:8   20, 40
94:8-11   95
94:8-23   168
94:12   769
94:15   614
94:16   37, 38
94:20   46, 69, 800
94:23   25, 27, 37, 38
95   179, 183, 184, 192, 194, 233, 236, 253, 254, 305, 319, 328, 329, 333, 343, 356, 371, 375, 390, 392, 393, 394, 412, 440, 444, 459, 524, 531, 537, 541, 552, 751, 753, 754, 811, 814
95-99   617
95-100   179, 180, 190, 286, 805
95:1-2   355
95:1-7   809
95:2   184, 285
95:3   183
95:3-5   225, 390
95:4-5   183, 192
95:6   184, 285, 319, 355, 531
95:6-7   236
95:7-11   372, 375
96   183, 286, 355, 809
96:1   183, 225, 228
96:1-13   286
96:2-3   278
96:4   230, 320, 341, 390, 392
96:4-5   52, 224
96:5   320
96:6   335, 372
96:7   678
96:7-8   356, 394
96:7-9   342, 359, 393, 465
96:8   358, 824
96:8-9   184
96:9   319
96:10   183, 192, 214, 224, 390, 440
96:10-12   188, 228
96:12   214
96:12-13   312
96:13   183, 184, 250, 252, 341, 343, 392, 440
97   183, 191, 236, 333, 391, 809
97:1   183, 355
97:2   187, 391
97:3   535
97:3-5   391, 408, 409, 410, 422
97:4   535
97:6   343, 535
97:7   184, 188, 192, 230, 231, 232, 250, 252, 320, 341, 357, 358, 390, 391, 392
97:7-8   183, 252, 373
97:7-9   393
97:8   183, 184, 187, 189, 225, 252, 278, 343, 359, 392, 417, 448, 824
97:9   229
97:10   189, 358
97:10-12   358
97:12   187
98   183, 319, 355, 360, 809
98:1   183, 225, 228, 229
98:2   343, 357
98:2-3   183, 225, 278
98:3   394
98:3-4   393
98:4   357
98:4-6   225, 465
98:5   836
98:6   183, 187, 260, 836
98:7-8   188, 214, 228
98:9   184, 250, 252, 343, 357, 392, 440
98:10-11   231
98:78   372
99   183, 191, 194, 319, 328, 393, 412, 417, 809
99:1   183, 187
99:2   184
99:2-3   188, 229
99:3   278

Index of Sources

99:4	183, 225, 343	107:41	121, 840
99:5	187, 355	108	293, 558, **565–67**, 603, 811, 813
99:6–9	236, 328	108–110	783, 859
99:7	391	108:3	836
99:8	189, 313, 394	108:7	562
99:9	355	108:10	563
100	183, 305, 355, 617, 809	108:11	560, 866
100:3	183, 192, 236	108:13	59
100:4	278, 285	109	94, 101, 103, 105, 109, 129, 655, **737–39**, 808
101	123, 218, 353, 472, 473, 477, 572, 574, 764, 765, 783, 812, 851, 859	109:1	840
101:4–5	409	109:2	50
101:5	683	109:2–3	101
101:7	43, 50, 54	109:6–20	737
101:7–8	21, 43, 409	109:16	121
101:8	25, 39, 40, 128, 824	109:17	736
102	109, 170, 547, 558, 608, 810, 824, 849	109:17–18	20
		109:18	736
102:1	120	109:22	120
102:1–12	129, 808	109:25	111
102:2–12	849	109:28	20, 736
102:24–28	849	109:30	593
102:25–28	339	109:30–31	593, 794, 802, 829
103	130, 131, 134, 783, 808, 844, 859	109:31	121, 839
103:3	109	110	359, 477, 495, 515, 525, 572, 573, 574, 576, **581–85**, 811, 814, 851
103:5	56, 339, 393	110:1	828
103:13–18	131	110:2	472
104	809, 859	110:3	472, 475, 629, 701
104:1	335	110:4	471, 472, 503
104:5–9	232	110:5–6	471
104:10	335	110:5–7	472
104:15	682	111	764, 809
104:30	393	111–118	858
105	764, 809	111:1	794
105–107	858	112	126, 655, 656, 705, 763, 764, 765, 766, 812, 815, 859
105:15	567	113	809
105:36	36	113–118	165, 795
106	547, 548, 558, 765, 810	113:7	121, 840
106:3	769	113:7–8	840
106:17	24	114	183, 184, 233, 319, 367, 390, 809, 814
107	107, 168, 808	114:1–2	234
107:17–22	134	114:2	183, 234
107:20	109		
107:22	824, 836		
107:33–43	809		

Psalms (cont.)

115	593, **690–94**, 695, 697, 810, 812, 814
115:9	836
115:12	836
115:12–15	771
116	130, 134, 166, 808, 844
116:4–6	131
116:10	120, 131
116:13	274
116:14	825
116:16	155, 571
116:17	824, 825
116:17–10	617
117	809
118	165, 169, 184, 213, 271, 279, 281, **297–302**, 317, 368, 378, 380, 383, 384, 534, 548, 556, **683–84**, 686, 703, 805, 809, 810, 812, 814
118:1–4	733
118:3	836
118:4	692
118:11	840
118:12	300
118:14	278, 335
118:19–26	702
118:25	683
118:26	771, 812
118:27	277, 280, 631, 824
119	109, 126, 128, 764, 765, 796, 808
119:21	77
119:29	50
119:37	50, 54, 59
119:51	77
119:53	32
119:69	49, 77
119:78	50, 77
119:85	77
119:86	50
119:122	77
119:133	37, 77
119:154	110
119:157	103
119:171–172	802, 829
119:175	802, 829
120	26, 48, 103, 109, 127, 128, 170, 185, 307, 351, 368, 535, 546, 547, 548, 648, 686, 795, 808, 810, 814
120–134	185, 368, 604, 814, 858
120–143	184
120:2	50, 101
120:2–3	25
120:3	50, 95
120:3–5	774
121	169, 185, 346, 355, 394, 547, 548, 604, **696–98**, 810, 812, 813, 814
121:1–2	185, 355
121:2	185
121:3–4	351
121:6	340, 393
121:7–8	185
122	169, 185, 217, 318, 367, 368, 501, 547, **684–90**, 695, 696, 698, 705, 783, 809, 810, 812, 813, 814, 859
122:1	785
122:1–2	826
122:3	312
122:3–4	344
122:5	185
122:6–7	342, 771
122:7–9	185
122:8–9	771
122:9	342
123	129, 169, 185, 307, 309, 321, 342, 355, 501, 547, 686, 810
123:1	185
123:3	259
123:4	75
124	307, 317, 351, 352, 355, 604, 617, 783, 810, 814, 859
124:1–5	355
124:3	24
124:6	771
124:6–7	259
124:8	185, 345
125	40, 75, 185, 217, 253, 307, 309, 312, 347, 350, 351, 352, 355, 394, 535, 547, 809, 810, 813, 814, 824
125:2	185
125:5	19, 39, 40, 128, 347, 774

Index of Sources

126	185, 217, 256, 257, 273, 310, 321, 336, 337, 344, 367, 368, 394, 411, 458, 501, 547, 550, 636, 810, 814	132:7	185, 355, 405, 647
		132:7–8	184
		132:8–10	286
126:1	393	132:9	344, 358, 394, 689, 695, 836
126:1–2	551	132:11–12	566
126:1–3	355	132:11–18	218, 459, 527, 528, 529, 687, 701, 811
126:2	362, 464	132:12	218, 355, 473, 575
126:4	393	132:13	824
126:5	550	132:13–18	184
126:6	455	132:14	285
127	703, 764, 783, 786, 810	132:15	121, 840
127A	185	132:16	319, 344, 358, 394, 689, 695, 836
127:1	59		
127:2	59	132:17	294
127:3–5	345	132:18	351, 352, 358, 394
127:5	769	133	124, 281, 344, 354, 394, 703, 764, 765, 783, 809, 814, 859
128	185, 394, 411, 455, 604, 655, **701–5**, 756, 759, 761, 764, 765, 772, 812	133:2	590, 836
		133:3	185, 749
128:4	342, 355	134	185, **694–96**, 814
128:5	772	134:1–2	683
129	185, 307, 312, 317, 318, 351, 352, 355, 604, 686, 687, **733–35**, 810, 812, 814	134:2	185, 785
		134:3	185
		135	809
129:5	351, 394	135:21	824
129:5–8	342, 352, 358, 774	136	809
129:8	682	137	262, 548, 558, 655, **728–33**, 812, 824, 859
130	169, 170, 308, 319, 342, 355, 394, 412, 501, 547, 548, 648, 687, 808, 810, 814	137:2	836
		137:7–9	774
130:4	307, 342	138	75, 130, 135, 808, 859
130:4–5	319	138–145	783, 859
131	169, 170, 308, 309, 319, 342, 352, 355, 501, 547, 548, 648, 687, 783, 808, 810, 814, 859	138:7–8	131
		139	109, 128, 785, 808, 859
		139:8	582
132	162, 180, 184, 194, 246, 271, 285, 286, **287–94**, 305, 321, 328, 331, 337, 344, 353, 354, 366, 368, 374, 384, 389, 393, 394, 411, 417, 440, 444, 468, 469, 476, 484, 511, **524–26**, 530, 545, 547, 572, 604, 638, 639, 646, 696, 751, 810, 811, 812, 813, 814, 851	139:9	629
		139:13–16	163
		139:19	101
		139:20	50, 56, 57, 101
		140	**24–25**, 103, 109, 127, 128, 613, 808
		140:4	27, 101, 615
132:1–5	217	140:5	101
132:6	647	140:5–6	101

Psalms (cont.)		149:1–2	358
140:6	75, 615	149:2	183, 192
140:9	614	149:3	836
140:9–12	737	149:4	370, 839
140:12	101	149:5	122, 358
140:13	121, 839	149:6–9	183, 225, 358
141	109, 128, 808	149:7–9	191, 192, 195
141:1	108	149:9	122, 183, 283, 335, 370, 412
141:2	824, 825, 831	150	809
141:4	37, 39	150:3	609, 836
141:8–10	12	150:4	288
141:9	19, 37, 38	150:5	609
141:9–10	25, 40		
141:10	737	Job	
142	109, 129, 606, 608, 808, 823, 867, 868	1:5	630
		1:21	773
142:4	101	3:8	20, 712
142:5	111	4:6	840
142:8	802, 829	4:8	38, 39, 61
143	103, 109, 129, 613, 808	5:6	39
143:3	101	5:17	656
143:6	614	5:23	461
143:12	101, 737	6:23	76, 117
144	54, 82, 109, 128, 811, 813, 851, 868	7:3	54
		10:3	117
144:8	50, 54	11:11	18, 39, 54, 58
144:9	836	11:13–19	762
144:9–10	802, 829	11:14	39, 40
144:10	101	12:13–16	659
144:11	50, 54, 102	13:4	844
144:15	769	15:20	76
145	131, 608, 785, 808, 844	15:27–28	116
146	131, 764, 808, 844	15:31	58
146–148	859	15:35	38, 39
146:5	769	16:8	60, 61
147	809	16:9–11	114
147:2	611	18:7	39
147:6	121, 840	18:12	39
147:7	611, 836	18:14	69, 70
148	809	19	113
149	122, 123, 183, 184, 191, 194, **245–46**, 248, 252, 352, 358, 359, 369, 390, 392, 394, 448, 543, 809, 814, 855	19:3	113
		21:8–13	660
		21:19	39
		21:19–20	39
149:1	122, 183, 225, 228, 794	21:20	247

Index of Sources

22:15	19, 20, 39	12:21–22	43
26:9	265	14:21	656
27:7	117	16:20	656
27:13	76	17:4	21, 38, 43
29–31	840	19:28	21, 37, 38, 39, 71
29:6	660	21:15	39, 41
30:1–17	114	22:8	39, 40, 61
30:1–31	7	24:24	712
30:2–8	116	28:14	656
30:8	116	29:18	656
31:3	39, 40	29:24	712, 717, 718
31:19–20	587	30:8	56
31:20	661	30:20	39, 41
31:38–40	273		
33:22	115	Ruth	
33:26–28	805	2:19–20	661
34:8	39, 40	2:20	681
34:22	39	4:11–12	660
34:36	39		
35:13	59	Ecclesiastes	
36:10	39, 41	3:17	440
36:21	39	10:16	656
37:22	433	10:16–17	656
38:10–11	232	11:9–10	582
38:36	147, 641		
39:20	335	Lamentations	
40:11–12	75	1:12	24
40:16	36	2:4	247
40:25–29	232	2:14	59
40:32–41:3	231	4:11	247
40:32–41:3 (Eng. 41:8–11)	390	4:20	472, 526
42:12	660	5	103, 558
Proverbs		Esther	
1:27	60	2:5	860
3:13	656		
6:2–3	40	Daniel	
6:12	8, 21, 37, 39, 58	3:26–45	558
6:12–14	28, 137	7	427
6:14	19	9:25–26	567
8:32	656		
8:34	656	Ezra	
10:10	30, 40	2	821
10:29	30, 39	2:41	818, 820, 822, 823
12:21	38, 39	2:63	731

Ezra (cont.)		15–16	285
3:8–9	622	15:19–21	640
5:1	515	15:20–22	620, 637
6:14	515	15:21	609, 623, 624, 641
8:15–20	838	15:22	511, 514
8:15–36	622	15:24	646
		15:27	511, 514
Nehemiah		16	188, 220, 286, 640, 645
3:15	306	16:4	618
5:1–13	797, 840	16:22	567
5:12	718	16:23–33	286
5:13	719	16:38	646
6:10–11	827	20:14	514
6:10–14	515	23:4	622
7–12	286	23:13	672
8	280, 384, 688, 833, 834	25:1	519, 607
8:1–2	688	25:1–3	515, 519
8:5	674	25:1–6	821
8:6	674	25:1–8	619
8:9	262, 298	25:2	607
8:9–12	259, 306	25:3	607
8:10	221, 288, 303, 384, 389, 834	25:7	822
11:17	818	26:1	823
11:22	820	26:4	305
12:4	515	26:16	306
12:22	286	26:18	306
12:24	818	26:19	823
12:27–43	282	29:23	581
12:37	306	2 Chronicles	
13:4–5	274	2:1	621
13:10–14	838	2:17	621
13:10–27	797	5–7	285
		5:12	619, 821
1 Chronicles		6:41	291
2:6	822	6:41–42	286
2:19	289	15:21	642
2:50	289	20	514
4:14	722	20:14	511, 519, 818
6:18	824	20:14–17	516
6:18–23	823	20:14–19	827
6:18–32	821	20:19	823
6:23	824	25:1–3	827
9:19	823	25:5	827
13:3	289	26:16–20	585
15	292, 517	29:14	619, 821

29:25	504	14:20–27	656
30:22	606, 822	21:3	833
34:12	620	25:7–9	656
34:12–13	623	28:13–19	656
34:13	621	28:13–26	762
35:13	619	28:19	656
35:15	821, 827	31:8–9	656
		32:1–5	834
		32:6	833
		34:8–9	656
		49:1	603
		51:1–12	844

Deuterocanonical and Pseudepigraphical Works

1 Enoch
- 60:24–25 — 427

1 Maccabees
- 4:52 — 168
- 14:41 — 515

2 Baruch
- 29:4 — 467

2 Maccabees
- 10:6–7 — 279, 280

4 Ezra
- 6:26 — 467
- 6:49–52 — 427

Judith
- 16:17 — 833

Psalms of Solomon
- 2:33–35 — 127
- 6 — 655
- 7 — 558
- 9 — 548, 558
- 10 — 655
- 12 — 127
- 13:5–9 — 127
- 14 — 127
- 15:7–15 — 127

Sirach
- 7:9 — 833
- 14:1–2 — 656

Testament of Naphtali
- 3 — 76

Tobit
- 3:8 — 76
- 10:11–12 — 660

New Testament

Matthew
- 12:43–45 — 7, 710
- 13:27–28 — 84

Mark
- 14:26 — 795

Luke
- 2:37 — 825
- 10:6 — 665
- 16:21 — 72

John
- 7:37 — 326
- 7:49 — 270
- 11:44 — 796
- 11:51 — 77
- — 498

Acts
- 21:26 — 167

Romans
- 3:10–12 — 555

Romans (cont.)		m. Sukkah	
9:21	560	4:1	694
		4:5	676
1 Corinthians		5:1–4	694
11:10	76	5:3	277
12:2	76	5:4	269
Galatians		m. Yoma	
4:9	76	7:1	674, 677
Hebrews		t. Roš Haššanah	
7:9–10	686	1:13	255
1 Peter		y. Sukkah	
5:8	865	55b	277

JOSEPHUS

Revelation	
9:1–11	433
12	427
13	427
17	427

Contra Apionem
1.22 — 694

RABBINIC WORKS

b. Sukkah
53a — 534

b. Baba Batra
74 — 467

m. Berakot
5:4 — 672, 681
6:1–3 — 682

m. Middot
2:5 — 269, 694

m. Pesaḥim
10:2 — 682
10:7 — 682

m. Roš Haššanah
1:2 — 261
1:14 — 261

www.ingramcontent.com/pod-product-compliance
Lightning Source LLC
Chambersburg PA
CBHW032126010526
44111CB00033B/133